DICKENS STUDIES ANNUAL

Essays on Victorian Fiction

DICKENS STUDIES ANNUAL

Essays on Victorian Fiction

DICKENS STUDIES ANNUAL

Essays on Victorian Fiction

VOLUME
45

Edited by
Stanley Friedman, Edward Guiliano,
Anne Humpherys, Natalie McKnight, and Michael Timko

AMS PRESS, INC.
New York

Dickens Studies Annual
ISSN 0084-9812
e-ISSN 2167-8510

Dickens Studies Annual: Essays on Victorian Fiction welcomes essay- and monograph-length contributions on Dickens and other Victorian novelists and on the history of aesthetics of Victorian fiction. All manuscripts should be double-spaced and should follow the documentation format described in the most recent *MLA Style Manual*. The author's name should appear only on a cover-page, not elsewhere in the essay. An editorial decision can usually be reached more quickly if two copies of the article are submitted, since outside readers are asked to evaluate each submission. If a manuscript is accepted for publication, the author will be asked to provide a 100- to 200-word abstract with the final version of the essay. The preferred editions for citations from Dickens's works are the Clarendon and the Norton Critical when available, otherwise the Oxford Illustrated or the Penguin.

Please send submissions to The Editors, *Dickens Studies Annual*, Ph.D. Program in English, The Graduate Center, CUNY, 365 Fifth Avenue, New York, NY 10016-4309. Please send inquiries concerning subscriptions and/or availability of earlier volumes to AMS Press, Inc., Brooklyn Navy Yard, 63 Flushing Ave.–Unit #221, Brooklyn, NY 11205-1073.

Dickens Studies Annual: Essays on Victorian Fiction is published in cooperation with Queens College and the Graduate Center, CUNY.

International Standard Book Number
Series ISBN: 978-0-404-18520-6

Vol. 45 Cloth ISBN: 978-0-404-18945-7
Vol. 45 e-ISBN: 978-0-404-90045-8

All AMS books are printed on acid-free paper that meets the guidelines for performance and durability of the Committee on Production Guidelines for Book Longevity of the Council on Library Resources.

AMS PRESS, INC.
Brooklyn Navy Yard, 63 Flushing Avenue–Unit #221
Brooklyn, NY 11205-1073, USA
www.amspressinc.com

Manufactured in the United States of America

CONTENTS

Preface   vii

Notes on Contributors   ix

DAVID PARKER

Pickwick and Reform: Origins   1

DIANNE F. SADOFF

Boz and Beyond: *Oliver Twist* and the Dickens Legacy   23

TIMOTHY SPURGIN

"Notoriety is the Thing": Modern Celebrity
and Early Dickens   45

ALEKSANDAR STEVIĆ

Fatal Extraction: Dickensian Bildungsroman
and the Logic of Dependency   63

GALIA BENZIMAN

"Feeble Pictures of an Existing Reality":
The Factual Fiction of *Nicholas Nickleby*   95

JEROME MECKIER

Dickens and Tocqueville: Chapter 7 of *American Notes*   113

ROSEMARY COLEMAN

How *Dombey and Son* Thinks About Masculinities   125

MATTHEW P. M. KERR

Floating Fragments: Some Uses of Nautical Cliché
in *Dombey and Son*   147

ANDREW MAUNDER

Dickens Goes to War: *David Copperfield*
at His Majesty's Theatre, 1914   175

JENNIFER CONARY
"Whether we like it or not":
Bleak House and the Limits of Liberalism 205

ZACHARY SAMALIN
Dickens, Disinterestedness,
and the Poetics of Clouded Judgment 229

JESSICA KUSKEY
Math and the Mathematical Mind:
Charles Babbage, Charles Dickens,
and Mental Labor in *Little Dorrit* 247

MATTHEW HEITZMAN
"A Long and Constant Fusion
of Two Great Nations": Dickens,
the Crossing, and *A Tale of Two Cities* 275

ERIN D. CHAMBERLAIN
Servants' Bright Reflections:
Advertising the Body in Victorian Fiction 293

ELIZABETH MEADOWS
Entropy and the Marriage Plot in
The Woman in White and *Lady Audley's Secret* 311

CAROLINE REITZ
Recent Dickens Studies: 2012 333

Index 399

Preface

Dickens's career as a published creative writer—launched in December 1833 with the sketch "A Dinner at Poplar Walk" in *Monthly Magazine*, and concluded a few months after his death in 1870 with the publication of most of the sixth of the intended twelve installments of *The Mystery of Edwin Drood*—lasted just short of thirty-seven years. But, as he hoped, interest in his work has long outlived him. This volume includes articles that suggest ways in which new information and new approaches can enhance our understanding of how Dickens and his contemporaries were read in their own time and in subsequent eras and how they continue to speak to the present.

We are, as always, very grateful to all who have submitted their work for our consideration and also to the outside reviewers whose generous contributions of their expertise and time have helped us in evaluating submissions and have frequently assisted authors in revising.

We offer special thanks to Caroline Reitz for providing an inclusive, thoughtful, and extremely useful survey of the multitudinous scholarly and critical works evoked by the bicentennial of Dickens's birth.

We appreciate the important practical assistance provided by various academic administrators at CUNY's Graduate Center: Interim Provost Louise Lennihan; Ph.D. Program in English Acting Executive Officer Carrie Hintz; and Nancy Silverman, Assistant Program Officer, Ph.D. Program in English.

We also are grateful to John O. Jordan and John Bowen, Co-Directors of The Dickens Project at the University of California, Santa Cruz; JoAnna Rottke, Assistant Director of The Dickens Project; and Jon Michael Varese, the Project's Director of Digital Initiatives, for placing on the Project's website the tables of contents for volumes 1-27 of *DSA*, as well as abstracts for subsequent volumes. (These items can be found on the Project's website: <http://dickens.ucsc.edu>. Click "Resources," and then click *Dickens Studies Annual*.)

We are indebted to Gabriel Hornstein, President of AMS Press, for his enthusiasm and support; to Jack Hopper, retired Editor-in-Chief at AMS Press, for his careful, expert assistance; to David Ramm, former Editor-in-Chief at AMS Press, for contributions facilitating the preparation of this issue; and to Albert Rolls, present Editor-in-Chief at AMS Press, for skillful guidance in completing this volume. Finally, we thank our valued editorial assistants, both of whom are doctoral students at the Graduate Center: Erin Spampinato, for useful help in the early phases of preparing the volume, and Laura Eldridge, for ably handling the middle and later stages.

—The Editors

Notes on Contributors

GALIA BENZIMAN is a senior lecturer at the Open University of Israel and specializes in British literature of the long nineteenth century. Her book, *Narratives of Child Neglect in Romantic and Victorian Culture*, was published in 2012 by Palgrave Macmillan. In 2008–09 she was a Fulbright Fellow at the University of California Dickens Project. She has published essays in *Studies in the Novel*, *SEL*, *Partial Answers*, *Dickens Quarterly*, *Journal of Narrative Theory*, and other journals.

ERIN CHAMBERLAIN has been an assistant professor of English at Washburn University in Topeka, Kansas, since 2008. Her teaching and research activities study the influence of public culture upon the private home in nineteenth-century British literature, in particular the literature written for and about women. Her current research includes the study of servant characters in terms of class, gender, and space as represented through the middle-class people and homes of the Victorian novel. She holds a Ph.D. from Purdue University in nineteenth-century British literature, as well as a master's degree from Ohio University and a B.A. from Hanover College.

ROSEMARY COLEMAN received her Ph.D. in English Literature from Rice University. She is currently working on an article comparing closural strategies in Dickens's novels.

JENNIFER CONARY is an assistant professor of English at DePaul University, where she teaches courses on nineteenth-century British literature, the British novel, Gothic literature, Austen, the Brontës, and Dickens. She has published articles on Benjamin Disraeli and George Gissing, and her current research interests include the Victorian bildungsroman and social problem novels.

MATTHEW HEITZMAN recently completed his Ph.D. at Boston College. His dissertation, "Revolutionary Narratives, Imperial Rivalries: Britain and the French Empire in the Nineteenth Century," examines the ways in which Victorian writers responded to the threat of French imperialism. His research interests include literature of the long nineteenth century, colonial and empire studies, transnational studies, and post-colonial theory.

MATTHEW P. M. KERR teaches English at Magdalen and Keble Colleges, Oxford. He has an article on *Persuasion* forthcoming in *Essays in Criticism* and is currently preparing his first monograph, on the subject of the sea and literary language between 1829 and 1914. His next project concerns John Stuart Mill's private library and the Victorian reader.

JESSICA KUSKEY earned her Ph.D. in English from Syracuse University and is currently Visiting Assistant Professor in the Literature Department at the University of California, Santa Cruz. Her essay on Dickens's *Our Mutual Friend*, titled "Our Mutual Engine: The Economics of Victorian Thermodynamics," won the SLSA Bruns Prize and recently appeared in *Victorian Literature and Culture*. She is currently at work on a book, tentatively titled "The Body Machinic," examining the mechanization of the labor process in Victorian literature and culture.

ANDREW MAUNDER is Reader in Victorian Literature at Hertfordshire University. He is editor of the series Varieties of Women's Sensation Fiction (2004) and, with Graham Law, author of *Wilkie Collins: A Literary Life* (2010). He is currently working on an essay collection "British Theatre and the Great War 1914-1919" to be published by Palgrave (2015) and is coordinator of a theater project which works to revive forgotten plays of the First World War.

ELIZABETH MEADOWS is a senior lecturer in English and the assistant director of Vanderbilt University's Curb Center for Art, Enterprise, and Public Policy. She was previously a visiting assistant professor of English at Mount Holyoke College, through an Andrew W. Mellon New Faculty Fellowship awarded by the American Council of Learned Societies. Her book project examines how Victorian authors use marriage to problematize the social and material power of literary form. Her chapter, "'You've Got Mail': Technologies of Communication in Victorian Literature," co-authored with Jay Clayton, is forthcoming in the *Oxford Handbook of Victorian Literary Culture*.

JEROME MECKIER, Professor of English Emeritus at the University of Kentucky, has published eight books, three of them on Dickens: *Hidden Rivalries in Victorian Fiction: Dickens, Realism and Revaluation* (1987); *Innocent Abroad: Charles Dickens's American Engagements* (1990); and *Charles Dickens's Great Expectations: Misnar's Pavilion versus Cinderella* (2002). He has also published numerous articles on nineteenth- and twentieth-century English literature. He served as sub-editor for the first seven volumes of DSA. His essays appeared in volumes 1, 21, and 26. He is a past president of the Dickens Society.

DAVID PARKER taught for the University of Sheffield, the University of Malaya, and Britain's distance-learning Open University and then served for over twenty years as the Curator of London's Dickens House Museum. After his retirement from the Museum, he was made an Honorary Research Fellow at Kingston University, London. In addition to publishing many articles on Dickens and other literary topics, he wrote *The Doughty Street Novels: Pickwick Papers, Oliver Twist, Nicholas Nickleby, Barnaby Rudge* (2002) and *Christmas and Charles Dickens* (2005). At the time of his death in February 2013, he was working on another book, to be called "*Pickwick* and Reform."

CAROLINE REITZ is an associate professor of English at John Jay College of Criminal Justice and the Graduate Center, CUNY. She is the author of *Detecting the Nation: Fictions of Detection and the Imperial Venture* (2004) as well as articles on Carlyle and Mill, Victorian literature of empire, Dickens, and contemporary female detective fiction. She is currently at work on a manuscript about fiction serialized in Dickens's journals and its imagination of national identity.

DIANNE F. SADOFF is a professor of English at Rutgers University, New Brunswick. She has published *Victorian Vogue, Representing Body and Subject in Psychoanalysis*, and *Monsters of Affection*. She also co-edited *Victorian Afterlife* and *Teaching Contemporary Theory to Undergraduates*. Her current project, "Beyond Waterloo: Pre-Histories of the Victorian Novel," examines the emergence of the Victorian novel from earlier nineteenth-century popular fictional modes.

ZACHARY SAMALIN is an assistant professor of English at the University of Chicago, where he specializes in Victorian literature. He is currently at work on a book manuscript, "The Masses Are Revolting," exploring the interrelation of disgust and aesthetics in various areas of Victorian culture, such as obscenity law, gastric medicine, slum tourism, and sanitary reform.

TIMOTHY SPURGIN is Associate Professor of English and the Bonnie Glidden Buchanan Professor of English Literature at Lawrence University. His writing has appeared in *The Chronicle Review* as well as *Dickens Quarterly* and *Dickens Studies Annual*. He has also recorded two series of lectures, *The English Novel* and *The Art of Reading*, for the Teaching Company.

ALEKSANDAR STEVIĆ is a junior research fellow in Literary Studies at King's College, Cambridge (UK). He received his Ph.D. in Comparative Literature from Yale University in 2012. His research focuses primarily on the French and English nineteenth- and twentieth-century novel and its links to intellectual and social history. Stević is currently completing a book on the history of the European bildungsroman, focusing on the work of Stendhal, Honoré de Balzac, Charles Dickens, Charlotte Brontë, James Joyce, and Marcel Proust, among others.

Pickwick and Reform: Origins

David Parker

Note: David Parker, at the time of his death in February 2013, was working on a book entitled "*Pickwick* and Reform" and had completed the initial chapter, which is presented here. The claims made in this essay were, of course, to be given further substantiation in future chapters.
—The Editors

While writing The Pickwick Papers, *Dickens seemed to be striving to compose just a captivating narrative, and in his 1837 preface to the first edition he refers to the book as "a mere series of adventures." In 1847, however, when* Pickwick *was included in a Cheap Edition of Dickens's works, he provided a new preface that considered the need for reform and proposed that fiction is vindicated by its promotion of "important social improvements." This change in attitude should not surprise us, since the period between the 1780s and the middle of Victoria's reign has been and still is regarded as an era in which reform of institutions, laws, customs, and morals was a primary issue. Moreover, despite the earlier preface's disavowal of serious intent, giving keen attention to "social improvements" was instinctive to Dickens, and* Pickwick *reveals not just denunciation of legal chicanery and abuses like those in parliamentary elections, but a central concern with reform. Although the supposedly contingent origins of* Pickwick *may distract readers from recognizing Dickens's interest in reform issues, the idea of jokes about the attempts of Cockneys—town-bred members of the middle class—to be sportsmen was historically related to challenges to privileges enjoyed by the landowning classes. The Pickwickians, in their adventures, are middle-class townspeople questioning these privileges.*

1.

ORIGINS

Something must be admitted from the start. During 1836 and 1837, while he was writing the monthly parts of the book, Charles Dickens was striving to make *The Pickwick Papers* nothing more than a captivating narrative. In the preface to the first edition, probably written in October 1837 when he was working on the final double number, he declared a simple intention, inviting judgment equally simple: "The author's object in this work, was to place before the reader a constant succession of characters and incidents; to paint them in as vivid colours as he could command; and to render them, at the same time, life-like and amusing." He was content for the book to be looked upon as "a mere series of adventures, in which the scenes are ever changing, and the characters come and go like the men and women we encounter in the real world" (*Pickwick* xcix).

Many a critic has taken Dickens at his word. That founding father of modern Dickens criticism, Edmund Wilson, insisted on seeing the early novels, *Pickwick* among them, each as "more or less picaresque and, correspondingly, more or less of an improvisation" (17). No organizing principle is to be sought, he advised. Alternative views have been proposed, to be sure, but Grahame Smith is not alone among the current generation of critics in wondering whether *Pickwick* can be accorded the status of a novel, featuring as it does too many "elements in excess of those required for the work's inner aims" (179). A loosely constructed narrative, that is to say, rather than a book addressing anything in particular.

In 1847, however, ten years after the last of the original monthly numbers of *Pickwick* went on sale, publishers Chapman and Hall launched a Cheap Edition of Dickens's works, starting with *Pickwick*. A new preface by the author concluded with a passage reviewing reforms of what he held to be amiss in the life of the nation—reforms effected since the novel had first appeared, and reforms yet to be achieved:

> I have found it curious and interesting, looking over the sheets of this reprint, to mark what important social improvements have taken place about us, almost imperceptibly, even since they were originally written. The license of Counsel, and the degree to which Juries are ingeniously bewildered, are yet susceptible of moderation; while an improvement in the mode of conducting Parliamentary Elections (especially for counties) is still within the bounds of possibility. But legal reforms have pared the claws of Messrs. Dodson and Fogg; a spirit of self-respect, mutual forbearance, education, and co-operation for such good ends, has diffused itself among their clerks; places far apart are brought together, to the present convenience and advantage of the Public, and to the certain destruction, in time, of a host of petty jealousies,

blindnesses, and prejudices, by which the Public alone have always been the sufferers; the laws relating to imprisonment for debt are altered; and the Fleet Prison is pulled down!

With such a retrospect, extending through so short a period, I shall cherish the hope that every volume of this Edition will afford me an opportunity of recording the extermination of some wrong or abuse set forth in it. Who knows, but by the time the series reaches its conclusion, it may be discovered that there are even magistrates in town and country, who should be taught to shake hands every day with Common-sense and Justice; that even Poor Laws may have mercy on the weak, the aged, and unfortunate; that Schools, on the broad principles of Christianity, are the best adornment for the length and breadth of this civilised land; that Prison-doors should be barred on the outside, no less heavily and carefully than they are barred within; that the universal diffusion of common means of decency and health is as much the right of the poorest of the poor, as it is indispensable to the safety of the rich, and of the State; that a few petty boards and bodies—less than drops in the great ocean of humanity, which roars around them—are not for ever to let loose Fever and Consumption on God's creatures at their will, or always to keep their little fiddles going, for a Dance of Death.

And that Cheap Literature is not behind-hand with the Age, but holds its place, and strives to do its duty, I trust the series in itself may help much worthy company to show.

With a few slight modifications, this passage—or most of it—was preserved in emended prefaces that Dickens supplied for the Library Edition of *Pickwick*, published in 1858, and for the Charles Dickens Edition, published in 1867 only three years before his death (*Pickwick* 887–88).

The burden of the passage is unmistakable, and not easily reconciled with the 1837 preface. Ten years later Dickens was allowing himself to suppose that fiction—not excluding *Pickwick*—is vindicated by its ushering in of "important social improvements," and that "Cheap Literature" does its duty by promoting such improvements. This is a view he never disowned.

It is unwise to trust Dickens's prefaces too much. Scrutinize them and you can see that, from time to time, the gaining of an immediate objective overrode other considerations (Parker passim). It is tempting, therefore, to suppose the shift of emphasis between 1837 and 1847 might be a result of Dickens's projecting more upon *Pickwick* than, strictly speaking, is to be found in it. As a writer and as a man, he had, we cannot but reflect, changed during the ten years which had elapsed since the completion of the first edition. It is scarcely surprising that, in 1847, the author of *A Christmas Carol* (1843) should be ready to think of himself as a campaigner for reform. It is scarcely surprising that the author already at work on *Dombey and Son* (1846–48) should be ready to think of himself as a literary craftsman carefully focusing his work.

It is least surprising that, by the 1840s, a writer of Dickens's generation should think the improvement of institutions, laws, customs, and morals a primary objective of his work, and go on thinking so for the rest of his life. Many early Victorian writers saw themselves as reformers, and were right—the best of them—to do so. They knew that the impulse to reform had arisen among an earlier generation, but they made it their own, and often made its promotion a central theme of their work in a way their predecessors rarely had. We could, to be sure, allow ourselves to see the 1847 preface as Dickens impressing a Victorian stamp of approval upon a text begun and nearly finished before Victoria ascended the throne. A freewheeling yarn in the Regency tradition it might be, we can suppose him to be suggesting—a "mere series of adventures"—but for all that a yarn instrumental in promoting "important social improvements." We cannot, however, dismiss out of hand the hypothesis that he was saying something more.

The promotion of "important social improvements" was certainly a task Dickens's generation set itself. We cannot deny that, between the 1780s and the middle of Victoria's reign, reform was an endeavor that dominated public life and imbued many a private life. The late Georgian and early Victorian understanding of this issue has been recognized and reaffirmed again and again by historians of succeeding generations. Published in 1938, the volume of *The Oxford History of England* covering the years 1815 to 1870, written by Sir Llewellyn Woodward, is entitled *The Age of Reform*. One of the most influential post-war studies of the era was published in 1959. Asa Briggs called his book *The Age of Improvement: 1783–1867*. After nearly half a century, the field was reviewed in a collection of essays published in 2003. Editors Arthur Burns and Joanna Innes called it *Rethinking the Age of Reform: Britain 1780–1850*. Primary source material needed to be looked at more carefully, they urged, information uncovered by research needed to be considered, detail needed correction, but Woodward's and Briggs's understanding of the era, as one in which reform was the central issue, remained substantially unchallenged.

My contention is that, for all his disavowal of an overview in 1837, Dickens, whether or not he articulated it to himself, saw what Woodward and Briggs invite us to see and made it manifest in *Pickwick*. The "mere series of adventures" was what he set out deliberately to contrive, but keen attention to "important social improvements" was something instinctive to him, as a man of his generation. Equipped with an amalgamating and synthesizing imagination, he was, moreover, no ordinary man of his generation, and this attention organized itself systematically, thanks to processes upon which, at the time, Dickens did not dwell. By 1847, however, responding to a shift in national mood, he began clearly to see more of what he had been doing ten years previously.

He had not simply dotted his text with fashionable grumbles, or with denunciation of abuses of which he had personal experience. No reader can, of course, miss the exposure in *Pickwick* of such matters as "the license of Counsel" (ch. 34), the "mode of conducting Parliamentary Elections" (ch. 13), the sharp practice of

attorneys such as Dodson and Fogg (chs. 20, 26, 34, 53), and the cruelty of the
"laws relating to imprisonment for debt" (chs. 21, 41–47). But we can minimize
the import of all this, if we choose, by noting how hectic and absorbing the "series
of adventures" is, and attributing the exposure to whims of no more moment than,
say, the topographical whims which persuaded the author to take the Pickwickians to Rochester or to Bath. Yet this, I believe, would be to neglect the intricacy
of Dickens's achievement. The reform he dwelled upon in the 1847 preface, I
intend to show, is central to the meaning of *Pickwick*, however much Dickens
neglected to speak of it in 1837.

His engagement with the Reform movement was all but inevitable (campaigners
for parliamentary reform capitalized the first letter of the word when using it to
denote their project, a practice I shall follow where it seems appropriate). In the
milieu in which he grew up, parliamentary reform was the political issue of the
day. Another great issue, the campaign for the repeal of the Corn Laws, agitated
the poor, proponents of free trade, and opponents of the landed interest, but among
members of the middle classes the predominant yearning was for their collective
voice to be heard and heeded. Grandson of domestic servants, son of a minor civil
servant turned journalist, Dickens was one of those seeking the suffrage through
constitutional reform. For him and for his father, moreover, the issue would have
been sharpened by parliamentary debates about Reform which began in 1831, a
year before the passing of the Reform Act of 1832, and continued afterwards as
Reformers struggled to see its provisions implemented. Father and son reported
these debates in the *Mirror of Parliament* and the *True Sun* (*Letters* 1: 2n, 10n).

Nor should we overlook a fact likely to have motivated Dickens, although he
never mentions it, perhaps anxious to hide origins he was not keen to admit. Until
he reached the age of twenty, he would have seen no sure prospect of voting
in parliamentary elections himself. At that age, when the 1832 act was finally
passed, he would have seen that he might one day do so after all. When in 1834 he
took chambers in Furnival's Inn, Holborn, at an annual rent of £35, he acquired
the new right to vote enjoyed by all borough householders paying £10 or more in
rent (*Letters* 1: 48n). His first opportunity to exercise that right would have been
in the general election at the beginning of 1835, scarcely more than a year before
Pickwick was launched.

Dickens was no root-and-branch democrat. The extension of the franchise in
the 1832 act evidently satisfied him, although the electorate was increased from
435,000 to no more than 652,000. The 1847 preface looks hopefully toward an
administrative "improvement in the mode of conducting Parliamentary Elections," but makes no complaint about the meager extension of the franchise in
1832. Further Reform legislation would be required in 1867 and 1884, plus a
series of Representation of the People Acts in the twentieth century, before universal adult suffrage was achieved, but that was something Dickens never sought.

He cautiously welcomed the 1867 act, which extended the franchise to about a third of adult males, only because most of them would be members of the middle class, who "will in the main be wiser as to their electoral responsibilities, and more seriously desirous to discharge them for the common good" than the mass of voters demanded by noisy populists (*Letters* 12: 172). It was the enfranchisement of middle-class men that he sought, something achieved, so far as he personally was concerned, in 1832. No reader of the works can miss his passion for treating the poor with sympathy, understanding, justice, and generosity, his indignation at failure so to do, but he never thought they should be given the vote. Their lot was to be improved by the intervention of responsible propertied voters, middle-class men not least.

Those eager to see Dickens as our contemporary in all but date—as a man espousing today's values—will resist accepting this or, if they do, be disappointed. But those who value Burkean incremental progress will applaud Dickens's cautious quest for improvement. If our views on the franchise differ from his, moreover, we can at least recognize his broader advocacy. From 1834, when he joined the staff of the *Morning Chronicle*, the leading Whig daily, Dickens became part of a team campaigning for all the other reformist measures that followed in the train of the 1832 act (Slater 36, 42). He was still reporting for the *Chronicle* when *Pickwick* was launched.

Students of *Pickwick* are discouraged from speculation about depth of purpose or meaning in the novel by what appears to be its contingent origin. My contention, however, is that its origin was less contingent than it seems in a twenty-first-century retrospect, and that it beckoned Dickens into a closer engagement with the reform movement. This is Dickens's account of the book's origin in the 1847 preface. In February 1836, he says, William Hall of Chapman and Hall put to him proposals for contributions to a "monthly something":

> The idea propounded to me was that the monthly something should be a vehicle for certain plates to be executed by Mr. Seymour, and there was a notion, either on the part of that admirable humorous artist, or of my visitor (I forget which), that a "Nimrod Club," the members of which were to go out shooting, fishing, and so forth, and getting themselves into difficulties through their want of dexterity, would be the best means of introducing these. I objected, on consideration, that although born and partly bred in the country, I was no great sportsman, except in regards of all kinds of locomotion; that the idea was not novel, and had already been much used, that it would be infinitely better for the plates to arise naturally out of the text; and that I should like to take my own way, with a freer range of English scenes and people, and was afraid I should ultimately do so in any case, whatever course I might prescribe to myself in starting. My views being

deferred to, I thought of Mr. Pickwick, and wrote the first number. (*Pickwick* 884–85).

The notion was Seymour's, not Hall's, as Dickens knew perfectly well (Parker 69, 71). Robert Seymour (1798–1836) was a successful graphic artist and illustrator, whom the less than venerable house of Chapman and Hall (founded in 1830) would have been pleased to publish. But, for all Seymour's eminence, the twenty-four-year-old Dickens was shrewd to question the marketability of a "Nimrod Club." For years, writers and print-makers, Seymour among them, had been poking fun at the misadventures of Cockney sportsmen—town-bred members of the middle classes—that is to say, trying their hand at country sports and muffing them. Poking more such fun was, by itself, never going to electrify the reading public. And Dickens's insistence that the text should lead was surely right. It would have been difficult to cobble together a story meeting the standards for such things that Dickens had already set himself, in response to a series of etchings made according to the artist's whim, without any notion of narrative sequence. Dickens's counter-proposal made commercial sense especially. It should have been welcomed, and there is no persuasive evidence that it was not. The freer range of English scenes and people he proposed, moreover, would enable him to exploit talents for which he was known, talents which he had been cultivating in the pieces that make up *Sketches by Boz*.

From the perspective of 1847 there could be no doubt. Dickens had taken his own way, triumphantly. His thinking of Mr. Pickwick had been a momentous event in the history of English literature. Sadly and shockingly, any tension there might have been between Dickens and Seymour, for all practical purposes, ceased to matter within weeks of the serial being launched. The illustrator committed suicide while working on the plates for the second monthly number. Dickens thereafter was dominant.

This is not to say, though, that Seymour left little or no mark on *Pickwick*. He left more of a mark, indeed, than Dickens chose later to acknowledge (Dexter and Ley passim; *Pickwick* xxii–xxix). We can see why this should have been so when we ask quite what it was that Dickens was being invited to participate in by Seymour's proposal, and by Chapman and Hall's initial endorsement of it. Seymour's plan, to poke yet more fun at Cockney sportsmen, was not just to exploit a joke hit upon randomly by its era, which ran the course such jokes do, and which was finally dropped when everyone got bored with it. It was a joke with a special significance for the era of Reform, and synchronized with it. It was a joke which may be said to represent that era. Seymour had made his name, it is worth remembering, not just by representing the misadventures of Cockney sportsmen, which indeed he had done to acclaim, in a series of little volumes from 1834, collected after his death in various larger volumes with such titles as *Sketches by Seymour*. He was also known for the political caricatures he had published, from 1830, in the *Looking Glass* and *Figaro in London*. And he had dwelled specifically upon

Reform in illustrations he had contributed to the 1832 comic poem, *The Triumph of Reform*, by W. T. Moncrieff. Cockney sportsmen jokes and agitation for parliamentary Reform were in fact complementary. Both had to do with privilege that went with land ownership, and with challenge to such privilege.

Perhaps so, it is tempting to say, but surely the point is how ineffectual the challenge from Cockney sportsmen was. Should not the genre be seen as a counterblast on behalf of the landowning classes? Think of Gillray's cartoons as well as Seymour's. We are shown Cockneys falling off horses, shooting badly and dangerously, getting into every kind of pickle on the riverbank. Was this not a way of insisting that the middle classes were unfit to be granted the privileges of the gentry and aristocracy? The landowning classes could certainly respond to the genre in this way. However, judging by its popularity and longevity, they were not its only consumers. Its nature and reception were in fact much more complicated. To begin with, without the mishaps of the Cockneys, there would have been no genre. The representation of Cockneys taking up hunting, shooting, and fishing, and simply doing well at them, would not have borne much repetition. No, the genre was an iconic configuration of social change, a meeting place at which all sorts of ambitions, prejudices, and anxieties converged and coexisted. Writers and print-makers could adapt it to their own sentiments. Enjoyers of the genre were likely to respond to the whole package, with individuals picking out details that suited them. Those against Reform could rejoice at spectacles of middle-class ineptitude. Those passionate for it could rejoice at spectacles of middle-class men undaunted by error as they seized new privileges. Those more cautiously for it could rejoice at spectacles of the incautious and precipitate coming to grief. And shifts in the public mood could be accommodated.

The genre, then, was based upon more than the supposition that townies can never shoot straight. The permutations of comic misadventure were so few, and the return to the theme so persistent, that we must suppose a deeper meaning attracted consumers of both text and print. It is to be detected in *Pickwick,* notwithstanding Dickens's refusal to confine himself to sporting mishap. Seymour (son of a cabinet-maker) and Dickens were both middle-class, both upwardly mobile within their class. Both sought audiences among the middle classes, and found them. Social mobility was their theme, something the Cockney sportsmen genre represented metonymically, something *Pickwick* represented synoptically.

To see how all this might be, it is necessary to remind ourselves of the development of the Reform movement. From the eighteenth century onwards, there were idealistic democrats demanding adult male suffrage—or adult suffrage *tout court*—because they could conceive of no other system so just. But the agitation for parliamentary reform was, for the most part, more modest and pragmatic. The stranglehold of the landowning gentry and aristocracy upon political power, through their domination of constituencies, was widely deemed inexpedient and archaic. The interests of the nation would be served, it was felt, as well as the interests of the newly enfranchised, if political power were shared with those to whom so much economic power was passing—the middle classes, whose wealth lay chiefly in things other than land ownership. And it was this, for all its limitations, that the 1832 Reform Act achieved. Votes were conferred upon propertied male adults. The industrial centers of the Midlands and the North were given a voice. The aristocracy and the gentry continued to dominate Parliament, to be sure, but were required to share power, and lost their stranglehold.

With some preliminary anticipation in the 1770s of what was to come, it was in the early 1780s that a multiplicity of groups and individuals began to lobby for parliamentary reform, in a campaign that was eventually to culminate in the 1832 act. In 1780, led by Christopher Wyvill, the Association movement took shape in London and the provinces, lobbying for constitutional reform. The Society for Constitutional Information was founded the same year. It sponsored an inquiry into the inequities of parliamentary representation, and it would eventually take the lead in the Radical movement, loudest of all groups in demanding Reform. William Pitt the Younger entered parliament in 1781. By the following year he was raising the matter of parliamentary reform in the House, and speaking at meetings of enthusiasts for Reform. As prime minister, in 1785, he proposed a reform bill which the House, needless to say, rejected. Pitt sought no more than reform of the conduct of elections, a gradual reduction in the number of rotten boroughs, and the creation of more county seats. But others sought more. John Cartwright, for instance, prominent in the Society for Constitutional Information, wanted universal manhood suffrage and the secret ballot (Mori 21–22).

It was more than a disinterested passion for justice that motivated Wyvill, Pitt, Cartwright, and the many others beginning to speak of Reform. The attention being paid to rotten boroughs, and to their cousins the pocket boroughs, indicates a growing awareness of something constitutionally amiss and in need of repair, and an awareness, too, that the old hegemony of the landed interest, conveniently served by such anomalies, might justly be challenged by rival interests

By the 1780s, economic change—creating new wealth, and new concentrations of wealth—was beginning to make the persistence of such boroughs, and the limitations of the franchise, ever more deplorable. The "industrial revolution" was not to emerge as a popular term before the 1840s, but what it signifies began to develop in the eighteenth century and escalated during its last two decades. The mechanization of the textile industry was boosted by successful challenges to Richard Arkwright's patents in 1781 and 1785, which made way for yet more mills to be added to those which had been proliferating in the north ever since the 1730s. Henry Cort's new combined puddling and rolling process, using coal as fuel and patented in 1784, made way for the production of wrought iron in the coalfields on an ever larger scale. Steam engines produced by James Watt and Matthew Boulton had, since 1776, begun to replace the notoriously inefficient Newcomen engines. In 1782 Watt patented his "sun and planet motion" design for steam engines, opening the way for rotary engines to supply power in factories.

As the evidence suggests, from 1782 on, industrial output surged (Ashton 125), thanks to these new technological developments. Improvements to the transport system were making it easier to convey raw materials and manufactured goods around the country, as well as to and from seaports. A network of turnpike roads linked most centers of population in England and Wales by the 1780s, and canals, constructed piecemeal since the middle years of the century, were beginning to cohere into a system. The opening of the Grand Trunk Canal in 1777, linking the Trent and the Mersey, had been a significant step towards the creation of what James Brindley, designer of the canal, called the "Cross," a web of navigable waterways centered upon Birmingham, and linking the four major ports of England: Liverpool, Hull, Bristol, and London. More than a hundred country banks were supplying manufacturers with the circulating capital they needed to take advantage of new technology.

In towns and cities transformed and expanded by the surge in economic activity—even in unincorporated boroughs denied parliamentary representation—a new mood of self-confidence arose among successful manufacturers, merchants, retailers, and professional men. The *Morning Herald and Daily Advertiser* of 1 February 1782 spoke of "the amazing wealth, industry, and prosperity of Sheffield, Birmingham, and Manchester, and other places that are governed by no higher officer than a constable." It was in Birmingham, around 1775, that the Lunar Society began to meet, including among its members Boulton and Watt, scientists Erasmus Darwin and Joseph Priestley, and Josiah Wedgewood, the pottery manufacturer—all of them fizzing with ideas, all as prone to political speculation as to scientific or technological. The Manchester Literary and Philosophical Society was founded in 1781 by Thomas Percival, physician, and Charles White, surgeon. Most of the original members were physicians, surgeons, or apothecaries, but, as the name of the society suggests, they were as eager to investigate every kind of topic as the more varied membership that succeeded them, and public affairs were not least among their concerns.

The struggle of middle-class men to enjoy country sports, in comic representations of Cockney sportsmen, mirrored the struggle of middle-class men, before 1832, to acquire political power and take their place at the nation's top table. There were exceptions and anomalies, but only gentlefolk found it easy to hunt and to shoot—even to fish—at the end of the eighteenth century and beginning of the nineteenth.

Formally, game laws had long banned virtually everyone but landowners from the enjoyment of shooting. Social standing and property qualifications determined the legal right to kill game. Since 1671, it had been granted only to possessors of real estate worth at least £100 a year, and to the eldest sons of such land-

Pickwick *and Reform* 11

owners. There were successful merchants and manufacturers, of course, who had bought estates and become landowners, and an elaborate process of "deputation," designed chiefly for gamekeepers, made it possible to get round the law, given determination. Nor would it have been easy to enforce the law on private land, and common land was not always strictly policed. But while exceptions and evasions made a marginal difference, they did nothing to reduce a sense of injustice.

Bizarrely, not only stag-hunting but also fox-hunting was subject to similar prohibitions, eagerly defended by spokesmen for the landowning classes. In 1799, the chief justice, Lord Kenyon, defended sporting privilege in court. Delight in fox-hunting and shooting, he said, induced gentlemen to live in the country, "and the consequence is, that their fortunes are spent in the country, and the manners of the people improved." Abolition of the game laws would result in "idleness in the lower classes of society," who would be tempted "to squander away their time which ought to be spent in their proper employments and callings" ("Law Report," *Times*, 23 April 1799). Packs of hounds, moreover, were almost all maintained, at considerable expense, by great landowners, who invited their social equals to join them on the field, and perhaps some tenants, but rarely city-bred members of the middle classes. Fifteen of the most successful packs in 1788 are identified in a *Times* report. The list begins with the packs of the dukes of Grafton and Beaufort, runs through twelve others maintained by magnates, and concludes with a single Hampshire subscription pack (*Times*, 8 January 1788).

Fishing was less beset by prohibition. No game laws regulated it and, from early in the nineteenth century, angling clubs proliferated. Yet their activities were being squeezed. Negotiating permission to fish was becoming more difficult. The public had no right to fish in non-tidal waters. Rights generally belonged to owners of the land bordering the water. The enclosure of common land—rapid during the second half of the eighteenth century and the opening decades of the nineteenth—took away common rights along many a stretch of water and reserved them for landowners.

The history of jokes about Cockney sportsmen is strikingly synchronized with the history of the Reform movement. The word "Cockney" had been used as an abusive term for townsfolk since the sixteenth century (*OED*), but depictions of such townsfolk making fools of themselves in country pursuits suddenly began to appear almost at the moment the demand for Reform began to be heard. The genre probably first found its way into print in an anonymous engraving, published in 1779 by Edward Hedges and Thomas Colley. Called *A Cockney at a Fox Hunt*, it depicts the fat Cockney tumbling from his horse after it has taken a fence.

But a text was probably more influential than this print—a text parallel to the genre, if not strictly belonging to it. William Cowper's comic ballad of 1782, "The Diverting History of John Gilpin," was one of those publications which manifested their hold on the public imagination with a rash of piracies, plagiarisms, and souvenirs. The poem first appeared anonymously in the *Public Advertiser,* was reproduced widely in chapbook and broadside form, and was not acknowledged as Cowper's work until he appended it to *The Task* in 1785.

It is a parody of a heroic ballad, not about country sports, but telling the story of a London shopkeeper, who agrees to his wife's proposal that they celebrate their wedding anniversary at the Bell in Edmonton. Mrs. Gilpin and other members of the family travel in a chaise, her husband on a borrowed horse. But the horse bolts, taking John Gilpin ten miles beyond Edmonton to Ware, and then back again to London, stopping neither on the way out nor on the way back. John Gilpin's means of locomotion, as Dickens might have put it, is not adopted for the purposes of sport. But he is a linen-draper, he chooses to travel as a landowning gentleman might, and that is his undoing. The subject matter, the manner, and the popularity of the poem all invite us to consider it in conjunction with the Cockney sportsmen genre.

And in 1782, when "John Gilpin" was first published, the nation was in the midst of that surge of economic, social, and intellectual activity that declared the entry of the middle classes as principal actors on the national stage. Can we suppose this was unconnected with loud and prolonged applause for a story of a city-bred shopkeeper discomfited by an unsuccessful effort to emulate the landowning classes?

"John Gilpin" opens with a mock-encomium of its hero:

> John Gilpin was a citizen
>   Of credit and renown,
> A train-band captain eke was he
>   Of famous London town.
>   (Cowper 9: 303)

But his middle-class status is made clear. He is a linen-draper, and the friend from whom he borrows the horse is a calendar—a tradesman, that is to say, who processes cloth by passing it between rollers. Values ascribed to the middle class insistently appear. John is pleased with his wife's proposal that they take their own wine to Edmonton: "though on pleasure she was bent, / She had a frugal mind." She fixes for the family to climb into the hired chaise, not at their own door, but three doors off—"lest all / Should say that she was proud" (Cowper 9: 304). John delays his departure on the expedition, and climbs down from his horse, because customers arrive just as he is about to set off:

> So down he came; for loss of time,
>   Although it grieved him sore,
> Yet loss of pence, full well he knew.
>   Would trouble him much more.
>   (Cowper 9: 305)

His failure to control his horse is pointedly emphasized by "Six gentlemen upon the road" who see in his mad career a bid to escape, and who raise a "hue and cry":

> Stop thief! Stop thief!—a highwayman!
> Not one of them was mute;
> And all and each that pass'd that way
> Did join in the pursuit.
>
> (Cowper 9: 311)

Nor is it just the content of the poem that calls for it to be seen as a sign of national change. It was offered to the *Public Advertiser*, not by Cowper himself, but by the son of Mrs. Unwin, his companion for many years. The retiring and self-effacing poet would scarcely have been so bold, but William Unwin's initiative helped the poem achieve the iconic status it did. Under the direction of Henry Samson Woodfall, the *Advertiser* had become famous for fearless and incisive commentary upon current affairs (*ODNB*). As early as 1760, a correspondent had spoken of trade giving "a new face to the whole nation," and had decried the absurdity of supposing "that so great a change as this in the people should produce no change in the Constitution" (Briggs 12–13). Between 1769 and 1772, the *Advertiser* had diverted readers with the pseudonymous Junius letters, denouncing the mighty while extolling democratic elections, freedom of the press, and the constitutional rights of the subject. Many suspect that Sir Philip Francis (1740–1818) was the author (*ODNB*). Cowper may have been startled by the success of a poem originating in childhood memories of his friend Lady Austen, but by appearing when it did and where it did, it both seized and shaped the public imagination.

"John Gilpin" has been declared the most popular poem of the 1780s (*ODNB*). And its popularity was undoubtedly intensified when, in 1785, the acclaimed actor John Henderson began to recite it at well-attended public readings in the Freemasons' Hall in London. This alone indicates that it was perceived as something more than a counter-blast against middle-class pretension on behalf of the landed interest. Though Cowper laughs at his protagonist, he is never harsh towards him. The animating spirit of the poem is glee at incongruity. We must suppose many of the poem's admirers were to be found among middle-class town-dwellers. Some must have shared John Gilpin's hunger for privilege rarely enjoyed by the middle classes, but all the same enjoyed the spectacle of his discomfiture. The poem is above all an oblique commentary upon a moment of change, inviting a broad range of disparate responses.

It was well that "John Gilpin" provided a model for oblique commentary, something that would be needed in the decades ahead. The American War of Independence (1776–83) put in power statesmen not in principle unsympathetic to

Reform, such as Rockingham, Shelburne, Fox, and—in the 1780s—Pitt. And in 1789 the French Revolution, greeted in Britain with applause as well as misgiving, inspired the foundation across the country of yet more clubs dedicated to Reform, in addition to a good many already thriving. Thomas Paine's tract *The Rights of Man* (1791–92) sold in huge numbers, unaffected by the charge of treason brought against him, or by his flight to France.

But the French Revolutionary Wars (1793–1802), and the Napoleonic Wars that followed them (1803–15), forced the Reform movement onto the defensive, and rendered it impotent. Events in France such as the September Massacres of 1792 prompted opponents of Reform to organize even before war was declared. The execution of Louis XVI and his queen (1793), and the Terror (1793–94), must have seemed confirmation of their judgment. Whatever else they were—and they were indeed a good deal else—the French Revolution and its aftermath comprised a violent wresting of power from the landowning classes, consequences swiftly barbarous, and the eventual passing of power to the bourgeoisie: a precedent the constitutional Reformers of Britain would not have wished to boast about.

Reaction to the revolution came swiftly. Founded in London in November 1792, the Association for Preserving Liberty and Property against Republicans and Levellers spawned similar societies in the provinces. Mobs in Birmingham and Manchester attacked the houses and chapels of Reforming Dissenters. Upon the declaration of war in 1793, a newly cautious Pitt ordered that the militia be made ready to combat domestic insurrection. Habeas corpus was suspended in 1794, and prominent radicals were charged with treason (although subsequently acquitted). In 1795 Pitt was able to pass what became known as the Two Acts, against treasonable speech or writing, and unlicensed public assemblies. The registration of printing presses was to follow, as well as acts against "unlawful Combinations and Confederacies." *The Age of Reason,* published by Paine in 1795, met with a very different reception from *The Rights of Man.* It was banned and burned. Paine's assault on Christian doctrine, indeed, prompted Durham miners to burn an effigy of the man himself. At the beginning of the wars, democratic politics fell victim as much to popular patriotism, as to anti-Jacobin repression organized by the government. Many who had once rejoiced at the French Revolution, such as Wordsworth and Coleridge, now began to deplore it.

The wars, moreover, re-tilted the balance of economic power. The landed interest grew richer and more self-confident, thanks to the dearth of corn imports from Europe, and to protection of the domestic product by tariffs. Merchants and manufacturers profited from the demand generated by a wartime economy, but suffered as a result of the loss of European markets.

From the early 1790s, open espousal of the cause of Reform became more risky. In January 1793 the antiquary Joseph Ritson—exaggerating if at all only slightly—tartly declared that he found it "prudent to say as little as possible upon political subjects, in order to keep myself out of Newgate" (Ritson 2: 7). The Two Acts of 1795 made it difficult for radical societies to campaign as once they had.

The case for Reform, however, remained as strong as ever. Something was amiss with the constitution and the franchise. If social cohesion was to be preserved, the aristocracy and the gentry needed to acknowledge that ownership of land could not be for much longer the primary qualification for political influence. With the middle classes largely silenced, open agitation for Reform was eventually taken over by the laboring classes, afflicted by low wages and high prices, and having little to lose. The mob took to the streets of London in 1810, when radical MP Sir Francis Burdett and radical author John Gale Jones were jailed. Three months before Waterloo, there were again riots in London—against the Corn Laws designed to protect the landed interest. Alas, working-class championship of Reform was rewarded neither by the Reform Act of 1832, nor by any other measure of the *Pickwick* era.

Middle-class yearning for Reform, however, even when deplored, could still be expressed through oblique commentary, and the Cockney sportsmen joke supplied the ideal vehicle for this. Writers and print-makers could spin their material whichever way they wished. Laughter could be substituted for open political commitment.

Graphic versions of the joke were more prominent and led the way. "John Gilpin" spawned a graphic tradition before it found textual imitators. Early chapbook and broadside editions were often embellished with crude woodcuts. A print entitled "Gilpin Going Farther than He Intended" appeared in *The Wit's Magazine* of July 1784. And a collection of six engravings illustrating the poem was published by Carington Bowles in London in 1785.

But the surge in such publications came after the Revolution of 1789, more particularly after the repressive measures enacted by the British government during the 1790s. *London Sportsmen, or The Cockney's Journal of the First of September,* was a series of engravings published as early as 1790. The tradition took hold of the public imagination, however, when Hannah Humphrey published a collection of four prints by James Gillray in 1800, entitled "Cockney-sportsmen marking game," "Cockney-sportsmen shooting flying," "Cockney-sportsmen recharging," and "Cockney-sportsmen finding a hare." *Cockneys Contemplating on the Exploits of the Day,* possibly by Charles Ansell, was another series of prints published in 1800. *The Cockney in a Slough* is a print published by Laurie and Whittle in 1804. A print by Henry Bunbury, *The City Hunt,* has been dated to 1810.

The textual tradition arose more hesitantly, and in periodicals prone to express the values of the landowning classes. Until the end of the Napoleonic Wars in 1815, it was customary for examples of the genre only to deride Cockney sportsmen, although, by featuring them repeatedly, they established such figures—unwittingly no doubt—as icons of social change. In the *Times* of 2 September 1789, for instance, we find a letter marking the opening of the partridge-shooting season, purportedly written by Watty Cockney, a character from Isaac Bicker-staff's comic opera of 1767, *Love in the City*. About a shooting expedition made by Watty and his City friends to the south-western fringes of London, the letter reports much ineffectual blazing away at chickens, cats, crows, pigs, and spar-rows, the killing of one of their own dogs, and the consumption of much alcohol. Published just as the French Revolution was declaring itself, the letter closes with a curious indication of the anxiety about undisguised public debate, which would precipitate the repressive measures of the next decade. Watty speaks of a dispute in the Cheshire Cheese tavern "concerning French Politicks"—a dispute, that is to say, about "whether or not, the present King of France ever had the tooth ach [sic]."

The *Times* of 3 September 1793, after war had started, likewise pokes fun gen-erally at "Cockney partridge shooting," with snippets about the shooting of spar-rows, donkeys, pigs, crows, and goats. A more elaborate piece in the *Times* of 2 September 1803 is entitled "A Cockney's Account of Yesterday." It tells of similar exploits but details humiliations too, such as the shooting of a scarecrow, the derision of onlookers, and the theft of their guns and dogs while the would-be sportsmen slept.

By 1805 the genre was finding its way into verse. Two poems in the *Gentle-man's Magazine* for that year ridicule Cockney country pursuits. "The Sports-man" tells of a Cockney who "went after game," but whose bag at the end of the day was found by the poet to contain cats, "And more, I must beg not to name." "The First of September" tells of two Cockneys out for sport, one distraught at having shot a cherub—only to be told it is an owl (*Gentleman's Magazine* 98: 845–46).

We can detect a change of mood, though, in Thomas Hood's poem *The Epping Hunt*, published in 1829 well after the end of the Napoleonic Wars. In the ballad tradition founded by "John Gilpin," it tells of the misadventures of a City grocer on a deer hunt, eventually thrown from his horse into gorse prickles, and obliged to remount upon an inferior nag. The mood change has much to do, doubtless, with Hood's genial imagination. Like Cowper, he was never one to carp ungener-ously. But the switch is not attributable just to the talent of a particular poet.

The occasion of the poem was one of those anomalies of which Cockney sports-men could take advantage. The Easter stag hunt in Epping Forest was a custom launched in 1226 by Henry III, who conferred upon citizens of London the right to hunt in the forests of Epping and Hainault. In the middle of the eighteenth century, the Lord Mayor evidently felt constrained to reassert this right. We read of him declaring that, "in Support of the Royal Charters granted to this City, he would hunt on Epping Forrest next Saturday" (*Daily Advertiser*, 5 April 1753). By 1785, though, Cockneys evidently dominated the occasion. "Not a horse was to be seen East of Temple-bar," we are told, "whose head was not turned towards Epping" (*London Chronicle*, 26 March 1785). And a report of 1828 speaks of "two or three thousand regular-bred cockneys" taking part (*North Wales Chronicle*, 17 April 1828).

In Hood's poem the sting of the genre is drawn not least by the delight in puns and other wordplay, for which he was justly famed. The glee at incongruity that marks "John Gilpin" is recovered. Fun is poked at the aspirations and poor horsemanship of John Huggins, the grocer, and of his fellow hunters, in verse drawing more attention to itself than to Cockney frailties. The assembled hunters include

> Butchers on backs of butchers' hacks,
>   That *shambled* to and fro!
> Bakers intent upon a buck,
>   Neglectful of the *dough*!
>
> Change Alley Bears to speculate,
>   As usual, for a fall;
> And green and scarlet runners, such
>   As never climbed a wall!
>   (Hood 2: 313)

The date of the poem goes some way towards explaining the recovery of equanimity. The national mood was changing, and the law was being revised. The Game Certificates Act of 1827 had begun the process of overturning land-ownership as the sole qualification for taking game. It made possible the purchase of an annual license for doing so, valid throughout England. Moderate Conservatives in Parliament, with William Huskisson and Robert Peel at their head, were seeking to change the die-hard image of the Tory Party by trimming the privileges of landowners and placating the middle classes. The provisions of the act would be extended by the Game Act of 1831, debated in parliament just a few weeks before the Lords rejected the 1831 Reform Bill. It was seen by many observers as part of the same historic process, in the way it finally abolished the monopoly of shooting enjoyed by large landowners. Possession of game was now vested in the owner of the land on which it was found, however small the holding. The principal mouthpiece of liberal Whig opinion applauded the way the Act hewed down "one of the greatest abominations in the country—the odious Game Code," and saw it as a blow to "the vilest remnant of the feudal ages" (*Morning Chronicle*, 21 October 1831). Country sports were opened up to anyone who could afford the license fee of three pounds, thirteen shillings, and sixpence, and get permission to shoot over any estate, however modest. The thrill of transgression that underpinned the Cockney sportsmen joke was thus abolished.

The 1832 Reform Act abolished its encrypted political meaning. *The Sporting Magazine*, founded in 1792, had long featured tales about the adventures and misadventures of fox-hunting gentlemen. But in 1831, a *New Sporting Magazine* was launched, addressed to all lovers of country sports. Between 1831 and 1834 it featured papers by R. S. Surtees—joint editor of the journal with Rudolph Ackermann—chronicling the exploits of Jorrocks, a fox-hunting London grocer. Jorrocks evolved into an iconic figure and won a following of readers at the moment of the triumph of Reform, during the year 1832 (Schachterle 8). Endowed with the passion, skill, and courage found among the best gentleman hunters, he lacks only their elegance of deportment and discourse. Such was popular interest that, in 1838, Surtees turned his papers into a book, *Jorrocks' Jaunts and Jollities.* In another, *Handley Cross* (1843), Surtees reflects the growth of subscription hunts—much less exclusive than those under the patronage of great landowners—and has Jorrocks made master of the Handley Cross foxhounds, no less. Thus, a genre which began life dramatizing problematic social change turned to comfortable contemplation of change accomplished.

The idea of putting inept Cockney sportsmen at the heart of the projected "monthly something," reminisced Dickens in 1847, "was not novel." It was a device that "had already been much used." He had preferred instead to take his own way, "with a freer range of English scenes and people." It is the language of practical decision-making, with an eye to sales. And it does not reveal, I believe, what his instincts at the time were telling him.

A clue to those instincts is offered by the perception that the date of the Great Reform Act—1832—is neatly straddled by the time scheme of the novel, which begins in 1827 and concludes in 1837. There were, to be sure, humdrum reasons why Dickens might have chosen 1827 as the date upon which to open the action. It was the year of the Game Certificates Act, which would allow him to involve his characters in field sports, from time to time, with no inconvenient hint of transgression. It was in 1827, moreover, that he, personally, had finally left Wellington House Academy to begin work as a clerk for solicitors Ellis and Blackmore—had begun as a fifteen-year-old, that is to say, to do adult work among adults, with every encouragement to develop an adult perspective upon the world around him. Launching *Pickwick* in 1836, and needing to start the action back in the past to allow time for things to happen, he is likely to have reflected that 1827 was as far back as he could go and be confident of the kind of understanding needed. He had been employed before, of course, but when he started to work with other boys at Warren's Blacking Warehouse in 1824, he had been barely twelve years old, a bewildered and disconsolate child fixated upon his own distress. As for finishing the action in 1837, Dickens made a choice which precluded any other date. The last double number was published at the end of September 1837, and is concluded in the present tense. The reading public had grown to love Mr. Pickwick and Sam Weller. So in his way had Dickens. He felt constrained to finish the book with a report on the present condition of its main characters. Yet even if we suppose the straddling of the 1832 act purely accidental, one thing remains true: it is a book of its era, the Reform era.

Nor need this surprise us. Before he launched *Pickwick*, Dickens had made his reputation (if not his name), with pieces in the periodical press subsequently collected in *Sketches by Boz*, the first series of which was published in February 1836 just days before Chapman and Hall broached what became the *Pickwick* project to him. The impact of these pieces upon the reading public had been due in part to native talent, in part to the choice of an unusual subject matter. In some of the later sketches, such as "The Black Veil" and "The Drunkard's Death," Dickens experimented with other genres, but all of those originally published between 1833 and January 1836 conformed to the subtitle he chose for the collection: "Illustrative of Every-day Life and Every-day People." It was urban life and urban people, moreover, that were illustrated, the life and the people of London. In the *Examiner* of 28 February 1836, John Forster, who had yet to meet Dickens, confessed to misgivings about the "caricature of Cockneyism" in the *Sketches*, but the *Court Journal* of 20 February commended Boz as "a kind of Boswell to society" and for his representation "of the middle ranks especially" (Slater 62–63).

Dickens depicted a wide range of Londoners in the *Sketches*, from criminals, through the poor and manual workers, through the shabby-genteel, up to members of the professional classes, but his specialty was urban middle-class folk, prosperous or not so prosperous, experiencing the tribulations, perplexities, and sometimes pleasures of life. Think of "Mr Minns and his Cousin," "Early Coaches," "A Christmas Dinner," or "The Bloomsbury Christening." The characteristic figure is a respectable Londoner, salaried or in receipt of unearned income, comically coping—or failing to cope—with the eventualities of life. None is a substantial landowner, none looks back to early years upon the family estate. The characteristic figure, that is to say, is a Cockney—the species of citizen, during the Reform era, most interested in reform.

Three of the sketches, moreover, all originally published in 1835, just three years after the passing of the 1832 act, comically call up the topic of reform. "The Parlour Orator" dwells upon the bewildering proliferation of reform issues and some of the stranger attitudes towards them. It features a blustering public-house controversialist, who will not allow a man to be called "a friend to Reform," just because he is "The abolitionist of the national debt, the unflinching opponent of pensions, the uncompromising advocate of the negro, the reducer of sinecures and the duration of Parliaments; the extender of nothing but the suffrages of the people" (274). The orator tells his dazzled audience that they are slaves, "bending beneath the yoke of an insolent and factious oligarchy; bowed down by the domination of cruel laws; groaning beneath tyranny and oppression on every hand, at every side, and in every corner" (275).

"A Parliamentary Sketch" features, among others, the old butler of Bellamy's Kitchen, the House of Commons's dining establishment, and solemnly attaches significance to his political views. Before the passing of the Reform Bill, the narrator advises us, he had ascertained "that Nicholas was a thorough Reformer. What was our astonishment to discover shortly after the meeting of the first reformed Parliament, that he was a most inveterate and decided Tory!" (189).

"The Election for Beadle" calls up the great issue of Reform obliquely. Ostensibly, it has to do only with parish affairs, but it is essentially a mock-heroic piece, and the grander arena comically evoked is the arena of national politics. It begins, "A great event has recently occurred in our parish":

> A contest of paramount interest has just terminated; a parochial convulsion has taken place. It has been succeeded by a glorious triumph, which the country—or at least the parish—it is all the same—will long remember. We have had an election; an election for beadle. The supporters of the old beadle system have been defeated in their strong hold, and the advocates of the great new beadle principles have achieved a proud victory. (34)

Hopes among the powerful of the parish for a "vestry-elected beadle" have been defeated. Parishioners, "fearlessly asserting their undoubted rights," have elected "an independent beadle of their own" (38). The principle of the open vestry, using the terminology of the day, has been triumphantly asserted, the principle of the select vestry soundly defeated. All the rate-paying householders of the parish have had their say, and the governing body of the parish has been thwarted in its attempt to choose without reference to popular opinion. Reflection of the issue of Reform would have been obvious to contemporary readers.

When he launched *The Pickwick Papers*, Boz was foremost among those of his era who depicted Cockney life—the Cockney life to which the reading public was ever more attentive, thanks to economic and political change. Dickens declined the invitation simply to represent yet more misadventures of Cockney sportsmen. That he would leave to others with more specialized talents, undeterred by so many precedents. By 1836 the thrill of transgression was gone from the genre, and the encrypted political meaning had become redundant. But whatever he would say later—exasperated by the claims of Seymour's widow about her husband's role in the project—Dickens would not do something different, with concessions. He would do something more. He would represent the diverse misadventures of Cockneys amid "a freer range of English scenes and people." Because, let there be no mistake, whatever else they are, the Pickwickians are Cockneys challenging the privileges of the landowning classes.

WORKS CITED

Ashton, T. S. *The Industrial Revolution, 1760–1830*. Oxford: Oxford UP, 1997.

Briggs, Asa. *The Age of Improvement: 1783–1867*. 2nd ed. Harlow, Essex: Longman, 2000.

Burns, Arthur, and Joanna Innes, eds. *Rethinking the Age of Reform: Britain 1780–1850*. Cambridge: Cambridge UP, 2003.

Cowper, William. *The Works of William Cowper.* Ed. Robert Southey. 15 vols. London: Baldwin and Craddock, 1835–37.

Dexter, Walter, and J. W. T. Ley. *The Origins of Pickwick.* London: Cecil Palmer, 1928.

Dickens, Charles. *The Letters of Charles Dickens.* Ed. Madeline House, Graham Storey, Kathleen Tillotson, et al. The Pilgrim/British Academy Edition. 12 vols. Oxford: Clarendon, 1965–2002.

———*The Pickwick Papers.* Ed. James Kinsley. Oxford: Clarendon, 1986.

———*Sketches by Boz.* Ed. Dennis Walder. London: Penguin, 1995.

Gillray, James. *Cockney Sportsmen.* London: Hannah Humphrey, 1800.

Hood, Thomas. *The Works of Thomas Hood.* 7 vols. London: Edward Moxon, 1862–63.

Moncrieff, William Thomas. *The Triumph of Reform.* London: Thomas Richardson, 1832.

Mori, Jennifer. *William Pitt and the French Revolution, 1785–1795.* Edinburgh: Edinburgh UP, 1997.

The Oxford Dictionary of National Biography (ODNB). 60 vols. Oxford: Oxford UP, 2004.

The Oxford English Dictionary (OED). 21 vols. Oxford: Oxford UP, 2012.

Parker, David. "The *Pickwick* Prefaces." *Dickens Studies Annual* 43 (2012): 67–79.

Ritson, Joeseph. *The Letters of Joseph Ritson, Esq.* 2 vols. London: William Pickering, 1833.

Schachterle, Lance. "The Serial Publication of R. S. Surtees's *Jorocks's Jaunts and Jollities.*" *Victorian Periodicals Newsletter*, no. 20 (June 1973): 8–13.

Seymour, Robert. *Sketches by Seymour.* London: Thomas Fry, n.d. (c. 1836).

Slater, Michael. *Charles Dickens.* New Haven: Yale UP, 2009.

Smith, Grahame. *The Novel and Society: Defoe to George Eliot.* London: Batsford, 1984.

"The Sportsman" and "The First of September." *Gentleman's Magazine* 98 (1805): 845–46.

Surtees, R. S. *Jorrocks' Jaunts and Jollities.* London: Methuen, 1951.

Wilson, Edmund. *The Wound and the Bow.* Boston: Houghton Mifflin, 1941.

Woodward, Sir Llewellyn. *The Age of Reform 1815–1870.* The Oxford History of England 13. Oxford: Clarendon, 1938.

Boz and Beyond: *Oliver Twist* and the Dickens Legacy

Dianne F. Sadoff

This essay argues that Charles Dickens's Oliver Twist *amalgamates popular narrative forms into a proto-Victorian fiction. Yet to invent that new fictional form, Dickens appropriated a melodramatic aesthetic and deployed the scenic imagination he had discovered while writing* Sketches by Boz, *his early descriptive newspaper and periodical pieces. Genre or mode mixing is crucial to the sketches' aesthetic, moreover, since the melodramatic mode in fiction promiscuously borrowed from the storytelling conventions of Gothic, farce, Newgate tale, and romance to create a historically situated, hybrid form. This essay argues that Boz generated the fame that enabled Dickens to create himself as novelist in* Oliver, *beyond* Pickwick's *picaresque; that celebrity then mobilized his later legacy, his afterlife in various literary modes and visual cultural genres.*

The literary mode of *Oliver Twist* has worried readers since the 1830s. The novel's seeming lack of plot, confusion about its subplots' relation to one another, characters' mysterious kinship, protagonist's passivity, and wild swings of mood and changes of atmosphere bewildered some nineteenth-century reviewers, and they continue to concern some of our contemporaries. George Henry Lewes, for example, called *Oliver* a "singular blend of different literary modes" (rpt. Collins 64–65). An anonymous reviewer thought it a "succession of sketches of character, scenes, and events" rather than a narrative with "a cunningly conceived plot, or a progressively arresting tale"; another noted, "the romance, novel, history, or narrative, or whatever else it may be called, of 'Oliver Twist,' is assuredly an invention *per se*" (rpt. *OT* 403; qtd. in Chittick 90). In the 1990s, Robert Tracy likewise complained that the novel's plot failed to develop, that its mode shifted dramatically as Dickens discovered Nancy's productive plot function (559). Recently, Robert Douglas-Fairhurst called *Oliver*'s plot "bewilderingly snarled," and Holly Furneaux, "short-circuit[ed]" (272; ch. 25). Yet Claire Tomalin, re-voicing a notion shared by critics before the twentieth century's last decade, claims that "*Oliver* was tightly plotted and shaped from the start" (74). Critical anxiety about Boz's plots and modes, however, opens a space for what I will argue here, that Dickens's scenic imagination in *Oliver* deploys a melodramatic modality so as to amalgamate popular narrative modes into a proto-Victorian fiction—a novelistic invention *per se* in which a coherent narrative emerges from 1830s subgeneric materials.

These nineteenth-century reviewers, like the late-twentieth-century critics who follow them, fret about the curious modal and hybrid quality of Boz's early narrative, which originated as the sketches, "Oliver Twist," in *Bentley's Miscellany*. Indeed, Dickens did not at first intend *Oliver* to become a novel at all; he began writing "Oliver" as a series of sketches about character, scenes, and events and, to link them together, borrowed plot points from popular fictional modes, the romance, Gothic, and Newgate tale. Yet his delivery of the sketches to Richard Bentley as one of the two novels he owed the publisher necessitated that they become a longer story (Wheeler 526–27). According to Kathryn Chittick, Dickens never fulfilled his contract with Bentley, for, having broken the agreement, he wrote just one narrative, which "rewrote the form of the novel itself" (71). Yet to invent that new fictional form, Dickens adopted in *Oliver* a melodramatic aesthetic and hybridized storytelling mode that he had discovered while writing *Sketches by Boz*, the earlier descriptive newspaper and periodical pieces that most closely resemble the early "Oliver" sketches. Bentley's shrewd business move triumphed, however, as *Oliver* itself became a popular novel whose hybridity made it especially appropriate for adaptation—and, indeed, remarkably easy to pirate. Coming to terms with *Oliver*'s plot, hybrid aesthetic, and fictional mode, demands that we shift our horizon of expectations somewhat, reframe our generic suppositions, and consider, as well, the early sketches' uses for Dickens as an emergent public entertainer.[1]

Boz's early *Sketches* and the *Miscellany* "Oliver" pieces invent a new fictional mode by accumulating visual scenes as interrelated scenarios connected by a thread of narrative logic that would, ultimately, enable the novel to disentangle its complicated plot. Genre or mode-mixing is crucial to the sketches' aesthetic, since the melodramatic scenic mode in fiction promiscuously borrows from the storytelling conventions of Gothic, farce, Newgate tale, and romance to create a historically situated, hybrid form, one that suits the developing style of the self-begetting writer, Charles Dickens. For Boz set in motion, as Dickens's career began, the celebrity that would enable him to create himself as novelist, that would mobilize his later legacy, his afterlife in various literary modes and visual cultural genres.[2] Boz's scenic aesthetic and his narrative mode-mixing also made *Oliver* appropriate for adaptation, whether on the nineteenth-century page or stage, or on the twentieth- or twenty-first-century screen. George Cruikshank's illustrations, various nineteenth-century theatrical dramatizations, and Dickens's public readings of Nancy's murder all remediate the parish boy's tale in visual or performative media and repurpose the story for new, often wider, audiences. In these remediations, the narrative may posit new psychological and social meanings for cultural consumers in different historical moments. Given *Oliver*'s narrative hybridity, it could be transformed into twentieth-century gangster or porn flick, stage or screen musical or melodrama, graphic novel, animated children's film, or heritage teleplay. And so it was.

But Boz—the name with which Dickens signed his early work—stubbornly disavowed his sketches' narrative hybridity, claiming that they were, in fact, realistic. In the 1836 preface to *Oliver*, Dickens asserted that he sought "to present little pictures of life and manners as they really are"; "our duty as faithful parochial chronicler," the *Sketches*'s narrator notes, is to depict the parish as a "little world of its own" (qtd. Miller 122; *Sketches* 13, 18). Dickens later claimed of Nancy's characterization, "IT IS TRUE" (*OT* 6). John Forster, perhaps Dickens's most important propagandist, eagerly supported Boz's fledgling career as well as the emergent realistic aesthetic his protégé trumpeted: "The observation shown throughout is nothing short of wonderful," Forster said of the *Sketches*; "things are painted literally as they are" (I: 65).[3] Yet the scenic imagination requires not only acute observation but also entry into a fantasized or imaginary scene that situates a spectator within a seen panorama. Freud called these scenes, when recalled, "screen memories." "Everything goes back," Freud said in an early letter, to the "reproduction of scenes. Some can be obtained directly, others . . . by way of fantasies set up in front of them. The fantasies . . . exhibit the same elements . . .—memory fragments, *impulses* (derived from the memory) and *protective fictions*" rearranged in new visual structures (*Letters* 239; Freud's emphasis). "It may indeed be questioned," Freud later said, "whether we have any memories at all *from* our childhood: memories *relating to* our childhood may be all that we possess" (*SE* 3: 318–22; Freud's emphasis).

These visual scenes are thus highly fictionalized representations. A sequence of scenes could be psychoanalyzed because they displayed the same elements but arranged them in a different visual context, their figures distanced from the scene-maker, estranged through temporal difference, yet made intimate through recollection. In scenes that exhibit childhood fantasies, Freud says, the subject "sees himself in the recollection as a child, with the knowledge that this child is himself; he sees this child, however, as an observer from outside the scene would see him" (*SE* 3:321)—much as Dickens might have viewed Oliver, David, and Pip as phantasms of his young self. Fantasy articulates these scenes into something like narrative units, Jean Laplanche and J.-B. Pontalis note, for fantasies are "scripts (or *scénarios*) of organized scenes which are capable of dramatization—usually in a visual form." The "subject is invariably present in these scenes," which form a *"sequence"* in which he has "his own part to play," "not only as an observer but also as a participant" (318, Laplanche and Pontalis's emphasis). Fantasy thus produces "the *mise-en-scène* of desire," a visualization or performance of the subject's own biological, familial, and wished-for or feared origins (332).

Like the fantasies and scenarios Freud describes, *Sketches by Boz* exhibits a limited repertoire of elements, figures, and tropes, often rearranged differently in a variety of visual scenes. Indeed, the *Sketches,* when published as a volume, form a story script of organized scenes picturing not only subjects but, in addition, a spectatorial witness who observes the scenic dramatization and sometimes participates in the performance. Sequenced as a scenario, Boz's *Sketches* represent the mise-en-scène of desire, which the "speculative pedestrian" calls "curiosity" and which articulates the hybrid scenes he observes and imagines into sequences (90). In "The First of May," our fantasizing ambler recollects the "old scenes of his early youth": "Magic scenes indeed," he sighs nostalgically, "for the fancies of childhood dressed them in colours brighter than the rainbow and almost as fleeting!" (169).[4] Peeping into his neighbors' windows even as their inhabitants stare back at him, the narrator enables both looker and looked at to mobilize curiosity's energy. The workhouse-master "eyes you, as you pass his parlour-window, as if he wished you were a pauper, just to give you a specimen of his power" (4–5); the parish's old lady, who sews near the window, "if she sees you coming up the steps, and you happen to be a favourite, . . . trots out to open the street-door before you knock," to sluice you with sherry (10). Whether a wish to strut or sate, the staring denizens of the parish, in miniature, and of London, as metropolis, mobilize the scenic look, in which figures related to the observer perform and dramatize themselves for the pedestrian—and sometimes reciprocate his conjuring gaze.

Yet the sketches, which invoke readerly affects of sorrow and sympathy as well as joy and laughter, depict not only scenes of urban conviviality but also of impoverishment, penury, and want. In "Mr. Bung's Narrative," the executioner of small properties pictures a devilish mother, who curses her naked children and strikes a hungry infant; the brutal, transported husband has left his children unprotected and their grandmother and mother to go mad in a "house of correction" or die in the workhouse (31). "If you had heard . . . and seen" this scene, Bung says, making us likewise observer of the scene, "you'd have shuddered as much as I did" (30). The tale's speaker performs as, and the *Sketches'* narrator ventriloquizes, the executioner, distancing himself from the scene of suffering with which Bung sympathizes; both speakers invite us to see these scenes, ask *our* bodies to shake, *our* hearts to "wring," as melodramatic sensation penetrates and saturates our bodies. Cruikshank's illustration repurposes the scene, jollifying its figures and rendering it grotesque, as he visualizes its "comedy of class struggle" and "melodrama" of victimage as an entertaining spectacle (Payne 26).

Our speculating perambulator visualizes the everyday scene as spectacle, a vision framed by and animated from his particular perspective, ready to be "imaginatively rehearsed" as memory or refashioned as fantasmatic invention (Walder xxx). In "Meditations on Monmouth Street," our metropolitan wanderer fits "some being of [his] conjuring up" with the second-hand clothes for sale in "the burial-place of fashions" (75). Performing a macabre dance, "rows of coats" and "lines of trousers," and "half an acre of shoes" start, jump, and stump through "a pleasant reverie" in which a man's whole life, fabricated by our fantasizing narrator, was "written . . . legibly on those clothes" (75). In his illustrations, Cruikshank fills hanging garments with apparent bodies, although no heads or limbs betray the beings that once occupied them. "[W]e saw, or fancied, we saw—it makes no difference which," the fantasizing ambler says. "We could imagine that coat—imagine! we could see it; we *had* seen it a hundred times—sauntering in company with three or four other coats of the same cut" (76–77; Dickens's emphasis). This scene pictures experience as entertainment, a vibrant life in which the narrator participates, making up figures, imaginatively joining them, requiring his readers to join, too, even as his scenes of suffering enable him and the reader to differentiate and distance themselves from figural suffering and mortality.

In sketches of trendy urban entertainments, Boz encounters—or invents—Dickens's first scenarios. At Greenwich Fair, he watches not only the costumed dances that Cruikshank etched but popular performances: take "rightful" and "wrongful heir[s]," rivals for a young lady's love; add dungeons, assassins, near-murders, imprisonment, a duel, the "ghost of the rightful heir's father," and you have a melodramatized script of *Little Dorrit*. In the sketch immediately preceding "Greenwich Fair," as our spectator-narrator surveys the crowd at Astley's and assesses its members' rank and status, he wishes all the performing "dramatis personae [were] orphans," since "[f]athers" are "great nuisances on the stage"; and so it turns out, the "hero or heroine" was bequeathed as an infant by "blessed mother" to "old villain," "&c., &c"; or he discovers, after "three long acts," that the hero is his "own child": "Those eyes! . . . It must be!—Yes—it is, it is my child!'—'My father!' exclaims the child; and they fall into each others' arms, and look over each other's shoulders, and the audience give three rounds of applause" (109). Here's a compact scenario of *Oliver Twist*, in which a villainous father-figure and/or a benefactor struggle in the streets over a boy, as the narrator hauls him, generally unconscious, from criminal to sentimental scene. Both over-the-top melodrama and direct address of actors to audience identify these performances not only as one of the many popular entertainments stuffed into the sketches but also as fantasmatic scenarios, as screens or protective fictions for memories and unspoken impulses.

This scenario, easily recognizable as what Freud would later call the "family romance," in which the child who questions his origin fantasizes his father noble rather than rude, or his mother an aristocrat's mistress, and so himself a child of gentry and his siblings bastards, imaginatively denigrates and declasses the parents even as it exalts their surrogates' class standing (Laplanche and Pontalis 160–61). In "The First of May," the strolling observer recounts his childish fancy that a dancing chimney sweep was a "nobleman's or gentleman's son," a belief he later grudgingly gave up, despite his joy at urban festivities (171). So, too, *Oliver* structures scenes of a family romance, yet its melodramatic scenario hybridizes romance, sentiment, and Gothic villainy in its mash-up of Victorian popular fiction.[5] Dickens's narrator justifies his hybrid aesthetic and its narrative sequencing:

> It is the custom on the stage: in all good, murderous melodramas: to present the tragic and the comic scenes, in as regular alternation, as the layers of red and white in a side of streaky, well-cured bacon. The hero sinks upon his straw bed, weighted down by fetters and misfortunes; and, in the next scene, his faithful but unconscious squire regales the audience with a comic song. We behold, with throbbing bosoms, the heroine in the grasp of a proud and ruthless baron: her virtue and her life alike in danger; drawing forth her dagger to preserve the one at the cost of the other; and, just as our expectations are wrought up to the highest pitch, a whistle is heard: and we are straightaway transported to the great hall of the castle: where a grey-headed seneschal sings a funny chorus. (117–18; ch. 17)

Here, the narrator beholds the scene of boyish suffering, of threat to girlish chastity, distantly observing yet identifying with figures for these youthful subjects; he invites the reader, too, to watch, to view the scene as spectacle even as he or she also participates in fantasizing it. Affects play upon these spectatorial bodies, as bosoms throb and fear sticks in the gullet. Fantasy's scenic logic transports the reader/spectator; melodrama alternates narrated threat with comedy and song; servants and vassals ultimately upstage aristocrats. Here, of course, the novel's narrator, unlike the sketches', parodies his aesthetic rationale, pointing out its over-the-top nature, as he disowns yet recognizes his tale's origins in the *Miscellany* sketches. Yet Dickens's treatise on melodrama functions like a screen memory: it conceals the scenario that *Oliver* performs, the scenes that make the narrator spectator of a fantastical noble and rude, even criminal, father; of caregivers who stand in for the dead, sexually naive mother; of the impoverished yet legitimate boy and his surrogate bastard siblings. This scenario declasses birth parents even as it imagines their substitute figures as evil aristocrats.

Dickens's melodramatized family romance serves his project to intervene in the ongoing 1830s debates about pauperism in England and, in particular, the displacement of responsibility for poverty away from abandoning fathers and onto pauper mothers. As Elaine Hadley demonstrates, nineteenth-century melodramatic plots and rhetoric addressed the social problems visible where issues of class and sexuality intersected. The decade-long New Poor Law debates in Britain deployed melodramatic posturing to speak about laboring, reproduction, and public policy on poverty. In its bastardy provisions, the figure of the impoverished mother is located in a melodramatic plot that serves to allay cultural anxiety about the dangers produced by modern economic and sexual arrangements in institutionalizing societies (Hadley 77–114, Hilton 353–54). Whether the threat is the Victorian workhouse or unemployment in the post-industrial workplace, the fear of falling out of the middle- or upper-middle-class feeds the cultural production of melodramatic plots and rhetoric even as those linguistic strategies seek to reassure bourgeois consumers that they will never suffer such a fate. Whether it affirms or contests dominant ideologies about individual consent and consensus within the material and social constraints of a bureaucratizing society, the melodramatic mode constitutes a Manichean logic, Peter Brooks says, that excludes the conceptual middle so as to legislate a "regime of virtue" by suppressing, even as it exposes, the very mediations it seeks to put in place (15).[6]

In *Sketches by Boz*, Dickens's melodramatic mode legislates a regime of virtue by proposing a social ethics of pauper sexuality. At the pawnbroker's shop, the gin-shops, and the criminal courts, our speculating onlooker testifies to the social problems visible where issues of class and sexuality intersect. Although Boz decries the forces of poverty which degrade London's laboring or lounging men, he is especially rhetorically indignant about the criminalization of poor women and mothers. Returning from an excursion, he beholds two "gaudily dressed" sisters emerge from a prisoner's van. One must be older, he surmises, since "fired" upon her "features as legibly as if a red-hot iron had seared them," she bears "the brand" of "two additional years of depravity"—the bodily sign that inscribes moral legibility (273). Both girls had been "thrown upon London streets, their vices and debauchery, by a sordid and rapacious mother," he hypothesizes, thinking their "progress in crime" like a "wide-spreading infection," a figurative "pestilence" (274). Here, the spectating Boz rehearses the hyperbolic tropes and bombastic rhetoric he has practiced throughout *Sketches* but fine-tunes them as the series concludes: "a tragic drama, but how often acted! Turn to the prisons and police offices of London—nay, look into the very streets themselves." Our moralizing narrator's exclamations, his grammatical imperative mode, demand the reader's attention, force him, too, to witness these filthy, diseased prostitutes, one shamelessly exhibiting herself, the other weeping with shame. "These things pass before our eyes day after day," within "the sphere of every man's observation," he declares to neglectful men and presents as a cautionary tale to women, yet "they are utterly disregarded." His melodramatic rhetoric piles up adjectives as he traces these girls' "career of vice": "hopeless at its commencement, loathsome and repulsive in its course, friendless, forlorn, and unpitied, at its miserable conclusion!" (273–74). The sketching eyewitness angrily commands his readers to "look into the very streets" and collectively pity the wretched pauper women he beholds (184). Situating the many men who daily and hourly view such scenes and trajectories of debauchery squarely within the middle ranks of metropolitan life, Boz hopes to strike a "strange chord" of sympathy "in the human heart" (194).

In *Oliver*, too, but especially in the early *Bentley's Miscellany* chapters published before the three-volume edition, the narrator sketches an ethics of bastardy, a morality that demands the person addressed and the reader witness the plight of foundlings and pauper mothers. Throughout his career, Dickens made illegitimacy a plot device: Esther Summerson's resemblance to, reunion with, and ultimate loss of her mother, now Lady Dedlock; Jo the crossing sweeper's continual moving on, in the streets and slums of London, and his ultimate death; Arthur Clennam's unveiled genealogy, which the narrator wishes would spare him from Mrs. Clennam's maternity. Yet illegitimacy also functioned in the later novels to articulate the regime of virtue that Dickens's narrators everywhere endorsed. As Dickens's career began, with *Oliver*, the narrator practices an angry rhetoric that forces the reader to attend to the illegitimate child's predicament: "What a noble illustration of the tender laws of England!" he yells when Oliver is presented to the workhouse board; "They let the paupers go to sleep!" The overseers, he sneers, fail "to turn their attention" to the workhouse, but, when they do, they discover "what ordinary folks never would have . . .—the poor people liked it!" (25; ch. 2). Boz's inflated rhetoric mocks the governors' perspicacity, authority, and supervision, as he mimics and ventriloquizes their disregard for figures they view as unremarkable urban dwellers. Throughout the sketches and the early chapters of *Oliver*, he pencils in spectacles of poverty: scenes of Smithfield, streets swarming, men and animals jostling, meat fetid; of "dirty and miserable" slums, shops decaying, kennels stinking, rats "putrefying," and houses towering over tiny peeping youngsters; "spectacle[s]" of pauper burial, with boys playing "hide-and-seek among the tombstones" (47, 49; ch. 5). Here, Dickens's narrator deploys a frequently repeated scenario, as his over-the-top rhetoric pictures an impoverished daughter's grave, with children gamboling on it; "it's as good as a play—as good as a play!" her mother chuckles merrily, likening a burial to a public entertainment much like those Boz inked in his first published sketches (48; ch. 5). Indeed, his first readers and reviewers thought Boz a "producer of public entertainments," and so not unlike the sketch writer, Theodore Hook, with whom he was often compared.[7]

Yet in *Oliver*, Dickens's melodramatic logic served not only to legislate an ethics of pauper bastardy but also to classify and widen his readership, much as Boz had assessed the audience at Astley's. Moreover, as I noted earlier, the melodramatic mode enabled Boz to fuse the popular narrative styles he appropriated as he began fashioning the novel, and the extraordinary variety of these subgeneric features served to make the tale especially suitable for the many kinds of adaptation it underwent even while it was being published serially. Melodrama, the most popular cultural mode purveyed by the nineteenth-century entertainment industry, offered Dickens a marketable genre with which to mobilize his new celebrity.[8] Melodrama's mise-en-scène featured larger-than-life spectacles of war, romance, natural disaster, and seafaring adventures, yet by the 1840s, melodramatizers would turn to the "social degradation of the contemporary city, with its heartless bailiffs, its alcohol[ism], homelessness, poverty, illegitimacy, and crime" (Hilton 625)—the scenes and settings so often pictured in *Sketches by Boz*. Theaters in both West and East Ends regularly dramatized the stories associated with scenes of laboring life, yet, whereas West-End box office, according to Michael R. Booth, depended on pleasing "an honest Englishman of the educated middle-class," East-End melodramas built class-conflict into their structures, pitting villains of higher social or economic class against working-boy heroes; "class bitterness" and status anxiety permeated the genre, and plots featured the "fearful fall into poverty" ("Melodrama" 103). Nevertheless, Booth notes, the taste for spectacle melodrama was "ubiquitous" and not necessarily determined by "income levels" or "class position"; staged spectacular drama and song thus reached a wide audience across the full spectrum of patent and illegitimate theaters (*Spectacular* 3).

The wide public vogue for *Oliver* meant it was immediately and repeatedly staged both during and after its publication. Our vulnerable boy was "on the boards" before the novel completed its serial run—as were many of Dickens's heroes from other novels—and so he was repurposed for mass audiences composed of people who may not have purchased serial numbers or rented book volumes: Britons who "were not readers" (Bolton 104). As George Rowell notes, these dramatizations expunged Boz's humor and blunted his observation, turning the tales into "melodramas, crude, sensational—and tremendously successful" (51). Despite, or because of, its popularity, Dickens despised George Almar's 1838 "serio-comic burletta" of *Oliver*, which appropriated "only the most forceful and inherently interesting scenes from the novel" and climaxed with Nancy's murder (Zemka 1, Barreca 90). As Forster reports, "in the middle of the first scene [Dickens] laid him[self] down upon the floor in a corner of the box and never rose from it until the drop-scene fell" (qtd. in Barreca 87). Although the Examiner of Plays sought to suppress production of this most popular of Dickens's tales with stage adaptors, the censorship proved largely ineffective (Bolton 104).

As his career closed, moreover, Dickens himself repurposed *Oliver*, hoping to gain yet another audience, widen his fan base, and earn additional income. He hoped, too, to recapture his tale from the theater, and, feeling anxious about "unauthorized" adaptations of his work, contemplated writing a theatricalization of *Oliver* himself (Zemka 12, Douglas-Fairhurst 307). Although he did not adapt *Oliver*, he did stage it in the public readings, a performance mode that Malcolm Andrews cannily calls "audio-visual Dickens" (viii). Dickens's first reading of Nancy's murder, however, frightened and delighted a private audience of invited guests:

> She staggered and fell, but raising herself on her knees, she *drew from her bosom a white handkerchief—Rose Maylie's—and holding it up towards Heaven, breathed one prayer, for mercy to her Maker. It was a ghastly figure to look upon. The murderer staggering backward to the wall, and shutting out the sight with his hand, seized a heavy club*, and *struck her* down!!" ("Sikes and Nancy" 393; Dickens's emphasis).

Afterwards, Dickens feted his friends with oysters and champagne, and sought advice about whether to go public with the murder.[9] Charley Dickens, who earlier had unknowingly overheard his father's rehearsal from the Gad's Hill library, had dashed outside and seen not a tramp beating his wife, as he expected, but his gesticulating father "murdering an imaginary Nancy" (Johnson 2: 1102–03). Forster cautioned against the Inimitable's descent to "the vulgarity of the stage"; the literary artist, he warned, must neither play "professional showman" nor perform "a public exhibition for private gain unworthy of a man of letters and a gentleman" (Johnson 2: 904–05). Anxiety about the term "gentleman" and the social position it names recurs throughout the literature on the public readings, especially when their propriety or Dickens's decorum were at stake.[10] But Dickens had decided: he would kill an imaginary Nancy regularly over the next three years, publicly staging as entertainment for mass audiences in London, the provinces, and America his own rise through authorship into the ranks of literary gentlemen.[11] Yet Dickens's readings failed to wrest *Oliver* from the theater, for, as Deborah Vlock maintains, early nineteenth-century popular theater and the emerging novel occupied a "hybrid novelistic-theatrical genre" or mode whose codes and conventions of dialogue, gesture, and movement shared a melodramatic aesthetic (18).

The Death of Nancy Sykes (1897), the American Mutoscope Company's mashed-up version of vaudeville and burlesque-house theatrical adaptations, repurposed the stage melodrama for an emergent cinema, again to specify a new audience—and to grant Nancy a wedding ring after all (Pointer 7). Looking back on cinema's prehistory, Sergei Eisenstein viewed *Oliver Twist* as modeling for D. W. Griffith the cinematic innovations of frame composition, close-up, and montage (213). Like Boz's early reviewers, Eisenstein, quoting T.A. Jackson, lauds Dickens's scenic imagination, his "'super-acuteness of physical vision'" and ability to make the "'whole picture aris[e] before us in sight, sound, touch, taste, and pervading odour, just exactly as in real life, and with the vividness that becomes positively uncanny'" (209). Eisenstein also hails *Oliver* as Griffith's blueprint for scenic "*montage exposition*" and for plot-based "*montage progression*," as he extolls cinema's capability to picture a new kind of sensationalized realism. Setting out scenes from *Oliver* as though they were a screenplay, Eisenstein intercuts scenes of Brownlow and Grimwig waiting for Oliver's return from the bookseller with those of his recapture by Sikes and Nancy, creating a parallel montage that "emotionally heightens" the tale's "tension and drama" (214–17). Eisenstein's focus on spectatorial sensation enables him to position Dickens as a "connecting link between the future, unforeseen art of the cinema, and the . . . past—the traditions of 'good murderous melodramas'" (217–24). For it was Dickens's appeal to his readers' "passions," to their sense of the "good and sentimental," their collective "shudder before vice," that made him Griffith's guide to the scenic and storytelling possibilities of the new century's spectacular melodramatic entertainment: cinema (206).

Although Eisenstein indulged in historical anachronism when he located Dickens prophetically between stage melodrama and film, he uncannily identified the spectacular medium of cinema as emerging out of spectacle melodrama by relying on the scenic multivalence that was already present in Dickens's sketches and early scenarios. Rick Altman quite wrongly criticizes Eisenstein for neglecting cinema's "debt to melodramatic stage adaptations" (148), for the Soviet filmmaker, like the Victorian entertainer, clearly valued the mode as capable of inaugurating historical shifts. Indeed, a newly constituted melodramatic mode in a new medium could legislate a new ethics of pauper bastardy, shape a sensational but realistic moral legibility, or picture a modern social ideal of economic justice. For Eisenstein, however, American filmmakers such as Griffith necessarily exhibited an "expressive reflection" of "American capitalism"; he and his compatriots, on the contrary, sought to forge "*montage trope*," an intellectually fused mise-en-scène that could bridge the "duality" they observed "behind the dynamic face of [capitalist] America," and so could fashion a characteristically Soviet dialectic to visualize an ideological commitment to mass political action—as Eisenstein did in the famous Odessa Steps sequence of *Battleship Potemkin* (1925) (196, 240). Recent critics, moreover, challenge Eisenstein's view of Dickensian novelistic and American cinematic melodrama as sentimental, moralistic, and bourgeois. For Daniel Siegel, Dickens's melodrama depicts and Griffith's melodramatic films montage moments of "hesitation" and narrative "arres[t]" to define the "condition[s] of historical consciousness" (375). Sue Zemka links nineteenth-century melodrama and an emergent cinema through Griffith's staging of Nancy's murder in a silent film of marital breakdown and domestic violence, *Brutality* (1912). Here, an unhappy couple watches a film of the murder, as they—and their spectators—experience not melodramatic sensation but modern unease, as the film exposes what Zemka calls bourgeois ideology's "emotional infection" (12).[12]

Dickens's over-the-top scenes and scenarios, his ethics of pauper bastardy, and a modernized melodramatic visual mode appealed once more to a mass audience a century later when social and economic upheavals roiled Europe. At this historical moment, the discursive intersection of issues of class and sexuality again sought to legislate a regime of virtue not in print but in radio drama and on the screen. Indeed, the post-World War II media helped allay anxieties caused by financial distress and wartime terror: Britons read more books, listened to BBC radio, and attended an emergent British cinema (Pointer 65). In 1945, David Lean, like Boz, made cultural consumers look at the pauper mother and her sexual degradation, but from his post-war historical perspective. Desperate over his failure to come up with a way to begin the screenplay, Lean appropriated the treatment sketched out by Kay Walsh, the film's Nancy and his then (but soon-to-be former) wife. After she trudges over a horizontal landscape, with melodramatic clouds and shadows that Lean superimposed on the film stock, the film's very pregnant Agnes braves the rain and thorns, sees the workhouse, and eventually arrives at its towering gates; later, she gives birth, looks at and smiles about her baby, dies without having wed, and speaks not at all through ten minutes of a soundtrack silent but for the wind's sigh, thunder's crash, rain's splash, bell's clang, and child's cry.

Here, the tale that protests against the 1834 New Poor Law becomes a script that would have evoked in its first spectators recollections of worry about financial exigency, the anxiety of women giving birth without the support of men, and fears about the institutional neglect of working-class want. Updating Dickens's rage at workhouse, bastardy clause, and female sexual fragility and fecundity for mid-twentieth-century spectators, Lean montages scenarios for British moviegoers still traumatized by the ravages of two world wars and the Great Depression's economic ruin, by the need to redomesticate children shipped to the country to avoid the Blitz, the need to reproduce and so improve the nation's diminished and impoverished population, as family romance became contemporary economic and political allegory.[13]

Throughout the film, Lean represents the bastard boy as a victim of institutions, authorities, and depraved paternal figures. He shoots Oliver's (John Howard Davies) vulnerable buttocks, often tracking in to something quite like a close-up. In the first such scene, Bumble's words, "And now, let me see the boy," usher in the scene of the urchin on his knees, and Bumble's and Mrs. Corney's (Mary Clare) astonished looks at the boy's behind conclude it. In medium shots, Oliver's rump centers the frame, drawing the spectator's look, as well as those of the authorities who observe. Later, in a scenario of caning, Lean pictures the apprentice's face in close-up, as whip whirrs on the soundtrack, hurt and pain etched on Oliver's countenance. Cutting among the characters present, Lean suggests Bumble's (Francis L. Sullivan), Sowerberry's (Gibb McLaughlin), and Claypool's (Michael Dear) perversity, pleasure in watching, and possible pederasty (Dellamora 70; Wills 599). Oliver's point of view (POV) shots underscore the pauper boy's suffering and his victimization, as, for example, Sikes's fist hits his face, and Lean cuts to black. At the film's end, Sikes (Robert Newton) drags Oliver up on the roof, and Lean shoots the ground and rooftops as adjacent on the frame's geographical plane, remediating and repurposing Cruikshank's etching to enhance spectatorial tension and narrative suspense. The boy's POV shot from rooftop heightens his and our fear and visually suggests his possible fall (like chimney pot from roof). This scene of childish susceptibility to physical and emotional harm produces Sikes's accidental self-hanging—and, edited as montage trope, his public execution.[14]

Roman Polanski's 2005 *Oliver Twist*, shot entirely on a purpose-built, back-lot set in Prague, uncannily replicates Lean's mise-en-scène, complete with painted backdrop of St. Paul's cathedral, smoking chimney pots, and cloudy skies. Yet Polanski's PG-13-rated *Oliver* repurposes Dickens's melodramatic scenario for twenty-first century family viewing. He made it, he said, for his own children— and, no doubt, for other young viewers in the highly valued 14- to 24-year-old market segment (Bouzereau, "Best"). Yet Polanski's background as orphaned son of Jewish parents incarcerated in a Nazi concentration camp uncannily echoes Oliver's childhood abandonment and pauperism; his youthful fears of discovery on the streets, the boyish Dickens's terror of display in the window of Warren's

Blacking, the screen memory Steven Marcus reads as represented by *Oliver's* hypnagogic scenes of Fagin with jewel box, Fagin and Sikes spying on sleeping boy (Scott B6; Marcus 370). Identifying with criminals and with the impoverished urchin, Polanski includes scenarios of Oliver's wonder in Brownlow's library, and of his benefactor's query: Will Oliver grow up to write books, to become an author?[15] With *Oliver Twist*, Polanski sought to use Dickens to consolidate his position as *auteur*, to widen his audience, to make classic fiction into popular film for consumption by boys less wounded than he—and thus, imitating Dickens, to dramatize his own successful mobility out of the class of pauper orphans, on the lam from Nazis and cops, into the ranks of major European filmmakers.

Yet Polanski's *Oliver* is really all about Fagin rather than the vulnerable boy. Although Fagin is "not so tender in the book," Polanski says, *his* villain is "lovable," a "father to the boys" in a scenario of all-male family romance (Bouzereau, "Twist by Polanski"). After Oliver (Barney Clark) gets shot during the bungled burglary, Fagin (Ben Kingsley) rubs salve into the wound, a compound he claims has passed from "father to son," and Oliver thanks him for his kindness; "I shall always remember," he moans, in a melodramatized scene of pain. And remember, he does. Faithfully restoring a Dickensian scene that Lean's screenplay expunged, in which the boy visits Fagin's cell, Polanski directs Oliver to reiterate: "You were kind to me." As the scene ends, the boy begs Fagin to get down on his knees, to say a prayer; "Forgive this wretched man," the child implores the heavenly Father, as abashed benefactor and ogling jailer watch, in montage. Here, Polanski identifies with both innocent victim and misunderstood street criminal who cares, as the filmmaker asks his spectator, too, to sympathize. As Fagin, moreover, Ben Kingsley becomes magician rather than pederast, caring father rather than criminal, and allows Polanski figuratively to cast himself as innocent and worthy of sympathy, as not guilty of criminality, of alleged sexual crime that caused him to flee the United States in 1977.

Carol Reed's 1968 musical, *Oliver!*, like Polanski's melodramatic all-male family romance and morality tale, rewrites class and criminality as they intersect with sexuality, but under the regime of commodity culture and class-stratified labor. Truncating the narrative in favor of numbers, Reed shoots nineteenth-century melodrama as musical entertainment that celebrates vice and overtly homo-eroticizes the vulnerable boy. A blond waif with trembling lip and pouty mouth, Oliver (Mark Lester) gets one of the film's two love songs, whose lyrics long for the absent pauper mother. Shot as 70-second pan across garret—a very long shot for this snappy musical—the sequence ends as Oliver weeps and warbles "Where Is Love?" In the tune "Oliver!" criminals constitute the all-male family romance, as the Dodger (Jack Wild) takes Oliver "home" to a "kind" and "respectable old gentleman," and the gang sings, "Consider yourself at home; consider yourself one of the family." This number and others paradoxically celebrate London labor and the London "breadline" or working poor: police, washer women with wagging hips, butchers, butter churners, newsboys, fishmongers, and chimney sweeps in pots who tumble out of doors and immerse their burning buttocks in tubs of water. The number ends with a carousel, as the city's laboring class becomes carnivalesque, a festive entertainment for the film's middle-class spectator.[16] In the number, "Pick a pocket or two," parodic, performative crime produces not booty but "untaxed income," and the boys watch on theatrical bleachers, becoming spectators of scenes of their own "core" poverty, the penury of those who perform no real work.[17]

If criminality is theatricalized and labor made festive, pauperism is effaced, as Lean's film's mid-century worries about world war's resulting penury morph into late-century anxiety about class stratification under the regime of capitalism. In "Who Will Buy?" Oliver stands on a balcony overlooking a brilliantly white Georgian crescent; here, Oliver is spectator, as high-angle and over-the-shoulder shots present the scene from his perspective. Reed's scenario cuts between song-and-dance and close-up of boy's happy face, as he trills, "Who will buy this wonderful feeling?"—a feeling he hopes to "tie . . . up with a ribbon" and enjoy at his "leisure." As Oliver watches the scene, the marketing class dances a choreographed paean to luxury goods and foodstuffs proffered by costermongers selling roses and violets, dairy wares, and ripe strawberries; butlers and cab drivers help gentlemen into hackneys, nannies tend babies as ladies frolic in the park. This spectacular number about upper-class conspicuous consumption recalls yet seeks to allay the worries expressed in "Food Glorious Food," when a horde of starving pauper orphans watches wide-eyed through a window as members of the Board of Governors gorge themselves. Yet Oliver's starring role in a merry musical entertainment means core poverty loses its bite.

The musical as genre invariably reassures its spectator that the hero will get his beloved at the narrative's end and so produces a happy heterosexual couple.[18] Yet rather than the boy-and-girl pair, "Oliver!" produces one fantasized family romance (without Dickens's bachelor pals) and one happy homosocial couple, as Oliver, Brownlow (Joseph O'Conor), and Mrs. Bedwin (Megs Jenkins) return home to exclusive wealth situated in Brownlow's suburban home, while Fagin (Ron Moody) and the Artful Dodger dance off together into the sunset, trilling "Once a villain, a villain to the end." By the late 1960s, the musical makes *Oliver* spectacle melodrama once more, legislating an ethics of upper-class virtue under late capitalism, as scarcity becomes abundance, exhaustion becomes energy, affective dreariness becomes intensity, and social fragmentation is displaced by a scenario of happy male couple and leisured surrogate parents.[19]

Repurposed for a European multicultural audience, Sarah Phelps's 2007 adaptation exposes as fraudulent the notion that melodrama may legislate an ethics of poverty under the regime of late capitalism. In this *"Oliver Twist* for our times,*"* capitalism has both begotten the criminal class and corrupted the gentry (Arnstein, "New Twist"): everyone's on the take in Phelps's rewriting. Mrs. Corney (Sarah Lancashire) manipulates Bumble (Gregor Fisher) into marriage so as to secure the "best wedding dress"; "I'm still your little bunny," she whimpers after a spat, going down on her knees toward his pants' zipper. Once hitched, she kicks Bumble in the buttocks, while howling with laughter. Against Monks (Julian Rhind-Tutt), she drives a hard bargain, demanding "forty guineas" in exchange for Agnes's locket; "seems the rich are as unable to control themselves as the poor," she sneers, making legible the class morality of this "modern" *Oliver* ("New Twist"). But, Monks, too, is on the take, hoping to maneuver Fagin into killing Oliver (William Miller), for a high price. His plot exposed, Monks melodramatically calls Oliver an "illegitimate maggot who would eat his way though what is mine." Fagin, too, follows the money, declaring Oliver his "prize" and mumbling from the gutter where Sikes has kicked him, "When I'm rich I won't have to associate with people like you."

Phelps denounces Dickens's melodramatic family romance as duplicitous, for her paternal figures are not caring but competitive. Declaring a "genuine fondness" for Oliver and his "boys," a fatherly Fagin (Timothy Spall), costumed with yarmulke and spouting Yiddish, feeds the gang sausages (but eats none himself, since he keeps kosher) and buys second-hand clothing for Oliver—but only to secure "deliverance" from the slums. Seeking to rationalize Dickens's bewilderingly snarled plot and the tale's murky kinship relations, Phelps collapses unruly subplots onto the figure of Brownlow, who becomes Rose's uncle and guardian, Monks's grandfather, and Oliver's great-grandfather. In this multigenerational family romance, Monks menacingly offers to marry Rose, who "could be mistress of this house" when Brownlow dies, since Monks will inherit: "I'm the young master," he boasts. Even the benevolent Brownlow (Edward Fox) is sinister; "you'd never want for anything again," he intones, cautioning Rose not to reject Monks. After the screenplay delightedly kills off Dickens's corrupt father figures, it exposes the gang as infected with sibling rivalry: the unprincipled magistrate, Fang (Rob Brydon), sentences Fagin to the gallows; Sikes (Tom Hardy) has presumably hanged himself, feet dangling in blue-lit sewers; cut to Pearly (Connor Catchpole), who sneers to the Dodger, "I'm big potatoes now; I'm leader."[20]

Borrowing iconic moments from Lean's opening scenario of rain and thunder, tree branches, and workhouse gates, Phelps addresses the social problems visible where issues of class and sexuality intersect, but she adds imperialism to the mix. Here, other socially vulnerable women figuratively replace the dead pauper mother; as befits a production by an all-female team, this melodrama's maternal figures counteract and seek to redeem capitalism's rapacity. When Oliver is shot during the burglary, Nancy (Sophie Okonedo), a black immigrant from the colonial periphery, cries, "I'll nurse him." This dimpled Nancy kisses, touches, and protects Oliver; when Sikes threatens her, she takes a stand, with the "child in [her] arms," as though she were the Madonna. But Nancy is not Phelps's heroine, even though she was Dickens's. Not Brownlow but Rose (Morven Christie) tracks the pauper, insisting on his truthfulness and ultimately detecting the secret of his birth. When Oliver disappears, Rose rages, as had Boz, demanding that spectators attend to her melodramatic rhetoric: "This and worse happens to children every day while we sit here eating our soup; I'm angry, so angry," she screams, exiting frame right. When Brownlow calls Nancy a "woman of the streets," Rose makes morality legible: she's "just poor." Both Rose and Nancy, moreover, are pictured as socially vulnerable because they are unmarried. When Rose and Mrs. Bedwin (Anna Massey) search the streets for Oliver, two laboring louts assume that Rose is a prostitute. He "don't fancy whores much," one sneers, thinking "little missy with her white gloves" a fraud; "Got me all sweaty," he yells after her, derisively.

Phelps's televisual classic serial also foregrounds its scenic aesthetic and narrative hybridity. "It's like something you might see on the London stage," Mrs. Corney says of Monks's melodramatized villainy. As the fifth and final installment of this television adaptation nears its end, moreover, melodrama reconstitutes a modernized family romance. Shot of crucifix; track to Brownlow, Rose, Oliver, and Mrs. Bedwin, who, lighting candles, bid goodbye to Agnes and Nancy; track to Rose's hand, taking Oliver's, and Brownlow's, the other; track to flowers on the altar, as the reunited figurative family exits the church. Later, happily ensconced in Brownlow's drawing room, Oliver and Rose play the piano; cut to Brownlow, his white hair having grown magically dark, grinning and bellowing, "Merry Christmas," as Oliver bows, directly addressing the BBC holiday-season audience. Here, Coky Giedroyc calls attention to the classic serial's "presentness," to television's medium-specific capability to transmit a performance simultaneously with the viewer's watching of it (Cardwell 83–85). Yet Giedroyc's quick cuts and hand-held camera shots, which capture the jostle and bustle on London's streets, and her reliance on close-ups, which solicit spectatorial sympathy and pity, also constitute a prestige televisual aesthetic. The candle lighting, the blue-lit day-for-night shots, the all-white set and costumes at Brownlow's (introduced by dissolve to white, as Oliver hits the floor at Fang's court), and the colorful heritage look of London celebrate authenticity, as the classic serial brands itself a quality niche product.

But this, of course, is not my story's end. The pauper's progress was repurposed for other niche audiences, as a new millennium demanded new forms of melodramatic scenario. Seth Donsky's *Twisted* (1996) adapts *Oliver Twist* as soft-core gay porn, which *New York Times* critic Stephen Holden called ghoulish, sentimental, and, yes, melodramatic (B5). Here, a homeless, black street boy, taken in by a gang of white male prostitutes and their autocratic yet pathetic pimp, is embraced by New York drug addicts, their pusher-lovers, and a drag queen with a heart of gold. In another porn rewrite, Jacob Tierney's *Twist* (2003), the vulnerable boy is beguiled by a pimp, adopted by adolescent gay prostitutes, and seduced by the drug scene in the hustler district of contemporary Toronto; a good girl— Nancy reborn—strives to save the little pauper. In a multicultural revamping, Tim Greene's *Boy Called Twist* (2004), a South African street kid, who's been mistreated in an orphanage, escapes to Cape Town and takes up with a Rastafarian Fagin and his gang of thieves. Although Juliet John suggests that updated Dickens sells best when the author is not identified as British, none of these niche films was widely seen, nor did any cross over into mainstream entertainment (239). In 2008, however, Walt Disney Pictures rereleased a twentieth anniversary DVD of George Scribner's *Oliver & Company*, in which boy becomes kitten, Dodger is a street-smart mutt; Fagin, the owner of pilfering puppies; and Sykes, a loan-shark.[21] One trailer for the film includes an online video game, so that youthful viewers can play along with the larceny. This *Oliver* has long enjoyed a popularity that Dickens, no doubt, would have envied. Finally, in the bicentennial year, 2012, *Oliver Twist* was again in production for the BBC, along with *The Mystery of Edwin Drood* and two new adaptations of *Great Expectations*, one scripted by Sarah Phelps (Lyttelton).

Remediated as a graphic novel, Will Eisner's *Fagin the Jew*, Oliver's orphan adventures reach another niche audience, contemporary readers who prefer their melodramatic print-narrative with pictures. Ironically mimicking the 1830s format in which Dickens first published, the graphic novel, like the sketch, is a "hybrid word-and-image form," Hillary Chute theorizes, but one in which verbal and visual narratives "register temporality spatially" but often "nonsynchronously," forcing its reader to overcome the "disjunctions between *reading* and *looking* for meaning" (452, Chute's emphasis). Eisner's frames, which include dialogue, and their surrounding white gutters overlay past, present, and future story tenses to complicate Dickens's scenario, to postmodernize its scenic sketch aesthetic. As a parody of Dickens's hybridized narrative mode, Eisner fills in Fagin's backstory, joining Newgate yarn, pomo-Gothic inheritance saga, and over-the-top romance with a focus on Jewishness: as it turns out, the fence, when a boy, was abandoned to the streets by his father, who, shot during a robbery, kindly bequeathed his criminal career to his son. In a postscript, Eisner conjures the adult Oliver recounting his marriage to Fagin's Jewish tutor's daughter, and thus his acquisition of both the tutor's and Fagin's fortunes. As Eisner parodies the bewilderingly snarled plot of his scenario's source novel, he spoofs the concept of "classic" text, identifying the comics page as a "material register of seriality" (Chute 454). Chutes's postmodernizing move nevertheless neglects that Victorian novel reviewers likewise attended to the "material indices of print" when they theorized the dominant prose form as a mass market cultural product (Dames 291).

Let us conclude this retelling of the Dickens legacy by recalling that some stories do cultural work not only for the historical moment of their production and first consumption but for later, and again later, historical periods, media, and cultural consumers. *Oliver Twist*'s scenic aesthetic and generic hybridity—its melodramatized mash-up of workhouse sketch, faux Newgate story, and Gothic disinheritance tale—make it call out for remediation. For Dickens's melodramatic scenarios offer to remediators of all kinds the logic of the sketches' multivalent scenic arrangements and provide an opportunity to reimagine Boz's scripts and fictional modes. Performing different cultural work for different audiences and historical moments, the remediated Dickensian scenario preaches and disseminates new social and ideological meanings for ever-wider modern audiences.

Seeking to complete the tale's "unfinished cultural business," *Oliver*'s adaptations and rewritings rehearse Dickens's stories' and sketches' "continuing historical relevance" (Braudy 331). Even as it helped launch Dickens's super-celebrity, *Oliver Twist*, deploying a melodramatic mode and scenic sketch aesthetic, sustains, augments, and exalts the Dickens legacy.

NOTES

1. Writing about the signature that Dickens affixed to his periodical, newspaper, serial, and book publications, Douglas-Fairhurst notes that "Dickens's twin identities [Charles Dickens and Boz] coexisted on the page" until the publication of *Dombey and Son* (1847–48). He reads *Oliver*, brilliantly, as "counterfactual storytelling," a fictional manner that takes on and turns away from a variety of popular tales (270). Amanpal Garcha recently argues that Dickens's sketches deploy a "plotless style" to represent urban "temporal rush" within a "stable, single, 'social body'" (25). I suggest an alternative way to account for the sketches' aesthetic and that mode's continuing popularity.

2. Douglas-Fairhurst notes that the word, "celebrity," was "first adopted in its modern sense in 1849," when Dickens began publishing *David Copperfield* (5).

3. Tomalin incorrectly represents the sketches as simply observations (32–50). Pykett, although her account is more nuanced than Tomalin's, focuses on the "theatre of the urban streets" (191).

4. Schlicke insists on the ways Dickens's belief in popular entertainments was integrated with his pleasure in childhood, but he resists viewing the narratorial perspective as necessarily nostalgic; nevertheless, he does not link this pattern to what Freud would call the "family romance," as do I (14–32).

5. Douglas-Fairhurst notes a possible biographical origin for Dickens's interest in this trope: his father's adoption of a "sham heraldic device," as a way to re-inscribe his upper-class social origins, and the son's inscription of himself, as "the young gentleman" in the "autobiographical fragment" (32).

6. See Goodlad for the post-1834 debates (79–85) and Hilton for the political, economic, and administrative contexts, including the law's uneven deployment after 1834 (588-99).

7. Quotation from Chittick (78); comparison to Hook, see Buller, Lewes, and an unsigned review from the *Spectator* (Collins 53, 65, 42).

8. Chittick identifies Dickens's "establishment of a market by repetition to satisfy an appetite created by that repetition" as indicated by his adoption of the name "Boz," as well as a numbering system for the sketches. John overstates this, claiming that Dickens undertook "active commercial efforts to forge a Dickens industry" (241). For a sympathetic reading of Dickens's need for his popularity to help establish professional authorship—and income—see Patten (9–27).

9. Schlicke notes that Dickens read "on many occasions in private, to gatherings of family and friends" (233).

10 See Andrews, esp. 255-56. Chittick makes it clear that this concern had been central since the early 1830s (18–23).

11 Schlicke, however, judges that, from the evidence of contemporary reading-goers, "it is doubtful whether [the public readings] brought his art to any large, previously untapped, sections of the population," even though they did "reinforc[e] his fame"(244).

12 Marsh convincingly views magic lantern storytelling as crucial to the Dickens-cinema genealogy (336). Stewart also revisits the Dickens/Griffith dyad.

13 John's impeccably researched "screen history" of *Oliver* focuses on the ways cinematic texts treat Fagin before and after the Holocaust; thus World War II creates, for her, a rupture in the ways film adapts the novel, making it a "culture-text," a "text that permeates the cultural consciousness" and whose genre may thus shift over time (211). Although she doesn't read the film's frames, shots, and montage, John's discussion of *Oliver* on the silent screen is particularly comprehensive (214–19).

14 Lean said the art director, John Bryan, "did a super Cruikshank" on the story, using the illustrations for set design of, detail in, and props for Fagin's den and Sikes's dive (Brownlow 209, 240).

15 Douglas-Fairhurst notes that Dickens inserted this exchange between Brownlow and Oliver—about whether the boy will become author or bookseller—"during one of his bitter disputes" with Bentley (332).

16 John uses these terms, too, to describe Reed's adaptation (228-30).

17 I take the terms for poverty (*core, breadline*) and wealth (*exclusive, leisured*) from Pantazis, Gordon, and Levitas.

18 See Altman, "Film Musical" (44).

19 For discussion of these binarisms in musical theater, see Dyer 24–25.

20 The London sewers, of course, were not built until after "the Great Stink" of 1858.

21 For a reading of the animated film as a celebrity star pop-song vehicle, see Napolitano.

WORKS CITED

Altman, Rick. "Dickens, Griffith, and Film Theory Today." *Silent Film*. Ed. Richard Abel. New Brunswick, NJ: Rutgers UP, 1996. 145–62.

———. "The American Film Musical as Dual-Focus Narrative." Cohan 41–51.

Andrews, Malcolm. *Charles Dickens and His Performing Selves: Dickens and the Public Readings*. Oxford: Oxford UP, 2006.

Anon. "Unsigned Review," *Spectator* 1838. Rpt. Collins 42–43.

Arnstein, Sven. "A New Twist on *Oliver Twist*." DVD.

Barreca, Regina. "'The Mimic Life of the Theatre': The 1838 Adaptation of *Oliver Twist*." MacKay 87–95.

Bolton, H. Phillip. *Dickens Dramatized*. Boston: G. K. Hall, 1987.

Booth, Michael R. "Melodrama and the Working Class." MacKay 95–109.

————. *Victorian Spectacular Theatre, 1850–1910*. Boston: Routledge & Kegan Paul, 1981.

Bouzereau, Laurent. "Best of Twist." DVD.

————. "Twist By Polanski." DVD.

Braudy, Leo. "Afterword: Rethinking Remakes." *Play It Again, Sam: Retakes on Remakes.* Ed. Andrew Horton and Stuart Y. McDougal. Berkeley: U of California P, 1998. 327–34.

Brooks, Peter. *The Melodramatic Imagination: Balzac, Henry James, Melodrama, and the Mode of Excess.* New Haven: Yale UP, 1976.

Brownlow, John. *David Lean: A Biography.* New York: St. Martin's, 1996.

[Buller, Charles]. "The Works of Dickens." *London and Westminster Review* xxix (July 1837): 194–213. Rpt. Collins 52–5.

Cardwell, Sarah. *Adaptation Revisited: Television and the Classic Novel.* Manchester: Manchester UP, 2002.

Chittick, Kathryn. *Dickens and the 1830s.* Cambridge: Cambridge UP, 1990.

Chute, Hillary. "Comics as Literature? Reading Graphic Narrative." *PMLA* 123.2 (2008): 452–65. Web. 15 Feb. 2012.

Cohan, Steven, ed. *Hollywood Musicals, The Film Reader.* London: Routledge, 2002.

Collins, Philip, ed. *Charles Dickens: The Critical Heritage.* London: Routledge, 1986.

Dames, Nicholas. "Realism and Theories of the Novel." Kucich and Taylor 289–305.

Dellamora, Richard. "Pure Oliver: Or, Representation without Agency." *Dickens Refigured: Bodies, Desires and Other Histories.* Ed. John Schad. Manchester: Manchester UP, 1996: 55–79.

Dickens, Charles. *The Adventures of Oliver Twist, or, The Parish Boy's Progress.* Ed. Fred Kaplan. New York: Norton, 1993.

————. "Sikes and Nancy." Kaplan 384–95.

————. *Sketches by Boz, Illustrative of Every-Day Life and Every-Day People.* Oxford: Oxford UP, 1957.

Donsky, Seth Michael, dir. *Twisted.* Perf. Ray Aranha and David Norona. Don Quixote, 1996. DVD.

Douglas-Fairhurst, Robert. *Becoming Dickens: The Invention of a Novelist.* Cambridge: Harvard UP, 2011.

Dyer, Richard. "Entertainment and Utopia." Cohan 19–30.

Eisenstein, Sergei, dir. *The Battleship Potemkin.* Perf. Aleksandr Antonov, Vladimir Barsky, and Grigori Aleksandrov. Corinth Films, 1998 [1925]. DVD.

————. "Dickens, Griffith, and Film Today." *The Film Form: Essays in Film Theory.* Trans. and ed. Jay Leyda. New York: Harcourt, 1977. 195–255.

Eisner, Will. *Fagin the Jew.* New York: Doubleday, 2003.

Forster, John. *The Life of Charles Dickens.* 2 vols. Collected, arranged, and annotated by B. W. Matz. New York: Baker and Taylor, 1911.

Freud, Sigmund. *The Complete Letters of Sigmund Freud to Wilhelm Fleiss, 1887–1904.* Trans. and ed. Jeffrey Moussaieff Masson. Cambridge: Harvard UP, 1985.

————. "Screen Memories." *The Standard Edition of the Complete Psychological Works of Sigmund Freud.* Trans. and ed. James Strachey et al. Vol 3. London: Hogarth Press, 1962. 301–22.

Furneaux, Holly. *Queer Dickens: Erotics, Families, Masculinities*. Oxford: Oxford UP, 2009.

Garcha, Amanpal. *From Sketch to Novel: The Development of Victorian Fiction*. Cambridge: Cambridge UP, 2009.

Giedroyc, Coky, dir. *Oliver Twist*. Writer, Sarah Phelps. Perf. Timothy Spall and Sophie Okonedo. BBC, 2007. DVD.

Goodlad, Lauren M. E. *Victorian Literature and the Victorian State: Character and Governance in a Liberal Society*. Baltimore: Johns Hopkins UP, 2003.

Greene, Tim, dir. *Boy Called Twist*. Perf. Jarrid Geduld, Bart Fouche, and Lesley Fong. Monkey Films and Twisted Pictures, 2004. DVD.

Hadley, Elaine. *Melodramatic Tactics: Theatricalized Dissent in the English Marketplace, 1800–1885*. Stanford: Stanford UP, 1995.

Hilton, Boyd. *A Mad, Bad, and Dangerous People? England, 1783–46*. The New Oxford History of England. Gen. ed. J. M. Roberts. Oxford: Clarendon, 2006.

Holden, Stephen. "A Specter of Dickens in a World of Hustlers." *New York Times* 5 Dec. 1997, nat'l. ed.: B5.

John, Juliet. *Dickens and Mass Culture*. Oxford: Oxford UP, 2010.

Johnson, Edgar. Charles Dickens: *His Tragedy and Triumph*. 2 vols. New York: Simon and Schuster, 1952.

Kucich, John, and Jenny Bourne Taylor, eds. *The Nineteenth-Century Novel, 1820–1880*. Vol. 3. The Oxford History of the Novel in English. Gen. ed. Patrick Parrinder. Oxford: Oxford UP, 2012.

Laplanche, Jean, and J.-B. Pontalis. *The Language of Psycho-Analysis*. Trans. Donald Nicholson-Smith. New York: Norton, 1973.

Lean, David, dir. *Oliver Twist*. Perf. Alec Guinness, Kay Walsh, Robert Newton, and Anthony Newley. Cineguild, 1948. DVD.

[Lewes, G. H. ?] "From a review of *Sketches*, *Pickwick*, and *Oliver Twist*." *National Magazine and Monthly Critic*. 1 (December 1837): 445–49. Rpt. Collins. 63–8.

Lyttelton, Oliver. "Jason Flemyng Joins Ralph Fiennes & Jeremy Irvine in Mike Newell's *Great Expectations*." *The Playlist*. 19 Aug. 2011. Web. 31 Jan. 2012.

MacKay, Carol Hanbery, ed. *Dramatic Dickens*. New York: St. Martin's Press, 1989.

Marcus, Steven. *Dickens from Pickwick to Dombey*. New York: Simon and Schuster, 1968 [1965].

Marsh, Joss. "Dickensian 'Dissolving Views': The Magic Lantern, Visual Story-Telling, and the Victorian Technological Imagination." *Comparative Critical Studies* 6.3 (2009): 333–46. *Ebscohost*. Web. 10 Feb. 2012.

Miller, J. Hillis. "Dickens, Cruikshank, and Illustration." *Victorian Subjects*. London: Harvester Wheatsheaf, 1990. 119–77

Napolitano, Marc. "Disneyfying Dickens: *Oliver & Company* and The Muppet Christmas Carol as Dickensian Musicals." *Studies In Popular Culture* 32.1 (2009): 79–102.

Pantazis, Christian, David Gordon, and Ruth Levitas, eds. *Poverty and Social Exclusion in Britain: The Millennium Survey*. Bristol, UK: Policy Press, 2006.

Patten, Robert L. *Charles Dickens and his Publishers*. Oxford: Oxford UP, 1978.

Payne, David. *The Reenchantment of Nineteenth-Century Fiction: Dickens, Thackeray, George Eliot, and Serialization.* Houndmills, UK: Palgrave Macmillan, 2005.

Pointer, Michael. *Charles Dickens on the Screen: The Film, Television, and Video Adaptations.* Metuchen, NJ: Scarecrow P, 1996.

Polanski, Roman, dir. *Oliver Twist.* Perf. Ben Kingsley and Barney Clark. R.P. Films, 2005. DVD.

Pykett, Lyn. "Charles Dickens: The Novelist as Public Figure." Kucich and Taylor 187–202.

Reed, Carol, dir. *Oliver!* Perf. Oliver Reed and Ron Moody. Romulus Films, 1968. DVD.

Rowell, George. *The Victorian Theatre, 1792–1914: A Survey.* Cambridge: Cambridge UP 1978.

Schlicke, Paul. *Dickens and Popular Entertainment.* London: Allen & Unwin, 1985.

Scott, A. O. "Dickensian Deprivations Delivered from the Gut." *New York Times* 23 Sept. 2005, late ed.: B6.

Scribner, George, dir. *Oliver & Company.* Perf. Joseph Lawrence, Billy Joel, and Cheech Marin. Walt Disney Feature Animation, 2008 [1988]. DVD.

Siegel, Daniel. "Griffith, Dickens, and the Politics of Composure." *PMLA* 124.2 (2009): 375–89.

Stewart, Garrett. "Dickens, Eisenstein, Film." *Dickens on Screen.* Ed. John Glavin. Cambridge: Cambridge UP, 2003. 122–44.

Tierney, Jacob, dir. *Twist.* Perf. Joshua Close, Nick Stahl, and Gary Farmer. Victorious Films, 2003. DVD.

Tomalin, Claire. *Charles Dickens: A Life.* London: Viking, 2011.

Tracy, Robert. "'The Old Story' and Inside Stories: Modish Fiction and Fictional Modes in *Oliver Twist*." Kaplan ed. *OT* 557–74.

Vlock, Deborah. *Dickens, Novel Reading, and the Victorian Popular Theatre.* Cambridge: Cambridge UP, 1998. Print.

Walder, Dennis. "Introduction." *Sketches by Boz.* Ed. Dennis Walder. New York: Penguin, 1995. ix–xxxiv. Print.

Wheeler, Burton M. "The Text and Plan of *Oliver Twist*." Kaplan ed. *OT* 525–37.

Wills, Gary. "The Loves of *Oliver Twist*." Kaplan ed. *OT* 593–608.

Zemka, Sue. "The Death of Nancy 'Sikes,' 1838–1912." *Representations* 110 (2010): 29–57. *LION.* Web. 12 Dec. 2010.

"Notoriety is the Thing": Modern Celebrity and Early Dickens

Timothy Spurgin

Dickens has often been identified as one of the first modern celebrities, but little attention has been paid to his own understanding of celebrity culture. Dickens was in fact a close and intelligent observer of that culture, and his fascination with celebrity marks much of his early work. In his treatment of characters like Mrs. Leo Hunter, Dickens locates the origins of celebrity culture in experiences of worthlessness and shame. Extending this analysis, he uses other characters, including the members of the Crummles troupe, to show how easily the pursuit of celebrity can become an end in itself. As he explores these issues, the young Dickens also reveals his own discomfort with the experience of celebrity and an increasingly powerful, perhaps understandable, wish to exchange it for a more respectable position and a more lasting sort of fame.

That Charles Dickens was one of the first modern celebrities, and perhaps the very first, has become something of a cliché. Once viewed as the precursor of Dostoevsky and Kafka, Dickens is now also seen as a forerunner of Andy Warhol and the Beatles. For Grahame Smith, Dickens is a "media personality, one of the most famous, and one of the first" (110). For Jane Smiley, he's "an object of fascination, a true celebrity (maybe the first true celebrity in the modern sense)" (v). And for David Lodge, he's the "first writer . . . to feel the intense pressure of being simultaneously an artist and an object of unrelenting public interest and adulation" (115). Recently, Juliet John has asserted Dickens's "claim . . . to be called the first self-made global media star of the age of mass culture" (7). Robert Doug-las-Fairhurst has written that Dickens "achieved, and to a large extent invented, a new form of literary 'celebrity'" (4–5). And Joss Marsh has described Dickens's "experience of celebrity" as "diagnostic, foundational, premonitory" (102).

In making such points, these writers draw on an emerging consensus about the definition of celebrity. According to this definition, celebrity is ephemeral and often insubstantial. It tends to fade over time, and it's not always linked to genuine achievement. Though people can be celebrated for leading armies or writing books, they can also be known for their wealth, their beauty, or their social connections. As a result, there can appear to be an inverse relationship between achievement and celebrity: it sometimes seems that the less you've actually accomplished, the more likely you are to attract attention to yourself.

With this definition comes a history, one that usually locates the origins of modern celebrity culture in the second half of the eighteenth century. Though historians of celebrity are alert to the changes wrought by photography, cinema, television, and the internet—to mention only a few of the larger forces at work here—they tend to stress the continuities between earlier experiences of celebrity and more recent ones. For these scholars, as Fred Inglis puts it, "the business of renown and celebrity has been in the making for two and a half centuries. It was not thought up by the hellhounds of publicity a decade ago" (3). In describing the emergence of modern celebrity, historians like Inglis have stressed two developments in particular. The first, implicit in the earlier definition of celebrity, is a growing sense of celebrity as distinct from lasting and genuine fame. Tom Mole offers a useful account of this development in his influential study of Byron's "Romantic celebrity," noting that the need to identify celebrity as an "inferior form of fame" goes hand in hand with a desire to "quarantine true fame from its contamination" (xiii).

The second crucial development in this history is the emergence of new sorts of relationships between celebrities and their admirers. This change is neatly described by novelist Matthew Pearl, author of *The Last Dickens*, when he observes, "Dickens set the stage for a whole new perception of intimacy with his readers. He also set the stage for the modern disjunction that comes from the realization that the celebrity who seems to be part of our lives is in fact another stranger." What Pearl captures here is the intensity of our relationship with celebrities, which includes not only an initial sense of closeness but also an inevitable discovery of distance and difference. Thinking again of Dickens, we might remember that in the days following his death, even the *Times* was moved to say that "[t]he loss of such a man . . . will be felt by millions as nothing less than a personal bereavement" (Chenery 506). We might also recall the surprises created by Forster's biography and, much later, by the mounting evidence of Dickens's affair with Ellen Ternan. People had thought of this great writer as a close friend, and he had encouraged them to do so, yet in the end he turned out to be something else again: "another stranger," as Pearl would have it, inaccessible and ultimately unknowable.

Despite the emphatic assertions of Pearl and others, there is no general agreement about Dickens's role in the history of celebrity. As we have seen, he is often given pride of place by Dickensians and other Victorianists, but the most distinguished historians of celebrity are more skeptical of his claims. In *The Frenzy of Renown*, still the most authoritative work on the history of fame, Leo Braudy identifies Laurence Sterne as "the first English author who can be called a celebrity" (13), making only three brief references to Dickens (see 449, 483, and 489). Fred Inglis does not go much further; in his *Short History of Celebrity*, he uses *Dombey and Son* as the basis for an argument about the rise of the urban bourgeoisie, but says very little about Dickens himself.[1]

In light of all this, it seems to me, the interesting question is not whether Dickens got there first. It's what celebrity meant to him and how it figured into his writing. In what follows, I hope to show that celebrity was not something that simply happened to Dickens while he was thinking of Mr. Pickwick. It was a recurrent subject of his writing, one that he proved capable of treating intelligently and ironically. Dickens's fascination with celebrity marks much of his early work, preceding his visits to America and his reading tours, the events usually used to establish his own credentials as a celebrity. In his early sketches and stories, and in episodes from books like *Pickwick* and *Nickleby*, the young Dickens explores the effects of celebrity on writers and their readers. Of his many insights, the keenest may be his recognition of the close connection between celebrity and humiliation. Dickens's middle-class characters often turn to celebrity culture in search of relief from feelings of worthlessness and shame. Yet instead of providing a cure for the disease of modern life, encounters with celebrity almost always carry harmful side effects and aggravate the original symptoms. As a result of such encounters, these characters may end up feeling and looking worse, not better, than ever before.

A fear of humiliation is not confined to the characters, however. The young author's anxieties are also exposed in these early writings, and by the time he gets to the middle of *Nicholas Nickleby*, in the winter of 1838–39, Dickens has begun to suspect that celebrity will rob him of his dignity and self-respect. He has also begun to hope that a public refusal of celebrity will help him to gain a more respectable position and more permanent sort of fame. It is not hard to understand Dickens's wish to protect himself from shame and ridicule, or to sympathize with his hopes of establishing the terms on which he might be observed, especially in light of his traumatic experiences in the front window of Warren's Blacking Factory, where he suffered so much unwanted observation.[2] And yet, even as we recognize Dickens's motives, we may also find something naïve and self-defeating about his attitude towards fame and celebrity. If celebrity can't provide a remedy for humiliation—and Dickens repeatedly shows that it can't—then how can fame become the antidote for celebrity?

* * *

Dickens's fascination with celebrity lies behind one of the great early triumphs of *The Pickwick Papers*: the public breakfast, hosted by Mrs. Leo Hunter, "to a great number of those who have rendered themselves celebrated by their works and talents" (198; ch. 15). This episode appeared in the sixth installment of *Pickwick*, not long after Dickens's breakthrough with Sam Weller, and much of its attention is focused on Mrs. Hunter herself. As her husband explains when inviting Mr. Pickwick to the breakfast, Mrs. Hunter not only "dotes on poetry," but is "wound up, and entwined with it" (199; ch. 15). Unlike many passionate readers, however, she is not content to worship her literary idols from a distance. She wants to mix with them, to know and be known by them, and indeed to display them as trophies: "it is her ambition," as her husband remarks, to "have no other acquaintance" but the "celebrated" (198; ch. 15).[3]

As Dickens mocks these pretensions, he also offers sharp insights into the connections between aesthetic taste, social distinction, and identity formation. Mrs. Hunter's preference for poetry not only sets her apart from her neighbors, but also gives her life a sense of purpose. At first, this may be hard to understand; for although Mrs. Hunter succeeds in drawing "half a dozen lions from London" to her breakfast, most of her guests are small-timers: "the young lady who 'did' the poetry in the Eatenswill Gazette," or Count Smorltork, "the famous foreigner—gathering material for his great work on England" (204, 206; ch. 15). Yet as we examine the situation, we can see that for Mrs. Hunter, the attention of such people is better than nothing. In her world, the only alternative to such attention *is* nothing—or, more precisely, an acute feeling of nothingness. As far as she's concerned, you're either a celebrity or a nonentity. There's no in-between.

On the morning of the breakfast, Mrs. Hunter appears dressed as Minerva, the goddess of wisdom, forcing her "full-grown" daughters into more "juvenile" costumes (206; ch. 15). She also reveals that her chief motive in hosting the breakfast has been to assemble a captive audience for the recitation of her own execrable poetry. Mr. Pickwick has been given fair warning of this by the uxorious Mr. Hunter, and the other guests have probably also seen it coming. In any case, Mrs. Hunter's "far-famed ode to an Expiring Frog" is

encored once, and would have been encored twice, if the major part of the guests, who thought it was high time to get something to eat, had not said that it was perfectly shameful to take advantage of Mrs. Hunter's good nature. So although Mrs. Leo Hunter professed her perfect willingness to recite the ode again, her kind and considerate friends wouldn't hear of it on any account; and the refreshment room being thrown open, all the people who had ever been there before, scrambled in with all possible dispatch: Mrs. Leo Hunter's usual course of proceeding, being, to issue cards for a hundred, and breakfast for fifty, or in other words to feed only the very particular lions, and let the smaller animals take care of themselves. (208; ch. 15)

Here, Mrs. Hunter exposes herself to a particularly awful form of humiliation. She's set herself up to be punished not only for her vanity, but also for her inability to accept her original place in the larger culture of celebrity. She has tried to exceed the usual boundaries of fandom—and, more importantly, to cross the line separating readers from writers—and for that, Dickens suggests, she must expect some sort of comeuppance.

In the end, however, none of these characters appears in a very good light. For if the hostess is needy and clueless, many of her guests are only superficially "kind and considerate." Indeed, the behavior of the guests reveals that they have no interest in "feasts of reason" and "flows of soul" (198; ch. 15). They're looking for an actual meal, for free food and drinks, and they don't seem to mind climbing over each other to get it. By exposing their own motives in this way, they may also open themselves to a kind of embarrassment. They have assumed that they could take advantage of Mrs. Hunter's hospitality without being dragged down to her level. But here, as Dickens extends his critique of celebrity culture to take in the "lions" themselves, we begin to see things differently. You can't eat the lady's breakfast, it seems, without also becoming part of her act.

* * *

Dickens continues to explore the ill effects of literary celebrity in "Some Particulars Concerning a Lion," a sketch published in May 1837 as a "stray chapter by 'Boz.'" The sketch centers on the exhibition of a literary lion at a dinner party hosted by "a lady of our acquaintance" (509). Boz describes himself as "anxious" to accept the lady's invitation and tells how he arrived early, hoping to gain "a full view of the interesting animal" (509). He also delights in exploring the increasingly familiar metaphors of lionization, equipping the lion with a "keeper," a "little prim man," who "mingle[s] among the crowd and spread[s] his praises most industriously" (510). The keeper "assists" in the guests' conversations (510), and when they are seated round the dinner table, he also takes responsibility for "putting [the lion] through the whole of his manoeuvers" (511). It is the keeper who decides when the lion has completed his routine, and the keeper who announces that the party is over--a "very dangerous feat," which Boz likens to "putting [your] head in the animal's mouth, and placing [yourself] entirely at its mercy" (511).[4]

Throughout the sketch, it should be noted, Boz remains a mere onlooker: detached, amused, and ironic. He is seated "nearly opposite" the lion at dinner (511), but never engages in conversation with him. After the party breaks up, Boz walks home alone, taking advantage of the chance to reflect on the conduct of the "genus of lions." Unlike the animals we see in the zoo, he explains, "biped lions" seek attention and are highly susceptible to flattery:

> While the other lions receive company and compliments in a sullen, moody, not to say snarling manner, these appear flattered by the attentions that are paid to them; while those conceal themselves to the utmost of their power from the vulgar gaze, these court the popular eye, and, unlike their brethren, whom nothing short of compulsion will move to exertion, are ever ready to display their acquirements to the wondering throng. (511–12)

Here, through his identification of "the popular eye" with "the vulgar gaze," Boz comes close to expressing some disdain for his audience. But what comes through most clearly is his contempt for writers who can't resist the temptations of celebrity:

> We have known bears of undoubted ability who, when the expectations of a large audience have been wound up to the utmost pitch, have peremptorily refused to dance; well-taught monkeys, who have unaccountably objected to exhibit on the slack wire; and elephants of unquestioned genius, who have suddenly declined to turn the barrel organ; but we never once knew or heard of a biped lion, literary or otherwise—and we state it as a fact which is highly creditable to the whole species,—who, occasion offering, did not seize with avidity on any opportunity which was afforded him, of performing to his heart's content on the first violin. (512)

In this carefully crafted sentence, Dickens not only expands the circus tent to include bears, monkeys, and elephants. He also contrasts their talents of these animals with the greater gifts of the lion. If all you can do is walk a tightrope or turn a barrel organ, then nothing much hinges on your decision to exhibit yourself. But if you can play on the first violin, you have an opportunity to move or transport an audience and should probably weigh your options more carefully.

In his recent biography of Dickens, Michael Slater has described this sketch as an "amusing in-joke" (99), noting that it's funny to see Dickens writing "as an awed spectator of a great literary lion," since "Boz himself was now an even greater lion than when he had described Mrs. Leo Hunter's *fête champêtre* in *Pickwick* VI" (99). In fact, Boz is never really "awed" by the lion, and his portrayal of the lion's act suggests something much more serious: a projection or displacement of Dickens's own fears for himself. Read in this way, the lion stands as an image of what Dickens fears he may be in danger of becoming. At this point in his career, as he's nearing the end of *Pickwick* and beginning the process of transforming *Oliver Twist* into something more like a novel, Dickens must know that he has no choice but to be lionized. He may even be ready to acknowledge that lionization has some appeal for him. After all, as Robert L. Patten has noted, most of his professional plans—his thoughts of careers in journalism, politics, or the theater—would have required some sort of reckoning with celebrity (see Patten 17–19). And yet, with his creation of the lion in this sketch, Dickens seems anxious to show that success won't go to his head. He wants to assure himself and his readers that he won't make the usual mistakes, won't submit to flattery or put himself at the mercy of hostesses and handlers. He is, at this point, still hoping to be the lion who stays out of the trap.

* * *

Similar anxieties are also on view in *Nicholas Nickleby*, where it becomes clear that Dickens is striving for something grander, something more permanent and more respectable, than mere celebrity. *Nickleby* is often described as a turning point in Dickens's career—it was, according to Forster, the book that established him as something other than a "marvel of fortune" (2: 274)—and the period surrounding its publication gave Dickens further opportunities to consider the vicissitudes of celebrity culture. For example, in February of 1838, his secret trip to the north of England, undertaken for the purpose of gathering information about the Yorkshire schools, was disrupted by his discovery that a local newspaper had printed a spurious "Autobiography of Boz." The "autobiography" overestimated his profits from *Pickwick* and overstated his salary as the editor of *Bentley's Miscellany*; and though Dickens eventually accepted an apology from the editor, he also told a friend that he was "annoyed at my private affairs being dragged before the public, and stated incorrectly in every particular" (see *Letters* 2: 367–68, 375).

Whatever Dickens's feelings may have been, he seems to have begun *Nickleby* with some determination to use the follies of celebrity as the basis for his comedy. These intentions are most obvious in his treatment of the Crummles troupe, but they can also be seen in earlier chapters, including the scene of the Kenwigses' anniversary party in the fourth installment of the novel. At first, this party may seem an unlikely occasion for an encounter with celebrity, since Mr. Kenwigs is merely a "turner in ivory" (165; ch. 14), lodging with his wife and daughters in a "bygone, faded, tumbledown street" near Golden Square (162; ch. 14). Like the other shabby gentlemen in early Dickens, Kenwigs is consumed by status anxiety, worried that his children will be cut out of a relative's will. And yet his anniversary party does include two local notables: the aforementioned relative, his wife's uncle, Mr. Lillyvick, who "collect[s] a water-rate" (165; ch. 14); and Miss Henrietta Petowker, of the Theatre Royal Drury Lane. In many other contexts, they might also be nonentities, but in this company, they are treated as distinguished guests and more specifically as "great lion[s]" and "public characters" (see 166, 168; ch. 14).[5]

Like most public characters, Mr. Lillyvick is preceded by his reputation—he's widely known to be cold and unfeeling—and in the moments before his arrival at the party, the other guests begin to make jokes at his expense. Surprisingly, the host will have none of it: "A man in public life expects to be sneered at," Mr. Kenwigs explains, adding that "it is the fault of his elewated situation, not of himself" (167; ch. 14). Thus, Kenwigs not only makes excuses for his wife's uncle, but also encourages his friends to imagine the burdens of celebrity. If you think it's hard being one of the crowd, he suggests, just think how it must feel to be in the spotlight. When Mr. Lillyvick finally turns up at the party, greeting his niece affectionately, the others are amazed, "quite absorbed in the sight" of a water-rate collector "leaving taxes, summonses, notices that he had called, or announcements that he would never call again for two quarters' due, wholly out of the question" (167; ch. 14). "It was pleasant to see how the company looked on," the narrator adds, "and to behold the nods and winks with which they expressed their gratification at finding so much humanity in a tax-gatherer" (167–68; ch. 14).

It's at times like these, Dickens suggests, that we're most vulnerable to the deceptions of celebrity. For although it may look as if Mr. Lillyvick is dropping his mask and revealing his true self, he's really just mounting another sort of per-formance—one designed to obscure his complicity in an unjust social order. As Dickens leads us to this conclusion, he describes the exhibition and reception of celebrity as an elaborate social ritual, in which each part is carefully scripted in advance. When offered a choice of seats, Mr. Lillyvick is supposed to say that he's "not particular" about such things (168; ch. 14). And when invited to "recite the Blood-Drinker's Burial," Miss Petowker is supposed to explain that she "dislike[s] doing anything professional in private parties" (171; ch. 14). Listeners and audi-ence members are then supposed to refuse these gestures of disavowal and find a way to get the celebrity back up on the usual pedestal. Mrs. Kenwigs understands this implicitly. "We are all so very friendly and pleasant," she tells Miss Petowker, "that you might as well be going through it in your own room" (171; ch. 14). With this, the line between the professional and the private is simultaneously erased and reinscribed: because Miss Petowker might as well be home alone, she should feel free to offer the recital she would normally reserve for the stage.

As Dickens explores these rituals, he reinforces another crucial point: namely, that celebrity culture originates in the peculiar anxieties of the urban middle class. The Kenwigses may be motivated by practical concerns about money and status, but they are also plagued by deeper feelings of insignificance and worthlessness. This is most obvious in Mr. Kenwigs's early defense of Mr. Lillyvick, which includes a crucial bit of hesitation: "'I have the honour to be connected with the collector by marriage; and I cannot allow these remarks in my—'" Mr. Kenwigs was going to say "'house,' but he rounded the sentence with 'apartments'" (167; ch. 14). This is a revealing moment, for it shows how pride in your connection to a rate-collector can immediately give way to embarrassment at the smallness of your lodgings. If celebrity culture offers itself to Kenwigs as a remedy for insignificance, it only makes him feel worse in the end.

Later, the rate-collector identifies Kenwigs as "a very honest, well-behaved, upright, respectable sort of man"—a good bourgeois, in short (170; ch. 14)—but not before recalling his initial opposition to the marriage of Kenwigs to his niece: "there was a very great objection to him," Mr. Lillyvick says, "on the ground that he was beneath the family, and would disgrace it" (170; ch. 14). Instead of resenting this reminder of his low origins, Kenwigs is pleased by it and apparently moved to join the general conclusion of his guests: that "in one of [the collector's] station the objection was not only natural, but highly praiseworthy" (170; ch. 14).

For people like Mr. Kenwigs, the experience of humiliation would appear to be perpetual. And because celebrity culture turns out not to be a remedy or cure for such feelings, the only way out would seem to be the one taken by Newman Noggs, the Kenwigses' upstairs neighbor and another one of their guests for the evening. Before being called away at the end of the scene, Newman busies himself with "sundry little acts of kindness for the children" and is "humoured in his request to be taken no notice of" (168; ch. 14). This strategy isn't foolproof—Newman is briefly "spoken about in a whisper as the decayed gentleman" (168; ch. 14)—but it allows him to keep his distance from the rest of the party and also to retain a small measure of dignity.[6]

* * *

By this point, several things are clear: Dickens knows where celebrity culture comes from, and he understands what it can do to people like Mrs. Hunter and Mr. Kenwigs. He also sees that the damage is not confined to such people, but also extends to lions and public characters like Mr. Lillyvick. What's more, he suspects that the only way to avoid the humiliations of fandom and celebrity is by following the example of Newman Noggs: hide in the corner and hope that others will ignore your retreat. For obvious reasons, as we've already noted, this is no longer a viable strategy for Dickens himself. And so, as he takes Nicholas through his engagement with the Crummles troupe, we can see him searching for an alternative strategy, another way of dealing with celebrity.[7]

For the members of this provincial company, celebrity is not simply a means to an end, a way of filling the house and paying the bills; in many ways, it's become an end in itself. In the words of Mr. Folair the pantomimist: "Notoriety, notoriety, is the thing" (362; ch. 29). These actors are eager to be recognized in the street, and they're proud of the fact that their likenesses have been "hung up for sale in the pastry-cook's window, and the green-grocer's, and at the circulating library, and the box-office" (286; ch. 23). They even treasure their appearances in local gossip columns. For example, Miss Snevellici's scrapbook, which she leaves open for Nicholas, contains "critical notices of [her] acting," as well as "complimentary allusions" to "honourable proposals" from a "young gentleman of immense fortune" (298; ch. 24).

The actors also take pride in their ability to control the machinery of celebrity, recognizing the existence of several different "mode[s] of getting popular" (362; ch. 29). Of course, the keenest insights into the workings of celebrity are reserved for the manager himself; for if Mr. Crummles is a rotten actor, he's also a brilliant publicist, with an instinctive feel for the dangers of market saturation. Fearing that Miss Snevellici has already put on too many bespeaks, he views Nicholas as a fresh "attraction" for a weary audience (296; ch. 24). Later, after Nicholas has announced his departure from the company, the manager asks the public to make "an early application for places" at the farewell performances—it being," as the narrator explains, "a remarkable fact in theatrical history, but one long since established beyond dispute, that it is a hopeless endeavour to attract people to a theatre unless they can be first brought to believe that they will never get into it" (378; ch. 30).

Not even Crummles can think of everything, however, and as Dickens takes us through these chapters, he underscores the irrationality and unpredictability of celebrity. Posters are displayed sideways and upside down, owing to the illiteracy of the bill-stickers (304; ch. 24). Critics are consumed by their own vanity (300; ch. 24), and the audience is easily distracted, as Nicholas discovers when helping Miss Snevellici with the canvassing for her bespeak:

> Some wanted tragedies, and others comedies; some objected to dancing, some wanted scarcely anything else. Some thought the comic singer decidedly low, and others hoped he would have more to do than he usually had. Some people wouldn't promise to go, because other people wouldn't promise to go; and other people wouldn't go at all, because other people went. (303; ch. 24)

To make matters worse, the public is often disrespectful and rude. The Curdles' servants, though initially eager to get a look at the "play-actors," soon dissolve into "whispering and giggling" (300; ch. 24). And when meeting the six little boys who are supposed to be her greatest admirers, the Infant Phenomenon is practically assaulted, as one of the boys is caught "pinching [her] behind, apparently with the view of ascertaining whether she was real" (302; ch. 24).

These scenes help to establish the fact that celebrity is a zero-sum game. The Crummles troupe appears to hold a place for everyone—even Mr. Crummles's pony is said to be "quite one of us," since "[h]is mother was on the stage" (279; ch. 23)—but the group is actually riven with conflict. Mr. Folair refers to the Infant Phenomenon as the "Infant humbug" (283; ch. 23), and when he and Mr. Lenville learn that Nicholas is writing a new piece for the company, they immediately begin angling for the best parts (see 291; ch. 24). Later, after Nicholas has begun to enjoy some success as an actor, Folair turns up again, this time bringing

a challenge from Lenville, who feels that he's being relegated to "second business" (362; ch. 29). In the course of this conversation, Folair also explains that
Lenville has had "half a mind" to pink Nicholas with a real sword during a performance of *Romeo and Juliet*: "All the town would have come to see the actor who
nearly killed a man by mistake," Folair says. "I shouldn't wonder if it had got him
an engagement in London" (362; ch. 29).

By this point, Nicholas is nearly finished with the actors. In the next few pages,
he receives a letter from Newman Noggs, warning him of "some treachery on
the part of [his uncle] Ralph" (365; ch. 29), and begins to hint at his imminent
departure from the company (see 366; ch. 29). These hints are the subject of a
striking illustration by Phiz, one that distances both Nicholas and Dickens from
the disreputable company (fig. 1). Placed in the center of the picture, Nicholas is
dressed in his street clothes and surrounded by people in silly costumes. Many
of the women are distressed by his announcement, but one of the men appears
to be giving it a thumbs up. Taken as a whole, the image makes an unmistakable
point: This company, plagued as it is by resentment and backbiting, cannot be a
permanent home for our hero. Nicholas simply does not belong here; he's better
and somehow finer than the others, and it only makes sense for him to bid them
farewell.[8]

Tellingly, this is not enough for Dickens. For instead of having Nicholas slip
away immediately, he affords his hero a few more chances to express his growing disdain for celebrity. Nicholas's final days with the actors begin innocently

Fig. 1. Hablot Knight Browne ("Phiz") "Nicholas hints at the probability of his leaving
the Company."

enough, with Mr. Crummles "taking prompt and energetic measures to make the most of him before he went away" (368; ch. 30). Yet Nicholas soon discovers that he and Smike have become the subject of unflattering rumors. Some of the rumors are clearly false—Smike is not related to a pickpocket who once hung around the coach stand at Covent Garden—but other bits of gossip strike closer to home: As one of the actors suspects, Nicholas has gotten into a "scrape" and is "run[ning] away from somewhere, for doing something or other" (371; ch. 30). The vague language of these rumors is funny, but their ability to arouse suspicion is not, as Nicholas's reaction makes plain: "'So these are some of the stories they invent about us, and bandy from mouth to mouth!" thought Nicholas. "If a man would commit an inexpiable offence against any society, large or small, let him be successful. They will forgive him any crime but that'" (371; ch. 30). Later in the same chapter, the connection between celebrity, vanity, and jealousy is reinforced in a scene involving Nicholas and Miss Snevellici. Sensing Nicholas's frustration with the other actors, Miss Snevellici invites him home to meet her parents and visit with their fellow lodgers, Mr. and Mrs. Lillyvick—originally known to us, of course, as Miss Henrietta Petowker. In what seems like a matter of minutes, the party erupts in discord, and Miss Snevellici's father, a lifelong veteran of the stage, is quarreling with his wife, flirting with other women, and boasting of his own meager celebrity: "Most men have seen my portrait at the cigar shop round the corner," he says. "I've been mentioned in the newspapers before now, haven't I?" (375; ch. 30). In earlier episodes, Nicholas had enjoyed a mild flirtation with Miss Snevellici (see 299, 302; ch. 24). Now, partly because of the unpleasant behavior of her father, he lumps her in with the odious Fanny Squeers (see 378; ch. 30).

That Dickens is also rejecting something he once might have embraced becomes obvious when Nicholas finally goes to take his leave of Mr. Crummles. The farewell performance has gone smoothly, despite the distractions created by the presence of "a London manager in the boxes" (378; ch. 30). But none of that really matters, since Nicholas has also received another distressing letter from London. And so, when the manager begs for "one last night more" (380; ch. 30), Nicholas insists that he must go: "I couldn't stop if it were to prolong my life a score of years," he tells Crummles. "Here, take my hand, and with it my hearty thanks.— Oh! that I should have been fooling here!" (380; ch. 30). These lines may reflect Dickens's impatience with his own digressiveness—he seems to realize that his reputation as a writer depends on his ability to construct a coherent narrative—but their main purpose is to announce a decisive renunciation of celebrity.

Nicholas hasn't minded rehearsing or appearing on stage, but he has been bothered by the infighting and bickering and rumormongering. He doesn't want to compete with others for attention and publicity, and he certainly prefers not to be associated with people like Mr. Snevellici. Through it all, Nicholas has often tried to see the actors as harmless, telling himself that they are "more calculated to provoke mirth than anger" (361; ch. 29). But underneath this good humor there has also been some annoyance—and with it, the potential for violence. Near the end of his run with the actors, after finally knocking down Mr. Lenville, Nicholas demands an apology, insisting that it must be delivered "humbly" and "submissively" (364; ch. 29). "Be careful, sir, to what lengths your jealousy carries you another time," he warns Lenville, "and be careful, also, before you venture too far, to ascertain your rival's temper" (364; ch. 29). Here, we see how an obsession with celebrity leads to professional and personal jealousy, which leads in turn to an outburst of anger and a show of force. Dragged into the spotlight, more or less against his will, Nicholas now has little choice but to warn his rivals and threaten his critics. They have driven him to this sort of behavior, and they must take care not to do it again.[9]

* * *

It's hard to know what to make of all this. For some critics, it's not just disappointing but discouraging. "Arguably," John Carey writes,

> this is where *Nicholas Nickleby* ought to have stopped, with Nicholas joining Crummles and becoming a professional actor (which is what young Dickens wanted to be). It is when Nicholas leaves the Crummles company and discovers the Cheerybles, in Chapter 35, that the novel starts to go soft. (xxiii)

Like Carey, Mark Ford sees the "Crummleses' banishment from the narrative" as being "in accordance with the overall drive of the book's last third towards a rather dispiriting normality" (xxvii), adding that before the introduction of the Cheerybles, the novel offers a "gloriously ardent sense of possibility and adventure" (xxiii). Following Carey and Ford, we might conclude that in taking Nicholas away from the actors, Dickens lost his nerve and began to trade in sentimentality. Had he allowed his hero to remain with Crummles, he might have produced a different sort of book—one with no Cheerybles, no Madeline Bray, and no creaky inheritance plot—and put himself, and perhaps the entire tradition of the English novel, on an entirely new footing.

Of course, this is not the only possible reading. For as we think about Nicholas's departure from the troupe, we might join G. K. Chesterton in applauding Dickens's decision to save his hero and himself for better things. Chesterton felt that *Nickleby* "coincided with [Dickens's] resolution to be a great novelist and his final belief that he could be one" (31). In support of such a reading, we might consider a much later scene, which briefly reunites Nicholas with the Crummles troupe. Here, Nicholas speaks with a new member of the company, a "literary gentleman," who has "dramatized in his time two hundred and forty-seven novels as fast as they had come out" (597; ch. 48). The hack dramatist asks Nicholas if he has ever heard a "definition of fame" and then offers one of his own: "When I dramatize a book, sir . . . *that's* fame—for its author" (597; ch. 48). Nicholas finds this appalling, and though he concedes that "Shakespeare derived some of his plots from old tales and legends," he also insists that

> whereas [Shakespeare] brought within the magic circle of his genius, traditions peculiarly adapted for his purpose, and turned familiar things into constellations which should enlighten the world for ages, you drag within the magic circle of your dullness, subjects not at all adapted to the purposes of the stage, and debase as he exalted. . . . if I were a writer of books, and you a thirsty dramatist, I would rather pay your tavern score for six months—large as it might be—than have a niche in the Temple of Fame with you for the humblest corner of my pedestal, through six hundred generations. (598; ch. 48)

Nicholas has never before used this sort of language, never spoken of the Temple of Fame or of things being exalted. Neither, for that matter, has Dickens. And so, with this speech, Dickens offers not only a denunciation of piracy and plagiarism, but also an assertion of his own claim to something grander than mere celebrity, something that might eventually place him in the same "magic circle" as Shakespeare.[10]

Unfortunately, our knowledge of Dickens's attitude toward celebrity can make it hard to sustain a Chestertonian enthusiasm for *Nickleby*. We know that Dickens eventually won the sort of fame he dreamt of, and we also know that he would not be the last great artist to hope that fame would prove to be a remedy for the humiliations of celebrity. We're familiar with the sorts of questions that surround the production of art in a modern celebrity culture: What if I want to be more than a flash in the pan? What if I can't resist the lure of celebrity? What if I find myself becoming an object of ridicule—or worse, an object of pity? We have heard it all before, and so we know what it means for a young writer to say, in the wake of his own enormous success, "I've gotta find some way to enjoy this that doesn't involve getting *eaten* by it, so that I'm gonna be able to go do something else"(Lipsky 33).[11]

Knowing all of these things, we can hardly blame the young Dickens for hoping not to be eaten by his own success. And yet, as we watch Nicholas Nickleby shake loose of the Crummleses, we must admit to knowing one more thing: that lasting fame, fame of the sort that Dickens might not even have allowed himself to imagine, fame of the sort that has come to no other writer in the last two hundred years, would not and could not release him from the bonds of celebrity. In his case, those bonds would prove to be unbreakable. He would not only live and work amidst appalling gossip—much of which would turn out to be true—he would live on in the midst of it, too. As long as people are reading *Pickwick* or *Bleak House*, *David Copperfield* or *Great Expectations*, they will also want to read about the blacking factory, Nelly Ternan, and the rest of it. There is no help for that now, and there never will be. This may be the most important thing for us to take away from Dickens's early writings on celebrity. For if his experience of celebrity was not entirely unprecedented, it was nevertheless profound. The young Dickens saw what celebrity culture offered to people like Mrs. Hunter and Mr. Kenwigs—which is to say, people like us. What's more, he showed how celebrity fails, and cannot help but fail, to deliver on such promises. In his early writings, we begin to recognize what celebrity culture would eventually do to fans, readers, and writers. It's our job, moving forward, to try and make sense of what it did to him.

NOTES

1. For Inglis's discussion of *Dombey*, see 79-82. For a detailed account of Sterne's pursuit of celebrity, see Peter M. Briggs's "Laurence Sterne and Literary Celebrity in 1760." Briggs argues that Sterne "differentiated between *kinds* of celebrity and the available paths to fame" and "deliberately chose to present himself . . . not as a literary candidate for slow fame but as a theatrical candidate for sudden fame" (90).

2. Dickens's memories of being exhibited in the window of the factory, and of drawing "quite a little crowd" of observers, are related in his autobiographical fragment (see Forster 2: 31–32). As Peter Ackroyd notes, these memories have often been likened to recollections of a "primal scene" (94). Following Ackroyd, Jane Smiley associates Dickens's memories with his later exhibitions of himself as a "phenomenon and a star" (172).

3. For many scholars, as we've already noted, this complicated relationship between closeness and distance is one of the defining features of modern celebrity. Chris Rojek puts it this way: "Bigots, forgers, criminals, whores, balladeers and thinkers have been objects of public attention since Greek and Roman times. . . . But they did not carry the illusion of intimacy, the sense of being an exalted confrère, that is part of celebrity status in the age of mass-media" (19). For similar arguments, see Inglis 156–57 and Mole 22–27. A powerful early version of this argument was advanced by film critic Richard Schickel, who suggested that modern celebrity culture had reached its logical conclusion in presidential assailant John Hinckley, Jr.'s obsession with Jodie Foster (1-22, 280-85).

4. The larger phenomenon of lionism has been most carefully analyzed by Richard Salmon. Salmon suggests that lionism is "the quintessential mode of nineteenth-century celebrity" (60), noting "its strongly gendered aspect" (69) and stressing its potentially unsettling liminality: "neither a fully interpersonal oral encounter nor a relationship of physical separation," he says, lionism "stands somewhere between the two communicational structures" (68).

5. Robert Douglas-Fairhurst explains that the term "public character" was "much in vogue during the 1830s" and was "routinely applied to anyone in the public eye" (312). That Dickens sees the term as applying to writers as well as to actors and public officials is

suggested by his later comments on the rate-collector's false modesty: "If [the collector] had been an author, who knew his place," Dickens tells us, "he couldn't have been more humble" (168; ch. 14).

6. Here, as before, Dickens anticipates the claims of many later theorists and historians of celebrity. The connection between modern celebrity and experiences of alienation, urbanization, and secularization has been noted, for example, by sociologists P. David Marshall and Chris Rojek. Marshall argues that the celebrity is "part of a system of false promise in the system of capital, which offers the reward of stardom to a random few in order to perpetuate the myth of potential universal success" (9), while Rojek describes celebrity culture as a distraction from "the fact of structured inequality and the meaningless of existence following the death of God" (90). Philosopher Mark Rowlands appears to offer a dissenting view when he describes celebrity culture as a symptom of our "inability to distinguish *quality* from *bullshit*" (28, emphases not mine), but he agrees that "this new form of fame seems driven by boredom—the ennui characteristic of a society that has become so comfortable that it is starting to feel uncomfortable about itself—and is attracted to the shiny baubles of the new and unfamiliar" (15).

7. For important and influential commentary on the Crummles troupe, see Michael Slater's introduction to the 1978 Penguin edition of the novel and Paul Schlicke's *Dickens and Popular Entertainment*. Slater establishes the actors' importance to the book by saying that "theatricality and role-playing are the living heart of *Nicholas Nickleby*, giving it such artistic unity and coherence as it can be said to possess" (15). Schlicke acknowledges his debt to Slater (50), but also attempts to move beyond the concept of role-playing, stressing the "extremely close affinity between theatres and other venues of popular entertainment" (64).

8. Looking at the illustration, we cannot help but be struck by the resemblance between Nicholas and Dickens himself. The artist Samuel Laurence produced at least two portraits of Dickens in this period, and engravings based on one of them were the first images of the author made available for sale to the public (see Xavier 462). That *Nickleby* coincides with a crucial moment in the development of Dickens's public image is further evidenced by the fact that the Laurence engravings would soon be supplanted by the famous "Nickleby portrait," painted by Daniel Maclise and adapted for use as the frontispiece to the first volume edition of the novel. For Robert L. Patten, the appearance of this portrait marks "the apogee of the first phase of Dickens's vocational career" (31–32).

9. Paul Schlicke offers "several explanations" for "Nicholas's sense of distance from the actors," including the character's "class-consciousness" (82). Though Schlicke admits that the Crummles troupe, and indeed much of nineteenth-century theater, is open to charges of "triviality" (83), he concludes that "in the end the players are inappropriately rejected" (85).

10. This is not the novel's only reference to Shakespeare, nor even its most revealing one. Shortly before Nicholas announces his imminent departure from the acting company, Mrs. Nickleby recalls her honeymoon trip to Stratford-Upon-Avon, where she dreamed of "a black gentleman, at full length, in plaster-of-Paris, with a lay down collar tied

with two tassels, leaning against a post and thinking" and also recalls that she was "in the family way with my son Nicholas at the time" (340; ch. 27). If Mrs. Nickleby is a fictional version of Dickens's own mother, as many biographers have suggested, then this speech amounts to a kind of literary annunciation scene, with the spirit of Shakespeare visiting the young mother to bring good news of her son.

11. The young writer in question is David Foster Wallace. Speaking with a *Rolling Stone* reporter while on a book tour for *Infinite Jest*, Wallace likened "getting a whole lot of attention" to "getting *heroin* injected into your cortex." Wallace added that "the reality is . . . being *in* a room with a piece of paper. And that all this, this is tangential stuff, and some of it feels real good and some of it doesn't. But this is all—that's—*that's* what's real, and the rest of this is just conversation around it" (Lipsky 191). This can't help but make us think of Wallace's eventual suicide and his struggles to finish his novel *The Pale King*. Though Wallace and Dickens are obviously quite different in temperament, their experiences do overlap. Like Dickens, Wallace is forced to juggle pleasure and disgust, temptation and fear. He also sees celebrity as not only "tangential" but unreal and hopes that what will sustain and satisfy him is the act of writing itself.

WORKS CITED

Ackroyd, Peter. *Dickens*. New York: HarperCollins, 1990.

Braudy, Leo. *The Frenzy of Renown: Fame and Its History*. Oxford: Oxford UP, 1986.

Briggs, Peter M. "Laurence Sterne and Literary Celebrity in 1760." *Laurence Sterne's "Tristram Shandy": A Casebook*. Ed. Thomas Keymer. Oxford: Oxford UP, 2006. 79–107.

Carey, John. Introduction. *Nicholas Nickleby*. By Charles Dickens. New York: Everyman's Library, 1993.

Chenery, Thomas. "[L]eading article in *The Times*." *Charles Dickens: The Critical Heritage*. Ed. Philip A. W. Collins. London: Routledge, 1971. 506–08.

Chesterton, G. K. *Chesterton on Dickens: Criticisms and Appreciations*. Intro. Michael Slater. London: Dent, 1992.

Dickens, Charles. *The Letters of Charles Dickens*. Ed. Madeline House, Graham Storey, and Kathleen Tillotson. 12 vols. Oxford: Clarendon, 1965–2002.

———. *Nicholas Nickleby*. Ed. Mark Ford. London: Penguin, 1999.

———. *The Pickwick Papers*. Ed. Mark Wormold. London: Penguin, 1999.

———. "Some Particulars Concerning a Lion." *Sketches by Boz and Other Early Papers 1833–39*. Ed. Michael Slater. Columbus: Ohio State UP, 1994. 508–12.

Douglas-Fairhurst, Robert. *Becoming Dickens: The Invention of a Novelist*. Cambridge: Harvard UP, 2011.

Ford, Mark. Introduction. *Nicholas Nickleby*. By Charles Dickens. London: Penguin, 1999.

Forster, John. *The Life of Charles Dickens*. Notes and Index by A. J. Hoppé. 2 vols. London: Dent, 1969.

Inglis, Fred. *A Short History of Celebrity*. Princeton: Princeton UP, 2010.

John, Juliet. *Dickens and Mass Culture*. Oxford: Oxford UP, 2010.

Lipsky, David. *Although of course you end up becoming yourself: A Road Trip with David Foster Wallace*. New York: Broadway, 2010.

Lodge, David. "Dickens Our Contemporary." *Consciousness and the Novel: Connected Essays*. Cambridge: Harvard UP, 2002. 114–34.

Marsh, Joss. "The Rise of Celebrity Culture." *Charles Dickens in Context*. Ed. Sally Ledger and Holly Furneaux. Cambridge: Cambridge UP, 2011. 98–108.

Marshall, P. David. *Celebrity and Power: Fame in Contemporary Culture*. Minneapolis: U of Minnesota P, 1997.

Mole, Tom. *Byron's Romantic Celebrity: Industrial Culture and the Hermeneutic of Intimacy*. New York: Palgrave, 2007.

Patten, Robert L. "From *Sketches* to *Nickleby*." *The Cambridge Companion to Charles Dickens*. Ed. John O. Jordan. Cambridge: Cambridge UP, 2001.

Pearl, Matthew. "*Bleak House*: The 3-D Concert Experience." *Slate*. 17 March 2009. Web. 15 October 2011.

Rojek, Chris. *Celebrity*. London: Reaktion, 2001.

Rowlands, Mark. *Fame*. Stocksfield: Acumen, 2008.

Salmon, Richard. "The Physiognomy of the Lion: Encountering Literary Celebrity in The Nineteenth Century." *Romanticism and Celebrity Culture*. Ed. Tom Mole. Cambridge: Cambridge UP, 2009. 60-78.

Schickel, Richard. *Intimate Strangers: The Culture of Celebrity in America*. With a New Afterword by the Author. Chicago: Ivan R. Dee, 2000.

Schlicke, Paul. *Dickens and Popular Entertainment*. London: Allen & Unwin, 1985.

Slater, Michael. *Charles Dickens*. New Haven: Yale UP, 2009

———. Introduction. *Nicholas Nickleby*. By Charles Dickens. Harmondsworth: Penguin, 1978.

Smiley, Jane. *Charles Dickens*. New York: Viking, 2002.

Smith, Grahame. *Charles Dickens: A Literary Life*. New York: Palgrave, 1996.

Xavier, Andrew. "[P]ortraits, busts, and photographs of Dickens." *Oxford Reader's Companion to Dickens*. Ed. Paul Schlicke. Oxford: Oxford UP, 1999. 462–65.

Fatal Extraction: Dickensian Bildungsroman and the Logic of Dependency

Aleksandar Stević

Focusing on Oliver Twist, David Copperfield, *and* Great Expectations, *this study explores the intersections of the Dickensian bildungsroman and the early and mid-Victorian debates about the sources of poverty and the legitimacy of charitable intervention in alleviating its effects. These debates, which culminated around the time of the New Poor Law, were the main venue in which political economists, social reformers, proponents of self-help, and advocates of organized charity exchanged arguments about the role of personal responsibility and environmental pressures in determining the individual's standing in the world. Their arguments were invariably driven by conflicting notions of individual agency: are the poor victims and in need of assistance, or vicious and in need of discipline? Even when not directly addressing the provisions of the New Poor Law and the effects of organized charity, Dickens's novels seek to negotiate some of the central tensions of these contemporary ideological conflicts: invariably focusing on orphans and the external factors that shape their fate, including both benevolent and tyrannical caregivers, Dickens's novels obsessively examine the meaning of dependency and guardianship. By organizing his plots around the moral and practical implications of social ascent by means of outside benevolent intervention, Dickens used the form of the bildungsroman to explore an alternative to the dominant ethics of self-sufficiency.*

Dickens Studies Annual, Volume 45, Copyright © 2014 by AMS Press, Inc. All rights reserved.

It has long been recognized that the rescue of helpless orphans is among the most persistent Dickensian fantasies. With precision worthy of Vladimir Propp's *Morphology of the Folktale*, Dickens's major bildungsromans fill the structural roles of villains and helpers, locating the center of narrative tension not in the relationship between the hero and the world but in the encounter between the hero's adversaries and his benefactors. And while Dickens's heroes are seldom fully relieved of agency, his bildungsromans nonetheless surrender a decisive amount of power to numerous external instances which limit the autonomy of protagonists.[1] *Oliver Twist* (1837–39), *David Copperfield* (1849–50), and *Great Expectations* (1860–61) all examine the proposition that one's place in the world—and sometimes even mere survival—is determined not by active efforts towards self-realization but by the care and terror exercised by various guardians. Oliver Twist is threatened by the brutal parish bureaucracy exemplified in Mr. Bumble, as well as by the criminal underground of Fagin, Sikes, and Monks, who are all strongly invested in corrupting, if not physically destroying him, until he is rescued through the benevolent interventions of Mr. Brownlow and Rose Maylie's circle. David Copperfield is saved from the terror and neglect of Edward Murdstone and his equally tyrannical sister Jane through the involvement of surrogate mothers like his nurse Peggotty and, in particular, his munificent if eccentric aunt Betsey. Even *Great Expectations*, a much darker variation on this familiar theme, and one which complicates the distinction between the bildungsroman hero's helpers and antagonists, seems nonetheless fixated on the possibility of elevation through benevolence. The *Times* recognized as much when the novel was first published:

> The hero of the present tale, Pip, is a sort of Oliver. He is low-born, fatherless and motherless, and he rises out of the cheerless degradation of his childhood into quite another sphere. The thieves got a hold of Oliver, tried to make him a pickpocket, and were succeeded in their friendly intentions by Mr. Brownlow. . . . The convict in the new story takes the place of Mr. Brownlow in the old, and supplies Master Pip with every luxury. In either tale, through some unaccountable caprice of fortune, the puny son of poverty suddenly finds himself the child of affluence. (Collins 445)

While the claim that "Pip is a sort of Oliver" certainly requires additional qualification, this review nonetheless recognizes a certain continuity in Dickens's preferred plot structures: repeatedly returning to the question of external forces that direct the hero's life path and define his social position, Dickens's novels obsessively examine the meaning of dependency and guardianship.

Traditionally, this interest in heroes by definition abandoned, neglected, and in need of help has been read as a sign of Dickens's fixation on childhood as an existential condition characterized by vulnerability and exclusion.[2] It is one of the aims of this essay to historicize this fixation. Helplessness, dependence, and passivity are the central categories of the interrelated Victorian debates about the status of the poor and the working classes, about crime, about charitable intervention, and about self-reliance. When Oliver Twist's and David Copperfield's protectors and detractors confront each other with contrary interpretations of the heroes' situation—Brownlow and Aunt Betsey acknowledging their helplessness, and Bumble and Murdstone accusing the boys of willfully falling into vice—they rehearse the familiar arguments known from the debates about the position of the poor in early Victorian England. Are they vicious and in need of discipline, or helpless and in need of salvation? Or, should they, perhaps, help themselves? By asking such questions, Dickens's novels participate in the contemporary debates that were primarily concerned with action, passivity, and individual agency.

However, in exploring the discursive conditions that pressured Dickens to turn a genre typically concerned with social and psychological aspects of a youthful protagonist's transition to adulthood into a tool for exploring abandonment and helplessness, I depart from the unusually persistent critical tradition that seeks to determine Dickens's status as a social commentator and the exact position he occupied on the ideological map of mid-nineteenth-century England. Once again, an early review sets the tone: "*Oliver Twist* is," argued Richard Ford in the *Quarterly Review* shortly after the novel was published, "directed against the poor law and the workhouse system, and in our opinion with much unfairness. The abuses he describes are not only exaggerated, but in nineteen cases out of twenty do not exist" (Ford 85).[3] While committed to reconstructing the discursive space within which Dickens's novels operate, I am interested in developing a decisively formalist version of literary historicism by examining the dialectical relationship between the logic of the bildungsroman plot and several historically conditioned views of agency and helplessness. Beyond explicit attacks on the Poor Laws and other instances of overt social commentary, how did the contrary propositions on agency which accompanied the discussions about poverty, pauperism, and crime, shape the narrative logic of the Dickensian Bildungsroman?

I. The State of the Laboring People

> *Considered in its moral and social aspect, the state of the labouring people has latterly been a subject of much more speculation and discussion than formerly; and the opinion that it is not now what it ought to be, has become very general.*
> —John Stuart Mill, *Principles of Political Economy*

By the mid-nineteenth century it had become common for commentators to decry the seemingly endless proliferation of debates on the status of the poor. According to an article published in *Westminster Review* in 1869, "it is not only that the subject [of pauperism and crime] is painful in itself, but it is worn threadbare. It has been treated so often, by so many able men, and in such a variety of aspects, as to leave little more to be said, nor the prospect of even grouping the facts in a new and more striking light" ("The Philanthropy of the Age" 437). The sense of saturation had been building for a long time. More than a decade earlier, Edward Cheney complained that "there never was a time when the condition of the poor engaged so much of the attention of the legislature, or occupied so large a portion of time and energies of individuals" (408). This immense intellectual and political effort was matched only by the financial expenditure required for the alleviation of poverty. As Henry Mayhew pointed out, in the first, incomplete, multivolume edition of *London Labour and the London Poor*, published in 1851–52, "the magnitude of the sum that we give voluntarily towards the support and education of the poorer classes, is unparalleled in the history of any other nation, or of any other time" (3:35).[4]

Mayhew's own unparalleled effort to penetrate the depths of urban poverty and provide a "cyclopaedia of the industry, the want, and the vice of the great Metropolis" (1,3) came on the heels of decades of institutional activity and public discussion. The intense interest in the poor peaked during the heated debates which led up to the Poor Law Amendment Act of 1834, and these can in turn be traced at least as far back as Jeremy Bentham's writings from the mid-1790s and Joseph Townsend's *Dissertation on the Poor Laws*, first published in 1786.[5] For a good hundred years, the poor and the working classes were objects of intense public scrutiny, scientific or pseudo-scientific study, fear, condemnation, sympathy, and ideological indoctrination, all culminating in a great amount of both legislative and charitable activity. Mayhew's own rhetorical apparatus reveals some of the paradoxes of this epistemological fixation on the lower orders: while unquestionably sympathetic to the plight of the urban poor, he appropriated the language of colonial exploration, presenting himself as "the traveller in the undiscovered country of the poor" and promising to illuminate a "body of persons, of whom the public had less knowledge than of the most distant tribes of the earth" (1:3). In order to be made visible, the lower classes are also thoroughly exoticized, simultaneously in plain sight in the heart of the metropolis and fundamentally alien: as if truly a faraway tribe, the poor are keenly examined, their habits obsessively observed, and they are, in the final instance, meticulously catalogued.

Predictably, the prominent position which the status of the poor occupied in the public discourse has also turned it into the central point of raging ideological conflicts. Social historians like David Owen, Derek Fraser, and F. David Roberts have done much to describe the complex interaction between the rising discipline of political economy, the traditional upper-class paternalism, religious attacks on poverty as a consequence of sin, and the spike in humanitarianism in the early nineteenth century.[6] And the closer one looks at these developments, the more apparent it becomes that the ideological disputes about the poor relief during the first half of the nineteenth century stem from a larger conflict between disparate notions of individual agency and personal responsibility, a conflict that Dickens's novels obsessively enact. Focusing on neglected children placed in the care of brutal guardians, anonymous benefactors, and ruthless criminals, the Dickensian bildungsroman as a form seeks to reconsider the central concerns of the poverty debates: like contemporary social commentators, his novels will repeatedly return to the limits of autonomous action and the relationship between individual choice and the pressure of external structures.

At least since the late eighteenth century, the central objection against the existing Poor Law arrangements, established during the reign of Queen Elizabeth, was that they provided too much relief too indiscriminately, thus promoting "idleness and vice" (Townsend 2).[7] The charge originally put forward by Townsend was not only reiterated in the ensuing debates, but also constituted the basis of public policy. Following this exact line of reasoning, the authors of the 1823 Charity Report severely criticized those who engage in the practice of indiscriminate charity: "Such a man by an indiscriminate alms-giving may be the promoter of idleness and beggary, a patron of deception and vice, and so far as he holds a premium for what is bad, an actual diminisher of the sum of good" (Ellis 98). A very similar line of argument was taken in the 1834 Poor Law Report which served as a basis for the new legislation (Roberts 110). As Townsend writes, offering an argument which will be restated countless times during the first half of the nineteenth century:

> It is universally found that where bread can be obtained without care or labour, it leads through idleness and vice to poverty. Before they discovered the gold and silver mines of Peru and Mexico, the Spaniards were distinguished among the nations of Europe for their industry and arts, for their manufactures and their commerce. But what are they now? a lazy, poor, miserable people. (14)

For early Victorians, like for Townsend, to be helped is to be relieved of agency. In the words of Samuel Smiles, the best-known Victorian popularizer of the widespread ideology of self-help, "Whatever is done *for* men or classes, to a certain extent takes away the stimulus and necessity of doing for themselves; and where men are subjected to over-guidance and over government, the inevitable tendency is to render them comparatively helpless" (Smiles 1). Although there is no reason to take a reductionist view of the rather diverse body of Victorian self-help literature—not everyone would subscribe to the Smilesean creed according to which reliance on others is outright detrimental—the fascination with self-reliance in the face of adversity nevertheless was a dominant theme. This is precisely why the Victorians have left us such an astounding number of terms that describe the care for the self, including *self-cultivation, self-education, self-training, self-culture,* and *self-formation.*[9]

"But Self-culture is possible," writes William Channing, "not only because we can enter into and search ourselves; we have a still nobler power, that of acting on, determining, and forming ourselves" (5). Although Channing's vision of this work on the self is certainly more complex than mere insistence on determination, he was nonetheless attracted to the sheer power of will as a factor in changing one's circumstances: "every condition has means of progress, if we have spirit enough to use them. Some volumes have recently been published, giving examples of histories of 'knowledge acquired under difficulties'; and it is most animating to see in these what a resolute man can do for himself" (10). The volume Channing most likely had in mind was George Lillie Craik's *The Pursuit of Knowledge under Difficulties* (1830) which, much like Smiles's later book, offered examples of men who have achieved great prominence in spite of the impediments of humble origin. Craik promises to describe "a body of examples, to show how the most unpropitious circumstances have been unable to conquer an ardent desire for the acquisition of knowledge" (1). In the words of Edwin Paxton Hood, who offered yet another version of this creed, "all the education that has ever been in the world, has been the result of self-determination, self-training, and self-reliance" (13–14). Whatever the complexities of Victorian attitudes towards self-help, this collective fascination with self-reliance meant that moral and every other form of responsibility was firmly located within the individual subject: "A man must act: whether he is necessitated to labour for his maintenance; or is freed by fortune from all apprehension, and from all constrained exertion; yet he must act" (Paxton Hood 2). For the early Victorians, this imperative of action regardless of one's circumstances, or rather, the imperative of transcending one's circumstances, could easily turn into the fear that reliance on others will diminish both the need and willingness to care for oneself. In the debates about poverty, this assumption was extremely influential. If you are helped, you will not help yourself.

Take the 1823 Charity Report and its attack on Anthony Highmore's book *Pietas Londinensis*, a book that seeks to familiarize the public with the work of charitable institutions "so that their utility may be readily seen and considered, their merits recommended to general patronage, their methods of reception more commonly known, and the requisites for the admission of patients obtained with greater facility" (ix). Highmore praises the Queen's Lying-In Hospital in the Bayswater area of London, pointing out that the hospital constituted the only institution in the area to which the poor could turn. Before the hospital was established, he contends, the patients had to walk so far to get help that it was not uncommon for women to give birth on the street while on their way to the nearest hospital (189-90). The authors of the *Charity Report* had a somewhat different view of the issue:

> We agree with Mr. Highmore that nothing can be more shocking than that women should be running about in such a state, totally unprovided; but we should ask him whether the occurrence of such events is not entirely due to the existence of Lying-in hospitals. If there were no such receptacles women would be left to their own prudence, and might, perhaps, reflect upon

the inconveniences that necessarily attend a state of pregnancy, and guide against them before-hand. (Ellis 114)

With such intense fear of the negative effects of charitable action, it was absolutely imperative for legislators who drafted the New Poor Law to ensure that welfare benefits were not easily accessible.[10] The most important measure put in place so that no unwarranted relief was offered was the so-called workhouse test, which severely limited the amount and kind of relief available to able-bodied men. In order to deter the laborers from seeking poor relief instead of employment, the only relief offered to those able to work was to be housed in the workhouses. As W. R. Greg noted in an 1853 article, "it was perceived by the authors of that admirable measure, that the only way of discouraging pauperism, and promoting energy and self-reliance, was by rendering the position of the pauper less comfortable and less desirable than that of the independent labourer" (63). With such arguments put forward, the reasoning of Mr. Bumble, Dickens's infamous workhouse administrator from *Oliver Twist*, seems somewhat less caricatural than it is usually considered. "The great principle of out-of-door relief is," argues Mr. Bumble, "to give the paupers exactly what they don't want; and then they get tired of coming" (179; ch.23).

Under these circumstances the arguments for poor relief, whether through state intervention or through private charity, had to take into account this pervasive individualistic philosophy. One necessary step was to suggest that there is such a thing as unforeseeable circumstances, but such suggestions were made timidly, and were usually prefaced by assurances that the charitable activity will not promote imprudence:

We are by no means advocates for imprudence; on the contrary, we hold self-reliance to be one of the principal ingredients for making a good and useful citizen ; but there are some accidents against which no foresight can guard. There are but a favored few who are not liable for sudden reverses ; and all of us may be suddenly stricken by death, or visited, with mutilation and disease in the very vigour of our days. ("Reports of the Society, 1838–1839" 343)

In fact, given the pervasiveness of the ideology of self-reliance, early nineteenth-century philanthropy had very limited rhetorical resources at its disposal when making the case for charitable intervention, unless, of course, it espoused moral and religious activism and explicit advocacy of self-help as a central part of the charitable effort. After all, if indigence is always a matter of individual failure, the primary form of helping the poor (and for many, the only acceptable form) was to help them acquire the moral qualities and the practical skills that would enable them to help themselves (Fraser 128).[11] And if one was to avoid what was in essence a missionary approach which dictated that the urban poor be saved from the state of moral depravity, one had to argue forcefully that the recipients of help have demonstrated their prudence. Dickens invariably took the latter path.

Advocating the cause of numerous charitable institutions, he was particularly vocal in his support for benevolent and friendly societies through which members of various professions sought to provide mutual aid in case of distress. Of course, such societies were the easiest to defend from the most common objections against outside assistance. As Geoffrey Finlayson has argued, those taking part in benevolent societies were in a sense *helping themselves*, since they were essentially participating in insurance schemes: "Friendly societies were, therefore, the most notable and widespread manifestation of providence: of the practice whereby the working classes—or a proportion of them—made provision for bad times in more favourable periods" (27). Dickens's rhetorical strategy in the speeches he offered at fundraisers for societies such as the Artists' Benevolent Fund or the Railway Benevolent Institution underscores this point. The emphasis is, without exception, that funds are being collected for those who have been prudent, and for the support of their widows and orphans. "I address you on behalf of those professors of the fine arts who *have* made provision during life, and in submitting to you their claims I am only advocating principles which I myself have always maintained" (*Speeches* 268). An analogous, though somewhat more complex (and more strained) argument is found in a request which Dickens, Carlyle, and Forster sent to Lord Palmerston on behalf of the daughters of one Mauritius Lowe. As Jude V. Nixon has demonstrated in a detailed case-study of the Lowes Memorial, in constructing the argument for helping the two poor elderly women whose father was once a close friend of Samuel Johnson, the signatories worked hard to demonstrate that the women met the test of worthiness: "they are gentlewomen in manners; by all evidence, persons of uniformly unexceptional conduct; veracity, sense, ingenuous propriety, noticeable in them both to a superior degree . . . they are very poor but have taken their poverty in a quiet, unaffectedly handsome manner, and have still hope that, in some way or another intolerable want will not be permitted to overtake them. They have an altogether respectable, or, we may say, a touching and venerable air" (Qtd. in Nixon 258). Given the extent to which poverty was associated with crime, idleness, and sin, it was imperative to establish the impeccable moral profile of welfare recipients, and to account for their inability to care for themselves.

The roots of this insistence on individual responsibility are complex. F. David Roberts has persuasively argued that the logic behind the New Poor Law was a matter of "consonance between the laissez-faire individualism of political economy and the self-reliant individualism of Victorian morality" (111). In other words, both religious moralism and free-market doctrines had good reasons to support a system that insisted on individual responsibility. For the former, unwarranted relief was morally corrupting; for the latter, it was interfering with the principle of the active pursuit of self-interest. Nominally, both doctrines allowed for the existence of the truly helpless, and hence acknowledged that there are situations in which relief could be administered without promoting imprudence. However, in practice the tendency of the legislators was to limit severely the definition of helplessness, and to attribute absolute responsibility to almost anyone: hence the insistence of the writers of the Charity Report that the availability of healthcare promotes recklessness. For the exact same reason, an enormous effort was necessary in order to put at least some limits on child labor and acknowledge that children are "not free agents."[12]

Clearly, to truly subvert this powerful ideological machinery, was to introduce an alternative understanding of agency. The most well-known (though by no means the most interesting) argument was put forward by Robert Owen, who simply decided to reverse the dominant ideological paradigm by denying all agency to individuals: "In those characters that now exhibit crime, the fault is obviously not in the individual, but the defect proceeds from the system in which the individual has been trained. Withdraw those circumstances which tend to create crime in the human character, and crime will not be created" (Owen 59).[13] Owen's view relieved the poor not only of the ability to act, but also to exert moral judgment.

By midcentury, one didn't have to be a utopian socialist to acknowledge the role of environment in perpetuating poverty and the many social evils associated with it. As Norris Pope has argued in *Dickens and Charity*, evangelical views have also evolved from an almost unanimous insistence that poverty is self-inflicted towards recognizing that "the connexion between the moral and physical condition of the poor was most intimate and inevitable" (Lord Ashley, Qtd. in Pope 202). And yet, as Pope's analysis shows, this shift in argument has only managed to displace the causes of sinfulness of the poor into the environment, without truly removing the stigma usually placed on the population of urban slums: "poverty, it would appear, could still be understood as a result of moral infirmity; but moral infirmity, evangelical reformers increasingly recognized, was largely unavoidable for the bulk of those individuals living in the worst slum environments" (203). The acknowledgment of environmental factors complicated the evangelical understanding of charity but did not do away with an essentially paternalist vision of the industrial poor as a class in dire need of a moral intervention from above.

A more far-reaching argument in favor of helping the poor was not that the circumstances have rendered them incapable of passing moral judgments, but rather that the poor were unable to escape their circumstances *in spite* of exercising proper moral judgment. It was Hugo Reid who provided this more sophisticated critique of both political economy and the New Poor Law, offering what will become a classical argument in favor of the welfare state, without completely obliterating individual agency. For Reid, it was precisely the failure of laissez-faire economics to create jobs and reduce poverty that invited state intervention: "if the natural operation of the law of demand and supply cannot supply to the people the bare necessities of existence, they ought to be interfered with" (16) As for the New Poor Law, Reid has essentially turned the tables on the deterrence argument: a brutal and essentially punitive poor law is in fact hurting the sense of self-respect and independence among the poor (15). Perhaps most importantly, Reid went on to reject forcefully the notion that either failure or success is self-incurred:

> But thousands—hundreds of thousands—are born or irresistibly forced into the condition we deplore, surrounded by circumstances which give them no possible chance of emancipation, and doomed to a painful struggle with the horrors of want, moral and physical suffering, disease, and crime, until they miserably sink—unless rescued by the strong arm of the state.
>
> The world is not all composed of "clever pushing fellows who get on," and "never-do-wells" who don't deserve to get on. The great majority of ordinary plodders who remain where they have been set, rise by good fortune they have done nothing to deserve,—or sink by the pressure of forces they could neither foresee nor withstand. It is for these—the mass—that we must legislate. (14)

The case in point: *Oliver Twist*. Although Dickens was by no means silent on the formative effects of deplorable surroundings, the plot of the novel hinges on the ability of benevolent figures to understand that Oliver is helpless, innocent, and in need of protection, despite all suggestions to the contrary. Other Dickensian heroes, like David and Pip, are not equally endangered, but their worldly prospects are equally dependent on outside intervention. In fact, in the midst of these conflicting accounts of agency and individual responsibility, the Dickensian bildungsroman repeatedly rehearses different scenarios in which external factors, variously understood as state bureaucracy, caring benefactors, malevolent conspirators, or simply the bizarre imagination of strangers, demonstrate the power to shape the hero's fate. In the face of so much insistence on self-reliance and the detrimental effects of what is deemed to be unwarranted help, Dickens remains fascinated with the power of benevolent intervention.

II. The Power of Benevolence

At the beginning of *Oliver Twist*, Dickens mounts a rather obvious parodic assault on the notion that help diminishes capacity for individual action:

> The fact is, that there was considerable difficulty in inducing Oliver to take upon himself the office of respiration,—a troublesome practice, but one which custom has rendered necessary to our easy existence; and for some time he lay gasping on a little flock mattress, rather unequally poised between this world and the next: the balance being decidedly in favour of the latter. Now, if, during this brief period, Oliver had been surrounded

by careful grandmothers, anxious aunts, experienced nurses, and doctors of profound wisdom, he would most inevitably and indubitably have been killed in no time. There being nobody by, however, but a pauper old woman, who was rendered rather misty by an unwonted allowance of beer; and a parish surgeon who did such matters by contract; Oliver and Nature fought out the point between them. (2–3)

Since there was no one to help newborn Oliver, he will have to fight for himself. This is a reductio ad absurdum of the position which advocated self-reliance of just about anyone. The authors of the Charity Report believed that the absence of medical assistance might promote prudence among women: here, the absence of proper care will force Oliver to fight for his life. This parodic undermining of the notion of free will is reinforced by the very structure of the novel's plot: the hero will escape the workhouse only to become an object of intense struggle between the competing worlds of Fagin and Brownlow. Much in the same way, the fate of David Copperfield hinges on whether he will be given up to the Murdstones or accepted by Betsey Trotwood. In Hugo Reid's terminology, these heroes have no possibility of "emancipation" unless saved by a "strong arm" of their bene-factors.[14] For both Oliver Twist and David Copperfield, the decisive question is which forces will take control over their lives.

Nonetheless, the central ideological intervention of the Dickensian bildungsro-man lies not in its insistence on the lack of agency, but in the subversion of the dominant understanding of relationship between agency and morality. The issue is not simply one of passivity and power to change one's own circumstances, but rather of the ethical benefits of charitable intervention. If one cannot control his own standing in the world, offering help and care is an imperative with beneficial moral effects for both the receiver and the giver of this care, hence the fascination with dependence on benefactors. This position anticipates the critique of liberal moral rationalism in the work of contemporary care ethicists:

> The liberal portrayal of the self-sufficient individual enables the privileged to falsely imagine that dependencies hardly exist, and when they are obvious, to suppose they can be dealt with as private preferences, as when parents provide for their infants. The illusion that society is composed of free, equal, independent individuals who can choose to be associated with one another or not obscures the reality that social cooperation is required as a precondition of autonomy. (Held 86)

And if dependency is, in fact, a crucial aspect of social reality, the ethics of individual choice no longer holds, or, at least, proves insufficient. The line of reasoning that contemporary proponents of care ethics seek to displace is the same one which has dominated the Victorian debates about the poor. As we have seen, indiscriminate compassion for the wretched was routinely attacked as a matter of irrational emotional attachment. For the writers of the Charity Report, the first step in seriously tackling the problem of poverty was to abolish injudicious benevolence. To the charge that such an approach might be seen as insensitive or even barbaric, they respond: "we have undertaken to reason the matter, in order to such as are guided by reason may open their eyes. We are not attempting to convince a sentimentalist, or a person who wishes to secure the constant existence of a stock of misery upon which to exercises his charitable feelings—but we wish to convince all who are open to conviction" (Ellis 105). Dickens, however, is self-consciously *not* open to conviction. Commenting on the frequent critical complaints against Dickens's sentimentalism, Steven Marcus writes: "yet at least one vital source of Dickens's power as a novelist can be located in his essential detachment, even alienation, from a kind of quasi-pragmatic apologetics on which the radical and liberal political intelligence so often relies" (Marcus 59). Dickens was working against moral rationalism, while trying to rethink the relationship between agency, external help, and individual accountability.

Novels like *Oliver Twist* or *David Copperfield*, with their explicit focus on benefactors, are critically concerned with the ethical and social value of caring. In fact, discriminating among caring, neglect, and pseudo-care is one of the central issues that the stories of Oliver and David address. Both the workhouse bureaucracy and the Murdstones mistake tyranny for care. "An ethic of care," writes Nell Noddings, "builds upon our desire to respond positively to need" (*The Maternal Factor* 103). The brutal refusal of Oliver Twist's ubiquitous "please sir, I would like some more" signifies not only unwarranted cruelty, but a misunderstanding about the nature of care. And while Oliver will end up severely abused, David Copperfield, after the death of his mother, will not arouse sufficient interest to become subject to terror:

> What would I have given, to have been sent to the hardest school that ever was kept!—to have been taught something, anyhow, anywhere! No such hope dawned upon me. They disliked me; and they sullenly, sternly, steadily, overlooked me. I think Mr. Murdstone's means were straitened at about this time; but it is little to the purpose. He could not bear me; and in putting me from him he tried, as I believe, to put away the notion that I had any claim upon him—and succeeded.
>
> I was not actively ill-used. I was not beaten, or starved; but the wrong that was done to me had no intervals of relenting, and was done in a systematic, passionless manner. Day after day, week after week, month after month, I was coldly neglected. (128; ch.10)

Following the same logic that informed the New Poor Law, both Mr. Bumble, with his refusal of Oliver's request, and Murdstone, with his insistence on "firmness," refuse to acknowledge the very existence of a need, either physical or psychological. Both Oliver and David understand this very well, and both are in active search for guardians who will acknowledge the need to care and to establish a close relationship. "God help me," cries David, "I might have been improved for my whole life, I might have been made another creature perhaps, for life, by a kind word at that season." (40; ch. 4) To become something else, David will have to acquire a new guardian.

Significantly, the care both Oliver and David will find is not entirely devoid of rational scrutiny. In both novels, the hero must account for himself and persuade the prospective benefactor that he is an innocent victim and should be rescued. Oliver pleads with Mr. Brownlow, "Don't turn me out of doors to wander the streets again. Let me stay here, and be a servant. Don't send me back to the wretched place I came from. Have mercy upon the poor boy, sir!" (104; ch. 14). David will face Betsey Trotwood with a very similar plea:

> I am David Copperfield, of Blunderstone, in Suffolk—where you came, on the night when I was born, and saw my dear mama. I have been very unhappy since she died. I have been slighted, and taught nothing, and thrown upon myself, and put to work not fit for me. It made me run away to you. I was robbed at first setting out, and have walked all the way, and have never slept in a bed since I began the journey. (163; ch. 13)

Although such professions of innocence and helplessness will not go untested—Brownlow will test Oliver by trusting him with money and books (a test he will fail, because he will be abducted by Fagin), while Betsey Trotwood will defer her judgment on David's fate until she consults the Murdstones—what the benevolent figures in these novels will decisively refuse to do is to operate under the *assumption of guilt*. Their reaction is rooted precisely in the "desire to respond positively to need" that Noddings has in mind. As we have seen, the association of need and guilt is the modus operandi of both malevolent characters in Dickens's novels, and of the prevailing moral philosophy: if you are in dire need of assistance you must have brought this need on yourself, most likely through some form of moral defect. As Mr. Lambkins, a member of the workhouse board, comments after Oliver Twist has asked for more food, "I never was more convinced of anything in my life, than I am, that that boy will come to be hung" (15; ch. 2). Contrary to this, benevolent figures have an intuitively different response to need, even if they express some reservations. Mr. Brownlow: "You say you are an orphan, without a friend in the world; all the inquiries I have been able to make, confirm the statement. Let me hear your story; where you come from; who brought you up; and how you got into the company in which I found you. Speak the truth, and you shall not be friendless while I live" (104; ch. 14). Later in the novel, when Oliver is caught after he was forced to take part in a break-in, Rose Maylie will afford him the same benefit of the doubt:

Aunt, dear aunt, for mercy's sake, think of this, before you let them drag this
sick child to a prison, which in any case must be the grave of all his chances
of amendment. Oh! as you love me, and know that I have never felt the want
of parents in your goodness and affection, but that I might have done so, and
might have been equally helpless and unprotected with this poor child, have
pity upon him before it is too late! (231; ch. 30)

In both cases, it is the initial emotional impulse that is to be trusted as the primary
guide towards a proper moral judgment.

Oliver Twist and *David Copperfield* will afford considerable attention to differentiating between care and other forms of interpersonal relationships which
might be mistaken for care. As Noddings points out, to care is to open oneself to
the needs of the other, not to shape the other according to one's own aspirations,
nor to project one's own needs and fantasies into the other: "When my caring is
directed to living things, I must consider their natures, ways of life, needs, desires.
And although I can never accomplish it entirely, I try to apprehend the reality
of the other . . ." (*Caring* 14). The narrative logic of Dickens's bildungsromans
reveals a similar ethical vision: empathizing with others is vital, but actively tampering with selves is decisively dangerous. In a novel like *David Copperfield*, to
be shaped by another is to be exposed to a violent and terrorizing action which
will rob you of individuality and even humanity, if it doesn't kill you first. Self-
fashioning is not a part of a process of social apprenticeship, but a mechanism of
exercising dominance over the weak. It is not surprising, then, that the first self to
be fashioned in the novel is that of David's mother, and that this shaping will be
performed by the novel's paradigmatic tyrant, Murdstone. "I knew as well," comments David, "that he could mold her pliant nature into any form he chose, as I
know, now, that he did it" (39). By the time David comes back from the school to
which he was sent, his mother has already fallen victim to the tyranny of Edward
and Jane Murdstone and remarks:

"He [Murdstone] is better able to judge of it than I am; for I very well know
that I am a weak, light, girlish creature, and that he is a firm, grave, serious
man . . . he takes great pains with me; and I ought to be very thankful to
him, and very submissive to him even in my thoughts; and when I am not,
Peggotty, I worry and condemn myself, and feel doubtful of my own heart,
and don't know what to do." (98; ch. 8)

David's own great fallacy is that he will reproduce this domineering relationship
with his "child wife," Dora, even if in somewhat less authoritarian terms: "What
other course was left to take? To 'form her mind'? This was a common phrase of
words which had a fair and promising sound, and I resolved to form Dora's mind.
I began immediately. When Dora was very childish, and I would have infinitely
preferred to humour her, I tried to be grave—and disconcerted her, and myself too"

(592; ch. 48). The formation is not only a failure but, more importantly, it offers a terrifying echo of Murdstone's words: "Yes, I had a satisfaction in the thought of marrying an inexperienced and artless person, and forming her character, and infusing into it some amount of that firmness and decision of which it stood in need" (43; ch. 4). The lessons David Copperfield is to learn will be concerned precisely with the limits of formative domination: "I found myself in the condition of a schoolmaster, a trap, a pitfall; of always playing spider to Dora's fly, and always pouncing out of my hole to her infinite disturbance" (593; ch. 48). Shaping others is the work of the Murdstones of this world, and the hero should have known better, especially given the fact that he has escaped Murdstone's formative efforts.

When Betsey Trotwood decides to take David out of Murdstone's hands, she does so precisely on the grounds of saving the boy from the fate that has befallen his mother: "'Mr. Murdstone,' she said, shaking her finger at him, 'you were a tyrant to the simple baby, and you broke her heart. She was a loving baby—I know that; I knew it, years before you ever saw her—and through the best part of her weakness you gave her the wounds she died of'" (182; ch. 14). Since shaping means domination, rescuers in both *Oliver Twist* and *David Copperfield* offer the heroes benevolence and the promise of respectable future, but never have the ambition of engineering their selves. Both Mr. Brownlow and Betsey Trotwood are really facilitators of self-realization.

The distinction is far-reaching, and seems to have something to do with Dickens's ambivalent attitude towards the ambition of the privileged and purportedly morally superior upper classes to discipline and shape the less fortunate. F. David Roberts has noted,

> Dickens, the many-sided reflector of life, could hardly not reflect paternalism, but he did so in a different manner and with strong doubts. His Cheerybles [in *Nicholas Nickleby*] and Pickwicks are not strictly paternalist. Their benevolence is diffuse and individual, not linked to the spheres of the lord's estate and the vicar's parish. It is a humanitarian, not authoritarian part of London's democratic life. (42).

To engage in extensive formative work on others, as Murdstone does with Clara Copperfield, is to slip into an authoritarian intervention.

One of the consequences of Dickens's fear of tyrannical formation is that the question of self-fashioning, so central to much of the bildungsroman tradition, is significantly displaced. For Balzac, Stendhal, Eliot, Hardy, and Joyce, the intensive work on the self constitutes the natural course of events, even if in some instances it ends in utter failure. From Lucien de Rubempré and Vautrin in Balzac to Daniel Deronda and Mordecai, bildungsroman heroes will often put themselves at the disposal of mentors who will shape and discipline them. Dickens, on the other hand, is far too wary of the detrimental consequences of subjection to allow dominant mentors to step in.

III. The Great Evasion

The rejection of self-fashioning is, however, only the first in a series of evasive gestures prompted by Dickens's commitment to a version of moral sentimentalism. The bildungsroman hero is lifted from his previous position defined by poverty and suffering by external forces that act as agents of care. As a consequence, active search for one's place in the world is displaced, marginalized, and sometimes completely suspended. Perhaps the advocates of self-help were not completely wrong: once the hero is saved, the questions of his education and profession are no longer relevant. The intensity of Dickens's commitment to care suppresses those elements which typically define the hero's socialization and drive the bildungsroman plot.

In *Oliver Twist*, which most explicitly explores victimhood and helplessness, such questions are barely asked. Agency exists in the novel primarily as resistance. As J. Hillis Miller writes, "Oliver wills to live, and therefore resists violently all attempts of the world to crush him or bury him or make him into a thief. But at the center of this fierce will, there is passivity, the passivity of expectation, of 'great expectations'" (43). Oliver will, of course, ask for more food (12), stand up for himself in the face of Noah Claypole's bullying (44), and escape to London to seek his fortune (54). But, more importantly, he will be auctioned by the parish, be taken by the Artful Dodger to Fagin, then be kidnapped by Nancy and Sikes and sought by Brownlow who will even offer a reward if the boy is found. Beyond the broadly defined struggle between the disreputable and reputable worlds, there are very few details as to what Oliver will become: the secret of his future is replaced with the secret of his origin, which will eventually attract most of the plot's energies.

Surely, Oliver's adoption by Brownlow contains a vague and unspecified promise of education (439; ch. 53), met, on the other side, by Fagin's attempt to shape Oliver into a criminal. But Brownlow's education of Oliver will never be described, and Fagin's attempt to turn him into a criminal will fail spectacularly precisely because Oliver cannot be shaped (205; ch. 24). In the colorful description of Steven Marcus, "he is active in the way that a ball batted back and forth between opposing sides is active: he is moved through space" (80). Because Oliver's self cannot be fashioned, the battle over his future will soon turn into a struggle for sheer physical control over the boy. Oliver is, as Dickens scholars have been noting for a long time, unchangeable, and a bildungsroman describing his development or education would be superfluous.[15] Dickens's narrator admits as much as he sketches a bildungsroman that could have been written:

How Mr. Brownlow went on, from day to day, filling the mind of his adopted child with stores of knowledge, and becoming attached to him, more and more, as his nature developed itself, and showed the thriving seeds of all he wished him to become—how he traced in him new traits of his early friend, that awakened in his own bosom old remembrances, melancholy and yet sweet and soothing—how the two orphans, tried by adversity, remembered its lessons in mercy to others, and mutual love, and fervent thanks to Him who had protected and preserved them—these are all matters which need not to be told. (439; ch. 53)

They need not to be told because everything is already settled. With Mr. Brown-low's adoption of Oliver (437; ch. 53), the respectable world has triumphed. After a series of false protectors, Oliver has found a proper guardian. He is reclaimed, his fate is sealed, and it will suffice to vaguely gesture towards his future. Development and education can find their way into the novel only as an afterthought.

But with Dickens, even as he leaves behind this notoriously static hero, even as he becomes interested in moral growth and psychological development, the change in guardianship continues to command a curiously prominent place in the narrative logic of his bildungsromans. In *Oliver Twist*, the fascination with rescuing the hero will simply preclude the possibility of a novel of education. Oliver is adopted and the novel ends. A decade later, in *David Copperfield*, the novel will continue for another five hundred pages after David changes hands, but it is difficult to miss that the moment in which Betsey Trotwood responds to David's plea to "befriend and protect" him in the face of the Murdstones (181; ch. 14), and in which she takes over as his guardian, is the real *peripeteia*. This reversal is, in fact, the condition of the bildungsroman to come: only under the benevolent eye of his new protectress can David hope to become someone. And although this will imply "another beginning" (184; ch. 15), and although David will become "a new boy in more senses than one" (193; ch. 16), the triumph of Betsey Trotwood over the Murdstones will also mark a moment of disinterest and disorientation. David has become a bit too much of a new boy, so new in fact that for a moment (though only for a moment) the question of his further development—of becoming, to use the Bakhtinian term—will seem as obsolete as it was in *Oliver Twist*.

It is true, once he is taken up by Aunt Betsey, that David will again face the prospect of proper schooling. Yet, as his education in Doctor Strong's school takes off, the narrative rapidly accelerates: "A blank, through which the warriors of poetry and history march on in stately hosts that seem to have no end—and what comes next! *I* am the head-boy, now; and look down on the line of boys below me, with a condescending interest in such of them as bring to my mind the boy I was myself, when I first came there" (229; ch. 18). A blank, indeed. Once again, the Dickensian education is contentless, and will simply serve as an indicator that the hero has achieved the proper status—"well educated, well dressed, and with plenty of money in my pocket" (243; ch.19). This triumph is a fait accompli, already inscribed in Betsey Trotwood's defeat of the Murdstones, and it is no surprise that David will step into the world with no distinct desires: "I suppose the opening prospect confused me. I know that my juvenile experiences went for little or nothing then; and that life was more like a great fairy story, which I was just about to begin to read, than anything else" (233; ch. 19). David is not only confused or unsure; he is devoid of any vision of the future. Facing his prospects with no ideas of his own, David will be sent on a journey, an "expedition" (235; ch. 19) to see the world.

In many ways this is the oldest trick in the book (especially if the book is a bildungsroman): to truly enter a process of education (or disillusionment, for that matter) you must step into the world. Wilhelm Meister, Lucien de Rubempré, Lucy Snowe, Jane Eyre, Roderick Hudson, Jude Fawley: all these bildungsroman heroes and heroines will embark on a voyage towards self-realization, however miserably such a voyage might end for some of them. Yet in *David Copperfield* the great journey towards self-understanding is really a trip to David's childhood maid Peggotty (234; ch. 19), a trip from one surrogate mother to the next, from one caregiver to another. The journey will involve a brief stop in London, but the detour only reinforces the sense that David's world is limited. In London he will go to the theater to see *Julius Cesar*, but Dickens will allow his hero to enjoy the metropolis for no more than a few passages before finding a way to evacuate him. David barely has had the time to express his fascination with the performance when Steerforth, a childhood friend, walks in and drags the hero and the story back to the predetermined path towards Peggotty (243; ch. 19). It is not terribly surprising that after this journey David will have no better vision of his life path than before it started: "My aunt and I had held many grave deliberations on the calling to which I should be devoted. For a year or more I had endeavoured to find a satisfactory answer to her often-repeated question, 'What I would like to be?' But I had no particular liking, that I could discover, for anything" (233; ch. 19). This indecisiveness will mean that a profession will have to be suggested by the aunt, who thinks that David should become a proctor.

> "What *is* a proctor, Steerforth?" said I.
>
> "Why, he is a sort of monkish attorney," replied Steerforth. "He is, to some faded courts held in Doctors' Commons,—a lazy old nook near St. Paul's Churchyard—what solicitors are to the courts of law and equity. He is a functionary whose existence, in the natural course of things, would have terminated about two hundred years ago. I can tell you best what he is, by telling you what Doctors' Commons is. It's a little out-of-the-way place, where they administer what is called ecclesiastical law, and play all kinds of tricks with obsolete old monsters of acts of Parliament, which three-fourths of the world know nothing about, and the other fourth supposes to have been dug up, in a fossil state, in the days of the Edwards." (292; ch. 23)

Once David gets the opportunity to examine Doctors' Commons, he will only add that he is "very well satisfied with the dreamy nature of this retreat" (301; ch. 23). A little out-of-the-way place and a dreamy retreat, in other words, the most obscure and obsolete of bureaucratic positions: such are the aspirations of Victorian England's indispensable bildungsroman hero. If the bildungsroman is habitually seen as the genre which explores the encounter with capitalist modernity, one must begin to wonder whether *David Copperfield* refuses such an encounter.

In fact, David will make something of a habit to turn the situations which offer the opportunity to extend his world into venues for turning to the past. When invited to a dinner party—the quintessential moment of entering the social world in Balzac or even Tolstoy—he shows very little interest in what he finds there. Writing about the French realist tradition, Bakhtin has famously described the bourgeois drawing room as the site of the great encounter between the private and the public: "the interweaving of petty, private intrigues with political and private intrigues, the interpenetration of state with boudoir secrets, of historical sequences with the everyday and biographical sequences" (247). On the opportunities such spaces offer, David has this to say: "There were other guests—all iced for the occasion, as it struck me, like the wine. But, there was one who attracted my attention before he came in, on account of my hearing him announced as Mr. Traddles! My mind flew back to the Salem House; and could it be Tommy, I thought, who used to draw the skeletons!" (317–18; Ch. 25) In *David Copperfield*, meeting old friends unmistakably displaces new prospects.

Among the most important victims of this evasive movement is David's literary career. Despite significant efforts by scholars like Mary Poovey and, more recently, Jennifer Ruth, to read *David Copperfield* as a representative instance of mid-Victorian interest in authorship as vocation, it is difficult to escape the fact that in the novel itself, literary profession is referenced rather than described or analyzed.[16] "I labored hard at my book," reports David Copperfield, "without allowing it to interfere with the punctual discharge of my newspaper duties; and it came out and was very successful" (588; ch. 48). It is very difficult to extract from this sentence David's (and Dickens's) understanding of literary production, much less ethical or economic views on which such an understanding might be based. One wonders, in fact, whether scattered references to hard work reflect any theory of profession, or indeed, any interest in the literary profession.

The scandal of *David Copperfield* is precisely that the profession has a name but no content. David's authorship will emerge suddenly in chapter 43, after some five hundred pages of text, and save for the fact that he has been working hard and doing well, it will remain a mystery. The status of the artistic profession in *David Copperfield* is essentially without precedent among the major European bildungsromans: we know about Stephen Dedalus's aesthetic theories, we read the poems of Lucien de Rubempré in Balzac's *Illusions perdues*, we even learn about the unsuccessful literary and artistic projects of Frédéric Moreau in Flaubert's *L'Éducation sentimentale*. We also witness the creative crises of James's Roderick Hudson, not to mention Thomas Mann's Adrian Leverkühn. With David Copperfield, we know nothing: no titles, no aesthetic theories, no literary preoccupations, except for a handful of references which suggest that David's penchant for storytelling can be traced to his schooldays and that his writing arises from personal experience (see e.g., 80; ch. 7, 699; ch. 58). As Alexander Welsh noted, "so slightly does the narrator of his own life touch upon his career that as readers we are a little taken aback and we have to remind ourselves that this is a novel about a novelist" (109). Nor is Dickens more interested in the practical side of a literary career that occupies such a prominent place in a novel like Balzac's *Illusions*: equally remote from the forces of the market and from internal development, "profession" in *David Copperfield* is an empty space.

There is, however, at least one familiar intervention that Victorianists routinely perform when faced with a passive hero—the equation of outward passivity with internal dynamism and moral reform. In a recent iteration of this view, Stefanie Markovits writes: "My claim is that in literature at least, if not in life, we are who we are, not by the virtue of what we do, but by what we have failed to do. Frustrated action—inaction—we is character building" (6). Or, in the words of Jerome Buckley, "[David's] autobiography describes the education, through time remembered, of the affections; his growth lies in the ordering of his 'undisciplined heart'" (37). The novel's ending certainly can be read in terms of moral self-realization: David has tried to turn the "undisciplined" youthful infatuation with Dora, who was to become his "child-wife," into an emotionally and intellectually fulfilling relationship. This attempt has brought David dangerously close to the kind of tyranny Murdstone previously exerted over his mother; by now, however, David has learned that he cannot turn Dora into a projection of his own desires: "It remained for me to adapt myself to Dora; to share with her what I could, and be happy; to bear on my own shoulders what I must, and be happy still" (595; ch. 14). This realization is almost immediately followed by Dora's death, allowing for the prospect of a mature commitment to Agnes, with whom David will be able to share far more.

But before we are fully seduced by the sense of closure the novel offers, and before we surrender *David Copperfield* to the traditional definitions of the bildungsroman as a chronicle of the journey towards maturity, we may want to take a more critical view of this decisive theme. Commenting on the moment in which David simultaneously realizes the inadequacy of his marriage to Dora and makes a renewed commitment to this marriage, Barbara Hardy writes: "Dickens is really only approaching, and then retreating from the idea of showing the disenchanted life. . . . He is touching on a marvelous subject for the psychological novel, but only touching on it. He chose to summarize, to evade, and then cut the knot with Dora's death" (131). The supposed attainment of maturity takes its place next to a series of evasive moves through which the narrative has already tried to suppress and even obliterate both the encounter with the outside world and the exploration of the hero's psychology. As we have seen, *David Copperfield* has demonstrated a profound lack of interest in artistic and intellectual development, it has refused to articulate the problem of professional ambition (unless the vague desire to be educated and avoid manual labor counts as ambition), it has offered us a hero with no plans for the future and with no unrealistic youthful projects, and it has finally denied us a psychological drama. What is left is a hero trapped in a circular movement within a predefined circle of friends and relatives—Aunt Betsey, Peggotty, Mr. Micawber, Steerforth. In fact, except for Dora and her father, Mr. Spenlow, who appear in chapter 23, practically all of the novel's chief characters are introduced to us by chapter 15. David's work as a parliamentary reporter and author, and his trip to the Continent late in the novel, introduce no new characters: the world of *David Copperfield* consists almost exclusively of relatives, childhood friends, and teachers. In other words, the world of the novel refuses to extend: it simply stops expanding once David grows up. The hero may have matured, but one wonders whether he has faced the world at all.

It is hardly surprising that a critic like Lukács was more than a little impatient with Dickens. Having described the bildungsroman's central problem as "the reconciliation of the problematic individual, guided by his lived experience of the ideal, with concrete social reality" (132), Lukács had little choice but to dismiss Dickens altogether: "He had to make his heroes come to terms, without conflict, with the bourgeois society of his time and, for the sake of poetic effect, to surround the qualities needed for this purpose with a false, or anyway inadequate, poetic glow" (107; see also Moretti 200). But reconciliation must be preceded by a conflict with social structures, a conflict David never enters. Dickens, however, sacrifices even more than mere outward action and the conflict with the organization of bourgeois society. The plot actually severely limits not only the forms of active engagement with capitalist modernity, but also the forms of self-exploration. The interpretation according to which *David Copperfield* chronicles the education of the protagonist's "undisciplined heart" has gained considerable traction precisely because a reading which would like to insist that the novel tracks some form of growth has very little else to cling to.

And yet, *David Copperfield*'s elaborate flight from the world and from the exploration of self-fashioning, reveals the profound stability of the novel's emotional and ethical coordinates. The difficulties of David's marriage to Dora stem from her inability to fully participate in his endeavors: "but that it would have been better for me if my wife could have helped me more, and shared the many thoughts in which I had no partner; and that this might have been; I knew" (595; ch. 48). It will soon become clear that this lack of "partnership" really indicates the absence of the caring relation: Dora is far too helpless to be able to respond to David's obvious need for care. The "child-wife" may not lack empathy, but Dickens makes it very clear that she cannot share in David's intellectual and artistic experiences. Agnes will fill this void: "I had always felt my weakness, in comparison with her constancy and fortitude; and now I felt it more and more" (700; ch. 58). She will take up the role of David's "guide and best support" (738; ch. 62) and rescue him from the misery of his continental tour by expressing support and encouragement. His response clearly outlines this dependency: "I wrote to her before I slept. I told her that I had been in sore need of her help; that without her

I was not, and I never had been, what she thought me; but that she inspired me to be that, and I would try" (699; ch. 58). The renewed commitment to Agnes will reinvigorate David's literary career, as he will produce yet another work of fiction with no known content and no known name: "After some rest and change, I fell to work, in my old ardent way, on a new fancy, which took strong possession of me. As I advanced in the execution of this task, I felt it more and more, and roused my utmost energies to do it well" (699; ch. 58). For David, to have Agnes next to him is to accept once again the status of "the cared–for," and to complete his pantheon of guardians by finally finding the one who can fully participate in his intellectual and emotional life.

At the end of the novel, we find David surrounded with protective figures: Agnes, Betsey Trotwood, and Peggotty (748; ch. 64). In the final chapters, he has slipped into "fame and fortune" (741; ch. 63), into a vague state of prosperity, as if this was a natural effect of the benevolence that surrounded him. As Carol Gilligan writes, "the ideal of care is thus an activity of relationship, of seeing and responding to need, taking care of the world by sustaining the web of connection so that no one is left alone" (62). But such an ideal is extremely difficult to maintain outside familial relations and domestic space, and *David Copperfield* will have to limit the hero's relations to those with which care is traditionally associated: a maid, a great-aunt, and a wife.[17] As the novel draws to an end, the circle of care has closed, obliterating in the process all other realities of life, external and internal.

IV. Epilogue: Fatal Extraction

Yet not everyone is cared for. The conclusion of *David Copperfield* stands in stark contrast to the close of *Great Expectations*. At the end of this novel— in the supposedly more optimistic version of the ending suggested by Bulwer-Lytton—Pip and Estella meet at the site of the burned down Satis House. What is left behind by Miss Havisham is quite appropriately a wasteland. At this site of Estella's tyrannical education, the place where she was "brought up by Miss Havisham to wreak revenge on all the male sex" (179; ch. 22), life can continue only after the lessons have been forgotten, or rather, superseded by the agony of her later life: "—now, when suffering has been stronger than all other teaching, and has taught me to understand what your heart used to be. I have been bent and broken, but—I hope—into a better shape. Be as considerate and good to me as you were, and tell me we are friends" (478; ch. 59).[18] Even as at the very end Pip and Estella leave behind what is left of Satis House, "the ruined place" (479; ch. 59), and seemingly step into a new life, we feel that we have witnessed a scene of mourning rather than of promise.

Great Expectations seems to deny us not only the final promise of serenity, but also the preceding drama: there will be no decisive confrontations between the Fagins and Brownlows of this world, as the novel has replaced the reassuring oppositions between rescuers and malevolent agents with much more opaque pretenders to the role of the hero's benefactor. It can easily seem that in *Great Expectations* destructive figures have risen to new prominence, uncontested by fairy godmothers and well-meaning old men. "Magwitch," writes J. Hillis Miller, "is a nightmare permutation of Mr. Brownlow and Mr. Jarndyce [from *Bleak House*]. He is the benevolent guardian, secretly manipulating the fortunes of the hero and protecting him, turned into a condemned felon who, like a horrible old dog, gloats over his victim" (255). Pip's unlikely benefactor certainly embodies some qualities of a diabolic demiurge, and his insistence that he "owns" Pip (317; ch. 39) may be taken as sufficient indication that Dickens's final bildungsroman has dissolved the familiar alignment between upward mobility and parental care. In *Oliver Twist* and *David Copperfield*, care is administered by surrogate parents who will rescue the heroes and secure for them a promise of respectable life. In *Great Expectations*, however, benefactors are not in any obvious way figures of care, and the promise of upward social movement has little to do with responding to need.

Pip will enter the world of Miss Havisham not in order to be educated or elevated—the lady of the Satis House has absolutely no interest in his education—but in order to serve as an instrument in her formative efforts directed at Estella. Rather than being saved from difficulty, Pip is to serve as a circus animal: "I only suffered in Satis House as a convenience, a sting for the greedy relations, a model with a mechanical heart to practise on when no other practice was at hand; those were the first smarts I had" (319; ch. 39).[19] Pip's entry into the world of Satis House, perceived by Pip and everyone around him as the beginning of his movement upwards, is really the moment in which he is turned into Miss Havisham's toy: "'I sometimes have sick fancies,' she went on, 'and I have a sick fancy that I want to see some play. There, there!' with an impatient movement of the fingers of her right hand; 'play, play, play!'" (58; ch. 8).

The irony here lies not in the fact that Pip was abused when he thought he was being introduced to the world, but in the fact that he was a tool in an even more sinister form of abuse. Miss Havisham's fashioning of Estella into a figure of vengeance and hatred (394; ch. 49) confirms Dickens's suspicion of apprenticeship. As Estella self-consciously points out, "I must be taken as I have been made. The success is not mine, the failure is not mine, but the two together make me" (302; ch. 38). Mentoring is, once again, a dehumanizing activity; as Miss Havisham reveals, "with my teachings, and with this figure of myself always before her, a warning to back and point my lessons, I stole her heart away, and put ice in its place" (395; ch. 49). Self-fashioning and care are decisively opposed, perhaps even more strongly here than in *David Copperfield*, as Miss Havisham's education of Estella consists primarily in destroying her capacity to empathize with others.

It is not an accident that Joe, the central figure of caring in the novel, literally cannot communicate with Miss Havisham: "I could hardly have imagined dear old Joe looking so unlike himself or so like some extraordinary bird; standing as he did speechless, with his tuft of feathers ruffled, and his mouth open as if he wanted a worm" (98; ch. 13). Completely dumbfounded by the appearance of Satis House, Joe will answer all of Miss Havisham's questions by talking to Pip, and he will fully recover only after they have left (99–100; ch. 13). Joe Gargery is, of course, grotesquely inarticulate, but that should not prevent us from appreciating the allegorical potential of this scene—between his caring innocence and Miss Havisham's project of subject-engineering, there can be no communication.

The problem of Pip's position is precisely that in *Great Expectations* care is associated with the poor and illiterate surrogate father, while the promise of social mobility lies elsewhere. As Vincent Pecora writes, "Pip's native guilt, inculcated by his resentful sister, is multiplied many times over as he comes to realize how far his 'expectations' as an heir to Miss Havisham have almost destroyed the one relationship in his life that suggests genuine kinship and fellow-feeling—his friendship with the illiterate blacksmith and abandoned father-figure, Joe" (182). The fact that Pip is not really the heir to Miss Havisham is of comparatively little consequence. The identity of the benefactor will be a source of much narrative excitement and ironic tension, but, more importantly, Pip has agreed in advance to be elevated by an anonymous force led by opaque motives. He has accepted to become a puppet before ascertaining the identity of the puppeteer, thus acknowledging the impersonal nature of the relationship with the benefactor.

In *Oliver Twist* and *David Copperfield* some form of emotional commitment, or at least a desire for such a commitment will go hand in hand or even precede social expectations. Buried in the bottling factory, David will fantasize about going "by some means or other, down into the country, to the only relation I had in the world, and tell my story to my aunt, Miss Betsey" (150; ch. 12), and he will struggle to imagine the aunt he never knew and to see her as a caring figure (151; ch. 12). In *Great Expectations*, however, to commit oneself to social advancement is to forgo the promise of care.

Toward the end, the novel will nonetheless seek to ameliorate this state of affairs: it will allow for the assumption that the unlikely benefactor is not simply a madman with a "fixed idea" (339; ch. 41) and the owner of a gentleman (317; ch. 39), but rather a hunted man in need of rescue. In fact, the attempt to save Magwitch from the certain death he was facing in England as an escaped convict will be by far Pip's most significant undertaking. And if the frightening and monstrous convict can be humanized, there must be a lesson there:

> For now, my repugnance to him had all melted away; and in the hunted, wounded, shackled creature who held my hand in his, I only saw a man who had meant to be my benefactor, and who had felt affectionately, gratefully, and generously, towards me with great constancy through a series of years. I only saw in him a much better man than I had been to Joe. (441; ch. 54)

Following this realization, the novel offers a proliferation of gestures of care: Pip will care for his ailing benefactor, and, after Magwitch's death, he will simultaneously fall into poverty and illness, only to be attended by Joe: "I was slow to gain strength, but I did slowly and surely become less weak, and Joe stayed with me, and I fancied I was little Pip again. For the tenderness of Joe was so beautifully proportioned to my need, that I was like a child in his hands" (461; ch. 57). This regression seems to turn the novel into something akin to a morality play: between forces of mobility and care, Pip chooses the former, only to lose everything and recognize the value of care.[20] The realization, however, comes too late to avert the dismal ending. Meddling with selves has already gone too far with Miss Havisham's toying with Pip and Estella, and with Pip's initially mysterious social elevation.

The prospect of creating the circle of care such as the one at the end of *David Copperfield* will be denied to Pip. After his defeat in London, he will attempt to go back home and marry his childhood friend Biddy, who throughout the novel represented the obvious alternative to Estella: "Biddy was never insulting, or capricious, or Biddy to-day and somebody else to-morrow; she would have derived only pain, and no pleasure, from giving me pain; she would far rather have wounded her own breast than mine" (128; ch. 17). Biddy has, however, already married Joe, entering a caring relation that will exclude Pip. This exclusion is underlined by the fact that their son will also be named Pip, symbolically displacing the novel's hero as the object of care.

Given such an outcome, nothing could be easier than arguing that *Great Expectations*, with its somber ending and grotesque benefactors, indicates an ideological shift in Dickens's understanding of benevolent intervention. Orwell has claimed that "*Great Expectations* is, in fact, definitely an attack on patronage" (35), and this claim is offered precisely in the context of a discussion about the benevolent figures in Dickens: "Hence that recurrent Dickens figure, the good rich man. This character belongs especially to Dickens's early optimistic period . . . and he is always a superhumanly kind-hearted old gentleman who 'trots' to and fro, raising his employees' wages, patting children on the head, getting debtors out of jail and in general, acting the fairy godmother" (35). For Orwell, the absence of such figures from *Great Expectations* indicates a new social vision: "The seeming inference from the rather despondent books that Dickens wrote in the fifties is that by that time he had grasped the helplessness of well-meaning individuals in a corrupt society" (36). However, Dickens and his original readers thought differently. It seems that neither Dickens nor his early reviewers saw *Great Expectations* as a particularly unsettling text. Dickens did describe the story as "grotesque" and "tragi-comic," but didn't think that these qualities distinguish it sharply from the much tamer *David Copperfield*, which he decided to reread in order to avoid repeating himself (Forster, 3: 362–63). Forster apparently agreed: "but the satire that thus enforces the old warning against living upon vague hopes, and paying ancient debts by contracting new ones, never presented itself in more amusing or kindly shape" (3: 367). Is it possible that *Great Expectations* shares more with stories of Oliver and David than one would normally assume?

No doubt, in *Great Expectations* Dickens was rehearsing a scenario which can easily be read as a reversal of his earlier bildungsromans. The novel has offered a new dealing of cards, a redistribution of narrative propositions so that benefactors are no longer innocent, well-meaning creatures but rather frightening puppet-masters. In many ways, Miss Havisham is an infinitely intensified version of Edward Murdstone, representing paternalistic terror gone wild. Yet the emergence of benefactors as grotesque monomaniacs doesn't so much undermine the commitment to benevolent intervention as much as it reemphasizes how vital the relationship between benevolence and ethics is: for Dickens, upward mobility makes sense only within the ethical context of care.

Pip will fail not because Dickens's assumptions about social mobility have changed, but because they have not. The outcome is different this time around precisely because the underlying presuppositions about permissible forms of benevolent intervention have stayed the same. If the prospect of social mobility now seems ironized and defeated, it is only because Dickens has always accepted it only conditionally, as a corollary of care. From the perspective of moral sentimentalism, once the relationship between mobility and care is dissolved, upward mobility is delegitimized. Relieved of the accompanying ethical attributes, social advancement will become an instance of destructive uprooting, a fatal extraction.

Here, the bildungsroman dissolves into a Gothic tale. In a novel like *Oliver Twist*, the bildungsroman was turned into a site of rescue. Yet both gestures are equally successful in turning the plot's focus away from the mechanisms of socialization. In *Great Expectations*, as Pip arrives in London, Herbert Pocket will step in as his guide in acquiring proper manners and in learning the ways of the metropolis. Yet this education is almost as elusive as the books of David Copperfield: we are informed that it takes place, but it has very little content. Herbert's course in etiquette will occupy only a marginal position in a conversation that focuses on the mystifying life of Miss Havisham (177–80; ch. 22). Because social advancement is placed under the auspices of an unknown authority, the novel's focus moves sharply away from the mechanisms which govern active pursuit of social position, and from the work on the self which usually follows such a pursuit. The mystery surrounding Miss Havisham, that MacGuffin of *Great Expectations*, successfully marginalizes the instruction in the ways of the metropolis. Benevolent or grotesque, benefactors are a singularly efficient device for evading the actual dynamics of social mobility.

NOTES

I am grateful to Maurice Samuels, Katie Trumpener, Alexander Welsh, and to the anonymous readers of this essay for their helpful suggestions.

1. For the purposes of this essay, I understand the bildungsroman as European modernity's central literary tool for exploring the process of entering adulthood, or, in more technical terms, the processes of individuation and socialization. In emphasizing this dual focus of the genre I follow the conceptualizations of the bildungsroman offered by Georg Lukács and Franco Moretti (see Lukács 132 and Moretti 15). I do, however, maintain some reservations with respect to their insistence on the opposition between self-realization and socialization as the defining characteristic of the genre. In my view, the relationship between these two processes has shifted throughout the history of the genre, and the emphasis on their conflict—although unquestionably justified in many instances—unnecessarily limits the range of problems the bildungsroman addresses. As this essay demonstrates, the vitality of the bildungsroman lies precisely in its ability constantly to reconceptualize the relationship between development and immutability, internal impulses and external pressures, and action and passivity.

2. See, for instance, Miller 252, Gilmour 114, Welsh 159, Peters 39ff., and in particular Wachs and Hochman.

3. Dickens's opposition to the New Poor Law was well known. See, for instance, Forster 1: 250. The view of *Oliver Twist* as explicitly concerned with the New Poor Law has gone virtually uncontested for the past century and a half. See for instance Gissing 67–68; House 92–93; Marcus 58; Schlicke 149–56; Fielding 49–65; Stokes 711–27. For various accounts of Dickens's ability to grasp fully social issues his novels were addressing, see Crotch 24, Orwell 34ff., House 50, and Eagleton 157–58.

4. Mayhew was, however, acutely aware of the flipside of this argument: "If the poorer classes require fifteen millions to be added in charity every year to their aggregate income in order to relieve their pains and privations, and the richer can afford to have the same immense sum taken from theirs, and yet scarcely feel the loss, it shows, at once how much the one class must have in excess and the other in deficiency" (3: 35).

5. For a detailed account of the eighteenth-century sources of these debates, see Fideler.

6. There is still considerable controversy about the exact role that strictly religious arguments, Bentham's pleasure/pain principle, or the work of political economists like Smith, Malthus, and Ricardo played in the poverty debates. I will, of course, seek to convey the complexity of this intellectual field, but the exact sources of particular arguments are not my primary concern.

7. On the views of vice as a cause of poverty, see Hollen Lees 88–93.

8. For a view that help and guidance should naturally follow work on the self, see Taylor 38.

9. Only *self-formation* can be traced back to 1700s, while other terms originated in the mid-nineteenth century. Victorian publications on the topic of self-reliance include Taylor's *Self-cultivation Recommended*, Capel Lofft's, *Self-formation; or, The History*

of an Individual Mind: Intended as a Guide for the Intellect through Difficulties to Suc-cess, Edwin Paxton Hood's, *Self-Formation: Twelve Chapters for Young Thinkers*, and William E. Channing, *Self-culture: An Address Introductory to the Franklin Lectures, Delivered at Boston, United States*; Channing was, of course, American, but his lecture went through at least four English editions before the mid-1840s.

10. I am much indebted to the detailed discussion of the New Poor Law provided in Fraser (31–55). See also Roberts 145ff., and Laybourn, in particular chapter 2.

11. Of course, this approach only revealed the inevitable paradox produced by the mixture of paternalism and individualism. The poor were simultaneously seen as free agents and as objects of paternalist intervention: the poor need to work on themselves, but in order to do so they must be pushed to internalize the ideology of self-help brought to them from above. Paradoxically, the very forces that promoted self-reliance saw the poor and the working classes as objects to be fashioned through the inculcation of the ideology of self-help. The paradox is obvious in *Principles of Political Economy*, where Mill postulated two approaches to poor relief, "the theory of dependence and protec-tion," and the theory of "self-dependence." According to the first, Mill argued, "the rich should be *in loco parentis* to the poor, guiding and restraining them like children. Of spontaneous action on their part there should be no need. They should be called on for nothing but to do their day's work, and to be moral and religious" (314). Accord-ing to the second, "the poor have come out of leading-strings, and cannot any longer be governed or treated like children. To their own qualities must now be commended the care of their destiny" (318). But even as he recognizes that the former approach will become increasingly untenable, Mill continues to treat the poor paternalistically. While acknowledging that "whatever advice, exhortation or guidance is held out to the labouring classes, must henceforth be tendered to them as equals, and accepted by them with their eyes open," Mill nonetheless immediately adds: "The prospect of the future depends on the degree in which they can be *made* rational beings" (319, my emphasis).

12. The conclusion of the Sadler Report of 1833, rptd. in Fraser 257.

13. For the classical analysis of the tension between the notions of individual freedom and social determinism in the early nineteenth century, see Gallagher 3–35.

14. When he speaks of the "strong arm" Reid, of course, has in mind state intervention, and Dickens took a similar view, suggesting that "a Public Charity is immeasurably better than a Private Foundation, no matter how munificently the latter may be endowed" (*American Notes* 36). In fact, Dickens himself argued in favor of "a Bill for taking into custody by the strong arm, of every neglected or abandoned child of either sex, found in the streets of any town in this kingdom" (Qtd. in Pope 180). The novels, however, never imagine a viable form of state intervention.

15. For a discussion of Oliver's incorruptibility, see, for instance, Gilmour 114 and Bal-dridge 184ff.

16. "While novels like *David Copperfield* and *Pendennis* tended to formulate their respons-es to the writer's market situation less directly than the essays in *Blackwood's* or *North British Review*, all of these discussions of literary men struggled to define the place the writer occupied in Britain's increasingly secular, capitalist society" (Poovey 102). See

also Ruth 59. On *David Copperfield* and literary professionalism, see Salmon, 35ff.
17. It clearly follows from this reading that *David Copperfield* radically circumscribes the social role of women by reducing it to that of a caregiver. While this is a significant issue, it is outside the scope of this essay to explore the implications of the limit that Dickens imposes on femininity.
18. This sentence appears in a somewhat different form in the original ending (482).
19. Wachs and Hochman have argued persuasively that "*Great Expectations* is, at one level 'about' the ethics of instrumentality" (174). However, they seem to read the novel primarily as a series of attempts to manipulate Pip psychologically by instilling in him a sense of guilt, a view that overemphasizes and simplifies the psychological thrust of the novel.
20. This realization is, however, foreshadowed by Pip's willingness to selflessly aid Herbert Pocket, taking up the role of Herbert's anonymous benefactor in chapter 37.

WORKS CITED

Bakhtin, Mikhail. "Forms of Time and Chronotope in the Novel." *Dialogic Imagination: Four Essays*. Ed. Michael Holquist. Trans. Michael Holquist and Caryl Emerson. Austin: U of Texas P, 1981. 84–259.

Baldridge, Cates. "The Instabilities of Inheritance in *Oliver Twist*." *Studies in the Novel* 25.2 (1993): 184–95.

Bentham, Jeremy. *Writings on the Poor Laws*. Vol. 1. Ed. Michael Quinn. Oxford: Clarendon, 2001.

Buckley, Jerome Hamilton. *Season of Youth: The Bildungsroman from Dickens to Golding*. Cambridge: Harvard UP, 1974.

Channing, William E. *Self-culture: An Address Introductory to the Franklin Lectures, Delivered at Boston, United States*. London: J. Cleave, [1838?].

Cheney, Edward. "The Charities of London: Comprehending the Benevolent, Educational, and Religious Institutions, Their Origin and Design, Progress, and Present Position." *Quarterly Review* 97 (September 1855): 407–49. Rptd. in *Poverty in The Victorian Age*. Ed. A. W. Coats. vol. 3. Westmead, UK: Gregg, 1973.

Collins, Philip. *Charles Dickens: The Critical Heritage*. London: Routledge & K. Paul, 1971.

Craik, George Lillie. *The Pursuit of Knowledge under Difficulties; Illustrated by Anecdotes*. London: Charles Knight, 1830.

Crotch, W. Walter. *Charles Dickens Social Reformer: The Social Teachings of England's Great Novelist*. London: Chapman and Hall, 1913.

Dickens, Charles. *American Notes*. Ed. Patricia Ingham. London: Penguin, 2000.

———*David Copperfield*, Ed. Nina Burgis. Oxford: Clarendon, 1981.

———*Great Expectations*, Ed. Margaret Cardwell. Oxford and New York: Oxford UP, 1998.

———*Oliver Twist*, Ed. Kathleen Tillotson. Oxford: Oxford UP, 1999.

———. *The Speeches of Charles Dickens*. Ed. K. J. Fielding. Oxford: Clarendon, 1960.

Eagleton, Terry. *The English Novel: An Introduction*. Malden, MA: Blackwell, 2005.

Ellis, William. "Eight Reports of the Commissioners appointed by Parliament to inquire respecting Charities." *Westminster Review* 2 (July 1824), 97–121. Rptd. in *Poverty in The Victorian Age*. A. W. Coats, ed. vol. 3. Westmead, UK: Gregg, 1973.

Fideler, Paul. *Social Welfare in Pre-Industrial England: The Old Poor Law Tradition*. Basingstoke: Palgrave Macmillan, 2006.

Fielding, K. J. "Benthamite Utilitarianism and *Oliver Twist*: A Novel of Ideas." *Dickens Quarterly* 4 (1987): 49–65.

Fielding, K.J., Ed. *The Speeches of Charles Dickens*. Oxford: Clarendon Press, 1960.

Finlayson, Geoffrey. *Citizen, State, and Social Welfare in Britain, 1830–1990*. Oxford: Clarendon, 1993.

Ford, Richard. "Oliver Twist; or, the Parish Boy's Progress." *Quarterly Review* 64 (June 1839): 83–102.

Forster, John. *The Life of Charles Dickens*. 3 vols. Philadelphia: Lippincott, 1872.

Fraser, Derek. *The Evolution of the British Welfare State: A History of Social Policy Since the Industrial Revolution*. London: Macmillan, 1984.

——, Ed. *The New Poor Law in the Nineteenth Century*. New York: St. Martin's, 1976.

Gallagher, Catherine. *The Industrial Reformation of English Fiction: Social Discourse and Narrative Form 1832–1867*. Chicago: U of Chicago P, 1985.

Gilligan, Carol. *In a Different Voice: Psychological Theory and Women's Development*. Cambridge: Harvard UP, 1993.

Gilmour, Robin. *The Idea of the Gentlemen in the Victorian Novel*. London: Allen & Unwin, 1981.

Gissing, George. *The Immortal Dickens*. London: Cecil Palmer, 1925.

Greg, W. R. "Charity, Noxious and Beneficent." *Westminster Review* 59 (January1853): 62–88. Rptd. in Poverty in *The Victorian Age*. Ed. A. W. Coats. vol. 3. Westmead, UK: Gregg, 1973.

"Great Expectations." *Times* 17 Oct. 1861: 6.

Hardy, Barbara. *The Moral Art of Dickens*. New York: Oxford UP, 1970.

Held, Virginia. *The Ethics of Care: Personal, Political, and Global*. Oxford: Oxford UP, 2006.

Highmore, A. *Pietas Londinensis: The History, Design and Present State of the Various Public Charities in and near London*. London: R. Phillips, 1810.

Hollen Lees, Lynn. *The Solidarities of Strangers: The English Poor Laws and the People 1700–1848*. Cambridge: Cambridge UP, 1998.

House, Humphry. *The Dickens World*. Oxford: Oxford UP, 1979.

Laybourn, Keith. *The Evolution of British Social Policy and The Welfare State c. 1800–1993*. Keele: Ryburn Publishing; Keele UP, 1995.

Lofft, Capel. *Self-formation; or, The History of an Individual Mind: Intended as a Guide for the Intellect through Difficulties to Success. By a Fellow of a College*. Boston: Crosby and Nichols, 1846. (1st ed., 1837).

Lukács, Georg. *The Theory of the Novel.* Trans. Anna Bostock. Cambridge: MIT P, 1971.

Mayhew, Henry. *London Labour and the London Poor. A Cyclopedia of the Conditions and Earnings of Those That Will Work, Those That Cannot Work, and Those That Will Not Work.* 3 Vols. London: Griffin, Bohn, 1861–62.

Marcus, Steven. *Dickens: From Pickwick to Dombey.* London: Chatto and Windus, 1965.

Markovits, Stefanie. *The Crisis of Action in Nineteenth-Century English Literature.* Columbus: Ohio State UP, 2006.

Mill, John Stuart. *Principles of Political Economy: With Some of their Applications to Social Philosophy,* vol. 2. London: Parker, 1848.

Miller, J. Hillis. *Charles Dickens: The World of His Novels.* Cambridge: Harvard UP, 1965.

Moretti, Franco. *The Way of the World: The Bildungsroman in European Culture.* Trans. Albert Sbragia. London: Verso, 2000.

Nixon, Jude V. "'Proud possession to the English nation': Victorian Philanthropy and Samuel Johnson's Goddaughter." *Dickens Studies Annual* 32 (2002): 247–75.

Noddings, Nel. *Caring: A Feminine Approach to Caring & Moral Education.* Berkeley: U of California P, 1984.

———*The Maternal Factor: Two Paths to Morality.* Berkeley: U of California P, 2010.

Orwell, George. *Collected Essays.* London: Secker and Warburg, 1975.

Owen, David. *English Philanthropy, 1660–1960.* Cambridge: Harvard UP, 1964.

Owen, Robert. *A New View of Society: Or, Essays on the Formation of the Human Character.* 3rd ed. London: Longman, 1817.

Paxton Hood, Edwin. *Self-Formation: Twelve Chapters for Young Thinkers.* 3rd ed. London: Jude and Glass, 1858.

Pecora, Vincent P. "Inheritances, Gifts, and Expectations." *Law & Literature* 20.2 (2008): 177–96.

Peters, Laura. *Orphan texts: Victorian Orphans, Culture and Empire.* Manchester: Manchester UP, 2000.

"The Philanthropy of the Age and its Relation to Social Evils," *Westminster Review* 35 (April 1869): 437–57. Rptd. in *Poverty in The Victorian Age.* A. W. Coats, ed. vol. 3. Westmead, UK: Gregg, 1973.

Poovey, Mary. *Uneven Development: The Ideological Work of Gender in Mid-Victorian England.* Chicago: U of Chicago P, 1988.

Pope, Norris. *Dickens and Charity.* New York: Columbia UP, 1978.

Reid, Hugo. *What Should Be Done for the People: An Appeal to the Electors of the United Kingdom.* London: Simpkin, Marshall; Edinburgh: Black; Liverpool: Webb; Nottingham: Dearden, 1848.

"Reports of the Society for the Suppression of Mendicity, 1838–1839," *Quarterly Review* 64 (October 1839): 341–69. Rptd. in *Poverty in The Victorian Age.* Ed. A. W. Coats. vol. 3. Westmead, UK: Gregg, 1973.

Roberts, F. David. *The Social Conscience of the Early Victorians.* Stanford: Stanford UP, 2002.

Ruth, Jennifer. *Novel Professions: Interested Disinterest and the Making of the Professional in the Victorian Novel.* Columbus: Ohio State UP, 2006.

Salmon, Richard. "Professions of Labour: David Copperfield and the 'Dignity of Literature.'" *Nineteenth-Century Contexts* 29.1 (2007): 35–52.

Schlicke, Paul. "Bumble and the Poor Law Satire of Oliver Twist." *The Dickensian* 71 (1975): 149–56.

Smiles, Samuel. *Self-help; with Illustrations of Character and Conduct.* London: John Murray, 1859.

Stokes, Peter M. "Bentham, Dickens, and the Uses of the Workhouse." *SEL: Studies in English Literature, 1500–1900* 41 (2001): 711–27.

Taylor, Isaac. *Self-cultivation Recommended: Or, Hints to a Youth Leaving School.* London: Fenner, 1817.

Townsend, Joseph. *A Dissertation on the Poor Laws: By a Well-wisher to Mankind.* *London*: Dilly, 1786.

Wachs, Ilja, and Baruch Hochman. *Dickens: The Orphan Condition* (Madison, NJ: Fairleigh Dickinson UP, 1999).

Welsh, Alexander. *From Copyright to Copperfield: The Identity of Dickens.* Cambridge: Harvard UP, 1987.

"Feeble Pictures of an Existing Reality": The Factual Fiction of *Nicholas Nickleby*

Galia Benziman

The attitude to children was a hotly-debated issue in late-1830s Britain, following the publication of parliamentary reports on child labor. Besides further investigations and debates, the shocked response also inspired various fictional descriptions. This essay examines the treatment of child abuse in Dickens's Nicholas Nickleby, *in which the brutal school scenes provide us with an opportunity to explore the interplay of fact and fiction in Dickens's early work. As Dickens declares in his 1848 preface, although the novel had presented but "faint and feeble pictures of an existing reality," a significant improvement in the Yorkshire schools followed its first publication. Were Dickens's pictures of reality indeed "feeble," and in what sense? In his representation of Dotheboys School, Dickens performs two contradictory missions: he aims to shock his readers and affect public opinion, while being intent on making his readers laugh even when describing brutal scenes involving victimized children. In order to find how these two paradoxical targets work together, I compare Dickens's narrative strategy—his humor, his avoidance of the theme of child labor, and his depiction of evil as individual aberration—with contemporary social-problem novels. Despite what we may construe as the other texts' greater political commitment, the essay discusses the way in which the seemingly apolitical aspects of* Nickleby *are strategically designed to affect a change.*

The complex relationship between fact and fiction in Charles Dickens's early work is an intriguing subject. It is of particular interest to examine the political implications of the tensions between Dickens's use of factual and fictional discourses in his early work in light of a specific example: the school scenes in his third novel, *Nicholas Nickleby* (1838-1839), which had an avowed basis in reality. These famously brutal scenes were based on material Dickens gathered as he visited certain Yorkshire schools in the late 1830s. They provide us with an opportunity to explore the interplay of fact and fiction as related to the mixture of realism and humor so typical of Dickens, especially at this stage of his career.

To distinguish between "fact" and its fictional narration is clearly an impossible task. Kenneth Burke has observed "how overwhelmingly much of what we mean by 'reality' has been built up for us through nothing but our symbol systems" (Burke 5; ctd. in Justman 834); and, as Stewart Justman comments, humans transform fact "and abstract and make fictions" in a way that allows representation to override fact. Reality is thus constantly mediated to us through representation (Justman 834). In examining a literary work's take on social reality, it is therefore useful to analyze what kind of mediation and manipulation the fiction in question employs. One kind of narrative mediation of reality conspicuous in Dickens's case is humor. In a transitional work such as *Nicholas Nickleby*, we can trace quite clearly the young author's movement between the comic and the real, as also between fictional and fact-based discourses, in a way that reveals how each of these modes excludes, overrides, sustains, and interacts with the others at the same time.

The political dimension of Dickens's work was a prominent critical concern already in the nineteenth century. A dominant evaluation until the 1930s was that his work had radical, even revolutionary, components, and he was often presented as an opponent of capitalism and bourgeois values.[1] However, the three highly influential readings of the late 1930s and early 1940s—George Orwell's "Charles Dickens" (1939), Edmund Wilson's "Dickens: The Two Scrooges" (1941), and Humphry House's *The Dickens World* (1941)—introduced a revisionary view. Orwell claimed that Dickens was far from being a champion of the proletariat (55) and that according to Dickens, change could occur only on the personal and moral level, and not in the political sphere (67). Orwell, however, did consider Dickens a subversive writer who "attacked English institutions with a ferocity that has never since been approached" (56). Offering a Freudian interpretive frame, Edmund Wilson's essay regarded Dickens's social critique as apolitical, originating in personal anxieties (42). Humphry House similarly pointed out Dickens's limitations as a social critic. Censorship, House asserted, had affected the entirety of his reformist writing and stamped it by middle-class morality (215-17, 219). Many subsequent critics have adopted a similar view of Dickens, especially Dickens of the early period, as an essentially middle-class writer, committed to middle-class values.[2]

Examined in their social and cultural context, the school scenes in *Nicholas Nickleby* offer us a unique case that demonstrates something of the complex relationship between fact and fiction typical of Dickens. This relationship should lead us to reconsider the view that in his early novels Dickens's social critique tends to be mild and at bottom committed to middle-class values. In his 1839 preface to the original edition of *Nicholas Nickleby*, Dickens indicates that the school scenes are based on fact—things he saw during the excursion that he made into Yorkshire with his illustrator, Hablot K. Browne (known as Phiz). Traveling under assumed names, Dickens and Browne visited the notorious boarding schools in this district to do background research for the novel and investigate the conditions and educational methods prevalent at these miserable institutions— establishments in which boys were cruelly flogged, starved, and taught little or nothing; establishments that probably appealed to those parents looking for a cheap and convenient way to dispose of their unwanted or illegitimate children (see *Dickens and Education*, 98-112). Stating in his preface that his objective was to call public attention to the cruelty of this school system, Dickens declared that in his descriptions of Dotheboys School he invented nothing, and that the shocking treatment of children in this kind of institutions involved "such offensive and foul details of neglect, cruelty, and disease, as no writer of fiction would have the boldness to imagine" (NN 3). He added that he even had to keep down and subdue some of the oppressive practices "lest they should be deemed impossible"; the fictional-yet-factual Dotheboys School of the novel was therefore, according to Dickens's testimony, only a collection of "faint and feeble pictures of an existing reality" (3)—a pale version of a reality that must be exposed and abolished. It is significant that Dickens reveals his alertness to the need to make the school scenes credible: if reality is too weird to be taken as fact, the descriptions have to be toned down in order to maintain at least an effect of the real. This is instrumental if the intention is not merely to entertain, but to produce a change. A strategic purpose thus subordinates, and shapes, artistic choices.

We can find further evidence of the strong factual basis of the school scenes in *Nicholas Nickleby* in the buzz of speculation about the real identity of the sadistic boarding school proprietor, Mr. Wackford Squeers, who, though invented by Dickens, was a portrait taken so much from life that much guesswork was done in this direction during the serial publication of the novel. In his preface to the book edition, Dickens had to protest against "more than one Yorkshire schoolmaster [who] la[id] claim to being the original of Mr Squeers" (3), some of these contenders even threatening to sue the author for libel. Squeers, Dickens argues, was not a one-to-one real character but a mixture of several, all very much like him; he was the representative of a class, an embodiment of the "race" of Yorkshire boarding school headmasters—all marked by their imposture, ignorance, and brutal cupidity. Yet according to Mark Ford, a common assumption at the time held that a certain schoolmaster, a William Shaw of Bowes Academy in Yorkshire, prosecuted and convicted of gross neglect of his pupils, served both Dickens and Phiz, the illustrator, as their chief model for the portrayal of the fictional Mr. Squeers.[3]

"Faint and feeble" versions of reality as they may be, Dickens's pictures of the horrors taking place at Dotheboys School were vivid and intense enough to arouse the desired public response. Critics and social historians have shown that following the publication of *Nicholas Nickleby*, parents started to dread the disgrace that would attach to sending their children to institutions run by incompetent and brutal taskmasters of the kind described in the novel (Adrian 237-41). The strong impact was the result of both the vividness of the description and Dickens's immense popularity: published in 19 monthly parts (with the last part being a double number) from April 1838 to October 1839 by Chapman and Hall, *Nickleby* had as many as 50,000 copies printed of its first number (Sutherland 74). As soon as the work was published as a book, this version, too, was an immediate success.

The social achievement was even greater. Not only parents dreaded the disgrace of the Yorkshire schools during the years following the novel's publication, but serious and prompt institutional intervention, too, brought about the collapse of most institutions of the kind Dickens had described. In the 1848 preface to the first cheap edition of *Nicholas Nickleby*, ten years later, Dickens was pleased to inform his readers that the number of cheap Yorkshire schools of the kind described in the novel has shrunk considerably since the original publication. He stated that the Yorkshire private-school teachers were, as a race, "blockheads and impostors"; those schoolmasters whom he had encountered were "the lowest and most rotten round in the whole ladder. Traders in the avarice, indifference, or imbecility of parents, and the helplessness of children"—yet now, he declared with pride, it was possible to refer to them in the past tense (5).

It remains a question whether Dickens's portrayal of the school in *Nicholas Nickleby* is indeed "faint and feeble," as he claims it to be. This somewhat unflattering self-description that Dickens offers here of his art, presenting it as a pale imitation of the real, may indicate that he believes that when an author is tackling social problems, questions of literary form and aesthetic achievement become subservient to the facts they are meant to denounce. Yet, we may suspect that for Dickens, the artistic achievement can never come second, and that his presentation of his fiction in the preface is therefore not entirely reliable. We should ask ourselves, how the uneasy relation between fact and fiction shapes Dickens's artistic representation so as not to make it entirely "feeble." Grounded as they were in an almost journalistic mission with a clear agenda—to expose and affect the Yorkshire cheap school system—Dickens's fictional and narrative choices in representing this reality are worth examining. The choices he makes may be taken as politically feeble, ambiguous, and undaring indeed, yet being made with an eye for persuading the readers and making a social impact, they are perhaps not as naïve or escapist as they might first seem.

If we wish to measure the feebleness or intensity of Dickens's fiction in relation to the "fact" that served as its origin—that is, the "existing reality" that had stimulated him to invent Dotheboys School to begin with—we face an inevitable obstacle. The facts, no matter from what perspective we try to gauge them, are bound to be mediated; even the allegedly nonfictional, factual reports about schools at the time cannot gain us direct access to the "reality" to which Dickens's preface refers. The little that we can tell on the basis of an abundance of such commission reports and statistical records—those records that use an emphatically factual discourse—is that many systematic, sadistic brutalities were performed against children in nineteenth-century British schools, and that certain cases resulted not only in severe traumas but also in permanent physical disabilities, sometimes even death.[4]

Social historians are almost unanimous that nineteenth-century schooling for lower-middle-class and lower-class children was intended as a medium for turning out obedient, tamed subjects. Harry Hendrick argues that school—being the institution imparting "knowledge"—served to preserve the children's inferiority by emphasizing their ignorance and dependence, inculcating their submissiveness toward the state and their own parents (31). It is worth noting that the deft indoctrination attributed by historians to the school system may overestimate the capacities of the system's actual representatives in the classroom. Cheap private schools for middle-class children of the kind described in *Nicholas Nickleby*, usually charging as little as nine pence a week, were often set up throughout the nineteenth century by individuals who had failed in their previous occupations as tradesmen or shopkeepers. These people frequently opened schools because they could find no better employment, and were usually utterly unqualified as teachers (Heyck 204-05, Hopkins 131). In one case, a parliamentary assistant commissioner was told of the principal of a school, not previously a teacher, who had had an accident and lost his memory—"so his friends set him up as a schoolmaster" (Horn 35). Private schools for middle-class children were notorious throughout the century for their inadequate teaching, the violent treatment they offered, and their poor diet (Walvin 112). Many of the teachers in similar establishments for working-class children were smiths or miners, who frequently could not even read (Kane 67). Until the early twentieth century, corporal punishment was taken for granted in all schools, even ones considered relatively humane (Hopkins 139). Besides the striking and caning of children, other prevalent punishments were the shackling of the child's legs, while making him or her walk round the room until tired; yoking offenders together by the neck; tying the elbows together behind the back; keeping children in after school, tied to the desk; and hoisting offenders to the ceiling in a basket (Hopkins 140). Legally, a teacher was in loco parentis, and the courts would uphold his right to inflict "the same punishment as a parent would be permitted" (Rose 182); and here we should note that until the late 1880s, parents were legally entitled to commit against their children almost any act of cruelty they could think of.

It is reasonable to assume, then, even without unmediated access to the scenes described in historical documents, that the violent episodes of child abuse in *Nicholas Nickleby*, although extreme, are no wild exaggeration on Dickens's part. We also know from various sources besides Dickens's 1848 preface that increasing public awareness and legislation gradually terminated the prevalence of such violent and neglectful practices in the course of the century.

However, in addition to historical evidence there is another valuable context by which we can evaluate just how "faint and feeble" Dickens's representation is—and that is the literary context. Several other works of fiction of the same period dealt with similar issues, yet Dickens's handling of brutality against children in *Nicholas Nickleby* differed from what we can find in other novels that sought to denounce social practices of neglect, abuse, and mistreatment of children in contemporary Britain.

Three choices that Dickens makes in *Nicholas Nickleby* are far from obvious—in fact quite unusual if examined according to the conventions of mid-nineteenth-century social-problem writing in Britain. One is his decision to ignore the wider social aspects of the collective exploitation of children, namely, the burning issue of child labor, which highly disturbed public opinion and legislators since the early 1830s. Instead, he chooses to treat only a local problem—that of the violence and cruelty at the Yorkshire schools—despicable and unsettling, no doubt, yet regional and far more narrow in scope and urgency for contemporary society than child labor. A second and related difference is that Dickens does not place the source of evil in any social or political context but in the idiosyncratic aberrations of one particular individual, Mr. Squeers, whose psychopathological drives are the sole origin of the phenomenon of child maltreatment in the novel. The third aspect that renders Dickens's treatment of child abuse distinct from other examples of social-problem writing is his preference to stage some unbearably brutal events as amusing, sometimes even hilarious scenes. To make his readers laugh often seems to be Dickens's primary target; the political wish to make them feel outraged may appear at such moments merely secondary, despite his professed commitment to social critique in the preface.

These three differences may suggest that Dickens's fiction is indeed more "feeble" in its critique of the social reality he wishes to denounce than other texts inspired by a similar impulse. Such a view—about which I suggest we should be cautious—would be compatible with the not uncommon critical opinion that Dickens, despite his critique of social injustice, is after all a relatively conservative spokesman of middle-class ideology.

Avoiding the issue of child labor—to begin with the first choice Dickens makes here—is a potential indication of an apolitical impulse. This avoidance is intriguing if only because of Dickens's otherwise deep, unflinching interest in the suffering of children. In two contemporary British novels published serially from late 1839 to 1841—that is, simultaneously with and immediately after *Nicholas Nickleby*, the case is quite the reverse. Frances Trollope's *Adventures of Michael Armstrong, the Factory Boy* (1840) and Charlotte Elizabeth Tonna's *Helen Fleetwood* (1841), although mostly forgotten today, were highly popular in the mid-nineteenth century and became famous even across the Atlantic. Both weave their plots around the horrors and damages of child labor. As the earliest

English social-problem novels, these texts, just like Robert Blincoe's 1832 *Memoir*, the first working-class autobiography depicting industrial labor, seem to have influenced later writers such as Elizabeth Gaskell and Benjamin Disraeli and were highly informed by fact. Blincoe cites his first-hand knowledge of factory life, whereas Tonna and Trollope base quite a few scenes and numerous details on parliamentary commissioners' reports that investigated the conditions in mills and factories and were published during the 1830s. Nonfictional accounts and autobiographies also served as a source from which Trollope and Tonna drew. In Trollope's case, some information was gathered during a fact-finding tour she made to Manchester in February 1839. She visited factories incognita, met labor activists and reformers, and interviewed workers.[5]

The early version of Blincoe's *Memoir* was compiled by the working-class journalist John Brown, who had recorded Blincoe's tale in 1825.[6] The famous, widely read 1832 edition was a revised and expanded version; following Brown's suicide, it was based on cooperation between Blincoe and John Doherty, himself a former child laborer, a working-class leader in Manchester, as well as a bookseller and printer (Reed 81). The book served to arouse public opinion against some of the practices of child employment and instigated a genre of autobiographical writing that had a wide impact. Simultaneously, some particularly horrifying cases publicized by the Ten-Hour Movement focused public attention. One child worker whose suffering became famous was Ellen Hooton of Wigan, who was allegedly forced to work in chains; her story (the "Wigan Case") caused a scandal. The comparison of the young girl's shackling to the oppression of slaves was readily made. Alongside the uproar caused by stories of children like Blincoe and Hooton, it was the routine of unexceptional cases that gradually came to be regarded as scandalous.[7]

In Blincoe's narrative there is a basic tension between the desire to portray himself, the main character, as unique, and the need to construct his persona as sufficiently representative in order to act as spokesman for his class.[8] Despite its interest in the child's interiority and point of view, the *Memoir* thus often shifts to the third-person plural, and its tone becomes impersonal. To provide information and make claims about working-class children at large are obviously the chief goals of this narrative. Blincoe thus refers explicitly to all those collectively deserted, destitute, famished, and tortured British children in whose name he is writing (Brown 91).

Similarly, Trollope and Tonna's novels were strongly realistic not merely in their narrative technique, but also in their emphasis on the extent to which they relied on fact. The avowed purpose of the two novels is political: they aim to expose the flaws of the socioeconomic system and stimulate their middle-class readers' awareness of the realities of working-class life and the pitfalls of charity and patronage. According to Sheila Smith, authors affiliated with the social-problem genre often use the novel "as though it were a popular form of Blue book in order to make their readers explore social problems and give them evidence to draw some conclusions."[9]

The ability of the novel to familiarize the working-class "other" and render his or her point of view carried political significance by potentially making readers more congenial to ideas of reform. Trollope and Tonna were well aware of this potential, as some of their narrators' direct addresses to the readers reveal. Trollope, for instance, declares at some point,

> Woe to those who supinely sit in contented ignorance of the facts, soothing their spirits and their easy consciences with the cuckoo note, "*exaggeration*," while thousands of helpless children pine away their unnoted, miserable lives, in labour and destitution, *incomparably more severe*, than any ever produced by negro slavery. (Trollope 186, her emphases)

Besides calling their readers to take a stand, the two authors also repeatedly assert the nonfictional dimension of their narratives. Trollope states that her intention was "to drag into the light of day, and place before the eyes of Englishmen, the hideous mass of injustice and suffering to which thousands of infant labourers are subjected, who toil in our monster spinning-mills. . . . The true but most painful picture has been drawn faithfully and conscientiously" (iii). Tonna similarly declares:

> Let no one suppose we are going to write fiction, or to conjure up phantoms of a heated imagination, to aid the cause which we avowedly embrace. Names may be altered, characters may be grouped . . .; but not an incident shall be coined to serve the purpose. . . . Vivid indeed, and fertile in devices must the fancy be that could invent a horror beyond the bare, everyday reality of the thing! Nay, we will set forth nothing but what has been stated on oath, corroborated on oath, and on oath confirmed beyond the possibility of an evasive question. (Tonna 43)

Like Blincoe's autobiography, these narratives claim to be telling a true story. Tonna, in particular, uses judicial discourse in order to present her narrative as legal evidence "corroborated on oath."

Significantly, unlike these writers, it is only in Dickens's preface that he attests to the factual basis of his fiction. No mention of that is made in the novel itself. It is also significant that, as mentioned above, unlike these other writers, he talks about schools, but avoids the theme of child labor. This avoidance—the first difference of the three we shall now discuss—is particularly intriguing because, unlike the other major novelists of his period, Dickens had first-hand knowledge of this phenomenon from his days as a boy operative at Warren's Blacking. He consistently refrained from writing about the subject not only in his fictional writing, but also in his journalistic work. Rosemarie Bodenheimer recounts how Dickens repeatedly postponed the writing of a piece against child labor requested by the editor of the *Edinburgh Review*, until finally it was too late to write it (62–63).

Throughout his career, with the exception of chapter 11 of *David Copperfield* and the "Autobiographical Fragment" (which he decided not to publish during his lifetime), Dickens was unable to revisit this traumatic period of his life, and never wrote "about children who worked—as he had done—in nondomestic jobs for regular wages" (Bodenheimer 63). It is intriguing that even in *Hard Times* (1854), the Dickens novel that most explicitly interrogates and denounces the social effects of the industrial scene, child characters are conspicuously missing from the description of the crowd of male and female laborers going in and out of the factory gates, in stark contrast to the noticeable presence of children among factory operatives in nonfictional descriptions of the period.[10]

Besides the discrepancy between Dickens's deep interest in child oppression and the absence of the theme of child labor from his work, it is important, in order to appreciate just how conspicuous this avoidance is, to be aware of the political climate of the late 1830s. The attitude to children was a hotly-debated issue in Britain during this decade, following the first publication of parliamentary reports that revealed the terrible living and working conditions of the lower classes and the masses of poor children in particular. The issue of child labor became a central target for debate in the public discourse—in Parliament and in the press. There was no consensus about the need to abolish child labor: a complex set-up of economic interests made it a very long and rough process until changes were brought into effect. Besides further governmental investigations and legislative initiatives, the shocked public response to the findings in the official reports also inspired new kinds of fictional descriptions of the oppression of the working-class, children among them, in contemporary industrial Britain. The rise of the new sub-genre of industrial novels such as Tonna's and Trollope's was a prominent cultural manifestation of this new political awareness.

In *Nicholas Nickleby*, toward the end of the 1830s, Dickens indeed chooses to write about the institutional abuse of children as a social crime that must be condemned in order to effect a change. Yet he completely ignores the more central, wide-scale problem so extensively talked about, and focuses instead on the regional problem of the Yorkshire school brutality, over which there is no controversy. There are critics who regard the function of the school in the novel as emblematic, and argue that it has underlying political significations. John Bowen, for example, contends that there is an economic parallel between headmaster Squeers's exploitative school system and Ralph Nickleby's shady business ethic, so that the depiction of the Dotheboys establishment is part of the novel's critique of capitalism (160). Leona Toker similarly maintains that the microcosm of Mr. Squeers's establishment shows the same devices of evil that are at work also within the larger social sphere. A "logical extension of the patterns prevailing in the society that has produced them, this school is like the world around it—only more so" (Toker 27). Just like the workhouse in *Oliver Twist*, whose evil is institutional and broad, Squeers and his establishment represent—as Dickens's preface to *Nicholas Nickleby* testifies—a group of evildoers, not just one abnormal individual. These interpretations notwithstanding, we can see Dickens's avoidance of the issue of child labor—especially if this theme is figuratively embodied in the school episodes—as a depoliticized way of tackling a social problem. If we were to argue that Dickens avoids the political dimension of social problems, we could make an opposite claim: that as a wide-scale, hard-to-solve social problem, the muted issue of child labor renders the analogous yet narrower Dotheboys School "like the world around it—only less so"—less, not in the quality of dehumanizing degradation with which the school provides its inmates, but in its quantity—that is, the scale of its significance and its relation to political, economic, systemic structures.

The avoidance of the issue of child labor is directly connected to the second difference between Dickens and his contemporaries mentioned above. Unlike other writers of social fiction, Dickens places the source of evil in one abnormal, hideous individual rather than in a social system based on ingrained injustice and exploitation. As Sally Ledger has argued, in *Nicholas Nickleby* (as also in *Oliver Twist*), "good and evil individuals shape the moral parameters of the novel" (593). This choice creates the impression that evil is not deeply rooted; it is enough to get rid of one disturbing, intolerable headmaster, and the horrors should then cease. This is indeed what happens in *Nicholas Nickleby* following the children's mutiny, which leads to the collapse of Dotheboys Hall. This representation of social facts seems less political, perhaps apolitical in nature, if compared to other Victorian social fictions based on contemporary social conditions and speaking for broad, systematic phenomena. Blincoe recounts his private history as a collective story, speaking for the many, and Tonna and Trollope repeatedly emphasize how the specific incidents of child abuse that they depict are not accidental or unique in any way, but serve as instances demonstrating broad and deeply-rooted social practices. Unlike these writers, and also unlike Disraeli in *Sybil, or The Two Nations* (1845) or Gaskell in *Mary Barton* (1848) and *North and South* (1855), even unlike the later Dickens of *Hard Times*—that is, unlike novelists who present the oppression and suffering of the weak and poor as rooted in some general social injustice—for Dickens in *Nicholas Nickleby* evil is individual, its origin purely psychological. The fact that the nature of this evil is clearly abnormal implies even further that social norms regarding children should not cause the readers any moral concern; it is merely a pathological aberration that is renounced. This kind of representation of evil contrasts with many social-problem novels' project of exposing the collective moral blind-spots of what society considers "normal"—for example, child labor.

The third aspect of Dickens's factual fiction that makes it conspicuously different from other representations is his masterly humor. We never smile when we read Tonna's descriptions of the horrible lives of child operatives in Manchester, nor when we follow the narrative of Blincoe's afflictions under his sadistic masters in the mills. Even in Trollope's *Michael Armstrong*, which uses comedy-of-manners conventions in its satirical depiction of the millocracy's family life, the tone becomes straightforward and grave as soon as the scene changes to the mill setting with its systematic and ongoing child abuse. Yet we laugh when we read Dickens's Dotheboys School's advertisement, tempting parents by the alluring promise: "no vacations" (40), a policy that one parent praises as the school's sound avoidance of those "ill-judged comings home twice a year that unsettle children's minds so" (49). And we laugh when Squeers voices his concern about the safety of his new pupils during the journey back to school, saying, as he places them in the back seat outside the coach: "I'm afraid of one of them boys falling off, and then there's twenty pound a year gone" (59); or when Squeers is looking at one of these pupils "to see whether he was doing anything he could beat him for: as [the boy] happened not to be doing anything at all, he merely boxed his ears, and told him not to do it again" (44); or when he refreshes himself in preparation for a particularly celebrative scene of flogging, making his appearance with a "diabolical grin" on his face, "a countenance of portentous import, and a fearful instrument of flagellation, strong, supple, wax-ended, and new,. . . purchased that morning expressly for the occasion" (155-56).

In *The Violent Effigy*, studying the treatment of cruelty in Dickens's fiction and letters, John Carey brings evidence to the hilarity with which Dickens would sometimes respond to other people's disasters, especially when these other people were of an inferior social standing. Seeing the comic side of lower-class death and suffering, Dickens's "flippant, educated tone" suggests a "disdainful callousness," Carey argues. Thus, when Dickens

> describes the suffering of the workhouse children in *Oliver Twist*, and of the pupils at Dotheboys Hall in *Nicholas Nickleby*, this is his regular voice, . . . [which] encourage[s] us to laugh at starving children, but we forget this and willingly co-operate with him . . . . Dickens . . . did not wish to provoke anger or reform so much as to retain a large and lucrative audience. . . . Thus the torturers become, in our eyes, genial managers of the entertainment. (Carey 70–71)

Indeed, if we are entertained by Squeers's malice, do we not become his accomplices? If we enjoy Dickens's irresistible humor in these passages, do we not secretly share something of Squeers's sadism?

However, if because of the humor, the narrow and consensual target, and the view of evil as mere personal aberration, we tend to regard Dickens's handling of social fact as largely depoliticized, there is still one important aspect of *Nicholas Nickleby* that we must acknowledge. The novel's unquestionable, decisive impact on fact is still something we have to account for. The comparison with other contemporary social-problem novels may lead us to think that Dickens's writing is in several respects less committed to a political critique and tends to be cautious in its method, consistently avoiding controversial targets. Yet the political effect of Dickens's factual fiction was nevertheless not feeble at all—perhaps all the more intense just because of what critics have often referred to as his middle-class conservatism. This alleged conservatism may be regarded as something quite different: a sophisticated, and highly effective, manipulation and mediation of "facts" and their translation into a fiction whose political dimension is better concealed. In a critical discussion of a given literary work's political engagement, it is important to address not only its explicit social outlook and ideology, but also its actual political effectiveness, as well as the implicit literary strategy that has made this effect possible.

In spite of all the potentially apolitical features of Dickens's writing, his factual fiction was immediately influential in arousing a strong public response and in achieving actual change. In this respect it was more powerful—less "feeble," if you like—than the more radical and strongly-committed fictional works produced by Dickens's contemporaries. The case of *Nicholas Nickleby* demonstrates that a critical evaluation of a literary text's political magnitude should take into account a complex multiplicity of variables. In fact, we can reexamine each of the three narrative choices that mark Dickens's art and see them, despite their seemingly faint and feeble political stance, as actually forceful in their political function.

That Dickens had a strategic, and not merely artistic, awareness of what he was doing is reflected in his declared need to keep descriptions of cruelty down so that they seem real to the reader, and in his references to "The Author's object in calling public attention to the system" in the preface (3). The urgent journalistic mission that had inspired the trip to Yorkshire was not abandoned as Dickens was writing his factual fiction. On the one hand, he is concerned that the horrors he is depicting might "be deemed impossible"; on the other hand, he does not wish to lose his readers' sympathy and ongoing interest. The three narrative choices discussed here make this double purpose possible.

First, by attacking a local, regional target such as the Yorkshire schools, Dickens sets up in front of his readers a social problem whose scope is clearly defined and that can therefore be treated pragmatically—as indeed it was. Other social-problem novels were probably also effective in influencing public opinion against child labor and other class-related problems, yet the phenomena they described were despairingly wide and all-engulfing. Actual restrictions and eventual abolition of child labor took an entire century to ripen. Historian Eric Hopkins claims that the process was so slow because Britain eventually abolished child labor only "when it became economically possible to do so" (38)—that is, when productivity grew to an extent that enabled the country to dispense with the contribution of child labor to the economy. This view, suggesting that objection to child labor on humanitarian grounds was not particularly effectual, is corroborated by the fact that even toward the end of the century, when the state could have dispensed with child labor altogether, this practice did not disappear. Although only about half as many children worked in the mines in England and Wales in 1881 as had done so in 1841, during the same period the number of children working as servants nearly doubled (Nelson 72). Industrial novels had little impact, it seems, on social reality. To critique the broad, deep-rooted socioeconomic reality of class division in industrial Britain—a structure that promoted the upper and middle classes, legislators included—was valuable ideologically, but far from effective practically. To begin with, then, Dickens's critique of the local, isolated problem of the Yorkshire schools had incomparably better chances of bringing about a change. Whether or not his avoidance of the subject of child labor had anything to do with his own childhood trauma, it is still likely that in depicting Dotheboys, Dickens felt that he was critiquing the wider, much-discussed phenomenon associated with children's suffering. This is shown, for instance, in his famous irritation with what he saw as the exaggerated resemblance between *Nicholas Nickleby* and Frances Trollope's *Michael Armstrong*. Other readers have often failed to observe such a strong resemblance; the accusation of imitation that Dickens hinted at can be better understood if we assume that for him, the Dotheboys experience and child labor were closely related themes.[11] The school and the factory share, for Dickens, the same patterns of child abuse that he, like Trollope, wishes to condemn. Choosing to tackle the problem through the depiction of a school could be merely a different method of addressing the same issue.

Second, we have established the view that the grotesque idiosyncrasy of Dickens's villains implies an apolitical staging of social evil as personal abnormality. However, is it not easier to make one's middle-class readers more indignant when the accused party is one guilty character, and not an entire social and economic system—a system that, exploitative as it may be, benefits these readers in various ways? Bowen's claim that there is an economic parallel between Squeers and Ralph Nickleby's capitalism (160) suggests that via the brutal headmaster, Dickens manages to critique broader issues than the mere running of an unspeakable school. We can take this claim further and suggest that through Squeers, an obvious villain, it is easier to denounce social hierarchies without antagonizing one's readers. Dickens's middle-class audience is not an accomplice to Squeers's sadism and does not benefit from the crimes performed by this hideous individual. The readers are not provoked by Dickens's critique of school brutality, whereas a more sweeping or deeper critique of child abuse as part of the overall British system, shown to be founded on economic exploitation, might have been too upsetting for them. To locate the source of social evil in one grotesque individual, as Dickens does, allows the readers to feel unambiguous disapproval of the wrongs done against helpless children in schools of this kind. Without antagonism among middle-class readers and legislators, change could occur more rapidly and willingly. Staging evil as abnormal is potentially more efficient than preaching against it as a widespread vice, a moral blemish on an entire society.

The third narrative choice that may seem to diminish the political determination of the text is Dickens's humor. Does its capacity to make us laugh indeed make Dickens's prose politically "feeble"? Do we slightly tend to sympathize with Squeers because we are amused by the compelling descriptions of his malice? These questions should be answered by examining what it is that we are laughing at. Here and elsewhere, Dickens never treats the victimized children as amusing; the target of his satire is always the perpetrator. The reason why we enjoy reading about Squeers's brutality is not that we secretly share his ruthlessness, but that through depicting him, Dickens manages to capture so brilliantly the grotesque, ugly, demeaning face of human cruelty. The function of humor here is not merely to entertain, but to augment the readers' sense of outrage. The purpose of humor—as Sigmund Freud argues in *Jokes and Their Relation to the Unconscious*—is often aggressive; a joke recruits the third party, the hearer (and in our case, the reader), making him or her "take sides with us" and with the critique we voice against our enemy (103). Satirical writing often uses humor when describing human suffering that is the result of evil actions, as a way to belittle the social agents or institutions that are responsible. In *Nicholas Nickleby*, Dickens manages to expose the ridiculous side of the power figures, the school headmaster and his wife, and defeat them not only aesthetically but politically, leading to their collapse both within the fictional text (closing down the school following the children's mutiny) and outside of it, through actual change produced by the readers' response. The effect of humor in a factual fiction of the kind Dickens creates in *Nicholas Nickleby* is therefore a subversive, political power par excellence.

What we have not mentioned so far in this comparison between Dickens and his contemporary social-problem novelists is his greater merit as an author. There is no doubt that Dickens's literary genius puts him high above the other authors listed here. This superiority is part of the reason why the overall impact of his texts would always exceed what we may regard as their measurable components. One of the central features that render Dickens so superior to other writers is his inimitable humor, a quality that has not always received enough attention from critical analyses of his work.[12] Yet it is not merely the humor that is distinctive, but the idiosyncratic way in which Dickens blends it with those textual elements that he perceives as not funny at all. The blend is not unlike the mixture of tragic and comic scenes that the narrator of *Oliver Twist*, in a famous passage, discerns in "all good, murderous melodramas." These mixed scenes, he states, usually appear "in as regular alternation, as the layers of red and white in a side of a streaky, well-cured bacon" (117; Ch. 17). Although "[s]uch changes seem absurd," Dickens's narrator believes that they "are not so unnatural as they would seem at first sight. The transitions in real life from well-spread boards to death-beds, and from mourning weeds to holiday garments, are not a whit less startling; only, there, we are busy actors, instead of passive lookers-on; which makes a vast difference" (118; Ch. 17). What makes the Dotheboys scenes so effective—and, arguably, in a way carefully contrived by the author for this purpose—is precisely this rapid transition from hilarious to sad moments and back again; from the "haggard faces" of lank and bony children, "darkened with the scowl of sullen dogged suffering," to the amusing account of the brutal administration of brimstone and treacle by Mrs. Squeers (97; ch. 8); and from the comic description of the children's peculiar breakfast, consisting of a "brown composition which looked like diluted pincushions without the covers, and was called porridge" (98), back to the sadness that strikes Nicholas as he observes the silent, desperate children sitting "crouching and shivering together, [lacking] the spirit to move about" (98; ch. 8).

This blend of moods seems to be a conscious strategy aimed at affecting the reception of the novel. Besides Dickens's proclaimed awareness of the necessity to tone down the descriptions in order to persuade his readers of the factual basis of his story, he seems to be also considering the emotional effect of his narrative. This effect has to do with the possibility that the school episodes, mediated though Nicholas's focalization and the omniscient narrator's perspective alternately, might be received and assessed differently by people who, unlike the author, have not been "there,"—that is, at Dotheboys Hall or at its factual Yorkshire counterpart. His narrator thus states that, despite its horrifying aspects, the scene of the suffering children that Nicholas has been witnessing, "painful as it was, had its grotesque features, which, in a less interested observer than Nicholas, might have provoked a smile" (97; ch. 8). The uninvolved observer, who is a stranger to the scene, might also find the children's appearance, in their "motley, ill-sorted" garments, "irresistibly ridiculous, but for the foul appearance of dirt, disorder, and disease, with which they were associated" (98; ch. 8).

Aware of both the horrifying and the grotesquely ludicrous sides of the scene, Dickens endeavors to perform two contradictory missions in this novel: on the one hand, he aims to shock his readers, affect public opinion, and bring about a social change. On the other hand, he is intent on making his readers laugh even while describing some highly sinister, brutal scenes. These two seemingly paradoxical targets manage to work together thanks to Dickens's command of creating the desired effect through his unique style of shifting and blending moods, and thanks to his success in exposing the degrading, preposterous side of the vicious power figures he satirizes. It is his very awareness and manipulation of the reader's response that makes Dickens's factual fiction so politically—as well as aesthetically—effective.

NOTES

1. On Marx and Engels's admiration of Dickens's commitment to social change, see Demetz 45. Another early favorable Marxist reading is Bernard Shaw's 1913 essay "Hard Times." Theodor Adorno's 1931 essay, too, emphasizes Dickens's critique of capitalism, claiming that the pre-capitalist elements in his novels dissolve "the very bourgeois world they depict" (172). T. A. Jackson's 1937 reading presents Dickens as a true revolutionary and a harsh critic of bourgeois society (150–52, 177).

2. On the tendency of subsequent critics to see Dickens as apolitical, see Sally Ledger 576. A reading of Dickens's politics that discussed the critical disagreement as to his social views and had some influence in underlining Dickens's sharp political awareness

and the vital place he assigned to class in the formation of character, was Monroe Engel's "The Politics of Dickens's Novels" (see esp. 945).

3.   For more on Mr. Squeers's factual origins, see Mark Ford's introduction to the novel
     (797–98n1).

4.   For some evidence on the shocking brutalities performed at schools, see Lionel Rose
     200, Eric Hopkins 129, and Pamela Horn 17.

5.   W. H. Chaloner provides a detailed account of Trollope's trip to Manchester (160–61).
     Some social-problem novelists, including Elizabeth Gaskell, visited factory work-
     ers personally; others based their novels mainly on Blue books (Elliott 388; see also
     Brantlinger 28–32).

6.   This early, less-familiar version was published serially in the radical paper *The Lion* in
     1828. See Elizabeth Reed's 2007 "Note on The Text," *Factory Lives*. 79–85.

7.   Hopkins 85. The Wigan Case is reported in the First Report of the Factory Inquiry
     Commission (*PP* 1833), 103–15. According to James Walvin, the material circulated
     by the Ten-Hour Movement and the reports published by Parliamentary commissions
     as of the 1830s supplied sufficient grounds for reformers to compare the condition of
     British child workers to that of slaves in the New World (51–53, 64).

8.   Regenia Gagnier persuasively demonstrates how nineteenth-century working-class
     autobiographers were chiefly concerned with their "image and status as atoms of the
     masses" (143).

9.   Smith 29. For more on the connections and mutual development of Blue books and
     fiction, see Brantlinger 28–32.

10. In a cancelled passage in *Hard Times* there is a reference to Rachael's dead little sister,
     who lost her arm in a factory accident. According to Joseph Butwin, Dickens deleted
     this single allusion in the novel to child labor during the final proof stage. There is
     no known reason why he deleted this passage (177–182). It should also be noted that
     although Dickens, as Bodenheimer observes (63), may not write about children who
     worked in nondomestic jobs for wages except in *David Copperfield*, he does consider
     other types of work by other children: Oliver Twist (who works briefly for the under-
     taker Sowerberry), Charley Neckett (in *Bleak House*), and Jenny Wren (in *Our Mutual
     Friend*). It is mostly the theme of children as industrial operatives that he avoids.

11. In 1839, when both *Michael Armstrong* and *Nicholas Nickleby* were serialized in
     monthly instalments, Dickens declined an invitation to dine with Frances Trollope ("To
     Frances Trollope," *Letters* 1: 499), and expressed his anger that Trollope's new novel
     was a reworking of *Nickleby* (*Letters* 1: 640). In two letters to Laman Blanchard dated
     9 February 1839, he referred to this matter: "If Mrs. Trollope were even to adopt Ticho-
     las Tickleby as being a better-sounding name than Michael Armstrong, I don't think it
     would cost me a wink of sleep." In the letter immediately following he added that he
     would "express no further opinion of Mrs. Trollope, than that I think *Mr.* Trollope must
     have been an old dog and chosen his wife from the same species" (*Letters* 1: 506–507,
     emphasis in the original).

12. Philip Collins has wondered "from how many discussions of Dickens in the learned
     journals would one ever guess that (as Dickens himself thought) humor was his leading

quality, his highest faculty, or indeed that he ever indulged in such an unelevated form of writing?" (Collins, *Critical Heritage*, 14).

WORKS CITED

Adorno, Theodor. "On Dickens' *The Old Curiosity Shop*: A Lecture." *Notes to Literature*. 2 vols. Trans. Rolf Tiedemann. New York: Columbia UP, 1992: 171–77.
Adrian, Arthur A. "*Nicholas Nickleby* and Educational Reform." *Nineteenth-Century Fiction* 4.3 (December 1949): 237–41.
Bodenheimer, Rosemarie. *Knowing Dickens*. Ithaca: Cornell UP, 2007.
Bowen, John. "Performing Business, Training Ghosts: Transcoding *Nickleby*." *ELH* 63.1 (Spring 1996): 153–75.
Brantlinger, Patrick. *The Spirit of Reform: British Literature and Politics, 1832–1867*. Cambridge: Harvard UP, 1977.
Brown, John. *A Memoir of Robert Blincoe, An Orphan Boy*. In *Factory Lives: Four Nineteenth-Century Working-Class Autobiographies*. Ed. James R. Simmons, Jr. Peterborough, ON: Broadview, 2007. 87–179.
Burke, Kenneth. *Language as Symbolic Action: Essays on Life, Literature, and Method*. Berkeley: U of California P, 1966.
Butwin, Joseph. "*Hard Times*: The News and the Novel." *Nineteenth-Century Fiction* 32.2 (September 1977): 166–87.
Carey, John. *The Violent Effigy: A Study of Dickens' Imagination*. London: Faber, 1973.
Chaloner, W. H. "Mrs. Trollope and the Early Factory System." *Victorian Studies* 4 (1960): 159–66.
Collins, Philip. *Dickens and Education*. London: Macmillan, 1964.
———. Introduction. In *Dickens: The Critical Heritage*. Ed. Philip Collins. London: Routledge and Kegan Paul. 1971. 1–20.
Demetz, Peter. *Marx, Engels, and the Poets: Origins of Marxist Literary Criticism*. Chicago: U of Chicago P, 1967.
Dickens, Charles. *Letters in Pilgrim Edition: The Letters of Charles Dickens*. Vol. 1 (1820–1839). Eds. Madeline House and Graham Storey. Oxford: Clarendon, 1965.
———. *Oliver Twist*. Ed. Fred Kaplan. New York: Norton, 1993.
———. *Nicholas Nickleby*. Ed. Mark Ford. London: Penguin, 1999.
Elliott, Dorice Williams. "Servants and Hands: Representing the Working Classes in Victorian Factory Novels." *Victorian Literature and Culture* 28.2 (2000): 377–90.
Engel, Monroe. "The Politics of Dickens's Novels." *PMLA* 71.5 (1956): 945–74.
Freud, Sigmund. *Jokes and Their Relation to the Unconscious. The Standard Edition of the Complete Psychological Works of Sigmund Freud*. Vol. 8. Trans. James Strachey. London: Hogarth, 1960.
Gagnier, Regenia. *Subjectivities: A History of Self-Representation in Britain, 1832–1920*. Oxford: Oxford UP, 1991.

Hendrick, Harry. *Child Welfare, England 1872–1989*. London: Routledge, 1994.

Heyck, Thomas William. "Walks of Life: Educational." *A Companion to Victorian Literature and Culture*. Ed. Herbert F. Tucker. Malden, MA: Blackwell, 1999. 194–211.

Hopkins, Eric. *Childhood Transformed: Working-Class Children in Nineteenth-Century England*. Manchester: Manchester UP, 1994.

Horn, Pamela. *The Victorian Town Child*. New York: New York UP, 1997.

House, Humphry. *The Dickens World*. London: Oxford UP, 1960.

Jackson, T. A. *Charles Dickens: The Progress of a Radical*. New York: International Publishers, 1987.

Justman, Stewart. "Political Fictions." *College English* 39.7 (March 1978): 834–40.

Kane, Penny. *Victorian Families in Fact and Fiction*. New York: St. Martin's, 1995.

Ledger, Sally. "From Queen Caroline to Lady Dedlock: Dickens and the Popular Radical Imagination." *Victorian Literature and Culture* 32.2 (2004): 575–600.

Nelson, Claudia. "Growing Up: Childhood." *A Companion to Victorian Literature and Culture*. Ed. Herbert F. Tucker. Malden, MA: Blackwell, 1999. 69–81.

Orwell, George. *A Collection of Essays*. New York: Doubleday, 1954.

Reed, Elizabeth. "Note on the Text." *Factory Lives: Four Nineteenth-Century Working-Class Autobiographies*. Ed. James R. Simmons, Jr. Peterborough, ON: Broadview, 2007. 79–85.

Rose, Lionel. *The Erosion of Childhood: Child Oppression in Britain 1860-1918*. London: Routledge, 1991.

Shaw, George Bernard. "Hard Times." *Bernard Shaw's Nondramatic Literary Criticism*. Ed. Stanley Weintraub. Lincoln: U of Nebraska P, 1972. 40–48.

Smith, Sheila M. "Blue Books and Victorian Novelists." *Review of English Studies* 21 (1970): 23–40.

Sutherland, John. "The Fiction Earning Patterns of Thackeray, Dickens, George Eliot and Trollope." *Browning Institute Studies* 7 (1979): 71–92.

Toker, Leona. "*Nicholas Nickleby* and the Discourse of Lent." *Dickens Studies Annual* 38 (2007): 19–33.

Tonna, Charlotte Elizabeth. *Helen Fleetwood*. New York: Scribner, 1852.

Trollope, Frances. *Life and Adventures of Michael Armstrong, the Factory Boy*. London: Henry Colburn, 1844.

Walvin, James. *A Child's World: A Social History of English Childhood 1800–1914*. Harmondsworth: Penguin, 1982.

Wilson, Edmund. "Dickens: The Two Scrooges." *The Wound and the Bow*. New York: Oxford UP, 1965. 1–104.

Dickens and Tocqueville: Chapter 7 of *American Notes*

Jerome Meckier

Abundant evidence has been presented elsewhere to show that Dickens took exception to Democracy in America *in both* American Notes *and* Martin Chuzzlewit. *Rather than recapitulate, I wish to suggest that the most famous early Victorian travel writer, who had a life-long interest in prison reform, also disagreed thoroughly with Tocqueville's earlier treatise* On the Penitentiary System in the United States and Its Application in France, *which had been translated in 1833. Throughout chapter 7 of* American Notes, *Dickens repudiated the French aristocrat's theories about incarceration and his notion of Philadelphia's Eastern Penitentiary as the ideal prison. Dickens rewrote the prison interviews in Appendix No. 10 of Tocqueville's opus, rejecting the Frenchman's positive findings and parodying his methodology. Thus may have been conceived the rationale behind the American chapters in* Martin Chuzzlewit: *en route to Eden and back, the hero in effect interviews a dozen or more American scalawags. The impressions they make upon him register opposite to their intentions, just as Dickens's disheartening interviews with Eastern Penitentiary inmates contradicted Tocqueville's upbeat testimonials. Dickens denounced the Philadelphia system as vigorously as Tocqueville had praised it. This mistaken judgment in Tocqueville's field of expertise, Dickens implied, not only discredited the so-called Separate System of solitary confinement but also compromised the aristocrat's entire critique of America's socio-political experiment.*

Regarding "the most significant of all early nineteenth-century European reports on America, Alexis de Tocqueville's *Democracy in America* (vol. 1, 1835; vol. 2, 1840), there appears to be no hard evidence that Dickens ever read it," Michael Slater concluded in his biography, *Charles Dickens* (177).[1] Along with other Dickens biographers, like Forster, Johnson, Kaplan, and Ackroyd, Slater overlooks the Inimitable's negative response to Tocqueville. Collectively, this amounts to a major oversight because much of Dickens's traumatic socio-political disappointment in 1842 stemmed from his failure to substantiate Tocqueville's claim that democracy was "the will of God," allegedly "the whole future" of civilization (*DA* 30, 38). A country of tobacco-spitting, dollar-worshipping, slave-owning chauvinists, Dickens angrily retorted, was bound to have become "senseless to the high principles on which [it] sprang, a nation, into life" (*MC* 435; ch. 22). America was not the next step forwards for humanity in some divinely sanctioned amelioration process. Instead, Dickens feared, it was jeopardizing the "very progress of the human race" and "the rights of nations yet unborn" (*MC* 435; ch. 22).

Abundant "soft" evidence has been presented elsewhere to show that Dickens took exception to *Democracy in America* in both *American Notes* and *Martin Chuzzlewit*.[2] Rather than recapitulate, I wish to suggest that the most famous early Victorian travel writer, who had a life-long interest in prison reform, also disagreed thoroughly with *On the Penitentiary System in the United States and Its Application in France*, a work attributed to Gustave de Beaumont and Tocqueville, but probably written mainly by Beaumont under Tocqueville's supervision and based on their joint notes and observations. This earlier treatise had been translated into English in 1833.

Dickens's visit to Philadelphia's Eastern Penitentiary is the focus in chapter 7 of *American Notes*. Most junketing Europeans toured this establishment. Dickens's investigation was probably inspired by Tocqueville's, but the visit went so contrary to his predecessors that it may be said to mark the beginning of the end for the novelist's daydream of discovering an ideal republic in America. Dickens disliked the prison at Cherry Hill intensely, and he disliked Tocqueville for having liked it.

Throughout chapter 7, Dickens talked back to Tocqueville. Vehemently, he repudiated the French aristocrat's theories about incarceration and his notion of the ideal prison, which are judged to be not just unsound but inhumane. Specifically, Dickens rewrote the prison interviews in Appendix No. 10 of Tocqueville's opus, rejecting the Frenchman's positive findings and parodying his methodology. Thus may have been conceived the rationale behind the anti-American chapters in *Martin Chuzzlewit*: en route to Eden and back, the hero in effect interviews a dozen or more American scalawags. The impressions they make upon him register opposite to their intentions, just as Dickens's disheartening interviews with Eastern Penitentiary inmates contradicted Tocqueville's upbeat testimonials.

Alexis de Tocqueville and Gustave de Beaumont, his close friend and fellow traveler, came to America in 1831-32 on a grant from the French government

to study prisons. Almost immediately, Tocqueville realized that it was imperative to produce a larger work, "an image of democracy itself" (*DA* 13); but first
he conducted prison inspections. In *On the Penitentiary System*, he idealized the
Separate System, which he and Beaumont encountered when they visited "the
most famous prison in the world—Cherry Hill, the Eastern Penitentiary in Philadelphia"; opened in 1829, the "international showplace for the Separate System"
had placed America in the forefront of nineteenth-century prison reform (Collins
117).

Under the Auburn System, implemented first at Mount Auburn in Massachusetts and then installed in Sing Sing prison in New York, convicts had to maintain
absolute silence but were allowed to emerge from their cells to work in groups. In
Philadelphia, prisoners remained isolated in separate cells—that is, solitary confinement—for their entire sentence, although they were given productive work to
do. Dickens denounced the Philadelphia system as vigorously as Tocqueville had
praised it. This mistaken judgment in Tocqueville's field of expertise, Dickens
implied, compromised the French aristocrat's entire critique of America's socio-
political experiment. His reflections on American manners and morals could not
be trusted either. Harriet Martineau believed that the Philadelphia system was
"the best yet tried" (qtd. in Collins 129), so that a blow against Tocqueville struck
her as well.[3] Most travelers to America "tended strongly to the Philadelphia plan"
(Collins 130). Dickens's abhorrence of it sets him apart from a consensus that
Tocqueville helped to build.

Tocqueville and Beaumont agreed with supporters of the Separate System that
"the best prison is that which does not corrupt" further (*PS* 49); thanks to the
"thick walls" separating prisoners' cells, "moral contagion" was "impossible,"
they argued. "Nowhere," Tocqueville emphasized, is the "vice" of mutual pol-
lution "avoided with greater safety than at Philadelphia, where the prisoners find
themselves utterly unable to communicate with each other; and it is incontest-
able that their perfect isolation secures the prisoner from all fatal contamination"
(*PS* 23). Thanks to their various occupations, the isolated prisoners acquire the
"means" that "will enable them to gain honestly their livelihood" when freed,
Tocqueville asserted (*PS* 24). Best of all, complete solitude paved the way for
remorse. Without distractions, Tocqueville maintained, the mind turns automati-
cally towards repentance and reformation. Consequently, the Philadelphia System
"produces the deepest impressions on the soul of the convict" and "must effect
more reformation than that of Auburn" (59). "When we visited" the inmates at
Cherry Hill, Tocqueville and Beaumont concluded, "not a single one of them"
failed to express "a kind of gratitude" for being able to labor and repent in solitude
(23).

A sense of community, Dickens believed, was essential to the individual's
sanity and sense of moral worth. In *American Notes*, he appears to be refuting
Tocqueville's views specifically when he rejects any preference for Philadelphia
over Sing Sing: "In its superior efficiency to that other code of regulations which

allows the prisoners to work in company without communicating together, I have not the smallest faith," he declared (*AN* 157; ch. 7). Even without visiting Sing Sing as Tocqueville had, Dickens felt the Frenchman had bungled the comparison. Dickens's curious phrasing: "to work in company without communicating together" speaks against solitary confinement. Sing Sing's prisoners labor as a unit. Even though they do not communicate, they maintain silence together— that is, in unison, as a group—which is better than prolonged silence in solitary, which Dickens believed drove men mad.

Titled "Philadelphia and Its Solitary Prison," chapter 7 of *American Notes* begins with a condemnation of the Separate System. Dickens found it "rigid, strict, and hopeless"—that is, it deprived its victims of hope. "I believe it, in its effects, to be cruel and wrong," he added. Its enthusiasts, he proclaimed, "do not know what they are doing" (*AN* 146; ch. 7) They are, Dickens implied, no better than Christ's crucifiers, of whom Jesus said, "Father forgive them, for they do not know what they are doing" (Luke 23:34). Dickens concluded chapter 7 with a rebuttal to Tocqueville's contention that the Philadelphia system "produced a more profound reformation" (qtd. in Collins 59). As if speaking directly to Tocqueville, Dickens voiced his "fixed opinion that those who have undergone this punishment [i.e., solitary confinement] MUST pass into society again morally unhealthy and diseased" (*AN* 156; ch. 7). Capital letters for "MUST" stress the psychological damage that solitary confinement caused and thus nullify emphatically Tocqueville's opinion that the Philadelphia system was more reformative. They also negate the Frenchman's confidence in solitary confinement as a barrier to contamination: of itself, the Separate System is said to have "unhealthy and diseased" results. Dickens recommended "abandoning a mode of punishment attended by so little hope or promise, and fraught, beyond dispute, with such a host of evils (*AN* 158; ch. 7).

Between the opening and closing condemnations of the Separate System in chapter 7, Dickens offered brief sketches of several inmates whom he considered victims of Cherry Hill; he deplored the lone hypocrite he encountered who claimed to have been reformed there. These sketches might have appeared in *Sketches by Boz* as a paper titled "Philadelphia's Solitaries" or "Victims of America's Solitary System." Characterizing the prisoners by nationality or occupation rounds out each one: simply numbering them as Tocqueville did, did not. As he would in *Chuzzlewit*, Dickens provides flesh-and-blood illustrations of the enormities he was opposing; he gives life and breath to the extremity of one wretch after another until the pathos becomes palpable. The author communicates to the reader a growing sense of outrage totally absent from Tocqueville who was unresponsive to the prisoners' plight. Nothing exceeds the misery Dickens says he witnessed in Philadelphia; "it remains" in his mind "in all its painfulness" (*AN* 152; ch. 7). Having "passed the day in going from cell to cell" (147), Dickens contended that he had learned more on Tuesday, 8 March 1842 than Tocqueville did in nearly two weeks of interviews.[4]

Before Tocqueville, it had never been "the practice of even the most consci-entious penologists to consult the prisoners" (Pierson 300). However, in Octo-ber 1831, as Appendix No. 10, "Inquiry into the Penitentiary of Philadelphia" indicates, the Frenchman conducted one-on-one interviews with some forty-five prisoners. Eleven years later, Dickens either came up with the idea of conducting prisoner interviews on his own, or, more likely, decided to reevaluate Tocqueville by employing his methodology against him, the implication being that chapter 7 of *American Notes* was telling the truth by rewriting correctly Appendix No. 10 of Tocqueville's study.[5]

Tocqueville's thumb-nail portraits seldom run more than three or four sen-tences. Nearly every prisoner interviewed expresses a favorable opinion of his situation, which Tocqueville recorded unquestioningly. Number 28, for example, "finds a kind of pleasure in solitude," while number 56 states that he "loves" it (*PS* 187, 189). The majority considers the chance to labor in solitude "a great benefit," as number 36 puts it (188). Formerly illiterate, number 32 has learned to read the Bible "fluently" (190). A self-taught shoemaker who turns out six pairs a week, number 67 is preoccupied with "philosophical and religious thoughts" (192). If there is a system which can make men "reflect and reform," number 41 observes, "it is this" (189).[6]

Dickens tells different stories. He begins with a description of the "black hood" that is "drawn over" the entering prisoner's head, as if in preparation for execu-tion (*AN* 148; ch. 7). The idea is to deny him any knowledge of where he is being taken. The prisoner is then led to the cell in which he is "buried alive" for the duration of his sentence.[7] Within two days, Tocqueville alleged, the prisoner gets over "the terrors" of solitude and seeks relief in labor from "a stinging con-science" (*PS* 39-40). The typical prisoner, countered Dickens, remains mired in "solitary horrors"; unaware of everything but his small cell, he hears no more of family, home, or friends but simply "grows old" (*AN* 149; ch. 7). Tocqueville's emphasis on relief, reflection, and reform is replaced by Dickens's grim, if some-what illogical, sequence: solitary confinement is like death by execution followed by burial while still alive; then one wastes away into old age.

Reminded of the wife he has not seen in six years, one of the first inmates Dick-ens interviewed "covered his face with his hands" (*AN* 149; ch. 7). A wretched German, three years into a five-year term, cries unrestrainedly throughout his interview. A prisoner allowed to keep rabbits in his cell nevertheless looks "as if he had been summoned from the grave" (150). A sailor, almost finished with his twelve-year sentence, "has lost all care for everything"; a more "helpless, crushed, and broken man" the visiting novelist cannot imagine (151). He was appalled by Tocqueville's opinion that Philadelphia's was the "mildest" punishment because it struck at "a man's mind only" (quoted in Damrosch 123). That is, it left the prisoner physically intact but supposedly increasingly receptive to "religious sen-timents" (*PS* 151). "I hold this slow and daily tampering with the mysteries of the brain, to be immeasurably worse than any torture of the body" (*AN* 147; ch. 7),

Dickens in effect replied. His summation of the German prisoner's woeful condition flatly contradicted Tocqueville's approval of solitary confinement as mental punishment: "I never saw such a picture of forlorn affliction and distress of mind," he insists. Dickens professed himself devastated by a "kind of misery" he "never saw or heard" before (150). Despite the hyperbole, his repugnance for solitary confinement sounds convincing. Without mentioning Tocqueville by name, the interviewer in *American Notes* makes both the Separate System and the Frenchman who endorsed it seem heartless.

Of the several inmates Dickens profiles, only a burglar with many prior convictions exults in his condition: "he declared that he blessed the day on which he came into that prison, and that he never would commit another robbery as long as he lived" (*AN* 150; ch. 7). Dickens found such "unmitigated hypocrisy" repulsive. He placed the burglar in the middle of the interviews in order to surround humbuggery with truthfulness. Instead of quoting the burglar directly, Dickens paraphrased his remarks, making them sound as phony as possible. Their insincerity undercuts one's confidence in prisoner number 1 in Tocqueville, who "considers his being brought to the [Philadelphia] penitentiary, as a signal benefit of Providence" (*PS* 192).[8]

Chapter 7 proceeds to condemn another instance of the Separate System in the prison Dickens later saw at Pittsburgh. As only a gifted novelist could, he imagined the "thoughts and feelings" of a newly incarcerated prisoner and dramatized the stages culminating in his "complete derangement" (*AN* 153; ch. 7). This experiment with interiority went beyond any travel writer's abilities and was before its time for novelists generally: a sliver of proto-modern fiction inserted in a Victorian's scrutiny of prison conditions in nineteenth-century Pennsylvania. When Tocqueville and Beaumont visited Pittsburgh's Western Penitentiary, their only complaint was that some of the inmates, who were supposed to be silent, "talked to one another unchecked" (*C-Span's* 122).

Admittedly, Tocqueville toured a brand-new facility, only a few years old. None of the prisoners he interviewed could have been incarcerated at Philadelphia for very long. Perhaps it was too soon to notice long-term ill-effects such as Dickens's sailor's inability to "look men in the face" and his incessant picking of the flesh on his hands (*AN 151;* ch. 7). Such behavior disconcerted Dickens, even though an attendant dismissed it as eccentricity: "'It is his humour: nothing more'" (*AN* 151; ch. 7). By 1842, Eastern Penitentiary had been in operation over a decade. Dickens opposed the theory of reform that underlay solitary confinement, not just the phenomenon itself; he would have objected to it under any circumstances.

The Eastern Penitentiary chapter anticipates *Chuzzlewit* in that it contains the first collection of Americans to appear in Dickens's writings. The anti-American chapters boil down to a sequence of hilarious interviews between a sensible young Englishman and a series of detestable braggarts and buffoons, a veritable rogues' gallery of ignorant, arrogant frauds who bring a country's deficiencies to life:

Brick, Choke, Diver, Fladdock, Pawkins, Norris, Kedgick, Kettle, Scadder, Chollop, Pogram, and Hominy. Tocqueville warned against the "tyranny of the majority" in a democracy; it suppressed freedom of opinion and resulted in sameness, "universal uniformity" (*DA* 315), but Dickens put faces on, and gave voices to, the nation's greed, thereby animating the country's selfishness and hypocrisy in ways that the French analyst's cultivated, even-handed prose could not.[9] Even Martin's two-chapter encounter with Mr. Bevan, the only admirable American he meets, is best read as one long interview (chs. 16-17). When they describe their country and their countrymen in glowing terms, Martin's interlocutors, Bevan excepted, prove as unbelievable as Tocqueville's prisoners—that is, self-incriminating. Their self-approval and consequent disdain for all things English are too lop-sided to credit, just as none of the prisoners Dickens interviewed (except for the burglar above) corroborated Tocqueville's absurdly contented solitaries.

Like his fellow Victorian travelers, Dickens shared the nineteenth-century's burgeoning awareness that the key to a society's merits were the provisions it made for its unfortunates: the poor, the sick, the deviant (i.e., criminals). One measured a country in terms of its hospitals and prisons. Dickens believed that Tocqueville had misled him, either over-praising the strengths of the new country's institutions or underestimating their deficiencies. *On the Penitentiary System* did both, extolling the Separate System as the epitome of enlightened reform when its treatment of inmates struck Dickens as almost criminal. No country that idealized the Eastern Penitentiary's philosophy of human nature, its conception of a human being, could be civilization's guarantor of liberty and freedom.

Noteworthy for its startling change of tone, the prison chapter sounds the first sour note in *American Notes*.[8] When Dickens replaced Tocqueville's upbeat bulletins with disconcerting prisoner interviews, he originated the "reviser's glance" (Meckier, *Innocent Abroad* 75); the parodic revaluator later trained it on his more sanguine rivals, darkening themes, characters, and situations in their novels that he deemed unrealistic.[11] Chapter 7 signaled Dickens's awareness that he would have to downgrade much of the travel writing that had "sparked his interest in the New World" as "a facsimile of utopia" (*Innocent Abroad* 75).

Years later, Tocqueville could still declare: "You know, I am half an American citizen" (qtd. in Damrosch 219).[12] Because his expectations had been higher, no doubt unrealistically so, Dickens, after 1842, could never echo the Frenchman's pledge of allegiance. The novelist who considered cellular isolation at Cherry Hill anti-social, uncivilized, and therefore as un-English as slavery, sailed home a reconstituted Englishman—no longer an ardent republican and less hopeful for radical reforms.[13] He stood for decency, fair play and, above all, compassion, cardinal virtues he felt that Tocqueville and advocates of the Eastern Penitentiary's Separate System egregiously flouted.

NOTES

1. Slater's second endnote refers to the "Battle of the Travel Books" chapter in Meckier, *Innocent Abroad*. "Based on a reading of *AN* and *MC*," Slater notes, this chapter "assumes...that CD not only knew De Tocqueville's work but was definitely engaging with it, as well as with Trollope and Martineau (on both of whom he is said to make 'an onslaught')"; "CD was...determined to show 'that he could evaluate a foreign country better than a Frenchman and two ladies had" (Slater 640, n.2). Outlandish though Slater makes this "onslaught" sound, it elaborates only slightly on Edgar Johnson's remark: "Dickens was convinced that he could understand [a kingless democratic republic] as neither of these ladies possibly could" (1:360).

2. Sylvère Monod asserted that Dickens "not unlikely" derived sanguine expectations from *Democracy in America* (Monod 36). The editor of *The Companion to Martin Chuzzlewit* cites half a dozen occasions where Dickens "may...have remembered" a passage from Tocqueville or pursued "a culture critique along the lines first articulated by Tocqueville," or where an implicit reference to Tocqueville resonates throughout an entire episode (Metz 222, 325). According to Forster, a letter from Dickens, 24 February 1842, virtually quoted a crucial passage from Henry Reeve's translation of *Democracy in America*. "I know of no country in which there is so little independence of mind and real freedom of discussion as in America" in Reeve became "I believe there is no country, on the face of the earth, where there is less freedom of opinion on any subject of reference to which there is a broad difference of opinion, than in this" (F 1:224-25; *DA* 117). On the eve of Dickens's departure for America, John Sherwood, an American journalist, found the novelist's study at Devonshire Terrace "piled high" with travel books on America by Basil Hall, Captain Marryat, Frances Trollope, and many others (Johnson 1:360). Tocqueville is never mentioned, but neither is Harriet Martineau, even though Slater realizes that Dickens is "most in dialogue [with her] in *American Notes*" (Slater 179). "The brunt of [Dickens's] displeasure...was reserved for Miss Martineau" (Meckier, *Innocent Abroad* 76). Perhaps Dickens was reading Tocqueville in America around the time he wrote Forster. That would explain the absence of Tocqueville's books from Dickens's library. For a full account of Dickens versus Tocqueville on a variety of subjects such as "irritable patriotism" and "love of money" (*DA* 104, 52), see *Innocent Abroad* 80-90.

3. One is surprised by the number of times the views of Harriet Martineau and Frances Trollope coincide with Tocqueville's. Between them, Richard Mullen, who edited Trollope's travelogue, and Seymour Martin Lipset, editor of an edition of Martineau, cite half a dozen instances where each is making comments "similar to," "almost identical with," or "like Tocqueville" (Lipset 3,13; Mullen xxv). Given what Lipset calls "congruence," Dickens often hit two birds with one stone.

4. According to George Wilson Pierson, Tocqueville made eight visits in twelve days, taking notes in pencil on small sheets of paper (Pierson 300-04). He talked "privately" with every prisoner (Sellin xvi).

5. Harriet Martineau claimed her support for "absolute seclusion" (i.e., solitary confinement) was based on "the confidence" she received from "a great number" of prisoners (Martineau 316-17). If she talked to them separately, none of these interviews is recorded and there are no portraits of individuals, just a summary of what she learned from "some" or was told by "others."

6. No correlation exists between a prisoner's number and the order in which Tocqueville recorded the interviews.

7. Dickens reused this phrase years later when noting that Doctor Manette had been "buried alive" in the Bastille for eighteen years (*TTC* 16; bk. 1, ch. 3). Grass conjectures that Dickens drew Manette from his memories of prisoners at the Eastern Penitentiary ("*Great Expectations*," 171).

8. Dickens's burglar and Tocqueville's prisoner number 1 reappear in composite as Uriah Heep, one of "two interesting penitents" (i.e., prisoners) whom Mr. Creakle, schoolmaster turned Middlesex jailer, shows David Copperfield. Heep outdoes the sycophant burglar when he maintains that "It would be better for everybody, if they got took up, and was brought here" (*DC* 712). He endorses "solitary confinement," which Creakle, echoing Tocqueville, calls "the only unchallengeable way of making sincere and lasting converts and penitents" (*DC* 712). Copperfield is certain that Heep is "exactly what [he] . . .had always been," a "hypocritical" knave (*DC* 720). According to David Paroissien, the Separate System encouraged prisoners to spout the "cant" its supporters liked to hear (Paroissien 37).

9. Dickens's Americans are alike in that they share the same failings; on the other hand, one cannot imagine a more grotesque collection of distinct, unforgettable rapscallions. Each is a variation on the theme of selfishness, yet each is marvelously individualized, paradoxically both representative and unique. Although Tocqueville "polished" his style in hopes of rivaling "the open-eyed clarity of the seventeenth-century [French] classics," his Americans always sound "stilted and formal in French" (Damrosch 154, xxi). A blend of journalism and creative writing, chapter 7 of *American Notes* allegedly "contains the travel book's real literary worth" (Grass, "Narrating" 52).

10. Dickens's dislike for "The Tombs," the city prison for New York (*AN* 31; ch. 7), is mild by comparison. In the chapter titled "New York," he first mentioned Sing Sing, calling it and Mount Auburn the "best examples of the silent system" (*AN* 142; ch. 7). In Boston, he approved of "the House of Correction for the State, in which silence is strictly maintained but the prisoners have the comfort and mental relief of seeing each other and working together" (*AN* 100; ch. 7).

11. See Meckier, *Hidden Rivalries* 2-3.

12. By the 1850s, Tocqueville's opinion of democracy's future, "especially in America," allegedly dimmed from "guarded hopefulness" to "pessimism" (Kaledin xiii). But in 1832 he and Beaumont returned to France as "ardent admirers of American institutions" which they believed "should be imitated in France" (Sellin xvii).

13. Rediscovering his fundamental Englishness did not prevent Dickens from drubbing the British national character as soundly as he had criticized the American. Notable examples: Dombey, Bounderby, Merdle, and Podsnap.

WORKS CITED

Beaumont, G. de and A. de Tocqueville. *On the Penitentiary System in the United States and its Application in France*. Trans. Francis Lieber. Philadelphia: Carey, Lea & Blanchard, 1833. [*PS*]

Collins, Phillip. *Dickens and Crime*. London: Macmillan, 1965.

C-Span's Traveling Tocqueville's America. Baltimore: Johns Hopkins UP, 1998.

Damrosch, Leo. *Tocqueville's Discovery of America*. New York: Farrar, Straus and Giroux, 2010.

Dickens, Charles. *American Notes*. Eds. John S. Whitley and Arnold Goldman. Hammondsworth, Middlesex: Penguin, 1972. [*AN*]

———. *David Copperfield*. Ed. Jerome H. Buckley. New York: Norton, 1990. [*DC*]

———. *Martin Chuzzlewit*. Ed. Michael Slater. London: Penguin, 1986. [*MC*]

———. *A Tale of Two Cities*. Ed. Norman Page. London: Everyman, 1994. [*TTC*]

Forster, John. *The Life of Charles Dickens*. 2 vols. New York: Scribner's, 1899.

Grass, Sean C. "*Great Expectations*, Self-Narration, and the Power of the Prison." Jan Alber and Frank Lauterbach, eds. *Stones of Law, Bricks of Shame: Narrating Imprisonment in the Victorian Age*. Toronto: U of Toronto P, 2009. 171-90.

———. "Narrating the Cell: Dickens on the American Prison." *Journal of English and Germanic Philology* 99 (2000): 50-70.

Johnson, Edgar. *Charles Dickens: His Tragedy and Triumph*. 2 vols. New York: Simon & Schuster, 1952.

Kaledin, Arthur. *Tocqueville and His America: A Darker Horizon*. New Haven: Yale UP, 2011.

Martineau, Harriet. *Society in America*. Ed. Martin Lipset. New Brunswick. NJ: Transaction, 1981.

Meckier, Jerome. *Hidden Rivalries in Victorian Fiction: Dickens, Realism, and Revaluation*. Lexington: UP of Kentucky, 1987.

—. *Innocent Abroad: Charles Dickens's American Engagements*. Lexington: UP of Kentucky, 1990.

Metz, Nancy Aycock, ed. *The Companion to "Martin Chuzzlewit."* Westfield, Hastings, UK: Helm Information, 2001.

Monod, Sylvère. *Martin Chuzzlewit*. London: Allen and Unwin, 1985.

Paroissien, David. "Victims or Vermin? Contradictions in Dickens's Penal Philosophy." Alber and Lauterbach 25-45. See Grass, Sean C. above.

Pierson, George W. *Tocqueville in America*. Gloucester, MA: Peter Smith, 1969. This is Dudley C. Lunt's abridgement of Pierson's 1938 publication titled *Tocqueville and Beaumont in America*.

Sellin, Thorsten, Introduction to *On the Penitentiary System*. Carbondale: So. Illinois UP, 1964. xv-xl.

Slater, Michael. *Charles Dickens*. New Haven: Yale UP, 2009.

Tocqueville, Alexis de. *Democracy in America*. Ed. Richard D. Heffner. Trans. Henry

Reeve. New York: New American Library, 1956. [*DA*]

Trollope, Frances. *Domestic Manners of the Americans.* Ed. Richard Mullen. New York: Oxford UP, 1984.

How *Dombey and Son* Thinks About Masculinities

Rosemary Coleman

*Fifty years ago Julian Moynahan observed that "*Dombey and Son *is a very disturbing book." It is no less disturbing today, as it lays bare Dickens's struggles with the vexed subject of bourgeois masculinity. The text becomes a kind of laboratory in which male bodies are anatomized and marked for punishment, or sanitized and marked for reward. It embodies a series of unsuccessful experiments in the theorization of an ideal masculinity—that is, a masculinity capable of both effective moneymaking and affective care-taking. The text's masculine constructions are, in fact, so serially ineffec-tual—the infantilized Dombey, the mutilated Carker, the castrated Bunsby, the androgynous and delusory men of the Midshipman—as to leave Dickens no alternative except desperately to provide, at the last textual minute, two simulacra of ideal male figures for this fictional world. In his final chapter, then, Dickens hastily and unconvincingly reconstructs two minor characters, Walter Gay as successful capitalist, and Mr. Morfin as domestic paragon, on whose frail shoulders the narrative will rest its unfulfilled needs for one whole man. Unable to fill its empty spaces, rejecting what it understands to be aggressive and dangerous masculinity, the novel leaves us in a zero sum world of waves and tears, stasis and replication, aberrant domestic arrange-ments, and androgynous males.*

Some fifty years ago Julian Moynahan observed that "*Dombey and Son* is a very disturbing book" (122). It is no less disturbing today despite, or perhaps because of the intervening years of critical attention to a novel whose complexity and apparent malleability have aroused multiple and contradictory interpretations. Moynahan, in his clever and perceptive essay, found *Dombey* disturbing in its "guilt-ridden submission to feminine softness," wherein a "Victorian patriarchy of stiff and tyrannical men of affairs surrenders to a matriarchy of weeping mothers and daughters" (130). It seems to me that the roots of the novel's disquieting aspects are more complex, that they lie in Dickens's attempts to deal with and define the vexed subject of bourgeois masculinity itself.

The novel can profitably be read as a series of anxious and ultimately unsuccessful experiments in the theorization of an ideal masculinity—unsuccessful because its theorizations are required to achieve contradictory goals: the need for a vitally energetic, confidently authoritative, virile male persona, in uneasy tandem with the felt necessity to repress, and indeed punish, that persona for the exercise of those selfsame desires and energies. Rooted in this disjunction, the text's masculine constructions are so blatantly and serially ineffectual as to give their architect no alternative except desperately and unconvincingly to allege, at the last textual minute, that his fictional world does indeed contain an ideal man—simultaneously emotionally whole, and wholly successful. Even so, Dickens is able only to finesse rather than to solve the enigma of masculinity, and then only by means of strategies and evasions mounted at the very margins of the text, and couched in the most vapid of phrases. The novel thus becomes a kind of laboratory in which masculine bodies are anatomized and marked for punishment, or sanitized and marked for reward—a laboratory in which the experiments are never successful.

Dickens was hardly alone in his uneasy dealings with the conundrum of masculinity.[1] In the late 1840s, as he was writing *Dombey*, social and economic changes, and the resultant cultural anxieties, created a heated if often subtextual conversation about bourgeois masculinity. As Michael Rosen remarks, this was a period "when one finds writing inundated with concerns about what is a manly man" (21). Herbert Sussman notes the ways in which England's new industrial age demanded the construction of "a new form of manhood and a new masculine poetic," accompanied by a "competition among multiple possibilities of masculinity," and an "instability in the configuration of male identity" (1,8). James Eli Adams examines Victorian "reconfigurations of masculinity," the "multiple, complex, and unstable constructions" of masculine identities (5,3). He notes the "passing of the old ideal of manhood," and the "loss of a central point of identity and social reference for large numbers of men across the class spectrum" (6). All these commentaries gesture toward a culture mirroring Dickens's own anxieties about the male body and its behaviors, a culture in which the novelist sought to theorize a working definition of masculinity capable of accommodating both his personal requirements and those of the larger society.

More recently, Nancy Armstrong theorizes a more extreme Victorian masculinity, one so savage as to be in need of a defense against its own violence. She
characterizes Victorian fiction as the medium in which attempts were made to
disguise the "despicable qualities of ruling-class masculinity," disguises accomplished by means of the transference of masculinity's worst features to a scape-
goated woman (81). Armstrong finds *Dombey* to be a particularly good example of
the construction of "a new ruling-class masculinity"—one achieved by "shift[ing]
the locus of aggression from male to female" (90), in this case from Dombey
to his second wife, Edith. She concludes that, at closure, the plot's humiliations
"knock the aggression" out of Dombey so that he can be incorporated into "an
ideal household," upon which Dickens "asks us to pity the man precisely because
he has lost his power to compete with other men and so dominate women"—that
is, a chastened Dombey becomes the "victim of his own masculinity" (91). But
surely Armstrong oversimplifies the ambiguities inherent in Dickens's construction of his protagonist, for a case can be made that Dombey is never fully able
to exemplify "a new ruling-class masculinity," and that his fate is very far from
an incorporation into an "ideal household." Moreover, the novel never intends
Dombey to be its only male experiment, and readers cannot ignore its attempts to
offer other alternatives. No matter how unconvincing and inconclusive those male
alternatives may be, the text nonetheless continues its efforts to transcend what
Armstrong calls "the murderous discrepancy between moneymaking and caretaking" in the bourgeois male (89)—efforts hardly limited to the transference of male
aggression to wayward women.

I read *Dombey and Son*, then, as a series of experiments in constructions of
masculinity—all of its males, in the end, are either emasculate or emasculated.
The body of the novel exudes such a fear of uncontrolled male sexuality and
aggression, of female power and temptation, that it is unable to conceive of a
whole man. To complicate matters further, a new difficulty arises at closure. In
preparing to take leave of the world he has created—one still rooted in ships and
trade, in profit and industry, in food stuffs and textiles—Dickens confronts the
fact that this world of economic realities must be managed and directed, that even
a world of fictional trade and industry requires a replacement for Paul Dombey
and his firm, demands in fact the construction of some version of the ambitious,
striving male. In addition, the world of domesticity and the family requires a
man who is scrupulous in loving and caring for his wife and children, who can
body forth some rendition of an ideal heterosexual domesticity. And so, in the
course of the text's closures, Dickens hastily folds into its margins a reconstruction of *two* minor characters on whose collective shoulders the narrative will rest
its unfulfilled needs for *one* whole man—that whole man so sorely needed to fill
the empty spaces of both the public and private spheres. I begin this essay, then,
with an examination of the text's masculine experiments and the ways in which
each of them fails. I end with an analysis of the kind of world with which Dickens
and *Dombey* leave us.

*

In a narrative in which the healthy, whole male body proves to be an impossibility, in which male sexual desire is severely punished, James Carker and Captain Bunsby exemplify the most extreme cases—the former ending in bloody fragments on a railroad bed, the latter in a state of paralytic panic, caught in the jaws of a female trap. Both men are the victims of their own aggressions and desires, their fates the result of their own erotic impulses—whereupon, too late, they realize that they themselves are the prey.[2] The feline Carker is both sexually potent and socially adroit—at cards, games, languages, and most of all at the manipulation of others. According to Mr. Morfin, his fellow manager at Dombey and Son, it is Carker who has actually run the firm for years: "extending and extending his influence, until the business and its owner were his football" (*Dombey* 840; ch 53).[3] Carker the Manager finally and purposely drives that business to ruin, but only after making himself enormously wealthy. He is the perfectly successful, ruthless Economic Man—a better model for Nancy Armstrong's "murderous" capitalist than his employer—until his overweening desire to destroy Dombey, and possess Dombey's wife, causes him to become a casualty of his own passions and an easy mark for Edith's intrigues. The sight of the vengeful Dombey as the thundering train approaches is the proximate cause of Carker's violent death, but the true cause of his bloody dismemberment is his surrender to lust and his desire to dominate and possess.

As he so often does, Dickens constructs a parodic version of the catastrophe suffered by Carker, the metaphoric and comic disintegration of a second man who is also a victim of his own sexual desires. Incapable of formulating Carker's devious plans and plots, Bunsby nonetheless demonstrates his own more direct erotic proclivities from the start, as he makes advances first to Susan Nipper, and then fatally to Mrs. MacStinger. She will take full advantage of his drunken lust, ultimately marching him in lockstep, heavily guarded, to the altar—a fate much like being hit by a speeding train in the eyes of the horrified Captain Cuttle, who witnesses his friend's final entrapment. Bunsby will be scrubbed down by day, and used up by night, at the hands of that indomitable domestic manager, Mrs. MacStinger. He will be as fully ravaged by matrimony as is Carker by the train. Both capitalist manager and ship's captain are failed experiments in the construction of a satisfactory masculinity—failed in a world in which sexual potency and desire equal disaster.

Dickens offers us still another parodic experiment in masculinity, but while Bunsby is merely a comic caricature, Major Bagstock is as much a figure of malice as of ridicule. The Major's entire life is conducted as a performance—an impersonation of the bluff, tough old soldier, the pillar of the Empire, the essence of virile masculinity. He purports to be a military version of the Regency beau—socially adept and sexually attractive—but in fact he is merely a sycophantic flatterer and vindictive liar. His bulging head, purple and enflamed, swells and dilates, but only gluttony and spite engorge Bagstock. Projecting what the easily deceived Dombey mistakes as "gentlemanly ease" (346; ch. 20), Bagstock watches and manipulates others as compensation for his own occluded sexuality. Possessing neither weapon nor war, the Major, old Joey B., embodies the text's parodic commentary on the problems and pitfalls inherent in the construction and performance of a whole masculinity. Unlike Carker and Bunsby, Bagstock survives the text's mutilations of desirous male bodies, an impotent, lesser version of the evil Quilp. A figure of ridicule, he will continue to boast and flatter, repeating his schemes and projecting his rancor into an endless, repetitive future.

There is very little mystery surrounding the fates of Carker, Bunsby, and Bagstock—the mystery of the text lies with Dombey himself.[4] Murderous capitalist or merely arrogant fool? Worldly and virile member of the ruling class, or awkward and impotent hollow shell? Emotionally abusive husband and father, or damaged victim of others' plots? At closure, healed and whole in warm, loving domesticity, or infantilized and isolated amidst tears and waves? Dombey is most often accused of wielding an overpowering will, manifested in arrogance, cruelty, and emotional frigidity. Charles Hatten charges him with exemplifying the capitalist's "monomaniacal sacrifice of domestic and paternal feeling to commercial and public advancement," thus reducing the family to a "savage and atavistic nightmare" (77). But perhaps Dombey can better be understood as a case of what James Eli Adams calls "the fragility of masculinity at the psychic level" (3). As Davidoff and Hall have noted, the Victorian masculine persona found its "puny strength" pitted against the power of a new and threatening economic environment and market. Far from "carrying the blustering certainty of the late Victorian paterfamilias, early nineteenth-century masculine identity was fragile," still being shaped (229). Dombey, then, can be viewed as another of the text's failed experiments in the construction of masculinity, a man attempting a performance as self-assured, dominant, ruthless mercantile magnate, but one who has never been able wholly to convince even himself of his own authenticity. His pride and rigidity merely serve as a carapace—an outer shell cradling his fragility, hiding and protecting him in his weakness and inadequacy. What might we learn about this man if Dickens's famous "good spirit" were to concentrate his powers on the removal of the Dombey mansion's house-top, and thus on the penetration of its owner's outermost shell? What "dark shapes" would issue from this home (*Dombey* 738; ch. 47); what kind of man would be revealed?

The spirit would expose a Paul Dombey who occupies only three rooms of the huge mansion he has inherited from his father, for he feels himself to be neither powerful nor substantial enough to fill his father's house. The mansion is divided into separate, isolated zones: Dombey's rooms, which are forbidden to his daughter, Florence; Florence's room, about which her father knows nothing, not even its location in the vast house; and the public rooms, shrouded like the ghosts of long-past social successes. The mansion contains only the dark, heavy furniture from a past era, none of it chosen by Dombey, but by his father—the same father who built the firm and created its wealth; the same father whose abilities and past successes enable his son to attempt the role of a "pecuniary Duke of York" (58; ch. 1). We see this son, described as "a strange apparition" (76; ch. 3), sitting in his darkened room, greedily and obsessively watching as his newborn son is nursed. Baby and wet nurse are commanded to appear twice a day in the conservatory which opens off Dombey's bedroom—he in the darkness, they in the lighted room, as if staged for his gratification. He is alone, always alone: "all his life, he had never made a friend" (103). Withdrawn, bereft of social skills, he is easy prey for flatterers—easily fooled and manipulated by his manager, Carker; by his sister, Mrs. Chick; by his new acquaintance, Major Bagstock; and ultimately by his second wife, and her mother.

This "merchant prince," secluded in a dim house whose expanses he cannot fully occupy or possess, is described by the narrator as "artificially braced and tightened as by the stimulating action of golden showerbaths" (69; ch 2). The reader is thus forewarned that should those artificial braces of pride and unearned wealth be removed, this outwardly rigid man will be left fearfully vulnerable. In fact, Dombey personifies what Herbert Sussman has characterized as Thomas Carlyle's "fantasy of masculinity," in which the male psyche is theorized as a "fluid interior or inner chaos," his vital energy and bodily integrity contained and protected only by a "rigid psychic carapace" (33). Sussman tells us that Carlyle conceptualized the male body as "a hard surface or 'plain' beneath which is a 'pestilential swamp,'" and the male psychic life as a "perilous passage over a surface that may at any time collapse into the miasmic waters beneath" (20). Dickens's Dombey is the very embodiment of Carlyle's theorization of masculinity, the male who requires the protection of a rigid carapace of pride lest he sink into the threatening miasma of his own inner desires. When misfortune cracks Dombey's hard shell, then his liquid center of raw emotions and powerful hungers will be exposed, and he will easily merge with, and be dissolved in Florence's water-world of tears and waves.

If the same good spirit were to remove the house-top from Dombey's mansion after his second marriage, a very different interior (although not a different man) would be exposed. The formerly darkened house is now ablaze with light, replete with satin and gilt and all manner of luxury. Dombey himself remains unable to own and fill the mansion's spaces, and so he crowds them with elegant new furniture, and adds an elegant new wife. She is intended not only to gratify her husband's sexual desires, not only to fill the house with the cries of a healthy new heir, but to fill the mansion's emptiness with her aristocratic self-possession, her grace and beauty, and her patrician friends. She must disguise Dombey's rigid insufficiencies with sumptuous dinners and at-homes, must contrive to impress his business acquaintances. Both mansion and wife are meant to create a facade of sophistication, a second protective carapace, an appearance of Dombeyan power and success. Almost immediately proving as incapable of filling or controlling his wife as he is of filling and commanding the expanses of his father's house, Dombey once again retreats to the safety and confinement of his three rooms on the ground floor. He is forced to assign Carker—already in charge of his business affairs —to the subjugation of the defiant, contemptuous wife over whom he has no command, forced even to hire a housekeeper to take charge of the domestic affairs which Edith disdains.[5] This putatively "murderous" representative of the new ruling class could hardly prove himself more ineffectual and powerless.

Unable to perform the role of authoritative husband, too distracted even to pretend to fulfill his role as mercantile magnate, Dombey demonstrates his impotence in both the private and the public spheres. At the mercy of his own inadequacies, racked by explosive jealousy, anger, and sexual frustration, he is emotional dynamite ready to be detonated—his responses constrained only by the rigid (now cracking) carapace of his delusory pride. His authority and power have always been mere poses of masculinity, poses assumed in order to clothe his nakedness and hide his impotence with what James Eli Adams has called "a mask of omnicompetence" (11). The remnants of that fragile mask will soon be torn from his face. When Edith publicly parades her defiance and contempt, and enacts her faux adultery, Dombey is exposed in all his powerlessness. The entire world knows he has been, in the words of Cousin Feenix's after-dinner anecdote, "bought and sold" (598; ch 36). Bankrupt and shamed by both marital scandal and financial disgrace, he loses the last vestiges of his protective shell of pride. Both house and House are in ruins—all the appurtenances of bourgeois masculinity forfeited. He wanders the gutted, ruined mansion, awash in remorse and guilt, reduced to abject weeping. Now he is indeed fully ready for Florence's return, ready to mingle his tears with hers, to be dissolved in and absorbed by her powerful aura, by her world of whispering waves.

Florence willingly provides tears and forgiveness, but she does not provide happy domesticity in the confines of a conventionally cozy home, nor does she conform to the pattern of Dickens's other "little women" who contrive cunning domestic fancies and inventions for miniature dollhouses. She is, in fact, sui generis in Dickens's canon—beyond nature, beyond culture, beyond the confines of idealized home and family.[6] She has morphed directly from abused daughter to powerful Oceanic Mother, with no stops along the way to play the role of little woman or Angel in the House. The text barely makes mention of the house to which she takes Dombey immediately after her return, nor is it ever described as a permanent home, ever represented as a domestic haven for an entity conventionally identifiable as the "Gay family." It is merely a stopover, an interim shelter from which father and daughter, now inseparable, can progress to their true home on the sea-beach, where the waves whisper endlessly of love and death. The text strains to direct us toward recognition of a triumphant Dombeyan moral transformation to loving paterfamilias, but instead provides a dark subtext of male abnegation and self-laceration. The childlike Dombey is neither familial caretaker nor authority figure, for at closure Dickens's novel abjures both conventional family and conventional world. There is only the mythic world of the Oceanic Mother, the immensity and timelessness of beach and sea.[7]

And so Dickens scuttles Carlyle's trope of the protectively hard male body; he stills Carlyle's cries of "Produce! Produce!"—and substitutes an abject Dombey murmuring "Little Florence! Little Florence!" The female Other, so deeply feared by Carlyle as to require erasure from his carefully constructed all-male literary worlds, reigns triumphantly over the world of the sea-beach.[8] Caught between the need for emotional fulfillment and safety, theorized as female and dangerous, and the desires of the sexual, aggressive body, theorized as male and fatal, Dickens struggles in the tangles of a web he cannot escape, in the confusion of a dissonance he cannot still. Finally he leaves us with an infantilized, enervated Dombey—leaves us with still another failure in the novel's series of male experiments.

The novel does, however, construct a group of contented and well-off men, happily insulated from harsh realities, dwelling at closure in a permanent state of homosocial conviviality.[9] The Midshipman, a shop purporting to sell maritime goods, belongs nominally to the public sphere in which productive male work is accomplished. In fact it is a cozy domestic space providing hearth and home for a collective of good-hearted, childlike men. By the end of the novel, the world of the Midshipman is carefully separated from that of Florence—women are not a part of this space.[10] Sol, Cuttle, and Toots may laud Susan Nipper's fecundity and perspicacity, may praise and deify Florence, but in the novel's closing pages neither woman participates in this male club of pipes, drams, and song—nor are the men of the Midshipman ever a part of the world of the tear-stricken, female sea-beach. As in Carlyle's fictional monastery, women are excluded from this enclave as the text makes its final arrangements. Even the married Toots in truth belongs to the Midshipman much more than to a nominal and unseen home with Susan, for his marriage is merely one of comic convenience.[11]

Cuttle's manifest sexual panic as he witnesses Bunsby's kidnapping by Mrs. MacStinger clearly marks the text's fear of female sexual power and male desire, and thus marks its need for a male haven like the Midshipman. Only virtuous male children in asexual adult bodies may inhabit this fairytale world, a world in which Sol Gills is a kind of semi-magical (though confused) patriarch, Captain Cuttle assumes the comic role of domestic/business partner, and Toots is their simple-minded child. The Midshipman's contented and domesticated homosociality thus contrives to distort the configuration of the conventional nuclear family while parodically echoing it. In addition, by skillful sleight of hand, Dickens avoids possible uneasiness with male intimacy and affective bonds. He simply obscures any hint of the homoerotic in clouds of pipe smoke and innocence, successfully androgynizing these men, while simultaneously displacing them to fairytale and childhood.[12] So here at last is the best of all possible worlds: an island of male safety and affluence (both Toots and Sol are wealthy) in a text otherwise awash in the fragmentation and dissolution of male bodies; an enclave of children-at-play while disguised as a place

of men-at-work. Dickens has ravaged the hegemonic ideology of middle-class masculinity—defined by marriage, heterosexuality, and economic production—and
replaced it with a celibate, homosocial family manque, happily at play.

Herbert Sussman tells us that early Victorian male writers, unable to imagine
"a manly life in their own time," amidst the demands and stresses of entrepreneurial manhood in industrial England, constructed all-male societies in marginal
spaces—spaces "central to the re-imagining of masculinity in this period." Such
a space allowed for "markedly different values" in an imagined zone beyond
bourgeois society, where "alternative masculinities may flourish" (45). *Dombey*'s
series of unsuccessful masculine experiments stands witness to the need for just
such an alternative space, inhabited by magically kindly men, free from the stains
of the "murderous" capitalist and the new ruling class. The men of the Midshipman offer warmth and community to each other, their maritime shop suggesting what Holly Furneaux calls "a renegotiation of available spaces and possible
domesticities" (53), but they cannot fill the empty spaces of the text marked "masculinity," cannot encompass the spatially scattered groups of individuals who
exist apart at the conclusion of the narrative, cannot offer "community" for the
world with which *Dombey* leaves us in its closing pages.[13] Both author and reader
realize that these men are no solution to the conundrum of masculinity, for they
live in a world of fantasy, a world in which "happily ever after" is possible only
for the androgynous. Their asexuality allows them to transcend what Sussman
calls "the central problematic in the Victorian practice of masculinity, the proper
regulation of essential male energy" (3)—that is, the regulation of ambition and
desire. The text must thus continue its attempts to construct a convincing model of
masculinity, to imagine a man who can deal with the responsibilities and realities
of the countinghouse and the warehouse, while simultaneously exhibiting sensi-
tivity and tenderness in his own house.

The construction of such a masculinity, with its internal contradictions and
inherent impossibilities, is attempted at the very margins of the novel where details
and specifics can be elided, where successes in marriage and business can be
alleged in a few well-worn phrases, or reported at second-hand just before the narrative's final return to the illimitable waves. Even so, this text proves itself unable
to construct one whole masculine model, and is thus compelled to assemble two
male simulacra, hastily sketched and pushed onto the stage at the last minute—
the first a domestic model, the second purported to be the ideal Economic Man.
In order to supplement the spectacular failures of Carker, Bunsby, and Dombey,
Dickens gives us the cursorily domesticated and newly-married Mr. Morfin, and
the unexpectedly ambitious and successful Walter Gay—two halves of a whole
man, both rushed post haste onto the final pages and stages of the novel, both
heretofore insubstantial supporting players, both vanishing in the final, climactic
mythology of Florence and the waves.

Clearly Dickens found himself unable to leave the world of *Dombey* without
the presence of some variety of conventional domesticity, the husband cared for

by the traditional Angel in the House who busily creates a harmonious home for her amiable man—even better for two men, one of them her brother. Equally clearly, there must be a model of (mildly) heterosexual, domestic masculinity to whom the Angel can minister. And so the text gives us Mr. Morfin, in his autumnal years rather suddenly married to Harriet, and John Carker, and thus a member of a newly-minted ménage à trois reminiscent of the Pinch-Pinch-Westlock arrangement in *Martin Chuzzlewit*. Heretofore we have known Morfin only as "the hazel-eyed bachelor," possessed of a violoncello but not of a first name. Constantly castigating himself for being an insensitive creature of habit ("we are so d___d businesslike," he moans [*Dombey* 559; ch. 33]), he has nonetheless behaved impeccably throughout the course of the novel. Sensitive and empathetic, virtuous and good-tempered, he possesses all the ideal qualities of the men of the Midshipman but, unlike them, is represented as neither delusory, confused, nor half-witted. Much older than Harriet, he avoids the trap of sexuality so greatly feared by this text—he is a "tender father" to her rather than a husband (561; ch. 33). He retires from the world of commercial capitalism after the fall of Dombey and Son, and devotes himself entirely to the role of family man. Unfortunately he is so insubstantial, so late to the domestic scene, that he cannot satisfactorily fill that unoccupied space of the text marked "caring male, domestic variety"—he only serves to mark its emptiness.

Nor, having left the world of money and trade, can Morfin fill the vacant space of the novel marked "ambitious-but-kindly man of business." He cannot stand as the replacement for the now infantilized Dombey, cannot assume the role of Captain of Industry or Mercantile Prince so necessary in an industrialized England which is required to answer Carlyle's call to produce. The text must thus construct a second supplemental masculine model: the competent, ambitious male; the successful yet sensitive director of the affairs of the public sphere; the newest member of the new ruling class. How then to represent this man who energetically and ambitiously pursues advancement and authority within the capitalistic system, yet still manages to project benevolence? How to simulate the role of reproductive husband, while in fact rejecting male sexuality and the desirous male body itself? In answer, Dickens offers a final solution to the masculine conundrum—that is, he simply asserts that such a man exists and flourishes, and that his name is Walter Gay.

Canny silences, suppressed contradictions, and strategic marginalizations are necessities in the rollout of this final model of masculinity, the heretofore "milky young man" (the phrase is Moynahan's [13]) who has been largely absent from the text, or unnoticeable when present. Walter is the supporting player who must now take center stage, who must play the role and fill the space that Dombey struggled and failed to play and fill, and then left so empty. The House of Dombey has crashed, but Dickens envisions neither a massive reform of the new ruling class, nor a massive collapse of the world of capitalism—rather, he hastily crafts a replacement so that things may continue as they were, with only minor adjustments. Goods must still be produced and bought and sold, ships must sail, profits must be made—and so there must be a man specifically designated to manage the realities of this material world. The new Walter Gay is intended to strike the necessary balance, to solve the contradictions between ambitious moneymaking and gentle caretaking. Walter's perfections are relayed to Cuttle and Gills at third hand by Mr. Toots, who is repeating Susan Nipper's rhapsodic impressions. Any doubts arising in the minds of readers are hastily glossed over, any possible disclaimers lost in bursts of Tootsian rhetoric. Walter himself does not speak after he escorts Florence to meet Edith, and even then his words are brief and perfunctory. We never witness him conducting business of any kind and yet, Toots tells us, he is "appointed . . . to a post of great trust and confidence at home, showing himself again worthy; *mounting up the ladder* with the greatest expedition; *beloved by everybody. . . .* [T]here is a foundation going on, upon which a—an Edifice . . . is gradually rising . . . another Dombey and Son will ascend . . . triumphant!" (974; ch. 62, my italics). Thus is the business future assured, production and profit guaranteed, and all things "economic" garnished and trimmed with the tissue and ribbons of benevolence.

Dragged to center stage at the last textual moment to represent the much-needed Economic Man, Walter can do so only because his moment there is so very brief. Dickens hurriedly takes leave of him somewhere in London, leaves him mounting up that ladder, presumably swelling to the manly proportions required to fill the empty space in the new ruling class, presumably becoming the new, improved model of the "pecuniary Duke of York." And so the ill-defined Walter, and the shadowy Mr. Morfin, constitute the proposed solutions to the domestic and mercantile disasters that have assailed this text's males. Dickens strives mightily to produce, by sheer bravado, an allusion to, and an illusion of a phallic, Carlylean Walter—a masculine construct capable of containing and organizing all the contradictions, excesses, and failures with which the text has contended. Walter will surely be able to align and combine domestic harmony, successful capitalism, and beneficent business practices. We simply must not look too closely.[14]

With its final paragraphs, however, the novel leaves us not with Walter and a promise for the future, but with a shattered, enervated man, obsessed with the guilt and grief of the past. Dombey has indeed been transformed in the course of this story, but he has neither evolved nor matured—and the distinction is important. He and Florence exist in a timeless myth, a romance of yearning and tears, a nirvana of his willing passivity and submission and her promise of blissful oceanic oneness. We are told that male energies and male striving continue to exist somewhere in London, that male happiness and celebration prevail at the Midshipman, that male domestic virtue flourishes in the Morfin home, but here on the sea-beach energy, celebration, and domesticity are non-starters. The disparate constellations of individuals with which the novel leaves us are unintegrated fragments of a world, divided and isolated from one another. Beset by contradiction and dissonance, the text subsides into the whispering voice of the waves—a female voice, a voice of death.

**

How best, then, to characterize this world constructed by Dickens and *Dombey and Son*? Steven Marcus specifies an obsessive concern with change as the principle that organizes the novel (298). He cites the revolutionary changes in Staggs's Gardens created by the "culture of the railroad": the affirmation of life, the "quality of energy and ferment," "the working out [of the novel's] theme of change . . . in the use of the railroad as agent and symbol of change" (309, 310, 311). So much is certainly true of Staggs's Gardens, but the worlds of the Midshipman, of Morfin in his pleasant house, and above all of the sea-beach, gesture not toward change but toward stasis and replication. Nor is Dombey's transformation from extreme rigidity to formless liquidity in any sense an instance of energy and ferment, or an affirmation of life and change. Ironically it is Florence, repeatedly described as ever unchanging, who undergoes the text's most radical alteration—from abused orphan to demi-goddess, an icon of myth but never of energy and progress.

Marcus's "energy and ferment" are real enough, but they pertain to a small segment of the novel's storyline, and not at all to its final arrangements. The text's representations of the next generation of children clearly point toward a future not of change but of replication. Little Paul and little Florence are mere replacements, the former a reiteration of his dead uncle, and the latter of her mother. Introduced as occasions for remorse and tears from Dombey, they are never intended to transform the future. The other children born into the world of the text are replications of their parents as well. Susan Nipper bears only daughters, two of them predictably named Susan and Florence, all three of them "repetitions of that most extraordinary woman," their mother (972; ch. 62). Mrs. MacStinger's daughter Juliana is "the image of her parent," one of a "succession of man-traps stretching out infinitely; a series of ages of oppression and coercion" (954; ch. 60), an augury of this world's unchanging generations of predatory females. Even the Toodleses' many children, born in the energy and ferment of Staggs's Gardens, promise only to replace their father and mother in perpetuating what the text implies will be the happy and contented working classes of England's future. Like their father, the sons will drive and fuel the railroads of the Industrial Revolution, but they will not foment any other revolution.

In *Dombey*'s world the class structure is static as well, thus assuring that there will be no real social or economic change. Walter, the putative reincarnation of a new and improved Dombey, will become a member of the ruling class, thus sustaining a prosperous and unchanged mercantile capitalism, as well as the success of the Empire.[15] He enters the world of capitalism just as Dombey and Morfin leave it, thus assuring a nice balance in manpower and economy, his rise compensating for his father-in-law's fall in this zero sum world. Moreover, Dombey in his dotage is supported, not by his son-in-law, but by Harriet Carker's largesse. Her money comes from her dead brother's ill-gotten gains, stolen originally from

Dombey himself and now returning to him in a neatly circular and closed process. Very little is gained or lost in this world in which the supply of talent and money remains constant, neither increasing nor decreasing.

The aristocracy, in the person of Cousin Feenix, is represented as enfeebled and aimless (although amiable)—the man and his class encapsulated in his wavering gait and vapid speech. Nonetheless, as Martin Wiener has pointed out, "the transference of power [from aristocracy to industrialists] protracted over a century, resembled a merger rather than a conquest; a marriage (in many cases literally) rather than a rape" (8).[16] The aristocracy continued to offer the attractions of blood and breeding, remaining an important factor in both the class structure and the marriage market. In still another layer of society—somewhere below the Feenixes and the Dombeys, between the haute bourgeoisie and the working classes—lies Mr. Feeder, representing a professional middle class. Feeder marries up to the ownership of the Blimber Academy, thus replicating his retiring father-in-law, and assuring that the school will continue to enact exactly the same educational horrors on the youth of England as before. Like the coat of paint applied to the Academy, the change in ownership is purely cosmetic. In addition, Major Bagstock will continue to spy on Miss Tox through the years to come; Mr. Morfin will play the violoncello as before. The men of the Midshipman will always sing their songs—continuing to thrive in that marginal zone where "alternative masculinities may flourish" (Sussman 45).

A text so dedicated to stasis and stability might be expected to depict, at closure, a world organized around a strong and solid center—whether a tightly-knit domestic unit like the home of David and Agnes Copperfield, or a blissful little community such as those portrayed at the closures of *Oliver Twist* and *Nicholas Nickleby*. *Dombey and Son* portrays no such center; it cannot organize its emasculated males and dangerous females around a single family, or a convincing scene of domesticity, or an integrated community. Just as Dombey's mansion consisted of walled-off, isolated zones for its divided inhabitants, so too do the novel's characters inhabit disconnected spatial zones at the end of the narrative. Suppose the spirit is once again summoned to fly over England, what would he see? Far below are tiny figures on an otherwise empty expanse of beach; far away from the beach a gutted mansion, empty warehouses and deserted offices; some place in London, a lone male figure climbing a (precarious?) ladder of success; near the waterfront a shop that does no business; finally, a school that perpetuates the ruin of young minds. There is very little interaction or communication among these disparate spatial points, little sense of these groups of individuals living in community with each other. The text attempts to take shelter in Florence's world of timeless myth, or in the happiness of the Midshipman fairytale, for it has been unable to construct either a convincing public sphere or a persuasive conventional domesticity.

Dombey and Son is frequently categorized as a domestic novel replete with harmonious pairings and happy endings. John Kucich notes the "warm reunions and restorations" which characterize the text's conclusion (215), while Lyn Pykett sees a triumph of bourgeois domesticity over "greed and materialism" (27). Catherine Waters believes the novel ends in a "celebration of domestic values," with "the consistency and stability of the home arranged by Florence" (56). Hilary Schor observes the narrative's domestic triumphs in which "[a]ll the daughters have brought home husbands to redeem their fathers' infirmity," leaving the reader with a "series of stronger houses" (69). Charles Hatten characterizes the text's closure as "a magical restoration of domestic harmony," marked by the "emergence of new and improved families" (79, 80). But where indeed do the magical restorations lie; where are the stronger houses? Have the daughters in fact "brought home" husbands who can redeem the fathers' infirmities?

It is certainly true enough that *Dombey* is a novel obsessed with pairing, and particularly with marriages both conventional and aberrant. In addition to matching Edith and Feenix, the text gifts even Miss Tox with a companion—in the Grinder she acquires a male she can dominate and correct and mold, thus creating a benign echo of the predatory relationship between Mrs. MacStinger and Captain Bunsby. But there is no convincing triumph of bourgeois domesticity, no magical restoration, in those couplings. Polly and Toodles are happy and happily reproductive, but the text's attitude toward the working-class Toodles family is one of condescending paternalism. Certainly the marriage of Cornelia Blimber and the avaricious Mr. Feeder, made for economic convenience, in no way qualifies as a triumph of blissful domesticity over greed and materialism, nor does Mr. Feeder himself model an ideal masculinity surpassing the father's infirmities. The reader may begin to wonder about the husbands these daughters have brought home to redeem the sins of the past.

Nor can we turn for reassurance to the domestic arrangements of Mr. Morfin and his family of Carkers. Intended to exemplify an ideal domestic masculinity, both Morfin and the marriage are so attenuated that neither can survive close scrutiny as redemptive triumphs. Neither do the men of the Midshipman qualify as redeemers of male infirmities, nor as exemplars of conventional family at all. Holly Furneaux places Cuttle and Gills "outside of both productive and reproductive economies," characterizing the society of the Midshipman as "a break with conventional expectations of what constitutes family," and as lacking "the accretion of the cultural meanings of the family house" (52). The critical references to conventional domestic bliss cited above, then, can only refer to the union of Florence and Walter. Theirs must be the "new and improved family," the "stable home," with Walter brought home to redeem masculine infirmities.

And yet, as Steven Marcus has remarked, there is something "very wrong" with the Walter/Florence relationship (355). It is Florence who proposes to Walter; they are united as brother and sister rather than husband and wife, and are immediately dematerialized—whisked aboard a ship bound for China. Apparently efficiently reproductive although lacking in virility, Walter becomes a father on the high seas, between chapters, and far, far away—so far out of the text's ken that the conjugal relationship is nonexistent, sexuality a nonstarter, the male body disembodied.

Davidoff and Hall point out that middle-class sexual passion was required "to be contained and hidden" (402), but Dickens and Walter take that precept to a new extreme. Even the conventional familial connections between husband and wife vanish almost altogether in the final scenes, as Walter simply fades from Florence's world. The important relationship throughout the novel is that between Dombey and Florence—there is no happy marital domesticity labeled "Gay," no "new and improved family" produced in the course of the narrative. The similarly reproductive but asexual pairing of Toots and Susan provides a comic gloss, gesturing toward a comparison with the peculiarities of the union between Walter and Florence. In the same way, the Bunsby/MacStinger marriage is a parody of the horrors of the Dombey/Edith pairing. All the males exhibit similar characteristics: Morfin's epicene qualities, Walter's asexuality, Toots's maimed manhood, Bunsby's paralysis, Cuttle's sexual panic, and Dombey's impotence in Edith's bedroom are all powerful reflections of this text's fear of female sexual power and male desire, powerful witnesses testifying that *Dombey* cannot be characterized as a novel of blissful domesticity and happy unions. Above all, Florence is not a daughter who has brought home a husband to replace her infirm father. Instead, she has brought home the infirm father.

***

Dombey and Son's darkness signals marked differences in both degree and kind from Dickens's earlier novels, for the text intensifies and exaggerates themes only embryonically present before, while simultaneously introducing new strategies in its attempts to exert control over dangerous male energies. The previous narratives present no shortage of mutilated male bodies, but never before has Dickens been so preoccupied with the hazards of maleness itself. Never before have his protagonists been so ravaged by their own sexuality, as well as by the manipulations of predatory females—powerful women uniformly triumphant in their ability to manipulate and punish men. Rose Maylie and Kate Nickleby possess none of Florence's mythic powers. Mrs. Nickleby and Cherry Pecksniff might aspire to Edith's sexual magnetism, might even believe that they possess it, but they only delude themselves. Nell's attractions make her the cynosure of all eyes, but her very magnetism dooms her, as her creator feels obliged to lay that budding and dangerously tempting body on its deathbed, its charms simultaneously idealized and neutralized in death.[17] Mrs. Gamp has powers and possibilities, but she is not allowed to become a Mrs. MacStinger; instead, Old Martin Chuzzlewit is deployed to discipline and control her in a textual world in which the Law of the Father still prevails. Nor has Dickens ever before been so severe with his principal male protagonist, leaving him torn with self-laceration and awash in tears. Oliver, Nicholas, Dick Swiveller, Tom Pinch, and both Martin Chuzzlewits are gifted with happy endings and compliant females. Even Augustus Moddle evades Charity Pecksniff, an escape not allowed to Captain Bunsby. In none of the earlier novels does Dickens so fully problematize, and then try to re-conceive masculinity and the male body as he does here; in none of them does he leave his textual world so entirely populated with emasculate and emasculated males.

This novel longs for, and then tries to supply, what Michael Balint has suggested is the goal of all erotic male striving: a return to the bond of unity between mother and infant, a sense of oceanic oneness, and a tranquil sense of well-being in which all needs are satisfied (50).[18] Supported financially by Harriet Carker, and emotionally by Florence, Dombey achieves oceanic oneness but at the extortionate price of infantilism. The narrative, like Dombey himself, desires and needs Florence while simultaneously recognizing and fearing her power to submerge and drown. That contradictory dread of, and need for the woman remains written at the heart of *Dombey and Son*, driving both character and plot.

Moreover, there is an empty place at the core of the novel, akin to the unfilled spaces and empty rooms of the Dombey mansion. A primary goal of the text has been the regulation of the male body, the control and punishment of male desire and ambition. And yet—encoded in the subtext of the narrative is the realization that the static world constructed at closure must include some degree of masculine striving and ambition, of masculine energy and virility. Despite its attempts to construct that kind of effectual, whole masculinity at its center, the novel ricochets between passivity and striving, between androgyny and virility. Sadly unable to fill its own empty spaces, *Dombey and Son* supplies the reader with worthless promissory notes marked "masculinity," but never manages to pay up. Rejecting what it understands to be hegemonic, aggressive, and dangerous masculinity, it can neither let go of it entirely, nor find a convincing replacement for it. Incapable of combining successful mercantile capitalism, beneficent business practices, and warmly emotional domesticity in one whole man, the text offers a compendium of fears and failures—an encyclopedia of marital aberrations and impossibilities; a laboratory of failed masculine experiments; an anatomy of peculiar domesticities. Small wonder that Moynahan dubbed it a "very disturbing book."

With his next novel, Dickens attempts a new masculine model, a new hero who—it will be asserted—can successfully contain and organize those contradictions so painfully outlined and then hurriedly glossed over in *Dombey and Son*. He constructs the Hero as Man of Letters—a man who functions successfully in both the public and private spheres, in both the masculine and the marriage plot. He gives us his favorite child, David Copperfield.

NOTES

1. Leonore Davidoff and Catherine Hall offer several criteria for middle-class Victorian masculinity: competence and success in business affairs; marriage, children, and ultimate authority in the family; emotional restraint, self-control, and self-discipline; and "contained and hidden" sexuality (402). For further discussions of masculinities, see Sussman, Kestner, Rosen, Adams, and Tosh. Kestner discusses what he specifies as the dominant fiction of masculinity, "the commensurability of penis and phallus [the phrase is Kaja Silverman's]"; that is, that "the male, by virtue of possession of the penis is part of the hegemonic, patriarchal order symbolized by the phallus/Law of the Father" (27). Kestner goes on to say that "the male believes in the penis/phallus equation even though it is not fundamentally valid" (28). Thus "masculinity" is based in a fallacy, mired in contradiction and anxiety.

2. While it is obvious that Carker is a sexual predator who intends to possess Edith, Bunsby's sexual nature and his intentions viz-à-viz Mrs. MacStinger are revealed only in a series of encoded gestures and descriptions. He "hugs" Susan as soon as he meets her—her "indignant" reaction telling the reader exactly how she interprets his intent (411; ch. 23)—and continues his attempts on her "fair form." Upon encountering an angry Mrs. MacStinger, he puts his arm around her, plies her with rum and water, and so soothes her that she allows him to escort him home. His drunken return to the Midshipman after being gone all night, and his conspiratorial wink at Cuttle, tell the story of what he considers to have been a sexual triumph over the willing Mrs. MacStinger (644-45; ch. 39).

3. All page references are to the Penguin edition of *Dombey and Son*.

4. I do not include Paul Jr. as one of the text's experiments in masculinity—Paul's significance in the narrative is his very refusal of masculinity. "Shall we make a man of him?" asks Dr. Blimber. "I had rather be a child," answers Paul (210; ch. 11). Clare Senior observes that he "cannot perform his gender," for he identifies with the feminine world of tears and waves (111), and Helene Moglen concludes that he rejects his gender identity in death (162). Anne Schwan has reinterpreted Paul in interesting terms, moving him from the margins of male gender identities to the center of the text's "critique of Dombey's hegemonic model of masculinity" (95). She analyzes the text's coded descriptions of Paul and concludes that he is an "early representation of a homosexual," a "symbol of masculine gender dissidence" (100), and that he thus presents a "queer vision" (101).

5. As Hilary Schor has noted, Edith is the text's most vivid and complex female character (67). She retains her integrity to the very end, neither apologizing nor asking for forgiveness. She has written her own story in a "sealed paper" (967; ch. 61) which she gives to Florence, drawing it from that bosom on which the text has been fixated throughout its course. To a large extent, she is the author not only of her own story, but of those of Dombey and Carker as well. Anne Schwan reads Edith through the text's codes of sexual fallenness and hysteria which mark her as "sexually deviant," resistant

to "Dombey's system of gender discipline," and thus a part of the text's "gender dissidence" (101).

6. In a fine reassessment of Florence, Kristina Aikens emphasizes the daughter's "sexual agency" (77), and reads her as a sexual being, with her own desires which "play out under the apparently innocent cover of the family" (81). Aikens further sees Florence's textual progression from a sexually desirous childhood and young girlhood to an "innocent" wifehood/motherhood, with maternity sanctifying and purifying her sexuality (78). It seems to me, however, that in the end the text empowers Florence as Oceanic Mother, rather than purifying her. It cannot, finally, discipline her into a patriarchal domesticity, nor mold her desire "into culturally acceptable forms" (Aikens 89). Rather, it leaves her in full control of her sea-beach world, and of her father—now her child. For other interpretations of Florence, and surveys of criticism about her, see Zwinger, Senior, and Schor.

7. Robert Newsom remarks that the text exhibits a "particular anxiety about going to pieces," that Dombey "is afraid of going to pieces and the world of the novel really justifies him in that fear" (204, 214). I would add that while Carker goes to pieces quite literally, Dombey is dissolved rather than dismembered, reduced to his liquid center of tears.

8. For an opposing view of where authority lies at closure, see Lisa Surridge's interpretation in which Dombey is "restore[d] to manhood and domestic authority." She concludes that the novel "thus foregrounds the primacy of male authority and the exclusivity of the home" (69, 70). See Sussman for an incisive analysis of Carlyle's *Past and Present* in which male "inchoate energy is channeled into productive work" and "chaste ties with other males" (54-55).

9. These homosocial arrangements are earlier and embryonically displayed at the close of *Oliver Twist*, with Mr. Losberne and Mr. Grimwig living together in a bachelor cottage in perfect harmony, as well as in the Cheeryble/Linkinwater ménage in *Nicholas Nickleby*.

10 Florence has previously lived in the Midshipman, but her marriage and ascension to mythic Oceanic Motherhood change her status irrevocably; she can no longer be a part of that world. At closure she visits the shop briefly with her father but she maintains a mythic silence. There is no mention of the possibility of future visits from either of them.

11. As Steven Marcus remarks, Toots is "as maimed in his manhood as he is in his intellect" (318).

12. Herbert Sussman notes the development of "an intensity of homophobic feeling in the 1840's" (5), and Donald Hall also points to an increased need for rigid definitions of effeminate and/or emasculate characteristics at this time (78). The men of the Midshipman are impervious to such homophobic suspicions.

13. For a contrasting view of the men of the Midshipman, see Natalie McKnight's *Idiots, Madmen & Other Prisoners in Dickens*. She reads the Midshipman as "the community that ultimately becomes central in this novel" (99), with the creative, chaotic energy of Gills, Cuttle, Bunsby, and Toots replacing "the static, ordered world of Dombey"

(108). McKnight emphasizes the fact that Cuttle creates a fairy tale for Walter and Flo, and helps to provide a world in which that tale can come true, culminating in their marriage. On the other hand, I emphasize the meanings of the final paragraphs of the novel, in which Florence's myth replaces Cuttle's fairy tale. The community of the Midshipman becomes "rejuvenated and stronger" (McKnight 101), but it remains marginal in that it is unable to organize and bring together the disparate worlds of this novel. Also, see Clare Senior for a somewhat more negative view of the energy of the men of the Midshipman; she concludes that "Gills could never survive in the city as Dickens represents it," and Cuttle lacks "useful function within the masculine sphere" (115).

14. Charles Hatten contends that *Dombey* is such a thoroughly domestic novel that it suffers a "loss of direct narrative access to the public sphere" (64). Whether the mythic Florence amidst the waves could reasonably be considered "domestic" or not, it is nonetheless certainly true that access to the public sphere is lost during the course of Dombey's disasters. That loss is precisely the reason for Dickens's hasty reconstruction of Walter as successful economic man.

15. Suvendrini Perera reads *Dombey* as a romanticization of colonial expansion even as it "decr[ies] its material agent, the expansion of capital" (607). In this interpretation, "the triumphant regeneration of expansionist mercantilism in *Dombey and Son* is undercut by a subtext that cannot dismiss the costly returns of empire" (620), and the novel's closure is marked less by Dombey's personal transformation "than by a forced realignment of the mercantile ideal with marriage and adventure" (616).

16. Wiener is here quoting Peregrine Worsthorne. Wiener points out that both the English aristocracy and the new bourgeoisie were essentially capitalists and thus there was no fundamental antagonism between the two, no need for the aristocracy to be destroyed.

17. I have made the case for this interpretation of Nell's death in a previous essay, "Nell and Sophronia—Catherine, Mary, and Georgina: Solving the Female Puzzle and the Gender Conundrum in *The Old Curiosity Shop.*"

18. For a further discussion of object relations, see Chodorow.

WORKS CITED

Adams, James Eli. *Dandies and Desert Saints: Styles of Victorian Masculinity*. Ithaca: Cornell UP, 1995.

Aikens, Kristina. "The Daughter's Desire in *Dombey and Son*." *Critical Survey* 17 (2005): 77–91.

Armstrong, Nancy. *How Novels Think: The Limits of Individualism from 1719–1900*. New York: Columbia UP, 2005.

Balint, Michael. *Love and Psychoanalytic Technique*. New York: DaCapo Press, 1986.

Chodorow, Nancy. *The Reproduction of Mothering: Psychoanalysis and the Sociology of Gender*. Berkeley: U of California P, 1978.

Coleman, Rosemary. "Nell and Sophronia—Catherine, Mary, and Georgina: Solving the Female Puzzle and the Gender Conundrum in *The Old Curiosity Shop*." *Dickens Studies Annual* 36 (2005): 33–55.

Davidoff, Leonore, and Catherine Hall. *Family Fortunes: Men and Women of the English Middle Class 1780–1850*. Chicago: U of Chicago P, 1987.

Dickens, Charles. *Dombey and Son*. Ed. Peter Fairclough. Harmondsworth: Penguin, 1970.

Furneaux, Holly. *Queer Dickens: Erotics, Families, Masculinities*. Oxford: Oxford UP, 2009.

Hall, Donald E. *Fixing Patriarchy: Feminism and Mid-Victorian Male Novelists*. New York: New York UP, 1996.

Hatten, Charles. *The End of Domesticity: Alienation from the Family in Dickens, Eliot, and James*. Newark: U of Delaware P, 2010.

Kestner, Joseph A. *Masculinities in Victorian Painting*. Aldershot, UK: Scolar, 1995.

Kucich, John. *Repression in Victorian Fiction: Charlotte Brontë, George Eliot, and Charles Dickens*. Berkeley: U of California P, 1987.

Marcus, Steven. *Dickens From Pickwick to Dombey*. London: Chatto and Windus, 1965.

McKnight, Natalie. *Idiots, Madmen & Other Prisoners in Dickens*. New York: St. Martin's, 1993.

Moglen, Helene. "Theorizing Fiction/Fictionalizing Theory: The Case of *Dombey and Son*." *Victorian Studies* 35 (1992): 159–84.

Moynahan, Julian. "Dealings with the Firm of Dombey and Son: Firmness vs Wetness." *Dickens and the Twentieth Century*. Ed. John Gross and Gabriel Pearson. Toronto: U of Toronto P, 1962.

Newsom, Robert. "Embodying Dombey: Whole and in Part." *Dickens Studies Annual* 18 (1976): 197–219.

Perera, Souvendrini. "Wholesale, Retail, and for Exportation: Empire and the Family Business in *Dombey and Son*." *Victorian Studies* 33 (1990): 603–20.

Pykett, Lyn. "*Dombey and Son*: A Sentimental Family Romance." *Studies in the Novel* 19 (1987): 16–30.

Rosen, David. "The Volcano and the Cathedral." *Muscular Christianity: Embodying the Victorian Age*. Ed. Donald E. Hall. Cambridge: Cambridge UP, 1994.

Schor, Hilary M. *Dickens and the Daughter of the House*. Cambridge: Cambridge UP, 1999.

Schwan, Anne. "The Limitations of a Somatics of Resistance: Sexual Performativity and Gender Dissidence in Dickens's *Dombey and Son*." *Critical Survey* 17 (2005): 92–106.

Senior, Clare. "'What the Waves Were Always Saying': Submerging Masculinity in *Dombey and Son*." *Dickens Studies Annual* 32 (2002): 107–127.

Surridge, Lisa. *Bleak Houses: Marital Violence in Victorian Fiction*. Athens: Ohio UP, 2005.

Sussman, Herbert. *Victorian Masculinities: Manhood and Masculine Poetics in Early Victorian Literature and Art*. Cambridge: Cambridge UP, 1995.

Tosh, John. *A Man's Place: Masculinity and the Middle-Class Home in Victorian England.* New Haven: Yale UP, 1999.

Waters, Catherine. *Dickens and the Politics of the Family.* Cambridge: Cambridge UP, 1997.

Wiener, Martin J. *English Culture and the Decline of the Industrial Spirit: 1850–1980.* Cambridge: Cambridge UP, 1981.

Zwinger, Lynda. *Daughters, Fathers, and the Novel: The Sentimental Romance of Heterosexuality.* Madison: U of Wisconsin P, 1991.

Floating Fragments: Some Uses of Nautical Cliché in *Dombey and Son*

Matthew P. M. Kerr

In Dombey and Son, *the sea is often present as a source both of metaphor and of experience. The shuttling between literal and symbolic registers which characterizes Dickens's use of the sea produces a kind of vagueness that has often been problematic for his critics, who complain that solid features of his nautical scenes continually risk dissolving into literary commonplace or cliché. This essay reconsiders some of Dickens's nautical clichés, refocusing attention on their constitutive vagueness. I argue that the slippery doubleness of the literary sea is what Dickens finds so appealing, and organize my discussion around two categories of nautical cliché: those related to water, and those related to solidity (especially wood). I challenge influential accounts of the novel, which praise solid aspects of the marine in* Dombey and Son: *"the real sea of ships and tar and tackling" (Carey 106). I go on to show that Walter Gay's association with woodenness alludes to nautical clichés and turns of phrase: a set of narrative possibilities Dickens hoped to keep in fluid contact with each other. In this way, I argue that if Dickens's nautical clichés were a problem, they were also a linguistic and imaginative resource.*

There is something about the way we understand water that makes it possible to think of the repetition of clichés as "a kind of brainwashing" (Zijderveld 13). Christopher Ricks writes that "the feeling lately has been that we live in an unprecedented inescapability from clichés. All around us is a rising tide of them; we

Dickens Studies Annual, Volume 45, Copyright © 2014 by AMS Press, Inc. All rights reserved.

shall drown and no one will save us" (357). Ricks's choice of words is telling: the nautical idiom he adopts lends subtle credibility to his claim that "the only way to speak of a cliché is with a cliché" (356)—a statement that is at once an appraisal and a recommendation. Like Marshall McLuhan, who writes that a cliché may provide "an active, structuring, probing feature of our awareness," and perform "multiple functions from release of emotion to retrieval of other clichés from both the conscious and unconscious life" (55), Ricks ascribes greater creative potential to the cliché than is typically acknowledged. When Ricks talks of "a rising tide" of clichés, or explains that a clichéd expression is "no sooner floated than sunk," he directs the reader's attention to the seam that connects conscious and unconscious forms of writing or thinking. This is because Ricks's terms encode the possibility of self-critique, or of being used "self-reflexively" (359, 361): "cliché rinsed and restored," as Geoffrey Hill puts it (48).

As the coasting sailor navigates by landmarks, so, writes Théophile Gautier, when "struggling to render what is most inexpressible in thought, what is vague and most elusive in the outlines of form," a novelist may work by reflexive borrowing (qtd. in Macfarlane 168). For Gautier, as for Ricks, cliché can be a way of "pushing back the boundaries of speech." If the sea tends to blur the originating voice into the voices of others, it also offers a figurative vocabulary for speaking about such intermingling. It is this strategy that I trace here, using Dickens's most nautical novel, *Dombey and Son* (1846–48), as case study. It is well known that, in this novel, the sea fostered Dickens's first ambitious attempt at fusing the details of a novel to a single symbolic idiom. However, a nagging feeling that Dickens was dabbling ill-advisedly in genre writing, or merely rehashing Romantic cliché, has prevented his marine writing (in this and his other novels) from being rigorously examined.

This essay by contrast reconsiders some of Dickens's nautical clichés, refocusing attention on their constitutive vagueness. In *Dombey and Son*, the sea is present as a source both of metaphor and of experience. The shuttling between literal and symbolic registers which characterizes Dickens's use of the sea produces a kind of vagueness that has often been problematic for his critics, who complain that solid features of his nautical scenes continually risk dissolving into literary commonplace or cliché. I contest this view, arguing instead that the slippery doubleness of the literary sea is what Dickens finds so appealing, and organize my discussion around two categories of nautical cliché: those related to water, and those related to solidity (especially wood). I first challenge John Carey's and Julian Moynahan's influential accounts of the novel, in which they praise solid aspects of the marine in *Dombey and Son*—what Carey calls "the real sea of ships and tar and tackling" (106)—demonstrating instead the uses to which Dickens put a feature of the novel that frequently troubles critics: Paul Dombey's indefinite murmurings about "what the waves were always saying." I go on in the next section to show that Walter Gay's association with woodenness, which might be thought of as one of the novel's firmer articles, in fact alludes to nautical clichés and turns of phrase: a set of narrative possibilities Dickens hoped to keep in fluid contact with each other. In this way, I follow McLuhan, arguing that if Dickens's nautical clichés were a problem, they were also a linguistic and imaginative resource.

Very Untrue

Critics writing about *Dombey and Son* since Kathleen Tillotson's landmark study *Novels of the Eighteen-Forties* (1954) have tended to position the sea at the literal and figurative center of the novel, taking it as a basis for further arguments about economy, empire, or sexuality, or as a means of revealing Dickens's new interest in planning and coherence, as seen in his use of intricate number plans. Mr. Dombey's wife, as she dies at the end of the first chapter is said (echoing Byron) to have "drifted out upon the dark and unknown sea that rolls round all the world," with Florence "clinging fast to that slight spar" (10; ch. 1). The death of Mr. Dombey's son Paul, in keeping with his short life, is similarly attended by "the restless sea" (194; ch. 14). Even the clerks at Dombey's firm appear "as if they were assembled at the bottom of the sea; while a mouldy little strong room in the obscure perspective, where a shaded lamp was always burning, might have represented the cavern of some ocean monster, looking on with a red eye at these mysteries of the deep" (182; ch. 13). Some, like Michael Slater and Philip Collins have suggested that Dickens's interest in careful plotting can be traced back earlier, to 1844 and *The Chimes* (see Slater, "*The Chimes*", passim). However, most critics, including Richard Altick, J. Hillis Miller, the Leavises, and Suvendrini Perera, accept the truth of Tillotson's thesis. "It is now generally agreed," William Axton declared in 1963, "that in *Dombey and Son*, 'the first masterpiece of Dickens' maturity,' Dickens solved the structural problems of the serial novel" ("Tonal Unity" 341). Behind or beneath the novel's profusion of detail "lies the abiding presence of the ocean," a "keystone" of narrative structure (Axton, "'Keystone' Structure" 42).

Among Dickens's first readers, however, were some who found certain elements of his novel more forced than felicitous. While *Dombey and Son* sold very well—"like the hottest of cakes," Slater ventures (*Dickens* 262)—the first number besting its predecessor *Martin Chuzzlewit* (1843–44) by more than twelve thousand copies, certain of the novel's earliest critics were behind in their appreciation of Dickens's accomplishment (Slater, *Dickens* 262). Specifically, the choice of the sea as a unifying metaphor perhaps seemed a bad one. In May 1848, for example, just after *Dombey and Son* was first published in a single volume, an anonymous reviewer in *Parker's London Magazine* dismissed Dickens's sea metaphors on the grounds that they were trite. The novel is, he writes, "full to over-flowing of waves whispering and wandering; of dark rivers rolling to the sea, of winds, and golden ripples, and such like matters, which are sometimes very pretty, generally very untrue, and have become, at all events, excessively stale" (rev. of *Dombey and Son*, 213).

The attack in *Parker's* is focussed chiefly on Paul Dombey, the novel's eponymous son, who repeatedly asks "what the waves were always saying," and whose thoughts return compulsively to the sea during the period he spends as a student (but chiefly an invalid) in Brighton: "A solitary window, gazed through years ago, looked out upon an ocean, miles and miles away; upon its waters, fancies, busy with him only yesterday, were hushed and lulled to rest like broken waves. The same mysterious murmur he had wondered at, when lying on his couch upon the beach, he thought he still heard" (214; ch. 14). When the reviewer calls Dickens "stale," he may have been thinking of the marine effusions of Byron, Scott, or Frederick Marryat. Or, perhaps, if he had read *Pictures from Italy* (1846), published the year *Dombey and Son* began serialization, he might have felt that Dickens was rehashing material from his travelogue, which contains passages professing faintly unconvincing admiration for Mediterranean sea views ("how blue and bright . . . How picturesque"), and passages in which the writer listens "all night" to the sea's "murmur beneath the stars" (410). Or perhaps he drew on the spate of unoriginal nautical melodramas flooding the stage at about this time, "come and gone like showers (and not very wholesome showers either)," according to Dickens himself ("Marylebone Theatre" 294). There are many possibilities. However, whatever the trope's origin, by choosing to focus on the literal and metaphorical sea, our reviewer claims, Dickens burdens his novel with a ponderous and predictable linguistic formula. He has failed to understand something essential about the sea's status in literature. The susurration of other voices that had previously taken up the same subject in the same way muffles Dickens's particular voice, its characteristic inimitability: Dickens is unable to redeem the sea's "staleness."

The pervasiveness of the sea in *Dombey and Son* (along with Dickens's other novels and journalism) means that it cannot be ignored altogether, but the investigation of commonplaces can produce criticism that is as worn out as the stock materials it busies itself analyzing. It is not hard to understand the disdain for Paul Dombey's quasi-mystical muttering in *Parker's*. By contrast, beyond pointing out the new care Dickens takes to form his novel around a key trope in *Dombey and Son*, few modern critics have found it worthwhile to write about the sea in Dickens at all; perhaps because, as David Trotter points out, in terms reminiscent of *Parker's*, "no critic or historian of culture likes an 'almost universal' meaning" (61). Accordingly, a reader curious about Dickens's representation of the sea finds him- or herself wading through such unhelpful theses as, "So much of what Dickens says about the sea and sailors is entirely straightforward" (Peck 72), or "The shipwreck metaphor and its function in *Dombey and Son* is quite obvious in its implication" (Palmer 18). Others have taken a different approach, and excused Dickens's vagaries by turning their attention to his personal love of the ocean: his (not uncritical) enjoyment of nautical melodrama and travel literature, his trips to Brighton or Broadstairs and his later more frequent trips to Boulogne, or his childhood near Chatham. Perhaps the sea in Dickens's novels represents a "deep and never-quite-extinguished response" to his past—a claim that is in itself the sort of critical vagary that, John Carey writes, can "make liberal intellectuals feel queasy" (41).

According to Carey, the problem is more complex. It concerns not just the badness of Dickens's metaphor, but the incommensurability of the literal and figurative senses in which he intends the sea to be read. The difficulty is that Dickens fails in *Dombey and Son* to reconcile what Carey considers the novel's conventional "religiosity," specifically Paul Dombey's talk of "the invisible country far away," and "the real sea of ships and tar and tackling." Hard features of the text such as "Captain Cuttle with his hook hand and salty language, Sol Gills' nautical instrument shop (The Wooden Midshipman), and the old sailor in battered oilskins who pushes Paul's wheelchair and smells like a weedy beach at low tide," Carey explains, "simply refuse to combine with the shadowy symbolic sea. Their sea is geographic and commercial, solid with detail from Dickens's childhood memories" (106).[1] Julian Moynahan is more strident than Carey, though essentially in agreement: "the vagaries of [Paul Dombey's] mental processes resemble the shapeless surgings of the sea," he writes (128). He characterizes "the essential movement of the book" in comparable terms: it proceeds unhappily "from complexity towards a weltering simplicity" (127). Dickens's mixing of metaphoric and literal reference to the sea represents to Moynahan a correspondingly confused logic. He wants Dickens to settle on something firmer—be it religious sentiment, or solid social critique—but is faced instead with a sentimentality he finds limply effeminate (Moynahan 129). What ought to have been the most solid part of Dickens's novel turns out to be its point of greatest fluidity.

The criticisms levelled by Carey and Moynahan are compelling—so much so that more recent criticism implicitly reflects their stance, either setting the sea aside, or treating it as a bit-player in more pressing discussions of gender (Nina Auerbach), the connection of free trade and sexuality (Clark), empire and gender (Perera, Helene Moglen), or mercantilism and modern forms of commerce (Jeremy Tambling). Such an approach has generated many important insights into the novel: for example, Garrett Stewart's brilliant exposition of the ways in which the "literary-historical capital" circulated by *Dombey*'s sea "is drawn on to reinvest colonial horizons with metaphysical glow" (204). This essay, however, seeks to return focus to the way in which Dickens writes about the sea and associated motifs. As such, I respond most concertedly to these earlier critics, whose claim that the sea in *Dombey and Son* is not worth considering has been so influential.

Both Moynahan and Carey dwell convincingly on the lack of coherence exhibited by Dickens's sea, which mingles tears and baptismal water with alluvial outflow, taking one fluid to be more or less interchangeable with any other. However, it is also worth asking in what ways the hardness critics wish for (evident in the implied solidity of Axton's metaphoric keystones, and Moynahan's dialectic of firmness/wetness) is countermanded. This seems especially important in light of the fact that, as Dickens protests in "Chatham Dockyard," childhood memories, even of spanners and spools of rope, might be anything but solid: the reassuringly ponderous things of the dockyard produce "vague mysterious awe," he admits, before any other feeling (290).

Let us consider one crucial example, reputedly the most banal metaphor of all, and the element that sits most uneasily with Carey: Paul Dombey's notion of "the invisible country far away." This cannot be considered a quirk merely of little Paul's fevered brain; it represents an afterlife of sorts, not least because it is also one of the most firmly settled tropes in Western literature—its banality is inseparable from its inertia. Until Dickens cancelled these paragraphs in proof, this is how the novel ended:

> The voices in the waves speak low to him of Florence, day and night— plainest when he, his blooming daughter, and her husband, walk beside them in the evening, or sit at an open window, listening to their roar. They speak to him of Florence and his altered heart; of Florence and their ceaseless murmuring to her of the love, eternal and illimitable, extending still, beyond the sea, beyond the sky, to the invisible country far away.
>
> Never from the mighty sea may voices rise too late, to come between us and the unseen region on the other shore! Better, far better, that they whispered of that region in our childish ears, and the swift river hurried us away! (967)

What Dickens means in such passages is deliberately vague. Even in the chapter entitled "What the Waves Were Always Saying," a reader hoping for clarification is bound to be disappointed. At the climactic moment Paul exclaims, "I hear the waves! They always said so!," but what they did say is kept secret (240). The feeling and the general idea Dickens wants to put across is, however, clear enough; Dickens speaks in familiar tones (as do the waves by this point) of misty beatitude.

This becomes explicit in light of some related texts. Consider Tennyson's use of the word *bourne* in his poem "Crossing the Bar" (1889).

> For though from out our bourne of Time and Place
> The flood may bear me far,
> I hope to see my Pilot face to face
> When I have crost the bar.
>   (Tennyson, *Poems* 254, lines 13–16)

To some the poem's first hearers, including his nurse, it seemed as if Tennyson had composed his own epitaph (*Tennyson's Poetry* 578). However, Tennyson's poem might be thought of as outside "Time and Place" in more ways than one. The "pilot-god trope," George Monteiro notes, has been "long a commonplace in the literature of many countries and nations of the Western world," appearing in works by Plato, Melville, Emerson, Emily Dickinson, Stephen Crane, and Walt Whitman, and popular hymns like Edward Hooper's "Jesus, Savior, Pilot Me" and Rood and Rexford's "Your Father's at the Helm" (42, 43). Tennyson's metaphoric "bourne," that is, springs not from one place, but several, which is appropriate to his depiction of death as passing from the bounded flow of a stream into a more oceanic mode of existence. The word *bourn* originally denoted a "limit or terminus" (*OED*), and it is used this way in *Hamlet*: "death, / The undiscover'd country, from whose bourn / No traveller returns" (3.1.78–80).[2] In Tennyson's lines, however, "bourne" is allowed freer play. It quickly yields to "bear," showing that Tennyson had in mind not only the way that life itself can demand endurance of what might seem unbearable, as Tennyson found the death of Arthur Hallam, but also the way we are borne through time as on a stream (a bourn). The combination of "bear" and "far" to make "bar" offers syntax and rhyme as a model of the continuity through change for which Tennyson hopes. "Bar" returns us to Hamlet's sense of *bourn* and marks the stream's end, though these variations demonstrate that what Tennyson imagines is a threshold and not an obstruction.

Though it is odd to think of him keeping company with Hamlet, Paul Dombey's murmurings could also be considered an aspect of the past of Tennyson's poem, as might Dickens's journalism: he used the bar as an image of oblivion several times, as in "Our French Watering-Place" (1854), "Out of the Season" (1856), "Travelling Abroad" (1860), and "The Calais Night Mail" (1863). And, of course, the image has other likely sources. Wordsworth's "Ode: Intimations of Immortality from Recollections of Early Childhood" (1807), for example, imagines children who linger near a sea of comparable profundity.[3] And, when Dickens writes that Paul Dombey's is "a fashion that came in with our first garments and will last unchanged until our race has run its course, and the wide firmament is rolled up like a scroll" (241), for example, he rehearses the visionary apocalyptic metaphors of Isaiah and Revelation (*King James Version*, Isa. 34:4; Rev. 6:14); "the swift river that bears us to the ocean" is the Styx to be crossed in death, as much as it is the Thames, or the Medway of Dickens's own private mythology (241). Acknowledging such provenance can have contrary effects. If Tennyson's meaning is firmed up (to the extent that his nurse immediately recognized it), it is also watered down: in other words, if the poem would work well as Tennyson's epitaph, it would work equally well as someone else's. In the case of both Tennyson's poem and Dickens's novel, however, our recognition of a common linguistic and literary past vouches for a common future, a possibility enabled by the literal and literary fluidity of their central figure.

If fluidity can be established by influence and allusion, it may take effect too within a single text. Matthew Arnold contends that another phrase of Hamlet's— "To take arms against a sea of troubles" (3.1.58)—demands to be read with much the same sort of half-attention, and can be liked only if it is not thought about too hard: "the figure there is undoubtedly most faulty, it by no means runs on four legs; but the thing is said so freely and idiomatically, that it passes" (Arnold 156). While his own metaphor is not "free," Carey and Moynahan would understand Arnold's implied claim that critics should not try to make too much of words like Shakespeare's or Tennyson's. The poet's particular expression turns out to be vaguely idiomatic, a part of speech that escapes critical consideration precisely because it is so readily understood. Shakespeare's words do and do not demand attention. They could just as easily be seen to look ahead to a more literal to-ing and fro-ing: Hamlet's departure with Rosencrantz and Guildenstern, and his return without them "ere we were two days old at sea" (4.6.15). It would, how-ever, take an unusually alert playgoer to notice such subtle linguistic recurrence.[4]

Dickens gives his reader more opportunity to notice a pattern when he writes of Florence Dombey's "sea of doubt and hope," Captain Cuttle's "sea of speculation and conjecture," and Mr. Dombey's consuming "sea of pride," in defiance of "the tides of human chance and change," expressed over a "dead sea of mahogany on which the fruit dishes and decanters lay at anchor; as if the subjects of his thoughts were rising towards the surface one by one, and plunging down again" (441; ch. 29, 421; ch. 28, 594; ch. 40, 856; ch 58, 455; ch. 30). Dickens's repetitions urge the reader to give attention to his "sea of" construction, rising in turn to the sur-face of his prose and dropping out of sight again before too much can be made of the swell. How to read the phrase on each recurrence remains uncertain, and not only because it may briskly unite apparent contraries like "doubt" and "hope." It is an innocuous figure of speech that calls to mind not just the novel's central metaphor, but also its key plot points. Language, that is, that would not normally be thought of as figurative—"sea of" is a species of dead metaphor—becomes obtrusively though ambiguously metaphorical because its literal referent is pres-ent in the text, and may or may not influence the text's idiom. The reader is left to guess how thoroughly to parse Dickens's phrasing: it is firmly established and fluidly ungraspable at once.

From one point of view, this banal language has become poetic. "How does poeticity manifest itself?," asks Roman Jakobson: "Poeticity is present when the word is felt as a word and not a mere representation of the object being named or an outburst of emotion, when words and their composition, their meaning, their external and inner form, acquire a weight and value of their own instead of refer-ring indifferently to reality" (378). It is unfair to take such a drastic line as this in Dickens's case since it is unclear whether or not these utterances about the sea enact *différance* or manifest a form of compositional indifference. Language as such is not exactly what the reader's attention is drawn to, but the relationship between sign and referent is called into question. Dickens may not, as Hill says, "rinse" his clichés, but they bring together a host of possible associations while avoiding the need to select between them. "Crossing the Bar" is also crossing into cliché: Tennyson's poem has done more perhaps than any other work of literature to turn this familiar motif into a commonplace verbal formula. *Dombey and Son* is more circumspect. Nevertheless, it is significant that the material features of the story reflexively (and often only partially) provide the vocabulary Dickens needs to make the hard facts mean something.

The material sea is encountered most directly by Walter Gay, who is aboard the *Son and Heir* when it is wrecked. Here, too, the reader meets with a "sea of doubt and hope." Axton considers the wreck to be the novel's "keystone"—the moment at which the "identity of [the novel's] literal and figurative dimensions of meaning" is most visible ("'Keystone' Structure," 42). With the wreck, Dickens connects together the novel's two key groups of characters—those under Mr. Dombey's auspices, and the knot of innocents centred on/at The Wooden Midshipman, the nautical instrument-maker—thematically parcelling up young Paul Dombey's watery end with that of Captain Cuttle, and Sol Gills's vanished heir, Walter Gay, thus offering shipwreck and salvage as a way of thinking about the fate of the novel's titular firm and the characters that trail in its wake.

In a sense, this is the sea Carey and Moynahan love best: a sea of wrecks and technical gewgaws. Yet here too Dickens is concerned, above all, with the sea's capacity to trouble a reader's firmest convictions. In the middle of the novel— chapter 32 of 62—the wreck is reported. Mr. Toots reads aloud to Captain Cuttle from the *Shipping Intelligence*:

> "the look-out observed, half an hour before sunset, some fragments of a wreck, drifting at about the distance of a mile. The weather being clear, and the barque making no way, a boat was hoisted out, with orders to inspect the same, when they were found to consist of sundry large spars, and a part of the main rigging of an English brig, of about five hundred tons burden, together with a portion of the stern on which the words and letters, 'Son and H—' were yet plainly legible. No vestige of any dead body was to be seen upon the floating fragments....There can be no doubt that all surmises as to the fate of the missing vessel, the Son and Heir, port of London, bound for Barbados, are now set at rest for ever; that she broke up in the last hurricane; and that every soul on board perished." (490; ch. 32)

Hans Blumenberg writes, paraphrasing Goethe, that "both progress and sinkings leave behind the same peaceful surface" (59). This is not wholly true for Dickens. Traces remain, and these are an invitation to invent: "debris is precious to him because it represents the best hope of rebuilding" (Rendall 3). We are told that "the words and letters 'Son and H—' were yet plainly legible" on the bits and pieces of the wreck found floating by a passing ship. But the *Shipping Intelligence*, Captain Cuttle, and we as readers are all led to misinterpret this scrap of text.[5] There is no "vestige of any dead body" there because the body we are concerned with is not dead. Dickens's word choice ("vestige," from Latin *vestigium,* footprint) alerts us that Gay has miraculously walked away, so to speak, Christ-like. The way

Captain Cuttle pronounces Walter Gay's name, "Wal'r!," stirs something in the memory of Mr. Perch, "who seemed to remember having heard in infancy that there was once a poet of that name" (252; ch. 17). He is thinking of the Royalist poet Edmund Waller whose patriotic verse "Of a War with Spain, and Fight at Sea" (1656) Dickens may also have in the back of his mind:

> Others may use the ocean as their road,
> Only the ENGLISH make it their abode:
>   . . .
> Our oaks secure, as if they there took root:
> We tread on billows with a steady foot.
>   (192)

Like the "Son and H—," the figure of Walter disappears as we read it; his footprints are miraculously present insofar as they are suggested by the text, and yet they signify equally an absence because there is nothing left on the surface of the water. Dickens reminds us that reading a serial novel is not like reading the shipping news: although the reader is told that there can be no doubt, doubt in this case is precisely the straw Dickens gives his reader to grasp.

When Dickens visited Chatham Dockyard in 1863, he imagined "writing a book" in the cab of one of the great cranes of the dockyard ("Chatham Dockyard" 295). In a sense, *Dombey and Son* anticipates such sentiments: a shipyard occasions thoughts of novelistic construction, while a shipwreck offers opportunities for narrative reconstruction. Paul Dombey, at his bedroom window, observes the sea and feels that "there were crowds of thoughts that mixed with these, and came on, one upon the other, like the rolling waves;" it is perhaps an indication of their otherwise unapparent affinity that Mr. Dombey's thoughts, as we have seen, follow similar patterns, "rising towards the surface . . ., and plunging down again" (206; ch 14). Dickens's brainwaves were also susceptible to the motions of actual waves: watching the Medway running into the sea, he ruminates that "everything within the range of the senses will . . . lend itself to everything beyond that range, and work into a drowsy whole, not unlike a kind of tune, but for which there is no exact definition" ("Chatham Dockyard" 289). In *Dombey and Son*, the sea spreads its ripples indistinctly, making it difficult at times to determine with "exact definition" where they begin and end. Solidity is not what Dickens primarily valued about the sea. Although the sea presses the original voice into shopworn patterns, such forms remained appealing to him; their fundamental vagueness cannot be thought of, with Carey, Moynahan, and others, wholly as a mark of authorial unconsciousness, because Dickens thought *with* such vagueness as well.

Wooden Midshipmen

With an uncertain sense of just how long his own text would endure, John Forster notes in his *Life* that one of what he calls Dickens's "prototypes" exists at the time of writing: "the Little Wooden Midshipman did actually (perhaps does still) occupy his post of observation in Leadenhall Street" (374). Forster's parenthesis gauges the durability not just of the figurine that served as a basis for the one positioned outside Sol Gills's shop, but also of his own textual recollection of it. (In fact, the midshipman is no longer in Leadenhall Street, but is now in the Dickens House Museum, where it can be seen, brightly painted, still staring through its sextant.) Its durability was a subject of interest to Dickens, too. On his way to Wapping in 1860—where he went, not "because I believe (for I don't) in the constancy of the young woman who told her seagoing lover . . . that she had ever continued the same," but to inspect workhouses—Dickens walked on, "past my little wooden midshipman" which really had "carried on the same," but only "after affectionately patting him on one leg of his knee-shorts for old acquaintance' sake" ("Wapping Workhouse" 43). Though it was not unusual for Dickens to feel haunted by his creations, it was rare that he could pat one on the knee. Of all the solid articles that clutter Dickens's novels, the wooden midshipman proved to be one of the most enduring.

As Dickens's allusion to the young woman and her seagoing lover of the ballad "Wapping Old Stairs" (ca. 1797) suggests, the kind of plot that the wooden midshipman introduces in the form of Florence and Walter's picturesque romance had also proved its tenacity. Yet, while Forster implicitly includes the Midshipman among the "vivid and life-like" creations of *Dombey and Son*, Dickens clearly felt by the time he visited Wapping in 1860 that the type of narrative suggested by the figurine could no longer be "believed" wholeheartedly. The novel sits on the cusp of these viewpoints. If a sense of doubt is crucial to the report of the wreck of the *Son and Heir*, it has throughout been important to Walter's character. Dickens was to settle on a version of the romantic plotting employed in "Wapping Old Stairs"—Walter turns out finally to be as wooden as his association with the figurine suggests—but throughout the novel Dickens makes an attempt to keep other possibilities in play. Moreover, he does so largely, and unexpectedly, by way of Walter's ties to the wooden midshipman. In particular, the several ways in which the midshipman's woodenness can be read allowed Dickens simultaneously to think of Walter as a stock figure and to imply a sense of hesitancy and knowingness, holding in reserve until the last moment the possibility that Walter will turn out differently than the reader imagines.

Walter Gay, Solomon Gills, and Captain Cuttle are introduced in their shop, named after the figurine that stands outside the door, whose immovability Dickens finds faintly laughable: "little timber midshipmen in obsolete naval uniforms, eternally employed outside the shop-doors of nautical instrument makers in taking observations of the hackney coaches" (36; ch 4). Still, as G. W. Kennedy points out (27), the shop is an emblem of cozy compactness of the sort Dickens loved, like the Atlantic packet *The Screw* in *Martin Chuzzlewit*, which under Mark Tapley's cheerful eye becomes so like a country pub that he can perceive "no great difference" (245; ch 17), or Bill Barley's place in *Great Expectations* (1860–61), which is "fitted out 'like a chandler's shop'," complete with a table on which he keeps "his grog ready-mixed in a little tub" (343, 344; ch. 23), or Mr. Tartar's quarters in *The Mystery of Edwin Drood* (1870). In Sol Gills's shop, "everything was jammed into the tightest cases, fitted into the narrowest corners, fenced up behind the most impertinent cushions, and screwed into the acutest angles, to prevent its philosophical composure from being disturbed by the rolling of the sea" (37; ch 4). Dickens tells us that "such extraordinary precautions were taken in every instance to save room, and keep the thing compact," though they also establish certain narrative expectations in the reader's mind (37; ch 4). Walter Gay's name would have suggested to readers that he was snugly recognizable, like one of Captain Marryat's heroes—Midshipman Easy, Jacob Faithful, and so on, or indeed like Jon Steadiman in *The Wreck of the "Golden Mary,"* the Christmas book Dickens wrote with Wilkie Collins in 1856. And, while he is not yet a sailor, Sol Gills's nephew "looked quite enough like a midshipman to carry out the prevailing idea" (37; ch 4).

In spite of Walter's garden-variety appearance, Dickens was unclear about exactly how solid or realistic to make his character when he began *Dombey and Son*. He wrote to Forster at the end of July 1846:

it would be a good thing to disappoint all the expectations that chapter [4] seems to raise of his happy connection with the story and the heroine, and to show [Walter] gradually and naturally trailing away, from that love of adventure and boyish light-heartedness, into negligence, idleness, dissipation, dishonesty, and ruin. To show, in short, that common, every-day, miserable declension of which we know so much in our ordinary life. (*Letters* 4: 593)

He wondered, however, if he could follow this course "without making people angry." By 22 November 1846 he told Forster that he was "far from sure it could be wholesomely done, after the interest he has acquired" (*Letters* 4: 658). In reference to the possibility that Dickens might have ruined Walter, George Gissing writes that "the hand was stayed where the picture would have become too painful alike for author and public." Gissing goes on to say that "the phrase about 'making people angry' signifies much less than it would in a novelist of to-day. It might well have taken the form: 'Can I bring *myself* to do this thing?'" (69).[6] Even if he finally gave the idea up, Dickens allows himself the option of diverging from the familiar pattern.

The popular literature of the sea that valorizes sailorly hearts of oak fascinated Dickens, and his personal love of this literature, together with a childhood spent around docks reading the *Terrific Register* in which "grisly accounts of the horrors that could occur in the aftermath of wrecks were commonplace" (Thompson 2), is evident in the solid details of *Dombey and Son*. The fascination that, for example, *Robinson Crusoe* (1719) held for Dickens has been widely noted.[7] David Copperfield's childhood reading, based on Dickens's own, includes "Roderick Random, Peregrine Pickle, Humphrey Clinker, Tom Jones, the Vicar of Wakefield, Don Quixote, Gil Blas, and Robinson Crusoe," half of which contain nautical themes; David also has "a greedy relish for a few volumes of Voyages and Travels," like Archibald Duncan's six-volume *The Mariner's Chronicle*, from 1804 (*David Copperfield* 53; ch. 5). The latter, William J. Palmer explains, "became *the* basic source for many of the other shipwreck narrative anthologies of the nineteenth century . . . including Cook's *Voyages* . . . and Hall's *Voyages*" (48). Walter Gay and his uncle recall shipwrecks, complete with dates and cargoes, as an introduction to their habits of conversation; these are reminiscent of eighteenth- and early nineteenth-century accounts of survivors collected in such volumes as Duncan's *Mariner's Chronicle*. Dickens also owned and drew readily from Charles Dibdin's *Songs, Naval and National* (1841) and Sir John Dalyell's three-volume *Shipwrecks and Disasters at Sea* (1812).[8] (Dalyell's works provided corroborating anecdote for Dickens's impassioned rebuttal of Dr. Rae's claim that Franklin's crew had turned to cannibalism in "The Lost Arctic Voyagers," published in *Household Words* in two parts on 2 and 9 December 1854.)

Walter and Sol's interest in shipwreck narratives, then, to some degree reflects Dickens's own. The *Daily News*, which Dickens briefly edited, and in which he still held an interest, published, along with his tabloid The *Household Narrative of Current Events* (an adjunct to *Household Words*), "regular sections devoted solely to shipping intelligence and disaster reports" (Dickens, *"Gone Astray"* 180–81). *Household Words* itself frequently published either narrative or statistical accounts of shipwrecks. For instance, "Lighthouses and Light-boats" (11 January 1851) and "The Preservation of Life from Shipwreck" (3 August 1850) protest against the shortcomings in training and practice of rescuers located along the coasts. "Life and Luggage" (8 November 1851), "A Sea-Coroner" (13 March 1852), "When the Wind Blows" (24 March 1855), and "Wrecks at Sea" (11 August 1855), all focus on the shocking frequency of shipwrecks. And, just as he had in Sol Gills and Walter's dialogue in *Dombey and Son*, in "The Long Voyage" (31 December 1853), Dickens's magazine printed miniaturized versions of the eighteenth-century shipwreck anthology, with true accounts of tropical and Arctic wrecks. News of this sort "was a staple of every London newspaper and most periodicals," as Palmer points out (55), and it is worth remembering that the fictional *Shipping Intelligence* from which Captain Cuttle hears of the wreck of the *Son and Heir* shares traits with Dickens's own periodicals.

At the same time, Dickens's first readers and numerous critics have noted that Walter would be equally at home treading the boards of a theater as the decking of a ship. Walter Gay's trajectory is highly redolent of the melodramatic portrayals of Jolly Jack Tars which achieved great prominence in the nineteenth century. The pair of boys who form the first glimpse that Nicholas Nickleby has of Crummles's theatrical troupe, "one of them very tall and the other very short, both dressed as sailors—or at least as theatrical sailors, with belts, buckles, pigtails, and pistols complete—fighting in what is called in play-bills a terrific combat," have perhaps more in common with Walter than the sturdily realistic survivors depicted in the periodical reports (278). Axton lays out in careful detail the resonances between *Dombey and Son* and various plays: a version of Dick Whittington produced by Dickens's acquaintance Albert Smith in 1845, and most significantly the enormously popular and influential *Black Ey'd Susan; or, All in the Downs* (1829) by another friend, Douglas Jerrold. The play was frequently performed. In September 1842, "the celebrated Nautical Drama" shared billing with a production of *Oliver Twist* at the Royal Victoria Theatre, where a certain Mr. Seaman first played Monks, before taking a turn as Captain Crosstree later in the evening.[9] The play comes up frequently in Dickens's journalism (see, for example, "Out of Town," and "New Year's Day"), and his assessments of it can be telling. Dickens reviewed a production at the Marylebone Theatre in *The Examiner* the year after he completed *Dombey and Son*, "at which the audience laughed and wept with all their hearts." He found it to be "a remarkable illustration of what a man of genius may do with a common-enough theme, and how what he does will remain a thing apart from all imitation" ("Marylebone Theatre" 294).

Dickens was right to say that the theme of Jerrold's play was "common-enough." The play, based on John Gay's ballad written almost a century earlier "Sweet William's Farewell to Black-Ey'd Susan" (1720), set a tight pattern for nautical melodrama throughout the century. J. S. Bratton writes, "In 1875 the Britannia presented the old plot unchanged in *The Sea is England's Glory* by F. Marchant; and in 1896 the Pavilion Mile End had it all out again in *Jack Tar*, by A. Shirley and B. Landreck, which bristles with nostalgic claptraps about the romantic tar" (52). Dickens himself staged an enthusiastic revival when Jerrold died in 1857. Ostensibly a benefit for the playwright's family, it may have been motivated by Dickens's love of the melodrama itself, and his convictions of the probable success of his staging, as much as by disinterested benevolence: Jerrold's family was in fact left well-provided for, and his widow asked Dickens outright to refrain from producing the play at all.[10] If, as I suggest above, Walter's Christian name alludes to Edmund Waller, his surname might be traced to the melodramatic convention initiated by John Gay; the minor mystery of Walter's parentage is partially resolved by these allusions (see Westland 93).

Axton suggests that Dickens repurposes both the dramatis personae of Jerrold's play and its structure, which he uses as a skeletal frame to model Walter's progress:

> Jerrold . . . uses a host of melodramatic clichés: the hero's timely return from the sea to his lover's arms, the grasping merchant, his hypocritical and

libidinous accomplice, the cock-sure sailor hero, the hard-pressed heroine of delicate sensibility, her spunky companion. . ., her idiot-lover. . ., and the hero's stridently nautical shipmates who repeatedly affirm in song their loyalty to nation and friend. ("Stereotype" 312)

Yet, even such explicit references are not made with the intent of clarifying Dickens's narrative aims. Dickens, for example, makes explicit allusion to *Black Ey'd Susan* in the character of Susan Nipper, called "the black-eyed" throughout *Dombey and Son*. There is little similarity, however, between Jerrold's Susan, a Penelope embattled by suitors while awaiting her husband's return, and Dickens's Susan. A comparison to Florence, who waits for Walter, just as Jerrold's Susan waits for William, would make more sense, but Dickens stops short of allowing such a direct equivalence. Indeed, the association is further loosened by a poster advertising the play, found in the lower left corner of the final illustration in the first volume publication: Phiz's illustration for the chapter "Chiefly Matrimonial" in which Cuttles's sailor friend is wed to his former landlady Mrs. Mac Stinger (fig. 1).

Fig. 1. Phiz's illustration of the wedding of Bunsby and Mrs Mac Stinger, with the poster for Black Ey'd Susan propped against the wall at bottom left. "Another Wedding," Dombey and Son, chapter 60. H. K. Browne ("Phiz").

Given the midshipman's status as an agreed-upon type, Walter's woodenness may have originated as a winking acknowledgment on Dickens's part that what he appeared to be introducing was a stock figure of balladic or melodramatic cliché. Sol's midshipman is, Dickens writes, "familiarly, the woodenest," his "suavity the least endurable," his garb the most ostentatiously stagey (36; ch 4). The reader is invited to compare the statue of the wooden midshipman to Walter, who is "firm and cheery" in his own right (729; ch 49). The figure's wooden face appears hardly "reconcilable to human reason," and Walter himself is similarly unbothered by thought, "not much given to analysing the nature of his own feelings" (118; ch 9). Repeatedly compared with both the shop's mascot and the shop itself, Walter may not be much different from the other movables that stock the shelves. The sense of *wooden* meaning "mentally dull; insensitive, inapprehensive; unintelligent, blockish" (*OED*), had been current since the sixteenth century, and Carlyle was fond of using the word as a synonym for *mechanical*. The term may also have had particularly nautical applications. "Would you learn the jargon of a Midshipman," wonders Hervey Brackbill, an early twentieth-century reporter and telegrapher.[11]

> "Catch a skag, settle down, and bone this gauge. You'll be savvy in a butt—
> before you have to caulk off—unless you're wooden." Which is to say:
> "Light a cigarette, settle down, and study this vocabulary. You'll know it in
> a short time—before you go to bed—unless you're an absolute blockhead."
> (451)

Brackbill goes on to define *wooden* as "unintelligent, stupid, 'dumb'" (455). While the origin of a usage like this is difficult to determine, it would not be right to assume that it is exclusively American, just because Brackbill is; throughout the nineteenth century, merchant crews were highly international and employed an argot of their own. Perhaps, then, it is no coincidence that the wooden midshipman in *Dombey and Son*, squinting through his "offensively disproportionate piece of machinery," is also perpetually winking (36; ch 4).

Given Walter's blockheadedness, another literary model may have helped Dickens to frame his character in light of a comparable marine definition of *woodenness*: Cruikshank's admonitory *The Progress of a Midshipman, Exemplified in the Career of Master Blockhead* (1820), a collaboration with, and comically fictionalized life of, Captain Marryat, which was nonetheless intended to disclose something about the midshipman as a type. Captain Marryat was arguably the most influential practitioner of naval novel-writing in the nineteenth century. He and Dickens were acquaintances, as, of course, Dickens and Cruikshank had been—Dickens wrote to Marryat, for instance, on 13 October 1842 to acknowledge receipt of *Percival Keene*, "over which I have been chuckling, and grinning, and clenching my fists, and becoming warlike, for three whole days last past" (*Letters* 3: 342–43).[12] It seems possible that Dickens would have been interested in his old illustrator's work with the Captain. Indeed, where Marryat had transmuted his youthful indiscretions, upon which Master Blockhead's are based, into a degree of bourgeois respectability, Cruikshank's midshipman is done in by his vices, as Walter threatens to be (Brantlinger 54).

If Dickens worried that his readers might be made angry, then it was not just because the decline of such a promising young man would be painful to observe, but also because the idea of the midshipman had settled into familiar shapes by this time, some of them heroic. I am not the only critic to consider the role some of these examples play in the novel; Ella Westland in particular carefully links *Dombey and Son* to *Black-Ey'd Susan*, Dibdin's *Songs*, and Marryat and Cruikshank's *Progress of a Midshipman*. According to Westland, "early Victorian readers of *Dombey* would. . . have been prepared by the mere mention of midshipmen for a story of youthful adventures and career success," an expectation Dickens was not at all sure he wished to satisfy (92). Westland goes on persuasively to examine some of the ways in which Walter could have reminded readers of "long-running maritime plots: the Midshipman's Progress and the Sailor's Farewell" (91), narrative conventions that sent their protagonists down contrasting tacks toward either salvation or infidelity, ruin or drowning (102). However, her suggestion that Dickens desired "to keep open an escape route for himself from the repressiveness of realism into the comparative freedom of popular culture" represented by "orally mediated traditions of story telling and song" (89) is less convincing. While it is right to say that Dickens evokes the narrative shapes of popular maritime fiction and melodrama, Westland is less clear about how this distinguishes Dickens's novel from any other since the form of the novel in this period, in spite of its variety, might still best be characterized by heterogeneity and inclusiveness. Nor does Westland explain why the *nautical* aspects of *Dombey and Son* in particular invoke such contradictory meanings.

Consider the term *midshipman*. The entry for the word is striking among the often terse definitions of nautical equipment and terminology William Falconer provides in his famous *Universal Dictionary of the Marine* (1769), which remained an essential resource for years despite having originated as a set of technical notes to Falconer's influential poem *The Shipwreck* (1762): by the 1784 edition of his *Dictionary*, Falconer required four pages to do *midshipman* justice. Falconer both implies the conventionality of the midshipman as a type and engages to correct some misapprehensions. He sketches out the duties and situation of a midshipman aboard ship, but also expounds at length upon the character of this species of young man, who "usually comes aboard tinctured with . . . prejudices," and "blinded by. . . prepossessions" gleaned from popular reading. According to Falconer, such young men come to sea for the first time full of mistaken opinions about "the genius of sailors and their officers. No character, in their opinion, is more excellent than that of the common sailor." However, every midshipman is eventually disabused of this misapprehension "and very soon surprised to find, amongst those honest sailors, a crew of abandoned miscreants, ripe for any mischief or villainy."

The sense given by Falconer that a midshipman will immediately upon embarking descend into a world of vice mimics Dickens's original vision of Walter's "miserable declension." Yet, in the end, Dickens and Falconer alike have it both ways because, not only the *ur*-midshipman of the *Dictionary*, but Walter too, embody at the outset a capacity for the kind of heroic innocence which the authors and the reader hold dear, and also the potential for dramatic decline. In this way, Falconer manages to describe a midshipman who is typical, and possibly typically heroic, but also allows the reader to keep in mind the various unpropitious ways in which such a person might change over time. Dickens thrusts onto Sol Gills an anxiety comparable to that he wished his readers to feel: "If I didn't know that he was too fond of me to make a run of it, and go and enter himself aboard ship against my wishes, I should begin to be fidgetty [*sic*]. . . I really should. All in the Downs, eh!" (38; ch 4). Dickens's original readers would have found it easy to discern in Sol's remark "All in the Downs" an allusion to the alternative title of *Black Ey'd Susan*.

If Dickens initially considered a trajectory for Walter something like the one Falconer gives his midshipmen, or Cruikshank gives his Master Blockhead, he finally settled on the kind of heroic myth that Marryat had been fond of depicting in his fiction. We do not know the reasons Forster gave to convince Dickens to maintain the conventionality of Walter's character. The editors of the Pilgrim edition of his letters suggest that there may have been too close a parallel discernible between an impecunious Walter Gay and Thomas Powell, an acquaintance who had embezzled money from Chapman and Hall and fled to America earlier in 1846 (Dickens, *Letters* 4: 593, 575)—a somewhat unconvincing explanation, given Dickens's willingness to lampoon even his friends in his novels; Forster himself was to appear as Podsnap in *Our Mutual Friend* (1864–65; see Slater, *Dickens* 523). Whatever his rationale, Dickens in the end capitulated and allowed Walter the heroic destiny he knew his public wanted, or at least expected (Forster 360). Walter's woodenness, however, is the pivot on which Dickens turned the two futures he had imagined for his character.

Carey suspects that such woodenness appears in Dickens—he has written engagingly about the proliferation of wooden legs in the novels—for the simpler but no less "pressing reason. . . that Dickens likes wooden men" (88).[13]   Indeed, Dickens was at times profligate in his application of the quality, so that, while Walter assumes some aspects of woodenness, Mr. Dombey also appears "like a man of wood, without a hinge or a joint in him," a likeness that suggests little about their respective characters (401; ch 26). Still, in the Victorian imagination there were good reasons to think that a wooden midshipman might be somewhat different from wooden men in general. Dickens makes the same association elsewhere. In "Some Recollections of Mortality" (1863), an indifferent nurse appears "like the figure-head of a pauper-ship," for example, and her charge dampens her "wooden shoulder" with tears (226). Lost in London as a boy, a rascal with "a stump of black-lead pencil" writes his mother's name and address on the young Dickens's white hat: "MRS. BLORES, WOODEN LEG WALK, TOBACCO-STOPPER ROW, WAPPING," the notorious haunt of sailors while ashore ("Gone Astray" 162). Dickens finds he cannot rub off the markings, and he was likewise never to rid himself of his predilection for wooden legs which, like Mr. Gamp's which leads him "walkin' into wine vaults, and never comin' out again 'till fetched by force," often appear to exhibit a life of their own (*Martin Chuzzlewit* 535). In *The Old Curiosity Shop* (1840–41), Quilp possesses "the effigy of some famous admiral," a ship's figurehead with a "mass of timber on its head, caved into the dim and distant semblance of a cocked hat," sawn off at that waist so that it resembles "a distinguished merman" (461). A comparable figure appears in "Our Watering Place," published in *Household Words* on 2 August 1851:

> One of those slow heavy fellows sitting down patiently mending a little ship for a mite of a boy, whom he could crush to death by throwing his lightest pair of trousers on him. You will be sensible of the oddest contrast between the smooth little creature, and the rough man who seems to be carved out of hard-grained wood – between the delicate hand expectantly held out, and the immense thumb and finger that can hardly feel the rigging of the thread they mend. . .—and yet there is a natural propriety in the companionship. (16)

If Walter's woodenness permitted a degree of irony, it could also suggest a sort of solidly English virtue. Two centuries after Edmund Waller made the association, "hard-grained wood" and British national identity remained firmly engrafted. Woodenness of heart was particularly associated with the British at sea who manned the nation's "wooden walls," as in the popular lines from "Hearts of Oak"—"heart of oak are our ships, jolly tars are our men"—which encouraged a metonymic cross-identification of the deck with the hands who manned it, and of the human heart with those decks. That "Hearts of Oak," written by David Garrick for the eighteenth-century opera of the same name, could be plucked from the boards of the West End to become the official march of the British Navy, suggests how central to both military power and a certain version of British identity this kind of hard, knotty virtue was thought to be. Walter's woodenness is finally keyed to reassuringly solid popular sentiment. A heroic return presented as melodramatic stagecraft is not at all the kind of hardness Moynahan or Carey have in mind. I have tried to suggest, however, that woodenness proves integral to the procedure by which Dickens connects two sorts of solidity: nautical bric-a-brac and the "miserable declension" Dickens thought characteristic of "ordinary life" are shown miraculously to be commensurate with no less ingrained cultural forms.

In developing his central symbol, Dickens had thought harder than most nautical writers, not just about what the sea might mean, but about what it meant to write about the sea. In an early scene that looks ahead to the wreck of the *Son and Heir*, set in The Wooden Midshipman, Sol and Walter find themselves immersed in familiar tales of shipwrecks, which they have memorized from popular accounts, finishing each other's sentences: "'Why, when the Charming Sally went down in the——' 'In the Baltic Sea, in the dead of night; five-and-twenty minutes past twelve when the captain's watch stopped in his pocket'." Steadiness is called for, however, and Sol urges Walter to maintain a moderate attitude to the sea: "'As to the Sea,' he pursued, 'that's well enough in fiction, Wally, but it won't do in fact: it won't do at all. It's natural enough that you should think about it, associating it with all these familiar things; but it won't do, it won't do'" (43; ch 4). Sol, of course, relishes the thought of the sea as much as Walter does, and looks about his shop with "stealthy enjoyment" even as he exhorts his nephew to caution. The "familiar things" Sol has in mind are the chronometers and sextants in The Wooden Midshipman, but Dickens is more interested in the way the sea shapes their conversation into conventional and familiar patterns.

Dickens admired the sea largely as Sol does, because he finds it at once absorbing and artificial, a fact and a fiction. He stresses this combination of qualities in "Gone Astray" when he recalls a nautical melodrama he had seen as a boy, featuring "a real man-of-war" (that nevertheless appears drastically undersized), which rolls onstage "in a very heavy sea," along with a "good sailor (and he was very good)," and a "bad sailor (and he was very bad)," who throws himself into the sea "from a summit of a curious rock, presenting something of the appearance of a pair of steps" (163–64). It is Dickens's point that by the mid-nineteenth century the sea was inseparable from the clichéd fictions Sol and Walter attach to it. Like Gills's shop, "wanting only good sea-room, in the event of an unexpected launch, to work its way securely, to any desert island in the world" (37), the "familiar things" Walter associates with the sea are not confined to the small circle of his makeshift family. Richard Altick writes that Dickens had picked up "the nautical songs Captain Cuttle quotes in mangled snatches. . . during his childhood among the old salts at Chatham and in the Dibdinesque naval dramas at popular theatres." "They had," he goes on to observe, "no intrinsic function in the novel but were merely employed to embellish a certain theme, in this instance Captain Cuttle's occupation" (84).

Dickens, however, was more interested in mangling than Altick's interpretation suggests. The reader learns later that the text Walter Gay recalls in his "hour of need" is not the New Testament, but the hodgepodge of popular sea tales he and Sol Gills recite near the beginning of the novel. "When he was a boy," Cuttle recalls, he loved "to read and talk about brave actions in shipwrecks—I've heerd him! I've heerd him!—and he remembered of 'em in his hour of need" (729; ch 49). Altick notes that Cuttle himself often makes similar substitutions, which might go some way to explaining Walter's confusion (84). In chapter 15, for instance, Cuttle recites to Walter a line from a popular song, though he claims it is one of Solomon's proverbs: "May we never want a friend in need, nor a bottle to give him!" (223).[14] It is, though, I suggest, Dickens's intention to direct attention to the links between pious reflection and popular recollection. "By the middle of the nineteenth century the good officer was both a good officer and an obvious Christian" in the public mind (Hamilton 386). While Walter Gay's creed is at the outset rather more obscure, by the end of the novel it has itself become one of The Wooden Midshipman's familiar things. If Walter's woodenness had initially allowed Dickens to entertain the possibility that his character might diverge substantially from his starting point in popular figures of ballads and nautical melodrama, he finally settled into those comfortable forms to which that same woodenness could be equally accommodated. The flexible ways in which Walter's woodenness can be interpreted encourage those alternatives to be read as narrative possibilities.

Hoarse Music

It is "by means of sheer repetition [that] clichés mould people's minds and souls in specific direction" (Zijderveld 6); perhaps this is why the waves that murmur and roll throughout *Dombey and Son* feel at once pregnant and vacant. Although their script seems, most prevalently, to be, as Garrett Stewart suggests, "a circumlocution for heaven" (198), they deliver their lines in two distinct ways. At one level, they reiterate the concerns of individual hearers. Thus Toots hears them murmuring about Florence's loveliness and Dr. Blimber hears them muttering about getting back to work. Yet when Paul finally hears the waves clearly, it does not seem to matter much what they are actually saying: "How fast the river runs, between its green banks and the rushes, Floy! But it's very near the sea. I hear the waves!" (240; ch 16). Such assonant trochees, all open vowels—"what the waves were always saying"—formally echo the unresolvable openness of the waves' repetitious speech. While the waves could be saying anything, perhaps they are saying nothing. The drone of "what the waves were always saying" threatens on repeated readings (which are inevitable, given the number of times the phrase appears in the novel) to submerge the sense of the passage in favor of its sound. Given how often critics have accused Tennyson of this sort of sacrifice, perhaps it is appropriate that it is Tennyson whom Dickens quotes in "Our Watering Place" when he wishes to give voice to the sea:

The poet's words are sometimes on its awful lips:

> And the stately ships go on
> To their haven under the hill;
> But O for the touch of a vanish'd hand,
> And the sound of a voice that is still!
>
> Break, break, break,
> At the foot of thy crags, O sea!
> But the tender grace of a day that is dead
> Will never come back to me.
> ("Our Watering Place" 18).

The repetitions in Tennyson's poem suggest that a person's hand might live on in their script, or in a particular trope, or turn of phrase. "What the waves were always saying" turns out to be vague in *Dombey and Son* largely because they were always saying it; the wornness, the woodenness, of this phrase either curtails its metaphysical aspirations or turns it into a kind of prayer. Nevertheless, Dickens returns to such tropes repeatedly and makes something of that very wornness and woodenness.

In this essay, I have concentrated on the extent to which Dickens's style can both comprehend and control the threats posed by the sea to originality and to the precision of figurative language. I have found that the sea's clichés do not merely accommodate, but are frequently a necessary precondition to Dickens's creativity. He liked to write by the sea.[15] Consider the image Dickens gives of himself in a letter to Foster announcing that he had commenced work on *Dombey and Son*: "BEGAN DOMBEY! I performed the feat yesterday—only wrote the first slip—but there it is, it is a plunge straight over head and ears into the story" (*Letters* 4: 574–75). He returned with Catherine to Brighton to finish writing the novel, spending a week there near the end of February 1848, and poured particular care into the conclusion, wanting to see his "one idea" through to the end. In the chapter plans for this final number, he notes his wish to "end with the sea—carrying through, what the waves were always saying" (see Slater, *Dickens* 274). In an 1851 letter he declared that "the freshness of the sea, and the associations of the place" had set him to writing "with great vigor" (*Letters* 6: 405).

However, "freshness" was not necessarily the most important thing about the seaside to Dickens. He again went to the seaside to finish writing *David Copperfield*, this time to Broadstairs. "I am within three pages of the shore," he wrote to Forster, "and am strangely divided, as usual in such cases, between sorrow and joy. . . . I seem to be sending some part of myself into the Shadowy World" (*Letters* 6: 195). He had already written to Macready in June that he hoped to "go down to that old image of Eternity that I love so much, and finish [*David Copperfield*] to its hoarse music" (*Letters* 6: 113). Dickens chose his words carefully. By combining an allusion to Byron's *Childe Harold* (185, canto 4, line 1644) with a reference to his own turn of phrase in *Dombey and Son*, where "the waves are hoarse with repetition of their mystery; [and] the dust lies piled on the shore" (611), Dickens suggests that writing about the sea can just as easily form itself into enduring patterns as the waves themselves. At least in this respect, his phrase supplies its own "image of Eternity." In all Dickens's novels, the endeavor to revive what at first appears inanimate is a major element of the fictional method. In *Dombey and Son*, the deadness represented by the wooden midshipman, its very linguistic and imaginative non-specificity, is the crucial antecedent of its renewal, and one reason why Dickens makes it his subject.

NOTES

1   I shall capitalize *wooden midshipman* when talking about the shop, but not when talking about the figurine more broadly.

2   Garrett Stewart also mentions these lines with relation to *Dombey and Son*, though his focus is on the "undiscover'd country" rather than the word *bourn* (199).

3   I am grateful to Seamus Perry for pointing this out.

4   For a brief but suggestive discussion of *Hamlet*'s marine idiom, see Raban 6–7.

5   For a reading of the shipping intelligence as it appears in *Bleak House* (and other novels), see Rubery 24–46.

6   Gissing uses the same phrase ("too painful") as Dickens does in his "mems" for the sixth number of *Dombey and Son*, in fact referring to the scene in which Florence is banished by her father to the upstairs room, though it is in this number too that Walter departs aboard the *Son and Heir*. See "Appendix B: The Number Plans," in Dickens, *Dombey and Son* 932.

7   See Kennedy for more on appearances of *Robinson Crusoe* in Dickens's novels.

8   For more on Dickens's reading of Dalyell and what Forster called the popular "books of African and other travel for which he had insatiable relish" (vol. 2: 42). Forster is quoted in Slater's editorial remarks to Dickens, *"Gone Astray"* 180–81.

9   For Dickens and *Black-Ey'd Susan*, see Axton, "Stereotype" 301–17. Axton guessed that Dickens would have seen T. P. Cooke in the role of William during the play's original run (312). On the nights *Black-Ey'd Susan* was not performed at the Royal Victoria, the slot was filled by Fitzball's *The Floating Beacon!; or, The Norwegian Wreckers*, another "popular and Romantic Nautical Drama." This line-up is documented in a playbill from 1 September 1842 in the John Johnson Collection of Printed Ephemera, Bodleian Library, shelfmark JJ Dickens Playbills.

10 For more on this zealous but unnecessary "getting up" of *Black Ey'd Susan*, see Slater, *Dickens* 429.

11 For Brackbill's biography, see "Hervey Brackbill (1901–1999)," *The Baltimore Sun*, 21 March 1999, http://articles.baltimoresun.com/1999-03-21/entertainment/9903220279_1_brack-woodlawn-evening-sun.

12 For more on their friendship, see Hawes.

13 For another detailed consideration of uses of wooden legs and other prosthetics in Victorian fiction, see O'Connor 102–47.

14 Altick claims these lines are from a song by Dibdin, "Friend and Bottle," but they also circulated anonymously in the form of broadsheet ballads.

15 See Forster's chapter on Dickens's "Seaside Holidays, 1848–1851," 374–90.

WORKS CITED

Altick, Richard D. "Varieties of Readers' Response: The Case of *Dombey and Son*." *Yearbook of English Studies* 10 (1980): 70–94.

Arnold, Matthew. *On the Classical Tradition*. Ed. R. H. Super. Ann Arbor: U of Michigan P, 1960.

Auerbach, Nina. "Dickens and Dombey: A Daughter After All." *Romantic Imprisonment: Women and Other Glorified Outcasts*. New York: Columbia UP, 1985. 107–29.

Axton, William. "*Dombey and Son*: From Stereotype to Archetype." *ELH* 31.3 (1964): 301–17.

———. "'Keystone' Structure in Dickens' Serial Novels." *University of Toronto Quarterly* 37.1 (1967): 31–50.

———. "Tonal Unity in *Dombey and Son*." *PMLA* 78.4 (1963): 341–48.

Blumenberg, Hans. *Shipwreck with Spectator: Paradigm of a Metaphor for Existence*. Trans. Steven Rendall. Cambridge: MIT P, 1997.

"Bourne." *Oxford English Dictionary*. 2nd ed. 1989.

Brackbill, Hervey. "Midshipman Jargon." *American Speech* 3.9 (1928): 451–55.

Brantlinger, Patrick. "Bringing Up the Empire: Captain Marryat's Midshipmen." *Rule of Darkness: British Literature and Imperialism, 1830–1914*. Ithaca: Cornell UP, 1988. 47–70.

Bratton, J. S. "British Heroism and the Structure of Melodrama." *Acts of Supremacy: The British Empire and the Stage, 1790–1930*. Ed. J. S. Bratton et al. Manchester: Manchester UP, 1991. 18–61.

Byron, George Gordon, Lord. *Childe Harold's Pilgrimage*. Vol. 2 of *The Complete Poetical Works*. Ed. Jerome J. McGann. Oxford: Clarendon, 1980.

Carey, John. *The Violent Effigy: A Study of Dickens' Imagination*. London: Faber and Faber, 1973.

Clark, Robert. "Riddling the Family Firm: The Sexual Economy in *Dombey and Son*." *ELH* 51.1 (1984): 69–84.

Collins, Philip. "*Dombey and Son*—Then and Now." *The Dickensian* 63.352 (1967): 82–94.

Dickens, Charles. *American Notes* and *Pictures from Italy*. Ed. Sacheverell Sitwell. London: Oxford UP, 1957.

———. "The Calais Night Mail." *Uncommercial Traveller*, 209–18.

———. "Chatham Dockyard." *Uncommercial Traveller*, 287–96.

———. *David Copperfield*. Ed. Nina Burgis. Rev. ed. Oxford: Oxford UP, 1997.

———. *Dombey and Son*. Ed. Alan Horsman. Oxford: Oxford UP, 2001.

———. *"Gone Astray" and Other Papers from "Household Words."* Ed. Michael Slater. London: Dent, 1998.

———. "Gone Astray." *"Gone Astray,"* 155–65.

———. *Great Expectations*. Ed. Margaret Cardwell. Oxford: Oxford UP, 2008.

———. *The Letters of Charles Dickens*. Pilgrim Ed. vol. 3, *1842–1843*. Ed. Madeline

House, Graham Storey, and Kathleen Tillotson. Oxford: Clarendon, 1974.

———. *The Letters of Charles Dickens*. Pilgrim Ed. vol. 4, *1844–1846*. Ed. Kathleen Tillotson. Oxford: Clarendon, 1977.

———. *The Letters of Charles Dickens*. Pilgrim Ed. vol. 6, *1850–1852*. Ed. Graham Storey, Kathleen Tillotson, and Nina Burgis. Oxford: Clarendon, 1988.

———. "The Long Voyage." *"Gone Astray,"* 180–90.

———. *Martin Chuzzlewit*. Ed. Patricia Ingham. London: Penguin, 1999.

———. *Nicholas Nickleby*. Ed. Paul Schlicke. Oxford: Oxford UP, 1990.

———. *The Old Curiosity Shop*. Ed. Elizabeth M. Brennan. Oxford: Oxford UP, 2008.

———. "Our French Watering-Place." *"Gone Astray,"* 229–41.

———. *Our Mutual Friend*. Ed. Michael Cotsell. Oxford: Oxford UP, 1989.

———. "Our Watering Place." *"Gone Astray,"* 9–18.

———. "Out of the Season." *"Gone Astray,"* 383–91.

———. "Some Recollections of Mortality." *Uncommercial Traveller*, 218–28.

———. "Travelling Abroad." *Uncommercial Traveller*, 83–96.

———. *The Uncommercial Traveller and Other Papers, 1859–1870*. Ed. Michael Slater and John Drew. London: Dent, 2000.

———. "Wapping Workhouse." *Uncommercial Traveller*, 41–51.

———. *The Wreck. The Wreck of the* Golden Mary. Ed. Melissa Gregory and Melisa Klimaszewski . London: Hesperus, 2006. 3–39.

[Dickens, Charles.] "Marylebone Theatre." *The Examiner* (12 May 1849): 294.

———. "New Year's Day." *Household Words* (1 Jan. 1859): 98–102.

———. "Out of Town." *Household Words* (29 Sept. 1855): 193–96.

Falconer, William. *An Universal Dictionary of the Marine....* New corr. ed. London: printed for T. Cadell, 1784. Eighteenth Century Collections Online (CW109378953).

Forster, John. *The Life of Charles Dickens*. Vol. 2. London: Chapman and Hall, 1873.

Gissing, George. *Collected Works of George Gissing on Charles Dickens*. Ed. Simon J. James. Vol. 2. Grayswood, UK: Grayswood, 2004.

Hamilton, C. I. "Naval Hagiography and the Victorian Hero." *The Historical Journal* 23.2 (1980): 381–98.

Hawes, Donald. "Marryat and Dickens: A Personal and Literary Relationship." *Dickens Studies Annual* 2 (1972): 39–68.

Hill, Geoffrey. "'The World's Proportion': Jonson's Dramatic Poetry in *Sejanus* and *Catiline*." *Collected Critical Writings*. Ed. Kenneth Haynes. Oxford: Oxford UP, 2008. 41–57.

Hillis Miller, J. "*Dombey and Son*." *The Dickens Critics*. Ed. George H. Ford and Lauriat Lane Jr. Ithaca: Cornell UP, 1961. 366–73.

Jakobson, Roman. *Language in Literature*. Ed. Krystyna Pomorska and Stephen Rudy. Cambridge: Harvard Belknap, 1987.

Kennedy, G. W. "The Uses of Solitude: Dickens and *Robinson Crusoe*." *Victorian Newsletter* 52 (Fall 1977): 25–29.

Leavis, F. R., and Q. D. Leavis. *Dickens the Novelist*. New Brunswick, NJ: Rutgers UP, 1970.

Macfarlane, Robert. *Original Copy: Plagiarism and Originality in Nineteenth-Century Literature*. Oxford: Oxford UP, 2007.

McLuhan, Marshall. *From Cliché to Archetype*. New York: Viking, 1970.

Moglen, Helene. "Theorizing Fiction/Fictionalizing Theory: The Case of *Dombey and Son*." *Victorian Studies* 35.2 (1992): 159–84.

Monteiro, George. "The Pilot—God Trope in Nineteenth-Century American Texts." *Modern Language Studies* 7.2 (1977): 42–51.

Moynahan, Julian. "Dealings with the Firm of Dombey and Son." *Dickens and the Twentieth Century*. Ed. John Gross and Gabriel Pearson. London: Routledge and Kegan Paul, 1962. 121–31.

O'Connor, Erin. *Raw Material: Producing Pathology in Victorian Culture*. Durham, NC: Duke UP, 2000.

Palmer, William J. "Dickens and Shipwreck." *Dickens Studies Annual* 18 (1989): 39–92.

Peck, John. *Maritime Fiction: Sailors and the Sea in British and American Novels, 1719–1917*. Basingstoke: Palgrave Macmillan, 2001.

Perera, Suvendrini. "Wholesale, Retail and for Exportation: Empire and the Family Business in *Dombey and Son*". *Victorian Studies* 33.4 (1990): 603–20.

Raban, Jonathan, ed. Introduction. *The Oxford Book of the Sea*. Oxford: Oxford UP, 1992. 1–34.

Rendall, Steven. Introduction. *Shipwreck with Spectator: Paradigm of a Metaphor for Existence*. By Hans Blumenberg. Cambridge: MIT P, 1997. 1–5.

Rev. of *Dombey and Son*, by Charles Dickens. *Dickens: The Critical Heritage*. Ed. Philip Collins. London: Routledge and Kegan Paul, 1971. 213.

Ricks, Christopher. *The Force of Poetry*. Oxford: Clarendon, 1984.

Rubery, Matthew. *The Novelty of Newspapers: Victorian Fiction after the Invention of the News*. Oxford: Oxford UP, 2009.

Shakespeare, William. *Hamlet*. Ed. Ann Thompson and Neil Taylor. The Arden Shakespeare. London: Thomson Learning, 2006.

Slater, Michael. *Charles Dickens*. New Haven: Yale UP, 2009.

———. "*The Chimes*: Its Materials, Making, and Public Reception." Diss. University of Oxford, 1965.

Stewart, Garrett. "The Foreign Offices of British Fiction." *MLQ* 61.1 (2000): 181–206.

Tambling, Jeremy. "Death and Modernity in *Dombey and Son*." *Essays in Criticism* 43.4 (1993): 308–29.

Tennyson, Alfred Tennyson, Baron. *The Poems of Tennyson: In Three Volumes*. Ed. Christopher Ricks. 2nd ed. Harlow, UK: Longman, 1987.

———. *Tennyson's Poetry*. Ed. Robert W. Hill, Jr. New York: Norton, 1971.

Thompson, Carl, ed. *Romantic-Era Shipwreck Narratives: An Anthology*. Nottingham: Trent, 2007.

Trotter, David. *Cooking with Mud: The Idea of Mess in Nineteenth-Century Art and Fiction*. Oxford: Oxford UP, 2000.

Waller, Edmund. *The Works of Edmund Waller Esqr. in Verse and Prose....* London: Printed for I. Tonson, 1729. Eighteenth Century Collections Online (CW115263685).

"Wapping Old Stairs." Roud Broadside Index B200307.

Westland, Ella. "Dickens's *Dombey* and the Storied Sea." *Dickens Studies Annual* 35 (2005): 87–108.

Zijderveld, Anton. *On Clichés*. London: Routledge and Kegan Paul, 1979.

Dickens Goes to War: *David Copperfield* at His Majesty's Theatre, 1914

Andrew Maunder

As a powerful symbol of education, culture, and "Englishness," Dickens had a busy time during the First World War. He was available as a cultural icon whose spirit and authority could be invoked for uses beyond the literary. In Britain, very few questioned the mobilization of Dickens in this way; the novelist's worth was self-evident. This was also the view of theater managers up and down the country who, worried about the slump in attendances, rediscovered Dickens's cultural (and commercial) value. This article focuses on a specific instance of how Dickens was put to work in the theatre during the War. In 1914, at His Majesty's Theatre in London's West End, Sir Herbert Beerbohm Tree produced a lavish version of David Copperfield, *adapted by Louis Napoleon Parker. The production was a hit, running for four months. Herbert Tree's star status was part of its appeal, but this version of* David Copperfield *can also be seen as an important piece of wartime propaganda. Dickens's work could be extended to a specific cultural and historical moment and reach out beyond its original boundaries. Thinking about this particular adaptation thus invites us perhaps to consider some of the strategies involved in dealing with the literary legacy of an author and his work.*

I.

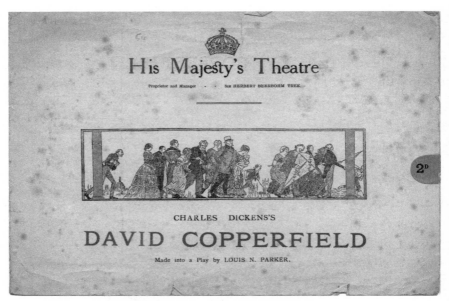

Fig.1. Cover of programme. Reproduced courtesy of Special Collections, Templeman Library, University of Kent, Canterbury.

On 24 December 1914, sixty-five years after *David Copperfield* began its weekly serialization, His Majesty's Theatre in London premiered *The Highway of Life: The Life and Adventures of David Copperfield*, based on Dickens's novel (fig 1.). The production, scripted by pageant-master Louis Napoleon Parker, and starring the theater's manager, Sir Herbert Beerbohm Tree, proved a hit. A major factor contributing to the success was the use of the play to serve patriotic purposes during a time of war. I wish to consider how this particular production achieved its effect. In 1914, many observers felt that the very qualities which gave rise to the term "Dickensian" were what the country was fighting for, and this new production helped encourage this idea.

Herbert Tree had made something of a career playing Dickensian characters, notably Fagin in *Oliver Twist* (1905) and John Jasper in *Edwin Drood* (1908). In 1914, his dual performances as Wilkins Micawber and Dan'l Peggotty confirmed his reputation as a powerful delineator of the novelist's larger-than-life creations. The impact of this *David Copperfield* production was considerable, and even the novelist's surviving family regarded it favorably. According to Kate Perugini: "all the actors and actresses breathe the very spirit of the man whose work although so simple and sympathetic is no doubt extremely difficult to arrange for stage pur- pose." It was unnecessary, she added, to say that the whole thing was done with "love and reverence" (Parker, *My Lives* 254).

In 1914, many observers echoed Perugini in marveling that the translation from page to stage had been achieved so harmoniously, especially since other stage versions of Dickens's novels had tended to fall rather flat. Tree's was obviously not the first version of *David Copperfield*. Philip Bolton has calculated that London had seen at least 138 by 1914 (343). The most recent of these, *Em'ly*, by T. Gideon Warren and Ben Landeck, had opened in 1903 but had closed early, widely dismissed as old-fashioned, with only Rosa Dartle—who came across as reminiscent of one of Henrik Ibsen's deranged heroines—providing much in the way of dramatic or psychological interest. In 1914, Herbert Tree faced the additional worry that even fewer people would come to see the play because of the wartime blackout, together with an accompanying belief that theater-going was inappropriate at a time of national crisis anyway (Wigram 128). In fact, the staging of *David Copperfield* at His Majesty's in the heavily-charged atmosphere of the winter and spring of 1914–15 made more impact than anyone expected. As well as reviving interest in Dickens and making him one of the war's major recovery stories, the production revealed *David Copperfield* to a new and younger audience who had not, so critics suggested, read the novel or indeed any of Dickens's works. These supposedly ignorant theatregoers would have encountered the story as one of His Majesty's Theatre's lavish entertainments and would respond to it against the backdrop of local and national preoccupations. That is, the wartime audience obviously experienced the story in a different context from that enjoyed by readers decades earlier, or those who had seen previous theatrical versions, the Adelphi's *Em'ly*, for example.

This article thus considers the way in which *David Copperfield*, a story which, to quote Mary Poovey, is itself wrapped up in acts of "transformation" (101), was reenvisioned for London audiences of 1914-15. While critics have noted the structural and aesthetic links between Dickens's fiction and the Victorian theater, the extent to which his novels continued to be adapted in the early twentieth century has received little sustained attention. Yet like *The Scarlet Pimpernel, Little Lord Fauntleroy*, and *Peter Pan*, other stage adaptations that became big theatrical successes in the early part of the First World War, at least two productions based on novels by Dickens—*David Copperfield* and *The Only Way* (adapted from *A Tale of Two Cities*)—assumed a cultural currency difficult to ignore. Moreover, as forms of theater, these stage adaptions were surprisingly controversial, forming the basis for heated debates about the wretched state of modern drama, as well as the apparent inability of dramatists to confront the war in any meaningful way.

Something of this latter mood is registered an article appearing in the *Bystander* in December 1914. Here the magazine's theater critic described the familiar fare on offer at London's theaters as "a tragical spectacle." He continued: "We are at war. Therefore there is on the theatre a vast responsibility. The amusement of the depressed population is a patriotic duty." But "[t]he theatre managers' idea of performing their duty is to revive '—,', '—', and, above all, '—'" ("Debacle" 345). Defending himself and his colleagues, Herbert Tree explained that it was "useless to attempt any serious work" because audiences weren't interested (qtd in Wigram 128). Another well-known performer, Julia Neilson, who with her husband, Fred Terry, revived *The Scarlet Pimpernel*, maintained that "playing 'the same old stuff' in some way stood for stability in a world that had suddenly become unstable." She later recalled, "A swing-over would certainly have been disastrous at a time when the nation as a whole was feeling unsettled—one section gone crazy over the 'new' ragtime and revue, another clinging desperately to the old tradition which Fred and I represented" (70–71). For the duration of the war, the actor managers—proud representatives of what Neilson called the "old tradition"—mostly helped keep out new work. Nor, to the chagrin of theater critics, did the public seem to mind. Theater-goers had been sustained for years by managers selling adaptations of popular novels, schooling them in a kind of popular theater criticism that compared novel to play and demanded little more than an appreciation of spectacle, of the "star" actor and his/her impersonation of the novel's chief characters.

The discussion that follows builds upon suggestions made by John Gardiner, Juliet John, and others that we should work to comprehend more fully the cultural legacies and folkloric appeal of Dickens's novels. Although the reach of the stage adaptations of Dickens's works in the novelist's own lifetime is not in doubt, the politics of their redeployment afterwards is still an undeveloped area of investigation. Yet, as David Mayer reminds us in an examination of Edwardian melodrama, this mode of enquiry can be productive. In approaching individual plays we need to consider not only where they were performed, and for whom, but also their cultural relevance, and the ways in which "current social problem[s]" were re-mediated to audiences. Mayer usefully poses a question that is of considerable relevance in understanding these novelistic and wartime recastings: "What was happening in the world outside the theatre, and what understandings of these events were early audiences bringing to performances?" (149; 146).

The remainder of this article follows the implications of these perspectives in relation to the Tree-Parker production of *David Copperfield* at His Majesty's Theatre in December 1914: firstly, by considering the "character" of His Majesty's Theatre and its program; secondly, by looking at how this theater's adaptation of *David Copperfield* might be understood in the context of issues of "stardom," "Englishness," and nationhood as they affected audiences at the time; and, thirdly, by thinking about some of the strategies commonly used to deal with the literary legacy of an author and his work. One of these strategies, to quote Gillian Beer, "is to liberate them, so that they become elements in a discourse and an experience which...they could not have foreseen. Rewriting sustains and disperses, dispels, restores and interrupts" (140). Dickens is a very plastic figure; one can mold him into all kinds of shapes. Accordingly, each generation has projected onto him its own views of what it considers valuable about the work and the history it represents, and has tried to legitimate its own views of history from his characters and plots. In 1914, at the same time as Dickens's favorite novel was being reworked to suit the performance style of Britain's preeminent actor-manager, it was being used as propaganda to prick the consciences of Britons at war and put to use as a national rather than personal autobiography. Before directly considering the wartime uses of Dickesns, however, I wish to examine the nature of both His Majesty's Theatre and the 1914 production of *David Copperfield*.

II. His Majesty's Theatre

His Majesty's Theatre opened in April 1897 in London's West End, on the corner of Charles II Street and Haymarket, surrounded by gentleman's clubs, exclusive shops, and government offices. Herbert Tree (knighted in 1912) part-owned and ran the 1,200-seat theater, assisted by Henry Dana, and sometimes by Maud Tree, Sir Herbert's long-suffering wife, who was also a well-known actor. Making much of its regal name, the theater, designed and decorated in the style of Louis XV, had long been associated with sophisticated and prestigious theatrical events, notably the annual Shakespeare Festival (1905–13) and the company's visit to Berlin in 1907 to perform for Kaiser Wilhelm II, a trip whereby Tree assumed the mantle of unofficial ambassador for British culture. It was common for admirers to speak of His Majesty's as the capital's "nexus of intellectual and social life," as Julia Neilson put it (50), and attendance at this theater was a "thrill" (Macqueen-Pope 31). For actor Cedric Hardwicke, Tree, despite his lisp and inability to remember lines, was "the undisputed leader of the London stage"; his theater, built with profits from the famous adaptation of George du Maurier's *Trilby*, "an Edwardian showplace" (43). Even George Bernard Shaw could not help but feel that entering His Majesty's "[y]ou feel that you are in a place where high scenes are to be enacted and dignified things are to be done" (116). Although in 1897 Edward, Prince of Wales, had been annoyed to see that Tree had had the cheek to dress the theater's powdered footmen in nearly identical livery to that worn by their counterparts at Buckingham Palace, such unofficial royal touches were part of the experience and proved "good for trade" as Shaw noted (*Our Theatres* 117). William Bridges Adams likewise recalled the "grand scale" on which the theater operated:

> The foyer was stately, the spring and curve of the tiers were purest theatre, and the proscenium they held in their embrace was full of promise: promise of wonders to be revealed when the great red and gold curtains parted and went hurtling upwards. . . . [Tree's] audience, once they had paid, were encouraged to feel they were his guests. When he took his curtain call he would survey them with his great, pale eyes and say a few words that seldom lacked pungency and wit. (379–81)

An oration by the poet laureate, Alfred Austin, delivered by Maud Tree on the theater's opening night, asserted its artistic purpose: to ensure that the weary theater-goer, "[l]leaving life's load of dullness at the door," might "come to dwell in Fairyland once more." According to a reviewer, Lady Tree went on to pledge a "magical medley": "Kings upon their throne/And Queens, though never one to match our own," together with exciting plays—"Bewildered innocence, taxed with very crime/And heroes entering in the nick of time" ("Mr Tree's New Theatre" 13). Although there was some overlap among the repertoires of His Majesty's and other West End theaters, the taste of affordable luxury offered to patrons made the theater distinctive, while what was shown or not shown represented a clearly-defined artistic policy catering to particular social and political assumptions. Drawing on Theodor Adorno's concept of the "culture industry," David Schultz has described the building as a "monument to the actor-manager who built it" but notes, too, that it was also "a monument to the fusion of conspicuous consumption and the prestige of the ruling bloc, the Society audience and taste-makers, for whom Tree and his brother managers posed as gentlemen-hosts" (231). In this sense, His Majesty's served a kind of civilizing function, as well as buttressing Tree as star performer and national treasure.

By 1914 Tree had was regarded as the country's leading actor-manager. He had cemented this reputation with a series of lavish productions which he cleverly masterminded and generally starred in. Great claims were made, in particular, for the theater's Shakespeare productions, notable for their heavily cut texts and splendid scenery, music, and costumes. The stagings proved very popular, and the idea that audiences attended His Majesty's as much to watch the past come alive as to listen was regularly commented on. Desmond MacCarthy recalled how in *Antony and Cleopatra* the transformation scene featured an enormous replica of the Sphinx: "This tableau was greeted, I remember, with louder applause than any part of the play" (*Theatre* 51). In 1906, an Italian visitor, Mario Borsa, likewise noted how the visual gimmicks—horses and wolfhounds in *Richard II*, singing and dancing in *Henry VIII*, hundreds of extras in the battle scenes in *King John*—sent audiences into "raptures" (187–88). So, too, did the deafening recreations of thunder and lightning, which Tree famously claimed were more convincing than the real thing (Blow 133). Other ultra-realistic revivals included *A Midsummer Night's Dream* (1900; live rabbits in the forest), *Much Ado About Nothing* (1905: tweeting mechanical birds), *The Merchant of Venice* (1908; gondolas); *Macbeth* (1911; flying witches). When Owen Nares, the matinee-idol who, in 1914, played the eponymous hero in *David Copperfield*, suggested that His Majesty's stage invariably "resembled one of the larger railway termini on Saturday night," he, too, was playing on Tree's reputation for filling the stage with as many bodies and buildings as possible (*Myself* 152).

An accompanying belief that West End audiences liked sensational theatre also played a large part in determining the contents of His Majesty's program. The Alfred Austin poem (cited above) is insistent that world-weary theater-goers come for "romance" and escapism: "With life ill-pleased you come not here to see/Man as he is, but as you'd have him be,/Tender yet strong, at Infamy aghast,/

And woman fond and faithful to the last" ("Mr Tree's New Theatre" 13). Thus Mario Borsa was struck by the rapidity with which "Tree, after a series of performances of *Julius Caesar . . .* don[ned] the doublet of D'Artagnan in a grotesque adaptation of the *Three Musketeers*." Borsa was puzzled by this shuttling backwards and forwards between the classical repertory and lurid melodrama but then realized that "[a]ctors of every country keep their eye on the main chance—it is only fair" (10-11). When quizzed about this, Tree's response was to retreat into a sort of defiant popularism. In 1917, William Courtney pointed out that as owner-manager having to fill "the vast auditorium of His Majesty's" Tree was "bound to consider the tastes not of sections, but of the public at large." Moreover,

> He always insisted on this fact. "I have to find something which will be agreeable to stalls, upper circle, pit, gallery—all at once." And directly we think of the many-headed public who keep theatres going, and the difficulty there is in finding a common focus for their ardent, unsophisticated enthusiasm and their uncritical approval, we shall begin to recognize the burden laid on theatrical *entrepreneurs*, and the necessary contrast between their point of view and that of irresponsible dramatic critics. (264–65)

Whether Tree was possessed of a gift for taking the public temperature or not, this awareness of audience, based largely on commercial lines, needs to be acknowledged when examining individual productions such as *David Copperfield* or His Majesty's productions more generally.

Critical reaction to Tree's work was always mixed. In the years running up to the outbreak of the Great War, critical encomia were still heaped upon the productions but there was some resistance to the Beerbohm Tree dominance. There was a growing feeling that he was less of an "artist" than a showman. "The scenery at His Majesty's is sometimes charming" noted Desmond MacCarthy, " but as everyone has been saying for years, amazing as the scenic effects often are, Shakespeare on that stage is smothered in scenery" (*Theatre* 51). For Tree's younger rival, Harley Granville Barker, the older man had become a mere "production manager" whose talent seemed to involve moving gorgeously costumed actors and elaborate props round the stage in a series of "complicated traffic control systems" (Salmon 107). Although some plays at His Majesty's had their origins in the so-called "New Drama"—notably 1912's *Pygmalion*—they were a long way from the works put on by the avant garde stage societies working outside the star system. Nor was there much sense of social or artistic reclamation of the kind being pushed through by William Poel for the Elizabeth Stage Society (1894–1905) or Granville Barker at the Court (1904–07), which tended to privilege the spoken word over grand spectacle and went in for minimalist set dressing. In contrast, everything about productions at His Majesty's remained impressively big, including the attendance figures: 127,000 saw *King John*; 220,000, *A Midsummer Night's Dream*; and 242,000 *Julius Caesar* (H. B. Tree 46). By August 1914 Tree still stood at the head of his profession but was suspicious, even paranoid, about other managers, believing that Barker's revolutionary season at the Savoy (1912–14) was "an attempt to seize the Shakespeare machine" (qtd. in Pearson 159). Tree, by now a pronouncing, somewhat self-important figure, who counted the Prime Minister, Herbert Asquith, among his friends, spoke angrily of those "who are naturally jealous of the national work I have done" (qtd. in Pearson 159). He was clearly not quite ready to step aside. This was despite the fact that the world was starting to have less use for him.

Receiving its London premiere on 24 December 1914, Louis Parker's adaptation of *David Copperfield* thus appeared at a theater that followed a clearly defined commercial and artistic strategy. Its world view was a melodramatic one in which virtue tended to triumph over evil. Plays were "improved" during rehearsal by Tree via a process of what Basil Dean, one of Tree's assistants, described as "'bespoke' playwriting [which] called for several fittings before the Chief was satisfied with his part" (105,110). Finished scripts accommodated Tree's old-fashioned acting style (slow delivery; rhetorical "points"; stage business); and his star status was assumed. The theatre relied on work from a range of playwrights— modern "names" like Shaw, Henry Arthur Jones, Sydney Grundy, and Stephen Phillips, as well as Shakespeare, but plays "founded upon . . . book[s]" as Tree put it, were also popular, being "freely adapted" by "play carpenters" including James Comyns Carr and Louis Parker (qtd. in Dean 110). The 1913–14 season discussed here included: Parker's *David Copperfield*; James Fagan's *The Happy Island*; revivals of *Julius Caesar* and *Henry IV Part 1*; Parker's Biblical epic *Joseph and His Brethren*, complete with live camel; Sheridan's *The School for Scandal*; David Belasco and John Luther's *The Darling of the Gods*; Shaw's *Pygmalion*; Parker's nautical drama *Drake*; and Pierre Frondaie's marital melodrama *The Right to Kill*. The plays often have a historical and/or foreign setting giving obvious scope for spectacular sets and exotic costumes; they invariably depict a range of sensational incidents—murder, seduction, adultery, suicide, forgery. Although not necessarily nostalgic, they address an audience that might pride itself on its sense of "Englishness" and "fair play," and might be supposed to sympathize with (or be susceptible to) the heroism of the swashbuckling hero in *Drake* or the distress of the young woman driven to suicide after a sexual assault in the Japanese-set *The Darling of the Gods* As Alfred Austin had promised in 1897, there is no sense of outright didacticism, but the content is designed to satisfy the audience's wish for moral imperatives, while the tone is constructed to "console" and "keep man's faith in nobleness alive" ("Mr Tree's New Theatre," 13). These plays are generally supportive of the middle classes, and assumptions about the important of family, loyalty, honor, and country are upheld.

III. *David Copperfield* at His Majesty's, 1914–15

Recently, the role of theater in London during the First World War has become the subject of some overdue critical attention. L. J. Collins has argued that "[t] heatre was much more than a diversionary and escapist tactic employed to provide temporary relief...the theatre was employed as a recruiting and propaganda agent, and raiser of funds" (3). This impulse was often represented by plays that showed ordinary people in realistic contemporary settings displaying extraordinary courage in confronting wartime challenges of life and death. In such popular plays as J. E. Harold Terry and Lechmere Worrall's *The Man Who Stayed at Home* (1914), Edmund Goulding's *God Save the King* (1914), and Leslie Stiles's *The Day* (1914) seemingly average men and women became the morally elevated heroes and heroines of wartime, willing to die for their country. Jane Potter has likewise pointed out that "the majority of authors, critics and dramatists reinforced beliefs in the righteousness of the cause." Their "vehicles of entertainment are inextricably linked to ideological motivations," while "the 'normalcy' they encourage is based on national and imperial imperatives" (118–19). As will be seen, one way in which this manifested itself was in the extent to which the British home was presented as facing new dangers, in which family life and spiritual values were consistently under threat. Spies and traitors feature as characters in many domestic dramas. And in their portrayals of seemingly average men and women outwitting them, playwrights suggested how the conflict might be won through pluck, selflessness, intelligence, and a strong community spirit.

Alongside the wartime thrillers and espionage dramas that dominated London's West End, a host of well-established older plays were also seen to offer a powerful antidote to feelings of despair or a lack of patriotic feeling. Seeing John Martin Harvey as Sydney Carton in the 1899 *Tale of Two Cities* adaptation *The Only Way* was still a psychologically powerful experience. As has been noted, Fred Terry as Sir Percy Blakeney and Julia Neilson in *Sweet Nell of Old Drury* (1900) also enjoyed enormous wartime success, the former famously carrying on when a bomb dropped outside the Strand Theatre on 13 October 1915 in the middle of Act 2 of *The Scarlet Pimpernel* (Steen 316). Also popular were Arthur Conan Doyle's celebration of the ordinary soldier in *Waterloo* (1895) and Lieutenant Colonel W. P. Drury and Major Leo Trevor's drama of military derring-do *The Flag Lieutenant* (1908).

The Lord Chamberlain's files indicate that *The Highway of Life, Being the Personal History of David Copperfield* was submitted for licensing and censorship on 27 July 1914, the intention being for it to open the autumn season at His Majesty's on 1 September. Judged by the censor to be "wholly void of offence," the performance license was awarded on 30 July. Yet when Britain declared war on 4 August the play was postponed in favor of a revival of Louis Parker's historical drama *Drake*, with Tree somewhat incongruous in the title role. The new Dickens adaptation seemed destined to be shelved. However, the next production at His Majesty's, a revival of *Henry IV, Part 1*, drew low audiences. Phyllis Monkman's performance of the "Pom-Pom Dance" in the revue *Everything New? Not Likely* at the Alhambra Theatre was much more popular than Tree's rehashing of Falstaff. Tree, whose imperialistic loyalties deepened during the war, and who was energetic in making recruiting speeches, could not quite believe "that even the splendid heroics of Hotspur and the philosophy of Falstaff are not so appealing at the moment." It was in this unpromising environment, together with the approach of Christmas, that Tree thought of *David Copperfield* again. "Dickens," he told an interviewer, "is still a power in the land and I believe I am right in saying that his works have had a greater sale than those of any author." By now events in Europe were moving fast and horribly enough to make people wonder whether they should go to the theater at all. The reports were impossible to ignore but Tree promised "to get away from the war and to turn to more pleasant topics" ("Sir Herbert Tree" 108).

Tree, therefore, would be the man to provide the public with a much-needed counterbalance to the current dehumanizing drift. In producing *David Copperfield* he would try to "transport" patrons into a charming Victorian fairyland of the "fifties." Tree then explained the new play in the following terms:

> The play begins in the garden of Betsey Trotwood at Canterbury, and it ends in the same scene. In Act I we have the introduction of Steerforth, the boathouse at Yarmouth, and we make the acquaintance of Mr Micawber and see him bravely trying the underdone mutton at Copperfield's lodgings. Then, amongst other things, we have the introduction of Agnes and her love affair, the incident of Uriah Heep, the pathetic romance and elopement of little Em'ly and Micawber's departure for Australia. There is the shipwreck in which we shall have a very effective storm scene and the death of Steerforth. And we have a happy ending. ("Sir Herbert Tree" 108)

Tree's précis suggests the play's convergence of interests—a kind of fusion of the Edwardian theater's continuing love for both melodrama, what J. C. Trewin calls "unrepentant make-believe" (3), and the supposed, comfortable familiarity of a much-loved literary classic, the locations of which Tree would, as usual, try to recreate.

The strategy worked. Reviews were mostly fulsome. John F. McDonald hailed the production as a turning point in the fortunes of wartime theater. It had allowed a depressed population to shake off the "dark consuming shadows" which had seemed to encircle them for the first months of the conflict (352). Yet not everyone liked it. For John Savoy, the play was disjointed: "a series of snapshots of a number of comic and serious episodes of the immortal story" (qtd. in Colby 146). On one level, there is nothing unusual here; the stage adaptor's task had always been to make pictures—or pictorial effects—out of words. But, on another level, Savoy's comments suggest "dumbing down." Dickens was getting the same kind of treatment that Shakespeare had received at Tree's hands. The high-culture *Athenaeum* was even more lukewarm, suggesting how "[t]he impression left is really more that of the best kinematograph . . . than of a play" (13). The *Times*, meanwhile, detected traces of an even lower art form, while also wondering what the theater-goers who flocked to His Majesty's ignorant of the novel made of it all: "Presumably they took it for a variety entertainment, with 'turns' by a comic patter gentleman with an egg-shaped head, another with a big kite, and a third who informed of a wreck outside, fell to shouting 'Ahoy, ahoy' presumably as an incantation" ("Christmas Plays" 9). It seemed to be a case of sacrificing the novel to the needs of the theater company, or at least to those of its manager, recalling for some Mr. Crummles's valuable pump and washing tub in *Nicholas Nickleby*.

Fig. 2. Permission courtesy of University of Bristol Theatre Collection / ArenaPAL

The most obvious significance of this *David Copperfield* adaptation, therefore, lies in the ways in which the story was redesigned to fit the production style of His Majesty's Theatre. As has been noted, a performance at His Majesty's was as much a pictorial as an aural experience, a conscious aesthetic strategy adapted to differentiate Tree's product from those of other theater managers. This was a three-act play, but there were twelve scene changes. These included the dining-room of the Golden Cross, a schoolroom, Peggotty's boathouse (fig. 2), and Betsey Trotwood's garden with a view across to the white cliffs of Dover (a garden filled with chestnuts, lilacs, and other flowers, all out of season). All the sets garnered the ovation Tree had come to expect. The stage was also typically crowded. While several characters are missing—notably Barkis, Rosa Dartle and the Murdstones—the play boasted a speaking cast of twenty-seven, plus extras ("fisher folk," "emmigrants").

The play's structural changes are equally striking. As in Dickens's novel, David appears in every scene, and part of the focus is still on what Rod Mengham has called his search for a "civic identity" (62). However, there is no attempt to reproduce the novel's first-person narrative or the psychological complexity that accompanies it. "No words can express the secret agony of my soul," writes the orphaned David in the novel (137; ch. 11). In contrast, when the play opens, David is already an adult. Little is made of the psychic damage brought about by his traumatic childhood—the beatings; his mother's willingness to sacrifice him—or its role in forming him. On stage, David's only striking psychological quirk is his dual love for Agnes and for Dora, who is never seen, although Jip, played by a real spaniel,

Fig. 3. Permission courtesy of University of Bristol Theatre Collection / ArenaPAL

is. Owen Nares, who played David, claimed in a 1915 interview that this quirk did not translate at all to the stage because it was "incomprehensible" to "modern minds." As he noted: "Heroes nowadays, although they may be burglars and assassins, must love only once. In novels, perhaps, a hero may have a mental and physical complement, but the simple David's division of affection does little more than puzzle the onlooker of 1915" ("David Copperfield" 73). In addition to questioning David's emotional reality, Nares found the hero's role in the play dull. On stage (Fig. 3) his function is to listen and react to other showier characters, alongside whom he comes across, so Nares felt, as a bit of a "prig." Nares, a matinee idol exempt from military service on the grounds of a weak heart, finally decided that the character would be most relevant to modern audiences if played as "the beau-ideal of the British hero," albeit old-fashioned in outlook: "I think of him as a flaming idealist, and doubtless he represented the clean-bred English boy and man of his era" ("*David Copperfield.* Reviews"72, 73)

Herbert Tree's approach to his roles exhibited no such agonizing. In 1914, the chance to play two Dickens's characters in the same production was the moment he had been waiting for. There are enough comments from those who saw Tree in the early 1900s to suggest that to be on the receiving end of one of his performances was to be struck not by booming actorly magnificence but by admiration for his skills in disguise. As surviving reports and photographs show (fig.4) he put these to good use in *David Copperfield.* Yet it also seems that Tree the actor thrilled to Micawber's egotism and dramatic vigor and to the character's unstoppable flow, which allowed him to dominate every scene. Micawber, as written by Louis Parker, is as uproarious and untethered as Dickens's original, but Tree, as his critics noted he was liable to do, made him into a clown. During the celebrated scene where David gives his first dinner party in his lodgings at Mrs. Crump's house in Buckingham Street, Tree's Micawber gets tipsy on punch. He then plays the spoons to accompany Mrs. Micawber's singing of "The Dashing White Sergeant" and falls off his chair. In many respects this was a fairly typical Tree performance, "a mixture of cheap effects and gleams of insight," as Desmond MacCarthy put it (175).[1]

In the final stages of the play, Tree's entrepreneurial nose persuaded him that the shipboard scene in which the Micawbers and Mr. Peggotty's entourage set out for Australia was ripe for some spectacular treatment in which he could indulge his taste for wires and trapdoors:
Scene II:

> *'Tween decks on an emigrant sailing-ship. At the back of the side of the ship, with port-holes and towards the left a large opening for the admission of goods, etc. Through this opening there is a view of Thames with, far away, Tilbury fort. In the centre the main mast, very broad. To the right of the main mast a companion downwards to the emmigrants' quarters.*

> ------------------------- *opening* ---------------

> *Down Companion*   *Up companion*

>   *Mast*

> *(Bales of goods, emigrants' luggage etc., etc., litter the floor. A special pile of luggage in the right corner at back. Also in front of the mast. There is*

a constant going and coming of emigrants, SAILORS, SHIP's OFFICERS, etc. Goods are being hauled in through the opening and carried down the companion C. GROUPS OF EMIGRANT FAMILIES are seated and lying, surrounded by their property.)

. . . (Mrs. MICAWBER comes up the companion, and crosses to the opening at the back. EM'LY comes shyly forward, DAVID crosses to her and silently presses her hand. DAN'L takes her sobbing from DAVID, puts his right arm round her, and leads her very slowly round behind the mast and so down the companion, where AGNES is still waiting, she stops them and tenderly kisses EM'LY.

Then Em'ly and Dan'l slowly disappear.)

(David has watched AGNES – he expresses joy, MRS. MICAWBER steps forward)

MRS. M. My dear Mr Copperfield, I do trust nothing untoward has happened to Mr Micawber!

DAVID. Make your mind easy, ma'am.

Mrs. M. Should anything have happened I must insist on being put ashore, or if that be inconvenient, I will gladly endavour to swim ashore, for I never will—

(MR MICAWBER'S head, very red and flustered appears over the bottom edge of opening at the back, like an angry red sunrise)

David: Look, ma'am.

Mrs. M. (*With a scream*) Wilkins! Are you drowned?

(MICAWBER clambers in. He has provided himself among other things with a complete suit of oilskin, and straw hat with a very low crown, pitched or caulked on the outside. Once on his feet, it is seen that he has acquired a bold, buccaneering air, not absolutely lawless, but defensive and prompt.)

(27, 33)

It wasn't easy to do, but Dan'l Peggotty's exit and Mr. Micawber's swift reappearance was the play's "sensation" scene. When Tree (as Peggotty) passed behind the mast with Em'ly, an extra wearing the same costume took over, completing the exit down the companion. Meanwhile Tree stepped into the ship's mast which doubled as a lift and travelled down under the stage. Tree's dressers stripped off his Peggotty costume. Now, dressed as Micawber, he was hauled upwards in another lift by stagehands and thrust his head through the opening at the back of the stage making audiences gasp. It was an impressive feat, but for Tree's harshest critics it was symptomatic of the actor's reliance on stage technology to cover up deficiencies in his own performance.

While the critical response to Tree's acting was mixed, so, too, was his decision to play two parts. On one hand, the decision was daring; on the other, it was seen as further proof, if any were needed, of the actor's egotism, propped up, as Owen Nares suggested, by "priceless sycophants" who were scared to tell him anything he did not want to hear (*Myself* 156). J. M. Barrie wrote a savage skit of Tree's performance for the revue *Rosy Rapture* (1916), as did the writers for another revue, *The Passing Show of 1915*, all latching onto the peculiar—unrecogniz-able—Norfolk idiom Tree adopted to play the fisherman.[2] But Tree's dual perfor-mances were, nonetheless, part of the production's selling point, an example of the kind of stunt casting whereby, as Michael Quinn has described it, the celebrity actor "displaces authority from the creative genius of the author . . ." (102). Tree as "star" actor-manager became the creator as much as Dickens. As Sydney Blow recalled, Tree "never seemed able to lose himself in a . . . part. It was always Mr Tree pretending" (131). But this was the point. The audience was being invited to admire Tree's skills in acting rather than be convinced that this *was* Micawber and Peggotty in front of them.

Elsewhere, it was said of Tree that he could never resist showing off but was also a lazy actor who relied on bits of "business" to cover up his deficiencies with the script and, where possible, to upstage everyone else. The production of *David Copperfield* was no exception. "I wish," noted the *Illustrated Sporting and Dra-matic News* watching Tree dressed up as Peggotty, "he could cure himself of the habit of being always audible even when he has no words to speak, for at such times by breathing heavily, or by emitting grunts and groans, or other noises from his throat he often distracts attention from what other actors are doing" ("*David Copperfield* at His Majesty's" 516). When news came of Em'ly's disappearance he was observed to "make a noise like the cooing of pigeons as he glares at space" (516). Tree's impulse to dominate caused his detractors to remark that if Tree was any good as Micawber it was because he was only playing a version of himself; the character's "flamboyant grotesqueness" and need for applause were Tree's own ("Things New" 11). Tree was "avid of public acclamation," as Julia Neilson recalled (48-49). He was also, as his manager, Henry Dana noted, "an optimist and an opportunist," again rather like Dickens's grandiose monster (qtd. in Beer-bohm, 106). And like Micawber, there was seen to be something hollow about him. When, after Tree's death in 1916, Maud Tree described her husband's doubling as "a *tour de force* which cost him not one instant's anxiety," noting that "he slipped from one part to the other with amazing lightness and facility," she was fulfill-ing her contract as Tree's devoted widow (qtd. in Beerbohm, 162). Yet associates who read these comments about Tree's malleability gossiped that Maude Tree was really thinking about her husband's double life, the fact that he, like Micawber, was a phony. He was a respectable actor-manager, scion of the establishment, who, for many years, had moved unobserved among his wife and their children in Chis-wick, his mistress Beatrice Pinney and their six children in Putney Hill, and the young female colleagues whom Tree allegedly propositioned in the famous Dome room perched at the top of His Majesty's Theatre (Wapshott, 9; 313).

This picture of Herbert Tree running amok obviously colored some critics' perceptions of *David Copperfield*. But there was also recognition that the stage adaption was not just about Tree's personal life; other processes were at work.

First, the 1914 production of *David Copperfield* celebrated Dickens as England's greatest novelist. Secondly, it celebrated Herbert Tree as the only living actor-manager with the resources to do this novelist justice, thereby accruing cultural capital for himself. Thirdly, it reflected its times albeit in an indirect way, mirroring something of the mood of Britain during the first months of the First World War. It is to these processes that I now want to turn.

IV. Dickens at War

When war finally came on 4 August 1914, triggered by the assassination of Archduke Franz Ferdinand, heir to the throne of the Austro-Hungarian Empire, that forced all the alliance systems into play, and Britain was gripped by what observers called "war fever." "[T]he whole nation", as Raymond Radclyffe recalled in 1916, jumped into "a white heat of enthusiasm. . . . Rich people discharged their men-servants, and tramped round gasworks with a badge on their arm and a flask in their pocket." Nor was it only the upper classes thus affected. As Radclyffe noted, "The patriotism of the poor was pathetic. They crowded the enlistment offices and a citizen army of a million men was soon enrolled" (199). Many commentators liked to evoke a sense of the country working together in the interests of a great national enterprise (whether this was true or not). What is also striking is the way in which, as soon as war broke out, Dickens was identified as someone who would help the nation. He would help the country find some backbone, as well as providing comfort. He was "the fire at which one can warm oneself," as Robert Lynd suggested in the *New Statesman* in November 1914 (137–38). There was a general feeling that Victorian England and its core values, especially as Dickens portrayed them through his characters, were a "Heritage" and a "History" capable of inspiring any decent-minded Britons to do their bit—even the hardened young person who spent his or her time listening to "ragtime" and lolling about in nightclubs.

Unsurprisingly, the Dickens Fellowship (established in 1905) was much to the fore in encouraging this idea, and much of its work during the war had to do with suggesting the novelist's continuing relevance. For example, for Walter Crotch, the Fellowship's president, it was foremost a matter of spirit:

Out there in the fields of Flanders and of France these men are shedding their blood in an heroic effort to vindicate the principles for which Dickens lived—the principles of freedom and unfettered independence for simple men. Junkerism denies and crucifies these things and consequently our master would have said Junkerism must be crushed. And the men who are giving their best of this purpose are emphatically the men of whom Dickens loved to write; whose simplicity he bade us value, whose strength he told us to rely on, whose uncomplaining endurance and selfless sacrifice have alone led this Empire up to greatness and have alone saved it, in this hour of supreme trial and adversity. (184)

Crotch's comments suggest some of the themes that readers thought Dickens expressed at this stage of the conflict. Many of Dickens's characters were deemed inspirational, and in this article Crotch went on to pick out Mark Tapley, Joe Gargery, Dick Swiveller, and Sam Weller as having their equivalents in the massed ranks of Lord Kitchener's volunteers, at the same time as embodying masculine behavior which men of any class would do well to follow. While one wonders how many working-class soldiers Crotch actually met, his attempts to dress them up as cheerful Dickensian archetypes, capable of being "jolly" in the most testing circumstances, are not as unusual as they might appear, especially when read alongside other propagandistic articles in the daily and weekly press.

It was also fairly easy to present Dickens the man as someone who, if alive, would have been actively involved in the war effort. As T. W. Hill noted in 1914, he was famously pugnacious, while also having "a passionate love of peace" (258). In his own lifetime he had also "proved" his patriotism "by placing one son (Walter) into the army and another (Sydney) into the navy" (257). Dickens also hated injustice, and he would thus have "flung himself into the task of raising men and money," unafraid to ask for more, as the *Times* noted on 6 February 1915 (the novelist's birthday): "[H]e would have been here, there and everywhere, reading, acting, speaking and making spare time in which to shoulder a musket himself and drill with a fiery enthusiasm; how he would have denounced the crimes of the Germans in Belgium, and what a trumpet call to the whole world his voice would have been" ("Some Thoughts on Dickens's Birthday" 9). Yet in several senses Dickens *was* still there. His youngest son, Henry, revived his father's practice of dramatized readings in order to raise funds for the Red Cross. Henry's son, Major Cedric Dickens, likewise appeared to be carrying on his grandfather's tradition of public duty until he was killed in action at Ginchy on 9 September 1916, aged twenty-seven. Amidst the mourning there was consolation for the Fellowship "that that great English name went with us into battle; that the blood of a Dickens was part of the victory" ("When Found" 255).

Another wartime project saw Dickens's writings being sent out the Front.[3] Whether the soldiers wanted them or not, there was a belief, loudly articulated by newspaper leader writers, that Dickens's works were eminently suitable for trench life—a life characterized by long hours of tedium and sudden, sporadic bursts of fighting—partly because of 'their cheery and optimistic outlook," as the *Observer* told readers in December 1915, "and also by reason of the fact that they can be picked up at any odd moment with the certainty of always being found entertaining" ("Dickens and Our Wounded Soldiers" 21). There were even suggestions that the Germans—the Nietzschean supermen—could be bested by flooding their country with copies of *A Christmas Carol*, thus letting Tiny Tim loose on the hearts and minds of the "Hun" ("Dickens v Nietzsche" 5).

This version of Dickens, or at least the bits of him which were taken to represent the whole, forms an important part of the backdrop for *David Copperfield* as shown at His Majesty's in the 1914-15 season. It is most obvious in the visual inflection of the production, itself an offshoot of Herbert Tree's own much-vaunted role as an interpreter of "History." Claiming to be almost a social document—an accurate representation of life as it once was—*David Copperfield* offered its audience a mythic version of Victorian England. This was a period that was nothing if not pretty: a riot of quaint cottages and eccentric buildings, flower-filled gardens, mullioned windows, with the theater orchestra playing (anachronistically) tunes by Edward Elgar ("Carissima"), Arthur Sullivan ("Storm Music from The Tempest"), Percy Fletcher ("Woodland Pictures"), and Sir Alexander Mackenzie ("Cricket on the Hearth")[4] as a soundtrack to the action. In an obvious sense, the production served as a form of propaganda. It employed ready-made symbols that were able to evoke powerful emotions about home and heritage at a time when war was forcing the country to confront the horrors of slaughter on the Western Front. Even the skeptical Owen Nares wrote of the play as "breathing the fine spirit of England" and felt that his own portrayal of David might help imprint on the young men of England a construction of masculinity which could constitute a summons to war, a Mark Tapley for the middle-classes to follow ("*David Copperfield*. Reviews" 160).

It is this kind of kind of missionary self-consciousness that makes the *David Copperfield* production worth a second look. It was fairly obvious that the onstage Dickens world was not the world of 1914—this was part of its appeal after all.

Fig. 4. Permission courtesy of University of Bristol Theatre Collection / ArenaPAL

The play absorbed the audience into its own world, rather than focusing directly on problems of the immediate wartime situation. But during the play's run, audiences must have needed to make a positive effort to avoid thoughts of the war when watching it, not just because the war was all-encompassing ("most people . . . can think of nothing else" noted the *Era* in 1914 ("War Plays and the Public" 9), but because the play's plot and characters were being overtaken by events— events that were not envisaged when novel and play were first conceived.

Tree never insisted on the play's extraneous meanings—although he did suggest its social relevance. But beneath its plots of seduction, betrayal, and the compromised morality of some of its characters (Steerforth, Heep) can be glimpsed something of the fears and anxieties of 1914. The adaptation registers something of the country's mood. For example, following the Dickens Fellowship, Herbert Tree was quick to stress the significance of Dickens's characters to the war effort: "We all know Micawber today. Every family has one. Even the theatrical manager must have something of the resilient fibre of the Micawber in the hope that something may turn up to his advantage" ("Sir Herbert Tree on his next production" 108). When Mrs. Gummidge tells Dan'l Peggotty, "I knows your sorrows and can be a comfort to you, and labour for you allus," (Parker, *Highway* 31) she speaks for all women who in real life were being asked to draw on extra reserves of strength. Equally, it is not too farfetched to think that audiences facing depressingly high casualty lists in the wake of the fighting at Ypres in October and November 1914 would have been attuned to the ways in which Little Em'ly's letter, read aloud after her elopement, turns her into a kind of spokesperson for all those who are missing: "I shall be far away. . . ."; "When I leave my dear home— my dear home—Oh my dear home!—it will be never to come back . . . . Try to think of it as if I died . . . and was buried somewhere" (Parker, *Highway* 39). These flickers of sentimentality were clear signals of the direction in which Tree was moving; tears, pathos, striking attitudes, and villainy had always attracted him, but wartime audiences were especially susceptible to these elements as well.

While *David Copperfield* offers nostalgia it also, of course, shows a world unsettled, or, as Mr. Dick suggests in the play's opening scene, is "mad. Mad as Bedlam." (Parker, *Highway* 2). Lives are thrown upside down, families are broken up, people disappear, friendships are betrayed, and homes are lost. Commentators at the time spoke of the conflict as "nothing less than an onslaught on civilization" ("The Task of the Allies" 256), a view that owed something to the sense of shock prompted by modern technology of machine guns, tanks, and airplanes. But there was also a sense, as Jay Winter points out, that this was "the last nineteenth-century war," and the strategic response was slow to change (178). In 1914 there would have been no prizes for recognizing Steerforth's class narcissism and betrayal as diametrically opposed to the masculine code of honor, stoicism and self-control needed to win the war. Notions of doing one's duty, playing fair, self-sacrifice, and communal feeling extending to social inferiors and the vulnerable were still much to the fore. None of these qualities distinguish

Steerforth's career, of course. By contrast, Ham Peggotty is the kind of ordinary working-class man celebrated by Walter Crotch and other Dickensians: incorruptible, physically brave, maintaining his integrity in the face of provocation.

This idea that the production scattered a series of metaphors for a country in crisis, that it had an "edge" to it underneath its prettiness, is also apparent in the play's other plot line. Characters are up against Uriah Heep. He, like Germany, is a rapacious enemy, whose motives are acquisitive and one who has been waiting a long time to put his plans into action. "Must teach 'em umbleness, Mister Copperfield. I am 'umble still," Heep tells David. "I hope I never shall be otherwise" (Parker, *Highway* 28). But, he continues, "there's one thing you forgot. Power! When I was quite a young boy, I got to know what 'umbleness did, and I took to it. I ate 'umble pie with an appetite. I am very 'umble to the present moment, Mister Copperfield, and thereby I've got Mr Wickfield under my thumb! Un-der-my-thumb!" (*URIAH puts his face to DAVID'S with an exultant leer*) (Parker, *Highway* 30). As in the novel, David's encounters with Uriah always contain an element of the physical. Here he "*[s]trikes URIAH across the face with his open hand.*" In response, Uriah "*catches*" David's hand "*and holds it in a fierce grip. So they stand facing each other.*" The curtain then falls (Parker, *Highway* 30). It was this fighting between good and evil that theater-goers were thought to want to see; melodrama with its simple dichotomies and eventual reassurances was just the genre for wartime. The audience of 1914–15 could recognize what needed to be defended—England's homes and its women—and the acceptable national identities that would enable this to happen. A case in point is Act 2, Scene 2, which opens with a clandestine meeting between David and Agnes in Canterbury:

Mr Wickfield's garden immediately under Canterbury Cathedral....The Cathedral towers up out of sight in the background. . . . The garden is closed in from the lane by a high red brick wall:

Canterbury Cathedral

	Lane	
		Door
Office Door	*Arbour of roses*	
Window		
House	*Sundial*	*Trees and shrubs*
Door		
	chair seat	
	table	

It is a lovely evening. The Cathedral catches the sunset, which during the scene fades upwards. Then the moon rises behind the Cathedral, is seen for a very short time and disappears behind the trees on the right. The Cathedral gleams white and ghostlike. The ORGANIST is playing and the stained glass windows are feebly lighted from within. Presently the blind of the office window is pulled down by URIAH, the office is brightly lit up...and now and again the shadows of MICAWBER and HEEP are seen on the blind. The curtains of the house windows are drawn and only a comfortable red glow shines through them. Every now and again a nightingale is heard, very very softly. And chimes . . . From the left enter DAVID COPPERFIELD and AGNES in close conversation.

AGNES: Speak quietly. Mrs. Heep may be listening. . . . She watches and listens all day long.

. . . MRS HEEP enters by the garden gate and hovers in the rose-arbour working towards the office door. . . . MRS HEEP nearly reaches the office door intently listening all the time, when an ill-judged movement attracts AGNES'S attention. She lays her hand on DAVID'S arm and points to MRS HEEP. . . . MRS. HEEP sniffs prodigiously and goes into the offices, where her shadow is seen on the blind excitedly pointing to the garden.

(21–25)

Several of the critics of 1914 responded strongly to the staging of this scene, some of them admitting being bowled over by its "serenity and grandeur," to quote the *Illustrated Sporting and Dramatic News* ("*David Copperfield* at His Majesty's" 516). The cathedral belongs, of course, to England and her long history, although the associations seem designed to rub off onto Dickens and Tree as well; they too have contributed to England's ongoing story. Yet Tree does not lose the dynamics of the novel altogether. The scene builds on relationships present in the text. The nightingale's chirps point to Agnes and David's undeclared love for one another at the same time as being a lament for a world now lost. Most obviously the scene points to Agnes's powerlessness at the hands of the Heeps. A sense of menace (helped by the stage lighting) hovers over the house. There is constant shadowing and surveillance. Agnes—young, loyal, and long-suffering—is watched and spied upon, her every move monitored. She is never alone.

If these are the experiences of Dickens's heroine, they were also those of the population of 1914–1915. If His Majesty's Theatre's audience had not experienced it themselves, they only had to pick up a newspaper to know Britain was being observed by a vast network of secret agents. Michael Macdonagh, a journalist for the *Times*, commented on the "spy peril" in his diary on 11 August 1914, noting how "London is said to be full of German spies" (15). Thousands of enemy aliens were lurking and listening everywhere: chauffeurs, hospital nurses, nannies, hairdressers, travelling salesmen, and waiters were all secretly recording and reporting back to their superiors in Berlin, sometimes using carrier pigeons.

The belief that all resident aliens had residual sympathies with the country of their birth and were acting as "the Kaiser's Eyes," as the *Daily Express* put it, was widespread and encouraged by large sections of the media ("How German Spies Work" 3). The *Daily Mail* reported how a "fully armed" convoy of "Motor Cycle Spies" had attacked a signalman at the quiet railway station at Chenies in Buckinghamshire (qtd. in Boghardt 74). On 18 November, Lord Curzon announced in the House of Lords that it was still the case that Britain was under siege from "a scheme of spymongering, in this country, conceived with ability and secrecy . . . and on a scale which . . . would startle every one of their lordships if they knew its ramifications" ("Parliament" 12). Bombs were found in the trunks of a German governess. In London, a woman travelling in a tram noted four Voluntary Aid Detachment (VAD) nurses behaving suspiciously and deciding that they were really German men, reported them to the police who arrested them. The fact that by December 1914 up to 400 people a day were still offering information on suspicious-looking foreigners to the London police suggests that the version of *David Copperfield* offered at His Majesty's was also tapping into a distinct line on Britain's defense at the same time as exploiting collective paranoia.

The reports on the "spy menace" show one element of the different fears and ideas that were being aired during the early stages of war, and also reveal the ways in which a play like *David Copperfield*, far from being a closed text, *could* be linked to diverse national issues. Yet this was not the only play addressing this theme. On stage at His Majesty's Theatre, David and Agnes were just two of a large number of characters forced to draw on reserves of strength to defend long-held and cherished British values. *Henry IV, Part I* which played just prior to *David Copperfield*, and which Owen Nares, who played Prince Hal, remembered chiefly for its "constant shouting, fighting and wearing of ill-fitting armour" (*Myself* 159) was taken by some politicizers as "a veritable call to youth to arms" ("Henry IV" *Stage*, 8). The *Era* wrote of it as a production which "voices the national spirit of the times, and makes its appeal to chivalry and patriotism" ("Henry IV," *Era* 5). For the *Standard* the revival was an "'allegory' of the change that has come over our own 'slackers' of today" ("Henry IV," *Standard* 6). A similar process was at work in *The Right to Kill*, which played immediately after *David Copperfield*, in which a worthy French officer (played by Tree) debates meting out rough justice on behalf of an abused Englishwoman. All can be said to have worked in a broadly similar way, attaching the theater and its management to the wider national wartime project.

These processes are also at work in Louis Parker's *Drake*—a play that critics noted His Majesty's Theatre inflicted ad nauseum on its patrons and that, as has been noted, was used to open the 1914 autumn season. The play, which had a speaking cast of forty-eight, encourages a similar sense of resolve, this time imparted by the eponymous hero (Tree again), the soldier, explorer, colonizer whose only resources for combating King Philip II of Spain's invasion fleet in 1588 are the Englishmen who serve in the country's navy. Drake/Tree makes this clear in a speech to the lily-livered politician Lord Burleigh on the eve of the Armada:

> Drake: [*Beginning quietly*] My Lord, do you thank God for your enemy's strength? Do you thank God that England must ever pipe the tune he calls? How long do you think England will hold, if she be as weak as you thank God for? Phillip has swallowed the Netherlands; anon, he may swallow France. Then England will be but a mouthful and cold-blooded Alva Stattholder of a Spanish province called Inglaterra! Shall we thank God for that? No, my Lord! But I thank God for stout oaks to build new ships with, for stout hearts to man them, and a stout will to teach Philip manners. The day shall come, my Lord, by heaven the day shall come!

                                                                         (14)

If, as Jim Davis has suggested, we accept the idea that melodrama—and both His Majesty's versions of *Drake* and *David Copperfield* fall into this category— "reflects a way of seeing specific to the age that fostered it" and that it "functions historically as a means of revealing ideological values common to particular communities" (369), then attempting to understand the thinking behind His Majesty's version of *David Copperfield* also means paying some attention to the time and place in which it was performed. One way of coming to terms with the play's moral and ideological stances is to try and understand how its first audience, the West End audience of His Majesty's Theatre (1914–15) would have viewed it. This audience, who, if we believe the press commentary, would not necessarily have read the original novel, encountered the play and its put-upon characters juxtaposed with other texts and subject to other national influences, including personal experience, which would have played a part in determining the response to the play. News—and gossip—whether reported by word of mouth or in print— together with other familiar plays worked intertextually to provide a kind of running commentary on the adaptation of Dickens's novel, with some of the audience able to fill in the gaps and complete what Peter Bailey has termed the "circuits of meaning" that run through any entertainment (138).

  It is for these reasons that back on stage at His Majesty's, as we move from the familiar generic elements of the play—the seduction of the working-class woman, the loss of home, the theft of property by a trusted employee, the daughter's sacrifice—other kinds of readings become possible. Like *Drake*, *David Copperfield* appealed partly to an idea of the national character, what David Lowenthal has termed "malleable steadiness," an "English virtue of an ever-evolving, never broken palimpsest" stretching through the centuries of the kingdom's history (185). It also helped conjure up a sense of powerful national history in which a national past is given voice in and enriches the present day. "[A]ll we can do just now is to keep a cheerful countenance," David counsels at one point, paraphrasing the message of both the British government and of many plays and revues of 1914–15 (Parker, *Highway* 7): keeping calm and carrying on were what was needed. Even Micawber's emigration scene, cited above, reinforces a patriotic theme, emphasizing Britain's links with her empire, embodying some of the aspirations of New Imperialism, and emphasizing new beginnings in the "land of the free" at the same time as it shows the "traitor" Uriah Heep being forcibly ejected (34).

The idea that something better will turn up is also borne out by the play's final scene which returns the audience comfortingly to where the action started: Betsey Trotwood's idyllic cottage. The characters exhibit reassuringly familiar manner-isms: Betsey is still chasing after donkeys, and Mr. Dick still flies his kite. After many months away, David has returned from overseas and becomes engaged to Agnes. "You," she tells both fiancé and audience, "will see us quietly happy; our anxieties are at rest, our home restored to us" (8). The old world has been preserved—something often suggested as one of the main motives for fighting the war (Tate xvii). This idealizing scenario is interrupted with the noisy return of Micawber from Australia. As he declares, it is a "joyful hour indeed when the exile can set his foot on the white cliffs of Albion, so nearer the spot made immor-tal by the Swan of Avon . . ." (10). Yet, just for once, it is tempting to see Micaw-ber's words not as "empty rhetoric" (Moore 12), but as sentiments designed to carry real emotional force. Certainly, the other characters seem pleased to see him. Betsey instructs Micawber to brew punch, "and we'll drink your health, and the healths of all our friends so far away" (13). A final patriotic egg is thrown into the nest as the characters sing *Auld lang syne*. This is clearly not Dickens as an anarchic, rebellious writer, but Dickens cast by Tree and Parker as a marvelously hygienic one, invested with an ability to heal old wounds, as well as carrying a profound sense of tradition.

The adaptation's ending is also, of course, in tune with the wider image of Dickens as the embodiment of conviviality—the Dickens of "feasts of turkey and sausage" as George Bernard Shaw described him (*Literary Criticism* 13). In an echo of the kind of mutually supportive society envisaged by Dickens, His Maj-esty's *David Copperfield* shows its audience the pleasures of community. The production counsels that true human values can be found across classes–a recur-rent trope in World War I plays but also one which echoes the "accommodat-ing" instinct Bert Hornback has ascribed to Dickens's original novel (835). Less sentimental audience members might also say that there is something inherently reactionary about all this, that the mis-en-scène and dialogue "hammer" into the audience at His Majesty's the politics "of the status quo," as Theodor Adorno put it: the overall effect is to reassure them that all is well in this old world (90). But there is also something mournful about it. What on stage is a story about recovery and a return to stability is also, of course, still a story about loss—at least for the audience of 1914 who are only temporarily transported back in time; they can never really experience life in the restorative world of mid-Victorian England.

However speculative this attempt to imagine the experience of watching Her-bert Tree's production of *David Copperfield* in the winter and spring of 1914–15 may be, we can at least begin to see the extent to which early twentieth-century stage adaptations and their producers raise a number of important questions about the angle from which war-time audiences viewed subjects like Dickens; about the disappearance from Dickens studies of a particular body of work, and about the ways in different generations have been fed his stories. The habit of adapting Dickens for the stage was not just a Victorian craze; the early-twentieth century continued to see adaptations of his novels performed on stage at regular intervals, even as cinema began to emerge. It was a fashion whereby adaptors pilfered novels to suit "star" performers but also, depending on audience and circumstances, repositioned characters and reemphasized certain plots. The First World War offers a particularly rich seam of this kind of work.

In 1914, the success of *David Copperfield* also demonstrated that Dickens's work could still attract theater-goers. Throughout the war, Dickens continued to be adapted and in such a way that the resulting adaptions had strong resonance for war-torn audiences, invariably playing to national opinion and the need for myth-making. Herbert Tree revived *Oliver Twist* in April 1915, another story of wrongs being righted, evil overcome, and female self-sacrifice. *The Only Way*, starring John Martin Harvey as Sydney Carton, toured Britain throughout the War, as did Bransby Williams's one-man show in which he impersonated Grandfather Small-weed, Scrooge, and others in variety theatres and music halls. In the revue *Money for Nothing* (1916), a gallery of Dickens characters, including Sairey Gamp and Betsey Prigg, now transmogrified into patriotic VAD nurses, take part in "The Ragtime Dickens Parade." *David Copperfield* was picked up again in Walter Hackett's spiritualist thriller *The Invisible Foe* (1917), in which knowledge of the novel is crucial to the unmasking of a white-collar criminal.[5] Critics have paid only limited attention to this aspect of Dickens's cultural legacy, but it deserves to be part of discussions of the ways in which the novelist's work was disseminated after his death and the various uses to which it was put.

NOTES

1. As MacCarthy noted, "Just as Dickens is a great novelist when describing the subtle sentiment of David Copperfield's relation to Steerforth, but not so in describing his relation to Agnes, so Mr Tree . . . fails in the obvious and triumphs in unforeseen opportunities. But he will insist on choosing plays . . . which while offering few such opportunities, afford boundless scope for indulgence in cheap appeals" (*Theatre* 175).
2. TREE—AS PEGGOTTY: Cheer up, mother. In a minute you shall see me play the Dickens with David Copperfield. . . .Yes the book was all about him—the play's all about me. I've brought in Ham too, but I've kept the fat for myself. All the world's my stage, the other men and women merely supers. Just listen to my dialect— (*Assumes PEGGOTTY'S voice*) —What a rough night it be for sure. (*Takes a drink*). The glasses

be going down rapid. . . .

COPPERFIELD. And so I'm really in Yorkshire after all.

PEG. No. Ma'sr Davy. This be Yarmouth.

COPPER. Forgive me, your accent misled me.

PEG. (*In TREE'S voice*) My accent! It's Yarmouth, I tell you. I learnt it from a bloater: I had a hard row to get it!

(*Business lighting candle*)

COPPER. Pray, Mr Peggotty, what are you doing with that candle?

PEG. Why, Mas'r Davy, that's for my little Em'ly. I've lit that there candle man and boy since she was six years old.

COPPER: But why, my good Daniel?

PEG. (*As TREE*) To remind her that the Saloon Bar closes by ten—(*As PEGGOTTY*) and not by no means she can't get a drink after that no how.

(*Passing Show* 19)

3.   One heavily-publicized wartime project in 1915 involved printing extracts from classic works into single sheets small enough to be put into envelopes. According to the organizer, Walter Raleigh, professor of English at Oxford University, the works chosen were those which "seem to me to symbolize the cause for which we are fighting." The first set included William Cobbett's description of the ride through the Winchester countryside in *Rural Rides*, Pericles's speech to the Athenians, and Dickens's description of the game of cribbage played by Dick Swiveller and the Marchioness in *The Old Curiosity Shop*. "There is no better expression of freedom in all its senses than English literature," Raleigh told the *Times* (30 August 1917). "I can almost imagine an intelligent German officer trembling and growing pale when he finds it in our trenches. By this token we shall conquer." ("Literature for the Trenches," 7). In subsequent sets, Dickens was represented by Mr. Micawber's transactions, Mrs. Wilfer's wedding day from *Our Mutual Friend*, the Circumlocution Office from *Little Dorrit* and Mrs. Lirriper's views about lodgings from the 1863 *All the Year Round* Christmas book.

4.   The use of these musical selections offers a good example of how in the twentieth century "the national past," as Patrick Wright argues, "is capable of finding splendor in old styles of political domination and of making an alluring romance" (254).

5.   In Hackett's play, a dying man, Richard Bransby, discovers that his brother, Stephen, not his nephew, Hugh, as was first thought, has robbed him of a large sum of money. He makes Stephen sign a confession and before dying hides it in the pages of *David Copperfield*. It is Richard's favorite book: "[W]hen I'm a bit low in my mind I like to read it, I find it sort of comforting." After Richard's death Hugh remains the chief suspect and faces disgrace until the play's final act, when Richard communicates the real facts to his daughter, Helen, from beyond the grave.

WORKS CITED

Adorno, Theodor W. *The Culture Industry: Selected Essays on Mass Culture*. London: Routledge, 1991.

Anon. *The Passing Show of 1915*. British Library. Add. MSs. 3221.

Ashwell, Lena. *Myself a Player*. London: Michael Joseph, 1936.

Bailey, Peter. "Conspiracies of Meaning: Music-Hall and the Knowingness of Popular Culture." *Past and Present* 144 (1994): 138–70.

Barrie, J. M. *Rosy Rapture* (1916). British Library. Add MSs. 3226.

Beer, Gillian. *Arguing with the Past: Essays in Narrative from Woolf to Sidney*. London: Routledge, 1989.

Beerbohm, Max. "From A Brother's Standpoint." *Herbert Beerbohm Tree: Some Memories of Him and of his Art. [By Lady Tree and others]. Collected by Max Beerbohm*. London: Hutchinson, 1920. 187–203.

Bingham, Madeleine. *The Great Lover: The Life and Art of Herbert Beerbohm Tree*. London: Hamish Hamilton, 1978.

Blow, Sydney. *Through Stage Doors*. London: Chambers, 1958.

Boghardt, Thomas. *Spies of the Kaiser: German Covert Operations in Great Britain during the First World War Era*. London: Palgrave, 2004.

Bolton, H. Philip. *Dickens Dramatized*. Boston: G. K. Hall, 1987.

Borsa, Mario. *The English Stage of Today*. London: John Lane, 1908.

Bridges-Adams, William. *The Irresistible Theatre*. London: Secker and Warbug, 1957.

"Christmas Plays: *David Copperfield* at His Majesty's." *Times*. (26 December 1914): 9.

Colby, Robert A. "Thackeray and Dickens on the Boards." *Dramatic Dickens*. Ed. Carol Hanbery MacKay. Basingstoke: Macmillan, 1989: 139–51.

Collins, L. J. *Theatre at War 1914–18*. London: Macmillan, 1998.

Courtney, William Leonard. "An Open Letter to an American Friend," *Herbert Beerbohm Tree: Some Memories of Him and of his Art. [By Lady Tree and others]. Collected by Max Beerbohm*. London: Hutchinson, 1920. 253–66.

Crotch, Walter. "The Immortal Memory of Charles Dickens." *Dickensian* 11 (July 1915): 183–86.

"David Copperfield." *Athenaeum*. (2 January 1915): 13.

"David Copperfield at His Majesty's." *Illustrated Sporting and Dramatic News*. (2 January 1915): 516.

Davis, Jim. "The Gospel of Rags: Melodrama at the Britannia 1863–74." *New Theatre Quarterly* 7 (1991): 369–89.

Dean, Basil. *Seven Ages. An Autobiography*. London: Hutchinson, 1970.

"The Debacle of the Arts." *Bystander*. (9 December 1914): 344–45.

Dickens, Charles. *David Copperfield*. Ed. Jerome H. Buckley. New York: Norton, 1990.

"Dickens v Nietzsche." *Daily Mirror* (16 January 1915): 5.

"Dickens and Our Wounded Soldiers." *Observer* (5 December 1915): 21.

Gardiner, John. "The Dickensian and Us." *History Workshop Journal* 51 (2001): 226–37.

Gosse, Edmund. "A Literary Bazaar," *Times* (29 March 1915): 11.

Hackett, Walter. *The Invisible Foe.* 1917. British Library Add. MSs. 1582.

Hardwicke, Cedric. *A Victorian in Orbit.* London: Methuen, 1961.

"Henry IV." *Era.* (18 November 1914): 5.

"Henry IV." *Stage.* (16 November 1914): 8.

"Henry IV." *Standard.* (16 November 1914): 6.

Hill, T. W. "Dickens and War." *Dickensian* 10 (October1914): 257–62.

Hornback, Bert. "David's Vocation as Novelist: Frustration and Resolution in *David Copperfield.*" Rpt. in *David Copperfield.* Ed. Jerome H. Buckley. New York: Norton 1990. 832–36.

"How German Spies Work." *Daily Express.* (29 September 1914): 3–4.

"Jingle." "The Theatre of Peace: Why It Should not Be Eclipsed by the Theatre of War." *Bystander.* 43 (19 August 1914): 432–33.

John, Juliet. *Dickens and Mass Culture.* Oxford: Oxford UP, 2009.

"Literature for the Trenches." *Times.* (30 August 1915), 7.

Lowenthal. David. *The Heritage Crusade and the Spoils of History.* Cambridge: Cambridge UP, 1998.

Lynd, Robert. "What One Reads," *New Statesman* (14 November 1914): 137–38.

MacCarthy, Desmond. "Tears Idle Tears: Colonel Newcome at His Majesty's." *The Speaker* (23 June 1906): 270–71.

———*Theatre.* London: MacGibbon and Kee, 1954.

Macdonagh, Michael. *In London During the Great War: The Diary of a Journalist.* London: Eyre and Spottiswoode, 1935.

MacDonald, Jan. *The New Drama.* London: Macmillan, 1986.

Macqueen-Pope, Walter. *Carriages at Eleven: The Story of Edwardian Theatre.* London: Hale, 1972.

Mayer, David. "Encountering Melodrama." *Cambridge Companion to Victorian and Edwardian Theatre.* Ed. Kerry Powell. Cambridge: Cambridge UP, 2004: 145-63.

McDonald, John F. "English Life and the English Stage." *Fortnightly Review* 97 (February 1915): 535–57.

Mengham, Rod. *Charles Dickens.* Plymouth: Northcote House, 2001.

Moore, Grace. *Dickens and Empire.* Aldershot: Ashgate, 2004.

"Mr Tree's New Theatre." *Era* (1 May 1897):13–14.

Nares, Owen. "David Copperfield. Reviews and Analysis." *Nash's and Pall Mall Magazine* 54 (March 1915): 71–73.

———. *Myself and Some Others.* London: Duckworth, 1925.

Neilson, Julia. *This for Remembrance.* London: Hurst and Blackett, 1940.

Parker, Louis Napoleon. *Drake. A Pageant Play.* London: John Lane, 1912.

———. *The Highway of Life, Being the Personal History of David Copperfield by Charles Dickens. Made into a Play in 4 Acts.* British Library. Add MSs. 1485.

———. *Several of My Lives.* London: Chapman and Hall, 1928.

"Parliament: Peers and the Spy Peril." *Times.* (19 November 1914): 12.

Pearson, Hesketh. *Beerbohm Tree. His Life and Laughter.* London: Methuen, 1956.

Poovey, Mary. *Uneven Developments: The Ideological Work of Gender in Mid-Victorian England*. Chicago: U of Chicago P, 1988.

Potter, Jane. "Hidden Drama by British Women: Pageants and Sketches from the Great War." *Women, the First World War and the Dramatic Imagination*. Ed. Claire Tylee. Lampeter: Edwin Mellen, 2000, 105–20.

Quinn, Michael. "Celebrity and the Semiotics of Acting." *New Theatre Quarterly* 6.22 (1990): 154–61.

Radclyffe, Raymond. "Corrupting an Empire." *English Review* 22 (February 1916): 189–204.

Salmon, Eric. *Granville Barker. A Secret Life*. London: Heinemann, 1983.

Schultz, David. "The Architecture of Conspicuous Consumption: Property, Class, and Display at Herbert Beerbohm Tree's Her Majesty's Theatre." *Theatre Journal* 51: 3 (1999): 231–50.

Shaw, George Bernard. *Our Theatres in the Nineties*. London: Constable, 1932.

———.*Shaw's Non-dramatic Literary Criticism*. Ed Stanley Weintraub. Lincoln: U of Nebraska P, 1972.

"Sir Herbert Tree on His Next Production." *Observer*. (6 December 1914): 8.

"The Soldiers Library." *Times*. (30 August 1917), 7.

"Some Thoughts on Dickens's Birthday." *Times*. (15 February 1915), 9.

Steen, Maguerite. *A Pride of Terrys*. London: Longman, 1962.

"The Task of the Allies." *English Review* 18 (September 1914): 248–61.

Tate, Trudi. Introduction. Ruby M. Ayres. Richard Chatterton V.C. *British Literature of World War I*. Eds. Andrew Maunder and Angela Smith. London: Pickering and Chatto, 2010. i–xx.

"Things New at the Theatres." *Sketch*. (6 January 1915): 11–12.

Tree, Herbert Beerbohm. *Thoughts and Afterthoughts*. London: Cassell, 1913.

Tree, Maud. "Herbert and I." *Herbert Beerbohm Tree: Some Memories of Him and of his Art. [By Lady Tree and others]. Collected by Max Beerbohm*. London: Hutchinson, 1920. 1–171.

Trewin, J.C. *The Edwardian Theatre*. Oxford: Basil Blackwell, 1976.

"War Plays and the Public." *Era* (26 August 1914): 9.

"When Found." *Dickensian* (October 1916): 255–56.

Wigram, Isobel, ed. *Beerbohm Tree's Olivia*. London: André Deutsch, 1984.

Winter, Jay. *Sites of Memory, Sites of Mourning: The Great War in European Cultural History*. Cambridge: Cambridge UP, 1995.

Wright, Patrick. *On Living in an Old Country. The National Past in Contemporary Britain*. London: Verso, 1985.

"Whether we like it or not": *Bleak House* and the Limits of Liberalism

Jennifer Conary

This essay reads Bleak House *as a critique of liberal individualism, especially the individual's role in affecting social change. I argue that Dickens accomplishes this critique through his use of the split narrative and multiple genres—primarily the bildungsroman and the social problem novel. In* Bleak House, *Dickens not only revises and expands the genre of the social problem novel, but he simultaneously deconstructs the popular Victorian narrative of individual progress presented by the first-person bildungsroman. Dickens's combination of the two genres through the use of the double narrative is what creates the potent pessimism of* Bleak House*'s social vision. By revealing the failure of the liberal paradigm on which both genres were founded,* Bleak House *hints at the terrifying idea that individuals have no power to change things for the better.*

As its title suggests and its famous opening confirms, *Bleak House* offers a gloomy outlook on mid-Victorian Britain. Although Charles Dickens had been attacking social injustices through the genre of the novel since the time of *The Pickwick Papers* (1836–37), it was not until 1852–53 with *Bleak House* that he began to evaluate the condition of England in his fiction through a more comprehensive and pessimistic lens. In his early novels, Dickens illustrated how social embarrassments such as the New Poor Law and Yorkshire schools could be combated and overcome by cheerful protagonists. While these novels do not present

Dickens Studies Annual, Volume 45, Copyright © 2014 by AMS Press, Inc. All rights reserved.

actual solutions to the social problems they highlight, they do provide means for their heroes to defeat their social impediments, even if those victories are only personal. *Bleak House*, however, breaks with Dickens's earlier investment in the popular Victorian narrative of individual-driven reform. Despite having Dickens's sunniest first-person narrator, the novel as a whole is plagued by a profound and unsettling doubt about the potential for individual agency, particularly in the area of reform. This, combined with the novel's expansive condemnation of a whole host of social problems, makes for an unusually pessimistic treatment of the "Condition of England" in the 1850s.

While many critics have noted the novel's role as a negative double for the Crystal Palace—a critical counter-narrative to England's great celebration of national and imperial progress[1]—I believe the novel goes much further in its cynical outlook on the potential for social improvement because of its lack of faith in the possibility of individuals affecting social change and its critique of the liberal reform paradigm wherein remedying social problems was understood to rely on curing defects in individuals. Critics who have proposed similarly pessimistic readings seem determined to locate a source of optimism in the novel, however much they may be disappointed by or critical of what they see as Dickens's retreat from a potentially radical representation of social problems. For example, while Lauren Goodlad recognizes what she labels "the diminished power of modern individuals" in the narrative (87), she sees Dickens as unable to move past the Victorian obsession with classical liberal thought, an impediment that forces him to fall back on a "defensive sentimentalization of the home" (106). Likewise, J. Hillis Miller sees the novel as a call to action for its readers, who should condemn the corrupt institutions Dickens describes and take Esther as their model for exemplary conduct (60). In a similar vein, Simon Joyce, in his reading of the hopelessness represented by the crossing-sweep Jo, makes an attempt to locate a source of hope in Esther, whom he sees as offering "a classically liberal Victorian reformism" (143). Bruce Robbins, in perhaps the most unusual effort towards resisting the novel's nihilistic elements, turns at the end of his pessimistic reading to a call for "responsible criticism" (158), placing the burden of political action on literary critics and his own readers. While these are all valid, insightful readings, they fail to give Dickens due credit for his radical vision of the workings of society because of their reluctance to see *Bleak House* as a novel that offers no hope for social change.

Caroline Levine, in her recent reading of *Bleak House* through the lens of network theory, comes closest to recognizing and accepting the utter bleakness of the novel. She argues that characters in *Bleak House* function more as nodes in a variety of networks than as individuals as such. According to Levine, "Characters are not centered subjects but points of social intersection. By hanging his novel not on individuals but on networks, Dickens is able to undermine the usual novelistic reliance on individual agency" (519–20). Unlike most other critics who address the novel's role as a social critique, Levine does not offer Esther or domesticity as an alternative to the failed institutions represented primarily in the third-person narrative. At the same time, she does not address the implications of Esther's first-person narrative on the lack of faith in individual liberty and on the individual's inability to affect meaningful change in the novel as a whole. Rather than reading Esther as one point in the novel's numerous networks, as Levine does, I see the combination of Esther's personal narrative with the expansive perspective of the third-person narrative as key to understanding the novel's troubling pessimism about the individual's role in society. *Bleak House* does not offer the home as a refuge from the gloom presented elsewhere in the narrative. Instead, Esther's account of her life provides a very personal perspective on the devastating effects of the removal of personal liberty that complements the critique made by the third-person narrator.

Moreover, while *Bleak House*'s despair-laden view of individual liberty is represented most obviously in the novel's topical references to corrupt social institutions, it is also built into the very structure of the narrative. Through the use of the split narrative with two narrators—one of whom writes in the paradigmatic genre of individual self-making, the bildungsroman—Dickens highlights the effect of the individual's lack of power and control over her own progress, for the narrative only reaches some semblance of completeness through combining (and often repeating) accounts of events told from two perspectives. The third-person narrator offers a scathing overview of England's various social failures, while Esther presents the story of a young woman who is robbed of all personal freedom, and whose strange account of her life reveals the anger and resentment created by her subordinate position as an illegitimate daughter with no chance at independence. Instead of offering a counterpoint to the pessimism of the third-person narrative, Esther's narrative reveals the inadequacy of the plan for social progress based on personal charity that the other narrative leaves as the only hope for saving the nation. Taken together, the two narratives offer an almost nihilistic view on the condition of England.[2]

This double critique of individual liberty in the context of national problems positions *Bleak House* as an unusual exception to the formula presented by other mid-century social problem novels. Unlike most other social problem novels written in the 1840s and 1850s, *Bleak House* rejects the usual "solutions" to social problems that were rooted in individual moral redemption, as is the case, for example, in Disraeli's *Sybil* or Gaskell's *Mary Barton* or *North and South*. Because Dickens represents social problems as systemic in *Bleak House*, he cannot resort to the sort of plot resolutions based in individual improvement commonly used by his fellow social problem novelists. Moreover, *Bleak House* to some extent "corrects" the limits of more traditional social problem novels, particularly the "Condition of England" or industrial novel, by addressing the multitude of social problems located in or created by the massive urban development of London and the residual (negative) influence of the aristocracy on English politics and national reform; by moving the problems of industrialism to the sidelines (the industrial North makes only a minor appearance through Mrs. Rouncewell's son, the Ironmaster), Dickens illustrates the ways in which the troubles of modern society plague the entirety of the nation, not just the manufacturers and laborers in the factory system.

Simon Joyce is, to my knowledge, the only other critic to recognize how far ahead of his time Dickens was in this expansive, pessimistic treatment of the "Condition of England" through the genre of the social problem novel (144), but he underestimates the radical nature of Dickens's attack on liberal individualism and ignores the importance of the form through which Dickens presents his critique. In *Bleak House*, Dickens not only revises and expands the genre of the social problem novel, but he simultaneously deconstructs the popular Victorian narrative of individual progress presented by the first-person bildungsroman. Dickens's combination of the two genres—the social problem novel and the bildungsroman—through the use of the double narrative is what creates the potent pessimism of *Bleak House*'s social vision. By revealing the failure of the liberal paradigm on which both genres were founded, *Bleak House* hints at the audacious and terrifying idea that individuals have no power to change things for the better—that both the domestic and the social might be too riddled with problems for there to be any hope for repair.

"Never meant to go right": Liberal Reform vs. Social and Narrative Determinism

As most recent critical works that address Victorian liberalism concede, "liberalism" is a frustratingly difficult term to define, in large part because the term encompasses so many abstract concepts that were espoused by groups with quite disparate political agendas.[3] Elaine Hadley, in her study of Victorian political liberalism, offers the following definition of the liberal individual: "For mid-Victorian liberalism, the citizen is a profoundly cerebral and privatized subject form, and yet he is simultaneously a citizen of the nation among many equivalent national citizens who all live their lives with political aspirations in the here and now, seeking effective change" (20). While Hadley provides an extensive and convincing fleshing-out of this definition in her book-length study, I am not so much interested in *political* liberalism as I am in the basic ideals that underpinned it. Following Hadley's lead, I turn to John Stuart Mill's *On Liberty* (1859) for the clearest articulation of mid-Victorian liberal values.[4] Mill provides the following definition of human liberty, the concept at the heart of mid-Victorian liberalism:

> It comprises, first, the inward domain of consciousness; demanding liberty of conscience in the most comprehensive sense; liberty of thought and feeling; absolute freedom of opinion and sentiment on all subjects. . . . Secondly, the

principle requires liberty of tastes and pursuits; of framing the plan of our life
to suit our own character; of doing as we like, subject to such consequences
as may follow: without impediment from our fellow-creatures, so long as
what we do does not harm them. . . . (50)

In sum, "The only freedom which deserves the name, is that of pursuing our own
good in our own way, so long as we do not attempt to deprive others of theirs, or
impede their efforts to obtain it" (50). This protectiveness of individual liberty,
combined with what Hadley identifies as the desire to seek "effective change,"
was the driving force behind liberal reform efforts that were aimed at saving the
nation one individual at a time.

In *Bleak House*, Dickens presents a cast of characters who appear to possess
liberty of action and thought and who frequently attempt to better their lives or the
lives of those around them. However, most of these characters are ultimately helpless in their ability to direct their own lives and ineffective in improving the lives
of anyone else. John Jarndyce and Esther Summerson, the two protagonists whose
reform efforts receive the most positive attention from the narrative and who work
the hardest to alleviate some of the misery they encounter, seem the most capable
of effective action. Jarndyce, with his mysterious and seemingly limitless fortune, goes about shedding light in the darkness through a variety of personal and
semi-institutional charities. In contrast to Jarndyce's charitable interests, Esther's
mission to bring improvement and good to the world is more limited in scope.
The seeming paragon of domestic wellbeing, Esther allows her optimism, cheerfulness, and household knowledge to influence those around her. When she does
leave the home to embark on missions of social improvement, she doesn't travel
far and limits her energies to only a few sufferers, such as Jo, Caddy Jellyby, and
the brickmakers' wives.

That Jarndyce's and Esther's projects are presented in a more favorable light
than those of characters such as Mrs. Jellyby or Mrs. Pardiggle seems to suggest
that the novel is advocating their means of bringing about social improvements—
a philosophy of social amelioration aimed at helping individuals very much in
line with mid-century liberal reform agendas such as Dickens's own project for
reforming former prostitutes at Urania Cottage.[5] Yet both Jarndyce and Esther
are almost entirely ineffective in their charitable efforts. For a novel that devotes
a great deal of narrative space to describing social problems and drawing attention to the need for reform, the reform narrative of *Bleak House*, which we would
expect to culminate in the improvement of at least *some* of the social problems
outlined, is surprisingly static. The two locations that receive the most attention
in the narrative—urban London and rural Chesney Wold—remain unchanged at
the end of the novel, the one still shrouded in legal, parliamentary, and literal fog,
the other "abandoned to darkness and vacancy" (767; ch. 67), inhabited more by
the dead than the living. While Esther and Allan Woodcourt retreat at the end of
the novel to the respite of their sunny second Bleak House, their marriage does

not serve as a symbol for class reconciliation or a brighter future for the nation, as it inevitably would in a traditional social problem novel; instead, the world they leave behind continues on its apocalyptic journey into darkness.

Perhaps more significantly, even Jarndyce's and Esther's small charitable projects fail, implying that, while institutions of justice such as Chancery and Parliament cannot bring about necessary social improvements, neither can individual efforts at doing good. All of Jarndyce's philanthropic connections are shown to be ineffective. That model project of telescopic philanthropy, Mrs. Jellyby's Borrioboolan endeavor, ends disastrously, its great, far-sighted advocate forced to redirect her energies into a new and, the narrative implies, equally unworthy cause. Mrs. Pardiggle's efforts at enlightening and converting the brickmakers come to nothing, as do Esther's attempts at kindness towards the same individuals. While Jarndyce seems to provide an inspirational presence for Gridley and, to a lesser extent, Jo, he can save neither, nor can he do anything to help George Rouncewell in his time of need.

Esther's efforts also end in defeat. Her altruistic attempt at saving Jo brings both her and her maid Charley near death and results in Esther's disfigurement, not to mention that Jo eventually succumbs to the illness from which neither Esther nor Woodcourt can save him. While Esther embarks with Inspector Bucket on a heroic journey through the wilds of London in a valiant rescue effort, she can do nothing to prevent the death of her mother. Gridley dies; Miss Flite continues her lonely, mad existence; and even Caddy Jellyby—one of the characters who benefits most from her interaction with Esther—ends the novel working to support her lame husband and deaf, mute child in much the same way that led to the exhaustion and early death of her would-have-been mother-in-law. Despite the narrative's persistent focus on Esther's and Jarndyce's good deeds, the charitable pair do very little to change anything in their world for the better.

Perhaps what is most telling about the inefficacy of the Jarndyce/Esther project for changing the world one person at a time, is their inability to save or even alter the fates of those closest to them. Esther and Jarndyce's attempts to save Richard end in failure, which suggests that charity at home is not the ideal means of reforming the nation. Jarndyce's strong personal example—he is, after all, the one member of the family not harmed by the suit—as well as his financial generosity, paternal advice, and patience, and Esther's cheerfulness, domestic wisdom, and genuine care cannot overpower the seductive siren's song of Chancery for Richard, who appears to have been mysteriously robbed of his liberty of thought.

Richard's demise also brings about the at least partial debilitation of Ada, who, as Christopher Herbert points out, exhibits, as do so many characters in *Bleak House*, a disturbing tendency towards self-destruction (109). Despite having been warned by Esther and Jarndyce about Richard's dangerous preoccupation, Ada nonetheless sacrifices herself in an attempt to help her doomed lover. She marries Richard with the slight hope of convincing him of his error, and then, after she loses faith in her own ability to complete this task, invests in the ability of her unborn child, if not immediately, then perhaps as an adult, to redeem his father from ruin. But just as Jarndyce and Esther cannot prevent Ada from proceeding on her wearying journey of self-sacrifice, Ada cannot prevent Richard from being consumed by his deadly obsession with the suit, and her child is never given the opportunity even to try. In the case of Ada and Richard, domestic warmth and care prove rather frail opponents to the potent darkness that permeates even the hearthside.

Esther's and Jarndyce's attempts at saving Richard and Ada, while noble and necessary (doing nothing to prevent their friends' demise would certainly seem heartless), are quixotic—doomed from the outset to failure—for they battle an invisible enemy that disregards the wills of its victims. The suit itself proves to have more willpower and liberty of action than do the ill-fated suitors, most of whom are born into the cause. As Jarndyce tells Esther, "[W]e can't get out of the suit on any terms, for we are made parties to it, and *must* be parties to it, whether we like it or not" (89; ch 8), an inability to "do as we like" (Mill 50) that violates one of the central values of liberalism. The very nature of the lengthy Chancery suits sets the suitors up for failure. Born into their "causes," they find that their lives are already caught in a legal web that also to some degree determines their identities (they are defined by the family names that bind them to their suits) before they ever have a chance to make a choice for themselves. All of the suitors—even John Jarndyce—are incapable of taking complete control of their lives because they are bound by the legal entrapment of the suits in which they are never given a choice but to participate.

Jarndyce's references to the suitors' entrapment are supported later in the narrative when he repeatedly insists that Richard cannot be blamed for his fall. Jarndyce says to Esther, "[Richard's] blood is infected, and objects lose their natural aspects in his sight. It is not *his* fault" (435; ch. 35). Like the disease that strikes Charley, Esther, and Jo, the lure of Chancery is an infection for Richard that is beyond his power to control and that causes blindness. And, like Jarndyce's evaluation of Richard, Miss Flite's account of her history identifies something beyond her power—the "cold and glittering devils" of Chancery (440; ch. 35)—as the reason for her derangement. Despite having seen her father, brother, and sister fall prey to the suit in which they found themselves entangled, and knowing full well that Chancery was the cause of their doom, Miss Flite finds herself helpless to resist the demons that haunt her. She knows her constant attendance at court will bring about her ruin, yet this knowledge does nothing to prevent her from becoming a slave to her suit.

This terrifying removal of one's ability to choose a path of action makes social reform according to the liberal model—one dependent on individuals being persuaded to improve themselves—irrelevant. An individual who has limited control over her actions or who has her fate essentially determined by her social conditions (say, her being born into a Chancery suit) cannot be reformed by any plan that depends on bringing about changes in individuals (such as the personal charity model Esther and Jarndyce seem to espouse). Richard cannot be saved by Jarndyce's warnings and social alternatives (the career paths he goes to great lengths to make available to his ward, for example) because Richard lacks complete control over his actions.

But if Chancery has such an irresistible draw—one that Richard and Miss Flite cannot resist—why does John Jarndyce remain immune to the enchantment of the suit into which he, too, is born? The only plausible answer the narrative provides is that Jarndyce's social position—his mysterious financial security—enables him to reject the charms of promised wealth the suit offers to those with no secure future. The reason Richard succumbs to the lure of the suit is that he believes it may grant him the gentlemanly independence he desires. Likewise, Miss Flite's far from wealthy family (her father and brother are builders, and she and her sister take in sewing work) is drawn in by the hope of wealth. Miss Flite only gives way to the suit after the demise of her father and siblings, when she "was ill, and in misery" (441: ch. 35) and thus, we would assume, prey to any promises of removal from her dire situation. John Jarndyce, who appears affluent enough to support a dozen destitute victims of Chancery in addition to his entourage of dependents, is offered no glittering future by the suit because his present state of affairs is already quite glowing; his presumably inherited wealth therefore makes him immune to the dangerous charms of the Chancery suit that is also his inheritance. This is no more his fault—his wealth seems inherent to him, for no mention is made of his ever having worked or earned his fortune—than the susceptibility to which Richard's and Miss Flite's precarious economic positions make them subject is theirs. In other words, although Jarndyce appears to exercise liberty of action in choosing not to be consumed by the suit, he is only able to do so because of the circumstances of his birth, over which he had no control.

What *Bleak House* suggests, in a radical rejection of the Victorian investment in self-improvement, is that an individual's agency—her ability to determine her own future and actions or even her ability to shape her own character—is severely limited. Characters find themselves in bad situations not so much because they themselves are bad, but because circumstances beyond their control determine their fates. For example, Jo's illiteracy and homelessness are conditions that have nothing to do with his character and cannot be altered by any act of individual initiative, and Guster's crippled physical and psychological state that keep her in a position of poverty and powerlessness result from the misfortune of being born into the Tooting baby farm, not from any personal flaw. Neither Jo nor Guster is shown to be morally depraved or in any way responsible for his or her bad situation. Both, in fact, are portrayed as worthy of sympathy, not condemnation, but neither is given the means to improve his or her position, nor does the kindliness of those like Mr. Snagsby who take pity on them make any significant difference in altering their lives for the better.

Even characters in less dire situations than Jo and Guster find themselves entangled in webs of causality that they enter by no choice of their own. What makes

Bleak House one of Dickens's most sophisticated novels—the remarkable inter-weaving of plots and characters and the multitude of connections between seem-ingly disparate events—also works to create an impression of a world in which an individual's actions are beyond her control, in which, as Caroline Levine has shown, individuals are all nodes in a series of networks (520). Esther is swept into the realm of Gothic romance, complete with a full-blown murder mystery, through a chance encounter with a woman bearing an uncanny resemblance to her, while visiting a country church neighboring the residence of a friend-of-a-friend who just happens to be the rejected suitor—rejected because of circum-stances resulting from Esther's birth—of her own aunt. George Rouncewell finds himself accused of a murder he did not commit because of his long ago friendship with a dissipated captain (the father of his student's guardian's betrothed), who happens to be of interest to a powerful lawyer, the executor to the aristocratic family for whom his [George's] estranged mother works and the same family that includes the former lover of his dissipated captain friend; a lawyer who holds rather dubious connections to an aged usurer, the brother-in-law to the man who holds possession of the will that eventually brings an end to George's student's chancery suit; a lawyer who holds George in a financial stranglehold, blackmail-ing him into turning over the evidence he needs in order to gain power over the former lover of the dissipated captain, which action and the reaction to that action leads to George's being accused of murdering said lawyer.

Dickens's convoluted arabesques of plot are dazzling and, at times, overwhelm-ing. The effect such intricate plotting creates is one of a mysterious and unavoid-able determinacy. All of the characters find themselves participants in a bizarre and uncanny labyrinth of action that they cannot gain a distant enough perspective on to understand—in fact, a single narrative seems incapable of explaining and unraveling the complexity of the characters' relationships. The interconnected-ness of the characters' lives and histories suggests that they are all minute actors in something much larger. The novel invites us to believe, like Mr. Snagsby, that "[s]omething is wrong, somewhere; but what something, what may come of it, to whom, when, and from which unthought of and unheard of quarter, is [a] puzzle" (315; ch. 25), the explanation of which exists already but will only be revealed with time, its outcome inevitable. Like the litigants in Jarndyce v. Jarndyce, we get the impression that when "the world go[es] wrong, it was, in some off-hand manner, never meant to go right" (9; ch. 1).

Aside from illustrating how masterful a novelist Dickens had become since the time of *Pickwick Papers* and *Oliver Twist*, the hopelessly overdetermined atmosphere that *Bleak House* creates has significant political ramifications. Unlike other mid-century social problem novels and in contrast to the generally held belief in the mid-Victorian period about the cause of social problems, *Bleak House* invokes a sense of social problems as resulting from deeply rooted flaws in the structure of society rather than in widespread individual defects. This view of social problems is radical both in its visionary nature and in its rejection of liberal reform. Josephine Guy, in her analysis of Victorian industrial novels, explains that the importance of individual agency was the prominent lens through which the mid-Victorians viewed their world, "ensuring that the problems which they identified in their society were invariably seen to have *individual* causes, and that the solutions which they subsequently advocated invariably recommended changes in the actions and beliefs of *individuals* (rather than changes in social structures)" (72–73). Amanda Claybaugh, in her study of the broader category of the "novel of purpose," agrees: "[S]tructural change took place, for nineteenth-century reformers, one individual at a time. This was true not only of the persons reformers were seeking to aid but also of the reformers themselves. Not only did each fallen woman or each drunkard have to be individually reclaimed, but each reformer had to recognize, individually, that slavery was wrong and factory work cruel" (24). In his description of Victorian intellectuals' attempts at explaining "the haunting spectacle of urban poverty," Daniel Born writes, "Thus went the frequent hypothesis: crime, poverty, and prostitution are the natural outcome of individual depravity; conversely, righteous individuals are sure to prosper" (33).

Novelists writing in the 1840s and '50s seem to have been unable to imagine or reluctant to represent social problems as stemming from anything other than individuals, hence their tendency to resort to solutions along the lines of Christian brotherhood or individual moral redemption (the solutions proposed by the endings of *Alton Locke* and *Mary Barton*, respectively). As Claybaugh writes of the reform agendas of *Uncle Tom's Cabin* and *Mary Barton*, "What must be reformed, in both novels, is not so much the slave or factory system but rather the individuals who profit from those systems, however remotely. Once these individuals come to feel sympathy, the systems themselves will wither away. And this is because sympathy is not only affective but also cognitive. To feel sympathy with a slave or a worker is to recognize that he or she is a person in some way like oneself, and this makes his or her sufferings unacceptable" (24). This description of how these two novels worked as reform texts is true of traditional social problem novels more generally: mid-century novelists wrote stories that encouraged readers to sympathize with *individual* characters in order to invite sympathy with liberal reform efforts that aimed at reforming the individuals who made social problems possible. But *Bleak House* does not fit this model.

While *Bleak House* invites sympathy with individual characters, Dickens presents no individual antagonists to blame for the suffering of the victimized characters. The novel certainly identifies a good number of morally corrupt characters whose selfish and at times malicious actions bring misery to their fellow Londoners, but it at the same time gestures towards something larger and more threatening as the cause of England's troubles. Unlike a novel such as *Little Dorrit*, in which social problems are illuminated but ultimate plot resolution is brought about by the bringing down of an identifiable villain, *Bleak House* provides no focused outlet for blame for the problems it presents. At the same time, the novel offers no triumphant heroes who might prove effective combatants of the social malaise. Because individuals do not hold complete control over their actions and lives, they cannot be held responsible for the general state of misery, nor do they have much power to change things for the better.

Perhaps more importantly, none of the novel's punishments for the characters who act in immoral or destructive ways brings about any general improvement in the social problems depicted in the narrative. Tulkinghorn's death makes absolutely no difference in setting anything right, nor does Krook's spontaneous combustion or Mrs. Snagsby's shaming significantly benefit anyone, much less society. Even Hortense's arrest for Tulkinghorn's murder is nothing more than an empty gesture towards achieving justice, a point she makes most clearly in her final speech before her arrest. After making Bucket admit that he can neither bring Tulkinghorn back to life nor restore Lady Dedlock's honor or Sir Leicester's pride, Hortense remarks on the meaninglessness of her arrest and expected execution: "You cannot do these things? Then you can do as you please with me. It is but death, it is all the same" (652–53; ch. 54). And Hortense's death *does* leave everything all the same, just as the end of Jarndyce v. Jarndyce changes nothing for the parties involved. Quite appropriately, Harold Skimpole, one of the most ethically despicable characters in the novel, receives no punishment whatsoever for his actions, and this, too, makes no difference to anyone.

Because there is no clearly defined source for England's social infirmity, one is tempted like Gridley (and like traditional mid-century social problem novelists), to attack individuals so as at least to have a recognizable opponent. Gridley complains of Chancery, "I am told, on all hands, it's the system. I mustn't look to individuals. It's the system. . . . But if I do no violence to any of them . . . I will accuse the individual workers of that system against me, face to face, before the great eternal bar!" (193; ch. 15). In this moment of frustration, Gridley seems to understand the ideological bind that the novel exposes: that the large social structures that affect individual lives are immune to the actions of individuals, leaving victims of "the system" like Gridley with no means of righting the wrongs that plague them. As Gridley recognizes, "the system" is a formidable opponent, for its slippery, shadowy, amorphous nature makes it terribly difficult to combat, especially if it cannot be seen through the blindfold of a liberal paradigm.

But *Bleak House* offers no means of removing this liberal blindfold. The social institutions that would seem the most effective way of battling the systemic problems to which the narrative gestures, come out as more villainous than any of the individual pseudo-villains and receive the bulk of the third-person narrator's wrathful satire. To return to one of the points with which I began, the novel seems to offer personal charity, especially through the examples of John Jarndyce and Esther Summerson, as the only possible alternative to the inefficiency and incompetence of the national institutions. However, as I have shown, the novel reveals this type of reform to be largely ineffective. More problematically, Dickens's use of Esther's first-person narrative lays bare the troubling effects of an individual's being born into a situation that grants her limited liberty of thought or action.

Instead of acting as a counter to the third-person narrative, Esther's story complements that narrative's pessimism by highlighting both the impossibility of an entirely altruistic and selfless form of charity as well as the psychological trauma of being a charitable recipient entrapped in a world where individual choices and actions do not matter.

"I felt that I had but one thing to do": Esther's Narrative and the Limits of the Liberal Bildungsroman

Esther's narrative reveals how powerless she is as a young woman without family or fortune. While she is central to most of the novel's plots, her agency is limited to her ability to retell her story; Dickens allows us to see Esther's liberty of thought through the use of first-person narration, but this freedom is at odds with her inability to achieve much liberty of action. Esther's first-person voice and generous actions make her appear as the character most capable of making a difference in the world, yet her narrative reveals, to borrow Mill's language once again, her inability "to frame the plan of [her] life to suit [her] own character" (50), a stifling lack of freedom that adds to the novel's pessimistic tone and underscores the third-person narrative's fatalism.[6]

Most of the criticism dedicated to Esther's portion of *Bleak House* focuses on the crippling effects of her illegitimacy and her relationship with her mother on her psychological development. For example, John O. Jordan's recent book-length study of *Bleak House* provides an excellent and surely almost exhaustive analysis of this aspect of Esther's character. While I agree with Jordan's and other critics' readings of the psychological trauma created in Esther because of all the problems surrounding her (lack of) connection to Lady Dedlock, I will instead address the broader issue of Esther's social position as it relates to the form of her narrative and her role in the world of *Bleak House*.

Esther opens her portion of *Bleak House* with a chapter titled "A Progress," and the form of her narrative—an account of her life that begins in childhood and moves through the various trials that end in her marriage—is that of a traditional bildungsroman, one that on the surface is not so different from *David Copperfield*, the novel Dickens wrote just prior to *Bleak House*. In its celebration of liberal freedom of thought and action, *David Copperfield* conforms to the way in which Franco Moretti defines the Western bildungsroman as "one of the most harmonious solutions ever offered to a dilemma conterminous with modern bourgeois civilization: the conflict between the ideal of *self-determination* and the equally imperious demands of *socialization*" (15). David works hard to establish his position in the world as a writer while maintaining his strong sense of middle-class identity; in the end, he is rewarded with the esteem of society and a happy domestic life with his wife and children. Susan Fraiman also notes the importance of liberal values in the history of the bildungsroman that she traces back to Goethe's *Wilhelm Meister*, but she identifies the origins of the bildungsroman with the story of a middle-class *man*, "an especially rugged or especially sensitive young man, at the leisure to mull over some life choices, not so much connected to people or the landscape as encountering or passing through them as 'options' or 'experiences' en route to a better place" (126)—a perfect description of David Copperfield. She argues that bildungsromans by women writers with female protagonists work differently.

Fraiman's definition of what is frequently termed the "female *Bildungsroman*" is more fitting for Esther's narrative in *Bleak House* than Moretti's implicitly masculine description of the genre. Fraiman explains,

> The myth of bourgeois opportunity has little place for the middle-class female protagonist, and to reinvent the genre around her is to recognize a set of stories in which *compromise and even coercion are more strongly thematized than choice*. Of course [male protagonists] get buffeted around as well and feel themselves in the hands of some higher power, but *willful self-making is still the keynote of their stories*, and self-regard is still the decisive factor. … [H]eroines … have, by contrast, a clearer sense that *formation is foisted upon them*, that they are largely what other people, what the world, will make of them. (6, emphasis added)

Fraiman's convincing analysis of how Georgian and Victorian female bildungsromans by women novelists work is surprisingly relevant to Esther Summerson's narrative—the creation of a male novelist—in *Bleak House*. Fraiman posits that the traditional masculine bildungsroman has been most frequently read with an obsessive attention to the hero's development at the expense of any acknowledgement of the social factors that affected or enabled that development (10). As in the case with the protagonists in other female bildungsromans, Esther finds that her personal destiny is not determined by self-will but by circumstances beyond her control, from her illegitimate birth to her appropriation by John Jarndyce. The very narrative structure of *Bleak House* highlights the impossibility of separating Esther's story from the social structures, events, and people that surround her, for her narrative is continuously broken up by a story in which she is presented as only a minor character.

In his unusual choice to write a first-person female bildungsroman, Dickens employs many of the narrative strategies used by nineteenth-century women writers to illustrate how entrapped Esther is because of the societal expectations for and limits placed upon women. Through his emphasis on Esther's powerlessness, Dickens, I argue, goes beyond the kind of negotiations with the traditional bildungsroman that Fraiman reads in the novels of Frances Burney, Jane Austen, and Charlotte Brontë. Instead, he presents a direct challenge to the narrative of individual self-determination in much the same way that Fraiman argues George

Eliot does in *The Mill on the Floss*. Fraiman argues that Eliot "estranges and ironizes" the individualist bildungsroman in *The Mill on the Floss* by illustrating "Maggie's inability to enter the story of self-culture" (139–40). Dickens accomplishes a similar critique by revealing in her own voice Esther's frustration with her inability to escape the cultural conversation that forbids her individual desires.

Esther begins her story with one of her most disingenuous claims: "I have great difficulty in beginning to write my portion of these pages, for I know I am not clever. I always knew that" (17; ch. 3). Not only does Esther lie about her intelligence, but she also distorts the truth (and drops her usually elegant prose) when she claims that she "always knew that," a point she immediately disproves by telling, in self-effacing terms that highlight rather than hide the resentment she still feels, how her aunt crushed young Esther's sense of self-worth. The difficulty with which Esther begins her tale of "progress" seems to arise not from her intellectual ineptitude, but from her unwillingness to begin a story that is still incredibly painful for her to recount.[7] For example, in describing how her birthday was "the most melancholy day at home, in the whole year" (18; ch. 3), adult-Esther jumps to the present to reflect, "[P]erhaps I might still feel such a wound, if such a wound could be received more than once, with the quickness of that birthday" (18; ch. 3). Unwilling to speak her own current pain, Esther confesses only that she "*might* still feel such a wound," when clearly she *does* feel the pain of having her birthday—the day that should have been devoted to celebrating her special, individual self—stolen from her because of her illegitimacy, a social position she did not choose. Esther's use of the conditional in this instance suggests that she feels exactly what she hypothesizes, for there is no other logical explanation for why she would include such a reference to what only "might" be her current feeling.[8]

Esther's account of her time with her aunt is the portion of the narrative most densely packed with her excessive self-deprecation, a narrative tic that can be read as an embittered parody of the discourse characteristic of the selfless angel Esther was forced to become. Dickens's use of Esther's ironic self-representation reveals the tension between her liberty of thought and her liberty of action, for Esther's view of herself and plan for her life are at odds with the identity and role that are given to her. Her aunt is the first character to define Esther's future; she says to Esther, "Submission, self-denial, diligent work, are the preparations for a life begun with such a shadow on it" (19; ch. 3). Esther's reaction to this edict is to repeat obsessively the story of her birthday to her doll and to attempt to internalize the life chosen for her: "I would try . . . to repair the fault I had been born with (of which I confusedly felt guilty and yet innocent), and would strive as I grew up to be industrious, contented, and kind-hearted, and to do some good to some one, and win some love to myself if I could" (20; ch. 3). This version of Esther is what many critics have accepted as her natural character, yet she reveals quite openly the struggle she endured to accept what she was told to become. This articulation of her plan to atone for her birth is immediately followed by yet another jump to the present, where adult-Esther confesses, "I hope it is not self-indulgent to shed these tears as I think of it [these painful moments with Dolly]. I am very thankful, I am very cheerful, but I cannot quite help their coming to my eyes" (20; ch. 3). Here, Esther reveals how much pain she continues to feel (despite reassuring us that she is thankful and cheerful). Her juxtaposition of her claims of thankfulness and cheerfulness with her confession of tears linked by "but" instead of "and" suggests that her tears are tears of sorrow over the burden placed upon her as a child rather than tears of joy.

Esther is presented with the opportunity to embrace the submission, self-denial, and diligent work that Miss Barbary foresaw when John Jarndyce enters Esther's life after her aunt's death. Instead of asking 14-year-old Esther what she would like to do with her life,[9] Jarndyce sends his attorney to lay out the terms of her future: that she will attend school (never leaving without Jarndyce's permission) and "apply herself to the acquisition of those accomplishments, upon the exercise of which she will be ultimately dependent" (23; ch. 3). She finds herself alone with no family and no fortune (Miss Barbary leaves everything she has to her servant, Mrs. Rachael), and Esther has no choice but to accept the future that Jarndyce chooses for her. Instead of voicing the joy that we would expect if Esther really were a domestic paragon delighted with her situation, she distances herself from narrating her feelings by switching to third-person: "What the destitute subject of such an offer tried to say, I need not repeat. What she did say, I could more easily tell, if it were worth the telling. What she felt, and will feel to her dying hour, I could never relate" (23; ch. 3). Esther never reveals what she said in this moment, nor does she express what she felt and still feels. This moment marks the beginning of her real "progress"—her departure from her miserable home—a new beginning that she should celebrate, yet of which she can only speak by splitting herself ("What *she* felt . . . *I* could never relate" [emphasis added]) and revealing nothing definite.

Fortunately for Esther, her time at school proves to be among the happiest periods in her narrative. She finally finds herself a part of a community of young women who are close to her social equals and who seem unaware of her scandalous origins. Yet Esther's six "happy, quiet" (27; ch. 3) years at Greenleaf exist as a near narrative omission: she mentions them only to bridge the time between her aunt's death and her removal to Bleak House. In the same way in which she began her narrative by denying her own significance, Esther transitions out of her brief references to her happy time at Greenleaf by attempting to write herself out of her story: "It seems so curious to me to be obliged to write all this about myself! As if this narrative were the narrative of *my* life! But my little body will soon fall into the background now" (27; ch. 3). Again, Esther's claim here seems more than simple self-deprecation. Once she leaves Greenleaf, Esther's life really *isn't* her own, and she has so little choice in what happens to her that her little body *does* in fact fall into the background. After this brief narrative interruption, Esther continues: "Six quiet years (I find I am saying it for the second time) I had passed at Greenleaf, s*eeing in those around me, as it might be in a looking-glass, every stage of my own growth and change there*, when, one November morning, I received this letter [informing her that she must leave Greenleaf]" (27; ch. 3; emphasis added). The repetition of the "six quiet years" and Esther's calling attention to that repetition emphasizes the importance to her of the time she so briefly discusses, and her description of being able to see *her* growth and *her* change through the mirror of her comrades perfectly illustrates how key this period was to Esther's development of a sense of self, one she is robbed of by the end of the sentence with the arrival of the letter that tears her away to a life she once again does not choose.

Upon arriving in London, Esther develops a new narrative tic as a means of coping with her altered situation: her strange references to and behavior towards Ada. While a number of critics have read Esther's hyper-affectionate treatment of Ada as Dickens's thinly-veiled inclusion of an unrealized lesbian romance,[10] Esther's response to Ada in the context of her narrative of powerlessness makes more sense as one driven by envy.[11] Reading Esther's relationship with Ada in this way once again aligns Dickens's novel with bildungsromans by women writers, who, according to Fraiman, create "a blurring or decentering of the 'major' narrative by alternative stories of female destiny, so that each text is less the telling of one life than a struggle between rival stories" (10). Privileged by her respectable parentage and independent fortune, Ada offers an alternative narrative trajectory guided by relative freedom and choice that Esther can never have because of her illegitimacy and financial dependence on John Jarndyce.

Esther is never asked whether she would like to serve as Ada's companion (she was trained at Greenleaf to be a governess and teacher), and the scene in which the two young women meet is one in which Esther very carefully includes but does not draw attention to the inequality between her and her new "friend." When Esther is brought before the Lord Chancellor, she receives a very different treatment from Richard and Ada as soon as her illegitimacy is revealed: "Mr. Kenge leant over before it was quite said, and whispered. His lordship, with his eyes upon his papers, listened, nodded twice or thrice, turned over more leaves, and did not look towards me again, until we were going away" (32; ch. 3). While the Lord Chancellor asks Ada whether she has considered Jarndyce's proposal for her residence at Bleak House and whether and why she believes she would find a happy home there, no one ever asks Esther these questions. Esther's way of managing this embarrassing dismissal is to attempt to mask her envy by infantilizing Ada in her retrospective account, apologizing to the reader for her inability to stop herself from calling Ada her "pet" and her "darling" in this scene. As soon as Esther must confess that she was brought in as a sort of elevated servant for Ada, she positions herself through her narrative as a fairly condescending caretaker of her child-like companion.

Esther's inferior social position at Bleak House is made even clearer when Jarndyce assigns her the role of housekeeper. While Esther develops into such an adept household manager that this role comes to seem natural to her, it is in fact something imposed upon her.[12] Esther records in detail the scene in which she is given her new job. First, she and Ada arrive at Bleak House and retire to their rooms to dress for dinner. Esther dresses quickly and then is approached by a maid with the keys to the house, whereupon Esther clarifies that this maid was "not the one in attendance upon Ada," subtly highlighting the class disparity between Esther and Ada in that Ada gets a lady's maid and Esther does not (65; ch. 6). She expresses her surprise to the maid, who replies, "I was told to bring them [the keys] as soon as you was alone, miss" (65; ch. 6). That Jarndyce orders the keys be brought to Esther when she is alone suggests that he is aware of the potential embarrassment Esther might feel for being assigned this job—one of a high-ranking servant, not of an educated woman.[13] Esther then records her reaction primarily through Ada, and only in negative terms: "[Ada] had such a delightful confidence in me when I showed her the keys and told her about them, that it would have been insensibility and ingratitude not to feel encouraged. I knew, to be sure, that it was the dear girl's kindness; but I liked to be so pleasantly cheated" (65; ch. 6). Esther implies that Ada was "pleasantly cheating" her in a polite attempt to smooth over her embarrassment, not just expressing her confidence in Esther's housekeeping abilities; as during earlier moments when Esther is forced into being something she would otherwise not be, she can only describe her reaction in terms of how she *doesn't* (or is not supposed to) feel: "it would have been insensibility and ingratitude *not* to feel encouraged."

Esther's new position as housekeeper provides her with the tool for her most characteristic tic: her reassuring shake of her keys whenever she catches herself feeling what she shouldn't. That Esther shakes her keys out of resentment and not out of domestic warmth is quite obvious the very first time she performs this action. At the end of her first night at Bleak House, she is left to muse over the possible future between Ada and Richard (a romantic future that Esther's social position forbids), her "shadowy speculations" on her birth (75; ch. 6), and the "idle dream," now dead, that Jarndyce was her father (76; ch. 6). As she kills off her hope for ways out of her current position, she returns to her childhood technique of repressing her desires, this time with the added reassurance created by the sound of her jingling keys: "It was all gone now, I remembered, getting up from the fire. It was not for me to muse over bygones, but to act with a cheerful spirit and a grateful heart. So I said to myself, 'Esther, Esther, Esther! Duty, my dear!' and gave my little basket of housekeeping keys such a shake, that they sounded like little bells, and rang me hopefully to bed" (76; ch. 6). Recognizing that the life Jarndyce chooses for her leaves no room for her own will, Esther attempts to crush that will by reminding herself of a duty created by her forced dependence on Jarndyce's charity.

The only time Esther directly speaks her dissatisfaction with her role at Bleak House is during her illness, when she can narrate through the safe medium of a fever dream. First, she describes her discomfort at seeing the various stages of her life melt into one another: "At once a child, an elder girl, and the little woman I had been so happy as, I was not only oppressed by cares and difficulties adapted to each station, but by the great perplexity of endlessly trying to reconcile them" (431; ch. 35). In a way that again echoes Fraiman's description of the plight of heroines in bildungsromans by women writers—characters who have "a clearer sense that formation is foisted upon them, that they are largely what other people, what the world, will make of them" (6)—what troubles Esther the most here is the difficulty of fulfilling all of the feminine roles that are expected of her, a burden that manifests most clearly at the height of her illness: "Dare I hint at that worse time when, strung together somewhere in great black space, there was a flaming necklace, or ring, or starry circle of some kind, of which *I* was one of the beads! And when my only prayer was to be taken off from the rest, and when it was such inexplicable agony and misery to be a part of the dreadful thing?" (432; ch. 35).

In the only moment in her narrative when Esther can openly focus entirely on herself, she relates her greatest horror as being bound to a system of which she desperately wants to be free. Just like all of the other characters in the novel, Esther finds herself caught in a tangled web of relationships and identities that she cannot escape. However, unlike the characters in the third-person narrative, Esther, as a first-person narrator, is allowed to voice her terror of this stifling existence, albeit briefly. Her recovery only binds her more tightly to the network from which she wishes to free herself, as it eventually leads to two of the most traumatic experiences in her narrative: her confrontation with and rejection by her mother, and her near-marriage to John Jarndyce.

Esther reveals part of her troubled feelings for Jarndyce through her circuitous method of referencing her own sexual desire. While Esther's bizarre means of introducing Allan Woodcourt into her story have frequently been read as evidence of stereotypical Victorian repression, the fact that she nearly erases her own (desired) marriage plot makes sense in the context of her story because her relationship with Woodcourt comes very close to being erased. From her first night at Bleak House, she is made aware that she is not to have the kind of romantic courtship that Richard and Ada are allowed; instead, she is taken in as Jarndyce's confidante and forced to watch Ada proceed towards a future that Esther seems to want but is not able to articulate.

In her retrospective narrative of how she became the happy Mrs. Woodcourt, Esther spends an inordinate amount of time describing just how bothered she was by the prospect of marrying Jarndyce. She carefully and repeatedly includes moments that highlight how strongly she felt for Woodcourt while telling the story that leads to her engagement to Jarndyce. Her account of her response to Jarndyce's proposal letter is incredibly detailed and, after a few necessary moments of self-reassurance, brutally honest. She describes what Jarndyce does *not* write in this letter: that he proposes only after Esther has lost her looks and learned of her illegitimacy, the conditions that make her essentially unmarriageable. She reflects on this omission: "But *I* knew it, I knew it well now. It came upon me as the close of the benignant history I had been pursuing, and *I felt that I had but one thing to do*" (538; ch. 44; emphasis added). She then gives her painful reaction: "Still I cried very much; not only in the fulness [sic] of my heart after reading the letter, not only in the strangeness of the prospect . . . but as if something for which there was no name or distinct idea were indefinitely lost to me. I was very happy, very thankful, very hopeful; but I cried very much" (538; ch. 44).[14] While Esther makes a feeble attempt to represent Jarndyce's offer as generous, she also characterizes the proposal as a form of blackmail. She had "but one thing to do"— no choice, no liberty of action—and she is forced to kill again whatever hopes she had developed for the direction of her life, this time giving them a symbolic burial in the burning of Woodcourt's flowers. Again, in a narrative that ends with praise of the generous and beneficent John Jarndyce, Esther recounts in surprising detail the pain that her guardian caused her when he decided to wield what little power he had in the form of irresponsible charity towards a powerless young woman.

Not only does Esther fail at her own attempts at affecting social change, but as the object *of* charity, she relates the devastating effects of being robbed of her will. The emotional turmoil that permeates Esther's narrative results not only from being deprived of social agency by her illegitimate birth, but also, more personally and painfully, by the way she is manipulated because of being a woman with no independent fortune and no family to look out for her welfare. In direct contrast to the traditional bildungsroman narrative of individual triumph, Esther's narrative reveals the extent to which some individuals cannot overcome the insurmountable odds stacked against them; her failed bildung serves as a critique of the power of "willful self-making" (Fraiman 6). What Esther wants for herself makes almost no difference in the path her life takes, and her narrative records her resentment towards everyone who disregards her will, particularly John Jarndyce.

Esther's sense of entrapment and her need to confess the intense pain Jarndyce put her through appear most strongly in her detailed accounts of Woodcourt's proposal and her distress at having to plan a wedding that she dreads. Moreover, when Esther finally records Jarndyce's "generous" transferal of her to the man she loves, she suffers an almost complete breakdown. Despite being unable to speak throughout the scene, she describes every part of Jarndyce's proud confession. The close of Jarndyce's triumphant speech is perhaps the most disturbing part of his character represented in Esther's narrative, and she records his words in detail:

"One more last word. When Allan Woodcourt spoke to you [proposing marriage], my dear, he spoke with my knowledge and consent—but I gave him no encouragement, not I, *for these surprises were my great reward*, and I was too miserly to part with a scrap of it. He was to come, and tell me all that passed; and he did. I have no more to say. . . . This day I give this house its little mistress; and before God, *it is the brightest day in all my life!*" (753; ch. 64; emphasis added)

To return to Mill, "The only freedom which deserves the name, is that of pursuing our own good in our own way, so long as we do not attempt to deprive others of theirs, or impede their efforts to obtain it" (28-29); in his treatment of Esther (and Woodcourt), Jarndyce abuses his power as a liberal individual by knowingly drawing out Esther's misery through preventing her from pursuing her own happiness. Before he leaves Esther and Woodcourt to their new home, Jarndyce makes a final request: "I know that my mistake has caused you some distress. Forgive your old guardian, in restoring him to his old place in your affections; and blot it out of your memory" (753; ch. 64). Clearly Esther does not grant this, for she records her entire traumatic experience seven years after its occurrence, when she claims to be the happiest of wives with the kindest of guardians.

As in the third-person narrative, little changes at the end of Esther's story. Esther has a future determined for her and is resigned to the role of housekeeper at the second Bleak House. Although she marries the man she desired, she does not bring about the marriage through any means of her own. In giving up Esther, Jarndyce reclaims the now impoverished and dependent Ada and the new Richard, requiring them to call him "Guardian," just as he did Esther. Esther, too, keeps her old, domestic nicknames, with Woodcourt calling her in the final scene "My precious little woman," "my dear," "my busy bee," and "My dear Dame Durden" (770; ch. 67). That Esther ends her narrative and the novel with a dash, not a period, is appropriate, for she clearly has not moved past the trauma of her experiences and is required to retell them.

Dickens's inclusion of so many unsettling indicators of Esther's discontent prevents her narrative from serving as an optimistic counter to the lack of hope for social progress in the third-person narrator's portion of the novel. Her story can hardly be called "a progress," for she does not recover from her traumatic experiences and instead seems doomed to relive them through the very act of narrating. Moreover, Esther's narrative suggests that personal charity is inherently flawed precisely because it is personal, a rejection of the personal-charity model for social improvement that the third-person narrative hints as the only alternative to the incompetence of institutional reform. In John Jarndyce, Dickens does not recreate the kindhearted wealthy man of his earlier fiction—a beneficent caretaker capable of creating a sanctuary from the gloom. Instead, through his creation of Esther Summerson, a masterful and entirely convincing imitation of a damaged psyche, he reveals the disturbing downsides to a world built on a liberal paradigm, one full of self-interested even if sometimes well-meaning John Jarndyces whose pursuits of individual happiness only come at the expense of others' liberty.

Through the combination of Esther's first-person anti-bildungsroman (her "progress" that makes no progress) and the third-person narrator's troubling account of the condition of England, Dickens offers in *Bleak House* a pessimistic forecast for the nation's future. His use of the split narrative and the combination of genres allows for a more thorough critique of the liberal values that underpinned both the bildungsroman and the social problem novel than would have been possible with a novel written in only one of these genres. Dickens makes the radical suggestion that a model for reform founded on the idea of changing individuals is entirely ineffective in a world in which individuals cannot escape the circumstances that define them or where individual action makes no difference in the greater scheme of things, a disconcerting exposure of the limits of liberalism that could only be achieved with such force through the unique and unprecedented form Dickens chose for this mid-century novel. Decades before any clear articulation of a theory of "the social" in England, *Bleak House* illustrates the inadequacy of liberal reform for the widespread systemic problems that plagued both the nation and the individual.

NOTE

1. See, for example, Tracy's "Lighthousekeeping" and Heady's "The Polis's Different Voices"
2. My argument about the parallel social critiques offered in the two narratives contrasts with other readings of the novel that see Esther's narrative as entirely different in focus from that of the third-person narrative. For instance, in comparing Hannah Craft's novel *The Bondwoman's Narrative to "Bleak House,"* Daniel Hack criticizes Dickens for the separation of his plots: "*Bleak House* presents this separation of mother and daughter as a personal tragedy, divorced from the social ones it describes" (750).
3. In *Living Liberalism,* Elaine Hadley illustrates the diversity of liberal identity by describing "the motley political party that consisted of old Whig families, former Peelite conservatives, Nonconformist northerners, intellectual agnostics, philosophical radicals, a younger generation of utilitarians, free-market ideologues, and, increasingly, any number of single-issue groups (Sabbatarian, nonsectarian)" (1).
4. Mill's *On Liberty* was not published until 1859, six years after *Bleak House.* However, like Hadley, who reads Anthony Trollope's 1855 novel *The Warden* through Mill, I believe that the slightly ahistorical application of Mill's definitions to Dickens's novel is legitimized by the fact that the ideas Mill espouses were already in wide circulation by the early 1850s.
5. This seems to be the most popular reading of the novel's reformatory agenda. Katherine Montwieler, for instance, writes, "Dickens suggests, by recognizing our shared suffering and mortality . . . we can begin to alleviate the pain of others. Dickens's hope then is that through the inclusion of scenes of suffering and paragons of good (and bad) readers, he can inspire his audience to look, to listen, and to act—to help others—as well" (239).
6. My reading coincides in many ways with Timothy Peltason's analysis of the power of Esther's will. However, while Peltason reads Esther's narrative as "the story of her progress in healthy self-love" (673), I argue that her narrative reveals her anger and frustration at never being allowed to have a will of her own.

7. For one of the earliest and most convincing applications of trauma theory to Esther's narrative, see Alex Zwerdling's "Esther Summerson: Rehabilitated." For a more recent reading of Esther's trauma, see Jordan's chapters "Voice" and "Psychoanalysis" in *Supposing Bleak House.*

8. Brenda Ayres, whose reading of Esther's dissatisfaction with her domestic lot shares much in common with my own, discusses this particular narrative trick that is so pervasive in Esther's narrative: "Regardless of what her desire is, [Esther] says that her desire does not matter. If so, why *indeed* hint at it in the writing? Erasing out of text any reference to her having desire would have been the true act of self-denial. What she erases, instead, is the specific desire itself as if she, as a woman, has no right to feel desire, but feel desire she does" (148).

9. As an illegitimate young woman raised in a middle-class household, Esther's options in life are, of course, limited. However, the fact that Esther is never even consulted about her future prospects highlights both the way in which Jarndyce sees her as lacking a will of her own and the general cultural assumption that women's fates were determined by their gender and class.

10. See, for example, Kimberle L. Brown's reading.

11. For an alternative yet complementary reading of Esther's use of Ada as a second-self, see Peltason (682–83).

12. An example of a critic who takes Esther at face-value in her relationship to domesticity is Laurie Langbauer: "With her basket of keys, [Esther] is also the embodiment of home in *Bleak House*, a warder who actually locks herself up: she monitors most closely her own emotions so that she can remain happily incarcerated within Bleak House" (150).

13. In her role as housekeeper at Bleak House, Esther in some ways resembles Agnes Wickfield in *David Copperfield.* However, Agnes is given the keys to her father's house as a child in a way that highlights the charm of her innocent sense of responsibility. She later is made to bear the full weight of that sense of responsibility when her father is no longer able to protect her or himself, but her role as housekeeper always remains a private relationship between her and her father. Esther, on the other hand, is assigned the role by someone she has just met and who has no family tie that would make her housekeeping anything more than a job, one for which she is paid in room and board.

14. Esther's language here echoes what she writes early in her narrative when she describes her reaction to thinking back to the painful time when she first formulated her plan to atone for her birth by winning love for herself: "I am very thankful, I am very cheerful, but I cannot quite help [tears] coming to my eyes" (20; ch. 3). This parallel suggests that Esther's self-sacrifice to Jarndyce pains her in much the same way that her concession to the identity her aunt impressed upon her did. In both instances, Esther claims to have feelings like those expected of her ("thankful," "cheerful," "hopeful,"), but her tears belie her underlying pain at having to become someone she would rather not.

WORKS CITED

Ayres, Brenda. *Dissenting Women in Dickens' Novels: The Subversion of Domestic Ideology*. Westport, CT: Greenwood Press, 1998.

Born, Daniel. *The Birth of Liberal Guilt in the English Novel: Charles Dickens to H. G. Wells*. Chapel Hill: U of North Carolina P, 1995.

Brown, Kimberle L. "'When I Kissed Her Cheek': Theatrics of Sexuality and the Framed Gaze in Esther's Narration of *Bleak House*." *Dickens Studies Annual* 39 (2008): 149–75.

Claybaugh, Amanda. *The Novel of Purpose: Literature and Social Reform in the Anglo-American World*. Ithaca: Cornell UP, 2007.

Dickens, Charles. *Bleak House*. Ed. George Ford and Sylvère Monod. New York: Norton, 1990.

Fraiman, Susan. *Unbecoming Women: British Women Writers and the Novel of Development*. New York: Columbia UP, 1993.

Goodlad, Lauren. *Victorian Literature and the Victorian State: Character and Governance in a Liberal Society*. Baltimore: Johns Hopkins UP, 2003.

Guy, Josephine M. *The Victorian Social-Problem Novel: The Market, the Individual and Communal Life*. New York: St. Martin's, 1996.

Hack, Daniel. "Close Reading at a Distance: The African Americanization of *Bleak House*." *Critical Inquiry* 34.4 (2008): 729–53.

Hadley, Elaine. *Living Liberalism: Practical Citizenship in Mid-Victorian Britain*. Chicago: U of Chicago P, 2010.

Heady, Emily. "The Polis's Different Voices: Narrating England's Progress in Dickens's *Bleak House*." *Texas Studies in Literature and Language* 48.4 (2006): 312–39.

Herbert, Christopher. "The Occult in 'Bleak House.'" *Novel: A Forum on Fiction* 17.2 (1984): 101–115.

Jordan, John O. *Supposing Bleak House*. Charlottesville: U of Virginia P, 2011.

Joyce, Simon. "Inspector Bucket versus Tom-all-Alone's: *Bleak House*, Literary Theory, and the Condition-of-England in the 1850s." *Dickens Studies Annual* 32 (2002): 129–49.

Langbauer, Laurie. *Women and Romance: The Consolations of Gender in the English Novel*. Ithaca: Cornell UP, 1990.

Levine, Caroline. "Narrative Networks: Bleak House and the Affordances of Form." *Novel: A Forum on Fiction* 42.3 (2009): 517–23.

Mill, John Stuart. *The Spirit of the Age, On Liberty, The Subjection of Women*. Ed. Alan Ryan. New York: Norton, 1997.

Miller, J. Hillis. "Moments of Indecision in Bleak House." *The Cambridge Companion to Charles Dickens*. Ed. John O. Jordan. Cambridge: Cambridge UP, 2001. 49–63.

Montwieler, Katherine. "Reading, Sympathy, and the Bodies of *Bleak House*." *Dickens Studies Annual* 41 (2010): 237–63.

Moretti, Franco. *The Way of the World: The Bildungsroman in European Culture*. London: Verso, 1987.

Peltason, Timothy. "Esther's Will." *ELH* 59 (1992): 671–91.

Robbins, Bruce. "Telescopic Philanthropy: Professionalism and Responsibility in *Bleak House*." *New Casebooks: Bleak House*. Ed. Jeremy Tambling. New York: St. Martin's, 1998. 139–62.

Tracy, Robert. "Lighthousekeeping: *Bleak House* and the Crystal Palace." *Dickens Studies Annual* 33 (2003): 25–53.

Zwerdling, Alex. "Esther Summerson Rehabilitated." *PMLA* 88.3 (1973): 429–39.

Dickens, Disinterestedness, and the Poetics of Clouded Judgment

Zachary Samalin

This article argues that, throughout his middle and late novels, Charles Dickens developed an explicit critique of the ideals of disinterestedness which continue to dominate discussion of the Victorian discourse of judgment. I make three specific claims about Dickens's development of a critical attitude towards the various kinds of objectivity and detachment that comprise disinterested judgments. First, through a careful reading of the motif of fog in Bleak House, *I argue that while Dickens initially relied on a visual rhetoric of obscurity and clear-sightedness to call for a disinterested critique of Victorian society, this rhetoric is both complicated and compromised by the novel's introduction of a poetics of smell; this alternative sensory modality for critical judgment registered a far more destabilizing and visceral sense of human implication in the physical and moral corruption of the world. Second, Dickens's ambivalent experiments with disinterestedness in* Bleak House *pave the way for a discussion of* Little Dorrit, *in which Dickens explicitly criticizes the visual rhetoric of disinterested and objective clear-sightedness he had earlier entertained.* Little Dorrit's *polemic alleges that Arnoldian endeavors to see the object as in itself it really is are in fact attempts to remain willfully blind to extant social relations among people. Finally, in addition to collapsing clear vision and disinterest into self-interest and obfuscation,* Little Dorrit *also offers readers ample room for speculation about alternative forms of judgment available to the Victorian critical imagination.*

Throughout his middle and late novels, Charles Dickens developed a pronounced and explicit critique of the ideals of disinterestedness that continue to dominate discussion of the Victorian discourse of judgment. While the century and a half since Matthew Arnold set the terms of the debate has yielded little enduring consensus as to the specific constitution of those ideals, the possibility of defining disinterestedness nevertheless maintains a captivating hold on modern scholarship; one is hard pressed to gesture with any precision towards other forms of judgment with which one might contrast this elusive ideal. Turning to Arnold himself offers little help, insofar as the pervasive "ulterior, political, practical considerations about ideas" he bemoaned as stifling the state of English critical intelligence would seem to be the only alternatives to the "free disinterested play of mind" he thought would set it aright (249–50). Yet there is a largely unremarked incongruity between the base and self-interested considerations Arnold eschews and a growing sense within Victorian culture that disinterestedness was neither a viable nor a desirable critical position from which to assess modernity. While this lack of enthusiasm for disinterestedness may have been in part factional, political, and petty, as Arnold urges us to believe, it ought to be seen as well in the context of more significant anti-Enlightenment currents in nineteenth-century thought which questioned both the plausibility and the motivation of calls for detached, objective, and disinterested attitudes; it is in this context that novels such as *Bleak House* and *Little Dorrit* belong.

There has been a notable effort over the last decade to recuperate the Arnoldian conception of disinterestedness, salvaging it from accusations of cultural escapism by complicating its internal mechanics. In this vein, Amanda Anderson's exploration of different "forms of detachment" to be found in the works of major Victorian authors reveals "the shifting and complex relations among objectivity, critical reason and aesthetic free play" which comprise Arnoldian disinterestedness (92–93). Focusing her attention on Arnold's ambivalence towards his own calls for objectivity and detachment, Anderson goes so far as to align Arnold with Dickens, citing their shared "general cultural anxiety about the moral ramifications of modern objectifying practices" (91). On this count, Arnold and Dickens are each understood to present strong cases for the value of a disinterested attitude for modern critical practice, while at the same time articulating often extreme reservations about the specific composition of this attitude. Yet, however nuanced and self-contradictory the relations underlying Arnold's call to "see the object as in itself it really is" might be, that call is incommensurable with Dickens's far more bombastic and negative critique of disinterestedness in *Little Dorrit*. Arnold's and Dickens's reservations differ in kind, and not merely degree. And this is in large part due to the fact that, for Dickens, the actual, lived possibilities for clear vision required to see the object—not as in itself it really is, but to see it at all—were felt to be severely restricted in a culture enshrouded in the obscuring and asphyxiating issue of noxious smokestacks, toxic storm-clouds, and an unceasing onslaught of miasmas and fogs.

In light of this unwholesome cultural atmosphere, this essay makes three claims about Dickens's development of a critical attitude towards disinterestedness and the various kinds of objectivity and detachment of which it is comprised. First, through a careful reading of the motif of fog in *Bleak House*, I argue that while Dickens initially relied on a visual rhetoric of obscurity and clear-sightedness to call for a disinterested and objective critique of Victorian society, this rhetoric is both complicated and compromised by the novel's introduction of a poetics of smell; this alternative sensory modality for critical judgment registered a far more destabilizing and visceral sense of human implication in the physical and moral corruption of the world. Second, reading the fog as both visual and olfactory, Dickens's ambivalent experiments with disinterestedness in *Bleak House* pave the way for a discussion of *Little Dorrit*, in which Dickens explicitly criticizes the visual rhetoric of disinterested and objective clear-sightedness he had earlier entertained. Bringing to the fore the underlying hermeneutic problems which had animated *Bleak House*, *Little Dorrit*'s polemic alleges that endeavors to see the object as in itself it really is are in fact endeavors to remain willfully blind to extant social relations among people, and to avoid self-implication in a negative social order. Finally, in addition to collapsing clear vision and disinterest into self-interest and obfuscation, *Little Dorrit* also offers readers ample room for speculation about alternative forms of judgment available to the Victorian critical imagination. Beginning on the far side of the affective neutrality inherent to disinterestedness, Dickens's late work moves towards a model of clouded judgment.

*

A dense condensation of epistemological, aesthetic, and social concerns, the "implacable November weather" of *Bleak House*'s opening pages marks the onset of the novel's searching inquiry into the nexus of obfuscation and exposure, depth and surface, knowledge and uncertainty. Everything in *Bleak House* is wrapped in a fog which has become a vehicle for a sharp critique of the obscurities of modern society — as morally nefarious as they are physically filthy and contaminating — and, on the most basic figurative level, *Bleak House* proposes to dispel its own fog. This endeavor to pierce the *Bleak House* atmosphere presupposes a certain causal relationship between vision and knowledge, in which sight leads to insight, a hermeneutic perspective which Dickens suggests is necessary in order to produce a critique of Victorian society. It is this visual and hermeneutic character of Dickens's critical project which led D. A. Miller to assert that, in *Bleak House*'s self-assessment, "the novel views the world in better, more clear-sighted and disinterested ways than the world views itself" (85). In Miller's now canonical reading, disinterested judgments and clear-sightedness stand together against the moral and perceptual obscurity of the fog, suggesting the novel's participation in the kind of distancing and objectifying critical practices Anderson describes.

Yet even as *Bleak House* uses its fog as a figurative vehicle to present a strong social critique, it also signals a much more complex shift towards the incorporation of a respiratory and olfactory revulsion as the foundation of critical judgment, and, notably, away from the primacy of vision. The heavy reliance on figures of inhalation, gagging, and smell in *Bleak House* would seem to indicate that, in the Victorian literary imagination, critical and aesthetic judgment were felt to be inextricable from the experiences of a revolting and even asphyxiating atmosphere. Put more succinctly, *Bleak House* exemplifies the shift towards a model of disgusted, as opposed to disinterested, judgment in Victorian culture. Even the opening description of a city lost in its own murk and mire can be read against the primary visual interpretation, in which the removal of the fog is a disinterested critical enterprise: "Fog everywhere. Fog up the river, where it flows among the green airs and meadows; fog down the river, where it rolls defiled among the tiers of shipping, and waterside pollutions of a great (and dirty) city" (11; ch. 1).

Far from providing the ingredients necessary for disinterestedness, the *Bleak House* fog is a figure of a "defiling," unwanted totality, declaring the need for its own removal or dispersal. The fog's role as an object intended to be dispelled, or negated, however, is complicated by its formal features — for example, the sense of all things being continuous and unified, fused with each other, even if grimy and obscure, and Dickens's loping, exhilarated cadence — which, despite the negative valence, speak to the fog's dual function as a source of both entertainment and condemnation:

> As much mud in the streets as if the waters had but newly retired from the face of the earth, and it would not be wonderful to meet a Megalosaurus, forty feet long or so, waddling like an elephantine lizard up Holborn Hill. Smoke lowering down from chimney-pots, making a soft black drizzle, with flakes of soot in it as big as full-grown snowflakes—gone into mourning, one might imagine, for the death of the sun (11; ch. 1).

From the start, then, the fog straddles a complex borderland, at once a powerful figure of socially critical disapprobation and a positive site of playful enjoyment invested with the imaginative energies characteristic of Dickens's writing. Indeed, throughout much of his late work, Dickens turned to and explored precisely this inherently contorted affective position, in which rejection is matched by assent, and repudiation intermingles with and is perhaps compromised by pleasure.

Moreover, if everything is in a fog, then the fog is also in everything: "Fog in the eyes and throats of ancient Greenwich pensioners, wheezing by the firesides of their wards; fog in the stem and bowl of the afternoon pipe of the wrathful skipper" (11; ch. 1). One does not merely watch this fog from across the moor— one breathes it in. Like the mixture of pleasure and displeasure, the internality of the fog to the people that it also enshrouds sorely complicates the initial sense that the fog must be dispelled, since it is not clear what form of gesture, rhetorical or otherwise, is appropriate to the negation of something located within as well as without. In order to account for the immanence of the fog, an element of self-accusation is necessary—though the tautological accusation of *Jarndyce v. Jarndyce* does not quite do the trick. As Miller has pointed out, "what is most radically the matter with being 'in Chancery' is not that there may be no way out of it...but, more seriously, that the binarisms of inside/outside, here/elsewhere become meaningless and the ideological effects they ground impossible" (62). The fog in *Bleak House*, Miller argues, is a critical figure of unwitting, seemingly inevitable complicity with a nebulous social order; a social order, no less, that constitutes the very substance of one's being. At this figure's extremity, there is Krook, whose alignment with nefarious society, morally and materially, finally burns him up into a thick greasy miasma, his body literally joining the fog. As Mr. Weevle notes of the "tainting sort of weather" that night: "It may be something in the air—there is plenty in it—or it may be something in himself, that is in fault" (466–67; ch. 32).

Since *Bleak House* fog is a respiratory phenomenon, albeit a suffocating one, the nose and mouth are the sense organs through which one experiences it, in addition to the eyes. In fact, a whole vocabulary of asphyxiation, distaste, and malodorousness pervades the book—Krook's combusted viscera taken for pork fat charring—distinct from the visual rhetoric of obscurity and illumination which has captivated readers like Miller. Moreover, and as has been often noted, the sense of smell in particular tends to evince just the kind of boundary confusion between inside and outside mentioned above. Writing in a psychoanalytic vein, for example, Robert Lougy has recently observed that smells of "death, excrement, and sex...permeate *Bleak House*" with an uncanny atmosphere of repulsion and attraction, arguing as well that "in *Bleak House*, smells move at will across boundaries or borders, threatening to smudge or blur desired distinctions" (478, 480). As an olfactory and respiratory phenomenon, the fog in *Bleak House* is itself a figure of such boundary confusion, with the novel condemning and repudiating the "defiled," "polluted" smog not only enveloping the whole filthy city, but also "inborn, inbred, engendered in the corrupted humors of the vicious body itself" (479; ch. 32). The critical function of the *Bleak House* fog derives its force from this olfactory and gustatory disgust directed at the porous, permeable human body, a body felt to be full of the same miasmatic foulness that constitutes the atmosphere outside it; rotten bodies aligned with the rotten world, in a kind of feedback loop of mutual contamination. Or, in the novel's own terms, if the combusted Krook's effluvia smells like chops, the meat had already turned: "I don't think—not to put too fine a point on it—that they were quite fresh, when they were shown the gridiron," Mr. Snagsby opines (32.467).

The heavy emphasis in Dickens on the lower senses of taste and smell complicates the conceptions of rationality and sensation, and man and animal, which had underpinned Enlightenment models of disinterested judgment. Dickens's exploration of the poetics of smell, however, is in keeping with Alain Corbin's observations that "the increased attention to social odors was the major event in the history of olfaction in the nineteenth century before Pasteur's theories triumphed," and that "the sudden awareness of the growing differentiation of society was an incentive to refine analysis of smells" (142–43). As modern French society demanded greater articulation of its stratification, Corbin argues, attention to smell heightened, and the attunement between social order and social odor was reinforced. A similar concatenation of the social and the sensory occurred in Great Britain as well, and texts which exhibit pronounced interests in teasing out subtle distinctions in the Victorian class structure not surprisingly often contain rich descriptions of smell and its consequences. Long before George Orwell's revelation of "the real secret of class distinctions in the West" in *The Road to Wigan Pier*, namely, "that the lower class smell" (128), Henry Mayhew had devoted pages and pages of *London Labour and the London Poor* to the yoked topics of stench and stratification. For example, the extended discussion of "the fried fish-sellers" quickly becomes a complex analysis of the interrelation of smell and intraclass prejudice. Noting how "even when the fish is fresh (as it most frequently is), and the oil pure, the odour is rank," Mayhew continues:

> The fried-fish sellers live in some out of the way alley, and not unfrequently in garrets; for among even the poorest class there are great objections to their being fellow-lodgers, on account of the odour from the frying. . . . The cooks, however, whether husbands or wives—for the women often attend to the pan—when they hear of this disagreeable rankness, answer that it may be so, many people say so; but for their parts they cannot smell it all. . . . A gin-drinking neighborhood, one coster said, suits "for people hasn't their smell so correct there." (70–71)

Mayhew highlights the social dimension of smell, especially as it relates to otherwise imperceptible differences in class position unrelated to cleanliness or disorder: "In one place I visited, which was, moreover, admirable for its cleanliness," Mayhew notes, "It was very rank" (70). This ability to sniff out invisible differences served as a justification for the maintenance of class difference, as Janice Carlisle argues in *Common Scents*, writing that the ubiquity of smell in "high-Victorian novels [of the 1860s] . . . reveal[s] the common sense of the middle-class as it was both enacted and obscured by the unremarkably ordinary practices of daily life" (22). For Carlisle, the fullest and most finely gradated representations of social difference emerge from "comparative encounters," moments of contact in which two characters measure their social standing through olfactory snap-judgments (3). Studies such as Carlisle's and Corbin's, as well as primary texts like Mayhew's, foreground the important and often unchallenged role that the sense of smell came to play in modern society as an arbiter of class division and a force of exclusion.

Unlike the stress olfactory studies like Corbin's and Carlisle's lay on difference and division, the fog in *Bleak House*, as a figure of olfactory disgust towards
a total condition, collapses the differences between individuals and classes, and
instead seems to permeate all corners of society with an alarming rankness. Following Edwin Chadwick's 1846 proclamation before the Select Committee on
Metropolitan Sewage Manure that "all smell is disease" (*Metropolitan Sewage
Committee*, 10), certain forms of olfactory experience merged with widespread
fears about the spread of cholera, both paranoid and legitimate. In this sense,
unlike Carlisle's comparative aromatic encounters, the function of the olfactory
motif in *Bleak House* is universalizing, since one noxious smell seems at once to
emanate from and to envelop all things. Even though the Victorian working class
was frequently associated with the spread of dirt and disease, the principal question raised by the fog in *Bleak House* is not one of differences among classes, but
a larger question of the distinction between man and animal, or between civilization and barbarity; such questions plagued Victorian society along much more
extreme and self-implicating olfactory lines than those which fueled the propen-
sity for discriminatory socioeconomic classification.

Victorian olfactory revulsion reached its apex during the Great Stink of 1858,
not quite five years after the publication of *Bleak House*, when a heat wave low-
ered the water level in the brackish Thames by a few inches, revealing well over
a decade's accumulation of human excrement; the weeks-long stench that ensued
was so intense that Parliament was evacuated, and legislature, previously mired
in a contentious bureaucratic limbo for years, was rapidly passed to commission
a modern sewer system and the Thames Embankment. As David S. Barnes has
written of the stinks in London and Paris, "beyond the emotions it provoked, each
of the two Great Stinks also represented a raw affront to the civilization and cultural stature of a great metropolis" (113). The concerns brought to the surface by
such extreme communal sensations reflect the intimacy between experiences of
olfactory revulsion and modern society's consciousness of the vulnerability and
culpability of its attainments. At the heart of this confrontation between sensation
and cultural anxiety lay society's realization of its self-implication in its own contamination; a dawning, gnawing sense that the byproduct of a burgeoning population, as it merged with the moral failings of a new mode of production, might be
enough to sully British civilization from the inside out.

The fog in *Bleak House* intermingles the self-implicating judgment endemic to
Victorian disgust with the figure of a putatively disinterested critical spectator. At
once a corporeal emanation "engendered in the corrupted humors of the vicious
body itself" (479; ch. 32), and a visual metaphor for a repressive social order, the
fog condenses into one figure two unreconciled sensory modalities attributed to
the process of critical judgment. Emphasizing the visual and cognitive dimension
alone, the fog of Chancery reads as an emblem of obfuscation, and the task of the
novel would be the application of the light of a disinterested critical rationality,
recalling again Miller's observation that "the novel views the world in better,

more clear-sighted and disinterested ways than the world views itself." The task
for a critic like Miller then becomes the demystification of the novel's fog-pierc-
ing disinterestedness. Yet we can see now that the fog is also an attempt to render
as "visible" not what is simply hidden from the eyes, but what is not properly
an object of vision: to turn taste or smell into sight. This presents an immense
challenge to the hermeneutically suspicious reader, like Miller, since an invisible
miasma or putrid stench made over into a discernible smokey haze is not so much
an obscuring figure but already one of exposure; specifically, exposure of the
ideological difficulties and aesthetic pressures of transforming an unrepresentable
kind of sensory experience into a representation or knowledge.

However ambivalent, the fog in *Bleak House* enacts a kind of demystification
so deeply embedded in the aesthetic process itself, that it deserves to be read in the
context of other grand critical projects of the nineteenth century which problematize unmasking, even as they take it as their central gesture. Like Nietzsche's critique of ascetic values in *The Genealogy of Morals* for their "hatred of humanity,
of animality" and of their "longing to escape from illusion," Dickensian critique
asserts that human sensation and emotion play a constitutive, ineluctable role in
judgment. Even while it renounces and denigrates the unpleasant sensory and
affective dimension of life, and even though it subordinates that dimension to an
ideal of disinterested reason and clear vision, Dickens's critique of wrong society
remains vitally rooted in the respiratory and olfactory experience of disgust.

*

In *Little Dorrit*, Dickens attacks the very forms of disinterestedness presupposed
by the figure of fog examined above. Even if, as Miller argues, *Bleak House*
attempts the impossible task of achieving disinterested exposure, exposure in
Little Dorrit now becomes the principal object of critique, an inversion that
Anderson has argued reflects his "deep ambivalence toward the very forms of
cultivated distancing that enable a systemic critique of the social totality" (70).
That is why "Sun and Shadow," the opening chapter of Dickens's most forcefully critical novel, *Little Dorrit*, which describes the golden disc of the sun
both illumining and desiccating the world, is functionally equivalent to the *Bleak
House* fog, only now the critique of vision as a dominant sensory modality has
been made explicit:

A blazing sun upon a fierce August day was no greater rarity in southern
France then, than at any other time. Everything in Marseilles, and about
Marseilles, had stared at the fervid sky, and been stared at in return, until
a staring habit had become universal there. Strangers were stared out of
countenance by staring white houses, staring white walls, staring white

streets, staring tracts of arid road, staring hills from which the verdure was burnt away. . . . The universal stare made the eyes ache. . . . The very dust was scorched brown, and something quivered as if the air itself were panting. (1; bk 1, ch. 1)

The passage shares its satirical yet exhilarated playfulness with the opening of *Bleak House*, as well as the emphasis on the connectivity of all things in society— and yet the terms have been pointedly inverted. Against *Bleak House*'s "flakes of soot . . . gone into mourning . . . for the death of the sun," *Little Dorrit* begins instead with an image of total exposure, of a world where the sun has brought all things together in a visual network of mutually constituting spectators and objects of examination: "Everything . . . had stared at the fervid sky, and been stared at in return, until a staring habit had become universal there." With vision exerting an exhausting, inquisitional dominance over the entire sensory realm, exposure is *Little Dorrit*'s starting point, and not the desired end to its critical project. More- over, this process of illumination and scrutiny, of "the universal stare," becomes the emblem of a systemically wrong society, and not the solution to its prob- lems. In a striking reversal of the "tainting sort of weather" characteristic of *Bleak House*, *Little Dorrit* begins with an image of an atmosphere that has been left gasping by the deprivations of exposure—"as if the air itself were panting."

Dickens connects the image of the brilliant sun, as it fixes everything in place, to the novel's economic fairy tale that "Mr. Merdle was . . . a Midas without the ears, who turned all he touched to gold," making a pronounced link between matters of socioeconomic value and the more diffuse thematization of visibility and exposure (206; bk. 1, ch. 21). Merdle, the financial fraud, has become the gold standard for modern society, a phony sun-king who guarantees the value of everything else simply by shining down disinterestedly upon it; in fact, we are told, "he was the most disinterested of men,—did everything for society, and got as little for himself out of all his gain and care, as a man might" (207; bk. 1, ch. 21). In a society where the sun is an immense golden coin, where visual perception and economic rational- ity overlap, Dickens suggests that sight becomes synonymous with the recognition of value: "The weightiest of men had said to projectors, 'Now, what name have you got? Have you got Merdle?' And, the reply being in the negative, had said, 'Then I won't look at you'" (207; bk. 1; ch. 21). Without Merdle, obscurity; though not the obscurity of Chancery, cloaked in secrecy and intrigue, but of a willed non- recognition. If perception and valuation coincide, then one cannot say whether something has no value because it is unseen or is unseen because it is without value. This exploration of the terms of recognition and appraisal is *Little Dorrit*'s main critical innovation, since it gives an account of the process by which areas and elements of society come to be deemed without value and beneath notice, and not merely a critique of one set of social values as opposed to another. By inter- rogating the mechanics at the root of judgments in society, *Little Dorrit* considers clear and disinterested vision a form of obfuscation.

Indeed, the novel consistently presents society's cultivated veneer of disinterest as a semi-willed blindness, describing a perceptual regime under which one sees because one refuses to look. Traversing social and psychological registers—from the Dorrit family's delusions of grandeur and Mrs. Gowan's aristocratic paranoia, all the way up to Merdle's mysterious complaint and the speculation epidemic— the novel understands clear-sightedness as a symptom of a refused confrontation with a repudiated social reality. As Raymond Williams observed, Dickens's critique of the social whole tended increasingly to target and dissect this form of negative, disinterested judgment, rather than focusing exclusively on inviting sympathy through the representation of economic deprivation: "The comfortable turn haughtily away, and from *Dombey and Son* onwards we see a social system in which the turning away is as much a product of circumstances as the distress" (224). Such turning away enables the putatively rational judgments within the solar world of the novel, where critical evaluations are underwritten by the refusal to acknowledge the falseness of society.

Dickens's scrutiny of this form of social evasion puts him in dialogue with a tradition in modern thought of understanding disinterested or detached attitudes in relation to conceptions of contempt. Less volatile and reactive than disgust, contempt can underwrite just the kind of supercilious sociality that Williams describes. Hobbes, for example, in his consideration of the political passions and their underlying motivations, described contempt as "a contumacy of the heart in resisting the action of certain things," a passion of resistance allowing the noble-minded to disregard those objects and people deemed to be "vile and inconsiderable" (28). As William Ian Miller has pointed out in *The Anatomy of Disgust*, Hobbes treats contempt as though it were the absence of emotion, a form of detached indifference, and yet insists on situating it alongside appetite and aversion, the twin engines of social intercourse in *Leviathan* that produce all judgments of good and evil (224). Unlike appetite or aversion, however, to experience Hobbesian contempt is to stifle all desire, rather than to excite it positively or negatively; objects which one desires or detests can enrapture or enrage, can be consumed or destroyed, whereas Hobbes suggests that contempt seals off the judging spectator from the push and pull of its objects, which are consequently designated as so low as to be unworthy of notice. Like Merdle's radiantly disinterested glow, Hobbesian contempt regulates the turning away which determines whether specific elements of society merit recognition or whether they are "inconsiderable." The subject is sealed up hermetically, and unwanted problems disappear.

Little Dorrit sharpens its indictment of disinterestedness by denying the possibility of contemptuously closing oneself off to the world. Moreover, the novel makes explicit the connections between recognition and disavowal through its critical presentation of Mrs. General's regimen for Amy Dorrit's socialization— what she calls, in a Hobbesian vein, "the formation of a surface" (2.5.398). After the family's rise to wealth frees them from the Marshalsea, but before the evaporation of their fairy tale fortune, Mrs. General's program for Amy's entrance into high society begins with the refusal to look, a sneering denial of recognition to unwanted elements of social reality. Gently chiding Amy that "it is scarcely delicate to look at vagrants with the attention which I have seen bestowed upon them, by a very dear young friend of mine," Mrs. General then, in keeping with her name, derives from the particular lesson a universal rule:

> Nothing disagreeable should ever be looked at. Apart from such a habit standing in the way of that graceful equanimity of surface which is so expressive of good breeding, it hardly seems compatible with refinement of mind. A truly refined mind will seem to be ignorant of the existence of anything that is not perfectly proper, placid and pleasant. (398; bk. 2, ch. 5)

In order to cultivate a discerning intellect, Amy's governess instructs her to disavow the existence of unwanted or uncouth realities; the proper functioning of the mind, she implies, depends upon acts of wishful negation. Yet while such negations may come cloaked in indifference, as with Mrs. Gowan "patting her contemptuous lips with her fan" while refusing to hear Arthur's words, Dickens also makes clear that Mrs. General's tutelage represents a mild case of a much broader psychosocial disturbance which is hardly impassive (.267; bk. 1; ch. 26). The novel repeatedly stresses the psychological violence—the denials, disavowals, splittings, projections, and other defenses—necessarily accompanying its characters' various disinterested attitudes and the social institutions they prop up. At the height of this, we find William Dorrit's menacing accusation of Amy for "systematically reproducing what the rest of us blot out"—for being vile without becoming inconsiderable, so to speak—not long before he collapses, mentally and physically, no longer able to straddle coherently the widening gulf between the fantasized world he actually inhabits and the denied realities on which that world depends (363; bk. 2; ch. 1). In Dickens's strong critique, acculturation becomes synonymous with the development of an aversion to the world, which takes shape as an aspirant disavowal.

The proper functioning of Mrs. General's program for "the formation of a surface" demands physically closing off the body, so that it presents an unbroken, impregnable shell to the external world. And, although Mrs. General criticizes Amy for turning her eyes to unwanted sights, it turns out that Amy's lips and mouth lie at the heart of the forms of refusal she promotes, recasting the tension between the visual and the oral or respiratory which we saw in *Bleak House* in more explicit terms. More than a merely metaphorical motto, forming a surface requires sealing up the mouth so that nothing unwanted can come in or go out:

> "I think, father, I require a little time."
> "Papa is a preferable mode of address," observed Mrs. General. "Father is rather vulgar, my dear....Papa, potatoes, poultry, prunes and prism, are all very good words for the lips: especially prunes and prism. You will find

it serviceable, in the formation of a demeanour, if you sometimes say to yourself in company—on entering   room, for instance—Papa, potatoes, poultry, prunes and prism, prunes and prism."

"Pray, my child," said Mr. Dorrit, "attend to the—hum—precepts of Mrs. General." (397; bk. 2; ch. 5)

By pronouncing words that "give a pretty form to the lips," Amy is supposed to avoid vulgarity, both physically and semantically; in fact, the semantic and the physical are here, on Amy's lips, indistinguishable. To understand what may seem like the rhetorical quirks of Dickens's socially critical vision, we have quite seriously to equate the maintenance of the openings and closings of the self with the maintenance of a larger social order beyond the individual. In the ideological fantasy of disinterest which Dickens skewers in *Little Dorrit*, puckering up and pronouncing one's plosives becomes a sociopolitically freighted act, at once an attempted means of encasing the self, of plugging oneself up, as well as a precondition for the production of a socially symbolic language of proper conduct. In this respect, the pattern of disavowal and blindness that Dickens examines throughout the novel begins with the initial disavowal of the body's own porosity and vulnerability—a garish vision of Society, shut down by its bilabial stops and holding its nose.

The language which Mrs. General urges Amy to adopt is a language of disgust, as contemptuous fantasizing about the body's impermeability to unwanted sights becomes indistinguishable from a seething repulsion which registers its own implication in unwanted social processes, breathing them in and breathing them out much as we saw with the *Bleak House* fog. Contumacy of the heart and gag reflex, it turns out, make use of the same language, a language that relies on the body, and yet repudiates bodies at the same time; a language of social squeamishness that depends on a visceral humanism. Interestingly enough, the mixture of physical and socially symbolic valences which Dickens affords his plosives would have found plenty of support within mid-Victorian linguistics, many of whom argued that the very origins of language were to be found in mankind's primitive, primal, onomatopoetic exclamations and ejaculations. At a historical moment when the study of language was beginning to understand itself as a science, and to focus exclusively on objectively knowable linguistic laws and universalizable phonetic notations, many Victorian philologists resisted the contemporary appeal of German proponents of *Sprachwissenschaft* and argued instead that language was rooted in the morphological contours of the human body and its guttural cries. Chief among these holdouts was the etymologist Hensleigh Wedgwood, whose essay on "The Origins of Language" (1866) left a lasting impression on the late work of his cousin and brother-in-law, Charles Darwin, yet was also derided by Max Müller in his *Lectures on the Science of Language* as arguing for "Bow-Wow" and "Pooh-Pooh" theories of linguistic origins. Indeed, in a subsection entitled "Pooh!" Wedgwood proposes that "the attitude of dislike and rejection is typified by signs of spitting out an unsavoury morsel," the foremost of which is, across a wide variety of cultures, the bilabial stop: "The sound of spitting is represented indifferently with an initial *p*, as in Maori *puhwa*, to spit out; Lat. Spuere, to spit; *respuere* (to spit back), to reject with disdain; *despuere*, to reject with disgust or disdain" (xlv). According to Wedgwood's onomatopoeic theory, the language of negative judgments arose from the sounds associated with the imitation of spitting in disgust and distaste—that is, with the letter *p*.

Throughout *Little Dorrit*, Dickens relies on the same sort of physical semantics that Wedgwood would propose a few years later, highlighting in particular the indeterminate fact that to purse one's lips can be at once to close off the body in disdain, and yet also to eject something already ingested across the body's borders and back into the world in disgust. Mrs. General's instructions for sealing oneself off from unwanted sights simultaneously enact a boundary confusion in which what is unwanted inside the body and what is unwanted outside the body meet in the mouth. With individual characters as well as in a broader thematic register, the novel equates the negotiation of the social, economic, and political spheres with the management of the permeability of the body through its breathing and smelling, as though both played a part in some larger homeostatic process. As an alternative to Mrs. General's imprisoning prunes and prisms, for example, one might turn to Pancks's perpetual "perspiration [as he] snorted and sniffed and puffed and blew, like a little laboring steam-engine," a respiratory process which seems to calibrate and pressurize him both morally and physically rather than to plug him up (1.13.124).

Dickens begins to thematize the body's respiratory porosity as early as the description of the "universal stare" in the novel's opening paragraph, the loping cadence of which comes to an abrupt halt when the assonant "staring white houses, staring white walls, staring white streets, staring tracts of arid road" crash headlong into a declarative bilabial stop: "The only things to be seen not fixedly staring and glaring were the vines drooping under their load of grapes." Dickens does not immediately explain why the grapes are singled out for exemption from the sun's universal gaze, and, in fact, they only gain a more than incidental association over three hundred pages later, at the start of the novel's second book:

> The air there was charged with scent of grapes. Baskets, troughs, and tubs of grapes, stood in the dim village doorways, stopped the steep and narrow village streets. . . . Grapes, spilt and crushed underfoot, lay about everywhere. The child carried in a sling by the laden peasant-woman toiling home, was quieted with picked-up grapes; the idiot sunning his big goiter under the eaves of the wooden chalet by the way to the waterfall, sat munching grapes; the breath of the cows and goats was redolent of leaves and stalks of grapes; the company in every little cabaret were eating, drinking, talking grapes. (361; bk. 2, ch. 1)

Falling outside the disinterested sunshine that consumes the opening pages of the novel, the grapes which open the second volume present a negative image of the first, with the "blazing sun" staring down from "the fervid sky" here offset by the "air charged with the scent of grapes," and the universal staring habit directly contrasting the olfactory and respiratory suffusion of breath "redolent of leaves and stalks of grapes." As night falls in the Alps and a thick fog descends on the prison-sprung Dorrit family's caravan, the novel's second beginning serves as a direct counterpoint to the first.

Far from suffocating, however, this alpine fog carries an entirely different affective valence than any of the examples considered above, suggesting that, in addition to its trenchant critique of the ideal of disinterested judgment, *Little Dorrit* also provides an alternative form of contemplative and critical judgment that is rooted in, and not pitted against, sensory experience:

> When [darkness] at last rose to the walls of the convent of the Great Saint Bernard, it was as if that weather-beaten structure were another Ark, and floated away upon the shadowy waves. . . . Up here in the clouds, everything was seen through cloud, and seemed dissolving into cloud. The breath of the men was cloud, the breath of the mules was cloud, the lights were encircled by cloud, speakers close at hand were not seen for cloud, though their voices and all other sounds were surprisingly clear...In the midst of this, the great stable...poured forth its contribution of cloud, as if the whole rugged edifice were filled with nothing else, and would collapse as soon as it had emptied itself. (362–63; bk. 2; ch. 1)

Like the fog in *Bleak House*, the cloud here is obscuring and respiratory, emphasizing the lack of distinction between what is outside and inside, the permeability of the body, and even, by the continuity between the "breath of men" and "the breath of mules," the animality of the human body. Yet, unlike *Bleak House* or Mrs. General's imprisoning pronunciations, this passage does not characterize this boundary confusion as either unwanted or foul, and instead lends a fantastic quality to the experience of dissolution. This is true despite, or because of, the fact that the fog is also full of the steam of animal dung, with "the great stable . . . pour[ing] forth its contribution of cloud," described as though it were defecating. Instead of the object of a critical revulsion, this very corporeal mountain fog is designated as a site of positive value, with the stable's steaming dung granted a foundational status, "as if the whole rugged edifice were filled with nothing else."

The desire for dissolution in *Little Dorrit* is not limited to taking in the mountain air. Quite the contrary, the Thames in the novel emerges as the focus of Arthur Clennam's and Amy Dorrit's depressive fantasies of drifting off and dissolving as a means of escaping the ordeal of professional, familial, societal, and romantic obligations. Maybe rivers are *loci classici* of this kind of idle fantasying, but the novel was being written and serialized in the three years leading up to the

Great Stink, when, as Dickens himself puts it in the novel, "through the heart of the town a deadly sewer ebbed and flowed, in the place of a fine fresh river"—a description not of the Thames during the 1820s, when the novel is set, but of the 1850s, long after it had become the whole city's cesspool. Still, not only does Amy stare longingly off the Iron Bridge into the murky future, but a heartsick Arthur actually fantasizes about floating off downstream, which for readers in 1857 would have meant immersing oneself in the sometimes visible excrement of nearly three million Londoners: "And he thought—who has not thought for a moment, sometimes—that it might be better to flow away monotonously, like the river, and to compound for its insensibility to happiness with its insensibility to pain" (169; bk. 1; ch. 16). Like being in a fog, the river here is a figure of alignment between container and contents, however grotesque. But the animus has once again been inverted in *Little Dorrit*, so that the dissolution of the physical body into its own muck, and the attendant loss of identity, are felt as potential alternatives to a wrong society that privileges false exposure, the primping and preening of Mrs. General's "formation of the surface," and, above all, "the odor of Circumlocution" (1.34.339). Against such putatively disinterested ideals, *Little Dorrit* provides us with a fully articulated poetics of clouded judgment.

*

Against the putative disinterestedness and clear-sightedness that *Little Dorrit* suggests retained dominance as prescriptive ideals within Victorian society, the novel asserts instead that judgment is inextricable from the the physical contours and sensory experience of the human body. In fact, the acknowledgment of the body's alignment with its environment is for Dickens the crucial step in producing a critique of modern society. Fog is no longer a figure of disinterested judgment, but rather an emanation of the judging subject's sense of its implication in the state of the world—that is, of the overlap between perception and valuation. Moreover, it is this very sense of self-implication that the disinterested attitudes we have examined attempt to abnegate, by isolating reason from sensation and feeling. At the broadest theoretical level, these questions of disinterestedness and self-implication are contortions of the same problem of acknowledgment of human involvement in the blighting of the natural world, and of the unavoidable humanness of nature. Far from the sentimental humanism often attributed to Dickens, *Little Dorrit*'s critical agenda runs surprisingly close to Adorno's discussion of ugliness in the *Aesthetic Theory*:

> In naively condemning the ugliness of a landscape torn up by industry, the bourgeois mind zeroes in on the appearance of the domination of nature at the precise juncture where nature shows man a facade of irrepressibility. . . .

This kind of ugliness will vanish only when the relation between man and nature throws off its repressive character, which is a continuation rather than an antecedent of the repression of man. (70)

Like Adorno, *Little Dorrit* also urges that the ugliness of modern society be understood as the excrescence of the repressive ugliness of the human relationships which comprise it. The natural world can only appear repulsive to a judging spectator, and what is deemed repulsive can only ever gesture back negatively to the alienated relations which constitute its substance—Amy Dorrit staring searchingly off the Iron Bridge, engulfed by the brute odor of the human river. Dickens's fogs and their spectators are figures for this dynamic confrontation between human and environment, a thematic site of interest which informed Dickens's sense of the deep connection between the novelistic project and the functions of criticism.

The specific shift in critical function from *Bleak House* to *Little Dorrit* reflects the substantial degree to which the prescriptive value of the disinterested spectator weakened over the course of the nineteenth century and was subjected to rigorous and explicit critique. Yet this weakening was, as *Little Dorrit* asserts, simultaneous with the development of ever more thorough and ever more disinterested methods for understanding society objectively. From one perspective the Victorian period articulated its needs through a complex set of appeals to the affective dimension of judgment, olfactory revulsion in particular, and from another perspective it developed progressively more efficient strategies for neutralizing, and not just responding to, those appeals; as though subordinating its own revulsion to retrospective disinterest was the solution to the problem. This double perspective provides an image of modern society as oscillating between irreconcilable modes of self-comprehension. At its most exposed and exposing, the Victorian discourse of judgment, embodied by Dickens's late works, radically questioned the inherited neutral epistemological rhetoric of disinterestedness, and approached a perhaps still unmatched understanding of the implication of human agency in society's own self-contamination and self-obscuring, its own suffocation, exhaust, and exhaustion.

WORKS CITED

Adorno, Theodor. *Aesthetic Theory.* New York: Routledge, 1984.

Anderson, Amanda. *The Powers of Distance: Cosmopolitanism and the Cultivation of Detachment.* Princeton: Princeton UP, 2001.

Arnold, Matthew. *The Portable Matthew Arnold.* Ed. Lionel Trilling. New York: Viking, 1949.

Barnes, David S. "Confronting Sensory Crisis in the Great Stinks of London and Paris."

Filth: Dirt, Disgust and Modern Life. Ed. William A. Cohen. Minneapolis: U of Minnesota P, 2005: 103–32.

Bromwich, David. "The Genealogy of Disinterestedness." *Raritan* 1 (1982): 62–92.

Carlisle, Janice. *Common Scents: Comparative Encounters in High-Victorian Fiction.* New York: Oxford UP, 2004.

Cohen, William. *Embodied: Victorian Literature and the Senses.* Minneapolis: U of Minnesota P, 2009.

Corbin, Alain. *The Foul and the Fragrant: Odor and the French Social Imagination.* Cambridge: Harvard UP, 1986.

Dickens, Charles. *Bleak House.* Ed. Stephen Gill. New York: Oxford UP, 1998.

———. *Little Dorrit.* Ed. Harvey Sucksmith, ed. Oxford UP, 2008.

Dowling, Linda. "Victorian Oxford and the Science of Language." *PMLA* 97. (2) (1982): 160–78.

Hobbes, Thomas. *Leviathan: With Selected Variants.* Indianapolis: Hackett, 1994.

Hume, David. *Essays Moral, Political and Literary.* Ed. Eugene F. Miller. Indianapolis: Liberty, 1987.

Kaplan, Fred. *Dickens: A Biography.* New York: Avon, 1988.

Lougy, Robert. "Filth, Abjection and Liminality in Charles Dickens's *Bleak House*." *ELH* 69 (2002): 473–500.

Mayhew, Henry. *London Labour and the London Poor.* Ed. Victor Neuburg. New York: Penguin, 1985.

McLaughlin, Kevin. "Culture and Messianism: Disinterestedness in Arnold." *Victorian Studies* 50.4 (Summer 2008): 615–39.

Metropolitan Sewage Committee proceedings. Parliamentary Papers. 1846.

Miller, D. A. *The Novel and the Police.* Berkeley: U of California P, 1989.

Miller, William Ian. *The Anatomy of Disgust.* Cambridge: Harvard UP, 1999.

Müller, Max. *Lectures on the Science of Language.* New York: Scribner, 1862.

Nietzsche, Friedrich. *The Birth of Tragedy and The Genealogy of Morals.* Trans. Francis Golffing. New York: Doubleday Anchor, 1956.

Orwell, George. *The Road to Wigan Pier.* New York: Houghton Mifflin, 1958.

Rind, Miles. "The Concept of Disinterestedness in Eighteenth-Century British Philosophy." *Journal of the History of Philosophy* 40.1 (2002): 67–87.

Ruskin, John. *The Storm-Cloud of the Nineteenth Century: Two Lectures.* New York: Wiley, 1884.

Sedgwick, Eve Kosofsky. *The Weather in Proust.* Durham: Duke UP, 2011.

Sen, Sambuda. "*Bleak House* and *Little Dorrit*: The Radical Heritage." *ELH* 65 (1998): 945–70.

Stolnitz, Jerome. "On the Origin of 'Aesthetic Disinterestedness.'" *The Journal of Aesthetics and Art Criticism* 20.2 (1961): 131–43.

Wedgwood, Hensleigh. "On the Origin of Language." *A Dictionary of English Etymology.* London: Trübner, 1872.

Williams, Raymond. "Social Criticism in Dickens: Some Problems of Method and Approach." *Critical Quarterly* 6 (1964): 214–27.

Math and the Mechanical Mind: Charles Babbage, Charles Dickens, and Mental Labor in *Little Dorrit*

Jessica Kuskey

While critics have remarked on Charles Dickens's decades-long association and friendship with Charles Babbage, we still lack close examination of the influence Babbage's wide-ranging work in political economy, mathematics, and mechanical inventions had on Dickens's literary production. Through analysis of Babbage's mathematical theory, his invention of the Difference Engine (the first programmable mechanical calculator), and Dickens's rep-resentation of Babbage in Little Dorrit, *I argue that our current conception of intellectual property derives from Victorian efforts to establish the mental labor of the "professional" as unalienated and self-directed through its op-position to the monotonous, repetitive labor imposed upon factory workers and on mechanized mental laborers. While critical attention to the novel generally focuses on its representation of speculative finance, the crucial role of math in this central plot element has yet to be taken seriously, as has the related mechanization of the characters most closely involved in the mental labors of mathematics and finance. The novel's representations of mechanized mathematical labor thus illuminate the ways Dickens as a novel-ist and Babbage as an inventor were similarly engaged with contemporary debates about mental labor, intellectual property, and the social utility of the professional.*

According to Thomas Carlyle's well-known declaration in his 1829 essay "Signs of the Times," his was a lamentably mechanical age: "Were we required to characterise this age of ours by any single epithet, we should be tempted to call it, not a Heroical, Devotional, Philosophical, or Moral Age, but, above all others, the Mechanical Age. It is the Age of Machinery, in every outward and inward sense of that word" (6). Carlyle is not simply critiquing industrialization, but accuses society of becoming thoroughly mechanized to the extent that individuals internalize this impulse and are now "mechanical in head and in heart, as well as in hand" (9). Among numerous supposed causes of this mental mechanization, Carlyle accuses math:

> Mathematics, the highly prized exponent of all these other sciences, has also become more and more mechanical. Excellence in what is called its higher departments depends less on natural genius than on acquired expertness in wielding its machinery. Without undervaluing the wonderful results which a Lagrange or Laplace educes by means of it, we may remark, that their calculus, differential and integral, is little else than a more cunningly-constructed arithmetical mill; where the factors being put in, are, as it were, ground into the true product, under cover, and without other effort on our part than steady turning of the handle. (9)

These "higher departments" of calculus and algebra were, in fact, widely reviled in Britain during the early decades of the nineteenth century for their allegedly detrimental effects on the mind of the student. According to many commentators, algebra's formulas and symbols not only cultivated mental laziness, but wreaked permanent psychic damage by installing mechanisms within the mind that converted it into a factory—"a more cunningly-constructed arithmetical mill"— motored by the logic of algebraical analysis. Whereas geometry was thought to discipline the mind to the practice of proceeding from first principles applied to empirical observations, algebra's reliance on symbolic language and abstract analysis seemed dangerous because it irreversibly mechanized the mind, ruining the student for the modes of inquiry pursued in other disciplines. Tapping into the nation's fear of the higher branches of math pursued on the continent, Carlyle claims algebra is one of the most insidious ways Britain's mechanical and industrial impulses have infiltrated its people, making them internally "mechanical in head and in heart" (9).[1]

Charles Babbage, on the other hand, thought algebra's potential to mechanize, streamline, and maximize the mind's mathematical production made it an important mental tool specifically appropriate for accelerating the mathematical pursuits of geniuses. While Carlyle criticized math for turning the mind into a "cunningly-constructed arithmetical mill" (9), Babbage saw the advantages in the organizational parallels between early industrial factories and algebraic processes. Babbage's extensive work in mathematical theory and as the inventor of the

Difference Engine—the first programmable computer—was far from unknown in Victorian Britain, especially after he achieved national fame in 1832 with the publication of *On the Economy of Machinery and Manufactures*.[2] As a member of his social circle, Charles Dickens was certainly aware of Babbage's work, but followed his beloved mentor Carlyle's disapproving views on mathematics and mechanization.[3] Some indication of Dickens's opinion of the Difference Engine can be gleaned from a letter written in August, 1846, criticizing

> the gentle politico-economical principle that a surplus population must and ought to starve. . . . I am convinced that its philosophers would sink any government, any cause, any doctrine, even the most righteous. There is a sense and humanity in the mass, in the long run, that will not bear them; and they will wreck their friends always, as they wrecked them in the workings of the Poor-law-bill. Not all the figures that Babbage's calculating machine could turn up in twenty generations, would stand in the long run against the general heart. (qtd. in Forster 235)

For Dickens, Babbage's Difference Engine represents the bureaucratic machinery of an unfeeling government. His generalizing move to lump together economics, mechanization, and mathematics as utterly opposed to the "sense and humanity in the mass" is characteristic of his Carlylesque humanist and anti-economic ideals. He is disgusted with the cold, political economic doctrines that reduce the poor and the hungry to an abstract, faceless "surplus population," ignored by governments and allowed to suffer and die with a Malthusian inevitability.

Dickens's faith in the "general heart" and condemnation of government bureaucracy became central concerns in his novel *Little Dorrit* (1855–57). Though critical attention to the novel generally focuses on its representation of speculative finance, the crucial role of math in this central plot element has yet to be taken seriously, as has the related mechanization of the characters most closely involved in the mathematical labors of industry, invention, and finance.[4] While it has become commonplace to observe that Babbage's efforts to secure government support for his Difference Engine are a likely source for the character Daniel Doyce's experiences with the Circumlocution Office, the novel in fact responds to Babbage's mathematical and mechanical work in ways much larger than critics have yet recognized.[5] Doyce is actually an amalgamation of Babbage and Babbage's theorization of a new class of professional inventors. Based in the prevalent assumptions that math—for better or for worse—inevitably mechanized the mind, Babbage proposed that algebra modeled a hierarchal division of labor that placed the genius inventor at the top, separating his supposedly self-directed, unalienated labor from all of the mechanized manual and mental labors of those below him in the labor process. While the division of labor generally and the distinction between mental and manual labor specifically were prominent features of most Victorian discussions of industrialism, Babbage's contribution was to produce a more nuanced division of labor among the components of mathematics, a wholly mental labor process. *Little Dorrit* revises this division of mental labor by transforming Babbage's personal conflicts with his partner Joseph Clement into the partnership between the genius Doyce and his mechanized accountant Arthur Clennam. The novel's representations of mental labor thus illuminate the ways Dickens as a novelist and Babbage as an inventor were similarly engaged with contemporary debates about mental labor, intellectual property, and the social utility of the professional. This essay's broadest concern is therefore to show how our current categorization of mental labor as uniquely productive of intellectual property derives from Victorian efforts to establish the mental labor of the professional as unalienated and self-directed through its opposition to the monotony, repetition, and supposed mindlessness of mechanical labor.

1: Dickens and Babbage, Babbage and Doyce

While critics have remarked on Dickens's decades-long association and friendship with Babbage, we still lack close examinations of the influence Babbage's wide-ranging work in political economy, mathematics, and mechanical invention had on Dickens's literary production.[6] Before I go on to analyze Babbage's mathematical and economic writings, I want to first describe him as a major figure in London society, whose unique and vibrant personality offers one among many links to the character Doyce from *Little Dorrit*. In 1828 Babbage purchased his London home at Dorset Street and began cultivating his reputation as a celebrated host. Dickens was often among the guests at Babbage's evening meetings, which became a highlight of the London social season and, as described by friend and fellow scientist Charles Lyell, were "very brilliantly attended by fashionable ladies, as well as literary and scientific gents, and where one meets with persons high in all professions, and with distinguished foreigners" (466). While Babbage enjoyed talking on a number of subjects, he was particularly eager to discuss science and explain his inventions and ideas to anyone who would listen. He proudly displayed the unfinished Difference Engine in his home (alongside his dancing lady automaton) as a prompt to visitors' inquiries and discussion of the thwarted invention. Harriet Martineau, another frequent guest, remarks, "All were eager to go to his glorious soirées; and I always thought he appeared to great advantage as a host. His patience in explaining his machine in those days was really exemplary. I felt so, the first time I saw the miracle, as it appeared to me" (271).

Despite his out-going and affable personality, Martineau recalls that "few men were more misunderstood" (270). Babbage was known for his somewhat odd personality, which Dickens made a decided effort to capture with his character Doyce. Lyell describes a particular evening:

We have had great fun in laughing at Babbage, who unconsciously jokes and reasons in high mathematics, talks of the "algebraic equation" of such a one's character, in regard to the truth of his stories, &c. I remarked that the paint of Fitton's house would not stand, on which Babbage said, "No; painting a house outside is calculating by the Index minus one," or some such phrase, which made us stare; so that he said gravely, by way of explanation, "That is to say, I am assuming *revenue* to be a *function*." All this without pedantry, and he bears being well quizzed for it. (363-64, original emphases)

Like Babbage, Doyce makes obscure mathematical jokes and is often the only one in the room who knows what he is talking about, typically saying things like, "But you know we always make an allowance for friction, and so I have reserved space to close in" (784; bk. 2, ch. 34). But Doyce is aware that his mathematical humor is generally impenetrable to listeners, and often seems to talk to himself for his own entertainment: "'In my calling,' said Daniel, amused, 'the greater usually includes the less. But never mind, never mind! Whatever pleases you, pleases me'" (195; bk. 1; ch. 16).

The parallel between Doyce and Babbage was first recognized by Anthony Hyman, and, following his lead, readers of *Little Dorrit* often point out that Babbage's fruitless efforts to secure government funding for his Difference Engine offer a source for Doyce's very similar problems with the Circumlocution Office.[7] Babbage's life was indeed consumed by his struggles with Parliament over his Difference Engine, struggles that he began following a dispute with his head engineer, Joseph Clement. When Babbage initiated the project of building the Engine in 1823, he made a series of drawings and plans and put Clement in charge of building them while Babbage spent the next two years abroad.[8] The elaborate Engine required Clement to make a large number of specialty tools, unique to the construction of this project, and without which the Engine could not be reproduced. While craft tradition held that all tools remained the property of their maker and user, this custom was inadequate in the case of the specialized lathes and machine tools required for the Difference Engine. Babbage and Clement fought over ownership of these tools, and their conflict came to a head in 1832 when Babbage refused to pay Clement's bills, forcing Clement to fire the entire staff of workers employed in building the Engine, and then demanded that the still unfinished machine be removed from Clement's workshop. Babbage attempted to resolve these property disputes by petitioning the government to take over ownership of the Engine and pay for its completion, a process that continued for the next two decades. Babbage did gain some small successes on this front, but never received enough funding to finish the project, and in 1852 received a final, decisive denial from Disraeli. While Babbage's struggles with Parliament were over financial resources, his constant source of frustration concerned the repeated failure of government officials and legislators to understand that the Engine deserved government funding because it could make a major contribution to the nation.

Anthony Hyman explains, "The Difference Engine was by no means the only project which was to run into difficulty and exceed its estimated cost. But where other projects could point to immediate public utility, it required considerable knowledge and intellectual effort to comprehend the significance of the Difference Engine" (56).[9]

Doyce also "perfects an invention (involving a very curious secret process) of great importance to his country and his fellow-creatures. I won't say how much money it cost him, or how many years of his life he had been about it, but he brought it to perfection a dozen years ago" (124; bk. 1, ch. 10). Doyce's struggles with the Circumlocution Office center on his difficulty penetrating government bureaucracy; he never states any intention beyond the simple desire to forge a line of progress and communication. The biting critique behind the Circumlocution Office lies in Dickens's frustration with bureaucratic red tape, which he felt had all but consumed the British government, a problem manifested most dangerously in the utter mismanagement of the Crimean War.[10] With the primary goal of preventing all comers from getting anything accomplished, "the Circumlocution Office went on mechanically, every day, keeping this wonderful, all-sufficient wheel of statesmanship, How not to do it, in motion" (111; bk. 1, ch. 10).[11] Thus committed to "not doing it," the Office constantly treats Doyce like "a public offender" for merely attempting to get something done, despite the fact that his intentions are entirely selfless: "he has been trying to turn his ingenuity to his country's service . . . to effect a great saving and a great improvement" (124–25; bk. 1; ch. 10). Critics usually interpret Doyce's calm persistence to return, time and again, to the Circumlocution Office as a sign of his nationalism, but I suggest this is better explained as an aspect of his character as a scientifically-minded inventor.[12] While Babbage had clear financial reasons for professing a selfless desire to benefit his country, Doyce is genuinely motivated by the invention itself and the incontrovertible fact that "The thing is as true as it ever was" (190; bk. 1, ch. 16). As he explains to Clennam, an invention is "not put into his head to be buried. It's put into his head to be made useful. You hold your life on the condition that to the last you shall struggle hard for it. Every man holds a discovery on the same terms" (190-91; bk. 1, ch. 16). Doyce is never motivated by economic gains or the allure of fame, but persists with "a calm knowledge that what was true must remain true" (192; bk. 1, ch. 16).

Doyce's problems with the Circumlocution Office are usually interpreted in light of Dickens's commentary on debates about patent law reform.[13] However, as Trey Philpotts has pointed out, the novel never even uses the word "patent," and by the time of its publication Dickens's earlier opinion on the patent debate had evolved from that expressed in his 1851 story "A Poor Man's Tale of a Patent."[14] Rather than offering a very specific comment on the patent issue, *Little Dorrit* engages much larger questions about mental labor, intellectual property, and the figure of the professional. This becomes apparent if we see Doyce as based not only on Babbage's personality and experiences, but also as a representation of the idealized figure of the inventor genius theorized in his mathematical and political economic work. As he declared in *On the Economy of Machinery and Manufactures*, "It is highly probable that in the next generation, the race of scientific men in England will spring from a class of persons altogether different from that which has hitherto scantily supplied them" (384). He claims that "the sons of our wealthy manufacturers," unlike the university-educated elite, will benefit from the combination of education and a thorough familiarity with the current mechanical strengths and needs of British industry (384). As he argued in *Reflections on the Decline of Science in England* (1830), the slow advance of British science was centrally related to the fact that "there exists no particular class professedly devoted to science" and that "the pursuit of science does not, in England, constitute a distinct profession, as it does in many other countries. It is therefore, on that ground alone, deprived of many of the advantages which attach to professions" (10–11). The advance of science was for Babbage thus crucially related to the attainment of class-based privilege achieved by a group uniquely formed by their mixed-class origins.

Doyce does not benefit from any economic privilege, but attains his status as a professional by spending approximately thirty years cultivating his knowledge and skill in engineering as a manual laborer: "he was the son of a north-country blacksmith"; he completed an apprenticeship with a lock-maker; he began a new apprenticeship with a working engineer "under whom he had laboured hard, learned hard, and lived hard, seven years"; following this, he "worked in the shop" for seven or eight more years; and, after relocating, he "studied, and filed, and hammered, and improved his knowledge, theoretical and practical, for six or seven years more" (190; bk. 1, ch. 16). While Doyce is no longer a manual laborer, but instead a factory-owner who directs the labors of others, his abilities as an inventor derive directly from his hands-on experience using machines and tools. His history as a mechanic is also the underlying factor explaining all of his peculiarities: "He spoke in that quiet deliberate manner, and in that undertone, which is often observable in mechanics who consider and adjust with great nicety. It belonged to him like his suppleness of thumb, or his peculiar way of tilting up his hat at the back every now and then, as if he were contemplating some half-finished work of his hand and thinking about it" (126; bk. 1, ch. 10).[15] The novel makes repeated references to Doyce's active thumbs, and his "certain free use of the thumb that is never seen but in a hand accustomed to tools" (123; bk. 1, ch. 10) constantly marks him as a manual laborer—as his workmen say, "a man as knows his tools and as his tools knows" (646; bk. 2, ch. 22).

While he clearly has an inventor's mental genius, Doyce's "plastic workman's thumb" (644; bk. 2, ch. 22) is crucial to his abilities as a creator and foregrounds the fact that the work of invention unites mental and manual labors, an important parallel to the new class of inventor that Babbage proposed would emerge from the educated sons of the nation's manufacturers.[16] The complex class locations and the tenuous relations between mental and manual labor that mark both

Doyce and Babbage's inventor clearly link them to the emerging figure of the professional, as well as to Dickens's and Babbage's participation in the cultural construction of this figure. As Clare Pettitt explains, in the first half of the nineteenth century, fiction writers and inventors alike "were attempting to transcend their mixed class origins and to form themselves as professions, and both were seeking recognition from the state" (155). This state recognition meant copyright and patent protections, and writers and inventors, including Dickens and Babbage, often worked together on their respective campaigns.[17] At this time when the category of mental labor was being hotly debated, this collaboration enabled writers and inventers to capitalize on similarities between their mental labors as acts of creation whose products had social use value. These reform campaigns, Pettitt explains, facilitated "in drawing together and defining the professions of writing and engineering at a time when the ownership and social status of such 'new' forms of labour was—indeed—uncertain and fluid" (79–80).[18] According to Jennifer Ruth, the tenuous nature of the new professional identity stemmed from its "contradictory class locations":

> How, then, to account for professionals who perform labor but also possess a kind of capital (mental capital in the form of measurable talent and the stored labor of knowledge acquisition)? The nascent professional also confounded assumptions about the relationship between economic and *social* class: if he did not look or act like a wage laborer, he nevertheless relied upon a wage or salary; if he did not possess financial capital (though he had to have *some* to embark on a professional career), he claimed what we would now call cultural capital. (4, original emphases)

Attainment of the new social identity of the professional was crucially tied to establishing the social utility and use value of the products of mental labor, while constructing this mental labor as categorically distinct from the manual labors usually associated with material production. Inventors and fiction writers alike had high stakes in these debates as they struggled to establish for themselves public roles as valued professionals whose labor was sharply distinguished from that of the mechanized wage laborer.[19]

I will extend the work of Pettitt and Ruth to show that with this emerging figure of the professional also emerges the construction of a hierarchical division of labor that separates the mental labor of the genius inventor from the increasingly mechanized labors of every other worker below him. This division of labor enables the ideological construction of the categories of mental and manual labor as mutually exclusive, and allows the professional's labor to be defined as non-alienated and directed by innate genius through an opposition to the supposedly mindless mechanization of the manual laborer. Through an analysis of Babbage's mathematical theory, political economy, and his invention of the Difference Engine, I will next examine Babbage's participation in these debates about professional labor and intellectual property through his imagined new class of inventor, which would later form the other component of Doyce's character.

2: Babbage and the Mathematical Mind

Babbage's proposal that a new class of inventor would emerge in Britain was based on his theorization of a division of labor modeled on algebra. This work began with his earliest writings, which defended algebra against the firm belief, widely held in Britain in the early decades of the nineteenth century, that the higher forms of math were dangerous because they mechanized the mind of the student. As historian of mathematics J. M. Dubbey remarks, "British mathematicians were riddled by irrational prejudice, unhealthy conservatism in choice of method and notation, cut off from their Continental contemporaries, and uneasy about unsettled internal disputes" (13).[20] Upon encountering this resistance as a Cambridge undergraduate, Babbage found ways to continue pursuing his interest in algebra by joining with other "radical" students, including John Herschel, in 1812 to form the Analytical Society. As he contentedly recalls, "Of course we were much ridiculed by the Dons; and, being put down, it was darkly hinted that we were young infidels, and that no good would come of us" (*Passages* 29). Babbage's defense of algebra was first articulated in 1813 when he coauthored with Herschel the Analytical Society's only publication, the *Memoirs of the Analytical Society*. In its preface he launches a compelling and forthright argument for the usefulness of algebraical analysis as an "instrument of reason" based primarily on "the accurate simplicity of its language" (i).[21] The symbolic communication which algebra enables is superior, he claims, because it omits the ambiguity and multiplicity of meaning unavoidable in language: "An arbitrary symbol can neither convey, nor excite any idea foreign to its original definition" (i). In addition, symbolic language is considerably abbreviated: it allows the mind to comprehend in a single formula the whole of a problem, whereas without the substitution of symbols the mind would be forced to continually move from component to component, constantly making an effort to re-familiarize itself with each part, and yet never able to grasp them simultaneously as a whole: "It is the spirit of this symbolic language, by that mechanical tact, (so much in unison with all our faculties,) which carries the eye at one glance through the most intricate modifications of quantity, to condense pages into lines, and volumes into pages; shortening the road to discovery, and preserving the mind unfatigued by continued efforts of attention to the minor parts" (i–ii).[22] For Babbage, algebra enabled the mind to become a more efficient producer of mathematical knowledge: translating language into symbols and organizing these symbols into formulae streamlined mental production, enabling the mind to comprehend more information at a glance.

While Babbage thought algebra could thus vastly accelerate British advancements in mathematical and scientific knowledge, he was also sadly aware that "The almost mechanical nature of many of the operations of Algebra, which certainly contributes greatly to its power, has been strangely misunderstood by some who have even regarded it as a defect" (*On the Influence of Signs* 9).[23] This conservative misunderstanding was based in fears that, as a result of algebra's supposedly permanent restructuring of the mind, long and concentrated use of symbolic language would dull or diminish other mental faculties. Conservatives like William Whewell argued that algebra ruined exactly those parts of the brain a university education was designed to cultivate. In his 1835 pamphlet "Thoughts on the Study of Mathematics as a Part of a Liberal Education," Whewell criticizes algebra for deadening the mind's receptivity to culture and moral cultivation: "a person inured to mathematical reasoning alone, reasons ill on other subjects, seeks in them a kind and degree of proof which does not belong to them, becomes insensible to moral evidence, and loses those finer perceptions of fitness and beauty, in which propriety of action and delicacy of taste must have their origin" (143).[24] While advocates like Babbage thought the mental advancements of algebra could produce a new, professional class formed to be the nation's inventors, the fact of the matter was that in first half of the nineteenth century Cambridge was in the business of producing cultured elites, not professional inventors.[25]

Babbage's claim that algebra allowed the mind to increase its productivity by rationalizing it like a factory placed mathematical thinking squarely in a realm of economic production and professional labor, also distinctly inappropriate for Whewell's elite students. Specifically, Babbage proposed that algebra could transform British invention by turning math into a capitalist labor process made increasingly productive and efficient through the same division of labor, deskilling, and mechanization that characterized the burgeoning industrial scene.[26]As early as his preface to the *Memoirs of the Analytical Society*, Babbage described math as a labor process that should be divided along lines separating intellectually stimulating from tedious, unrewarding, and therefore "mechanical" labors: "The ingenious Analyst who has investigated the properties of some curious function, can feel little complaisance in calculating a table of its numerical values; nor is it for the interest of science, that he should *himself* be thus employed" (viii; original emphasis). In contrast to the mental stimulation the "ingenious Analyst" enjoys in investigating "some curious function," the task of calculating tables was entirely undesirable for Babbage because it is boring and tedious. As he later recalled in a letter to Sir Humphrey Davy, "The intolerable labour and fatiguing monotony of a continued repetition of similar arithmetical calculations, first excited the desire, and afterwards suggested the idea, of a machine, which, by the aid of gravity or any other moving power, should become a substitute for one of the lowest operations of human intellect" (212). Babbage thereby hit upon his idea to invent the Difference Engine to take over the mechanical aspects of mathematical labor, relieving humans of this distinctly inhuman labor.[27]

Babbage decided that in order to design his Difference Engine he would first have to learn as much as he could about machinery, and these industrial tours became the basis for his most well-known text, *On the Economy of Machinery and Manufactures* (1832). Perhaps the most influential experience Babbage describes in his *Economy* occurred in France, where he observed Baron de Prony's organization of mathematical laborers along an intelligence-based division of labor. Inspired by his reading of Adam Smith's *Wealth of Nations*, De Prony divided his workers into three sections. In the first, the "most eminent mathematicians" investigated analytical expressions and devised formulae; "This section had little or nothing to do with the actual mathematical work" (194). In the second section, "persons of considerable acquaintance with mathematics . . . convert into numbers the formulæ put into their hands by the first section,—an operation of great labour" (194). The third section received the completed formulae and filled in the tables "using nothing more than simple addition and subtraction" (194). Their labor "may almost be termed mechanical, requiring the least knowledge and by far the greatest exertions," and Babbage looks ahead to the time "when the completion of a calculating-engine shall have produced a substitute for the whole of the third section" (196, 195).[28]

Babbage thus saw in de Prony's workers a full-scale enactment of the division of labor produced by algebraical thinking wherein the "eminent mathematicians" were freed from "the actual mathematical work" and "great labour" assigned to the deskilled and devalued second and third sections, who had "no knowledge of arithmetic beyond the two first rules which they were thus called upon to exercise" (195). In observing de Prony's system, Babbage finds a parallel between this divided mathematical labor and the process through which a manufacturer invents new machinery: "he makes drawings of his plans of the machinery, and may himself be considered as constituting the first section. He next requires the assistance of operative engineers capable of executing the machinery he has designed . . . and these constitute his second section" (195–96). Babbage's comparison is far more than just a convenient analogy. In both scenes of invention, algebra transforms a complex real-world problem into an abstraction, and divides the abstract labor of inventing (machines or formulae) from the decidedly more laborious tasks of everyone beneath the inventor in this hierarchical division of labor.

This parallel between algebraical thinking and the labor of mechanical invention is made clear by Babbage's associate Dionysus Lardner, who wrote an article about the Difference Engine for the *Edinburgh Review* in 1832. Amidst Babbage's well-known disputes with Parliament over the Engine's funding, Lardner's goal was to explain to the general public the social utility of the mechanical notation that was the product of its mathematical labor:

> the mechanical notation derives a great portion of its power as an instrument of investigation and discovery [because] it enables the inventor to dismiss from his thoughts, and to disencumber his imagination of the arrangement

and connexion of the mechanism. . . . When once the peculiar conditions of the question are translated into algebraical signs, and "reduced to an equation," the computist dismisses from his thoughts all the circumstances of the question, and is relieved from the consideration of the complicated relations of the quantities of various kinds which may have entered it. He deals with the algebraical symbols, which are the representatives of those quantities and relations . . . and, by a process almost mechanical, he arrives at the required result. The various parts of the machinery under consideration being once expressed upon paper by proper symbols, the enquirer dismisses altogether from his thought the mechanism itself, and attends only to the symbols. (316)

Lardner goes on to give an example, drawing on Babbage's personal experience inventing the Difference Engine. Though he omits their names, Lardner's anecdote about an inventor who was "assisted by a practical engineer of considerable experience and skill" would have quickly recalled to his readers the infamous relationship between Babbage and his engineer Joseph Clement, who was charged with building the Engine based on Babbage's design (316). As Lardner tells the story, while the two were working on the Difference Engine,

A question arose as to the best method of producing and arranging a certain series of motions necessary to print and calculate a number. . . . To accomplish this, the engineer sat down to study the complicated details of a part of the machinery which had been put together; the inventor at the same time applied himself to the consideration of the arrangement and connexion of the symbols in his scheme of notation. . . . Here the powers of the practical engineer completely broke down. By no effort could he bring before his mind such a view of the complicated mechanism as would enable him to decide upon any improved arrangement. (316)

The inventor (Babbage), however, "without any extraordinary mental exertion," was able to quickly locate the problem and propose a solution simply by examining his plans and using the "symbolic instrument with which he conducted the investigation" (316). The inventor and the engineer are engaged in the same project: they encounter the same problems and questions and are both engaged in highly skilled and innovative labor. The difference between them is that while the engineer works on the concrete construction of the physical invention, the inventor translates all of this into the realm of abstraction. For Babbage, algebra accelerates the work of invention by producing a division of labor founded on the opposition between the abstract and the concrete, and it is this difference that separates the labor of the inventor from every other class of labor beneath him, ranging from the highly skilled mental labor of the head engineer, down to the mechanized factory workers laboring under the invention as a finished product.

While Babbage's algebraical division of labor is based in separating abstract and concrete as distinct realms of labor, he also theorizes about another foundation for the division of labor because of conflicts with Clement, who was charged with transforming Babbage's abstract plans into a concrete reality. Scholars have pointed out that as a direct result of this conflict over ownership, Babbage made a special effort in his *On the Economy* to differentiate the role of the *manufacturer* (the inventor) from the *maker* (the engineer). As Joseph Bizup explains, Babbage's goal was to prioritize the mental labor of innovation from the solely manual labor of production: "The conflict between Clement and Babbage thus touches on the more general question of whether ownership in an industrial society derives (as Clement held) from production and use or (as Babbage maintained) from initial conception and design" (60–61). Harry Braverman goes further, crediting Babbage as the first to separate *conception* from *execution* (316–18).[29]

However, neither Bizup nor Braverman fully recognize that in Babbage's theorization of the division of labor between manufacturers and makers, the categories of mental and manual labor that he mobilizes are ideological constructions. Lardner's anecdote shows Clement's labor to be just as investigative, innovative, and intellectual as the inventor's, but Babbage aims to categorize invention/conception as purely mental labor, and execution/production as entirely manual in order to gain advantage in his struggles with Clement over ownership and intellectual property. While he argues that invention and scientific innovation are motored by a dialectical interaction between abstract and concrete labor, he also aims to naturalize property rights and exploitative social relations by dividing mental from manual labor, constructed as discrete and mutually exclusive modes of work.[30] He collapses his dialectic between abstract and concrete labor into the ideological opposition between mental and manual labor in an effort to align his inventor with the emerging figure of the professional. In their struggles for copyright and patent protections, writers and inventors alike were engaged in establishing the mental labor of the professional as non-alienated, self-directed, and therefore productive of intellectual property. Central to this endeavor was the construction of their mental labor as non-alienated through its contrast to the mechanized factory laborer, as well as the categorization of the products of their labor—books and machines—as containing unique intellectual property through their contrast to the infinitely reproducible material products of industrial machines. While Babbage attempts to separate neatly the mental labor of innovation from the manual labor of production, the fact remains that all labors—from invention to mechanized factory work—contain both mental and manual elements and that material production and mental production are both potentially innovative and potentially subject to mechanization. The ideological stakes of these categories of mental and manual labor—in the early nineteenth century and now—are that they mark certain forms of labor and certain products of labor as innovative, creative, and productive of intellectual property, while devaluing all others. The figure of the professional and the debates about mental labor thus secured property rights for certain laborers by denying them to others.

3: *Little Dorrit*: Math, Mechanization, and the Division of Labor

While Babbage thought the algebraical division of labor could accelerate the progress of science by separating abstract from concrete labors, Dickens criticizes this division as the most dangerous problem with speculative finance. In this final section, I return to *Little Dorrit* to examine its critique of the mechanizing effects of mathematical and financial labor. The novel's idealized representation of Doyce's professional labor as selfless and thus unalienated is usually read in relation to Amy Dorrit's domestic labors, which are so selfless that they result in her complete vanishing of self.[31] I want now, however, to examine the opposition between the supposedly unalienated labor of the professional and the mechanization of the other mental and manual laborers beneath him in a hierarchical division of labor, modeled on Babbage's theorization. The novel establishes Doyce's labor as unalienated precisely through its opposition to the mechanization of the financial and mathematical laborers beneath him; however, despite this idealization, the novel's structural use of Doyce as its deus ex machina reveals the deep tensions in Dickens's thinking about his own professional labor as inescapably grounded in the economic self-interest of a market society.

Doyce is positioned at the top of the hierarchical division of labor: he is the inventor and delegates to everyone beneath him the tedious, repetitive, and thus mechanical aspects of the labor process. This hierarchy of mental and manual labor is imaged in the organization of the Bleeding Heart Yard factory: Clennam's mental and mathematical labors are placed at the top of the hierarchy as his office is located in the factory's attic above the manual labor of the factory workers who labor alongside the factory's actual machinery. Doyce, however, lacks a fixed place within Bleeding Heart Yard, which places him outside of the scene of labor and disconnects him from the exploitation of the unseen factory workers as well as the general misery of Bleeding Heart Yard's unemployed. The manner in which Doyce discusses his inventions also obscures their connection to the actual labor of the factory, thus presenting his work as entirely self-directed by his innate genius, rather than crucially connected to a larger production process, and absolutely selfless in being unmotivated by financial gains. When he describes his inventions to Clennam, for example, he emphasizes their usefulness, rather than his own ingenuity: "He never said, I discovered this adaptation or invented that combination; but showed the whole thing as if the Divine artificer had made it, and he had happened to find it" (496; bk. 2, ch. 8).[32] Critics have often remarked that, with this passage, Dickens distances Doyce from messy issues of property, commercial value, and self-interest in order to show that he works for the work's sake.[33] In addition to denying Doyce's embroilment in economic self-interest, the passage also erases the labor of everyone else in the Bleeding Heart Yard factory upon which his escape from alienation depends. Doyce's freedom and also his genius—both its practical daily operations and his professional status—depend on their separation from the labor that is directly connected to the profits gleaned from Bleeding Heart Yard rents and factory labor. In addition to the hierarchy that distances Doyce's mental labor from the manual labor of factory workers, his disinterested and unalienated genius is further separated from the mental labors of the novel's mathematicians who deal most directly with these financial matters. Clennam and Pancks are thus represented as mechanized both to mark them as tainted by the concern with money from which Doyce is protected and to mark their mental labor as categorically distinct from Doyce's. Just as Babbage early on in his career had come to see the mental labor of the mathematician as separable into the interesting and rewarding aspects that he found desirable as well as the repetitive, tedious, and thus mechanical aspects he hoped to one day delegate to his Difference Engine, so too does the novel distinguish Doyce's unalienated genius from other forms of mental labor by mechanizing the mental labors Doyce delegates to his mathematical employees.

Whereas Pettitt attributes Doyce's position in the division of labor to the novel's concern with the separation of "property and labor," I see the partnerships of divided labor in the novel as a revision of Babbage's separation of abstract and concrete labor (191). The division of labor between Pancks and Casby is often described as the separation of the Works from the Winder—the difference between a machine and its operator—and in other places as the separation of the Proprietor and his Grubber—a class-based distinction between management and labor. This division of labor transforms Pancks, the novel's most overtly mechanized character, into an engine: "a little coaly steam-tug will bear down upon it, take it in tow, and bustle off with it; similarly the cumbrous Patriarch had been taken in tow by the snorting Pancks, and was now following in the wake of that dingy little craft" (151–52; bk. 1, ch. 13). As a result, his entire body is composed of mechanical elements, like a steam engine made filthy by constant use: "He was dressed in black and rusty iron grey; had jet black beads of eyes; a scrubby little black chin; wiry black hair striking out from his head in prongs, like forks or hairpins. . . . He had dirty hands and dirty broken nails, and looked as if he had been in the coals; he was in a perspiration, and snorted and sniffed and puffed and blew, like a little labouring steam-engine" (150–51; bk. 1, ch. 13).[34] Further down the hierarchy, Meagles is reduced to mere tools: his "arithmetical solidity belonging to the scales and scoop" are emblematic of his fixation on his financial labors of measuring and doling out (199; bk. 1; ch. 16). While we see almost nothing of the Bleeding Heart Yard factory workers, whose mechanized manual labor is perhaps a foregone conclusion in *Little Dorrit*, it is primarily the mental labors involved in financial work which mechanize characters so as to establish a hierarchical distinction of quality between forms of mental labor.

Doyce and Clennam's partnership is premised on a division of mental labor between Doyce's inventive genius and the mechanized, routine monotony of bookkeeping in which Clennam immerses himself. Pancks describes Clennam's job as "not a partner in his [Doyce's] mechanical knowledge, but in the ways and means of turning the business arising from it to the best account . . . a question of figures and accounts" (199; bk. 1, ch. 16). Clennam throws himself wholeheart-edly into "mechanically discharging" (270; bk. 1, ch. 23) his duties, including the tedious, senseless pursuit of the Circumlocution Office: "and so the work of form-filling, corresponding, minuting, memorandum-making, signing, counter-signing, counter-counter-signing, referring backwards and forwards, and refer-ring sideways, crosswise, and zig-zag, recommenced" (497; bk. 2, ch. 8). The list structure of this sentence and the rigidity of its elements force onto the reader the boredom, monotony, and tediousness of Clennam's labors. When Clennam finishes updating and organizing their accounts, Doyce examines them "as if they were a far more ingenious piece of mechanism than he had ever constructed, and afterwards stood looking at them, weighing his hat over his head by the brims, as if he were absorbed in the contemplation of some wonderful engine" (644; bk. 2, ch. 22). And it is at this point that he cautions Clennam against speculating: "'If I have a prejudice connected with money and money figures,' continued Doyce, laying that plastic workman's thumb of his on the lapel of his partner's coat, 'it is against speculating. I don't think I have any other. I dare say I entertain that prejudice, only because I have never given my mind fully to the subject'" (644; bk. 2, ch. 22).

But Pancks the steam engine *has* given his mind fully to the subject. He assures Clennam that the Merdle speculation is safe and strongly encourages him to invest: "Be as rich as you honestly can. It's your duty. Not for your sake, but for the sake of others. . . . Poor Mr Doyce (who really is growing old) depends upon you. Your relative depends upon you. You don't know what depends upon you" (561; bk. 2, ch. 13). In addition to Clennam's own self-interest, Pancks argues he has a responsibility to get rich for the benefit of his family and society, but particularly for Doyce, who lacks financial motivation and self-interest: "Manage it better. . . . Recompense him for his toils and disappointments. Give him the chances of the time. He'll never benefit himself in that way, patient and preoccupied workman. He looks to you, sir" (559; bk. 2, ch. 13). This final statement—"He looks to you, sir"—implies that rather than being entirely without self-interest, Doyce has in fact delegated the labor of money-making to Clennam.

When Pancks infects Clennam with speculation fever, he begins by seeming to criticize the other investors who joined in the Merdle speculation without first checking the math:

"[Y]ou see these people don't understand the subject. . . . Know nothing of figures. Know nothing of money questions. Never made a calculation. Never worked it, sir!" . . .

"If they had," observed Clennam, who was a little at a loss how to take his friend, "why, I suppose they would have known better."

"How so, Mr Clennam?" Pancks asked quickly, and with an odd effect of having been from the commencement of the conversation loaded with the heavy charge he now fired off. "They're right, you know. They don't mean to be, but they're right. . . . I've gone into it. I've made the calculations. I've worked it. They're safe and genuine." (558–59; bk. 2, ch. 13)

Clennam and Pancks both assume that any trouble with the Merdle speculation— any dishonesty, any deception—would be revealed by the calculations. What these calculations could not predict, however, is that eventually Merdle kills himself, exposing the deception and causing a run on the bank, and all of their money is lost. Pancks is driven almost insane by the inexplicable fact that the scheme went bad despite his "incontrovertible figures" (731; bk. 2, ch. 30).

"I can prove by figures" added Mr Pancks, with an anxious countenance, "that it ought to have been a good investment. I have gone over it since it failed, every day of my life, and it comes out—regarded as a question of figures—triumphant. The present is not a time or place," Mr Pancks pursued, with a longing glance into his hat, where he kept his calculations, "for entering upon the figures; but the figures are not to be disputed. Mr Clennam ought to have been at this moment in his carriage and pair, and I ought to have been worth from three to five thousand pound." (730–31; bk. 2, ch. 30)

Pancks hits upon the exact problem: while his math is correct, he has only regarded the issue "as a question of figures," with no attention to the concrete reality behind those figures. As Babbage explained, algebra condenses the entirety of a real-world problem by translating it into an abbreviated symbolic language. For Dickens, however, as expressed in the letter quoted in my introduction, math and political economy both dangerously remove the full complexity of a real-world problem from one's view, allowing cold, unfeeling, government bureaucracy to reduce its poor and starving people to faceless, abstract "populations."

This is the primary critique which Dickens launches in *Little Dorrit* against financial speculation: it exists entirely in the abstract and is thus potentially disconnected from the realm of hard work and production of actual value. It offers the tempting promise of money begotten of money, but also the very real danger that one's investment could disappear in a puff of smoke. In the case of the Merdle speculation, his death reveals that there was no real-world enterprise backing up the investments, and he had embezzled everyone's money. Pancks, the "unhappy arithmetician," remains confused by the inexplicable fact that material reality fails to correspond with his abstract figures. Perpetually flummoxed, he keeps seeking consolation in his "infallible figures which proved that Arthur, instead of pining in imprisonment, ought to be promenading in a carriage and pair, and that Mr Pancks, instead of being restricted to his clerkly wages, ought to have from three to five thousand pounds of his own at his immediate disposal" (759; bk. 2, ch. 32).

While Pancks assures us repeatedly that his calculations are correct, at the end of the novel—in what is arguably the single most frustrating passage for *Little*

Dorrit's readers—Doyce suddenly returns to announce that he has found a mistake in the math: "There was an error in your calculations. I know what that is. It affects the whole machine, and failure is the consequence. You will profit by the failure, and will avoid it another time. I have done a similar thing myself, in construction, often" (784; bk. 2, ch. 34). Doyce, who has been absent from England for months (and from the novel for a dozen chapters), suddenly reappears to free Clennam from debtor's prison and undo the financial damage to their business. Though he begins by saying that there was an error in their calculations, in fact it is Doyce's own money, earned through his work as an engineer for Russia, that actually solves Clennam's financial troubles. While most readers express irritation at Doyce's odd remarks and Dickens's weak solution to the novel's need for a happy ending, critics fail to take Doyce's reference to math seriously, or at least to read it as anything more than a metaphorical platitude.[35] Given the novel's larger obsessions with the mechanizing effects of mathematical and financial labor, Doyce's description of his plot resolution as a mechanical solution to a mathematical problem seems a far more deliberate and complex matter than critics have accounted for.

The "error" Doyce discovers in the calculations is not a mathematical error, but the error Pancks and Clennam committed in viewing the world entirely through mathematical abstraction, which dangerously obscured the fact that there was nothing behind Pancks's calculations or the Merdle speculation in the first place. The relation Doyce describes between Clennam's abstract calculations and the construction of a material machine based on these calculations quickly draws to mind Dionysus Lardner's descriptions of the division between Babbage's abstract mathematical work as the inventor and his engineer Clement's concrete production of the Difference Engine. In that case, while the engineer was unable to solve a problem by examining the machine itself, Babbage was quickly able to determine a solution through examining his plans and using the "symbolic instrument with which he conducted the investigation" (Lardner 316). As the inventor, Babbage has access to an all-encompassing view, while Clement is unable to apprehend the entirety of the situation at one glance. Doyce's statement that "I have done a similar thing myself, in construction, often," reminds us that, in participating in the mechanical labors of calculation, Pancks and Clennam could not see the entirety of the speculation—"the whole machine"—in their minds. They were thus assured by a narrow look at their calculations that the entirety of the speculation was operational and that its real-world application was extant. In this way, we are reminded that Doyce's view of the speculation is the all-encompassing view of the products of the labor process available only to the inventor genius, while anyone with a more limited view of only their own limited contribution is thus by definition alienated in contrast.

But this explanation of the calculations does not resolve the critics' other complaint. Doyce's return usually receives harsh criticism as an all-too-convenient deus ex machina, and most readers are unsatisfied when Dickens "lower[s] Doyce from the rafters with enough money" to offer a far too easy conclusion to the novel's rich complexity (Jarvie 109). I'd like to address this by considering the double meanings of words like "contrivance," "device," and "mechanism" as both plot and actual material tools. While Doyce is arguably the most idealized character in the novel, he is given this task of unsatisfactorily tying up the plot primarily because he functions in the novel as a stand-in for Dickens himself.[36] In this role, Doyce unites the two camps engaged in campaigning for recognition of the social value of the professional—inventors and fiction writers. As professionals themselves, both Babbage and Dickens were personally invested in establishing the social value of their mental labor as exclusively productive of unique intellectual property. However, the economic value of Dickens's novels depended specifically on their combination of both the unique products of literary genius, and their reproduction of familiar plot elements.[37] These mechanical plot devices thus exist in tension with Dickens's vision of himself and other professionals as producing unique intellectual property through their unalienated innate genius—attributed by Doyce to the gifts of "the Divine artificer."[38] The fact that the novel uses Doyce as its deus ex machina and uses the money he made from his inventions to provide a happy ending for his friends (and for Dickens's readers) foregrounds the text's acknowledgement that even this most idealized, selfless character can never be entirely free from the economics of capitalist production. This tension is thus symptomatic of the larger fact that Victorian cultural debates about the figure of the professional, the construction of his mental labor as socially valuable, and the legislative affirmation of his exclusive rights to intellectual property are all achieved through establishing and maintaining a delicate and purely ideological opposition between the fantasy of his unalienated mental labor and the mindlessness and mechanization of the factory worker.

NOTES

1 Carlyle continued his critique of mathematical thinking in *Latter-Day Pamphlets* (1850), particularly "Jesuitism," where he laments "That poor human symbols were higher than the God Almighty's facts they symbolised; that formulas, with or without the facts symbolised by them, were sacred and salutary; that formulas, well persisted in, could still save us when the facts were all fled!" and then rails against the "reverent or quasi-reverent faith in the dead human formulas, and somnolent contempt of the divine ever-living facts" (354, 359).

2 With his partially completed Difference Engine and later plans for an Analytical Engine, Babbage is credited with inventing what would have been the first computer. Though not the first to devise a mechanical calculator, his invention would have been the first that could be programmed.

3 Herbert Sussman and Gerhard Joseph sum up evidence of Dickens's friendship with and intellectual interest in Babbage: "Dickens not only owned a copy of Babbage's

Ninth Bridgewater Treatise but also knew the author quite well. He attended Babbage's regular Sunday gatherings (*Letters* 2: 307) and invited Babbage to his own house for dinner parties (*Letters* 4: 134; 6: 113). They sat in the audience for worthy causes (*Letters* 3: 428n.) and corresponded about such controversial matters as the Corn Laws (*Letters* 2: 307), taxation (*Letters* 2:251), and the Society of Authors (*Letters* 3: 477). Dickens also visited the home of Babbage's champion, Ada Lovelace (*Letters* 3: 458)" (626n1, [Pilgrim *Letters* are cited]). According to John Picker, Dickens read Babbage's *Ninth Bridgewater Treatise* carefully, referenced it in *Dombey and Son*, cited it in a speech in 1869, and, "Dickens's stated forecast of 'widest diffusion' for his works had an implicit model in Babbage's theory of vocal diffusion" (39).

4   This financially-focused attention to *Little Dorrit* began with Jeff Nunokawa, whose work was highly influential in drawing critical interest to the economics of Victorian novels. Important contributors to this larger conversation who likewise center their readings of *Little Dorrit* on the speculation plot include Nancy Henry, Gail Turley Huston, Paul Jarvie, and Claudia Klaver.

5   Jay Clayton's passing remarks about the Babbage-Doyce connection are typical (96).

6   While Babbage has become a familiar figure in Victorianist literary and cultural studies, critics fail to historicize his writings adequately, and are more likely to project their own critical agenda onto his texts than to take Babbage at his own word. Sussman and Joseph's hasty assessment of the creative interchange between Dickens and Babbage is typical in its ahistorical identification of a range of post-modern concepts concerning the human machine relation (618).

7   The following overview of Babbage's efforts to gain funding for the Difference Engine is heavily indebted to Anthony Hyman's detailed and careful study of Babbage and to Babbage's autobiography, *Passages from the Life of a Philosopher*. On the parallels to Daniel Doyce and the Circumlocution Office, Hyman writes, "It would be unreasonable to suggest that Babbage's experience was the sole source of inspiration . . . but certainly the treatment of Babbage for daring to develop a calculating engine was a primary inspiration" (193–94). Other scholars who don't point to Babbage, still feel Doyce must have been based on *someone*: John Lucas argues that Dickens intended Doyce as "an amalgam of Carlyle's ideal poet and Ruskin's thinking-worker" (279). Janet Larson agrees, emphasizing his Carlylean origins (162).

8   Hyman explains, "Clement was a highly skilled mechanic but had not previously been responsible for so large a project. Before leaving England, Babbage was already worried that Clement was less than straightforward, suspecting him of developing and constructing at his employer's cost special lathes and other tools valuable in constructing the Difference Engine but intended to remain in Clement's workshop" (122).

9   The Difference Engine's function was to calculate tables, and it promised to save great deal of time, energy, and money in the cost of labor, in addition to offering increased reliability and accuracy. In Babbage's time these long and extensive tables of figures were necessary for many fields, primarily navigation, which required volumes of astronomical tables. Multi-volume sets of tables had been published but contained numerous errors. As Babbage's colleague Dionysus Lardner explained, "The surveyor,

the architect, the builder, the carpenter, the miner, the gauger, the naval architect, the engineer, civil and military, all require the aid of peculiar numerical tables, and such have been published in all countries"; however, "the existing supply of tables, vast as it certainly is, is still scanty, and utterly inadequate to the demands of the community" (269, 283).

10 See also Dickens's Carlylesque raillery against "Red Tapeosophy" and "the Right Honorable Red Tape, M.P." in his short piece called "Red Tape" in *Household Words* (15 Feb. 1851).

11 See Ruth Bernard Yeazell's article "Do It or Dorrit" for a discussion of "doing it" in the novel.

12 For example, Doyce "naturally felt a preference for his own country, and a wish to gain distinction there, and to do whatever service he could do, there rather than elsewhere" (190; bk. 1 ch. 16). These scattered remarks have been overemphasized by critics like Amanda Anderson, when in fact their primary function is in Dickens's critique of government bureaucracy. The Circumlocution Office created problems for inventors that are specific to Britain: "When they take their inventions into foreign countries, that's quite different. And that's the reason why so many go there" (126; bk. 1, ch. 10). Doyce is lured away from his native land by "a certain barbaric Power with valuable possessions on the map of the world, [which] had occasion for the services of one or two engineers, quick in invention and determined in execution" (643; bk. 2, ch. 22). The fact that Doyce's powers of mechanical genius are eventually used by Russia only emphasizes the link between the Circumlocution office and Dickens's critique of the British government's bungling of the Crimean War, which, given the backdating of the novel, is exactly the "occasion" for which they would need the service of an engineer like Doyce. When he returns at the end of the novel, Meagles explains that "Dan is directing works and executing labours over yonder, that it would make your hair stand on end to look at. He's no public offender, bless you, now! He's medalled and ribboned, and starred and crossed, and I don't-know-what all'd, like a born nobleman. But . . . he must hide all those things under lock and key when he comes over here. . . . Britannia . . . won't give her children such distinctions herself, and won't allow them to be seen when they are given by other countries" (782–83; bk. 2, ch. 34). In Babbage's *On the Economy* he rails against England's prohibition against inventors and engineers traveling to other countries.

13 Clare Pettitt states, "As in 'A Poor Man's Tale of a Patent', Dickens deflects class antagonism from Doyce himself, who remains untainted by self-interest or radicalism"; "Doyce is not based on a person, but on a debate—the patent and copyright debates, to be precise" (192; 196).

14 According to Philpotts, "Evidence in *Household Words* suggests that by at least 1853 Dickens had second-thoughts about patent reform and had begun to concur with the small group of engineers, manufacturers, and economists who wanted to abolish the patent system altogether. . . . [T]he technical issue of patent reform, mostly of interest to a few inventors, would have become subsumed by a larger question: why are these important inventions not being used? And if England fails to use them, what other

country will? When Doyce observes that matters are 'quite different' in foreign countries, he is voicing common fears, not obsolete ones of 1852" (158, 166).

15 While Babbage delighted in talking about his machine to anyone who would listen, he lacked the mechanical skill of a working engineer, which enables Doyce to successfully explain his mechanical work to an audience of non-experts: "He had the power, often to be found in union with such a character, of explaining what he himself perceived, and meant, with the direct force and distinctness with which it struck his own mind. His manner of demonstration was so orderly and neat and simple, that it was not easy to mistake him" (495–96; bk. 2, ch. 8).

16 The *Oxford English Dictionary* on "plastic" as an adjective: "That moulds. Characterized by or capable of moulding or shaping clay, wax, or other soft or formless materials."

17 On Dickens's participation in the Author's Society and other copyright organizations, see Poovey (112–13), Pettitt (185), and Hyman (203–04).

18 Pettitt characterizes the early nineteenth-century category of mental labor as "uncertain and fluid": "The nineteenth century represents a critical period in the history of the debate about mental labour. How far do men and women 'enter into' their labours? How far should that trace of their identity of corporeality be rewarded financially? And how long before that trace fades away and allows the invention—be it literary of mechanical—to revert to the possession of the general culture?" (1). She goes on to explain that "for writers and inventors in the early nineteenth century, it was crucial that the law held out a promise of future value for their inventions, as only such an investment in futurity could mark them out as different from 'common labourers' who sold their work on a daily basis" (3).

19 Ruth explains the ideological stakes of the professional for a capitalist society: "The professions enable capitalism by falsely holding out the promise of unalienated labor to everyone. Yet they also destabilize it because by holding out the promise of gratifying work, they remind us that work should be gratifying" (22–23).

20 The British universities' resistance to algebra stems from the quarrel and resulting accusations of plagiarism between Newton and Leibniz over who developed calculus. As a result of national loyalty to Newton, British mathematicians were trained exclusively in Newtonian notation, and thus lagged behind Continental advancements, unable even to read their different style of notation. Moreover, in the decades following the French Revolution and during the wars with France, it was impossible for any expression of interest in French science to be interpreted apolitically, especially in the conservative university environment. In this context, it makes sense that Babbage's student cohorts seemed radical. On the political causes of the stunting of early-nineteenth-century British mathematics, see Hyman (20–30) and Dubbey (10–30).

21 Dubbey explains the distinction between arithmetical and symbolic algebra: previously algebra had been considered only as arithmetical, with letters and symbols replacing the numbers. Algebra may be defined to be the science of general reasoning by symbolic language (100).

22 These arguments advocating the mental benefits of algebraical analysis were also advanced by Dugald Stewart, whose *Elements of the Philosophy of the Human Mind* was

a great influence on Babbage as an undergraduate (*Passages* 474). Stewart develops an "analogy between the mechanical arts and the operations of scientific invention" in order to propose that, just as "the natural powers of man have been assisted by the use of tools and instruments," mechanisms can similarly be devised as "aids to our intellectual faculties" (1: 82): "In [algebra], where the use of an ambiguous word is impossible, it may be easily conceived how the solution of a problem may be reduced to something resembling the operations of a mill—the conditions of the problem, when once translated from the common language into that of algebra, disappearing entirely from the view; and the subsequent process being almost mechanically regulated by general rules, till the final result is obtained" (2: 106).

23 William Ashworth reads Babbage's early writings as evidence that Babbage and Herschel set out to industrialize the mind and arrived at algebra with this intention, arguing that "Herschel and Babbage's stress on systematization and economizing mental labor had led them to Lagrange's algebraic calculus. . . . with its emphasis on abbreviation, symmetry, and unity, Lagrangian calculus sat well with their industrial agenda" (641). Mine is a more biographical argument in recognizing that Babbage was first interested in math; that he was engaging pre-existing rhetoric about its educational benefits and dangers; and that it was not until after he left Cambridge and started work on his Engines that he began to tour factories to learn more about machinery. I do not go as far as Ashworth in claiming that Babbage's earliest and foremost intention was to mechanize the mind.

24 Whewell reprinted his pamphlet as an appendix to *On the Principles of English University Education* (1835), and later extended the arguments in *Of a Liberal Education in General and with Particular References to the Leading Studies of the University of Cambridge* (1845). In the latter publication, he developed the comparison between algebra and geometry to argue that, while geometry is preferable for teaching students to reason from first principles, algebra is too advanced for university students and an inappropriate substitute for geometry. He was concerned that "Analysis, pursued without a proper geometrical and arithmetical foundation, has in it no clearness or light. The student who is led on in such a course, is immersed in a mist of symbols, in which he only here and there sees a dim twilight of meaning" (54–55). Whereas in "geometrical reasoning, we tread the ground ourselves, at every step feeling ourselves firm, and directing our steps to the end aimed at," in "analytical calculation, we are carried along as in a rail-road carriage . . . without having any choice in our progress in the intermediate space" (41).

25 As Dubbey remarks, "The feeling that mathematics was only a charade, a useful exercise for sharpening the wits, prevailed with few exceptions" (14); "There was very little possibility of a professional career in mathematics" (20).

26 Critical assessments of Babbage have generated much confusion over the direction of influence and the chronological order in which he theorized algebraical thinking and developed his knowledge of industrial factories. As an undergraduate in the 1810s, Babbage was already endorsing algebra on the basis that it rationalized the mind's productivity and organization, and therefore even before he developed his knowledge

of factory production his thinking was already shaped by industrial capitalism's values and priorities. When he later began touring industrial factories in the 1820s, Babbage assumed the factories were enacting the scientific principles that he had already argued were latent in the pure facts of mathematics—as opposed to the capitalist ideologies which he had read into mathematics. Specifically, because he already saw algebra as modeling a division of labor, Babbage naturalized the social relations he witnessed in factories by describing the industrial division of labor as enacting a principle of pure mathematics. He concludes, "the arrangements which ought to regulate the interior economy of a manufactory, are founded on principles of deeper root than may have been supposed, and are capable of being usefully employed in preparing the road to some of the sublimest investigations of the human mind" (*On the Economy* 191). Andrew Zimmerman similarly aims to understand how Babbage was able so capably to theorize industrial factories at a time when large-scale industry was still comparatively undeveloped, and argues that Babbage mobilized a "machine ontology" deriving from capitalist social relations that pre-existed the prevalence of large-scale machinery.

27 The most recent scholars to interpret Babbage's efforts argue that he set out to model his Engine on the human brain. Schaffer claims Babbage set out to make machines "intelligent," and he capitalizes on the ways Babbage's language of "intelligence," "memory," and "anticipation" borrows concepts from human brain functions: "In 1838 he confessed that 'in substituting mechanism for the performance of operations hitherto executed by intellectual labour . . . the analogy between these acts and the operations of the mind almost forced upon me the figurative employment of the same terms'" (204–08). This interpretation discounts the central role Babbage ascribed to the Engine's human programmer, which Babbage actually argued in his *Ninth Bridgewater Treatise* offered an explanation for miracles in that God had programmed them at the time of Creation. Laura Otis unpersuasively fits Babbage into her schematic union of bodily and machinic networks, arguing from scanty textual evidence that Babbage had an interest in the human brain and nerves and that he modeled his Engine's organization on the nervous system's structure (32–33).

28 Rather than recognizing that the division of labor functions to de-skill the workers of the other classes and devalue their labor, for Babbage the application of the division of labor to mental processes naturalizes the resulting social relations and class divisions because he sees each performing the labor "for which his natural capacity and acquired habits have rendered him most fit" (379). In addition to "possess[ing] much more skill," Babbage notes that the workers who perform the higher mental functions of inventing machinery "are paid much more highly than that class who merely *use it*" (371, original emphasis). This naturalization of class divisions and the value of workers' abilities as natural traits preexisting the imposition of capitalist labor allowed Babbage to make his most original contribution to classical political economy, now known as the "Babbage principle." As explained by Harry Braverman, "In the mythology of capitalism, the Babbage principle is presented as an effort to 'preserve scarce skills' by putting qualified workers to tasks which 'only they can perform,' and not wasting social resources.' It is presented as a response to 'shortages' of skilled workers

or technically trained people, whose time is best used 'efficiently' for the advantage of 'society'" (81–83).

29 Braverman explains, "Mental labor is carried on in the brain, but since it takes form in an external product—symbols in linguistic, numeric, or other representational forms—it involves manual operations such as writing, drawing, operating writing machines, etc.—for the purpose of bringing this product into being. . . . The progressive elimination of thought from the work of the office worker thus takes the form, at first, of reducing mental labor to a repetitious performance of the same small set of functions. The work is still performed in the brain, but the brain is used as the equivalent of the hand of the detail worker in production, grasping and releasing a single piece of 'data' over and over again" (316–19).

30 Babbage theorizes the realms of the abstract and the concrete as comprising a dialectic. As new technologies emerge to take over more aspects of the labor process, the mind is able to do more, the genius to reach farther, and what was once out of reach now becomes common knowledge. The tasks undertaken by inventors thus draw an ever-shifting line motored by technological development. In *Reflections on the Decline of Science in England* Babbage explains, "In mathematical science, more than in all others, it happens that truths which are at one period the most abstract, and apparently the most remote from all useful application, become in the next age the bases of profound physical inquiries, and in the succeeding one, perhaps, by proper simplification and reduction to tables, furnish their ready and daily aid to the artist and the sailor" (17–18).

31 Critics often follow Poovey in examining the mental labor of the professional in relation to domestic labor. Pettitt claims that while Doyce's labor is unalienated, Amy Dorrit's is "emphatically alienated": "Work seems to threaten the basis of identity, unless it can be represented, as is Doyce's invention, as unalienated" (196–97).

32 Doyce's focus on his invention's usefulness is an idealized version of the professional fiction writers' efforts to establish their lack of self-interest: "In claiming professional status, the members of the Guild of Literature and Art, most prominently Dickens, Bulwer Lytton, and Forster, all placed a strong emphasis on the *instrumentality* of literature, claiming that literary interventions in public life could have a direct, practical effect" (Pettitt 157, original emphasis).

33 Doyce's way of doing business is tellingly counterpointed in the novel by the Merdle business, which is shown in the end to be an empty shell of self-interest, greed, and pursuit of value. Julian Markels says Dickens deliberately "focus[es] the idealization of Doyce on use-value labor before it is alienated into surplus" (42). Paul Jarvie points out that Doyce's partnership with Clennam is an additional way Dickens separates Doyce from the actual business of the firm and the fact that his factory makes things in order sell them for profits (112).

34 Later in the novel Pancks is electrically powered: "His little black eyes sparkled electrically. His very hair seemed to sparkle as he roughened it. He was in that highly-charged state that one might have expected to draw sparks and snaps from him by presenting a knuckle to any part of his figure. . . . Where he got all the additional black prongs from, that now flew up all over his head like the myriads of points that break out in the large change of a great firework, was a wonderful mystery" (373–75; bk. 1, ch. 32).

35 Amanda Anderson is particularly angry about Doyce's remarks: "Perhaps Doyce is just being nice, but this is a blatantly false analogy in several respects. Drawn in by the speculative tendencies of his age, duped by the forces of global capitalism and the idea that all can share in his profits, Clennam's was no simple mechanical misjudgment. It was the result of pervasive and systematic forces that simply cannot be 'avoided in the future.' An ideal of purposive labor held within the bounds of situated judgment is not sufficient to take on the unavoidable conditions of modern social and economic reality" (89). In identifying an "analogy" in Doyce's words, Anderson follows Larson's similarly irritated evaluation of the passage: "In Doyce's neatly molded reconciliation speech in II.34, he needlessly, almost perversely teaches Clennam to learn from failure; he compares Arthur's disastrous investment to a mechanic's faulty calculations, as though the mind were a machine; and, although he is admirably forgiving, this deus ex machina 'perfectly arranges' things so that Arthur can dismiss the past" (164). Anderson and Larson both assume that Doyce's reference to "calculations" is a translation of the financial endeavor into a mechanical one, and with this assumption both take Doyce's language to be metaphorical, and seem to miss the connection to the actual mathematical calculating with which Pancks is obsessed. My intention is to take Doyce at his word and give the passage a bit more credit.

36 Houston calls him "Dickens's alter ego" (80). Pettit argues that the connection between Doyce and Dickens is indicative of "Dickens's own troubled self-perception as an artist" (193). Jarvie similarly concludes that "Doyce doubles Dickens in this creative role, his ability to 'combine what was original and daring in conception with what was patient and minute in execution,' and throws the weight of Dickens's own role as a generative artist, and successful middle-class entrepreneur, who lives, like Doyce, by the products of his personal labor, behind the case for use-value in the novel" (105–06).

37 Peter Garrett's examination of Dickens's multiplot novels takes seriously the mechanical nature of certain elements of their plotting, and compares *Little Dorrit*'s plot machinery to Doyce's factory's "straps and wheels; which, when they were in gear with the steam engine, went tearing round as though they had a suicidal mission to grind the business to dust and tear the factory to pieces" (261).

38 See Houston's comments on letters written by Dickens during the composition of *Little Dorrit* in which he complains about his difficulty keeping up production of the novel on the exhausting schedule demanded by serialization (78–79). See Poovey on the "factory-like" conditions of Victorian literary production (104–05).

Works Cited

Anderson, Amanda. *The Powers of Distance: Cosmopolitanism and the Cultivation of Detachment*. Princeton: Princeton UP, 2001.

Ashworth, William J. "Memory, Efficiency, and Symbolic Analysis: Charles Babbage, John Herschel, and the Industrial Mind." *Isis* 87.4 (1996): 629–53.

Babbage, Charles. *Passages from the Life of a Philosopher*. 1864. Reprint edition. London: Pall Mall, 1968.

————. *On the Economy of Machinery and Manufactures*. 1832. 3rd ed. London: Knight, 1833.

————. "On the Influence of Signs in Mathematical Reasoning." *The Transactions of the Cambridge Philosophical Society*. Cambridge: Smith, 1826. <www.books.google.com>.

————. "Preface." *Memoirs of the Analytical Society*. 1813. Charles Babbage and John Herschel. *Science and Reform: Selected Works of Charles Babbage*. Ed. Anthony Hyman. Cambridge: Cambridge UP, 1989. 11–34.

————. *Reflections on the Decline of Science in England*. London: Fellowes, 1830.

————. To Sir Humphrey Davy. 3 July 1822. *Science and Reform: Selected Works of Charles Babbage*. Ed. Anthony Hyman. Cambridge: Cambridge UP, 1989. 43–51.

Bizup, Joseph. *Manufacturing Culture: Vindications of Early Victorian Industry*. Charlottesville: U of Virginia P, 2003.

Braverman, Harry. *Labor and Monopoly Capital: The Degradation of Work in the Twentieth Century*. New York: Monthly Review P, 1974.

Carlyle, Thomas. "Jesuitism." *Latter-Day Pamphlets*. No. 8. Aug.1, 1850. *Thomas Carlyle's Collected Works*. Vol. 19. London: Chapman and Hall, 1869. 353–404.

————. "Signs of the Times." 1829. *A Carlyle Reader: Selections from the Writings of Thomas Carlyle*. Ed. G. B. Tennyson. Acton, MA: Copley, 1999. 3–24.

Clayton, Jay. *Charles Dickens in Cyberspace: The Afterlife of the Nineteenth Century in Postmodern Culture*. Oxford: Oxford UP, 2003.

Dickens, Charles. *Little Dorrit*. 1855–57. Eds. Stephen Wall, Helen Small. London: Penguin, 1998.

————. "A Poor Man's Tale of a Patent." *Household Words* 19 Oct. 1850. *Charles Dickens: Selected Journalism, 1850–1870*. Ed. David Pascoe. London: Penguin, 1997. 408–13.

————. "Red Tape." *Household Words* 15 Feb. 1851. *Charles Dickens: Selected Journalism, 1850–1870*. Ed. David Pascoe. London: Penguin, 1997. 420–26.

Dubbey, J. M. *The Mathematical Work of Charles Babbage*. Cambridge: Cambridge UP, 1978.

Forster, John. *The Life of Charles Dickens*. Vol. 2. Boston: Estes and Lauriat, 1871.

Garrett, Peter K. *The Victorian Multiplot Novel*. New Haven: Yale UP, 1980.

Henry, Nancy. "'Rushing into Eternity': Suicide and Finance in Victorian Fiction." *Victorian Investments: New Perspectives on Finance and Culture*. Eds. Nancy Henry and Cannon Schmitt. Bloomington: Indiana UP, 2008. 161–81.

Houston, Gail Turley. *From Dickens to Dracula: Gothic, Economics, and Victorian Fiction*. Cambridge: Cambridge UP, 2005.

Hyman, Anthony. *Charles Babbage: Pioneer of the Computer*. Princeton: Princeton UP, 1982.

Jarvie, Paul A. *Ready to Trample on All Human Law: Financial Capitalism in the Fiction of Charles Dickens*. New York: Routledge, 2005.

Klaver, Claudia. "Natural Values and Unnatural Agents: *Little Dorrit* and the Mid-Victorian Crisis in Agency." *Dickens Studies Annual* 28 (1999): 13–43.

Lardner, Dionysius. "Babbage's *Calculating Engine.*" *Edinburgh Review* 59 (July 1834): 263–327.

Larson, Janet. "The Arts in These Latter Days: Carlylean Prophecy in *Little Dorrit.*" *Dickens Studies Annual* 8 (1980): 139–96.

Lucas, John. *The Melancholy Man: A Study of Dickens's Novels.* Sussex: Harvester Books, 1980.

Lyell, Charles. *Life, Letters and Journals of Sir Charles Lyell.* Vol. 1. London: J. Murray, 1881.

Markels, Julian. *The Marxian Imagination: Representing Class in Literature.* New York: Monthly Review P, 2003.

Martineau, Harriet. *Autobiography.* 1877. Ed. Linda H. Peterson. Peterborough, ON: Broadview P, 2007.

Nunokawa, Jeff. *The Afterlife of Property: Domestic Security and the Victorian Novel.* Princeton: Princeton UP, 1994.

Otis, Laura. *Networking: Communicating with Bodies and Machines in the Nineteenth Century.* Ann Arbor: U of Michigan P, 2001.

Pettitt, Clare. *Patent Inventions—Intellectual Property and the Victorian Novel.* Oxford: Oxford UP, 2004.

Philpotts, Trey. "Dickens, Patent Reform, and the Inventor: Daniel Doyce and the Question of Topicality." *Dickens Quarterly* 9.4 (1992): 158–69.

Picker, John M. *Victorian Soundscapes.* Oxford: Oxford UP, 2003.

Poovey, Mary. *Uneven Developments: The Ideological Work of Gender in Mid-Victorian England.* Chicago: U of Chicago P, 1988.

Ruth, Jennifer. *Novel Professions: Interested Disinterest and the Making of the Professional in the Victorian Novel.* Columbus: Ohio State UP, 2006.

Schaffer, Simon. "Babbage's Intelligence: Calculating Engines and the Factory System." *Critical Inquiry* 21.2 (1994): 203-27.

Stewart, Dugald. *Elements of the Philosophy of the Human Mind.* Vol. 1. 1792. Vol. 2. 1814. *The Collected Works of Dugald Stewart.* Ed. William Hamilton. Edinburgh: Constable, 1854.

Sussman, Herbert, and Gerhard Joseph. "Prefiguring the Posthuman: Dickens and Prosthesis." *Victorian Literature and Culture* (2004): 617–28.

Whewell, William. *Of a Liberal Education in General; and with Particular Reference to the Leading Studies of the University of Cambridge.* Part I. *Principles and Recent History.* 2nd ed. London: John W. Parker, 1850.

———. "Thoughts on the Study of Mathematics as a Part of a Liberal Education." 1835. *On the Principles of English University Education.* London: John W. Parker, 1837.

Yeazell, Ruth Bernard. "Do It or Dorrit." *NOVEL: A Forum on Fiction* 25.1 (1991): 33–49.

Zimmerman, Andrew. "The Ideology of the Machine and the Spirit of the Factory: Remarx on Babbage and Ure." *Cultural Critique* 37 (1997): 5–29.

"A Long and Constant Fusion of the Two Great Nations": Dickens, the Crossing, and *A Tale of Two Cities*

Matthew Heitzman

This essay explores Dickens's treatments of the Channel Crossing in his journalism and considers them in relation to his drastically different representation of it in A Tale of Two Cities. *The Crossing was a richly cognitive experience for Dickens in which he could reconcile a sense of dual fidelity to England and France, and cultivate a sense of simultaneous connection to both countries.* A Tale of Two Cities *departs radically from this paradigm, depicting the Channel Crossing as a dark and sinister event, and Charles Darnay is arrested in both England and France for the crime of crossing the Channel. This essay argues that the novel responds to contemporary Anglo-French political tensions in the wake of an assassination attempt on French Emperor Napoleon III in 1858, and that its pessimistic depiction of the Crossing and the public denunciations of Darnay reflect Dickens's despair over the nationalist rhetoric that followed the attack and the popular will in both countries to secure a clean divide between them.*

Charles Dickens opens *A Tale of Two Cities* (1859) with a sensational midnight journey to the English Channel. As the narrative begins, Jarvis Lorry, a clerk for Tellson's Bank in London, is en route to the Channel aboard the Dover Mail, traveling to France to aid Alexander Manette, one of the bank's clients, who has just been released from prolonged incarceration in the Bastille. The opening scene seems drawn straight out of Gothic melodrama: an icy mist creeps in from the coast, the passengers secrete themselves under layers of dark clothing, and paranoia reigns on the nighttime ride. Jerry Cruncher, an emissary from Tellson's, is nearly shot when he approaches the coach unannounced with a message for Jarvis Lorry, and Lorry replies to it in code, concealing his response from the carriage's other passengers, who feign sleep in order to better eavesdrop.

Why would Dickens open *A Tale of Two Cities* with such a dark, enigmatic scene along the English coast? The culture of secrecy and suspicion he sketches certainly fits with his portrayal of the widespread distrust of the Revolutionary period and the rise of the Terror; but he begins with an ecology of fear and mistrust along the English border, casting the coast as a dangerous and sinister place, and making the journey between England and France seem perilous and suspect. Indeed, the novel's protagonist, Charles Darnay, is twice arrested *because* he crosses the Channel. In England, he is charged with treason, accused of crossing the Channel in order to pass state secrets to the French. In France, he is denounced as an emigrant, condemned for seeking refuge in England, thus avoiding Revolutionary retribution. Darnay's crossings generate consternation on both sides of the Channel, marking the Channel itself as a contested space in the novel.

That depiction is totally at odds with how Dickens typically wrote about the Channel Crossing. For Dickens, the Crossing tended to be a jarring but ultimately positive and transformative experience. He relished its narrative potential: the surreal disorientation of moving across the Channel at night, the abject horror of seasickness, and the sheer trial of the enterprise. Dominic Rainsford argues that Trans-Manche narratives reached their apex with Dickens and reads the violence of the Crossing as part of a rigorous process for Dickens by which France is rendered familiar:

> All in all, the process of getting to France is lavishly traumatic for Dickens, but being there is perfectly comfortable. It seems that Dickens plays up the Channel-crossing process, but this only goes to make France, once he gets there, surprisingly familiar and unthreatening. Dickens seems to be an Englishman for whom France is not really very foreign—or, perhaps for whom France is no more foreign than England. (67)

Dickens knew the Channel Crossing well. By the 1850s, he was a part-time resident of both England and France, and shuttled routinely between them. As Rainsford suggests, Dickens's depiction of the Crossing is indicative of his dual familiarity with England and France; Rainsford regards the Channel as a threshold space for Dickens, a line of national demarcation that the novelist crosses and *then* finds himself in either England or France, the Crossing being an experience that separates the two nations in space and time.

This analysis will suggest instead that the Channel functions as topological space for Dickens: its geography doesn't separate England and France in his mind.

Rather, it offers Dickens a rare opportunity to feel a fleeting sense of simultaneous connection to both countries. Dickens varies how he represents that simultaneous connection—he occasionally imagines England and France overlapping or collapsing into one another as a result of the disorientation of the Crossing, and at other times depicts them as mirroring or "doubling" one another along the Channel. But what registers for Dickens in each case is the impression that on the Channel he is connected to both at once.

Jonathan Grossman has recently argued that Dickens's international perspective shifted significantly in the mid-1850s as he began to cultivate a sense of "international simultaneity" in his works, no longer viewing travel as a discrete process by which characters go abroad, have life-changing experiences, then return "home" forever shaped by them, a schema that separates territories in space and time. Instead, Grossman suggests that with the publication of *Little Dorrit* (1857), Dickens's spatiotemporal perception changed, a shift in accord with changes in the ways in which passenger transportation systems networked people, connecting them across international space and "in shared, synchronized time" (179).

A consideration of Dickens's treatments of the Channel Crossing gives us a model to conceptualize further the spatiotemporal change Grossman identifies. The Channel was a space in which time and geography tended to break down for Dickens, and was characterized by his sense of simultaneous connection to multiple national spaces. As Grossman suggests, recognizing the ways in which Dickens registered and cultivated a sense of synchronous national connection allows for a critical reassessment of Benedict Anderson's seminal work on the development of nationalism, challenging the idea that the simultaneous "homogenous, empty time," which Anderson argues is essential to the development of the nation-state ends at the national border (26).

I will first consider Dickens's depictions of the Crossing in his journalism, arguing that his personal recollections always return to the idea of national stasis. The Crossing itself is brutal and unsettling, but Dickens tends to find a sense of national equipoise on the Channel, a way to reconcile his dual fidelity to England and France, and a form of national belonging that de-privileges the border. My discussion will also consider the relationship between England and France in Dickens's journalism more broadly, suggesting that his representations of the Channel Crossing are indicative of a desire in his nonfictional writing to imagine less difference and distance between the two nations. Finally, I will offer a local historical context for *A Tale of Two Cities*, a way to understand why the Channel operates as a national barrier in the novel, and why Charles Darnay's multiple crossings produce so much anxiety in both England and France. My essay will suggest that *A Tale of Two Cities* responds to a diplomatic crisis between England and France that unfolded just before Dickens began to serialize the novel, and that significantly altered the politics of the Crossing and the Anglo-French relationship.

On January 14, 1858, three Italian republican nationalists attempted to assassinate French Emperor Napoleon III by throwing bombs at his carriage as it arrived at the Paris Opera. The emperor was unharmed, but 156 people were injured, eight of whom later died. It was quickly learned that the would-be assassins had been political refugees in England, and had planned and trained for the attack in Birmingham, even going so far as to design and to construct the bombs in consultation with a Birmingham manufacturer before shipping them to the continent. The architect of the attempt was an Italian revolutionary named Felice Orsini, who hoped that the Emperor's death would set off a series of popular uprisings in Europe that would eventually lead to Italy's independence.[1]

The assassination attempt set off a diplomatic crisis between England and France, and the Channel became a political briar patch, laced with the anxieties of both countries, and a space for each side to expiate its guilt. The French directed their embarrassment and sense of vulnerability towards it, raging that the political refugees who committed the crime had been able to cross both ways, and compensating for the insecurity the attack generated by threatening to invade England. The English responded with a mixture of nationalist bravado and contempt for the invasion threat, and mitigated a sense of responsibility by marking the Channel as the space in which the refugees *became* would-be assassins. The political fallout from the assassination attempt raised the Channel in the public consciousness in both England and France, and cast it as a space for the competing nationalisms of both countries.[2]

That formulation would have been anathema to Dickens, and this reading will suggest that *A Tale of Two Cities* responds to both countries' nationalist rhetoric in its depiction of the multiple trials of Charles Darnay, who is persecuted on both sides of the Channel for the crime of crossing it. Dickens's dark depiction of the Crossing in *A Tale of Two Cities* suggests a degree of pessimism on his part that those who feel a sense of fidelity to both England and France could ever escape popular repudiation, and a degree of despair that the rich sense of simultaneous national connection he felt on the Channel could ever be sustained in political fact.

Writing the Channel—Dickens and The Crossing

As Dickens began to spend more time in France, primarily along the coast in Boulogne, he came to appreciate the forms of cultural exchange he saw there. Remarking on the number of English tourists in Boulogne in "Our French Watering-Place," published in 1854, Dickens observes: "But, to us, it is not the least pleasant feature of our French watering-place that a long and constant fusion of the two great nations there, has taught each to like the other, and to learn from the other, and to rise superior to the absurd prejudices that have lingered among the weak and ignorant of both countries equally" (241). Boulogne's proximity to the Channel allows English and French citizens to intermingle freely and frequently, overcoming their biases against one another; but Dickens imagines a transformation in space as well as sentiment, a "fusion of the two great nations" along the coast. Boulogne becomes a multinational space in Dickens's mind: it reaps the benefits of both nations and blurs the distinctions between them.

Dickens registered a similar sense of civic and geographical blending on the Channel itself. In "The Calais Night Mail," published as part of *The Uncommercial Traveller* series (1861), Dickens narrates the surreal experience of crossing the Channel in the dark on the tiny, turbulent night-mail packet:

> What is going on around me becomes something else than what it is. The stokers open the furnace doors below, to feed the fires, and I am again on the box of the old Exeter Telegraph fast coach, and that is the light of the forever extinguished coach-lamps, and the gleam on the hatches and paddle-boxes is *their* gleam on cottages and haystacks, and the monotonous noise of the engines is the steady jingle of the splendid team. Anon, the intermittent funnel roar of protest at every violent roll, becomes the regular blast of a high pressure engine, and I recognize the exceedingly explosive steamer in which I ascended the Mississippi when the American civil war was not, and when only its causes were. A fragment of mast on which the light of a lantern falls, an end of rope, and a jerking block or so, become suggestive of Franconi's Circus at Paris where I shall be this very night mayhap (for it must be morning now), and they dance to the self-same time and tune as the trained steed, Black Raven. (214–15)

Dickens is interested here in the phenomenology of travel, rendering his Channel Crossing as a series of cognitive associations. The physical experience of moving across the Channel allows him to skip imaginatively between disparate geographies and memories. The impression is that time and geography become malleable in the turbulence of the midnight crossing, as Dickens flashes between the Mississippi of years ago and a circus from hours hence, all based on the stimuli of the moment. The resonances among the experiences fascinate Dickens here, the parallel impressions he is able to draw in the dark, strange no-space of the Channel at night, and the momentary thrill of mentally being in two places at once.

The Crossing facilitates this "doubling" of place. In "The Calais Night Mail," Dover and Calais blend into one another amid the violent disorientation of the Crossing. Fighting seasickness, Dickens stands on the deck of the packet-ship looking expectantly for Calais:

> Malignant Calais! Low-lying alligator, evading the eyesight and discouraging hope! Dodging flat streak, now on this bow, now on that, now anywhere, now everywhere, now nowhere! . . . Even when it can no longer quite conceal itself in its muddy dock, it has an evil way of falling off, has Calais, which

is more hopeless than its invisibility. The pier is all but on the bowsprit, and you think you are there—roll, roar, wash!—Calais has retired miles inland, and Dover has burst out to look for it! (212)

Just as Dickens expects to see Calais, he finds Dover. At the beginning of this Crossing, the two cities start as national beacons, markers for how far Dickens has traveled across the Channel, but they soon collapse into one another. They end up not opposed to one another but in a more symbiotic relationship, balancing one another as Dickens cycles through a series of complementary emotional pairs: love and hate, hope and despair, revulsion and attraction. His emotions mimic the ebb-and-flow of the unsettled crossing, and help to emphasize that he feels the same pull towards both cities. In "The Calais Night Mail," he personifies both, often treating them as a pair of near-forgotten mistresses. He quips at the opening of the piece, "It is an unsettled question with me whether I shall leave Calais something handsome in my will, or whether I shall leave it my malediction. I hate it so much, and yet I am always so very glad to see it, that I am in a state of constant indecision on this subject" (211).

The Channel Crossing only exacerbates Dickens's love-hate relationship with Calais. He loves it when he can see it; hates it when it disappears. When he finally arrives at the French customs station, Dickens manically declares that his was a case of mistaken ambivalence, a simple matter of disorientation: "Calais *en gros*, and Calais *en détail*, forgive one who has deeply wronged you.—I was not fully aware of it on the other side, but I meant Dover" (216). Dickens's affection is of course based on proximity. He is a capricious paramour who loves whichever city he is closest to at the time. He doubtlessly loves them both equally when in the middle of the Channel; but his connection to both, his sense of fidelity to both, is the key dynamic here. His playful rendering of his affection for both cities as a love-hate relationship underscores how much Dickens *does* feel affection for both cities, and the Channel Crossing briefly lets him reconcile his dual fidelity, as he casts each as equal and constantly collapses them into one another.

His sense of dual fidelity to England and France is the opening conceit in "Our French Watering-Place" as well. Dickens begins the piece by suggesting, "having earned, by many years of fidelity, the right to be sometimes inconstant to our English watering-place already extolled in these pages, we have dallied for two or three seasons with a French watering-place" (230). Dickens's faithfulness to his family's summer home in Broadstairs gives him the right to be faithful to his family's summer home in Boulogne. Dickens feels an obligation to nurture both connections, and casts his dual fidelity as an affective scale that must be balanced. Dickens also refers to an earlier encomium to Broadstairs ("our English watering-place already extolled in these pages"), an article entitled "Our Watering Place," published in *Household Words* in August 1851. He would eventually publish both articles side by side in *Reprinted Pieces* (1858) as "Our English Watering-Place" and "Our French Watering Place," an editorial decision that suggests how aligned the two locales were in his mind, and how much he was striving to represent a sense of balance between them.

Dickens's compulsion to see England and France as equals along the shared space of the Channel can also be seen in his article "A Flight," published in *Household Words* on August 30, 1851, as a response to the debut of the South Eastern Railway Company's new "tidal trains." It is a deeply impressionistic account of a Channel Crossing made in conjunction with the new service. The "tidal" express trains were designed to make the journey from London to Paris (via Dover and Calais, or Folkestone and Boulogne) in only eleven hours by coordinating London departures with the tide. This meant that departures were irregularly scheduled, but that it was also possible to travel from London to Paris in the same day.

The tidal-train service shaved only an hour and a half off of the Night Mail's service, but the Night Mail typically left London at 8:30 p.m. and arrived in Paris around 9:00 a.m. the next morning. With the tidal train, one could stand in London and Paris *in the same day*, which is exactly what Dickens does in "A Flight." The piece begins with Dickens waiting for his train to depart London. In order to characterize the experience more deeply, he emphasizes precisely what time of day it is, in part because he's stuck waiting on a particularly sultry London morning. He quips, "Here I sit, at eight of the clock on a very hot morning, under the very hot roof of the Terminus at London Bridge, in danger of being 'forced' like a cucumber or a melon, or a pine-apple" (26). This jibe sets a ribald tone for the piece, but it also privileges the role of chronology in the text. When Dickens arrives in France at the end of what was still a long journey, he reflects on and, to a degree, relishes the fact that it is still the same day:

> When can it have been that I left home? When was it that I paid "through to Paris" at London Bridge, and discharged myself of all responsibility, except the preservation of a voucher ruled into three divisions, of which the first was snipped off at Folkstone, the second aboard the boat, and the third taken at my journey's end? It seems to have been ages ago. Calculation is useless. I will go out for a walk. (34)

Dickens walks Paris in a traveler's haze, "pushing back this morning (if it really were this morning) into the remoteness of time, blessing the South Eastern Company for realizing the Arabian Nights in these prose days, murmuring, as I wing my idle flight into the land of dreams, 'No hurry, ladies and gentleman, going to Paris in eleven hours. It is so well done, that there really is no hurry!'" (35). Dickens savors the sureality of the experience, the sublime confusion of travelling from London to Paris without a sense of rupture, either from the manic "hurry" that he typically associates with the Crossing, or from the clean divide between night (London) and day (Paris) that came from crossing on the Night Mail. Dickens relishes the reverie, the feeling of poetic timelessness in a prose world, and is in no rush to let go of his spatiotemporal disorientation.

Dickens *was* in a rush to compose the work, so much so that he wrote "A Flight" before having even taken the tidal-train service. Dickens composed the account from notes taken by his sub-editor, W. H. Wills, who took the trip during the summer of 1851.[3] His urgency to produce the piece suggests how enamored Dickens was with the idea of the new service, and his cavalier blending of fact and fiction (not an unusual practice for Dickens in his journalism) underscores that it was what the journey itself represented that mattered most for Dickens, since the trip was a pronounced departure from the traditional experience of crossing the Channel.

Dickens structures "A Flight" to mimic the new experience of the tidal train: opening the work on a sleepy, sultry London morning, crossing the Channel in bright day, and arriving in Paris with enough time to savor a nighttime walk in the city. Dickens centers the article with a Channel Crossing, imagining the moment in which the packet approaches the French coast:

> And now I find that all the French people on board begin to grow, and all the English people begin to shrink. The French are nearing home, and shaking off a disadvantage, whereas we are shaking it on. Zamiel is the same man, and Abd-el-Kader is the same man, but each seems to come into possession of an indescribable confidence that departs from us—from Monied Interest, for instance, and from me. Just what they gain, we lose. (31)

Dickens imagines an autochthonic connection between the individual and his or her native soil; the traveler is nurtured by and grows in proximity to his or her home country. But Dickens's imagery also suggests symbiosis: the English are shrinking *as* the French grow. He registers it as a parallel experience, suggesting there is a fixed amount of national energy that must be shared in common, and which, presumably, would be equally balanced midway across the Channel. Once again, Dickens imagines the Channel Crossing as part of a geographic schema that strives for stasis, one that suggests a comfortable middle space in which competing national connections are resolved or balanced. His model here segregates the nationalisms: the French are connected to France, the English travelers to England, but the Channel is still the space that mediates opposing forms of national affinity. Dickens's Channel is topological space, defined not by the distance between two points, but by the traveler's relationship to them—a space in which it makes sense to feel connected to and pulled towards two difference places at once. It is not a barrier space for Dickens, but rather an opportunity to overcome the quintessential burden and experience of those who travel and call two places home—you are always not in one of them. The Crossing, for a moment, allowed Dickens to negotiate a split sense of self, and to reconcile his sense of dual national fidelity.

Crossing the Line—Orsini's Bombs and the Channel as *Cordon Sanitaire*

The Channel was a psychogeographic safe-haven for Dickens, and crossing it gave him a brief sense of nationalist equilibrium. This would have made Felice Orsini's failed attempt on Napoleon III in January 1858 particularly traumatic for Dickens. Dickens was by no means fond of Napoleon III himself, but the political fallout from the assassination attempt marked the Channel as threshold space in public discussion, a highly invested line of nationalist demarcation in the public imaginations of both England and France.

For the French, the issue was the ease with which Orsini and his accomplices could cross the Channel before the attack and, in some cases, flee back across it following its failure. Napoleon III's government targeted England's culture of political asylum. On February 1, 1858, the *Times* reprinted a speech delivered to the emperor by one of his generals, General Barazine, in which Barazine raises the prospect of invasion as a response to the attack:

> This odious and cowardly attempt has filled our hearts with indignation and rage against those who, by giving an asylum to these sanguinary anarchists, have made themselves their accomplices. In expressing our wishes that your Majesty's life, so intimately connected with the repose and prosperity of France, may be ever preserved from all parricidal attempts, it does not suffice the army to form a rampart round its Sovereign; it is ready to shed its blood in all places to reach and annihilate the artisans of regicide. ("The Revival of Liberty")

Barazine uses the Channel to recast the issue of national culpability, making the central issue not the French army's failure to protect the emperor, but the English government's willingness to grant the refugees asylum. Asylum equals complicity, a formulation that shifts responsibility across the Channel, and seeds the origins of the crime on English soil. The invasion threat also charges the Channel, making it a challenged space that the French army might cross at any moment.

The English offered a concomitant response, also using the Channel as a means to deflect national guilt. On February 2, 1858, the *Times* editorialists suggested,

> It is much easier to catch a man at a bridge than to catch him in the open country, far simpler to identify him as he steps out of a boat than when he is at large in a multitude. A refugee more or less is lost in the swarms which flock to us from every territory in Europe. We cannot, until he betrays himself by some significant act or word, distinguish the conspirator dealing in bombs and daggers from the harmless dancing-master eating the bread of labour in a foreign land. Orsini might be in England for any purpose; he could hardly be in France except for purposes of evil. When he and his colleagues set out

on their infamous mission with grenades in their pockets their objects might indeed be said to acquire some notoriety, but not before. It was in the very act of quitting our shores that their criminality assumed a notable shape. ("England Gets Rather Hard Measure in the Matter.")

The Channel is the centerpiece in this geojudicial schema, the threshold at which the refugees' whispered plotting becomes intent, and the Crossing itself is the moment in which speculation becomes sinister, and politically frustrated refugees become worthy of surveillance. This formulation absolves England of much of the responsibility for policing political exiles, and mitigates any guilt that the refugees *became* criminals in England. Both sides use the Channel to mark a clean line of national culpability, and to cultivate a Manichean sense of guilt and innocence.

For France, this was coupled with the need to allay a feeling of vulnerability after the attack. That anxiety was evident in an anonymous pamphlet, entitled *L'Empereur Napoleon III et l'Angleterre* that was published in France and reprinted in the *Times*, and was thought to be authored by Napoleon III himself. Midway through the work, the author strives to illustrate how dangerously revolutionary French refugees have become as a result of political shelter in England by quoting Félix Pyat, a French revolutionary, who in 1858 was in exile in England. In his own pamphlet, written in England and smuggled into France, Pyat promises, "in spite of all your precautions—notwithstanding your walls of China, your line of Customs, your *cordon sanitaire*—we pass, we penetrate, we arrive in the cottage, in the hands, eyes, hearts, of the operatives and peasants, and the people read us notwithstanding all" ("The Emperor Napoleon III and England"). Pyat blends the dual fears of the imperial government, evoking the imagery of geographical transgression in order to illustrate the pervasiveness and power of revolutionary thought. He morphs two forms of circulation, people and ideas, and makes threshold crossing in all forms a political seditious act.

The French government began to monitor both forms of circulation much more aggressively. In the wake of the attack, Napoleon III's government moved to suppress any periodical not supportive of the emperor's leadership, and to restrict movement across the Channel from England. The Imperial government targeted the politically dispossessed, passing the *Loi de sûreté générale* or, as it was popularly called, the *Loi des suspects*. The legislation, adopted on February 27, 1858, in effect established a suspect class, consisting of anyone who had been accused of political dissent since 1848. Among its provisions, the law stipulated that anyone who had been complicit in the Revolutions of 1848 and 1851, and had subsequently fled France, would be subject to arrest or deportation to Algeria if they returned to France (Wright 414–30).

This group's standing soon became untenable on both sides of the Channel. For its part, Prime Minister Palmerston's government finally relented to French pressure and introduced the Conspiracy to Murder Bill, which made it a felony to plot in Britain the assassination of someone abroad. Palmerston's bill was eventually defeated, but its circulation facilitated the arrest of a French refugee living in England named Simon Bernard. Bernard, a French-language teacher, was arrested on February 14, 1858, exactly one month after the attack on Napoleon III. This suggests that his arrest was partially a diplomatic gesture designed to encourage *détente* between England and France. Bernard was charged with shipping the weapons used in the attack from England to France, an accusation that continued to deepen the public perception of the border as a dangerously porous space.

Bernard's trial at the Old Bailey was a popular sensation in England. His attorney, Edwin James, positioned the case as an opportunity for the English jury to reject public and political pressure from France, and to demonstrate that they were not cowed by the threat of invasion across the Channel.[4] He urged,

> I implore you to let the verdict be your own, uninfluenced by the ridiculous fears of French armaments or French invasions. . . . You, gentlemen, will not be intimidated by foreign dictation to consign the accused to the scaffold; you will not pervert and wrest the law of England to please a foreign dictator? No. Tell the prosecutor in this case that the jury-box is the sanctuary of English liberty . . . tell him that, though 600,000 French bayonets glittered before you, though the roar of French cannon thundered in your ears, you will return a verdict which your own breasts and consciences will sanctify and approve, careless whether that verdict pleases or displeases a foreign despot, or secures or shakes and destroys forever the throne which a tyrant has built upon the ruins of the liberty of a once free and mighty people. ("The Attempted Assassination of the Emperor of the French")

James flips the dynamic of the case. Instead of making the principal issue whether England has a legal responsibility to punish its refugees for complicity in crimes abroad, which asks the jury to consider the ways in which England and the Continent have become connected, James makes the case an opportunity for England to assert its independence from the Continent. Furthermore, by alluding to the border threat, James reinforces the border itself in the public imagination, marking it as a barrier, a line of demarcation and national difference.

James's nationalist rhetoric worked. After a brief deliberation, the English jury acquitted Simon Bernard of complicity in the assassination attempt, rejecting the legal premise that he could be held accountable for a crime committed across the Channel that he did not directly take part in. The diplomatic crisis between England and France eventually died down, in no small part due to the execution of Felice Orsini in France, but the nationalist posturing on both sides raised the Channel in the public consciousness of both nations, and marked it forcefully in the popular imagination as a contested threshold between England and France, a space that was far too easy to cross for refugees, would-be assassins, and imagined invaders. Additionally, public discussion after the assassination attempt focused on sounding the distance between England and France, and insisting on a clean separation between them.

A Compulsion to Cross—Charles Darnay and the Channel

Dickens for his part followed the events surrounding the assassination attempt. When Palmerston's Conspiracy to Murder Bill was finally defeated, Dickens wrote to French actor François Régnier, "there is great excitement here this morning, in consequence of the failure of the Ministry last night, to carry the Bill they brought in, to please your Emperor and his troops. I, for one, am extremely glad of their defeat" (*Letters* 8: 522). Dickens responds specifically to the political pressure from France, alluding to the invasion threat, and signaling his disgust at the nationalist bluster that prompted the bill. He also followed Felice Orsini's trial in France and was troubled by Orsini's remorselessness at trial, writing to John Delane, the editor of the *Times*, on February 28, 1858, "I think the attitude of that miserable man Orsini, on his trial, as sad a picture, almost, as this world has to shew at the present time. 'Sir,' said a noble gentleman to me when I was last in Italy: 'in this country of mine, the greatest social misery is to have a son'" (*Letters* 8: 525–26). The horror for Dickens was that political oppression in Italy gave rise to someone like Orsini, and that social inequality could make acts of violence and political martyrdom inevitable. This aligns with his perspective on revolutionary violence in *A Tale of Two Cities*. In the novel, Dickens recognizes that the first French Revolution was the result of extended class oppression and social equality, but his sense of the long narrative of revolutionary upheaval is that it only leads to more violence and new forms of oppression: the excess of the *Ancien Régime* becomes the brutality of the Terror.

A Tale of Two Cities is also shaped by the nationalist rhetoric that followed Orsini's attempt on Napoleon III, and can be read as a response to it. *A Tale* stands apart from Dickens's typically playful and imaginative renderings of the Crossing and his will to see it as a rich, sublime space connected to both nations, not an inviolate line between them. In the novel, Dickens duplicates the public paranoia and nationalist bluster that followed the attack. He does so through his depiction of Charles Darnay, a thinly-veiled double for Dickens himself, whose familial obligations compel him to cross the Channel repeatedly, and whose crossings generate much of the narrative tension in the text and twice lead to Darnay's arrest, once in England and once in France. Darnay feels a sympathetic connection to France even after he has fled it, confessing to Jarvis Lorry:

> My dear Mr. Lorry, it is because I am a Frenchman born, that the thought (which I did not mean to utter here, however) has passed through my mind often. One cannot help thinking, having had some sympathy for the

miserable people, and having abandoned something to them…that one might be listened to, and might have the power to persuade to some restraint. (245; bk. 2, ch. 24)

Darnay's sympathy pulls him across the Channel pre- and post-Revolution. First, in order to make amends for his family's past abuses, and later to rescue his former servant, Monsieur Gabelle, who has been arrested by the Revolutionary government for handling the financial affairs of an aristocrat.

His pre-Revolutionary crossings lead to his arrest in England. He is accused of spying for Louis XVI and crossing the Channel to pass information on British military deployment.[5] The attorney general at Darnay's trial at the Old Bailey foregrounds the issue of national security, imploring that

> the jury, being a loyal jury (as he knew they were), and being a responsible jury (as he knew they were), must positively find the prisoner Guilty, and make an end of him, whether they liked it or not. That, they never could lay their heads upon their pillows; that, they never could endure the notion of their children laying their heads upon their pillows; in short, that there never more could be, for them or theirs, any laying of heads upon pillows at all, unless the prisoner's head was taken off. (69; bk. 2, ch. 3)

As with the Simon Bernard trial, the verdict is seen as a moment of national testament, a chance for the jury to prove its national loyalty and to protect England from an external threat from France. Dickens also draws on public anxiety about the Crossing itself by centering Darnay's supposed treasonous acts there. One of the chief witnesses against Darnay, Roger Cly, testifies that he met Darnay on the Channel Crossing and witnessed him passing lists of information on the British army to Frenchmen in Calais and Boulogne. Cly's character is part of Dickens's larger critique of nationalism in the Old Bailey trial scene. Cly is later discovered to be an actual spy, but he testifies at Darnay's trial as a "patriot" and "true Briton" (71; bk. 2, ch. 3). Cly uses the rhetoric of patriotism to mask actual sinister intent, just as the defense attorney in Bernard's case uses it to color how the jury views all the evidence presented at trial.

All of Darnay's actions are placed in the worst possible light due to the heady mixture of fear and nationalism cultivated at the Old Bailey. The virtuous Lucie Manette is forced to testify that she not only saw Darnay pass papers to two Frenchmen on the packet-ship, but that when she first met Darnay on the Crossing, he made a provocative and potentially treasonous statement to her. She recalls his assessment of the American Revolution: "He tried to explain to me how that quarrel had arisen, and he said that, so far as he could judge, it was a wrong and foolish one on England's part. He added, in a jesting way, that perhaps George Washington might gain almost as great a name in history as George the Third" (75; bk. 2, ch. 3). Darnay's sense of the social grievances in France makes him acutely aware of the injustices that have lead to the American Revolution. His gibe about George Washington is an attempt to make Lucie understand the historical underpinnings of the American war, but nationalism trumps nuance at the trial, and Darnay's statement is seen as proof of treasonous intent.

Darnay is ultimately acquitted at the Old Bailey, and the manner of his acquittal points to an alternative for Dickens to the nationalist monomania that drives the trial. Darnay is saved because he has a "double," Sydney Carton, an Englishman whose physical resemblance is enough to sow reasonable doubt in testimony that it was Darnay who crossed the Channel. Darnay's trial is about fear of those who make the Crossing, and Dickens offers a resolution that aligns with how he tended to view that passage and what he found therapeutic about it—that it was a moment when England and France came to "double" or collapse into one another in richly uncertain ways, and when the disorientation of the journey made it impossible to say, for certain, which nation was which.[6]

But *A Tale of Two Cities* still signals Dickens's pessimism about the political climate between the two countries at the time of the novel's composition. He is careful to paint both England and France as stubbornly nationalistic and, in France's case, to evoke the judicial discourse that followed the assassination attempt itself. Darnay is arrested when he returns to France, indicted, as in England, *because* he crosses the Channel. In France, he is denounced for emigrating, a crime that strips him of all rights and titles, reducing him in title to the act itself ("the Emigrant Evrémonde"). He is condemned because he is a political refugee, rendered abject because he has sought refuge in England, the identical crime made punishable under Napoleon III's *Loi des suspects*.

In his second trial, Darnay's defense is that he fled France and returned there before it was a crime to do so. He testifies:

> He had voluntarily relinquished a title that was distasteful to him, and a station that was distasteful to him, and had left his country—he submitted before the word emigrant in its present acceptation by the Tribunal was in use—to live by his own industry in England, rather than on the industry of the overladen people of France. (293; bk. 3, ch. 6)

After the French Revolution, emigration allowed members of the French aristocracy and clergy to evade arrest and condemnation. On October 23, 1792, the Revolutionary Government formally dispossessed emigrants of their land and titles, and made any return to France a capital crime. Darnay's defense is that he fled France before the term, *émigré*, became synonymous with the country's most suspected class and returned to France before it was a crime to re-cross the Channel.[7] Darnay also stresses that he severed his fiscal connection to France before leaving, ceasing to benefit financially from his family's estate holdings; in other words, that he made a clean break from France.

Darnay is also asked at his trial if it is true that he married in England, and he replies, "true, but not an English woman" (293; bk. 3, ch. 6). Darnay's response further deepens the sense that for Dickens the real issue that is on trial is whether or not Darnay's emigration has resulted in an intermingling of cultures and cultural resources. The French Tribunal probes for evidence that England and France have not become more blended as a result of Darnay's crossing; indeed, he is finally acquitted when Doctor Manette testifies that Darnay had previously been placed on trial in England for treason against the English government. Manette testifies regarding Darnay:

> So far from being in favour with the Aristocrat government there, he had actually been tried for his life by it, as the foe of England and a friend of the United States —as he brought these circumstances into view, with the greatest discretion and with the straightforward force of truth and earnestness, the Jury and the populace became one. . . . At every vote (the Jurymen voted aloud and individually), the populace set up a shout of applause. All the voices were in the prisoner's favour, and the President declared him free. (295; bk. 3, ch. 6)

Darnay's indictment in England perversely allows for his acquittal in France. Dickens seems to draw on the adage that "the enemy of my enemy is my friend." In this case, Revolutionary bloodlust—the blind eagerness to punish any member of the *Ancien Régime*—is trumped by the Tribunal's nascent sense of nationalism. The fact that Darnay stands trial in England positions him as an enemy of the aristocracy in a way that no amount of personal testimony could ever do. The French jury is largely unreceptive to his claims that he has renounced his aristocratic standing and is poised to condemn him as an aristocrat nonetheless, until they learn of his trial in England and are then eager to use the jury box as a moment to denounce the English government instead. It is the natural conclusion for a trial in which the more salient issue seemed to be sounding the distance between England and France, rather than assessing the crimes of the aristocracy.

The first two trials in *A Tale of Two Cities* replicate the Anglo-French political dynamic following the assassination attempt on Napoleon III in 1858. Dickens portrays the English and French people, represented by their juries, as rigidly nationalistic and deeply invested in establishing a clear line of separation between England and France, and also deeply distrustful of those who do desire to cross between the two countries. Darnay is twice acquitted for the crime of crossing the Channel, but is eventually condemned anyway. He is denounced ultimately as an aristocrat, but his conviction suggests pessimism on Dickens's part that someone like Darnay could ever completely escape popular repudiation.

Darnay does, of course, escape capital punishment. He is saved, once again, by his double, a conclusion to the novel that signals both Dickens's despair that someone like Darnay, who does feel a sense of connection and obligation to both sides of the Channel, could be condemned for it, and Dickens's hope that salvation can be found in similarity, and that England and France will recognize their resemblance, just as Carton grudgingly does over the course of the novel. Carton's vision on the scaffold, which concludes the novel, is of the day when Darnay is able to safely cross the Channel again. He imagines Darnay returning to the Place de la Révolution with his two children, one who carries Carton's name, signaling rebirth, and another who carries Lucie's, and who, Dickens writes, fulfills the promise of the novel's title and "chattered in the tongues of the Two Cities that were blended in her life" (219; bk. 2, ch. 21). This is Dickens's only direct reference to the novel's title, and it underscores how much his aspiration for it was linked, once again, to the idea and hope of a greater cultural blending between England and France.[8] Dickens is not telling the tale of two different cities with his novel, each resolutely and irreconcilably separated from the other; he's imagining a process by which they could become whole. Little Lucie blends England and France together far more completely than her parents' habitation in both ever could, and fuses "the two great nations" in a way that Dickens typically only glimpsed in the sublime, surreal disorientation of the Crossing.

NOTES

1. Gregory Vargo's dissertation also links *A Tale of Two Cities* to the Orsini affair. He reads the refugee crisis and Simon Bernard's trial as part of an ongoing debate in England regarding the significance of the 1848 French Revolution and the Chartist Movement, and a desire to see England as separate from continental political uprisings. Vargo does not deal directly with the Channel, but he does note that Bernard's arrest revived rhetoric on English exceptionalism: "the refugee question foregrounded the ways England was distinct from the continent as a haven from tyranny while paradoxically highlighting connections between European revolutionaries and British radicals" (304). For a broader historical account of Orsini's attempt, see Porter (170–99) and Finn (181–83)

2. Recent criticism has offered a series of contemporary geopolitical contexts for *A Tale of Two Cities*. Deborah Wynne (2006) reads the novel's focus on famine and crowd scenes in relation to a religious revival that Dickens witnessed while on tour of Ireland in 1858. Grace Moore and Priti Joshi both link the novel to the 1857 Indian Mutiny (First War of Indian Independence). Moore sees a complex displacement at work in the novel, viewing Dickens's depiction of the Parisian mob as informed both by his frustration towards the British government's neglect of the working-class, as well as a more sober, sympathetic assessment of the Indian Mutiny following revelations of British atrocities in response to the uprising (131). Joshi sees the novel less as a specific response to the events of the Mutiny than as a work animated by them, part of a broader moment of English national self-articulation. Joshi's reading is particularly evocative, for it suggests "that the Indian Mutiny focused and strengthened Dickens's yearning

for a unified British identity and his conviction that such an identity is forged in a foreign landscape" (84). But Joshi's analysis also demonstrates the ways in which critical assessments of *A Tale of Two Cities*, even as they establish a wider geographic context for the novel, tend to insist upon a somewhat conservative definition of "the nation" for Dickens, one that aligns with the contours of the island. This essay suggests that while the Anglo-French relationship may have been a special case for Dickens, it certainly complicated his sense of national identity and belonging.

3. Dickens wrote to Wills on August 13, 1851, "I am now going at once to do the 'Flight to France.' I think I shall call it merely 'A Flight'—which will be a good name for a fanciful paper. Let me have your notes by return. Don't fail" (*Letters* 6: 459).

4. James was Dickens's model for Stryver in *A Tale of Two Cities*, according to Edmund Yates (30–31).

5. Military deployment was a major concern during the post-assassination political crisis. The French invasion threat led to fears in England that British soldiers would need to be recalled from India, where they had been dispatched to combat the Indian Mutiny, in order to better secure England's southern coast.

6. For a discussion of Carton's significance in the novel as barrister, see Petch. Petch moves beyond the doubling issue, examining Carton in the context of English professional culture.

7. In the Penguin edition of *A Tale of Two Cities* Richard Maxwell dates Darnay's departure from England as August 14, 1792, before it became a crime to return to France; but he is brought to trial in December 1793, after the passage of the law (481n).

8. Dickens considered a number of titles for the novel: *Buried Alive*, *The Thread of Gold*, and *The Doctor of Beauvais*; he finally settled on *A Tale of Two Cities* in March 1859.

WORKS CITED

Anderson, Benedict. *Imagined Communities: Reflections on the Origin and Spread of Nationalism*. Rev. ed. London: Verso, 2006.

"The Attempted Assassination of the Emperor of the French." *Times* 17 April 1858. *Times Digital Archive* 1785–1985. 26 May 2012.

Dickens, Charles. "The Calais Night Mail." *The Dent Uniform Edition of Dickens' Journalism*. Vol. 4. Ed. Michael Slater and John Drew. Columbus: Ohio State UP, 2000: 209–218.

———. "A Flight." *The Dent Uniform Edition of Dickens' Journalism*. Vol. 3. Ed. Michael Slater. Columbus: Ohio State UP, 1999: 26–35.

———. *The Letters of Charles Dickens*. Vol. 6: 1850–1852. Ed. Graham Storey. New York: Oxford University Press, 1965.

———. *The Letters of Charles Dickens*. Vol. 8: 1856–1858. Ed. Madeline House and Graham Storey. New York: Oxford University Press, 1965.

————. "Our French Watering-Place." *The Dent Uniform Edition of Dickens' Journalism.* Vol. 3. Ed. Michael Slater. Columbus: Ohio State UP, 1999: 229–241.

————. *A Tale of Two Cities.* Ed. Richard Maxwell. London: Penguin, 2000.

"The Emperor Napoleon III and England." *Times* 10 March 1858. *Times Digital Archive* 1785–1985. 26 May 2012.

"England Gets Rather Hard Measure in the Matter." Editorial. *Times* 2 Feb. 1858. *Times Digital Archive* 1785–1985. 26 May 2012.

Finn, Margot. *After Chartism: Class and Nation in English Radical Politics, 1848–1874.* Cambridge: Cambridge UP, 1993.

Grossman, Jonathan. *Charles Dickens's Networks: Public Transport and the Novel.* New York: Oxford UP, 2012.

Joshi, Priti. "Mutiny Echoes: India, Britons, and Charles Dickens's *A Tale of Two Cities.*" *Nineteenth-Century Literature* 62.1 (June 2007): 48–87.

Moore, Grace. *Dickens and Empire: Discourses of Class, Race, and Colonialism in the Works of Charles Dickens.* Burlington, VT: Ashgate, 2004.

Petch, Simon. "The Business of the Barrister in *A Tale of Two Cities.*" *Criticism: A Quarterly for Literature and the Arts* 44.1 (Winter 2002): 27–42.

Porter, Bernard. *The Refugee Question in mid-Victorian Politics.* Cambridge: Cambridge UP, 1979.

Rainsford, Dominic. *Literature, Identity and the English Channel: Narrow Seas Expanded.* New York: Palgrave, 2002.

"The Revival of Liberty in France." *Times* 1 Feb. 1858 *Times Digital Archive* 1785–1985. 26 May 2012.

Vargo, Gregory. "Social Protest and the Novel: Chartism, the Radical Press, and Early Victorian Fiction." Diss. Columbia University. Ann Arbor: ProQuest/UMI, 2010. (Publication No. 3420878).

Wright, Vincent. "Loi de sûreté générale de 1858." *Revue d'histoire moderne et contemporaine* 16. 3 (July–Sept. 1969): 414–30.

Wynne, Deborah. "Scenes of 'Incredible Outrage': Dickens, Ireland and *A Tale of Two Cities.*" *Dickens Studies Annual* 37 (2006): 51–64.

Yates, Edmund. *Recollections and Experiences.* Vol. 2. London: Bentley, 1885.

Servants' Bright Reflections: Advertising the Body in Victorian Literature and Culture

Erin D. Chamberlain

This essay examines the literary and cultural representations of Victorian servants and how their bodies and beauty are tied to the spaces in which they live and work. In particular, I argue that the idealized functional nature of the servant's body (as demonstrated through advertisements from the period) became the perceived way for the public to determine the effectiveness of management skills employers exerted over their domestic workers. These representations also illustrate the complicated tensions confronting employers wanting to establish a social superiority over their servants by noting differences in individual appearance, health, and cleanliness while at the same time needing these same servants to stand as representatives of the high quality of their households through those very same means. Whether servants perform their duties well or poorly, their bodies are presented by authors and advertisers as a reflection and ultimate success or failure of the productive and beautiful Victorian home.

In an advertisement for Brooke's Soap (fig. 1), a young, pretty maidservant polishes the pots and pans in her mistress's kitchen. She is neat, tidy, and efficient. The kitchen is likewise spotless—all is order and harmony, not only in the arrangement and general cleanliness of the kitchen, but in the countenance of the girl as well. Of particular note are the objects surrounding her. Each pot and pan mirrors one part of the maid's body. There are six different images of the girl's face, images which do not correspond to her facial expressions. Her arms and legs are also visible, thus illustrating her appearance through the reflections in the shining cookware. A view outside shows a sheet on a clothesline with the Brooke's slogan, "Won't Wash Clothes," while at the bottom of the whole picture is the phrase, "Makes Bright Reflections." Underneath the advertisement, a caption promises "will do a day's work in an hour." However, it is unclear whether the makers of Brooke's Soap are promising that the soap or the maid will complete these tasks so quickly. Even the phrase, "Makes Bright Reflections" could be associated with both kitchen objects and the servants hired to clean them. The shiny pots and pans act as mirror images for the maid, who in turn has a "bright," clean countenance of her own. The ad's promises—that the household (objects and servants included) will sparkle after the use of Brooke's soap—raises many questions about the place of the servant in the middle-class household. This ad

Fig. 1. "Brooke's Soap," *Illustrated London News* 29.iii (1890). Reprinted in De Vries, 93. (Courtesy John Murray).

uses the servant's body (broken into parts) to promote an appearance of the home highly sought after by the aspiring middle classes, emphasizing the role appearance plays in acquiring this ideal lifestyle as represented by advertisers.

Published in 1890, the ad is an excellent example of the desire for a well-managed household, and suggests how consumers could purchase not only a supposedly effective product, but also the domestic order portrayed in the advertisement. The mass consumption of products targeted at the growing middle classes was in full swing by the late nineteenth century, as was the emphasis made between a clean home and its healthy inhabitants. The intent of the ad to sell soap is evident, and yet the way in which this household is portrayed reveals a great deal in terms of the class tensions taking place in late Victorian society, particularly among the ambitious middle classes and the servants they employed. These tensions are explored through prevailing concerns over health, and the necessity of beauty and cleanliness in the domestic household.

Everyone was subject to the poor health conditions of the nineteenth century, but the working classes were particularly vulnerable to poor sanitation and the spread of disease. In an effort to amend the public health issues, several reports were made in the late 1830s by sanitary reformers like Southwood Smith, Neil Arnott, and J. P. Kay, whose Poor Law Commissions illustrated the seriousness of the problem throughout British society. Most prominently, however, Edwin Chadwick's Report on the *Sanitary Conditions of the Labouring Population of Great Britain* (1842) fueled great public health reforms. The 1848 Public Health Act authorized a central Board of Health to set up local boards, whose responsibility it was to assure proper drainage and water supply. The bill also allowed authorities to regulate waste disposal and the construction of burial grounds. However, these reforms and others took many decades of further legislation to improve the health conditions throughout England.

It is no wonder, then, that employers sought out only the healthiest servants to invite into their households. After all, servants were the ones who kept their houses clean, prepared their food, and lived in the closest proximity to all matters dealing with health and hygiene. When employers were concerned about the health and strength of their servants, it was also for their own and their children's welfare, and not exclusively for that of their servants. Indeed, some of the limitations placed upon servants were for health reasons. Circulating reports in newspapers suggested that servants who went to visit their own working-class families in poorer neighborhoods on an occasional Sunday brought back with them diseases from those households and districts. Many employers assumed that the poorer segments of London carried the greatest risk for disease and ill-health.[1]

For example, one such employer showed his Irish maid-of-all-work, Bridget, a newspaper, and said that "it was servants who carried small-pox and fever into the houses of their employers, through visiting the miserable homes of their own people when they got out on Sundays, and that it was advisable that such visits be prevented" (Greenwood 29). So not only were employers and servants often at odds about class position and servant mobility, but the emergence of these divisions and debates was reflected through the fear of disease, as servants could at any time "infect" their masters and mistresses with their own lower-class status.

For women in particular, the discussions on class and health were rarely mentioned without an additional emphasis upon their beauty or lack of it. And yet unlike the "infectious" definition usually associated with servants, health had a far different meaning for middle-class women than it did for upper-class ones. The middle-class mistresses were of special significance because they ran the households, governed the servants, and as such were targeted heavily by advertisers. Often in the advertisements of the period, women's clean and healthy bodies were the sign of a superior class stature, played out in the ads for soft skin, white hands, and a noble profile. The illustrations of middle-class women show them as beautiful, in perfect health, and at leisure in a luxurious home. For the upper classes, however, purity of health seemed a reward to which they were entitled because of their naturally superior class status. This look of health encouraged those wanting to leave the lower classes to seek it first. Advertisements from the later nineteenth century often placed upper-class women in spaces meant to display a more decorative, artistic, noble household as represented by the sense of leisure and beautiful objects surrounding these women. Above all, this type of woman is visible and admired by those who surround her. Her physical beauty has a glow that affects her entire sphere and creates a home for all in her presence. In this situation, the individual health and beauty of the woman acts to shape the interiors of the home and those who reside within its walls.[2]

While the middle-class ideal of health emphasizes as an addition an attractive appearance, I would argue that representations of the ideal servant in art, literature, and advertising overwhelmingly discourage this connection. For the servant, health is about neatness, cleanliness, and respectability—without the danger of too much beauty. It is about having the type of health defined by their ability to perform their duties in the household, to keep the space free from disease, and to be functional rather than ornamental. The look of health for servants includes a purity that does not infect others morally or physically. It is a lack of sickness, achieved through hard work, virtue, and obedience. In this context, as with the mistress, the servant's body is very much tied to the domestic space. This body ideally should blend into the household and take no visible credit for its happy, orderly state. While the bad, "contagious" (both morally and physically) servants are often blamed for any negative effects they have upon the household, when servants function well they become essentially an extension of the home. They lose their individuality as their bodies reflect, but do not (as with the mistresses) influence, the interior spaces of the home. Their bodies show only a collective form of healthy, active workers, who make highly visible the well-functioning household, thus leading to an appearance among the middle classes of the time and space for the higher-class pursuits of leisure.

Advertisements in particular establish a difference between the bodies of servants and those of middle-class women. Again, the portrayals of servants illustrate a functional purpose. Rather than focus upon the state of their skin or the beauty of their profiles, these ads often define them either as another part of the household that needs fixing or as experts on the household's needs, able to distinguish the good from the bad products on the market. In this latter case, servants are given a degree of authority over the middle-class consumers, but only to sell the product. Maids are an ideal choice for providing testimonials because they are the ones laboring in the home, and, if a product is purchased, testing it out. One advertisement promoting a cookbook asks, "Do You Know How to Cook Fish?" (fig. 2), as the cook looks directly at the audience.

Fig. 2. "Do You Know How to Cook Fish?" *The Graphic* 6.ix (1890). Reprinted in De Vries, 82. (Courtesy John Murray).

The servant in this ad serves two purposes: with her experience in the kitchen, she understands what it takes to cook well. Thus, her support of this cookbook lends it a great deal of credibility. However, the ad also implies that by using the cookbook, the mistress may be able to eliminate the need for a cook altogether. In this ad the servant is interchangeable with the product *and* she provides the testimonial necessary for its success. These dual purposes illustrate the tensions existing when attempting to define the servant's place in this domestic space. To associate her skills with another object in the home suggests that, like the book in question, she can be purchased and used to improve the household itself. Function, then, is a critical part of the success or failure in the quest for the desired—and desirable—middle-class household. This ad stresses that good servants have the skills and strength to produce good meals, and their bodies always reflect functionality over leisure.

These two definitions of health that stress the functional strength of a servant or the ornamental beauty of an employer seemingly at leisure are descriptions recognizable in the makeup of the household itself. Consider, for example, the numerous household manuals which were produced for growing numbers of people aspiring to join the middle class. *Cassell's Household Guide* professed two hopeful outcomes for householders who follow its advice: economy and luxury. A more specific example will be found in its objectives in selecting furniture. The *Guide* states that "in the articles on Furniture, information will be given as to what sort of furniture in each part of the house will be found most economical, durable, and pleasing, both in colour, material, shape and texture" (1). What is most important about a household and its objects, the manual argues, is not only its value (is it *economical*?) and quality (will it *last*?), but also its appearance (is it *pleasing*?), both to the inhabitants of the home and any visitors judging it from a less intimate perspective. These descriptions of the qualities for an excellent choice are relevant not only to the objects within that home, but to the people as well in their varying class positions and interactions with one another.

With these views in mind, it is fitting to return to the "Makes Bright Reflections" of the Brooke's Soap advertisement. In terms of space, the kitchen is perhaps the most practical in the whole household. In the ad a strong sense of order prevails; the dishes are neatly put away and the maid smiles as she works efficiently. Most striking is the way in which these objects reflect the activity and more importantly—the body—of the servant. Each pot and pan represents a part of the servant's body. Some of the dishes are meant for serving, intended to be seen in other parts of the household while others are everyday objects to be used only in the space of the kitchen. Each of these objects has a level of visibility or invisibility within the Victorian household. The maid's body is transposed onto all of these objects, thereby associating her with the same perceptions that outside visitors may connect to the home, and, by association again, its mistress. For example, the maid's cleanliness and her work within the kitchen show the results of her labor. When she exchanges the space of the kitchen for the display of the dining room, her bright efficiency coupled with the bright objects is a performance, her moment of visibility. However, any success she gains will be attributed to the home and mistress, rather than to the individual maid. The servant's presence brings about the order of the household (with the help of Brooke's Soap), but on the surface this presence does not bring about order—she works under the influence of her mistress and the products purchased for her use. The mirror images reflect not the industriousness of this particular maid, but rather her objectification and functionality as another part of the domestic institution. When the pots and pans are clean, the maid is likewise obedient.

The appearances of the servants, therefore, are a reflection on the home and its beauty and function rather than on the maids themselves. The ideal servant also avoids another situation: looking too much like her mistress. This situation is not unlike one described by the Mayhew brothers in *The Greatest Plague of Life: or,*

The Adventures of Lady in Search of a Good Servant (1847). Caroline Sk—n—st—n, the "Lady" described in the title of the book, goes through servant after servant, claiming that all the bad servants always enter her employment. Her servants are perpetually incapable: she hires alcoholics, thieves, vain beauties, novel readers, foreigners and gossips who are all in some form or another lazy—or so Caroline asserts.

One servant in particular, Rosetta, is at fault because she is too young, pretty, and preoccupied with improving her complexion and wearing fine clothing. Shortly after Caroline hires her, the "unpretending chrysalis had changed into a flaunting fal-lal butterfly" (89). After justifying her own money spent on new caps for herself, Caroline watches in dismay as her maid mimics her behavior in less expensive fashions:

> But I declare, no sooner did I get a new cap to my head, and one that I flattered myself was quite out of the common, than as sure as the next Sunday came round, that impudent stuck-up bit of goods of a Miss Susan would make a point of appearing in one of the very same shape and trimming—only, of course, made of an inferior and cheaper material. (89; ch. 7)

Susan is the name Caroline gives Rosetta because she believes Rosetta sounds too much like the name of a Duchess—too "stuck-up," Caroline again complains. Her fear of being mistaken for her beautiful maid is even realized when a police officer, seeing her cap from behind, believes she is Rosetta and winks familiarly at her on the street (90).

Elizabeth Langland and other critics have noted the significance of differences in dress between mistresses and their servants as distinct markers of social status. Rosetta's attempts to dress like her employer are not simply a flattering imitation, but an attempt to be perceived as an equal. This attempt, adds Langland, is of much greater importance to the social structure than it may seem: "If one signifies status by dress, one can never dress above one's station. How one dresses constitutes the person and class. . . . The 'great evil' arises because someone will have successfully imposed on a society that fancies sufficient its mechanisms for distinguishing rank" (35-36). What Caroline considers proper dress for herself—clothing that enhances her own beauty—in imitation by Rosetta becomes a reflection of her poor character. A competition arises between the two that should not, according to this representation, be a problem by nature of the social divisions that naturally exist.[3]

Rosetta has as much ambition for social climbing as her mistress, and her beauty gives her a better chance of succeeding than Caroline. When she first hires Rosetta, Caroline describes the ideal servant whose dress should indicate her lack of ambition:

> When the conceited bit of goods came after the situation, she looked *so* clean, tidy, and respectable, and had on *such* a nice plain cotton gown, of

only one colour—being a nice white spot on a dark green ground,—and *such* a good, strong, serviceable half-a-crown Dunstable straw bonnet, trimmed very plainly; and *such* a nice clean quilled net-cap under it; and *such* a tidy plain white muslin collar over one of the quietest black-and-white plaid shawls I think I ever saw in all my life, that I felt quite charmed at seeing her dressed *so* thoroughly like what a respectable servant ought to be. (86; ch. 7)

Not only does Rosetta's appearance suggest her respectable character, but the types of clothing Caroline chooses to emphasize are significant. Her gown is plain and simple, her bonnet "strong and serviceable"—as she also expects servants to be. She wears a "quiet" shawl and above all else looks clean and healthy. Like the servants depicted in advertisements of the later nineteenth century, her appearance depicts function, not fashion. Rosetta's role will be to labor at *producing* a fashionable home, but not to embody it herself. To the outside observer, she appears to fit this character, and Caroline hires her solely on the basis of this appearance. She hopes to put her on display in the household alongside her other objects so that her superior management skills are also visible when visitors arrive. Rosetta's plain appearance is the "correct" look for a respectable servant, and Caroline desires to purchase the commodity of Rosetta's labor as depicted through her body and overall obedient appearance.

Once Rosetta enters the household, however, appearances change. Not only does Caroline believe that the new servant is too showy in her dress, but Rosetta displays a fascination with her complexion that literally spills over into the kitchen—the one space in the home designated for practicality in order for the rest of the household to run smoothly. Caroline is continually frustrated because, "do what I would, I couldn't prevent the conceited peacock from poking her nasty, greasy bottles of rose hair-oil and filthy combs and brushes all among the plates and dishes over dresser" (88; ch. 7). She later finds that her maid has been reading "The Hand-Book of the Toilet," which "soon told me that the dirty messes I had been continually finding in all the saucepans, were either some pomatum, or cream, or wash, which she had been making for her face or hands" (88; ch. 7). Constantly looking at her own reflection, Rosetta engages in behavior very different from that of the Brooke's Soap maid. While similarities exist in the mirror imagery of both servants, Rosetta uses this space to improve her own personal beauty. The Brooke's Soap maid *becomes* beautiful because of her labor to improve the household and serve her employers. She merely reflects the success of the household. Rosetta, however, uses the kitchen objects for her own gain. When she makes her desires central, the objects surrounding her lose the ideal state of a pristine kitchen and home.

This scene also highlights what happens when ideologies collide in the kitchen. Facial creams and washes do not belong in her kitchen, Caroline believes, because her maid makes them for herself. The negative consequences of such actions should be noted as well. When Rosetta does something for herself—improving her body in order to raise her social status—only a mess is left behind in the kitchen. The order of the home is upset because the maid attempts to move beyond the sphere of invisible servitude. The body of the maid and the space of the kitchen are inextricably linked in middle-class ideology, and when Rosetta brews recipes that will make her more visible to others, the "natural" consequence is reflected in the chaos of the home, and by extension the changing class structure of Victorian society.

Having a pretty servant not only causes disorder within the household, but invites outsiders into the private space of the family. A standard hiring practice of servants in the Victorian period included forbidding servants to have followers. For the especially beautiful servants, as Caroline complains, this is especially difficult to enforce:

> Though, really, when I came to reflect, in my calm moments, upon the girl's conduct, there was every excuse to be made for the poor ignorant thing; for being cursed, as the philosopher says, with—what some people would have called—a pretty face, and having been only a year or so up from the country, it was but natural that the silly creature should have been tickled by the flattery of the pack of fellows who, to my great horror, were continually running after her. (90–91; ch. 7)

In the Mayhews' novel, George Cruikshank's illustration "Followers!" (fig. 3) quite comically demonstrates the nuisance having such a visibly beautiful servant can cause. Instead of enhancing the beauty of the home, the servant distracts and brings unwanted strangers to its door. It is interesting that Caroline here describes the pretty face of the servant not as an advantage, but rather as a curse and something to be pitied.

The influence of people upon the spaces around them is evident in these texts, and yet the idea that one shapes the other is not shared by all. In *The Poetics of Space*, Gaston Bachelard suggests that a house ought to be nothing more than an object, "dominated by straight lines, the plumb-line having marked it with its discipline and balance." It should be a space of rationality, one that "resists metaphors that welcome the human body and the human soul" (48). And yet in many of these representations it does not. The humanity that defines the intimate space of the home can also show us the human perceptions and desires projected onto that space.

Advertising is an excellent way to examine the ideology of the middle class, as it imagines the "dream world" that Bachelard suggests emerges despite all physical boundaries (48). Advertising both teaches and reflects the wishes of these would-be social climbers, creating a lifestyle with their own unique principles. The position of the servant in these advertisements is often a conflicted one. One type of servant who does emerge throughout, however, is the servant-as-reflection of the household. If the household is in disarray, so is the servant. An illustration

Fig. 3. George Cruikshank, "Followers!!!" Augustus and Henry Mayhew. *The Greatest Plague of Life*, between 90 and 91.

of this connection can be seen in an ad for Southall's Patent Window Cleaner (fig. 4).

Two female servants are pictured at work cleaning the windows of their employers' homes. The window to the left is clean and in perfect order, while the one

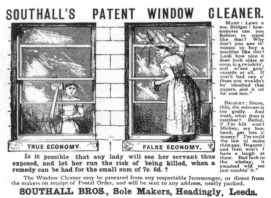

Fig. 4. "Southall's Patent Window Cleaner," *The Graphic* 3. iii (1883). Reprinted in Leonard De Vries, Victorian Advertisements, 91 (Courtesy John Murray).

on the right—the one in which the "Patent Window Cleaner" is not in use—is cracked and dirty. What is more interesting about this view, however, are the two housemaids. The first woman on the left is inside the home, while the second maid (whose Irishness lowers her even further in class status) stands dangerously outside the home on the ledge to reach the more difficult places. Readers are left to assume that this is why the window is cracked, but it should be noted that neither this maid's position nor the window is in the "right" state. Both reflect a damaged household, which the ad claims can be miraculously repaired with its product.

However, it is not simply the physical positions of the women nor the corresponding views provided of the homes that signify the would-be social status of both the employers and their servants. Their appearances also reflect the true or false economy of their cleaning methods. The woman on the left is younger and prettier than the one on the right, her features smaller than her counterpart, whose body is bulkier and nose longer than the first. The latter woman is old and ugly, inferring a bad household through the depiction of a bad maid. A dialogue between the two women printed to the right demonstrates their true and false characters. On the left Mary says to Bridget,

> "'Laws o me, Bridget! howsomever can you fashion to stand like that? Why don't you axe th' missus to buy a machine like this? Look how nice it does both sides at once, in a twinklin', and wi'out goin' outside at all. If you'd had one o' these you wouldn't ha' smashed that square, and it ud ha' cost less.'

To which Bridget responds,

> 'Shure, thin, the mistress is too gra'dy. And troth, what does it matthur? Bedad, if I'm kilt won't Mickey, my husband, get lots o' money? I'm tould the law ul make thim pay. Begorra! and then won't I have a laugh at them. Bad luck to the winday, it smashed wid me just touchin' it.'" (fig. 4)

Bridget's comment that her mistress is too "gra'dy" exhibits the failure of her mistress to buy quality household products *and* to avoid hiring a low-quality servant whose sole aim is to take advantage of her employers. The positioning of Bridget on the window ledge displays the mistress's poor management of the space within. Neither the servant nor the window perform their proper functions. The ad's implication that both mistress and servant are greedy for money also positions Bridget as a substitute figure for her mistress. She reflects the greed of her mistress by wanting to get "lots 'o money" from the law, just as her employer hires cheap products and labor to save money. Thus, through the poor quality of the window cleaner and servant the mistress's character is on public display because of the objects she does or does not possess.

What should also be examined in this advertisement are the inconsistencies displayed over traditional views of female strength within class boundaries. The typical stereotype of the upper-class woman dictated that her features be more delicate, her body weaker, and her beauty greater than her lower-class counter-part. Mary is small, slight, pretty, and, as can be assumed by looking at her body, weak. Bridget is older, more muscular, unattractive, and so strong the window breaks with one touch of her most indelicate hand. Mary's body reflects the higher class because it is the weaker of the two.[4] These class definitions are confirmed through the text as well. Mary is concerned with getting the window clean while staying indoors, but also, and more importantly, saving her mistress money. She aims to protect the property of her employers, unlike Bridget, who only thinks about how much money she can get for herself (or her husband) should she be injured or killed in a fall. Beauty or the lack of it becomes a means by which we can discern the servants' characters through the level of their productivity.

But what is really being affirmed here has less to do with the house*maids* than the house*holds*. Consider that the maid furthest left—the good and thoughtful one—stays indoors while the second stands dangerously outside of the home. This picture suggests that the domestic space should be a place of security and propriety. To be connected to the home only through a ledge—outside looking in—puts both the maid and the home in peril. The employers cannot be assured of any long-standing loyalty to them. This housemaid looks out for herself. Not in any way the archetypal loyal servant often depicted in literature, she embodies the popular belief of the untrustworthy servant, not really committed to her employ-ers and ready at a moment's notice to leave and improve her own socio-economic status.

Bridget's response to Mary clearly categorizes her as one of the "greatest plague" servants discussed during the height of the servant problem. In many fictional representations, the solution was often to hire servants with little beauty or other physical attractions. In *The Life and Adventures of Michael Armstrong* (1840), Frances Trollope explores this by depicting the respectable servant as essentially unattractive. In the novel, Lady Dowling employs a collection of female servants consisting of the "ugliest set of neat and carefully dressed middle-aged women that ever were found assembled together" because she is "deeply sensible of the dangerous attractions of youth and beauty in her own sex" (3; ch. 1). A female servant's looks could surpass those of the mistress in beauty, and by extension, class. The servant attracts others to her individual body in a way completely disconnected from her functional role in the home, and her appear-ance is often represented as disruptive to its peace. Returning to Rosetta, she is so beautiful that all the guardsmen and other men in the neighborhood chase after her. The authors of these two novels examine how youth and beauty are powerful attractions, and if embodied by the "wrong" people (the servant class), they may allow them autonomy and ascension into a higher ranking class.

However, the terms of classification must necessarily change when evaluating servant types like Bridget and Mary. This is a significant distinction because it often appears in the advertisements of the late nineteenth century. Maids who use the advertised product are almost always depicted in a positive—and hence more attractive—light, and yet many novels of the period, besides those just considered, show us the exact opposite: a trustworthy servant is not a beautiful one. It would appear, then, that these two genres follow two different systems of servant classification. The advertisements suggest that healthy, beautiful appearances serve as a positive confirmation of the product's success in improving the home. Much of the fiction, on the other hand, asserts that beauty is a sign of an individualistic, independent, ambitious servant. This beauty separates rather than connects her to the household, and thus is regarded suspiciously with greater frequency as the century continues.

Indeed, many literary texts traditionally represent servants as either invisible or too visible for their own good and those who employ them. Bruce Robbins notes that servants rarely appear as protagonists in Victorian fiction, but instead function solely as "mere appendages of their masters" (x). Instead of developing their servant characters, Victorian writers, Robbins suggests, use them as plot devices or to offer additional insights into the primary characters:

> Moreover, all that has been represented of these prefabricated tropes is their effects, their momentary performance of useful functions. It is as expository prologues, oracular messengers, and authorial mouthpieces, rhetorical "doublings" of the protagonist, accessories used to complicate or resolve the action, that servants fill the margins of texts devoted to their superiors. (x)

In fulfilling their functions, the actions of servants thus become very important. However, they draw unwanted attention to themselves when their dress, beauty, and health bring them out of the shadows. If it is not to the advantage of those who employ them, suddenly the supposed entitlement of social position must compete with those who should, as many representations suggest, be mere "appendages" but instead have the potential to *look* equal and independent from those who desire a higher social superiority.

The definition of beauty within defined class boundaries is further emphasized when a servant exists outside of the home—and thus beyond the values (and valued) lifestyle of the middle class. In yet another Pears' Soap ad (fig. 5), two servants and a chimney-sweep are depicted near the threshold of the home. The two on the left (one a very young girl) stand washing the steps, presumably with Pears' Soap. Their positive attitude comes across when they greet the passing chimney sweep with a "Good morning!" and ask, "Have you used Pears' soap?" Evidently not. A striking contrast exists between the two women and the sweep. Despite the fact that all the workers here are employed in cleaning duties, only the two women on the left actually have clean bodies and bright countenances. They are connected to this household in a way the chimney-sweep is not. He is on the move, pointedly located next to a ditch of water that moves up the road. He carries the dirt of several households on his body, but more important than this, he moves it *away* from the households. This worker will not reflect the household, and so moves along up the road, transient and in opposition to the purity of the home.

The ideal of cleanliness and the necessity for purity in the domestic space are again represented in another soap advertisement, this one quite different from the

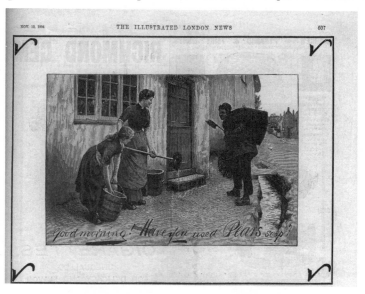

Fig. 5. "Pears' Soap," Illustrated London News 105 (Nov. 10, 1894): 607.

earlier Brooke's Soap illustration (fig. 1). Figure 6 shows a dirty kitchen before the product has been used. Note that the pots and pans are filthy, the kitchen is in disarray, and the maid is not in her proper space cleaning, but rather is outside the entire household as she runs indoors to attend to her duties. She provides a striking contrast to the maid from the "Makes Bright Reflections" ad. The reflections themselves have changed. Unlike the illustration in Figure 1, in which the maid can see her shining reflection in all her cookware, the scene from Figure 6 shows only two reflections: the monkey holding up a mirror to his image, and a dirty mirror in the corner. The pots and pans do not provide any reflections of the maid (as they do in the former ad) because she is as unkempt as the space around her. What all of this adds up to, finally, is the idea that servants are connected to the functional space of the home in a way their employers are not, and that if the physical space of the household is in chaos, it may be safely assumed that the servants are as well. The advertisers do not promise to fix the character of the servant directly, but do suggest they can be influenced by the right amount of cleanliness and calm in the home.

The use of mirrors and reflections in these advertisements explores a broader theme in popular culture and literature that depicts the servant as another part or

Fig. 6. "Brooke's Soap," *Illustrated London News* 90 (Apr. 2, 1887): 398.

object within the domestic space to be used. Instead of a traditional mirror that might reflect the individual beauty of those who gaze into it, these servants and their reflections (or lack thereof) in the cookware instead demonstrate the productivity and characters of the workers. This is an intriguing contrast to the some of the servants portrayed in literature. There are a number of servants in *The Greatest Plague*, for example, who seem to be causing the mayhem rather than mirroring it. These two contrasting representations of the invisible servant (without individual identity) versus the chaotic troublemakers are widespread stereotypes of this particular class of domestic workers. They are either too weak to fix a broken household or the ones contributing to its destruction. And even in these failed households, many portrayals in periodicals and literature simply point to the employers as ultimately responsible for managing the behavior of their servants, once again removing all individual autonomy from their employees. These popular representations idealize the servant as a functional object incapable of ordering his or her own life with precision, calm, cleanliness, health, and beauty without the help of the employer and a wonder product that will easily fix all the very complicated domestic ties of the Victorian household and its inhabitants.

NOTES

1. For more information on the public health acts, see Hamlin's *Public Health in the Age of Chadwick,* 156–87 and Haley's *The Healthy Body and Victorian Culture,* 3–22.
2. In a different context, Ann Colley has said much the same thing, that "articles do not define interiors; bodies that move and feel their way among these objects do" (40). For more on this argument, see Colley.
3. John Burnett similarly describes the importance of a servant's appearance by noting that "dress and function . . . proclaimed in an outward and visible way the degree of success in life that their employer had attained and, by implication, conferred upon him membership of the class" (136). A servant's appearance should reflect that of the household and its employers rather than detracting from the home or competing with one's employers.
4. The Mayhew brothers ridicule middle-class obsession with appearances in a hilarious anecdote on the shaping of social classes after Caroline has given birth to her first child. She is told by her mother that "noses might be grown to any shape, like cucumbers, and that it was only for the mother to decide whether the infant nasal gherkin should be allowed to run wild, and twist itself into a 'turn up,' or should, by the process of cultivation, be forced to grow straight, and elongate itself into a Grecian" (111; ch. 8).

WORKS CITED

Bachelard, Gaston. *The Poetics of Space.* 1958. Trans. Maria Jolas. Boston: Beacon, 1994.
"Brooke's Soap." *Illustrated London News* 90 (Apr. 2, 1887): 398.
Burnett, John, ed. *The Annals of Labour: Autobiographies of British Working-Class People 1820–1920.* Bloomington: Indiana UP, 1974.
Cassell's Household Guide to Every Department of Practical Life: Being a Domestic Encyclopedia of Domestic and Social Economy. 2 vols. London: Cassell, Petter and Galpin, 1878.
Colley, Ann. "Bodies and Mirrors: The Childhood Interiors of Ruskin, Pater and Stevenson." *Domestic Space: Reading the Nineteenth-Century Interior.* Ed. Inga Bryden and Janet Floyd. Manchester: Manchester UP, 1999. 40–57.
De Vries, Leonard, ed. *Victorian Advertisements.* London: Murray, 1968.
Greenwood, James. "The Maid-of-All-Work." *Toilers in London, by One of the Crowd.* London: Diprose & Bateman, 1883. 26–32.
Haley, Bruce. *The Healthy Body and Victorian Culture.* Cambridge, MA: Harvard UP, 1978.
Hamlin, Christopher. *Public Health and Social Justice in the Age of Chadwick Britain, 1800–1854.* Cambridge: Cambridge UP, 1998.
Langland, Elizabeth. *Nobody's Angels: Middle-Class Women and Domestic Ideology in*

Victorian Culture. Ithaca: Cornell UP, 1995.

Mayhew, Augustus, and Henry Mayhew. *The Greatest Plague of Life: or, The Adventures of a Lady in Search of a Good Servant by One Who Has Been "Almost Worried to Death."* London: David Bogue, 1847.

Robbins, Bruce. *The Servant's Hand: English Fiction from Below*. Durham: Duke UP, 1993.

Trollope, Frances. *The Life and Adventures of Michael Armstrong*. London: Henry Colburn, 1840.

Entropy and the Marriage Plot in *The Woman in White* and *Lady Audley's Secret*

Elizabeth Meadows

The sensation novel's exciting effects on its readers have been the topic of critical concern since the inception of this novelistic subgenre in the 1860s. Yet the repetition of sensational thrills that characterizes Wilkie Collins's The Woman in White *and M. E. Braddon's* Lady Audley's Secret *has paradoxically entropic effects: a state of reduced energy, agency, and volition for characters and readers alike. The depletion of agency within sensation novels constitutes a genre-defining strategy that calls attention to the determining power of formal conventions of nineteenth-century novelistic closure and social conventions of normative sexuality, which are deeply intertwined in the marriage plot that dominates Victorian fiction. Braddon and Collins make the binding power of conventional plot structures into the subject matter of plot as their sensation novels portray and enact the loss of energy that defines entropy. This essay examines how the entropic plots of* The Woman in White *and* Lady Audley's Secret *theorize the formal requirements of sensation to interrogate the relations among literary and social conventions and human bodies.*

In 1859, the first number of Wilkie Collins's *The Woman in White* appeared in *All the Year Round*, ushering in a decade filled with sensational works of art,

Dickens Studies Annual, Volume 45, Copyright © 2014 by AMS Press, Inc. All rights reserved.

drama, and literature. During the 1860s, novels that used an alternating rhythm of suspenseful secrets and sensational revelations to evoke thrills of fear and gasps of shock became common enough to provoke a furious response criticizing such novels as dangerous stimulants; one reviewer declared, "Excitement, and excitement alone seems to be the great end at which they aim" (Mansel 482). In the vigorous critical debate still swirling around Victorian sensation novels, scholars follow the tradition established by such reviews, focusing on sensation novels' power to excite emotional and physiological responses.[1] Yet the initial shock in Collins's novel offers another way to read the effects of sensation on both characters and readers. As Walter Hartright, hero and master-narrator, walks alone through the midnight darkness of Hampstead Heath, his erotic reverie about his future pupils is abruptly terminated when an unknown woman clad in white reaches out to touch his shoulder. Even as it sets in motion the novel's compelling plot, the shock of this touch brings "every drop of blood...to a stop" (Collins 23). Collins here figures the outset of narrative as a cessation of movement; a deathly loss of energy paradoxically stimulates narrative drive. This moment encapsulates Collins's innovation in his first blockbuster success: the creation of the entropic plot, in which the repetition of sensational thrills leads to a state of reduced energy, agency, and volition for characters and readers alike. Nor are the entropic effects of sensation unique to Collins's novel. Mary Elizabeth Braddon's *Lady Audley's Secret*, another early example of the genre, features a hero whose actions spring from his loss of agency. The deterioration of agency that characterizes the protagonists of Collins's and Braddon's novels nonetheless enables a cheerfully domestic ending that unites narrative order and social convention in marriage. *The Woman in White* and *Lady Audley's Secret*, the most canonical of the novels that critics grouped under the rubric of sensation, reveal the entropic losses entailed by the teleological energies that drive the marriage plot of the nineteenth-century realist novel.[2]

In their depletion of individual energy and agency, sensation novels follow the second law of thermodynamics: the law of entropy, which declares that the level of available energy in a closed system must decline. The codification of the laws of thermodynamics took place during the central decades of the nineteenth century and became, like the emerging theory of evolution, a foundation for conflicting narratives of cultural progress and decline. While the conservative first law of thermodynamics assures us that the energy of a closed system remains constant and thus provides a foundation for a hopeful narrative of progress, the second law's insistence on the dissipation of *usable* energy revokes the hopeful narrative, declaring that systems inevitably move from order to disorder. As Anna Maria Jones points out, critical studies of the conflict between Victorians' optimistic reading of the first law and their dire apprehensions regarding the second law share a "chronological logic that links it [the conflict] to the degeneration theories of the late-nineteenth century" ("Conservation of Energy" 67).[3] Victorian responses to sensation novels make it possible to situate the subgenre within this critical narrative, reading such novels as an early symptom of the cultural degeneration that preoccupied Victorians more and more as the century moved towards its end.

By describing the depletion of energy within sensation novels as "entropic," I do not mean to suggest that sensation novels participated in the cultural formation and dissemination of thermodynamic principles, nor to determine the place of the entropic plot of sensation on a continuum from guaranteed progress to inevitable decline. Rather, I use the term "entropic" to characterize the plot of sensation because "energy" and "entropy" carry formal implications particularly useful in discussing the relations among the form of the sensation novel, its dominant themes, and its embodied effects on its readers. As Bruce Clarke points out, before energy became a thermodynamic term, it served as a "common literary and philosophical term" denoting "emotional and textual as well as physical intensity, intellectual as well as bodily vigor, and in particular, rhetorical force" (21). Straddling the border between abstraction and materiality, energy's duality emblematizes the contradictory nature of form, which, as Angela Leighton elegantly reminds us, "is an abstraction from matter, removed and immaterial," but that "is also subtly inflected towards matter. . . . it holds off from objects, being nothing but form, pure and singular; at the same time, its whole bent is towards materialization, towards being the shape or body of something" (1). In thermodynamics, energy's "bent . . . towards materialization" leads to the increase of disorder, a movement from a higher energy state to a lower, a phenomenon that Clausius coined the term "entropy" to describe.[4] In order to be used, energy must be harnessed, embodied in machines like looms or steam engines that produce material goods or have physical effects, yet the second law of thermodynamics decrees that this productivity is matched by a corresponding loss. Entropy names the process through which abstract form becomes material, at the price of inevitable losses, whether of energy, will, or interiority.[5]

In *The Woman in White* and *Lady Audley's Secret*, these losses take on literary form as the lack of interiority typical of characters in the sensation novel.[6] This lack is more than just a characteristic that distinguishes such works from the realist novel. The depletion of individual will and agency within sensation novels constitutes a genre-defining strategy that calls attention to the determining power of formal conventions of nineteenth-century novelistic closure and social conventions of normative sexuality, which are deeply intertwined in the marriage plot that dominates Victorian fiction. Peter Brooks's *Reading for the Plot* demonstrates the politically and thermodynamically conservative power of the comic ending of marriage, which restores social order and a steady state through the successful discharge of dangerous energies produced in and by the plot. Collins and Braddon explore the implications of such plotting under the law of entropy, to suggest that the materialization of textual energies in the conventional generic bodies of plot constitutes a diminished rather than a restored order or "thermodynamic plenum" (Brooks 123). In *The Woman in White* and *Lady Audley's Secret*,

Collins and Braddon forge links between sexuality and the diminution of energy, between marriage and the abdication of agency, between sensation and the evacuation of interiority. Both authors represent the depletion of will through images of unbreakable chains that constrain the actions of their characters. Form and theme cohere in this appropriation of a dominant trope for plot, so that the use of chains to figure the loss of agency in both novels exemplifies the entropic conversion of formal literary conventions into narrative theme.[7] Braddon and Collins make the binding power of conventional plot structures into the subject matter of plot; their sensation novels portray and enact the loss of energy that defines entropy.

In this essay, part of a larger project on Victorian forms and formalism, I argue that the entropic plots of *The Woman in White* and *Lady Audley's Secret* make the literary and embodied effects of conventional forms of narrative and social organization their central theme. In addition to drawing on and contributing to various scientific and social discourses, the sensation novel reflects on the Victorian realist novel's imbrication of the cultural form of marriage with the problem of narrative closure. The entropic plots of *The Woman in White* and *Lady Audley's Secret* theorize the formal requirements of sensation to interrogate the relations among literary and social conventions and human bodies.

A "Passive Force": Sensation, Sexuality, and the Marriage Plot

In the first and most powerful shock of *The Woman in White*, Walter's encounter with Anne Catherick on Hampstead Heath, Collins uses sensation and sexuality to generate an entropic plot that charts the decline of individual energy and unravels an energetic narrative model based on the arc of male sexual arousal and climax.[8] When the anonymous Woman in White reaches out to touch Walter, his response is both deathly and sexual: his blood freezes in his veins, to which he responds by "tightening [his fingers] round the handle of [his] stick" (23).[9] With a "forlorn woman" "utterly and helplessly at [his] mercy" and his hand on his stick (26), Walter seems to embody an energetic model of plot in which "arousal...creates the narratable as a condition of tumescence" (Brooks 103). Yet even as Walter's words and gesture call our attention to the erotic potential energy of this moment, his initial sense of total control facilitated by gender and circumstance transforms into a recognition that he has no power over the nameless woman or himself: "no earthly right existed on my part to give me a power of control over her" (26). Alone at night with a woman, Walter's sexualized fantasy of control flips over into recognition of his inability to act as he chooses, deflating the plot of "tumescence." In its place, Collins installs a plot paradoxically driven by the hero's initial loss of will, a loss repeated, multiplied, and reflected upon throughout the rest of the novel.

While Walter implies that his volition has been bled away by his erotic response to the chilling touch of "the Solitary Woman," the threat that eros poses to agency is even clearer for women (26).[10] Of all the characters, Laura Fairlie, the double and half-sister of Anne Catherick, suffers the most complete depletion of will and individuality. Her uncanny resemblance to Anne enables Count Fosco to exchange the two women's bodies for each other: Anne's body substitutes for Laura's in the grave, while Laura's body takes Anne's place in the mental asylum. The theft of Laura's identity, her incarceration in the asylum, and her ensuing state of near-imbecility literalize the legal erasure of her identity in marriage and take the "norm of the submissive Victorian wife" to an extreme (Ablow 169–70; Miller 172), but her dire situation results from her own choice as much as from legal and cultural constraints on women. In love with Walter and engaged to Sir Percival Glyde, Laura chooses to abdicate the power of choice, declaring, "'I can never claim my release from my engagement'" (Collins 163); she can only admit that she loves another and allow Sir Percival to choose. She reassures Sir Percival that this love can never be expressed in any other way: "'No word has passed… between myself and the person to whom I am now referring for the first and last time in your presence, of my feelings towards him, or of his feelings towards me—no word ever can pass'" (170). Rather than repressing her desire for Walter, Laura explicitly avows her love for him—but only in order to subject herself to Sir Percival's will. Laura's sole independent decision is an abdication of agency expressed through a declaration of illicit love.

Marian Halcombe, Laura's half-sister on the distaff side, calls Laura's determination to relinquish her right to choose a "passive force in her character…hidden from me—hidden even from herself, till love found it, and suffering called it forth" (167). An abdication of agency that is both the product of her sexual awakening and her chosen means of erotic expression, the "passive force" Laura exerts depletes her of any further power of expression or choice. In her journal, Marian makes it clear that this entropic force transforms Laura: "She used to be pliability itself; but she was now inflexibly passive….it was so shockingly unlike her natural character to see her as cold and insensible as I saw her now" (176). Collins's choice of adjectives—"inflexibly passive," "cold and insensible"—implies that Laura's sexual desire for Walter deanimates her, rendering her living, human flesh marmoreal and corpsely. Because of the "passive force" of Laura's entropic passion,[11] when she marries Sir Percival, she is already a dead woman walking down the aisle.

The depletion of volition that Collins portrays as the unexpected corollary to sensation and sexuality reaches its apotheosis in marriage. Not only is Laura metaphorically dead when she weds Sir Percival, her second marriage to Walter also occurs when she is "socially, morally, legally—dead" (413). While such an erosion of female agency in marriage is hardly surprising, given the doctrine of coverture, Collins shows marriage atrophying male agency as well. Walter's union with the dead is a culmination of multiple images of marriage between a spectral woman and a man drained of volition. In her hypnagogic vision at Blackwater Park, Marian proleptically envisions Walter "kneeling by a tomb of white marble;

and the shadow of a veiled woman rose out of the grave beneath, and waited by his side" (274). Marian's vision then materializes in the sensational graveside scene that closes "The Second Epoch," when Walter visits Laura's grave and sees two women draped in veils moving slowly toward him in a solemn procession that figuratively recapitulates the marriage ceremony. When the veil drops to reveal Laura, alive and breathing, standing by her own tombstone, her persistent association with whiteness, through both her choice of clothing and her resemblance to the titular woman in white, makes her simultaneously bridal and ghostly, "Medusa *and* virgin bride" (Dever 108).[12] Walter's rhetoric emphasizes the deathly power that Laura wields over him at this moment of reunion: "the springs of my life fell low" at the sound of the veiled woman's voice, as she takes "possession of me, body and soul" (410). Collins represents the meeting between Walter and his beloved as deathliness and possession, showing that his hero's vital energies are sapped through this figurative marriage to the dead.

By depicting sexuality as a diminution of energy and agency consummated in matrimony, Collins expands the critique of Victorian marriage from its effects on female agency and identity to its effects on individuality and volition more generally. Through Laura and Walter, Collins shows sexuality causing the loss of agency, and this causal relation revises the link between sex and death that dominates Victorian literature.[13] Moralizing narratives like Elizabeth Gaskell's *Ruth* use death as the punishment for or result of sexuality outside the bounds of marriage; in transcendent narratives like Emily Brontë's *Wuthering Heights*, union in death figures or replaces sexual union in this world. In contrast to both, Collins's entropic narrative reveals a deathly sexuality that diminishes agency and individuality, not *even* but *especially* when it terminates in matrimony. In the deathly marriages of *The Woman in White*, Collins critiques the normative telos for sexual desire—an end central to Victorian culture and institutionalized in countless Victorian novels. Collins's morbid images portray marriage as an ossified and ossifying institution, in which sex becomes the necessary death of the individual, placing the body in a chain of reproduction to ensure the stability and continuation of the social order.[14] Repeatedly representing the scene of marriage as the culmination of a morbid sexuality that entropically depletes individual energy and will, Collins suggests that the marriage plot itself is a formal convention as powerfully binding as the chain of events that traps both characters and readers of sensation fiction.

While Collins portrays the entropic effects of sexuality to critique the power of the marriage plot in Victorian literature and culture, Braddon challenges the dominance of the realist marriage plot through her depiction of the entropic evacuation of her hero's will. Braddon begins by suggesting that female sexuality poses a threat to male agency. In his quest to explain the disappearance of his beloved friend George Talboys, Robert Audley turns detective, seeking the connection between Lucy Graham, now Lady Audley, and George's supposedly dead wife, Helen.[15] On the verge of uncovering evidence that Lady Audley is indeed Helen

Talboys, Robert Audley exclaims to himself, "'how these women take life out of our hands'" (237; vol. 2, ch. 8). In context, this exclamation condemns women's eagerness to betray each other's interests; Robert is commenting on how eager Miss Tonks is to discredit Lucy Graham. Yet shortly afterward Robert slips into a dream, in which he sees a "pale starry face…and knew it was my lady, transformed into a mermaid, beckoning his uncle to destruction" (246; vol. 2, ch. 9). Despite having "my lady" in his power, Robert still sees her as a form of alluring and monstrous female agency, suggesting that his earlier comment bears a more literal meaning: women take life away from men.

Robert's nightmare image of Lady Audley bears a hidden resemblance to Clara Talboys, sister to his missing friend, a resemblance all the more striking because of the explicit contrast between the two women: Clara's "grave and earnest face [is] so different in its character to my lady's fragile beauty" (274; vol. 2, ch. 11). This physical difference clearly indexes a deeper moral difference between the two women, yet Robert groups them together in his condemnation of female agency depleting men of life and liberty of action. Robert blames his unwontedly energetic pursuit of the hidden cause of Talboys's disappearance on feminine energy, declaring that "women were at the bottom of all mischief" because they "are *never lazy*. They don't know what it is to be quiet. They are Semiramides, and Cleopatras, and Joan of Arcs, Queen Elizabeths, and Catharine the Seconds, and they riot in battle, and murder, and clamour, and desperation….Look at this business of poor George's! It's all woman's work from one end to the other" (207; vol. 2, ch. 6). Mythical and monstrous whether they are mermaids or monarchs, women are sexually compelling forces that drive men into energetic activity that is nonetheless a deprivation of volition. The imagery of Robert's diatribe against women who "agitate the universe and play at ball with hemispheres" when they "make mountains of warfare and vexation out of domestic molehills" reveals the entropic costs of the perverse and chaotic energies that women generate (207; vol. 2, ch. 6). Even though Robert's pursuit of Lady Audley's secret jolts him out of a torpid existence of reading French novels and smoking cigars, he repeatedly ascribes his transformation into an upstanding, hard-working subject to a sexualized and monstrous female agency external to himself and embodied in Lady Audley and her opposite, Clara Talboys.[16]

Just as Robert complains that women transform "domestic molehills" into "warfare and vexation," reviewers disparaged sensation novels for adding a dangerous admixture of bigamy and other marital crimes to the domestic scene of the realist novel. Robert's critique of feminine agency replicates the terms of the critical outcry against sensation novels, particularly those by women, encouraging us to interpret the external agency that Walter submits to and Robert rails against as, respectively, Collins's "mechanical talents" and Braddon's corrupt plotting ("Saturday Review" 249).[17] Through Robert's misogynistic tirade, Braddon's detective reflects upon the form of the debased and feminized genre of sensation, even as he acknowledges his own subjection to its depleting and entropic power.

Although Robert attacks the formula of sensation novels, Braddon's novel follows a formula equally essential to the domestic realist novel. Despite Lady Audley's seductive charms, Robert withstands her plotting and finally incarcerates her in an asylum in Belgium, and this incarceration merely exaggerates the narratives meted out to heroines who must abandon the plot of vocation to complete their marriage plots.[18] Elaine Showalter points out that "Lady Audley's real secret is that she is *sane*, and, moreover, representative" of women in Victorian culture, whose struggles against the limitations imposed upon them could easily be diagnosed as insanity (*Female Malady* 167).[19] But Lady Audley is also "representative" of a narrative arc that shapes the fate of women in novels acclaimed for their brilliant and sympathetic psychological realism. I am here referring to heroines such as George Eliot's Dinah Morris, Dorothea Brooke, and Gwendolen Harleth, who must all accept a narrower orbit for their energies as the price of narrative closure.[20] When Robert forces confinement on Lady Audley, he refers his agency in the matter to an external force that is not just sensational plotting, but a narrative structure that dominates the Victorian realist novel. Braddon preempts the critique of sensation to challenge the realist novel of character by calling attention to the binding power of the conventional marriage plot.

"Morbid Phenomena": The Embodied Effects of Literary Form

"Make 'em laugh; make 'em cry; make 'em wait." This famous dictum on the art of the serialized novel "makes" readers dance to the tune of the text; the rhythmic alternations of suspense and revelation unleash physical energies in the form of readers' laughter and tears, while simultaneously channeling readers' volition through the nervous tension of expectancy. While central characters lose energy in the form of agency and interiority, shocking sensations hurry readers toward the inevitable end, absorbing and exhausting readers' energies through formal strategies designed to grab and hold their attention (and their wallets). The deterioration of agency that both readers and characters undergo manifests itself thematically through Walter's, Marian's, and Robert's various self-reflexive meditations on the compulsions of plot. Like Robert's tirade against monstrous female agency in *Lady Audley's Secret*, these meditations preempt the critique of sensation. This metacritical dimension intertwines the strategies of sensation with those of domestic realism to demonstrate the embodied and material power of literary form.

The physical power sensation novels wielded over their readers preoccupied Victorian critics, who ascribed the genre's pathological power to its formal structure as much as to its portrayal of domestic crime. In a review that has become canonical for its virulent condemnation of sensation novels, Henry Mansel declares, "works of this class manifest themselves as belonging . . . to the morbid phenomena of literature—indications of a widespread corruption, of which they are in part both the effect and the cause; called into existence to supply the cravings of a diseased appetite, and contributing themselves to foster the disease, and to stimulate the want which they supply" (482-83). Designating literature as "morbid"—causing disease—Mansel posits a profound connection between bodies and texts; his metaphors of disease, addiction, and ingestion assume that readers are subjected to uncontrollable physical processes, "cravings of a diseased appetite" that drain readers of agency just as Walter and Robert are drained of will.[21] In "Sensation Novels," an article almost as frequently cited in current scholarship as Mansel's, Margaret Oliphant addresses the morbid form of sensation novels: "The violent stimulant of serial publication—of *weekly* publication, with its necessity for frequent and rapid recurrence of piquant situation and startling incident—is the thing of all others most likely to develop the germ" of a diseased literary appetite (568). By this account, the regular repetition of shocking occurrences becomes a formal structure necessary to the sensation novel that deprives readers of choice, making them into embodied creatures driven by somatic responses rather than conscious will. Sensation fiction's direct appeal to the body and the uncontrolled physical response of its readers combine to emphasize how corporeality is shaped by narrative forms.

Collins places multiple reflections of the readerly effects of sensation within his novel. In one instance, Marian's meditation on memory becomes a reflection on the demands of serial publication, which requires that readers maintain interest in events to come based on memory of previous plot events. As the *Examiner*'s review makes clear, Collins stimulates such feats of memory and attention in his readers through an "enthralling" mastery of linear causality: "Of every page the chief interest is made to depend entirely upon memory of what has gone before and expectation of what is to follow" (549). Within the narrative, the importance of memory in linking past, present, and future becomes the subject of concern for Marian when she consults her journal to verify her memory of events and then writes: "It was almost as great a relief to my mind as to Laura's to find that my memory had served me…as faithfully as usual. In the perilous uncertainty of our present situation, it is hard to say what future interests may not depend upon the regularity of the entries in my journal, and upon the reliability of my recollection" (284). The "future interests" that "depend upon the regularity" of her journal entries mirror the serialized narrative's dependence on "memory of what has gone before and expectation of what is to follow." Thus Marian's anxiety about regularity, recurrence, and recollection transforms the structural requirements of the genre into the subject matter of plot even as it reproduces critics' anxieties about the morbid power of literary form. Furthermore, Marian's journal recasts what should be a record of her inner self into a manifestation of the lack of interiority that becomes a central theme of both sensation novels and the charges leveled against them. Acknowledging the compelling power of Collins's novel yet lamenting the way characters' interiority and individuality are sacrificed to the exigencies of the sensational plot, another reviewer asserts that Collins "does not attempt to paint character or passion" but uses characters "simply and solely with reference to the part it is necessary they should play in tangling or disentangling his argument" (*Saturday Review* 249). When Marian worries about her memory, she calls our attention to how the journal functions not as a record of her inner thoughts and feelings, but as a resource for "disentangling" Fosco's plots. Collins exposes the exigencies of the form through the entropic transformation of the readerly effects of sensation into narrative content.

Marian's journal is just one of the multiple first-person narratives that constitute the novel, and Collins's use of this formal strategy paradoxically depletes characters of interiority. At the outset of the novel, Walter makes the instrumental nature of these narratives clear, introducing them as a substitute for, improvement on, and supplement to a case at law. He asserts that each narrator is a "witness" who will "present" part of "one complete series of events," so that "the Reader shall hear" the case as a "Judge might once have heard it" (9). His claims make the multiple ensuing narratives into a form of testimony, and the critic in the *Saturday Review* picks up on Collins's invocation of the courtroom to argue that it deprives characters of interiority:

> None of his characters are to be seen looking about them. They are not occupied in by-play. They are not staring at the spectator, or, if they are, they are staring listlessly and vacantly, like witnesses who are waiting to be called before the court, and have nothing to do until their turn arrives. There they stand, most of them, like ourselves, in rapt attention, on the stretch to take their share in the action of the central group—their eyes bent in one direction—their movement converging upon one center—half-painted, sketchy figures, grouped with sole relation to the unknown mystery in the middle. (249)

The listlessness and vacancy that characterize the "witnesses" stem from their "rapt attention" to the central "mystery" that governs the plot they both participate in and represent. In the courtroom, the power and knowledge of representation that each narrator possesses, Walter above all, become the very means of subjecting characters and narrators to the needs of the plot.

Not only are characters and narrators deprived of interiority in sensation novels, but readers are similarly drained of will; as the review above makes explicit, characters are "like ourselves, in rapt attention" on the plot.[22] While the first-person narratives of eighteenth-century epistolary novels such as *Clarissa* and *Evelina* seem to offer a window into characters' inner lives, thus underwriting the realist status of the novel and the interiority of the subject, the first-person narratives of *The Woman in White* draw readers and characters together into a form of narrative spectatorship that bleeds off their agency and also creates the embodied effects that give the genre its name.[23] Collins's adaptation of epistolarity to produce characters lacking interiority draws on a technique central to the rise of the realist novel of character only to reverse its effects, revealing this realist strategy's sensational potential through the interplay of knowledge and ignorance within and among the multiple narratives.

Although Braddon does not employ the same narrative technique as Collins, her novel shares with Collins's a persistent emphasis on the image of chains—a metaphor for plot that calls attention to its constraining power. Near the end of *The Woman in White*, Walter uses this metaphor to describe the narrative as it draws to its close: "Two more events remain to be added to the chain, before it reaches fairly from the outset of the story to the close" (620). Despite Walter's assumption of narrative and editorial control in the Third Epoch, this phrase reminds us that earlier Walter wondered whether he was "linked . . . to a chain of events . . . [he is] powerless to snap asunder" (78).[24] In Braddon's novel, even before the mysterious disappearance of George Talboys spurs Robert into his detective endeavors, the narrator calls our attention to a seemingly unimportant letter, wondering "that so simple a thing . . . would one day come to be a link in that terrible chain of evidence afterwards to be slowly forged into the...criminal case" against Lady Audley (52; vol. 1, ch. 7). This moment of proleptic wonderment casts the plot of the novel as a series of links in a chain, slowly forged episode by episode in each serial portion yet to come, and also evokes the image of a courtroom through referring to the "evidence" in a "criminal case."[25] After Talboys disappears, Robert obliquely warns Lady Audley that he is pursuing her by expatiating on the power of "'Circumstantial evidence...that wonderful fabric which is built out of straws collected at every point of the compass'" and declaring that the accumulation of minute details forms "links of steel in the wonderful chain" of evidence (119-20; vol. 1, ch. 15). Braddon's choice of metaphors here links the courtroom and its chains of evidence with the textual "fabric" of narrative itself. Like Robert's evidence, the text of the sensation novel is made up of "infinitesimal trifles" that gain significance by their juxtaposition with others in the "chain" (119; vol. 1, ch. 15). The logic of circumstantial evidence is the logic of narrative: the insistence that every "trifle," no matter how small, will have ramifications later in the plot. Although critics complain that the sensation novel's plot is too much like a chain, Robert's speech reveals that such chains equally bind the realist novel, in which the accumulation of "infinitesimal trifles" is essential to the interlocking chains, Roland Barthes's famous five codes, that constitute the classic realist text (*S/Z* 18–21; 28–30).

In both *The Woman in White* and *Lady Audley's Secret*, chains function as a concrete image that insists upon the "temporal and causal continuity" of plot (Kendrick 25). Causality, as theorists of narrative from Forster to Barthes have made clear, is the principle of narrative that converts random events into plots; forging causal links between events through the "confusion of consecution and consequence" that is "the mainspring of narrative" (Barthes *Image* 94). In sensation novels, this "confusion" becomes the means of evoking embodied responses from readers. When Walter and Robert call attention to the chains of causality that constrain their actions, the chain becomes a figure not just for causality or the sensation plot, but also for the material power of literary form. Collins's and Braddon's entropic conversion of abstract principles of causality and temporality into narrative content reflects on how narrative techniques and formal strategies affect the living, human bodies of their readers.

The "Dark Road" and the Ends of the Entropic Plot

Readers of sensation, however, are not the only people subjected to the power of narrative structures. In addition to depicting the entropic power of the marriage plot and the embodied effects of literary form, Collins and Braddon portray the compulsions of dominant plot structures usurping authorial agency as well. The compulsions of form become clearest in the relentless teleological drive that both novels display and question through another recurring figure for the arc of the plot: a road or a journey that ends in an empty space. In *The Woman in White*, both Walter and Marian sense that they are caught up in a series of events moving toward a predetermined end. In Braddon's novel, Robert repeatedly asserts that his pursuit of Lady Audley's secret is not the result of his own desire, but of a force that directs his actions, moving him on a foreordained path that leads to an end he can neither foresee nor control. Walter, Marian, and Robert's shared sense of an inevitable end becomes a reflexive meditation on the binding power of convention in determining the ends of any plot.

In Marian's hypnagogic vision of Walter's adventures in the wilderness of Central America, Collins endows his narrators/characters with a multilayered metatextual awareness of the entropic power driving the sensation plot. As Marian lies in a daydream, she sees death repeatedly menacing Walter, and each time the dream-Walter turns and reassures her that he will survive:

> 'I shall come back....I am still walking on the dark road which leads me, and you, and the sister of your love and mine, to the unknown Retribution and the inevitable End....'
> 'Another step...on the dark road....'
> 'Another step on the journey....'
> 'Darker and darker...farther and farther yet....The Pestilence that wastes, the Arrow that strikes, the Sea that drowns, the Grave that closes over Love and Hope, are steps of my journey, and take me nearer and nearer to the End.' (273–74)

Marian's vision suggests that even as she participates in and then narrates the events that make up the plot, she is both aware of and observing how characters' actions are determined by the demands of the narrative's drive toward a prede-termined, "inevitable End," which for most Victorian novels is marriage. When Marian wakes to discover that Laura has finally met Anne Catherick, she writes: "a growing conviction that the complications which had long threatened…had suddenly closed fast around us both, was now beginning to penetrate my mind. I could not express it in words—I could hardly even realise it dimly in my own thoughts. 'Anne Catherick!' I whispered to myself, with useless, helpless reiter-ation—'Anne Catherick!'" (275). In Marian's "useless, helpless reiteration," the Woman in White of the title becomes the signifier for the sense of being bound by "complications" leading to an "inevitable End." Marian's narrative is second in length and importance only to Walter's, and as a narrator trapped within a plot whose end is beyond her control, Marian articulates the subjection of authorial agency to the demands of narrative conventions.

In *Lady Audley's Secret*, Robert expresses his feeling of being trapped in the plot in terms remarkably similar to those that Marian uses. Using images of both chains and roads to describe his situation, he asks:

> "Why do I go on with this…when I know that it is leading me, step by step, day by day, hour by hour, to that conclusion which of all others I should avoid? . . . Should I be justified in letting the chain which I have slowly put together, link by link, drop at this point, or must I go on adding fresh links to that fatal chain….Am I bound to discover how and where he died? or being, as I think, on the road to that discovery, shall I do a wrong to the memory of George Talboys by turning back or stopping still? What am I to do? What am I to do?" (157; vol. 2, ch. 1)

Like Marian, Robert gives voice to a "useless, helpless reiteration" of a sense of powerlessness created by his awareness of being chained to walk a road that ends, he thinks, in death. The chain of circumstantial evidence, with which he threat-ened Lady Audley, enmeshes him as well. Like Walter in Marian's vision, Robert later meditates on his sense that an external force compels his actions: "I try in vain to draw back or to stop short upon the road, for a stronger hand than my own is pointing the way to my lost friend's unknown grave" (167; vol. 2, ch. 2). As the plot thickens, Robert again declares, "It is not myself; it is the hand which is beckoning me further and further upon the dark road whose end I dare not dream of" (172; vol. 2, ch. 3). The "dark road" is the developing plot of the novel, lead-ing to the eventual and inevitable revelation of Lady Audley's bigamy, attempted murder, and—the real shocker—hereditary insanity. If we look at how Braddon deploys this image in another instance, this connection between the "dark road" and the teleology of the plot becomes clearer. Later in the novel, Robert's unex-pected encounter with Clara Talboys reminds him that he must return to his task, and the narrator informs us that this reminder also "brought him back to that consciousness of his own helplessness, in which he had exclaimed—'A hand that is stronger than my own is beckoning me onward on the dark road that leads to my lost friend's unknown grave'" (257; vol. 2, ch. 10). In each case the road is the same, as is the invisible hand, but the destination is either the "end I dare not dream of" or the "unknown grave." This oscillation perfectly describes Braddon's narrative of sensation and suspense, in which readers are sure they have already divined the secret that Lady Audley has murdered George Talboys to conceal her bigamy, only to discover that the real secret is her insanity.[26]

Yet the novel does not end with the revelation of her insanity, nor with Robert's discovery that George was not murdered after all. So what is the "hand" that draws Robert on, and what is the "end [he] dare not dream of"? To begin with the second question, the novel ends with a chapter titled "At Peace," in which we learn that Robert's "dream of a fairy cottage [has] been realised" in the material form of "a fantastical dwelling-place of rustic woodwork" that Robert inhabits with his wife Clara and her brother George (445; vol. 3, ch. 10). As if to call attention to the conventional nature of this ending that embodies dreams and fairy tales, Braddon ends by citing religious authority as the basis of closure. She writes,

I hope no one will take objection to my story because the end of it leaves the good people all happy and at peace. If my experience of life has not been very long, it has at least been manifold; and I can safely subscribe to that which a mighty king and philosopher declared, when he said that neither the experience of his youth nor of his age had ever shown him "the righteous forsaken, nor his seed begging their bread." (447; vol. 3, ch. 10)[27]

Braddon's circumstances at the time of writing add bite to her justification of the happy ending that fiction demands. Considering that Braddon was living with a married man and writing to support her married lover's legitimate children as well as the many children she bore him out of wedlock, her reference to her own "manifold" experience makes ironic her deployment of Psalm 37 to certify the believability of the final idyllic chapter. Braddon's final paragraph cedes authority for the closure of *Lady Audley's Secret* to the Bible, a text central to both the gender ideology that informs the Victorian realist novel of marriage and the institutions that shape the material conditions of existence for Victorians themselves. Here, novelistic convention and institutional authority combine to diminish authorial agency, making Braddon's happy ending a matter of form, dictated by the rule best articulated by Oscar Wilde's Miss Prism: "The good ended happily, and the bad unhappily. That is what Fiction means" (26). Robert's invisible hand is fiction itself.

While ending with the restoration of a fictional order founded on biblical authority may seem to contradict the inevitable disorder of entropy, reading the ending of *Lady Audley's Secret* in light of the opening of the novel reveals another entropic aspect of Braddon's text. The novel begins with an extended description of Audley Court; it is the habitation of decay, of secrets, of history. This space is profoundly anentropic in its juxtaposition of multiple periods, its preservation of the past within the present, for while entropy is the measure of disorder, it is also the foundation of temporal order. Because the second law of thermodynamics decrees that disorder always increases over time, the measure of entropy marks the inevitable progression of time. In its initial refusal of time, Audley Court disobeys the second law; the closing chapter, with its cheerfully contemporary bourgeois idyll, restores the law of entropy to its rightful place. Entropy tells us we cannot go back or unknow what we have learned, and Robert's reluctance to pursue the secret (which he thinks he already knows) is symptomatic of a desire to escape the second law. In the end, he cannot, so Braddon rewards him with an ending that demonstrates how narrative order is founded on entropy, that bleeds off authorial control just as the preceding chain of events has drained characters and readers of interiority and volition. Braddon's ending illustrates Seymour Chatman's claim that "the working out of plot (or at least some plots) is a process of declining or narrowing possibility. The choices become more and more limited, and the final choice seems not a choice at all, but an inevitability" (46). The biblical certification for Braddon's happy ending emphasizes how the apparent constriction of narrative choices fundamental to novelistic closure conscripts the reader into accepting socially determined ends as natural and right.

Collins's ending dramatizes the process by which realist narratives empty out multiple forms of individual agency and replace interiority with compelling stories. Sir Percival's "Secret"—its centrality marked by its insistent capitalization— is the object of obsessive desire for Marian, Walter, and, through their narratives, the reader. However, this central secret turns out to be, like the well at Audley Court, completely empty. When Walter finally discovers Sir Percival's "Secret," it is a "blank space" in a church register instead of the record of a marriage, and Walter triumphantly exclaims, "That space told the whole story!" (509). The compelling "Secret" that has driven the plot of the novel is an empty space that Walter fills in with the sensational narrative of illegitimacy. Walter's discovery of the "Secret" leads to Sir Percival's death by fire, so that Walter's narrative can display "at the end, stark and grim and black, in the yellow light…his dead face" (521). In the penultimate scene in the novel, Walter sees Fosco's corpse in the Paris Morgue, exposed to the "flippant curiosity of a French mob," and claims that "the truth itself was revealed to me" in the "strange mark on his left arm"—another empty space where an inscription should be (623). Knowing the secret of Pesca's association with Fosco, Walter can fill in the empty space that is both Fosco's "unowned, unknown" corpse and the effaced mark on the corpse's arm with a story that is both sensational and providential. In both scenes, Collins shows sensational narratives produced by and producing spectacular human bodies, violently emptied of animation, will, life itself.

But it is not only sensational narratives that produce bodies emptied of interiority and identity. Rather than ending with Walter and Laura's marriage, or the retribution embodied in Fosco's corpse, Collins's novel exceeds the bounds of the marriage plot to suggest that such bodies are its unspoken end product. The entropic plot ends by linking the master-narrator's "faltering" pen with the unnamed, though not unidentified, body of a child. Even though Sir Percival's "Secret" turns out to be insignificant in that it does not enable Walter to unravel the plot against Laura, it does enable Walter to marry her, which of course leads to the eventual production of a legitimate "'*Heir of Limmeridge*,'" triumphantly identified as such by Marian immediately before Walter's "pen falters in [his] hand" on the last page of the novel (627). Replacing the infant's name with his social position transforms the living child into a body identified only by its function in a chain of ownership, so that the "Heir of Limmeridge" becomes both an empty space, a body lacking individuality and agency, and a placeholder within the sequence of proprietors of the Limmeridge estate. While Fosco's body is "unowned, unknown," this body is known only by a relation to ownership that overrides all other forms of identity. Although Collins violates the boundaries of the marriage plot while Braddon emphasizes their constricting force, both novelists' entropic plots reveal that narratives of progress and decline are inextricably linked, as the teleological energies that impose order on events come at the price of individual agency and will. The significance of the entropic plot of sensation lies not only in its status as a harbinger of fin-de-siècle cultural degeneration or its participation in various social and scientific discourses, but also in its insistence on the entropic and material effects of literary form.

NOTES

1. Elizabeth Meadows wishes to thank Vanderbilt University's Robert Penn Warren Center for the Humanities and the American Council of Learned Societies for support essential to the development and completion of this article. And with good reason. Such comments lend themselves to compelling historicist analyses of this novelistic subgenre's relationships to discourses of disease, madness, memory, affect, gender, and mass culture in studies by Jenny Bourne Taylor, Ann Cvetkovich, Pamela Gilbert, Nicholas Dames, and Nicholas Daly.

2 Examples of sensation novels in the 1860s include Ellen Wood's *East Lynne* (1861), Wilkie Collins's *No Name* (1862), Mary Elizabeth Braddon's *Aurora Floyd* (1863), Charles Reade's *Hard Cash* (1863), and Charles Dickens's *Great Expectations* (1860–61). Although these novels share a focus on secrets and criminality within the domestic sphere, Jonathan Loesberg points out that the genre of the sensation novel is constituted as much by literary reviews "that insistently grouped [novels by Collins, Braddon, and Wood]…together among a varying list of other novels" as by the thematic features of the novels themselves (115). D. A. Miller calls *The Woman in White* the first and best sensation novel (148), while Pamela Gilbert credits *Lady Audley's Secret* with starting the craze for sensation (8).

3 The literary and cultural implications of thermodynamics are the focus of Ted Under-wood's *The Work of the Sun* (2005), Barri Gold's *ThermoPoetics* (2010), and Anna Maria Jones's "Conservation of Energy," in which she challenges the "entropic focus" of this cultural narrative by arguing that Victorians' anxieties about undisciplined en-ergy were as pervasive as their fears of entropic decline (68).

4 Rudolf Clausius deliberately crafted the term to mirror "energy" and to call on the idea of a *"trope*—the linguistic torsion that transforms literal into figurative usage," a transformation from one state to another (Clarke 25).

5 The entropic effects of embodiment are evident in Nicholas Dames's account of sensa-tion and memory, in which memory transforms from an abstract mental and emotional process to a physical and embodied one, and thus becomes unreliable: "as memory gains a mechanical apparatus, it gains the ability to break down" (173).

6 Critics have long recognized that sensation novels feature intricate plots at the expense of fully developed characters. Anthony Trollope outlines (and then challenges) this conventional distinction in his *Autobiography*: "The novelists who are considered to be anti-sensational are generally called realistic. I am realistic. My friend Wilkie Collins is generally supposed to be sensational. The readers who prefer the one are supposed to take delight in the elucidation of character. Those who hold by the other are charmed by the continuation and gradual development of a plot" (146; ch. 12).

7 Walter Kendrick points out that for Victorians roads and chains are figures for plot itself (20).

8 Brooks elaborates the model in *Reading for the Plot*; Jay Clayton and Susan Winnett point out how Brooks's narrative model relies on a model of male sexuality. Interest-ingly, Clayton points out that Brooks's model of desire in narrative does not move us beyond formalism—it places two structures in apposition, but makes no causal claims about the relation between the two "formal patterns" (39), while Winnett cri-tiques Brooks for promulgating a model that is both "situational" and "thematic," even though we are "asked to regard it as an issue of form rather than of theme" (511). The sensation novel's thematization of form places the genre at the heart of a debate about how literary interactions of theme and form could or should shape social situa-tions.

9 D. A. Miller reads Walter's gesture as an attempted "reaffirmation" of a "violated... gender identification"; made uncertain of his manhood by his nervous response, Walter has to reach for the closest thing resembling it (152). True, but it is also a response to a violation of his agency, represented in his fantasy of marriage and upward class mobil-ity, as well as an erotic response.

10 Mary Poovey points out that the Victorian belief in a spermatic economy, through which sexual consummation drains men of vitality, is "anchored" in a "model of the human body" as a "closed system containing a fixed quantity of energy" (36). Here Collins reveals sexuality's entropic effects, not at the moment of climax, but in the experience of sexual arousal.

11 As Herbert Tucker points out in another context, "passive" and "passion" are etymo-logical relatives (18).

12 Veils are a common feature of wedding ceremonies in a number of cultures. In the Victorian period, the popularity of the white gown and veil was stimulated by Queen Victoria's choice of this color for her wedding gown, a choice replicated by her daughters to be recorded and circulated in royal wedding photographs (Landsell 13).

13 In her introduction to *Sex and Death in Victorian Literature*, Regina Barreca declares that the "dialectic of sex and death" is "one of the most influential patterns in Victorian poetry and prose" (7).

14 See Lee Edelman's critique of Jean Baudrillard's "The Final Solution" in *No Future: Queer Theory and the Death Drive*. According to Baudrillard, sexual reproduction implies mortality for the individual as the price of guaranteeing survival in the form of the child. Edelman points out that death is the "corollary of [sexual] difference" in a system that depends on transmitting its values and valuables to legitimately reproduced offspring (62).

15 Over the course of Braddon's novel, Lady Audley changes her name many times: Helen Maldon marries and becomes Helen Talboys, renames herself Lucy Graham, marries again to become Lady Audley ("my lady"), and finally submits to confinement in an asylum under the name Madame Taylor. Braddon's narrator most often calls her "my lady"; I use "Lady Audley."

16 In "From Do-Nothing to Detective," Vicki A. Pallo maps Robert's upward trajectory from a lazy dilettante into an ideal of industrious Victorian manhood. While Pallo emphasizes Robert's newfound power as a detective, I focus on the entropic and externally imposed nature of his transformation.

17 In the *Saturday Review*, an anonymous reviewer damns *The Woman in White* with faint praise of Collins's "mechanical talents" (249); Gilbert shows how Victorian critical discourse constructed the sensation novel as a debased because feminized genre that spread contagion through the social body (3).

18 As Rachel Blau Du Plessis points out, the intertwining of these two plots characterizes the male bildungsroman, in which the hero finds both a proper vocation and wife. However, in the female bildungsroman, the two plots do not reinforce each other in reaching a simultaneous resolution. Instead, the heroine must sacrifice her vocation, should she be so unfortunate as to have one, for her marriage, should she be lucky enough to find someone to marry her (Du Plessis 284–87).

19 In *The Female Malady* Showalter uses the example of *Lady Audley's Secret* to suggest "'insanity' is simply the label society attaches to female assertion, ambition, self-interest, and outrage" (72).

20 It is no coincidence that Cleopatra is one of the examples of monstrous agency in Robert's internal monologue. Cleopatra appears as a slothfully sexual model of femininity that Lucy Snowe must reject in Charlotte Brontë's 1853 novel *Villette* (223-24; ch. 19). Later, in Eliot's *Middlemarch* (1871-2), Dorothea appears as a dangerously alluring Cleopatra when Will Ladislaw finds her in "the hall where the reclining Ariadne, then called the Cleopatra, lies in the marble voluptuousness of her beauty" (188; bk. 2, ch. 19).

21 Mansel and other Victorian critics are not anomalous in their assumption that reading impacts the body. In D. A. Miller's classic analysis of *The Woman in White*, he cites

its physical effects: accelerated heart rate and respiration, increased blood pressure, the pallor resulting from vasoconstriction, and so on" (146). More recently, Anna Maria Jones's choice of the term "masochistic" indexes the physiological register in theorizing readers' engagement with sensation novels' systematic alternation of secrecy and shock (*Problem Novels* 22).

22 Daly also notes the identification of readers with characters that this review creates (48–49).

23   According to Ian Watt, such narratives purport to place the reader "in contact not with literature but with the raw materials of life itself *as they are momentarily reflected in the minds of the protagonists*" (193, emphasis added).

24 In "The Sensationalism of *The Woman in White*," Walter Kendrick points out how Collins uses the image of a chain to describe his narrative in the Preface, while Walter calls his assembled narratives a chain near the end of the novel (Kendrick 24–25). While disparaging other authors of sensation, Kendrick reads Collins's novel as a sensational text that uses realism to deconstruct realism's mimetic status (21–22, 31). While I am greatly indebted to Kendrick's insights, I am more interested in how the emphasis on chains in *The Woman in White* and *Lady Audley's Secret* blurs distinctions between form and content and how the chain comes to represent narrative and social structures that deplete the agency of characters, readers, and authors.

25 This reference to a "criminal case" is also disingenuous, since Robert decides to have Lady Audley certified insane and incarcerated in an asylum to avoid the publicity attendant on any legal action against her (377, 380).

26   ike Dr. Mosgrave in the novel, I would characterize Lady Audley's actions as evidence of rational self-interest rather than insanity. It is Lady Audley herself who declares that she has inherited insanity from her mother, a diagnosis only partially confirmed by Dr. Mosgrave's reconsidered opinion that she has "latent insanity" (379; vol. 3, ch. 5).

27   Braddon is quoting Psalm 37, which also reassures us that "the meek shall inherit the earth" (37:25, 37:11).

WORKS CITED

Ablow, Rachel. "Good Vibrations: The Sensationalization of Masculinity in *The Woman in White*." *Novel* 37 (Fall 2003/Spring 2004): 158-80.

Barreca, Regina, ed. *Sex and Death in Victorian Literature*. Bloomington: Indiana UP, 1990.

Braddon, Mary Elizabeth. *Lady Audley's Secret*. 1862. Ed. and intro. David Skilton. Oxford: Oxford UP, 1987.

Barthes, Roland. *Image-Music-Text*. Trans. Stephen Heath. New York: Hill and Wang, 1977.

———. *S/Z: An Essay*. Trans. Richard Miller. New York: Hill and Wang, 1974.

Brontë, Charlotte. *Villette*. 1853. Ed. and intro. Helen Cooper. London: Penguin, 2004.

Brooks, Peter. *Reading for the Plot: Design and Intention in Narrative*. Cambridge: Harvard UP, 1984.

Chatman, Seymour. *Story and Discourse: Narrative Structure in Fiction and Film*. Ithaca: Cornell UP, 1978.

Clarke, Bruce. *Energy Forms: Allegory and Science in the Era of Classical Thermodynamics*. Ann Arbor: U of Michigan P, 2001.

Clayton, Jay. "Narrative and Theories of Desire." *Critical Inquiry* 16 (1989): 33–53.

Collins, Wilkie. *The Woman in White*. 1860. Ed. and intro. Matthew Sweet. London: Penguin, 2003.

Cvetkovich, Ann. *Mixed Feelings: Feminism, Mass Culture, and Victorian Sensationalism*. New Brunswick, NJ: Rutgers UP, 1992.

Daly, Nicholas. *Sensation and Modernity in the 1860s*. Cambridge: Cambridge UP, 2009.

Dames, Nicholas. *Amnesiac Selves: Nostalgia, Forgetting, and British Fiction, 1810–1870*. Oxford: Oxford UP, 2001.

Dever, Carolyn. *Death and the Mother from Dickens to Freud*. Cambridge: Cambridge UP, 1998.

Du Plessis, Rachel Blau. "Endings and Contradictions." *Narrative Dynamics: Essays on Time, Plot, Closure, and Frames*. Ed. Brian Richardson. Columbus: Ohio State UP, 2002: 282-299.

Edelman, Lee. *No Future: Queer Theory and the Death Drive*. Durham: Duke UP, 2004.

Eliot, George. *Middlemarch: A Study of Provincial Life*. 1871. London: Penguin 1994.

Gilbert, Pamela. *Disease, Desire, and the Body in Victorian Women's Popular Novels*. Cambridge: Cambridge UP, 1997.

Gold, Barri. *ThermoPoetics: Energy in Victorian Literature and Science*. Cambridge: MIT P, 2010.

Holy Bible. The King James Version. Nashville: Thomas Nelson Publishing, 1984.

Jones, Anna Maria. "Conservation of Energy, Individual Agency, and Gothic Terror in Richard Marsh's *The Beetle*, or, What's Scarier Than an Ancient, Evil, Shape-Shifting Bug?" *Victorian Literature and Culture* 39 (2011): 65–85.

———. *Problem Novels: Victorian Fiction Theorizes the Sensational Self*. Columbus: Ohio State UP, 2007.

Kendrick, Walter. "The Sensationalism of *The Woman in White*." *Nineteenth-Century Fiction* 32 (1977): 18–35.

Landsell, Avril. *Wedding Fashions 1860–1980*. Aylesbury, Bucks: Shire Publications, 1983.

Leighton, Angela. *On Form: Poetry, Aestheticism, and the Legacy of a Word*. Oxford: Oxford UP, 2007.

Loesberg, Jonathan. "The Ideology of Narrative Form in Sensation Fiction." *Representations* 13 (1986): 115–38.

Mansel, Henry. "Sensation Novels." *Quarterly Review*. 113 (April 1863): 481–514.

Miller, D. A. *The Novel and the Police*. Berkeley: U of California P, 1988.

Oliphant, Margaret. "Sensation Novels." *Blackwoods Edinburgh Magazine* 91:559 (1862): 564–84.

Pallo, Vicki A. "From Do-Nothing to Detective: The Transformation of Robert Audley in *Lady Audley's Secret.*" *Journal of Popular Culture* 39 (2006): 466–78.

Poovey, Mary. *Uneven Developments: The Ideological Work of Gender in Mid-Victorian England.* Chicago: U of Chicago P, 1988.

Rev. of *The Woman in White. Critic* 21.259 (Aug. 25, 1860): 233–34.

Rev. of *The Woman in White. Examiner* 2744 (Sept. 1, 1860): 549.

Rev. of *The Woman in White. Literary Gazette* 5.110 (Aug. 4, 1860): 57–58.

Rev. of *The Woman in White. Saturday Review of Politics, Literature, Science and Art* 10.252 (Aug. 25, 1860): 249–50.

Showalter, Elaine. *The Female Malady: Women, Madness, and English Culture, 1830–1980.* 1985. New York: Penguin, 1987.

———. *A Literature of Their Own: British Women Novelists from Brontë to Lessing.* 1977. Princeton: Princeton UP, 1999.

Taylor, Jenny Bourne. *In the Secret Theatre of Home: Wilkie Collins, Sensation Narrative, and Nineteenth-Century Psychology.* London: Routledge, 1988.

Trollope, Anthony. *An Autobiography.* 1883. Ed. and intro. David Skilton. London: Penguin, 1996.

Tucker, Herbert F. *Tennyson and the Doom of Romanticism.* Cambridge: Harvard UP, 1988.

Underwood, Ted. *The Work of the Sun: Literature, Science, and Economy, 1760–1860.* New York: Palgrave Macmillan, 2005.

Watt, Ian. *The Rise of the Novel: Studies in Defoe, Richardson and Fielding.* Berkeley: U of California P, 1957.

Wilde, Oscar. *The Importance of Being Earnest.* 1895. Ed. Michael Patrick Gillespie. New York: Norton, 2006.

Winnett, Susan. "Coming Unstrung: Women, Men, Narrative, and Principles of Pleasure." *PMLA: Publications of the Modern Language Association of America* 105 (1990): 505–18.

Recent Dickens Studies: 2012

Caroline Reitz

This essay surveys Dickens scholarship in the year 2012, summarizing and commenting on nearly 150 critical articles, books, and worldwide celebrations of the bicentenary of Dickens's birth. While the broad and often overlapping categories below indicate the difficulty of grasping such a rich and diverse body of scholarship, there are some areas of particular interest this year, such as a new understanding of the global nature of Dickens Studies and a new access to Dickens's journalism, which has begun to revise significantly our understanding not only of writing outside the novels but of novelistic mode, as well. The scholarship surveyed is organized into the following categories: the Bicentenary, Global Dickens, Victorian Print Cultures, Sexuality and Gender, The City and Modernity, Dickens Adapted, Childhood, Disability, Things, Sentiment and Affect, Dickens and/as the Public, and Biographies and Biographical Criticism.

The Dickens made me do it.

It is the only answer I have to a question frequently asked of me, and which I asked of myself, in the past year and a half: why? Why agree to review *all* of the scholarship about Dickens, and not just in any year but in the *bicentenary* year, a year in which I'm sure even the guy delivering mulch on my street published a monograph on Dickens and sustainable landscaping. When I say that "the Dickens" made me do it, I mean Dickens as the kind of author against whom, once he has entered your world (or you his, one is never quite sure which), resistance is futile. I mean being compelled by the enormity of his work: the dizzying numbers (147 orphans in his writing, 152 named characters in *Bleak House* alone, 14,000 letters in the Pilgrim volumes), the simultaneous journalism, advocacy, editing, and theater careers alongside the novels. To agree was to indulge a fantasy of Dickensian omniscience, hoping to stand, Bucket-like on London Bridge and apprehend the lawless river of the bicentenary. It was so tempting to try to cordon off even a bend in that river by saying "I have grasped 2012." Tempting and hopeless. If, as David Paroissien writes in an "Editorial" for *Dickens Quarterly*, "Charles John Huffam Dickens—the man and his work—both prove too comprehensive and too energetic to remain confined to a single period" (10), imagine trying to cram him into a single review. While this review hopes to be true to the range and vitality of Dickens Studies in the bicentenary year, I have without a doubt missed a large number of texts, exhibits, adaptations, special issues, panel discussions, and performances, both great and small. I will be apologizing to colleagues at conferences for the rest of my life. It is also, somewhat surprisingly, clear that, given a 30-hour day, or an additional year, I could go on happily reading and watching Dickens-related material from 2012. Resistance is futile.

Before I introduce the semi-functional categories of this review, I want to echo a sentiment of Review Essays Past. There is a startling range in the scholarly and popular engagement with Dickens, from challenging philosophical explorations (Benjamin, who gets the most hits this year, Kierkegaard, and Freud—to say nothing of Deleuze and Derrida—are all here) to a quite moving consideration of Dickens's "unparalleled portraiture of self-destruction" by the former archbishop of Canterbury, Rowan Williams, at a wreath-laying ceremony in Westminster Abbey on Dickens's birthday (114).The depth of our interest in Dickens is also startling. Since Dickens was a writer of almost immediate celebrity, we have been talking about him in one way or another for the greater part of these 200 years. As a result, the scholarship is embedded with the history of these long conversations; every argument here is also the history of the argument, whether that is over Dickens's representation of women or his affair with Ellen Ternan or the limits of his representation of human psychology. (Howard Jacobson, Booker Prize-winning author of *The Finkler Question*, takes Dickens's side on this one: "what others saw as caricature I saw as true, what they called exaggeration I called bounteousness," 8.)

This long conversation is made manifest in projects like Ashgate's *A Library of Essays on Charles Dickens*, six volumes of collected criticism about Dickens published in honor of the bicentenary. Series Editor Catherine Waters explains that from "the publication of his first sketches in the *Monthly Magazine* in the 1830s, and especially after the phenomenal success of *Pickwick*, Dickens attracted the attention of contemporary reviewers and critics who variously praised his humor and pathos, condemned his sentimentality, marveled at his poetic imagination or objected to his lack of realism" (xiii). The scholarly conversation in 2012 reflects the mixed verdicts critics have and have had towards Dickens. Is Dickens an artist or a businessman? A feminist or a creator of "legless angels"? A dreamer or a practical social reformer? A citizen of the world or a border patrolman? We even debate the bicentenary: Florian Schweizer, director of the newly restored Dickens Museum, asks, "will the bicentenary be seen as a public relations bubble created by the media, a commercial cash cow for clever product developers, a legacy-building celebration of Dickens heritage or simply a reconnection of Dickens with his readers at all levels?" (210). Rightful questions to be asked during a year which also saw the Olympics and the Queen's Diamond Jubilee, when the sun seemed never to set on celebrations of British heritage. What we don't debate in 2012 is Dickens's relevance, something we take for granted now, but shouldn't; Robert L. Patten's *Charles Dickens and "Boz"* and Michael Slater's *The Great Charles Dickens Scandal* both mention their struggles as young scholars to argue for Dickens's academic importance.

Add to this history of debate a kind of perspectival whiplash, perhaps appropriate for scholarship in a Google-earth age. Dickens criticism in 2012 can be intensely local: Michael Allen's detailed investigation into the specific location of Tom-all-Alone's, Lyn Squire's look at what Edwin did with the ruby and diamond ring after he and Rosa agreed to separate, or the careful, continuous emendations to the indispensable Pilgrim letters (covered in *The Dickensian*; Jenny Hartley mentions that about 20 new ones are discovered every year). But it is increasingly likely to be global: as Paul Schlicke explains, "celebrations for Dickens's two-hundredth birthday have been truly global in scope" ("The Dickens Bicentenary" 378). This, Michael Hollington says in his Foreword to Gillian Piggot's *Dickens and Benjamin*, is appropriate, as Dickens is now regarded "not just as the quintessentially 'English' writer he was felt to be, not without reason, by previous generations, but also as a literary and cultural giant of international and indeed global significance" (xiii). Indeed, Deborah Logan, writing to introduce an edition of *Victorians Journal* dedicated to Dickens, notes that this edition is "nearly as international, in terms of scholarly affiliations" as a recent previous edition that was based exclusively on international scholars in Victorian Studies (4). There are Dickens stamps, Natalie McKnight reports, "in Botswana, Antigua, Barbados, St. Vincent, and, of course, the U. K. and the U.S" (9). The British Council's Global Dickens Read-a-thon on Dickens's birthday encompassed countries from Albania to Zimbabwe. There is no particular Dickens that means Dickens in 2012 (some eras favor the early works, some the later ones), and the Dickens Universe focused on *Bleak House* in 2012: square in the middle. The pronounced interest in publication history that forms one of the sections tends to be interested in those early years when Dickens is establishing himself, in the words of Robert L. Patten, as an "industrial-age author." Nevertheless, there are probably more references to Dickens's final complete novel, *Our Mutual Friend*, than to any other single work.

For a writer "as restlessly ubiquitous these days in our culture as he ever was in his life" (Andrews, Editorial 3), it is hard to develop sure-footed categories of analysis. It goes almost without saying that most individual works belong rightly to at least two. After a shortcut across the globe of the Bicentenary, this review starts out with the "six key themes" of the Ashgate *Library*, topics which Waters suggests "have become central to Dickens studies, particularly over the last two decades": Global Dickens, Victorian Print Cultures, Sexuality and Gender, The City, Dickens Adapted, and Childhood. At the risk of making that section as "unknowable" as Dickens's London, I squeeze the topic of "Modernity" in with "The City" as many accounts of Dickens's representation of urban life are also reflections on modernity. A section on Disability is placed after Childhood to reflect the concern with the vulnerable that is a hallmark of Dickens's writing and reflects the rise in this type of analysis. The remaining categories are Things, Sentiment and Affect; Dickens and/as the Public; and Biography and Biographical Criticism. But, as you'll see, works on disability ask questions about the relationships between those bodies and things or about sexuality; critics focused on things look at how they enable Dickens to problematize sentiment and sexuality in an industrial age. The imbrication of these categories suggests the richness of the conversation.

Bicentenary

"How does it feel to be an adjective?" *Cloud Atlas* author David Mitchell asks, addressing himself to Dickens in a tribute in *The Dickensian* (10). Many bicentenary events asked what it means to be "Dickensian," such as a poetry contest hosted in conjunction with a symposium on "What Dickens Means to Me" and a conference on "Dickens and Childhood" at the Victoria and Albert Museum. (Winning poems were published in the September volume of the journal *English*.) The idea of "the Dickensian" was one of the main themes of the "*A Tale of Four Cities*" Conference, a weeklong event in London, Paris, Boulogne/Condette, and Chatham/Rochester (for the outsize Dickens, even four cities are actually six). As Robert L. Patten reports, the conference presentations were "old themes being revisited in new ways—verbally, visually, auditorially, experientially, cinematically, comparatively" ("*A Tale of Four Cities* Conference" 176). (There is an additional account of the conference's high spirits and grisly weather in the Spring issue of *The Dickensian*.)

The bicentenary was so sprawling that it had its own (still-operating) website (www.Dickens2012.org), and as Schweizer, also the Project Director for Dickens 2012, says gratefully, its own significant budget that withstood widespread belt-tightening. Paul Schlicke's review of bicentenary events begins on February 7, when the Prince of Wales and the Duchess of Cornwall visited the Charles Dickens Museum on 48 Doughty Street and then went on to Westminster Abbey, joining members of the Dickens family and scholars, to hear readings by the actor Ralph Fiennes (who plays both Magwitch and Dickens in recent films), biographer Claire Tomalin, and the Inimitable's great-great grandson Mark Dickens.

The British Council worked with over 50 countries worldwide to coordinate a range of educational and cultural events celebrating the bicentenary (382), including the touchingly appropriate "What the dickens?" educational program developed by the Author's Licensing and Collecting Society (ALCS) and the National Schools Partnership, "aimed at inspiring and encouraging creative writing in schools and nurturing an appreciation of the importance of copyright" (380). Two Dickens descendants (Gerald and Ian), "completed a fund-raising walk, retracing the steps of Nicholas Nickleby and Smike over seventy-five miles from London to Portsmouth" with the proceeds going to a Dickens statue (381). Many writers remarked that all this memorializing would have made Dickens uncomfortable, as his last wishes were to have a simple funeral and to live through his works.

Despite those desires, the festivities continued around the globe. In Lowell, Massachusetts, a seven-month event featured over 75 performances, speakers, and community and family events. In Delhi, Jamia Islamaia University held a Pickwick Festival; The Royal Society for Medicine sponsored a Dickens Day fundraising for the Great Ormond Street Hospital for Children. There were also special versions of ongoing annual celebrations: the 39th "Dickens on The Strand" in Galveston, Texas, and the 34th "Great Dickens Christmas Fair and Victorian Holiday Party" in San Francisco. There were even events in Myrtle Beach. (That really says something when the same artist is being celebrated in Delhi and in Myrtle Beach.) Gad's Hill Place, Dickens's "childhood dream" and home at the end of his life, was open for the first time to the public and there were dozens of major museum exhibits: Southern Methodist University hosted "Charles Dickens: the First Two Hundred Years"; The Museum Strauhof in Zurich, "The Mysteries of Charles Dickens"; The Free Library of Philadelphia, "From the Desk of Charles Dickens: Celebrating the Great Writer at 200"; the de Beer Gallery of the University of Otego, NZ, "Celebrating CD 1812-1870: A Man of His Age"; The Lilly Library at Indiana University's "Conducted by Charles Dickens: An Exhibition to Commemorate the Bicentennial of his Birth"; and The British Library, "A Hankering after Ghosts." "Most comprehensively of all," Schlicke writes, "the Museum of London recreated the atmosphere of Victorian London through sound and projections, providing a journey to discover the city that inspired his writings" (385). There are simply too many mentions in print and online of what Dickens means to us in the bicentenary year, but I was delighted to watch youtube clips from the British Council's January 2012 conference in Berlin on "What would Dickens write today?" featuring an interview with A. S. Byatt. (the answer is: XXX).

My own uncommercial travels in both New York and London took me to The Morgan Library & Museum's "Charles Dickens at 200," where the highlight was a display of Dickens's manuscripts and letters. The New York Public Library had an exhibit titled "Charles Dickens: The Key to Character" featuring treasures from the Berg Collection and an extended lecture series featuring Victorian scholars from the greater New York area. The Roundabout Theatre Company staged a revival of Rupert Holmes's musical *The Mystery of Edwin Drood* (my review of which will not run in *Victorian Literature and Culture*, mercifully, until 2013). Lee Jackson's *Walking Dickens' London* was a terrific companion for following Dickens's footsteps—and thankfully did not lead to Dickens World.

Nancy Aycock Metz's "Recent Dickens Studies: 2010," published in the 2012 volume of Dickens Studies Annual, looks both at the recent past of Dickens scholarship and towards the future of the bicentenary. It is fitting to mention her review of Dickens studies for 2010 between the section on the bicentenary and "Global Dickens" as she writes with a "consciousness of how strongly this body of research reflects Dickens's soon-to-be-celebrated global impact and significance" (261). Indeed, Metz suggests that 2010 was "notable" for the "scholarly conversation around the concept of 'cosmopolitanism'" (262) and sees this as a window into his cross-cultural appeal, or "why, 200 years after his birth, worldwide communities continue to form and thrive around his potent art" (262). Metz divides her review into the following categories: Biography, History and Reference; Dickens the Writer/Dickens and His Readers; Sources, Influence, Intertextual Engagements; Language, Structure, Style, and Genre; Gender, Family, Children, Education; Social Class, Economics, Politics and the Law; Urban and Cosmopolitan Contexts; Science, Technology, and the Arts; Ethical and Philosophical Approaches; and Adaptation. My favorite sentence in Metz's comprehensive and sure-footed review suggests that one of the reasons for this "worldwide" interest is that there are so many different versions of Dickens: "Here Dickens appears as abandoned child, domineering husband, word wizard, popular artist, professional author, editorial journeyman, practical jokester, ethical teacher, powerful magus, master craftsman, generic innovator, collaborative writer, savvy entrepreneur, promoter and underminer of the Victorian domestic ideal, poet of the city, cosmopolitan, intelligent conversant with scientific, philosophical, and political thought, endlessly adaptable 'portable property'" (352).

Global Dickens

As the works in this section illustrate, Global Dickens concerns far more than the reception of Dickens around the world, or representations of the world in Dickens. Fueled by technological developments and a variety of different aesthetic forms, Global Dickens is scholarship on the publication of *A Tale of Two Cities* in revolutionary China, a first-person account of Dickens's influence on the Indian novelist in English (Lakshmi Raj Sharma's "Charles Dickens and Me"), or the Radio 4 serial *The Mumbai Chuzzlewits*. Ayeesha Menon's three-part serial aired on January 1–15, 2012, and features a Catholic family in Mumbai. The works here illustrate Dickens's international stature, but also raise questions: is trying to apprehend the "Global Dickens" a form of intellectual imperialism?

Only the final chapter of Jonathan H. Grossman's engrossing *Charles Dickens's Networks: Public Transport and the Novel* is about Dickens's novels beyond England's shores (*Little Dorrit*). I am justifying its presence at the head of the Global Dickens section, however, as the public transportation revolution it explores provides the kind of movement and understanding that makes "global Dickens" both possible and imaginable. In a panel discussion in 2011 (the transcript of which was published in *Dickens Studies Annual* in 2012), Grossman explains that the "sense of contemporaneous, synchronous, connected global existence" did not exist "as strongly in the eighteenth century" ("Dickens on Broadway" 25). Grossman's book is about what changes occur in the nineteenth century in order to be able to "imagin[e] community in an era of systems and networks" (7). *Charles Dickens's Networks* is at once a huge argument—this joint moment in the history of public transport and the Novel (specifically Dickens's *Pickwick*) altered how we experience and represent time and space—and a small one—his analysis is chiefly of *Pickwick, Master Humphrey's Clock*, and *Little Dorrit*. He addresses this limited focus in the afterword; he could have included many Dickens novels, most immediately *Dombey and Son*, which chronicles the disruptions of the emerging railway system. But these three works show the arc of Dickens's "role in synthesizing and understanding" the transport revolution; from *Pickwick* to *Master Humphrey* to *Dorrit*, Dickens shows us the "community's coming together, then at a subsequent recognition of its tragic limits, and, finally, at the working out of a revised view that expressed the precarious, limited omniscient perspective by which passengers came to imagine their journeying in the network" (3). Grossman distinguishes between a communication system "to which medium his novels belong" and "the passenger transport system, about which they have so much to say" (7), and they say it with "certain narratological complexities" such as "omniscient narration, simultaneity, serialization, and multiplottedness" (7).

Grossman reads *Pickwick* as a road novel at a crossroads. Set in the late 1820s, Dickens's novel provides a comprehensive look at "virtually every aspect of the stage-coaching system" but it is written in 1836–37 when the "steam railways had arrived and begun obliterating this world" (11). *Pickwick* "projected the public transport system's essential aim—the coordinating of people's journeys in space and time—into a collective vision of individuals as synchronically engaged in interconnecting journeys and a model—across history—for community in contemporaneity" (12). In so doing, Dickens "draws a circle around a community newly becoming linked together" (27) and makes "shared the perceived arena of people's circulation" (28), resulting in the "standardization of our merged movement"(35). Two things are particularly important here: one, that the system gets "subordinated to its individual users' purposes" (46), and two, serialization. Serialization is a crucial part of how Dickens achieves this, Grossman argues: the "story's serial delivery" materializes "the novel's formal capacity to express individual fates collectively networked as they proceed from a shaping past toward an unwritten future. That meaning of serialization had to be created historically, and that is what *Pickwick* accomplished" (68).

When Grossman turns to *Master Humphrey's Clock* and *The Old Curiosity Shop*, the shared sense of possibility takes a turn for the worse. The joyous mobility of *Pickwick* becomes tragedy as the *Clock* offers "the possibility of dropping out of the network altogether." Nell's falling out of the Passenger Transport System is a falling out of "communal time and space" (104). Dickens shows that "the same forces holding together a community [can] ironically rip it apart" (92). As the railways evolve, transport is less about shared-but-still-individual movement and "makes individual journeys indivisible" (99). Grossman claims that locating Dickens in the passenger transport revolution answers some open questions for Dickens scholars: *Pickwick*'s notorious formlessness can now be read as "structured by its coaching trips" (38); the surprise ending of *Old Curiosity Shop* within its *Master Humphrey* Frame (141) becomes a recognition of limits to sharing; and the seemingly opposed journeying and carceral narratives of *Little Dorrit* can be read as working together. Traditionally, readings of the "carceral" engage the journeying but only "to expose the journeying as labyrinthine and dead-ending" (157). Grossman instead sees the carceral and the journeying plots as "a toggling of perception in which one seesaws between equally plausible realities" (157–58).

Grossman reads *Little Dorrit* as representing a new perspective that reveals international simultaneity, "a synchronized, 'universal' standard time," which is made possible by "the international reach of the passenger transport system" (166). This is new for Dickens as he envisions the "individual plots of his characters as unfolding simultaneously in an international arena" (175) and reconfigures his internationalist view from British protagonists simply traveling the world to a sense of simultaneity, "a zone of human contact, a space shared in time" (186). This reading reconsiders not only Dickens's, but also Benedict Anderson's ideas (expressed in his *Imagined Communities*) about time, which is not for Dickens, Grossman argues, "homogenous [and] empty" but international, springing from "an interlocking global passenger network, from railroads and route maps, steam ships and timetables" and so not "to be filled in by a national community" (187). This risks fragmentation (as opposed to community), but Grossman points out that *Little Dorrit* does not suggest the failure of community as much as it illustrates "the density and extensivity of people's interconnections exceeds their capacity to grasp them" (195).

In the Introduction to the Ashgate volume *Global Dickens*, John O. Jordan and Nirshan Perera attempt to grasp such interconnections, or, in other words, how the Chuzzlewits came to Mumbai. The writers collected in this volume all write in English but are "from many different cultures, national origins and geographical locations, often from outside what one might think of as the Anglo-American critical mainstream" (xv). Jordan and Perera suggest that the works combine to make manifest, what, "until recently, has been less than fully evident to students and scholars of his work" or what might surprise readers who have seen him "as an English novelist, even as a novelist of Englishness": Dickens is "a writer of global stature, substance and impact, and it is this perspective that the present volume seeks to bring into sharper focus" (xxi).

One of the obstacles to seeing Dickens as global has been his strong association with London (though the idea of London as a familiar, knowable space takes a beating in the "City" section below). Walter Bagehot's oft-quoted description of Dickens—he "is like a special correspondent for posterity"—obscures the fact that he spoke and wrote French, travelled frequently to France and also made trips to North America, Italy, and Switzerland, and sent his family abroad (sons to Germany, India, Australia). "Although his motives for sending them abroad were complex," Jordan and Perera write, "these expeditions by his sons are another indication of their father's awareness of and engagement with the world beyond England's borders" (xvi). But of course he "also travelled imaginatively" (xvi). From a childhood in the busy port town of Chatham, with all its comings and goings, to his readings of the *Arabian Nights* and *Don Quixote* to his philanthropic interests involving emigration plans to his work as editor in reviewing and approving "for publication articles and new fiction that brought the outside world closer to his English readers" (xvi), Dickens was not just a writer "of a globalized space, but a citizen of one" (xvi).

Jordan and Perera explain that Dickens was knowledgeable about world affairs, kept "abreast of liberal political movements on the Continent and [was] familiar with their exile communities in London," not to mention his correspondence with writers in several countries (xvi). We are more familiar with Dickens's complex relationship with the United States, and a forthcoming two-volume work edited by Michael Hollington, *The Reception of Charles Dickens in Europe*, will make a "major contribution to the understanding of Global Dickens" (xix). But this attention enables Jordan and Perera's collection to cover essays on China, Australia, Japan, South America, Israel, India, and Africa. Such contributions, they explain, reveal "the instability of Anglo-American instantiations of Dickens when he is rethought as a global author" (xxii).

While Global Dickens is "one of the most promising future directions of Dickens studies" (xxviii), this has also been part of the past; Jordan and Perera remind us that in his own time, Dickens was read in the Australian outback or around the campfires in California gold country. The essays considered below on the Russian Dickens show how he has been a permanent fixture in their literary constellation since his earliest days as an author, while the concluding essay in the section, on cannibalism and Victorian ideas about both heroism and medical service, reminds us of the fear and misunderstanding that needed to be cleared up before there could be a section celebrating Global Dickens.

In "Global Dickens: A Response to John Jordan," Juliet John responds not to Jordan's introduction to the Ashgate volume but to his 2009 essay for *Literature Compass*. In that piece, Jordan argues that with our new tools, such as the Global Circulation Project, and an increasing emphasis on globalization studies, we can satisfy our desire for "more complete knowledge of Dickens's global influence" (502). John warns, however, that "the more we know, the more difficult it is to compose a convincing meta-narrative about Dickens's global significance" (503). This does not mean that the "enterprise lacks value," but that scholars will need to accept "localized, relatively undisciplined knowledge" (503). "The progress of global literary studies," she writes, "may then require us to let go of a model of professional academic discipline that could be seen as a form of methodological and intellectual imperialism" (503). Certainly the bicentenary makes clear that the global circulation of Dickens "depends in large part on the big and small screen as well as on the internet" (503), not to mention new media, creative writing, cultural institutions, and video links (505)—forms that are outside of what we have traditionally considered within our discipline. John celebrates this interest in global Dickens as "a return to scholarship as dialogue, dialogue that includes and indeed analyses languages other than English, and media other than books" (506).

Two significant essays in *Dickens Studies Annual* provide a broad context for understanding Dickens in Russia in the nineteenth and twentieth centuries. In "A Kindred Writer: Dickens in Russia, 1840-1990," Julia Palievsky and Dmitry Urnov explain that for about 150 years, "in spite of the variable ideological and literary climate in the country, Dickens's status as the greatest English novelist was unequivocally recognized" (210). The idea of him being "a kindred writer," not just a popular one, comes up repeatedly in Russian scholarship on Dickens (211). At the heart of this kindred feeling is "the utterly emotional sympathy for 'the insulted and injured,' to use Dostoevsky's title, which Russians treasured in their own literature" (211). This essay is based in part on work done by two Russian scholars, Mikhail P. Alekseev and Dr. Igor M. Katarsky, whose comprehensive research covered the history of translations and critical interpretations of Charles Dickens in Russia from the late 1830s through the early 1960s, as well as the question of Dickens's influence on Russian writers (210). *Pickwick* appeared first and then, generally, within two to three months of the publication of any new novel, a Russian translation was available (210). Irinarkh Vvedensky translated the material liberally, "inserting uniquely Russian phenomena and even adding passages. . . . and yet the Russian reading public accepted these translations as 'the true Dickens'" (210).

Palievsky and Urnov explain the concept of *narodnost*, "a distinctive national quality intrinsically present in art and specifically in literature" (212) and a goal of Russian art. While Russian readers have sometimes seen a tension between Dickens's representations of "social evils" and his idealization of a "bourgeois ideology" (212), of "all Western writers, it was Dickens who served as an example of true *narodnost*" (213).

Palievsky and Urnov go through a sample of major Russian authors and their relationship to Dickens's work. Nikolai Gogol saw in Dickens "greater expressivity of every narrative detail" which shaped his writing but brought down on him censure by "conservative critics" (215). In an interesting example of the two-way road of influence, Ivan Turgenev's *A Sportsman's Sketches* parallels *Pickwick* (216) and Dickens included translations of three stories from *A Sportsman's Sketches* in *Household Words* (218). Dickens and Turgenev were acquaintances. Dickens's portrait was the only one of a writer in Leo Tolstoy's study and he cited *David Copperfield* as making the "strongest impression on him" of any book—period (219). Tolstoy characterized Dickens's description of the storm in *David Copperfield* as the finest piece of writing in the world's prose literature (219–20). At the end of his life, Tolstoy remarked, "Dickens is the kind of genus that is born once in a hundred years" (222). Sometimes called "the Russian Dickens," Fyodor Dostoyevsky read Dickens in Russian and French translations, whereas Tolstoy read him in English (223). In recent years, there has been some discussion of a purported 1862 meeting in the *All the Year Round* offices between Dickens and Dostoyevsky, but the report of such an encounter has been exposed as a hoax (Michael Slater removed mention of it from the paperback version of his biography). It is tempting, however, to imagine (as Eric Naiman does in his *TLS* article) a conversation between writers with so much in common: concerns for the poor, a special interest in children and the oppressed, and narrative structure (222).

For Anton Chekhov and Maxim Gorky's generation, Dickens was a classic writer. Of the many articles written for the centenary in 1912, one was by the father of Vladimir Nabokov. In the early 1920s, an adaptation of *The Cricket on the Hearth* ran for several years, starring Mikhail Chekhov, the writer's nephew (226). Simon Callow wrote, in "Playing Dickens," that this production "was one of the great triumphs of the Moscow Arts Theatre Studio" (7). In 1934 the Moscow Arts Theatre produced *The Pickwick Club* with *The Master and Margarita* author Mikhail Bulgakov, who was both a coauthor of the stage version and acted in the play (226). In the Soviet Union, centralized control over publishing and problems of translation shaped access to Dickens's works (227), but there are well-known references to Dickens in Victor Shklovsky's *On the Theory of Prose* (1929), as well as in the work of Mikhail Bakhtin (227).

Picking up from where the previous essay leaves off, Tatiana A. Boborykina's "Dickens in Post-Soviet Russia" begins with the work of scholar Igor Katarsky and his "portrait of 'The Soviet Dickens'" (234). This was a time when "ideology ruled over art," but "in today's Russia [Dickens] seems to be a different writer, not because anything has changed about him, but because a lot has changed in the eyes of those who read and those who analyze" (234). Dickens's works have been published, printed, and reprinted in large numbers during the last two decades, "unlike the situation in Soviet times, when getting hold of each book of Dickens, not to say a complete collection, was a piece of luck and an event" (234). Today, "it is not a problem: one can buy editions in Russian, English, or both languages in most bookstores or . . . on the internet" (235).

Boborykina cites Joseph Brodsky's Nobel speech in which he said that it would be harder for a man to kill someone if he had read Dickens. Underscoring Dickens's potential as a "spiritual teacher" (236), Boborykina writes that it "is literature and Dickens's work, in particular, that may touch the sleeping soul and teach it how to laugh and to cry, and how to be a human being" (236). While it might sound stereotypically Russian to stress "the soul," teaching Russian students sounds a lot like teaching American students. Boborykina concludes with a discussion of her class on Dickens, who used to be a fixture on Russian syllabi. Today her students started out "all prejudiced against [Dickens] as dull, too long, old-fashioned, and boring" (256). But after taking them through some *Sketches*, Sikes's flight in *Oliver Twist*, and *The Cricket on the Hearth*, she comments, "Dickens for them has been the most modern, modernist, existentialist, surrealist, great, real, vivid, cool, awesome writer" (256).

Darren Bevin takes us to a different time and place; Dickens's interest in the Alps is the focus of his "Mountain Thoroughfares: Charles Dickens and the Alps." In the mid-nineteenth century, everything from railroads to Romantic poets to Ruskin contributed to a vigorous interest in the Alps (151). Dickens's letters in the 1840s reveal his interest in this landscape, particularly as a refuge from the city (152). From scenes in *Little Dorrit* to his 1867 work *No Thoroughfare* (Bevin reads this in the context of the 1865 Whymper mountaineering tragedy), the Alps remained an interest for Dickens. Bevin's essay centers on Albert Smith, an admirer and acquaintance of Dickens who dramatized both *The Battle for Life* and *The Cricket on the Hearth*, and who "fulfilled his long-held ambition of climbing Mont Blanc" in 1851 (152). This adventure resulted in *Mr Albert Smith's Ascent of Mont Blanc*, which ran for 2,000 shows over six years, including one for the Queen (153), making it one of the most "popular and successful entertainments of the nineteenth century" (153). It had such modern features as a performance gift shop selling "sledges and alpenstocks," sheet music, and "stereoscopic views of the dioramas" (155). Smith was accused of having a 'purely mercantile' (155) interest in Mont Blanc. He then responded with *The Story of Mont Blanc* (1853), which Dickens read and recommended to Catherine while he was on a nine-week tour of Switzerland with Wilkie Collins and Augustus Egg.

At the *A Tale of Four Cities* conference, Klaudia Hiu Yen Lee gave a talk on the translation of Dickens into Chinese. She explores this subject in her "*A Tale of Two Cities* and Chinese Literary History." Between 1907 and 1914, seven of Dickens's novels were translated and published in China. Lee suggests there is little hard data, but the multiple editions and different formats of Chinese editions of Dickens "suggest a healthy demand for his works" (25). Chinese intellectuals were interested in the social function of his work, and prose fiction in particular was seen to be especially conducive to "nation-building exercises" (26). Realism appealed to Chinese intellectuals since it seemed to be, quoting Martson Anderson, "the most progressive of Western aesthetic modes" (27). *A Tale of Two Cities* was first translated by Weit Yi and published in the Chinese political journal *The Justice*, established in 1912 by Liang Qichao and noted for its anti-revolutionary stance. So why, Lee asks, did "it feature Dickens's novel of revolution in the wake of the 1911 Revolution and the founding of the Chinese Republic?" (25) Lee describes a tension between revolutionaries, like Sun Yat-sen, and reformers, like Liang, and how they might appropriate or process the lessons of the French Revolution (28). Liang was a reformist who could engage in "debates with the revolutionaries on the applicability of revolution to China's historical development" (29). Lee's reading explains how the translation of *Tale* highlights the violence of the mob to strengthen the antirevolutionary message (30), while also reducing the complexity of a character like Madame Defarge, who is violent in the original, but also a character whom Dickens suggests has been a victim of violence herself (33). The translation eliminates some of the contradictions, making us mindful of "the socio-political condition of the target culture" in the "reception of a literary text" (34).

The condition of "the target culture" is central to Kylie Mirmohamadi and Susan K. Martin's *Colonial Dickens: What Australians Made of the World's Favourite Writer*, which examines "what Australians thought of Dickens rather than what Dickens thought of Australia" (2). The writers explain that their "project has been situating the role that reading Dickens played in the transmission, circulation and re-negotiation of the English language and English literature, which was so key in the cultural work of imperialism, and the concomitant shifts in reading subjectivities that occurred in the Southern lands" (2). Dickens, who was himself so influenced by *Thousand and One Arabian Nights*, is, according to these writers, a kind of Shahrazad figure for Australia: "as her narratives were held up as protection from the daily threat of annihilation, Dickens was seen by many of the colonisers of Australia as a . . . bearer of what they saw as civilization in the cultural wilderness of a new and uncharted world, as well as a means of forging new and changing colonial identities" (5). This might look like a study of the way "Melburnians overlaid their conceptual maps of the local urban environment with a template of London, often etched from the pages of Dickens's novels" (51) or ways in which *Oliver Twist* shaped "urban fears and anxieties surrounding crime and punishment in Sydney" (84). The Australian context can also de-familiarize the familiar in Dickens. While some people credit Dickens with the creation of modern Christmas, an 1883 essay in the *Queenslander* notes that "England's festive fare—the turkey, rum, sugar, spice, currants, raisins and citron peel—are the 'product of every clime except her own'" (48). Like many of the works reviewed, as we shall see in the next section, this book makes excellent use of the periodical press. A particularly fascinating chapter describes how the regional press "encoded" Dickens "into the everyday places and vocabularies of Australian country and mining towns" (71).

Not all works on global Dickens are about literal places; some works, consider, like Grossman's, consider Dickens's interest in how an emerging sense of geographical space shaped a sense of one's individuality. Dominic Rainsford's "Out of Place: David Copperfield's Irresolvable Geographies" uses that novel as a way of looking at Dickens's exploration of the individual's relation to the world. Always in motion, "Dickens was acutely aware of the difference it may make to live on one spot on the earth's surface rather than another, and the problems involved in conforming our ideas of self and duty to geographical space" (193). Rainsford cites the work of Sabine Clemm on *Household Words* and John Jordan on Global Dickens in his claim that Dickens is interested in "the vulnerability of personal placement" (197) and that "any place in the Dickensian world can reveal itself to be a provisional and vulnerable structure" (205).

A fear of what one might encounter out in that wider world is the subject of Marion Shaw's "The Doctor and the Cannibals." Shaw considers the cultural anxiety about and interest in cannibalism, arguing that for the English imaginary it is "a marker of what lies outside Western civilization" (121). It is this anxiety as well as the Medical Reform Committee of 1837 and the Medical Reform Act of 1858 that provide the context for her reading of Allan Woodcourt in *Bleak House*. The doomed Franklin mission that left England in 1845 in search of the Northwest Passage was the subject of a government report. The report, based on interviews with Eskimos, found reason to suspect cannibalism in the final days of the expedition. We know that Dickens's and Collins's play, *The Frozen Deep*, is a strenuous denial of those charges and an insistant argument for British heroism in such circumstances. Shaw argues that Dickens's construction of Allan Woodcourt is a similar argument for British fortitude; Woodcourt is a ship's surgeon and he performs heroically when his ship is wrecked.

Victorian Print Cultures

Shaw's article on cannibalism demonstrates in brief the interplay between fictional, dramatic, and governmental texts. One of the major scholarly trends in 2012 was the expansion of the textual archive, manifest in Global Dickens, but specifically in terms of our access to the enormous world of Victorian journalism. While the emphasis of this section is on Dickens's professionalization as an author and then as an editor of two journals, the second half covers the diversity of print culture, including what we might, using Gerard Genette's term, call paratext: advertisements, prefaces, and illustrations. This nuanced attention to the diversity of Victorian publishing produces a new concern with form. Works considered at the end of this section focus on Dickens's novels in relation to British painting and to lyric verse. Sambudha Sen's book on "the making of the Dickensian aesthetic," discussed below, examines how the popular "subliterary" forms with which his work is in dialogue produced his "novelistic aesthetic" (12). Mentions of two new editions of relatively rare collections of Dickens's early writing conclude the section, the longest of this review.

The Dickens Journals Online project (www.djo.org.uk), built and supported by John Drew and his colleagues at the University of Buckingham, was launched on Dickens's birthday, "digitzing almost thirty-thousand pages of mid-Victorian journalism," including full facsimile access to *Household Words, Household Narrative, Household Words Almanac,* and *All the Year Round* on a searchable, interactive site, for which there have been over 900 volunteer correctors (Horrocks 358–59). Anyone who has tried to access these materials previously knows what a godsend this is. On a practical level, one of the "main achievements of the project" is the "text-to-speech facility" which allows "access to the richness of Dickens's journalism for both blind and visually impaired users" (359–60). On a more abstract level, it puts real body behind the increasing scholarly recognition of Dickens's substantial journalistic career and how that affects our understanding of the man and his writing not just of his journalism, but of his fiction as well. Clare Horrocks, writing about Dickens Journals Online in *Victorian Periodicals Review*, provides a brief look at the March 2012 conference to celebrate the official launch of the site. "Charles Dickens and the Mid-Victorian Press, 1850–1870" was held at the University of Buckingham and plenary lectures were given by Michael Slater, Joanne Shattock, Laurel Brake, Louis James, Iain Crawford, Holly Furneaux, John Tulloch, Patrick Leary, Judith Flanders, Robert Patten, Catherine Waters, and John Sutherland. A collection from the conference was published in 2013 and contains papers from these talks as well as several in addition. Michael Slater provides the foreword and rightly points out that most of Dickens's journalism was inaccessible until the Dent Uniform Edition (1994–2000), and this accompanied a rise in periodical studies. In Introduction to the conference collection, John Drew points out how central Dickens's contributions as a journalist and editor were to the periodical literature of England and to his own professional success. But he also suggests that the conference's attempt to focus at once on a single contributor and an entire "complex cultural phenomenon" ("The Press") is "surely a kind of epistemological mismatch" (vii). How does "the Inimitable" look when studied in terms of the collaborative editing and writing that is a feature of his journals? That these questions must now be asked and these relationships and texts analyzed shows how central this part of Dickens's career has become to our understanding of Dickens and the Victorian period. The books and essays that follow in this section are part of our enlarged understanding of Victorian print cultures.

One of the major books published in 2012 was *Charles Dickens and "Boz": The Birth of the Industrial-Age Author*, by Robert L. Patten, who, as we'll see below, also wrote the introduction for the Ashgate volume *Victorian Print Cultures*. This book grows out of a long career spent studying Dickens, and the wealth of data and cultural context provided here make such an extensive excursion into the Dickensian weeds deeply rewarding. Patten explains "industrial-age" authorship as the product of "a set of publishing and more general cultural conditions that coalesced during the first half of the nineteenth century in Britain," conditions that included innovations in manufacturing and transportation, advances in the legal system that secured authors' rights, growth in the advertising industry, and a rise in literacy and leisure time (3). In short, "it became possible to produce writers of worldwide renown and commercial viability" (3). Patten's particular interest is to find the "author" in this web of "the print culture industry" (3). In so doing, he is drawing not only on historical data, but also on theoretical framings of this question from John Locke (the idea of an individual is necessary for conceiving of author, buyer, and seller) to Michel Foucault ("What Is an Author?"). Dickens is the perfect object of study because when he came of age, "writing was a central occupation of the industrial era" (22), but "in Britain 'authorship' was a peculiarly unstable and variegated concept" (16). Indeed, Patten suggests that in the 1830s Dickens was still "conceiving of himself as a writer, actor, producer, and potential lawyer" (53). By his death, he had, of course, achieved the international stardom we observed in the previous section.

Patten provides a great deal of information on the early, formative business arrangements with Bentley and then with Chapman and Hall (as well as with Cruikshank and Phiz). This is important context for understanding the emergence of "Boz" not only as a writing and an editorial identity, but, also, Patten suggests, as a genre: "an illustrated serial representing contemporary middle- and lower-middle-class life" (76). The arc of Patten's argument is that Dickens works hard to build Boz and then has to work hard to kill him off, to become Charles Dickens. Woven into this story are readings of Dickens's early writings that show a thematic resonance with issues of buying, selling, and plagiarizing (think of Oliver as both a boy and a book, and his fateful run-in with Brownlow at the bookseller's stall) as well as how his childhood experiences might have shaped his understanding of education, "that fundamental building block of industrial literacy" (24). The autobiographical fragment is here understood as "part of a concerted, lifelong effort by Dickens to understand, and in so doing inscribe and promulgate, a narrative about how authors are born" (26). If "Boz" in some part is born in the Blacking factory, "Boz" is also partly born on the street; the "speculative pedestrian" of the first sketches will carry through to the "Uncommercial Traveller" persona of his later journalism. While we know Dickens to have been a bold and forceful editor and businessman, Patten's focus on these formative years shows how "Boz" crafted his appeal by keeping a low profile politically (54) and writing more about "local than national issues" (56). There were "few relevant models of authorship by which to steer" (79). William Hazlitt and Walter Scott had financial difficulties, though William Harrison Ainsworth and Edward Bulwer Lytton offered brighter prospects. Patten notes that the 1841 census listed authors as "Other Educated Persons" and that they did not get their own category until 1861 (83).

Patten continues thinking about both Dickens's career and the dramatic changes to the publishing industry in his introductory essay to the Ashgate collection *Dickens and Victorian Print Cultures*. After *Pickwick*, "a publication event that changed the print market for subsequent fiction" (xv), Dickens wanted to "be seen as a national treasure (as indeed he was)" and his writings "to be understood as a service contributing to the national good (as they were) and to be rewarded for diligent and honest professional labour, as doctors and clergy were" (xv). Patten provides an invaluable history of how we came to see all of the "correspondence, manuscripts, proofs and other papers" as part of the Dickensian archive (xvi). He makes the important point that this understanding is only possible because of the work of scholars like Humphry House, John Butt, and Kathleen Tillotson, who did their work when "the New Criticism was in vogue and historical/contextual studies were strongly rebuked" (xvi–xvii).

Patten groups the essays into eight sections, and while space precludes any consideration of the contents, the section titles indicate what objects of study make up "print culture": Books and Authors; Serialization; Illustration; Circulation; Readers; Dickens as Editor; Contemporaneity; and Social, Cultural and Political Impact. The "bottom line is that reading material became extensively available in various formats, got cheaper as the century progressed and helped to shape an avid reading public and culture of literacy" (xxi). Dickens's early success with *Sketches*, *Pickwick*, and *Oliver Twist* proved that "there existed a substantial market for piecemeal publications that might be issued inexpensively over time and sold again when gathered up as a whole" (xxiv). Essays collected here on working class readers, on the socio-economic make-up of his public reading audiences, and on the role of illustrations help flesh out the range of ways in which and by whom these texts were consumed. Dickens "democratized the circulation of fiction. His formats were the vehicles for transmitting those works, as the Globe was the format for transmitting Shakespeare's plays" (xxxi). Patten writes, "This was in fact a revolution in publishing"(xxiv).

As research into these details of print culture develops, certain ideas about Dickens are being revised. A previous emphasis on "the dictatorial Dickens" can be "significantly modified by subsequent generations of students finding all kinds of exceptions, from additions to plates made after Dickens approved the general design to derelictions by illustrators which Dickens let go by without correction, to inattention that seems to apply . . . to his relations with his artistic collaborators in the last decade" (xx). This is a point underscored by Drew and his coauthors Hazel Mackenzie and Ben Winyard in a series of essays published in 2012 in conjunction with the launch of Dickens Journals Online. (Printed facsimiles of the first volumes are also being released.) One can't read a magazine like *Household Words*, they argue, "as though it was simply an outlying part of the Dickens empire" (51). The essay in *Dickens Quarterly* on volume 1 (March 30, 1850– September 21, 1850) provides an overview of the journal's "house style, namely a willingness to blend if not transgress genre boundaries" (52). The installments that comprise the first volume ("semester") had a particular emphasis on Public Health and sanitary reform, as well as more poetry than in subsequent semesters. But there was no set pattern, as "the unpredictability of subject matter for leading articles was clearly a deliberate strategy" (53). (The authors mention the supplement to the journal, the *Household Narrative of Current Events*, and suggest that much research still needs to be done about this text and its relationship to Dickens's views.) One of the subjects that links the diverse material, Drew, Mackenzie, and Winyard suggest, is travel writing: "the traveler's voice is flexible but singular—and this is one of the more striking ways in which Dickens's original notion of the omnipresent 'Shadow,'" the image Dickens shared with Forster in a letter, "succeeds in permeating through the series of apparently closed structures presented by the end-stopped articles and magazines of which *Household Words* was constituted" (60). "Given the elements of the emergent house style—investigative fieldwork, narrative innovation, a variable and frequently ironic tone, the sense of theater and audience—one might, correctly, predict that dry, monologic scientific writing" would be avoided in *Household Words*. However, Drew, Mackenzie, and Winyard explain that "writers about science in Victorian periodicals understood the need for a precise understanding of storytelling strategies" (62). "Dickens championed a democratically accessible science," they write, and "the scientific processes underpinning industrial and technological advances in Britain also receive treatment" (64).

Any treatment of *All the Year Round* notes both continuities and changes from its predecessor. Mackenzie, Winyard, and Drew continue their review of the first volumes by reading the start of the journal "as an unforeseen by-product of Dickens's marital crisis" and a legal dispute with publishers Bradbury and Evans that led to "a business decision prompted by personal feelings and animosities" (271). But the timing, they note, was "serendipitous" (271). By starting in early 1859, *All the Year Round* had a head start on a wide range of competitors, both monthly and weekly, that began to crowd the marketplace, among them: *Macmillan's Magazine* (November 1859 onwards), the *Cornhill Magazine* (December 1859), *Temple Bar* (1860), *St James's Magazine* (1860), the *Sixpenny Magazine* (1861), *Robin Goodfellow* (1861), and *Bow Bells* (1862).

It is tempting to think of Dickens at this point in his career as consumed by the novels and the readings (not to mention his personal life), but the aforementioned essay provides an excellent correction. It shows how these first months of this new journal "represent the point in its editor's career when the fate of his journal mattered most to him, and his role as magazine owner-editor-writer was at the forefront of all his professional activities" (251). This is not to say that he took his novelist's hat off; *A Tale of Two Cities* opens all 26 weekly numbers of the first biannual volume of *All the Year Round* (254). Its first six months "were crucial in developing a new, more literary, and less 'newsy' profile for its contents, and setting new benchmarks for sales and distribution," including "a comprehensive and eye-catching national advertising campaign" (253).

The article takes us through notable and representative contributions to this new journal. Despite Gaskell's not wanting to publish another novel with Dickens, her "Lois the Witch" is one of the other extended pieces of fiction in this first volume. Collins is a more frequent contributor, and his sense of the journal's "voice," "in terms of [its] register and address," shows why "Collins was to prove such a congenial contributor over many years" (256). While poetry remained a feature in the journal, this essay provides an interesting discussion of the struggle to include that as a characteristic element. The question of the politics of this journal is frequently debated: Dickens did not want to cover the American Civil War, but he did have a serious interest in foreign policy. Dickens was a notable supporter of the Italian nationalist movement (262). The authors here provide an interesting perspective on the journal's war coverage, arguing that the journal prioritizes "the specifics of good governance and liberal administration over the glamour of military exploits" (264). And the interest in foreign affairs reflected a growing sense that there was a new world opening up, one in which "migration through necessity and travel for business and pleasure result in a kind of perpetual flux" (266). One of the opportunities that access to this archive can provide is a chance to identify the authors of the pieces. In 1997, Drew suggested that the article "Dress in Paris" (*All the Year Round*, February 1863) was a translation by Dickens from a recent French work *La Nouvelle Babylone*. John Bowen's 2012 "Ellen Ternan: Traductrice?" responds to Drew's claim that in translation it is "hard to judge authorship." But Bowen wonders if maybe Ellen was the translator as "the very modesty of the additions seems uncharacteristic for Dickens" (81), and Ellen, as Mrs. Wharton Robinson, later translated a travel guide from the French (82).

John Drew subjects Dickens's journalism to deeper analysis in his "Texts, Paratexts and 'e-texts': the Poetics of Communication in Dickens's Journalism." Arguing that Dickens's work as a journalist constitutes "a self-conscious poetics of communication" (73–74), Drew charts Dickens's movement from a "linear model of press management" to a "sense of the editor's role . . . as a more cyclical and circular model" (69). Dickens's job involves as many roles (editor, creator, service provider, content manager) as the journal's forms, issued at three "distinct frequencies" and in three different formats. Drew also addresses the question about what role the journals play in a commodity culture. The journals "can be read on one level as an enlightened attempt to restore lost aura, and reanimate a sense of wonder" and yet on the other as "the phony spell of a commodity" (77). "In Dickens's hands," Drew explains, "I read this duality as a redemptive mythology against industrial materialism and 'the iron binding of the mind to grim realities' rather than a fetishising of the commodity" (77). Drew sees "consumers of Dickens's weekly magazines" (now and then) as part of shared community through new "publishing practices that have brought author and reader into anonymous communion in the first place" (89).

John Drew thinks about Dickens's journals in relation to e-texts. Michaela Mahlberg's "Corpus stylistics—Dickens, Text-drivenness and the Fictional World" places Dickens scholarship squarely in the digital age. Mahlberg's essay illustrates "how computer-assisted methods can support the analysis of linguistic devices and the effects they create in the text" (94) by "reading" enormous amounts of data, which seems particularly relevant to a writer like Dickens who has such a large volume of writing. For example, one might choose a characteristic

Dickensian device, such as his emphasis on external features, and get data on examples of noses in *Bleak House*. Similarly Dickens's use of character "tags" can be read as a cluster ("the repetition of a specified number of words in a sequence"), such as "and his nose came down" in *Little Dorrit*, a phrase associated with the character Rigaud. One can also use the data analysis to find suspensions, which are a "span of (narrator) text which interrupts a span of quoted speech" (110). Mahlberg argues that such examples demonstrate how "computer-assisted methods can contribute to the study of characters " or of rhetorical strategies in Dickens (112). Trey Philpotts, in a panel discussion about the future of Dickens Studies, suggested that "quantification will be the next big thing in literary studies and in particular in Dickens studies" (17).

As noted throughout this review, works in all subject areas are making use of the accessibility of the wider textual archive. Robert Terrell Bledsoe's *Dickens, Journalism, Music: Household Words and All the Year Round* is a perfect example. It is a meticulous analysis of the coverage of music in Dickens's two journals as well as in the human relationships that provide a context for understanding Dickens's development in this area, specifically his friendships with Henry Fothergill Chorley and Frederick and Nina Lehmann. Bledsoe's work seeks to correct the traditional assumption that Dickens, beyond musical theater, is not terribly interested in music. He was part of a musical family, married into a musical family, and introduced his children, particularly Mamie and Katie, into a social world full of musicians (181). Bledsoe explains that while "both journals aim at improving taste and morals," the earlier *Household Words* emphasizes "music's social role and its public functions" whereas *All the Year Round* is more concerned with educating its readers about "the classical canon" and creating discerning critics (1). In addition to being an object of interest for Dickens the editor, music, Bledsoe argues, is important to Dickens's sense of memory and therefore central to his "fictional imagination" (2). Music suggests to Dickens, Bledsoe claims, the "essence of Christianity, as opposed to a narrow construction of its letter" (3). The coverage of music takes on the journal's characteristic eclecticism, with articles on subject matter from odd musical instruments to the musical world of St. Petersburg to the street music of London. Bledsoe gives special attention to Chorley's writings on the music of Wagner, which Chorley called "nightmares imposed on a helpless and astray public" (131).

Katie Lanning's essay "Tessellating Texts: Reading *The Moonstone* in *All the Year Round*" also makes Dickens's journal the context for her reading of Collins's novel, which was serialized in *All the Year Round* in 1868. Though Lanning's focus is on *The Moonstone*, she shows how reading the novel would have to "tessellate" between the text and the journal's paratext, such as advertisements. This understanding of the novel's original serialized context, Lanning argues, makes it "possible to read the role of *Robinson Crusoe* in *The Moonstone* as a kind of Victorian product placement" (12). David Parker's "The *Pickwick* Prefaces" examines the four versions of the preface Dickens wrote for *The Pickwick Papers*

(67) and what they might reveal about Dickens's authorial self-fashioning. *Pickwick* Illustrator Robert Seymour, whose proposal for the etchings led to *Pickwick*, killed himself in the middle of the run; Dickens had difficulties with Seymour's family. Parker argues that if we look at the prefaces "as a series . . . we hear discordant voices in them" (67). Initially, Dickens characterizes *Pickwick* as a "monthly something" (71) but he grows "bolder about the value of the book" (72). In the 1858 preface "Dickens wanted to impress readers, not with the cheapness of his books, but with their standing as works of narrative art" (72). Ultimately, his 1867 preface emphasizes "the durability of his reputation" (72).

There were a range of essays this year on Dickens and his illustrators, some attempting to clarify the historical record. Leon Litvack's "Marcus Stone: A Reappraisal of Dickens's Young Illustrator" aims to correct some critical misunderstandings of one of Dicken's illustrators in order "to restore him to his rightful place in the Dickensian firmament" (214). Stone did the wrapper design and illustrations for *Our Mutual Friend* (1864–65). His work has generally been dismissed due to both his distinct naturalist style (more "Ruskin" than "Cruikshank") and his quasi-dependence on Dickens after the death of Stone's father, Frank (at Tavistock House, the Dickenses had the Stones as neighbors). Q. D. Leavis rather harshly said that "'Dickens had better have left the bereaved Stone family to starve' . . . than to have employed Marcus Stone as his book illustrator" (248). Stone's appointment has been understood as "a charitable act on the part of Dickens" (221). But the handsome plates that accompany the essay provide support for the argument that Stone was both responding to Dickens's direction and working through his own legitimate concerns as an artist. Litvack argues that Stone cannot be considered self-taught, despite such claims (including Marcus's own) (219). There was not formal training, but he grew up amidst his father's circle of artists: Cruikshank, W. P. Frith, Augustus Egg, Edwin Landseer, and William Holman Hunt.

An essay on Phiz's illustrations for *Little Dorrit* explores the conversations between text and image. In "A Note on Costume and Historicity in *Little Dorrit*," Bryan Osborn suggests that despite the opening words being "Thirty years ago," Dickens does not try too hard to stick to the novel's 1825–26 setting. "It was widely felt to be what it probably is," Osborn explains, "a mid-century inquest on Victorian society" (47). While Dickens is meticulous about period features of dress in his language, such details are not matched by Hablot K. Browne (Phiz)'s illustrations. Most of the costumes in Browne's illustrations to *Little Dorrit* suggest "the period roughly between 1840 and 1850" (49) leaving room for the reader to think about the questions this raises. Aileen Farrar does just this in her "Charles Dickens and Hablot K. Browne." *Bleak House* is famous for its dual narration, and Farrar's consideration of the role of Browne's forty illustrations for the novel adds to our sense of how "collaboration of text and image" also produce "multiple perspectives" (36). Farrar reads a dialogue between author and illustrator that "smudges the boundaries of epistemological reality and probes the period's confrontation between power and self" (36). Her discussion includes Browne's dark plate illustrations, a technique he developed resulting in "a dual imagistic style" (38), where "the dark plate and lithographic etchings" can be read as foils in this narrative (38), and which, she notes, began appearing around the time in the serial publication that Esther experiences blindness (43). It underscores Esther's new understanding of her role in an optical economy, which generates "the crushing weight of the external eye and the oppression of being watching" (43). This interaction between pictorial and textual narrators, according to Farrar, can "redefine boundaries and thus find a balance between traditional narrative authority and advancing methods of perception . . . anticipating an incipient aesthetic that relies on a synthesis of narrative techniques and modes of thought" (47).

Not all conference proceedings are as grand as Yale University Press's book from the *Dickens and the Artists* exhibition at the Watts Gallery in Surrey (from June 19 to October 18, 2012). The resulting book, with beautiful images and detailed essays by different writers, covers both Dickens as an art critic and his influence on artists. Mark Bills, the curator of the Watts Gallery, locates Dickens within the art world of his day, touching both on the intensely visual nature of Dickens's writing, the role of Hogarth in his imagination, his work with illustrators, and his close friendships with artists such as Daniel Maclise, August Egg, Clarkson Stanfield, Marcus Stone, and William Powell Frith (3). Stanfield was not only a friend, Leonée Ormond writes, but provided sets for Dickens's theatricals and illustrations for the Christmas books, as did Maclise (39, 41). Hilary Underwood documents the influence of Dickens's works in such paintings as Frith's *Dolly Varden* and William Holman Hunt's *Little Nell and her Grandfather*. Dickens's subjects, Underwood writes, "were at their most popular in the 1840s, when they were part of a broader taste for literary narrative genre paintings" (82). She also notes that "modern-life genre painting from Frith to Luke Fildes," though it is "profoundly Dickensian," does not "depict Dickens subjects" (83). Pat Hardy looks at Dickens's influence on social realists, including Fildes, Hubert Herkomer, and Frank Hull and suggests that Dickens's work galvanized this group to develop a "coordinated response, in subject matter, form, composition and reception to the social issues of the late 1860s and 1870s." Rather from painting from literary sources, this group emphasized eye-witness scenes (155).

Scholarship this year explored the many forms in which Dickens wrote and published, as well as the different aesthetic forms that shaped his work as both a writer and an editor. Joseph P. Jordan sees his book, *Dickens Novels as Verse*, both as belonging to the recent conversation about form, in part initiated by Stephen Best and Sharon Marcus about surface reading, and also as returning to Orwell's provocative comment on the "unmistakable mark" of Dickens's fiction being the "unnecessary detail" (8). In both his book and an essay in *Dickens Quarterly*, Jordan makes a bold argument that repeated patterns in Dickens novels have value even when that value is not the traditional one of being linked to a theme. The typical way of reading repetitions, such as the image of fog in *Bleak House*, is to assume it can provide a window into the overarching themes Dickens wants to address. This is not what Jordan is doing in his readings of patterns in *A Tale of Two Cities* (where he looks at the image patterns of wheeled vehicles), *Our Mutual Friend* (wooden things), and *Great Expectations* (hands). He chooses these texts in particular because they are well known for their repetitions. The repetitions are important but nonsubstantive, or in his terms "a pattern that is insignificant in the literal sense —a pattern that doesn't signify anything—is not therefore insignificant in the metaphoric sense—is not therefore dismissible as a factor in the experience of a work" (4).

We grant this part of the reading experience to lyric verse, Jordan explains, but not to novels. The patterns he identifies in Dickens's novels are "as humble as alliteration is, as meter is, in a line of verse" (8). In Jordan's reading, attention to these repetitions provides a balance to the Dickensian sprawl that makes novels seem both as if they are "bursting at the seams" and "bounded and tight" (7). "The incidental patterns of topics in Dickens novels perform the same function" as these poetic devices do: "they make the variously distinct elements of the novels more of a piece even as, because the patterned elements are so many and densely intertwined, they augment the book's feel of multifariousness" (7). His *Dickens Quarterly* 2012 essay is an appendix to the book and offers a close reading of word choice at end of these much-discussed first chapters to argue for "a kind of structural girding" (278).

Sometimes, such structure is impossible. Saverio Tomaiuolo's *Victorian Unfinished Novels: The Imperfect Page* takes up famous unfinished novels, with a chapter on perhaps the most famous of them all: *The Mystery of Edwin Drood*. While *Drood* is unfinished because of Dickens's death, Tomaiuolo suggests that in some ways *Drood* is about the problem of narrative closure itself, about a "principle of 'de-composition'" (55) that runs throughout the novel. From George Eliot's 1857 observation (in a letter to John Blackwood) that conclusions "are the weak points of most authors, but some of the fault lies in the very nature of a conclusion, which is at best a negation" (12) to contemporary theorists such as D. A. Miller and Peter Brooks, closure has been a thorny problem. It has not, however, troubled the "Drood-finishing industry," as Tomaiuolo describes the many theatrical and literary attempts to provide a sense of the ending for Dickens's last novel. Nevertheless, *Drood* is "pervaded by a paradigm of dissolution and decomposition that characterizes and determines its thematic and narrative structure"(52). Such an emphasis on decomposition speaks to our understanding of that novel's association of moral decay with structural decay, very suggestive of the kinds of connections between theme and aesthetics that Tomaiuolo wants to make.

Gavin Edward's "Dickens, Illiteracy and 'Writin Large'" adds to our sense of how Dickens's material and thematic concerns influenced one another—how "the treatment of writing and reading *in* the novels" relates to "the writing and reading *of* the novels" (28). His essay examines Dickens's increasing interest in illiteracy in such novels as *Bleak House* and *Great Expectations*, as well as in the Christmas number for 1865 *Doctor Marigold's Prescriptions*. He places this interest in the context of the change in the material forms of Dickens's own texts from "manuscript to corrected proof, from proof to published edition, and from editions designed for reading to prompt-copies for public Readings" (27). Edwards also considers Dickens's understanding of the wide spectrum of illiteracy, of the relation of print/typography to handwriting, and to what kinds of *writing* would be useful for his public Readings, evident in his prompt-copies.

Rachel Malik also looks at *Great Expectations* and how its thematic concerns relate to its publishing history in "Stories Many, Fast and Slow." Malik argues that Dickens's interest in both speed and slowness in that novel (think of Pip racing off to Satis House versus the long periods of time that elapse in the story) have everything to do with the rapidly changing world of Victorian publishing. Malik explains the "horizon of the publishable" as a "constitutive set of relations between publishing practices" and commercial, legal, educational or media institutions. Fascinatingly, in light of the range of work done on the conditions and form of Dickens's publication, Malik suggests that this serialized view of the novel is overtaking traditional understandings of "the novelistic" (480). She argues that "the full range of editions and versions . . . shape the possibilities of the novelistic during this period, including Dickens's narrative style itself" (481).

Sambudha Sen's *London, Radical Culture, and the Making of the Dickensian Aesthetic* locates the development of Dickensian novel in the radical print and visual culture of the early nineteenth century. Like Sally Ledger in her *Dickens and the Popular Radical Imagination* (2007), Sen sees the "satiric techniques that developed in the radical journalistic tradition" as central to Dickens's writing. However, Sen's argument departs from Ledger's "instrumentalist" view of Dickens's writing. Unlike "mobilizing pamphlets", "Dickens's entertainment-oriented novels worked in very different domains and were likely, therefore, to produce very different kinds of political effects" (9). If Dickens was changing minds, it was gradual and indirect in the mind of a reader who read "in her leisure time for pleasure rather than political education" (9). Sen's book features two traditions of representation that influenced this aesthetic: the "radical expression" of literary and visual satire (Thomas Paine, William Hone, William Cobbett, and George Cruikshank) and popular visual culture (from Hogarth's *Industry and Idleness* to the panorama and the stereoscope), and one foil—William Makepeace Thackeray. While Sen insists that this is not a book on Thackeray and that he wants to avoid "that long-established tradition of scholarship that locks the two greatest male novelists of Victorian England in a rigid binary relationship" (11), Thackeray's frequent worrying about the "Art of Novels," the possible contaminating affect of the popular subliterary forms that formed a rich resource for Dickens, and his "self-conscious rejection" of these resources throw Dickens's methods into relief.

What follows is a discussion of the "politics of caricature" in *Bleak House, Little Dorrit*, and *Vanity Fair* or the problems of selfhood within a radical culture represented in *Great Expectations* and *Pendennis*. In a chapter that really belongs in this review's section on the City, "Re-visioning the City," Sen looks specifically at non-literary forms. He starts with the camera obscura introduced in Pierce Egan's *Life in London* that "detaches not only the represented scene but also the viewer/reader from the city itself." Hogarth's "A Full and True Account of the Ghost of Tho. Idle," which is the last plate of *Industry and Idleness*, features a broadsheet from the Tyburn hanging. Unlike the camera obscura, it is the kind of print commodity that "owes its existence" to its "integration with the human traffic on the streets" (75). Two forms that also "helped to produce the urban aesthetic" were the panorama and the stereoscope. Sen argues that Dickens's writing, as opposed to Thackeray's, deliberately responds to these non-literary "popular expressive resources" (93).

Space precludes attention to new editions of Dickens's work, with a few notable exceptions. Robert C. Hanna's *Dickens's Uncollected Magazine and Newspaper Sketches* is a labor of love, begun many years ago and representing an important resource to those scholars who have come of age understanding that Dickens was not only a novelist but a writer in several domains over his entire working life. The sketches collected here are intended to be as the first audience saw and read them, and as such Hanna does not provide annotation. Hanna offers brief introductory essays to provide a framework for approaching the material. *Sketches of Young Gentlemen and Young Couples with Sketches of Young Ladies by Edward Caswall* collects Dickens's sketches that he wrote on types of gentleman and then later on couples in honor of Victorian's marriage to Albert. (Caswall's sketches of young ladies appeared first.) Dickens wrote these anonymously for Chapman and Hall, the publishers of *Pickwick*, as he was under contract with Bentley, his *Oliver Twist* publisher, and not supposed to publish anything with a rival. Dickens's authorship was not revealed until Forster's biography was published in the years after Dickens's death. These texts are rarely reprinted now, but, as Paul Schlicke's introduction explains, sketches were "the dominant mode of publication in the 1830s" (viii). The illustrations for all the sketches were done by Phiz. In these works, Schlicke suggests, the observer is not Benjamin's flâneur, but rather an ordinary city-dweller (x). Caswall went on to have a career as a writer and, later, a priest; Schlicke provides an interesting context for these sketches in the scientific debates of the time, as the preface of the *Sketches* "set forth the classification of young ladies according to the Linnaean system" (xii). Dickens's sketches contain "the marvelously lively imaginative details which constitute the hallmark of his characterization (xvi). While there has been some alternate readings about the treatment of gender in these works, Schlicke argues that "both the ladies and the gentlemen come in for Boz's genial mockery" (xvi). Phiz's illustrations, "the unifying ingredient of the three volumes" (xxii), "offer a revealing glimpse of courtship rituals and gender relations at the outset of the Victorian era" (xxv).

Sexuality and Gender

Dickens's representation of gender relations has been debated almost since these early publications (and certainly since *Oliver Twist*). Lillian Nayder's introductory essay to the Ashgate volume *Dickens, Sexuality and Gender* sums up the tension in studies of sexuality and gender in Dickens's work: "Though he proves willing to draw on conventional ideas of sexuality and gender to serve his ends— artistic, political, personal—and to idealize or vilify his characters, he also represents those ideas as inadequate and confining" (xiii). The essays published in 2012 range from new looks at familiar characters (Agnes, Estella) to work on queer Dickens, expanding and in some cases challenging the work of Eve Sedgwick and Sharon Marcus. Some readers find him definitely a feminist, or at least, building on Michael Slater's influential 1983 work *Dickens and Women*, capable of "complicated psychological portraits" (xiv). Other scholars find the Angel in the House very hard to shake. Nayder notes that scholarship further "complicated this picture" (xiv) by focusing on the "construction and instability of the categories themselves" (xiv). These essays understand gender to be about more than women, looking at the construction of masculinity in Dickens, or at the relationship between gender and other categories of analysis such as class and race. Nayder argues that the "ability of gender ideals to cut across social classes—or, rather, the energy Dickens and his contemporaries devote to making gender ideals *seem* universal—testifies to the political significance of these constructs" (xvii). Taken as a whole, Nayder explains, contemporary scholarship illustrates Dickens's "ability to occupy conflicting positions" (xxvi).

Maria Ioannou's reading of *Great Expectations* is not conflicted; she sure-footedly asserts in her "'Simply because I found her irresistible': Female Erotic Power and Feminism in *Great Expectations*" that this novel has "a central feminist core" (142). While it is a work "filled with mutilated women," it not only condemns male violence, but also "develops, in Pip, a form of masculinity that accepts a woman's sensual power and appeal" (142). Ioannou links the novel's "examination of the idea of the gentleman" with the "scrutiny of gender codes in the novel" (143). Miss Havisham and Estella are both explained by the external forces that shaped their characters and need to be seen in context of "the confines which restricted women to a life centered on feeling" (145). Ioannou argues that Pip's "relationship with a sexually powerful woman" is central to "his maturity rather than an obstacle to his development" (146). Precious McKenzie Stearns's "'Sex and the City': Charles Dickens's Working Women in *Martin Chuzzlewit* and *Our Mutual Friend*" similarly sees Dickens's representation of working women in *Martin Chuzzlewit* and *Our Mutual Friend* as positive. The characterizations of Mrs. Gamp and Jenny Wren contribute to an understanding of the challenges faced by women working in "the masculine realm of business." If we have traditionally seen Dickens's female characters as either angels or grotesques, Mrs.

Gamp and Jenny Wren occupy both an economic and a domestic sphere and as such have a "free thinking, free-moving privilege . . . compared with the caged birds of the middle class" (150).

Katie R. Peel's "'Make Her Pay': Fanny Dorrit's Disruption in Charles Dickens's *Little Dorrit*" reformulates Eve Sedgwick's triangle to show "relationships among women that are not nurturing, but are a matter of business" (125). Fanny, Peel argues, "sets a socioeconomic goal for herself" (127). Peel uses the work of René Girard and Gayle Rubin, as well as performance theory, to broaden Sedgwick's triangle; she argues that Fanny Dorrit "uses her husband in order to form a relationship with his mother" (126). But this is not Adrienne Rich's continuum; it is not nurturing: "the only thing nurtured in this triangle is a desire for vengeance" (127) or in Dickens's words Fanny's "demolition of the Bosom." Fanny is a dancer and Peel uses Erving Goffman's and Joseph Litvak's theories of theatricality to argue that "Fanny performs in nearly every aspect of her daily life" (132). This performance both "destabilizes and adheres to Victorian social standards" (138) and "affects our reading of larger systems at work in the text, including those of gender, class, and narrative" (128).

Victorian social standards are embodied by *David Copperfield*'s Agnes, typically dismissed, in Orwell's famous phrase, as that "legless angel of Victorian romance." Mark Eslick asks us to take another look at Agnes in the context of the Victorian interest in the Madonna figure or "Mariolatry," the cult around the Virgin Mary. Though Dickens may "have rejected Catholic Mariolatry," Agnes's "distinctly Catholic associations suggest that he was emotionally open to imagery not found in the Church of England" (62). One of the Protestant objections to Mary was that the celebration of her power seemed to minimize or "infantilize" Jesus (63). Also "popular anti-Catholicism denounced Marian images and invocations as signs and symbols of a dangerous, foreign religion" (63). But as Eslick points out, Mary's virtues "closely resemble the Victorian paradigm of the feminine ideal known as the Angel-in-the-House" (63). Dickens is critical of Mariolatry, particularly in *Pictures from Italy*. Eslick contends, however, that Agnes is certainly a Victorian angel and therefore in dialogue with the Madonna figure, especially as aspects of her characterization are "fundamentally religious" (67) and she is repeatedly associated both in the text and in illustrations with the church.

Studies of gender in Dickens involve scrutiny of masculinity as well. Nicholas Shrimpton's "*Great Expectations:* Dickens's Muscular Novel" looks at the novel in the context of the cult of "Muscular" novels, started by George Alfred Lawrence's *Guy Livingstone* (1857) and to which, Shrimpton suggests, Dickens had to respond. Shrimpton distinguishes between the "Muscular Christianity" associated with Charles Kingsley and the "Muscular pagans" (127), to whom Lawrence belongs. Shrimpton also looks back to Coleridge's account of "Manliness" in his *Aids to Reflection in the Formation of a Manly Character* (1825). Muscular novels were less interested in F. D. Maurice's and Kingsley's religious treatments and more in line with Macaulay's essay on "Machiavelli" and its association of civilization with a fighting spirit (129–30), an idea also picked up in Carlyle's *Past and Present* (1843). This context in part explains why "hand-to-hand combat is a conspicuous feature" (Shrimpton 135) of *Great Expectations*. Fights include, of course, Pip and Herbert Pocket, Orlick and Joe, Magwitch and Compeyson, Pip and Bentley Drummle, who dies, like Guy Livingstone, after being crushed by his horse (137). Interestingly, Shrimpton argues that "Dickens provokes these expectations [of a muscular plot] in order to disappoint them. Though Pip is muscular, his muscularity is of no use to him in the crises of his adult experience" (137). His love for Estella makes him miserable and his "considerable physical feat" of rowing Magwitch 20 miles down the Thames results in failure (138). Shrimpton concludes that "Muscularity as an idea, like the Muscular Novel as a format, is fully acknowledged in *Great Expectations*. It is also very scrupulously interrogated" (140).

Holly Furneaux's "Dickens, Sexuality and the Body; or, Clock Loving: Master Humphrey's Queer Objects of Desire" is part of multiple critical conversations from Thing Theory to Queer Theory. It explores "Dickens's investment in the imaginative, emotional and erotic appeal of objects" (41). Furneaux also links her concerns with the surface reading debate, as attention to "what texts present on their surface" is fitting "for an author like Dickens, so concerned with the material" (44). Furneaux's essay focuses on the rich image of the clock in *Master Humphrey's Clock*, noting that it is both "the mechanism for the generation of narrative throughout" (45) as well as a "porous body" offering "a device for understanding the interpenetrability through which social connection operates" (57). As such, it helps Dickens resist "a thesis of the mechanistic as inevitably dehumanizing" (50) because, as the storytellers come and go from the clock with their manuscripts, "Dickens models his relationship to his readers through a tale of intimacy between the human story teller(s) and machine" (48). It is in this openness to "non-naturalised opportunities of a cyborg world" that he is "queerest." The clock itself is a queer image with "its phallic casing . . . combined with a womb-like interior, apparently endlessly expandable in relation to the male storytellers' need for their texts to be brought to term" (58). Furneaux argues that Dickens's "skepticism towards what constitutes the 'natural'" allows him to question whether "attributes and responses perceived to be natural or innate, especially in terms of gender and sexuality, are really so" (51).

Kim Edwards Keates similarly explores how Dickens adaptations and neo-Victorianism address questions of gender blade-running. In "'Wow! She's a Lesbian. Got to be!': Re-reading/Re-viewing Dickens and neo-Victorianism on the BBC," Edwards looks at the work of neo-Victorian novelist Sarah Waters with a "queer, revisionist lens." Seeing in her form of neo-Victorianism a way "to reinterpret the overlap of contemporary feeling and historical understanding" (172), Edwards argues that Andrew Davies's *Bleak House* (BBC 2005) "straighten[s]" Esther but opens up possibilities in the representation of "the queer temporalities of Lady Dedlock," particularly in the portrayal of her relationship with her maid Rosa.

Jane Griffith, covering almost all the categories of this review, takes the idea of form—here serialization—to think about the gendering of urban space. Her essay "Such a Labyrinth of Streets: Serialization and the Gendered View of Urban Space in *Bleak House*" argues that the text's original publication format shaped the representation of public space. Each installment, Griffith explained, would have either a "cartographic" or "extra-cartographic" perspective. While such perspectives are also in the unified text, the placement of them in the serial draws attention to the distinction between the perspectives. The extra-cartographic is gendered male and performed by the male omniscient narrator; for Esther space is always a map. In other words, "men question space; women take space at face value" (249). What this means is that Esther's narration is shaped by a sense that space is stable whereas the omniscient narrator understands the city's instability (250).

Stacy Floyd's "The Specter of Class: Revision, Hybrid Identity, and Passing in *Great Expectations*" is, as the title suggests, focused on class, but she puts her discussion of the novel's "exploration of identity crises" (100) in the context of "passing," a term used in considerations of gender and race. Floyd argues that class, too, is "embodied" and therefore can be discussed in terms of passing. Floyd uses Judith Butler's work on gender to discuss Dickens's class passing as both "performance" and "performativity," noting that Dickens's extensive interest in the theater is an important context. *Great Expectations*, Floyd argues, "offers an image of identity formation as dialectic, with past, present, and emerging selves reflecting on and communicating with one's constant revision of subjectivity" (101). Both Floyd and Furneaux argue that Dickens is just as interested in hybrid figures, Pip or the clock, as he is in locking anyone into a category.

The scene where Sissy confronts Harthouse in *Hard Times* has long troubled Dickens critics. Victor Sage's "Girl Number Twenty Revisited: *Hard Times*'s Sissy Jupe" looks at performance and subjectivity in his reading of Sissy's grammatically correct dressing down of Louisa's seducer. It is faulted for being unrealistic and even ridiculous, most memorably by George Bernard Shaw who said "this is the language of a Lord Chief Justice, not of the dunce of an elementary school in the Potteries" (qtd. in 325). But Sage wants us to revisit this attitude and his essay shows how just looking at "a notion of linguistic decorum" misses "the nature of self and performance in this novel" (326). Sage suggests that *Hard Times* develops "a notion of the displaceable, mobile, and, as we shall see, even the substitutable, self" (326) and sees in Sissy's acting as Louisa's representative a radical "substitution of self" (330). Katharyn Stober's "'Another Thing Needful'" also makes a case for revisiting *Hard Times*. If the standard take on that novel is that it is a show down between fact and fancy, decidedly in fancy's favor, Stober wants an "alternative reading" that demonstrates "the interdependency of the two" (127). Noting that it is "industry, not fancy" that "pulls Stephen from the mine shaft" (130), and that Sleary's circus ultimately "decreased fancy and increased commercialism" (131), Stober argues that "fancy here is meant to alleviate the stress of productive work and industry, not replace it" (133).

The City and Modernity

The City was a focus of bicentenary celebrations, and several scholarly works provide rich detail of the city in which Dickens lived and the city as it lives in Dickens's writings. Using Walter Benjamin as a major lens through which to examine Dickens, in books and essays scholars consider how Dickens thought through, with, and against the city and what urban life portended for the future. Given both the concrete reality of the city and its rich field for metaphoric considerations, the works here range from material history to philosophy. Judith Flanders makes a major contribution not just to our understanding of Dickens's London but also to another conversation active in the bicentenary: what it means to be Dickensian. In *The Victorian City: Everyday Life in Dickens' London* Flanders historicizes the characterization in a rigorously detailed history of Dickens's London, arguing that "it was not until the twentieth century, as social conditions began to improve, that 'Dickensian' took on its dark tinge" (1). For his contemporaries, "Dickensian" might mean "comic . . . good cheer" or "merely life" (1). Alternately cheerful and dark, Dickens's London was full of life—as is the book itself; it is teeming with dozens of topics covering how Victorians traveled in (and out of) the city, who and what gets sold, performed, and policed on the street, as well as public health (industrial waste meets human waste) and urban planning issues. Dickens's characters wander in and out of the streets of Flanders's book. Here is Pecksniff traveling by heavy stage, there is Pleasant Riderhood's leaving shop (as well as a description of what a leaving shop is). That London is itself a character is a familiar idea in Dickens scholarship. Author David Mitchell explains in a short piece in *The Dickensian* that Dickens's "strongest character is London itself" (10). Flanders's book also makes use of greater access to the journalism to show how Dickens was thinking about and through the city on multiple levels: in his fiction, in his journalism, and as a citizen.

There is both an incredible festivity and an aching sorrow in Flanders's account. Chapters on street performance and street theater, ranging from the insanely elaborate funeral for Wellington to spontaneous animal shows, add a new dimension to understanding the role of theatricality in the development of Dickens's imagination. One understands the anger that fuels some of Dickens's sharpest writing when learning that the government's response to the 1831 Cholera epidemic was a Day of Fasting and Humiliation (as some noted, what good would it do for the starving to fast?). The evolution of government responsibility for "maintaining the health of its citizens" (213) is in part due to the attention Dickens paid to these issues. Flanders concludes with Arthur Clennam and Little Dorrit descending the stairs of the church, newly married, and entering the "usual uproar" of the busy London street.

If Flanders's book provides a broad and deep consideration of Dickens's London, Helen Amy 's *The Street Children of Dickens's London* offers a more pared-down look at one of the groups we associate with Dickens: vulnerable children. Amy's book covers the many different populations involved in the lives of "street children," from the children themselves (laborers, entertainers, prostitutes, caretakers) to the investigative journalists and the "charitable" organizations that were involved in their care. With its significant selection of images and a section of brief biographies of the relevant actors, this would be useful reading for a high school or college class.

There are many cities in Dickens, from the four cities of the bicentenary conference to the cities considered in the Global Dickens section. The works this year also revealed new discoveries about Dickens's London. Ruth Richardson's *Dickens and the Workhouse: Oliver Twist and the London Poor* tells the story of the relatively recent discovery that Charles Dickens's childhood London residence, 10 Norfolk Street, was just down the road from the Cleveland Street Workhouse. This is a work of both detailed scholarship and advocacy; Richardson argues, persuasively, that the "old Workhouse in Cleveland Street should be recognized as a key source of inspiration for the most famous workhouse in the world: the one featured in *Oliver Twist*" (300). Despite being the only surviving Georgian workhouse in the London region, it was under the threat of demolition since the closing of the Middlesex Hospital to which it had become attached. There has been much speculation over the years about Dickens's source for the workhouse, but Richardson presents convincing evidence that shows "how closely *Oliver Twist* fits the regime at Cleveland Street." She also finds traces in Dickens's other writings that manifest his "careful observations concerning the life-cycles of shops" (264) in that neighborhood, from a pawnbroker's shop to the shop across the street from the workhouse run by a real man named Bill Sykes (301).

Richardson opens with the relatively unknown early years Dickens spent in London and "the unexplained silences about his family's association with the street" (3). While Dickens revealed little of his childhood directly, the "autobiographical fragment" he shared with Forster neglects any mention of the time on Norfolk Street, despite Dickens having lived there for two different periods, from 1815 to 1817 and 1829 to 1831. Certainly, the London location was not something to brag about. Richardson's careful analysis shows how this eastern part of Marylebone abutted the rough neighborhood of St. Giles, which kept it affordable for "marginally viable families like the Dickenses" (48) and artists (the Landseers and the Havells lived around the corner). Richardson tracks down important characters, such as John Dodd, who ran the corner grocery and served as the Dickenses' landlord during both their residences and who, himself, survived near bankruptcy (103). Dodd left "an unexpected gift from the past" (113) in a detailed inventory for 10 Norfolk Street listing the fixtures in the house. Richardson visited 10 Norfolk Street and "can report that quite a surprising proportion of the materials listed in the Schedule can still be found *in situ*" (113).

The role that this house and this neighborhood played in Dickens's self-fashioning is embodied in one item from the archive Richardson presents: Dickens's calling card from the period of his second residence on Norfolk Street. The card has his name and below that "Short Hand Writer," in a kind of calligraphic flourish foreshadowing the famous signature. Below his professional title is his address, and Norfolk Street is listed as Fitzroy Square, which "would have looked socially good to anyone who did not know the area too well" (189). The card shows the mixture of dissemblance, aspiration, and confidence that marks this period in Dickens's life. Richardson's work ends with an extended reading of *Oliver Twist* and provides an invaluable context for understanding all the very many things going on in this novel: social critique, topical reference, authorial self-fashioning, and reporting. It also conveys a convincing sense of the anger and injustice felt in response to the New Poor Law; Richardson argues that when you add to the Poor Law the Anatomy Act of 1832 which enabled paupers' bodies to be used for dis-section at medical schools, it became bracingly clear "that entering a workhouse was to become a kind of social death" (231). Richardson suggests that this was on Dickens's mind in his emphasizing the absence of Oliver's mother's body at the novel's conclusion: "there is no coffin in that tomb" (236). "It is part of the subtext of the novel," Richardson writes, "that the poor young woman who dies in its opening pages was being dissected while her son was being starved" (236). Dickens's time in Marylebone is also part of his subtext: "While the Marshalsea and the blacking factory are perfectly understandable silences, the omission of Marylebone, despite its focal importance in his own biography and that of his family, is altogether less explicable"(287). While Richardson's book does not provide that explanation, she provides a rich context for understanding the role of that location in Dickens's development.

Michael Allen, author of last year's *Charles Dickens and the Blacking Factory*, has an essay on a very specific question in Dickensian topography: where is Tom-all-alone's, the slum in *Bleak House* that is so metaphorically laden that its pre-cise location on a map has gone unanswered? Allen's "Locating Tom-all-alone's" emerges from his research into the business arrangements and personnel issues of Warren's Blacking Factory and of George Lamerte, whose father married Dick-ens's Aunt Mary (34–35). Lamerte was part of an extended German Jewish fam-ily, though George left that behind in marrying Dickens's aunt. Allen speculates that Dickens might have gone with George to see Henry Worms, a shopkeeper, in the dicey neighborhood of Fox Court (entered from Gray's Inn Lane), also men-tioned in Mayhew's *London Labour and the London Poor*, as well as in *Oliver Twist* and "On Duty with Inspector Field." Fox Court is what, Allen argues, is pic-tured in the famous Hablot K. Browne illustration. He provides a convincing read-ing of the "gibbeted black doll" hanging in that picture as being a common trade sign for marine stores; Worms had a marine store in Fox Court (42). Owners of such stores were often receivers of stolen goods, and indeed Worms appeared in the dock at The Old Bailey in 1823 (43). Allen's article follows Henry Worms's transportation and subsequent career of petty crime in Australia, with all sorts of Dickensian resonances with Fagin and Magwitch.

While Flanders's and Richardson's books were published for the bicentenary, Jeremy Tambling's "Introduction" to Ashgate's volume *Dickens and the City* provides a useful history of the long conversation about the role of the city in Dickens's life and writing. Tambling explains that "Dickens knew other cities," but also that "his writing of London is qualitatively different from any of the others" (xii). While Dickens is famously seen as the special correspondent for posterity, Tambling asks how Dickens's "presentation of the city is selective, and its reality is constructed" (xix), as well as how "London constructed Dickens" (xx). Tambling sees the "Dickensingly" (a word he prefers to Dickensian) city as "a text, as a place of multiple communications . . . which baffles narrative and enables other forms of narrative" (xxi).

Tambling notes the influence of German philosopher Walter Benjamin (1892–1940), specifically *The Arcades Project*, on Dickens studies. Two book-length studies, as well as several articles published this year (including one by Tambling, discussed below), explore this connection. In the introduction to Ashgate's *Dickens and the City* Tambling states that Benjamin sees in the nineteenth-century city "the triumph of urban capitalism . . . [and] 'modernity' in action" (xx). Or it could be a failure of the modern: Tambling emphasizes a fundamental unknowability at the heart of the city. There is similarly a Foucauldian lens on Dickens, in which the city is subject to "a double perception, which sees lives as laid open, and yet secret, as under the power of surveillance, and yet marked by forms of life which elude control" (xxii). Dickens, Tambling explains, saw "the city as prisonous" (xix). Tambling "loosely" categorizes work on the city in Dickens in three types: "those which treat London as a literal fact, and those which see it as a symbolic landscape, or series of landscapes: its river, its roads, its fog, its endless streets, perhaps as a Gothic landscape. There are those which regard the city as a text, readable or threatening unreadability. And there are those which, using Benjamin, see the city as the expression of modernity" (xxii).

Tambling's essay in *The Dickens Quarterly* is the latter. Locating his discussion in terms of both Baudelaire's and Benjamin's writings, Tambling defines modern as being "able to see both the historical and the new, and to be able to distinguish them" (197). "This double situation, of being able to see something, and not see it," Tambling argues, "is at the heart of Dickens" (200). His "Dickens, Benjamin and the City: The 'Object Riddled with Error,'" opens with an argument for using the word Dickensingly instead of Dickensian; part of what is hard to understand about the notion of "the Dickensian," a seemingly sure-footed adjective, is that "Dickens's novels become, increasingly, the record of encountering bafflement" (197). Examples of characters or places that manifest this bafflement are Pip, George Silverman, John Harmon, John Jasper, Esther Summerson, "Tom-all-alone's," and Jo. Tambling traces this phenomenon primarily through *Bleak House,* reading words like "unaccountable," "undistinguishable," and "unintelligible" as reflecting a Benjaminian alienation, "disallowing any reconciliation between the self and the world, and rendering all speech about the city an attempt to say something about the unintelligible" (205). Tambling reads Benjamin's "dialectical image" in the tension between past and present, Chancery and the world of Fashion, and then in "the boredom of the dandy" (Steerforth is an example), or Lady Dedlock's famous boredom. Benjamin writes in *The Arcades Project* that "boredom is the threshold to great deeds," and Tambling explains "it is never a single state, always anticipative. . . . To read it requires considering the dialectical image; it means confronting what there is as not single, but the object riddled with error" (211).

Julian Wolfreys's *Dickens's London: Perception, Subjectivity and Phenomenal Urban Multiplicity* is in deep conversation with Benjamin's *Arcades Project* (and, for a few pages, Tambling's reading of Benjamin, (Wolfreys 212–18). As such, it is both a challenging and innovative work of literary criticism. Dickens is "no mere, faithful copyist of the city," but rather, to use Benjamin's phrase from "Theses on the Philosophy of History," its "most astute materialist historiographer" (qtd. in 205). Wolfreys begins by asserting that "as soon as there is London, fiction, narrative, and storytelling take place" (xviii), drawing a rich (and humorous) parallel with the figure of *Hard Times*'s Josiah Bounderby, who "exists as a 'state of mind predicated on a fiction" (xix). What follows is both an argument about London and its unknowability. The book has "alternative contents" called "enargia" that run from A to X? and comprise a series of images and scenes (sketches might be more appropriate) of London from Dickens's own words. Some letters are more literal: K is for Krook's. Some are more metaphoric: H is for Heart, about St. Paul's Cathedral. As to why there is no Z, Wolfreys explains: "Dickens's London, like the list of entries one can only begin to imagine under such a title, never reaches an end, any more than Engels's imagined pedestrian" (xx). This sense of (serious) play is evident in other formal choices. There is no introduction—no one can "take in everything at once"—but "in lieu of an introduction" there is a chapter at the end, very much echoing Dickens's choice to provide a "Postscript in lieu of a Preface" at the end of *Our Mutual Friend*.

In this chapter, Wolfreys does not so much explain the text that has come before as offer a reflection on representation as "re-presentation." Wolfreys asks what Dickens's "critical engagement with, and re-presentation of, London" can mean, period, and mean to us, as twenty-first century readers reading about a nineteenth-century city (204). He explains: "the topoanalysis is always that reading where place and subject are read in relation to one another, as place becomes meaningful and, in turn, determines subjectivity and, often, the meaning of being, and what it means to dwell" (204)—and to lose oneself—in the city.

Gillian Piggot treats the relationship between Dickens and Benjamin at length in her book *Dickens and Benjamin: Moments of Revelation, Fragments of Modernity*. In the foreword to this book, Michael Hollington refers to "the Benjamin approach to Dickens" (xv), and we see his point that "the two names have been increasingly invoked and linked by critics and theorists of literary and cultural studies, especially in connection with approaches to urban experience" (xiii).

Such an approach also allows Dickens to be viewed through "a European lens" (3). A key moment in this "connection" is Theodore Adorno's 1931 essay on *The Old Curiosity Shop*, which Piggott argues is "implicitly influenced by Benjamin's theory of allegory" (6). Despite their differences in terms of geography, historical moment, and genre, Piggot explains that the writers "share a common vision of modern existence" (1) and "a mutual concern with how consciousness is affected by industrial patterns of time and urban contexts." Piggot argues that "they wanted to understand the spiritual or religious crisis that resulted from an increasing emphasis upon the material world, material culture, commodities" (1). Both men "turn to memory in an attempt to redeem the lost content of experience" (7). For Benjamin this is Proust, and for Dickens, *David Copperfield*.

Piggot expands on Hollington's famous essay "Dickens the Flâneur," as well as on Peter Ackroyd's sense of Dickens's keen relationship to the city's "state of flux, heterogeneity, complexity and energy" (8) as she locates Dickens within Benjamin's mixture of despair at the "fallen world of modern capitalism" (14) with "present hope for a different future" (14). "Dickens's tendency to show both an extraordinary excitement and welcoming of modernity as well as his regret and fear about the loss it involved, is," she writes, "echoed in Benjamin" (207). Piggot suggests that where we have traditionally seen the Dickens of *The Old Curiosity Shop* influenced "by the Christian biblical and emblematic tradition, by Carlyle and Calvinism," we should see an "affinity" with the German Romantic/Judaic "comprehension of the material/political world as an imperfect reality to be violently overcome" (15). Like Tambling's sense of the representation of bafflement in Dickens, Piggot explains that his characters experience "the urban in a way that anticipates Benjamin's 'theory'" of the new urban *chockerlebnis* (shock experience) (84–85). The "crowd" is emblematic of the urban, and in Dickens we have both the fearful crowd in *Barnaby Rudge* and the more threatening mob in *A Tale of Two Cities* (181). But Piggot, pace Benjamin, reads the crowd as a "dialectical image" "where past and present are brought together in a temporal montage" (186).

Ben Moore also views the city "as Benjamin proposes, as dialectical image" (348) in his essay, "'When I went to Lunnon town sirs': Transformation and the Threshold in the Dickensian City." Moore's notion of "threshold" is from Benjamin's *Arcades*, and he considers "the nature and function of the threshold . . . in Dickens's London" with special focus on *Great Expectations*. "Thresholds," Moore explains, are "places where transformation between opposing or contradictory states occurs" (336), and they are also productive of narrative (339). Noting that Pip's name is a palindrome (342), a kind of threshold idea in itself, Moore provides a few representative examples. The comic song "When I went to Lunnon town sirs" in chapter 15 of the novel "is positioned on the edge of language. . . . where the excess of nonsense over sense overwhelms comprehension" (338). In the passage where Pip has hidden the bread-and-butter down his leg to take to Magwitch on the marshes, Joe "marks his surprise" by, in Dickens's words, stopping "on the threshold of his bite." According to Moore, this is "a moment that contributes to producing the pervasive guilt" for which the novel is famous (339).

A quotation from Benjamin's *Arcades Project* serves as the epigraph for Hadas Elber-Aviram's "The Labyrinthine City: *Bleak House*'s Influence on *Perdido Street Station*," which looks at Dickens's influence on contemporary urban fantasy, particularly China Mieville's *Perdido Street Station*. Elber-Aviram uses Foucauldian concepts of the carceral and the heterotopia to draw parallels between *Bleak House*'s London and Mieville's "New Crobuzon." Urban fantasy, Elber-Aviram argues, is the inverse of urban realism, but notes that such realism "flirts with the fantastic in its representation of the city" creating "an unmistakably fantastic metropolis, but tethers it to 'a real city,'" (270).

Luke Thurston's *Literary Ghosts from the Victorians to Modernism: The Haunting Interval* is not necessarily a work about the city, but is very much about this idea of a threshold and the kinds of ideas that exceed the normal boundaries of "discursive narration" (5). Thurston's subject is ghosts, and he starts with an intriguing moment in literary critical history for Dickens studies. Near the end of his life, Gilles Deleuze takes as a reference point for his *Immanence: Une Vie* the scene in which Rogue Riderhood hovers between life and death in *Our Mutual Friend*. "The Dickensian text," Thurston explains, "plays host to a 'spark of life' . . . registered by the philosopher as a point of vitality *in excess of* a discursive structure, something precisely inconsistent with the sphere of narrative signification" (5). Dickens's musing on Riderhood's threshold state "opens a virtual or spectral space where reality itself becomes hypothetical, experimental, speculative" (13). This "spectral space" resists narration, and it emerges "as the primary source . . . of the incessant power and undying fascination of the ghost story" (7). For Thurston, the ghost is a "singular ontological manifestation on the edge of the void, in excess of consistent reality" (53).

While Thurston's work extends into Modernist writers, he reads *Our Mutual Friend*'s famous "Postscript: in Lieu of Preface" as well as Dickens's 1866 story "The Signalman" in the first chapters. The "Postscript" tells of the Staplehurst railway crash that puts both Dickens and the manuscript to *Our Mutual Friend* on death's door (32). Thurston sees "the suspension of the railway carriage on the verge of nothingness—it 'seemed impossibly balanced in the act of tilting" writes Dickens in a letter—[as] an uncanny figure for the suspension of narrative discourse at the point of apparition or anamorphic intertextuality" (33). In addition to the Staplehurst disaster, Thurston reads "The Signalman" in the context of the communication revolution reflected in the rise of the telegraph, as well as anticipating ways in which the story is "telephonic." As with the death of Riderhood, Thurston sees "something illegible" in the story's opening scene, "something fundamentally at odds with the narrative dimension as such" (36). This opens an "interval" or "deep trench" in the narrative's otherwise "flat discursivity" (37–38).

The illegible aspects of Dickens's final complete novel also interest Stephen James. His "Repetition, Rumination, Superstition: The Rituals of *Our Mutual Friend*" takes the sometimes criticized repetitive rhetoric of the novel and sees Dickens thinking about thinking, or a "proto-psychoanalytic understanding of how voluntary, compulsive, and self-perpetuating inclinations pattern and govern the workings of the mind" (217) in language or in Bradley's repetitive thoughts. (It would be interesting to have James and Joseph P. Jordan on panel together about *Our Mutual Friend.*) A similarly philosophical consideration of the working of the mind is found in Shale Preston's analysis of Scrooge as a Kierkegaardian "demonic" individual in his "Existential Scrooge: A Kierkegaardian reading of *A Christmas Carol*." While *A Christmas Carol* is not often subjected to rigorous analysis, Preston sees Scrooge as a perfect example of "the demonic" individuals who is "essentially in dread of the good and as a consequence close themselves off from freedom" (743). Scrooge's boyhood, Preston explains, is marked by a lack of love and of security that threatens to lead to a kind of non-being. His miserliness is a "neurotic coping mechanism" (745) for a profound death-anxiety. Christmas, then, is "not a time of joy but rather a catastrophic event which threatens to completely engulf him in non-being" (746). Preston sees the evening's dream-travels as a kind of panic attack. "The role of anxiety in *A Christmas Carol* is to awaken Scrooge to his being," according to Preston, and "by revealing death as a definite and meaningful eventuality, it forces Scrooge to acknowledge his freedom. In doing so, he finds faith "(750).

Explorations of the city, both on the streets and within one's mind, are in many ways also explorations of modernity, and this was a significant focus of scholarship in the bicentenary year. Some authors, such as Gillian Piggot, think Dickens's modernity is so pronounced that it makes us question the use of the adjective "Victorian" to describe him; other scholars, such as David Paroissien, remind us that 25 of Dickens's 58 years were not strictly *Victorian*. "In this respect," Paroissien writes, "Dickens's viewpoint remains very much that of Janus, a figure able to look both into the past and into the future" (9). Juliet John, the editor and author of the introduction to *Dickens and Modernity*, the *Essays and Studies* volume for 2012 brings together an "eclectic" (9) collection of essays especially devoted to Dickens. As such, some of the contributions to this volume are discussed in other sections. John recognizes Dickens's "consonance in the post-Victorian world" but wonders "how modern was Dickens?" (1).

It depends on which Dickens we explore, she suggests. In the centenary, the "cheery" Dickens of *Pickwick* and *A Christmas Carol* were celebrated; in the bicentenary, we recognize that "state of uncertainty and instability we associate with the nebulous but resonant concept of modernity" (3). Seeing Dickens through the lens of modernity also asks us to see him less as the great entertainer and more of a literary artist (7). But John also points out that Dickens would resist the distinction: "in Dickens, a communal, nostalgic, organic view of the world co-exists and indeed grows out of a very modern sense of instability, mobility and radical uncertainty" (15). If the Dickensian viewpoint is Janus-faced, it is appropriate to conclude this section with two pieces by distinguished Dickens scholars, one who starts with Dickens and looks forward and one who looks back. In "Dickens and the Circus of Modernity," Michael Hollington sees the circus "as a utopian alternative to modernity" (134). He looks at Dickens's interest in the circus in *Hard Times* as a paradigmatic alternative to a grim utilitarianism and locates it in a larger aesthetic context including Picasso and Spanish modernism, Ramon Gomez de la Serna's *El Circo* (1917) a book that, in the year's continuing interest in all things Benjamin, was reviewed by him (139), Charlie Chaplin, and Angela Carter's *Nights at the Circus*. In his essay "Dickens and Ben Jonson," Jeremy Tambling begins with Dickens's literal engagement with Jonson: his performance as Bobadill in Jonson's *Every Man in His Humour* in 1845. Tambling argues here that Dickens's connection to Jonson (in part through Charles Lamb) is an important one that sheds light on Dickens's relationship to the city, such as his interest in Bartholemew Fair, or to shared character-types, such as the Braggart, or to the theater as a form uniquely suited to capturing the often ambiguous energy of London. Dickens, like Jonson, had a "fascination with people's self-creation out of language" (25).

Dickens Adapted

In 2009, her annual review of Dickens studies, Shari Hodges Holt noted the prevalence and variety of Dickens adaptations from graphic novels to biofiction. For a writer who was almost immediately pirated, adapted, performed, and parodied, adaptations of Dickens's works on the page and on the stage have almost always been part of the Dickens world. "Almost from the beginning Dickens lost sovereignty over Dickens," John Glavin explains, "to his considerable chagrin but to the world's profit" (xxii). This is fittingly, then, another of the Ashgate *Library*'s main topics, and Glavin is the editor and author of the introductory essay for *Dickens Adapted*. Unlike the other volumes in the series, *Dickens Adapted* is, understandably, comprised of recent works (the oldest is from 1996), reflecting both technological advancements (large and small screen are two of the categories) but also the arrival of this as a field of study in itself: "Adaptation Studies." Thomas Leitch's opening critical piece observes, as Glavin explains, "in the last two decades adaptation studies have finally broken through the corseting, hitherto dominant, metric of fidelity" (xv). Without the burden of mimesis, Glavin argues, "adaptation studies have begun routinely to generate analyses not only of intellectual distinction but even of surprise" (xv). Film, television, theater, and fiction, such as the novels *Jack Maggs* or *Mister Pip*, emphasize "what is new and original . . . not merely echo" (xvi).

Glavin humorously asks, "have I talked myself out of an introduction?" (xvii), when he claims that we don't "read Dickens differently, see the books in a new

light, because of these later achievements" (xvii). Shari Hodges Holt would dis-
agree, remarking in the "Dickens on Broadway" panel discussion, "I would argue.
. . for the future, we take a more intertextual approach that incorporates the adaptations into the study of their original sources" (27). But Glavin's essay does ask,
"why is it Dickens, of all novelists writing English, who turns out to be for adapters the gift that keeps on giving? How and why did Dickens become an adaptation
bonanza?" (xviii). Glavin uses terms from archaeological restoration to make an
argument that adaptation is more like restoration than conservation: "conservation, or preservation, protects the older structure, stabilizing and maintaining its
integrity. Restoration reanimates the structure, transforming it so that it enters
the present in a robust and relevant way, thereby extending what might be well
termed its life" (xix).

It is particularly interesting in light of the bicentenary, not to mention the
Olympic and Jubilee year, to contemplate the relationship of both Dickens and
adaptation to the heritage industry. Dickens "is the nineteenth century's supreme
purveyor of nostalgia" (xxi). According to Glavin, "heritage seems to overlap
what Walter Benjamin invokes with his resonant term reproduction. I not only
inherit heritage, I can reproduce . . . it, as I desire" (xxii). Glavin does distinguish *Jack Maggs* and *Mister Pip* from other kinds of adaptations, using Harold
Bloom's formulation in *The Anxieties of Influence*: "they take on, they swerve
from—Bloom's formulation—they don't rejoice in, the original" (xxii–xxiii).
Adapters on the other hand "find identity explicitly through interdependence,
embracing affiliation" (xxiii). Glavin concludes with an arresting point—for millions, Dickens *is* the big and small screen Dickens: "the books may indeed remain
exemplary on the plane of the literary, but Dickens Adapted has now ascended
into myth" (xxiii).

While Adaptation Studies might generally be oriented toward the present, there
are still discoveries from the past. There were almost 100 films based on Dickens
during the Silent Period (1896–1927), according to Graham Petrie, and a "lost"
version of *Oliver Twist* was recently found in the Serbian Film Archive in Bel-
grade. In his essay, "A 1919 Hungarian Film of *Oliver Twist*," Petrie reviews
director Marton Garas's version (with Serbian intertitles). There were originally
six twelve-minute reels and, unfortunately, the two missing reels contain the key
scenes of Oliver asking for more and Sikes's murder of Nancy. Nevertheless,
Petrie argues, the film can be followed, with an interesting frame of a flashback to
a character reviewing a legal document. This explains "the reasons for Monks's
pursuit and persecution of Oliver—reasons not provided till a relatively late stage
of the novel and a technique employed elsewhere, to the best of my knowledge,
only in Alan Bleasdale's 2005 television version of the book" (32). Around the
same time, G. K. Chesterton was adapting Dickensian characters and themes in
his Father Brown mysteries. Ewa Kujawska-Lis's essay "Charles Dickens and
G. K. Chesterton—Admiration in Many Forms" gives flesh to our understanding
of Chesterton as "an ardent admirer" and scholar of Dickens, both in his *Charles*

Dickens (1906) and his *Appreciation and Criticisms of the Works of Charles Dickens* (1911), previously written as prefaces to the novels and believed to be "among the best ever written" (350). Kukawska-Lis reads "The Flying Stars" Father Brown mystery, showing how the mixture of humanitarian concerns and humor are adaptations of Dickens's themes.

Dickens's interest in the theater is well known, but Robert C. Hanna's guide to his amateur theatricals demonstrates just how deeply and consistently involved with the theater he was (something Simon Callow considers in his biography discussed below). Published in two parts in *The Dickensian*, Hanna's study provides a guide to 32 plays in which Dickens acted (or possibly acted), giving identification of the playwright, Dickens's role, and the performance date(s), location(s), and performance types. Plot summaries are also identified. In another two-part essay on Dickens's involvement in the theater, Marc D. Cohen explains "How Dickens Co-opted the British Theatrical Adaptation Industry in 1844." Cohen "builds on the work of Peter Bracher and H. Philip Bolton," as well as on the legal context of the 1830s and '40s in order to demonstrate how Dickens's exerted "control over the unpreventable theatrical adaptation of his books on the London stage in 1844." The key year is 1844 because that is when Dickens started authorizing adaptations (127). Cohen argues that "Charles Dickens was a much more ingenious and active defender of his literary works from would-be 'pirates' than previously known" (126).

In 1838, Dickens was feeling particularly frustrated. Cohen explains how Dickens, anticipating the piracy of *Oliver Twist*, offered Frederick Yates at the Adelphi Theatre to adapt it himself. This went against his principle that the novels should not be adapted. Yates instead "opened an unauthorized adaptation of *Nicholas Nickleby* at the Adelphi" (130). Theater managers were friendly with Dickens but under no obligation to negotiate with him. "This, Dickens must have realized, would have to change" and his solution, according to Cohen, "was to create a commodity—authorized adaptations—that he could grant like a royal patent to agreeable managers" (133). When Yates died in 1842, Dickens saw an opportunity to work with Edward Stirling, a playwright who "showed relative fidelity to the original narratives" (136). While he didn't get any money, with the 1844 *A Christmas Carol* "Dickens achieved his first major victory in his project to co-opt the major players in the Dickens adaptation industry of Britain" (138). A victory meant that he received credit for the play's source material, the play was not produced until the narrative was published in full, the play had fidelity to the book, and this supported production came out first. Dickens "had managed to lower the metaphorical pirate flag of the Adelphi Theatre" (138). Dickens would go on to work with additional producers and directors and also to authorize more adaptations, including dramatizations of *The Chimes* and of *The Cricket on the Hearth*, which was so popular that "at one point in January 1846 there were at least seventeen versions of this tale playing simultaneously in the metropolis" (246).

Joss Marsh and Carrie Sickmann provide a thorough account of a "genuine revolution in theatre history and to the Dickens 'adaptation industry'" (151) in their essay "The Oliver! Phenomenon; or, 'Please, sir, we want more and more!' They suggest that the first "monster" musical continues to dominate in part because of its "invitation to tourism, its celebration of Britishness and its remembrance of the Second World War" (163). Paradoxically given the original text's representation of the city, "Oliver!" is a 'love song to London' (164), with a set "so spectacular" that, as one critic remarked, "you come out humming the sets" (161). In addition to an account of the continued popularity of the musical, the essay tells the rather Dickensian story of creator Lionel Bart, the "Cockney Pied Piper" who "burst on to the London stage in 1960 with the full force of new freedoms behind it . . . the freedom to say to life and society, 'Please, sir, I want some more'" (158).

Appropriation is a more apt term than adaptation for Neo-Victorian Studies, though both suggest a fluid, active engagement with Victorian culture. A special issue on Dickens of *Neo-Victorian Studies* originated in a bicentenary conference at the University of Portsmouth (the city of Dickens's birth). Called "The Other Dickens," the resulting collection focuses on "those aspects of Dickens's life and work that have been the subject of recent revision, reappraisal, and transformation." As Charotte Boyce and Elodie Rousselot explain, this perfectly suits a neo-Victorianism that "conveys the idea of celebrating while contesting, of looking back while moving forward" (2). If an ongoing question of the bicentenary has been "what is Dickensian," neo-Victorianism sees that signifier as both "an eminently knowable and assimilable version of the 'Victorian'" and "mutable and mobile, capable of supporting contradictory representations" (3).

While each article in this special issue could find its way into other sections (childhood, disability, the bicentenary), I will treat them together here in order to show the range of Neo-Victorian Studies and the rich product of the collision between "Dickensian commemoration and neo-Victorian nostalgia" (10). Lillian Nayder, author of *The Other Dickens* (2010), turns to biofiction with "Tangible Typography," which is an excerpt from a forthcoming novel, *Harriet and Letitia*, about the friendship of Letitia Austin, Dickens's younger sister, and her sister-in-law Harriet Dickens, who was deserted by her husband, Dickens's brother Augustus (179). Harriet was blind and Nayder's fiction invites the reader to draw analogies between "Harriet's literal and Charles's metaphorical blindness" (10), as well as to learn about a moment when Dickens was thinking of publishing editions of his work for the blind. Dana Shiller's "The Pleasures and Limits of Dickensian Plot" locates contemporary postmodern, postcolonial revisions of *Great Expectations* in the ongoing question about Dickens's narrative structure. What is the stronger legacy of Dickens's novel: plot or randomness? Shiller uses Charles Palliser's *The Quincunx* (1989) and Lloyd Jones's *Mister Pip* (2006) to show one of the legacies of Dickens's two-ending novel is that "one narrative may take many forms" (100). Indeed, another essay in the issue also looks at the inheritance of *Great Expectations*. Amber K. Regis and Deborah Wynne's

"Miss Havisham's Dress: Materialising Dickens in Film Adaptations of *Great Expectations*" looks at the costuming of Miss Havisham in three films, David Lean's *Great Expectations* (1946), Billy Wilder's *Sunset Boulevard* (1950), and Alfonso Cuarón's *Great Expectations* (1998). The character of an aging woman "trapped in, and fixated on, the past," Regis and Wynne suggest, "lends herself to neo-Victorian interpretation because she embodies the idea of a visible commentary on the past" (36), specifically ideas about "the novel's portrayal of perverse and uncanny femininity" (35).

Elodie Rousselot's "*A Christmas Carol* and Global Economy: The Neo-Victorian Debt to the Nineteenth Century" considers Margaret Atwood's recent nonfiction book *Payback: Debt and the Shadow Side of Wealth* (2008), especially her final chapter in which she rewrites *A Christmas Carol* from "the perspective of financial and environmental disasters set in the early twenty-first century" (59). Atwood's Scrooge is visited by three "Spirits of Earth Day" who show him "the real cost of his indulgent lifestyle to the environment" (60). Rousselot asks both why Atwood would choose *A Christmas Carol* and what this choice might mean for understandings of the Victorian period. Appropriation and adaptation are, like the idea of heritage, "not history at all, but a version of the past made to best suit the needs of the present" (Boyce and Rousselot 5). It is just this question—how Dickens's posthumous fame speaks to "the apprehensions of our own cultural moment"—that Karen Laird takes up in her essay "The Posthumous Dickens: Commemorative Adaptations, 1870–2012." Laird looks at three moments—1870, 1912, and 2012—and explains that "as three generations of writers rewrote Dickens to suit their epoch's authorial ideal, Dickens's personae evolved from a benevolent patriarch to a restless, tormented, and sometimes vindictive genius" (13). This bicentenary period, Laird writes, "has been unique in mythologizing 'The Fallen Dickens'" (14).

Childhood

The strong association of Dickens and childhood has complicated the legacy of him as an artist, with some critics dismissing him as a children's author and others seeing the resulting sentimentalism as his Achilles' heel. But, as the works discussed here suggest, this continues to be a rich area for scholarly work. There are many aspects to the association between Dickens and childhood, from Dickens's own famous, and famously concealed, childhood to his representation of children and childhood in his writing (and thus his contribution to the bildungsroman genre) to his advocacy for children as the unique victims of social and personal injustice. Laura Peters's introductory essay for the Ashgate volume *Dickens and Childhood* covers the range of work in Dickens studies and locates Dickens's understanding of children in the context of what the Victorians understood by the term "child" (xiii). Dickens inherits a Romantic understanding of "childhood as a special spiritual state of innocence" (xiii) that is "in contrast to the grim, bleakness of the Calvinistic doctrine" (xiii). This is a complicated legacy, for concomitant with this Romantic idea is the "Noble Savage" as representing "the childhood state of man" (xiv). This enables a critique of capitalism (the system turns street children into urban savages) while also placing ideas about childhood at the center of British imperial ideology. "At the intersections of discourses on family, nation, race and empire," Peters explains, "the child provides a suggestive figure" (xviii). Peters notes how Dickens's own experience of childhood is tied up with the exotic, such as his devotion to *Robinson Crusoe* and the *The Arabian Nights*. While we have noted the role of his early reading in the preponderance of travel writing in his journals, there is a tension between the journeying and the desire to have all the places to which he has "never been . . . Damascus, and Bagdad, and Brobdingnag . . . Lilliput, and Laputa, and the Nile, and Abyssinia, and the Ganges, and the North Pole" be kept "intact" (xix).

Scholars find similar tensions expressed in Dickens's efforts on behalf of children, such as greater educational opportunity and limited working hours. Dickens representation of street children make visible the uncomfortable realities of poverty and illegitimacy; but his work famously celebrates the Victorian hearth as "a site of morality" (xvi), the kind of ideological investment that perpetuates structural violence. Though Dickens is associated with the family ideal, Peters points out that the critical conversation in Dickens Studies includes "transnormative" families that "exist in opposition to the 'natural' and 'complete' family of husband, wife and children" (xvii). "This body of work," she explains, "challenges the restrictive definitions of the family" (xvii). Critics also see in Dickens's "poignant and . . . powerful pathos" for the "solitary, vulnerable child" a fertile ground for work in disability studies (xxi), considered below.

Dickens's famous preface to the novel most associated with vulnerable children, *Oliver Twist*, explains what he sees as a deliberate departure from the overly romanticized pictures of criminal life typical of Newgate fiction in order to show instead its true squalor. But Oliver's superhuman resistance to the criminal life challenges Dickens's commitment to portraying its "miserable reality" (Wagner 69) In her essay "The Making of Criminal Children: Stealing Orphans from *Oliver Twist* to *A Little Princess*," Tamara S. Wagner argues that this "seeming incongruity" has been part of the novel's "literary legacy" (69). Wagner suggests that in addition to his suffering, however, Oliver also "prefigures the more active child criminals" of subsequent fiction (68). "As the novel alternately pinpoints and sidesteps the question of criminal responsibility," Wagner explains, "Oliver's immunity rears its head as a recurring problem" (70), but it also conveys an ambiguity that was central to Victorian discourses on endangered children (69–70). This is also true in the character of Jack Dawkins, or the "Artful Dodger," who is both a victimized child and, in Fagin's representation of his trial and his preference for adult clothing, a mini-adult masterfully and humorously in charge (72).

Wagner points out the ways in which Dickens's novel complicates notions of essential morality. Monks's inherent badness and Oliver's inherent goodness are complicated by their blood relation. Similarly, Fagin sees Oliver's middle-class good looks not as an inner purity but as a mask that can be strategically deployed, and thus Fagin is "able to identify and trade on the bourgeois culture that singularly fails to protect the vulnerable members of its society it is nonetheless so ready to sentimentalize" (76). If essential morality is questioned, it becomes harder to read the "dubiously attractive vitality" of other child thieves. Wagner's essay traces this legacy of *Twist* in Charlotte Yonge's *The Clever Woman of the Family* (1865) and Frances Hodgson Burnett's *A Little Princess* (1905). The former inherits *Twist*'s insistence on childhood innocence, victimized by an adult world, whereas Burnett's book implies, in keeping with other Edwardian works, that maybe children don't particularly need adults.

The final section of the *Dickens and Childhood* Ashgate volume is titled "The Child as a Theoretical Vehicle" (xi). One approach used in the study of Dickens's representation of childhood is psychoanalysis. Several works this year were interested in exploring trauma theory, and, while they begin here in the childhood section, they extend to readings of trauma outside of this focus on childhood/children. Indeed, one of Dickens's arguably most traumatic moments happens at the end of his life, with the Staplehurst disaster (discussed below). Madeleine Wood's "Whispers and Shadows: Traumatic Echoes in Paul Dombey's Life, Death, and Afterlife" is a psychoanalytic reading of the resulting trauma from the death of Fanny Dombey. According to Wood, her "death in the first chapter of the novel inscribes parental loss as a primal moment that is subsequently constituted through a series of differential repetitions," such as Paul's death, which she sees as a result of the "affective violence created by Dickens in this opening scene" (89). Wood builds on the work of French psychoanalyst Jean Laplanche, who "reconceptualized Freud's early trauma theory," emphasizing Freud's idea of *nachtraglichkeit* (translated by Laplanche as "afterwardsness"). This understanding makes "a trauma . . . always a *post*-traumatic disorder" (83) as well as productive for "a narratological analysis." In *Dombey and Son* Dickens "creates repetitive echoes that collectively point towards the fundamental familial conflicts" (84). Along the same lines, Carolyn W. de la L. Oulton's essay "'Shall memory be the only thing to die?': Fictions of Childhood in Dickens and Jerome K. Jerome" suggests that it is only in the retelling of one's childhood after the fact and through fiction that such experience gains importance. She makes this point through a comparison of *David Copperfield* and the autobiographical fragment sent to Forster with Jerome's *Paul Kelver* (1902). Jerome, who was 11 at the time of Dickens's death, was "strongly influenced by the myth Dickens himself had largely created, of the special intimacy existing between him and his readers" (112).

Another essay that looks at the narrative implications of trauma is Jerome Meckier's "Twists in *Oliver Twist*." While it is famously a novel of many twists, Meckier looks at one in particular, the surprising recovery of Rose Maylie from her "withering" (116) illness. In restoring Rose rather than letting her die, Dickens, Meckier argues, "in effect postponed his emergence as a full-fledged realist from June 1838, the date for installment 15, until 30 Jan 1841, when, in installment 39 of *The Old Curiosity Shop*, he killed Little Nell" (116). Dickens's choice to let Rose live has complex explanations (he kills Nancy because he could not kill Rose or save Mary Hogarth) and simple explanations ("he flinched" 121). Meckier puts this decision in the context of the multiple traumas Dickens was "facing through print" (122). At the same time as Mary Hogarth's sudden death, Dickens is writing the part of *Pickwick* about the Fleet prison, a section that carries intimations of a buried secret about the Marshalsea. Kay Young, too, is interested in trauma: the trauma of being "born a motherless child" (234). In her "'Wounded by Mystery': Dickens and Attachment Theory," Young looks at Esther's narrative in *Bleak House* to argue that Dickens foreshadows insights of Attachment Theory and psychoanalysis (234).

David Ellison's "The Ghost of Injuries Present in Dickens's *The Signalman*" extends the reading of trauma in Dickens's 1866 ghost story beyond the immediate context of the Staplehurst railway accident to include an older injury: the editorial struggle with Elizabeth Gaskell over his editing an early installment of *Cranford* and her death just five months after Staplehurst. Ellison begins by noting that trauma, like anachronism, is "a break in the mind's experience of time" (650) and that critics, since Edmund Wilson, have found "in trauma a skeleton key to unlock Dickens" (653). Ellison recaps the dispute between Dickens and Gaskell in which he changed the text Captain Brown was reading when he was killed by a train from his own *Pickwick* to Hood's *Poems*. In holding a serial installment, this is a scene not only about an industrial accident, but about new "industrial changes to literary production" (658). "The Stapleurst derailment (an experience linking Dickens with the train, death, the serialized literary commodity text, and a threat to identity)," Ellison argues, "recalled an intensified version of Gaskell's contested section of *Cranford*" (659).

Disability

Identity as both threatened and threatening is central to the works discussed here, which take the question of disability as at least one of the categories of their analysis. Gareth Cordery's "Remaking Miss Mowcher's Acquaintance" looks at the "grotesque eccentric" from *David Copperfield* (11), who was based on the real Mrs. Seymour Hill. Hill complained to Dickens that he made her seem like "some kind of procuress for Steerforth and his fellow roués" (11). By way of apology, Dickens made changes to her characterization, and this is where, according to Cordery, the critical consideration has remained. Cordery, however, wants to see Mowcher, "itinerant hairdresser and cosmetician," and

her non-normative body as a "site for examining issues of gender and domesticity" (19). Seeing her in a new light allows her character to express "her and
David's hidden and forbidden sexual desires" (20), something not generally
available to disabled characters. While the text and illustrations increasingly
associate Mowcher with the hearth, she also can work and move about the city.
As she violates separate spheres, she raises the question, "does one have to be
disabled in order to inhabit both spheres simultaneously?" (27). Ellison notes at
the end that Dickens's "heroic apology to Mrs. Hill"—making Mowcher instrumental in seizing Littimer at the end of the novel—can also be read as making
her an effective instrument of the state, and less subversive than she might otherwise be (29).

  Just as Cordery argues that Mowcher's disability makes it both harder and easier
for her to cross boundaries, Helen Williams maintains that Quilp, the misshapen
villain of *The Old Curiosity Shop*, similarly can "resist the labels assigned to his
disability" by being a sexual being (124). Her essay "'Blank Epochs': Narratives
of Disability in Charles Dickens's *The Old Curiosity Shop* and Dinah Mulock
Craik's *John Halifax, Gentleman*" compares Dickens's work with Craik's as
"each work features a disabled narrator describing a disabled character" (115).
For both Craik and Dickens, Williams explains, a "realistic mode of representing disability did not exist" (124). Williams reminds us that this "inability to talk
realistically of disability" extended to medical writing. An article in the *British
Medical Journal* on dwarves published in 1891, used the character of Quilp as
an example to back up an "assertion that there was a link between 'the development of the intellectual, the moral, and the physical'" (125).) Williams concludes
that despite the attempts of such writers as Craik, Dickens, and [Wilkie] Collins,
the disabled figure in Victorian literature remained without an openly articulated,
autobiographical self" (125).

  Mary Ann O'Farrell's "Blindness Envy: Victorians in the Parlors of the Blind"
adds another complication to the discourse of disability as she looks at Victorians' attitudes towards the blind in terms of their intense relationship to material
culture. This has gone overlooked, O'Farrell suggests, because it is very easy to
abstract blindness, to read it as metaphorical or disembodied. But in fact, what
"Victorians envy in the imaginary blind" is an intense relation to things (513).
Blindness envy "bespeaks a craving for a more tactile and bodily . . . relation to
materiality" (514). O'Farrell reads, among other works, Dickens's *The Cricket
on the Hearth*. When toymaker Caleb Plummer gives his blind daughter a box of
eyeballs to put in sockets, O'Farrell suggests that Dickens is exploring the idea of
bodies as things—and things not being what they seem (518).

Things

This section looks at works that both take up "thing theory" itself as well as works that are interested in material objects in Dickens's writings. Juliet John, in her essay "Things, Words and the Meanings of Art," explains thing theory as an attempt to counter a widespread critical assumption of the 1980s and 90s that "things in Victorian literature, as products of an industrial marketplace, were most meaningfully understood as commodities" (116). Citing critics such as Bill Brown and Elaine Freedgood, John notes that "the assumption that things function simply as commodities in literary texts is no longer a widespread or even respectable critical position" (116). While it has long been a truism of Dickens scholarship that his people and things "are difficult to distinguish," the critical conversation now is shaped by the challenge of differentiating "in Dickens's world between artefacts and 'stuff', commodities and things, art and commerce" (128). Dickens "is fascinated by how things mean" and views them in a relational way, "never existing in isolation" (117). John describes the history of Laura Bridgman, the deaf, dumb, and blind girl, whose process of learning to read from objects to metal type to words is discussed by Dickens in *American Notes* and shows, according to John, "how a knowledge of things becomes a knowledge of a language system" (118–19). John interestingly considers the history of Dickens's celebrity as a "form of objectification and commodification in itself" (126), something several critics ponder in this bicentenary year, and argues that he was aware not only of "the mutually constitutive relationship between literary and material culture" (130) but also of his powerful role in it.

Clayton Carlyle Tarr's "Knots in Glass: Dickens and Omniscience from Boz to Bucket" puts a familiar conversation about Dickensian omniscience in a broader light as he historicizes Dickens's use of glass in his fiction. Tarr suggests that while we may have vilified omniscient narration in the wake of readings of panopticism in Victorian literature, "omniscience at the character level can benefit both narrative and social progress." (33). By "exploiting glass objects to achieve narrator-like access to private spaces," Tarr argues, "omniscience is not an ethereal authority reserved only for narrators, but rather can be a real prospect for both characters and perhaps the author himself" (33). Tarr's essay opens with a useful discussion of Alain-René Lesage's demon, Asmodeus, from *Le Diable Boiteux*, who can lift up rooftops and is a familiar figure in the nineteenth century for omniscience. Citing the importance of Isobel Armstrong's *Victorian Glassworlds* (2008), in which she claims, "The novel is founded on glass culture," Tarr takes us through the history from a window tax instituted in 1696, to 1833 Parliamentary votes to uphold the tax "resulting in significant protest that escalated into the Coldbath Riot" (36), and, of course, the 1851 Great Exhibition at the Crystal Palace. Tarr explains crown glass and the "bull's eye" (what results from where a blown glass globe attaches to the rod). The bull's eye distorts the image, thus serving as "an apt metaphor for how we see in Dickens's novels . . . as deceptive and illusory to willing imaginations" (45). Tarr charts an evolution in Dickens from the limited perspective of an embodied narrator to those more omniscient characters whose observations are facilitated by lanterns and skylights. The "roving reporter in *Sketches By Boz* is regulated by the physical limitations of embodied narration" (38), but by the time Dickens gets to *Bleak House* Bucket "achieves real-world Asmodean omniscience" when he looks through skylights and "uses the illuminating and focusing power of lanterns . . . to highlight his subjects while at the same time blinding them from any view of his corporeal presence" (52).

Jolene Zigarovich's look at Dickensian things focuses on the tombstone. Her "Epitaphic Representation in Dickens's *Our Mutual Friend*" notes that even though that novel is all about death and includes a character named "Headstone," the tombstone has been "a largely neglected preoccupation of Dickens's later novels" (141). Zigarovich provides multiple contexts, such as Dickens's declining health, Wordsworth's "Essay upon Epitaphs" in which the poet "critically evaluates epitaphs and poetic practice" (143), and Dickens's own publication in *All the Year Round* of Collins's *The Woman in White* with its plot centered on a wrongly marked grave. As many of the works in this section do, this essay emphasizes the relationship between material objects and writing. Zigarovich "unpacks various forms of epitaphic rhetoric" (141), including both the novel's dedication to Sir James Emerson Tennent as "a memorial of friendship" and the narrator's "curious post-script," which invokes Dickens's (and the manuscript's) close brush with death in the Staplehurst railway disaster. "Dickens admits that the train accident and the subsequent trauma," Zigarovich explains, "are signs of the recognition of his mortality, of his own impending epitaph that reads 'The End'" (161). *Our Mutual Friend* "takes the epitaph for its thematic condition: it at once articulates and disarticulates, is about ends and the suspension of ends, about death and the preservation of life" (144).

Jay Clayton's essay "The Dickens Tape: Affect and Sound Reproduction in *The Chimes*" is a perfect bridge from thinking about things to thinking about affect as he thinks about sound *before* it could be turned into a material object. "In the absence of recordings," Clayton writes, "we must take the measure of Dickens's voice in other terms, find a different kind of tape to tie up the bundle of meanings and memories that sounds in his texts evoke" (20). Clayton reminds us that "until Edison's wax cylinders changed everything, sound was primarily a medium for communication, not for the preservation of the past" (20). Clayton puts his reading of *The Chimes* in the context of affect theory and explains affect as "comparatively unstructured, non-narrative and free-floating bodily intensities" that allow critics "to attend to emotional states without reinstating a feeling subject" (21–22). The bells in *The Chimes* "produce the *affect* of belonging, not more crisply defined emotions" (27).

Sentiment and Affect

While some of the work discussed here invokes affect theory explicitly, this baggy category encompasses the range of work done on Dickens's relation to the sentimental tradition, on his understanding and representation of emotion and ethics. Brad Fruhauff's "The Devil You Know: Sentimentalism and Gothic Threat in *The Pickwick Papers* and *The Old Curiosity Shop*" looks at what he sees as "two sides of a single intersubjective coin": sentimentalism and Gothic (77). If ethics is "a description of the self's relation to" an other, these two literary conventions can engage ethical questions of otherness" (77). Gothic moments in the texts seem to suggest that the "world is inhospitable to ethical action or goodness, while sentimental response counters this anxiety with a common hope precisely that ethical actions matter" (77). The "short, interpolated narratives" of *Pickwick*, Fruhauff suggests, draw from both traditions (78), whereas *The Old Curiosity Shop* "stages a confrontation between a sentimental protagonist and a grotesque Gothic villain" (81). Fruhauff posits that Dickens, in these early works, is using eighteenth-century genres to open "a crucial ethical field of intersubjectivity," and, as he continues to write, he uses them "to develop a more mature, realistic sentimentalism" (87).

Dickens's relationship to the sentimental tradition of the eighteenth century is the subject of Valerie Purton's book *Dickens and the Sentimental Tradition: Fielding, Richardson, Sterne, Goldsmith, Sheridan, Lamb*. Purton's work is an attempt to address what she perceives has been a dismissive attitude toward Dickens's novels as "sentimental" (xiii), hoping to "rehabilitate the adjective 'sentimental' as a useful critical concept" (xiv). In the way that Juliet John's *Dickens's Villains* (2001) and Sally Ledger's *Dickens and the Popular Radical Tradition* (2008) "reclaim melodrama by revealing its radical roots" (xviii), Purton's book "seeks to make a similar argument for at least some examples of sentimentalism" (xviii), seeing it as deployed "for a precise rhetorical and cultural purpose" (xvi). Purton provides a broad context of writings about sentiment to which Dickens would have had some access, from dramas of Richard Steele to a translation of Goethe's *The Sorrows of Young Werther* in Elizabeth Inchbald's *Farces*, "which he relished as a child and acted in as an adult" (6).

In a chapter on "Dickens and Nineteenth-Century Drama" Purton argues that "the safe confines of the sentimentalist tradition gave Dickens access to potentially deviant modes of vision. Creating on stage the heroes of *Not So Bad As We Seem* and *The Frozen Deep*, he acted out, in publicly acceptable form, subversive impulses which threatened to engulf him both as man and as writer" (75). *The Frozen Deep*, a "monument to sentimentalism" (83), was also a way of exploring his unhappiness as a married man. "Critical attacks on Dickens's sentimentality increased," such as George Henry Lewes's in the *Fortnightly Review*, in the second half of the century, "as the tenets of novelistic realism took hold" (152).

Rae Greiner's look at "Dickensian Sympathy," a chapter from her book *Sympathetic Realism in Nineteenth-Century British Fiction*, also begins in the eighteenth century with Adam Smith's *The Theory of Moral Sentiments* and suggests that "Dickens's rowdy cast of characters, with their trademark noise and extravagance, seem . . . inimical to the rational, well-mannered sympathy Smith prescribes, an up-tempo riot to Smith's slow jam" (87). It is instead "Humean emotional contagion, vibrating unstoppably from one body to the next," that would seem "to animate the typical Victorian text" (87). Greiner reads the struggle for sympathy with an other in the language, grammar, and syntax of Dickens's writing, specifically *Nicholas Nickleby*, *Little Dorrit*, and *Our Mutual Friend*, where "sympathy with the living meant dwelling in their sentences rather than in their skins" (89). But language often fails, for characters are "baulked" and unable to express themselves. Greiner provides an impressive reading of Magwitch's famous "click in the throat" as an example of "that which the sympathetic imagination must make sense of once human language splinters into the otherwise meaningless noise of syllables torn apart" (96). Greiner also sees Dickens in the context of translation, particularly in terms of his representations of class, challenging our understanding of him as a realist transcriber of London life. Translation requires making sense of other characters' fragments of speech or unfinished sentences.

The question of how Dickens handles the representation of emotion has always been an aspect of Dickens Studies. Nancy Engbretsten Lind's "'The Mind of the Heart': Mr Dick's Percipience" makes the point that "Dickens has more realistic handicapped characters in his fiction than any other writer of his period" (18). Dickens's representation of Mr. Dick as an "empath" (20) illustrates his "awareness of people 'outside' the social norm and, in their extraordinary knowingness, perhaps beyond it" (20). Maria Bachman, however, begins with Eliot's (in)famous contention that Dickens represented the external rather than the inner life. "Affective Economies and Charles Dickens's *The Haunted Man*" looks at Dickens's representation of emotion in the context of sociologist Marcel Mauss's "theory of the gift economy" (53) in order to show how Dickens could see his books as both a commodity and as "gifts [that] had an emotional value over and above their commercial value" (53). According to Bachman, Dickens indicates that characters in *The Haunted Man* are shown to "catch" emotions from one another, something "only recently . . . scientifically proven with discovery of 'mirror neurons' and the concept of neural WiFi" (55). Dickens "anticipates the findings of modern neuroscience by treating the mind as 'embodied'—our mind is shaped by our bodies and by the types of perceptual experiences we have as we navigate through and interact with the surrounding world" (60).

Shu Fang Lai looks at "Dickens and Emotions" in the context of the period's interest in physiognomy and phrenology, building on studies such as Michael Hollington's survey of "physiognomics" in *Oliver Twist* (89). We know that Dickens would have been familiar with *Human Physiology* by Dr. John Elliotson, who was Dickens's close friend and family doctor. Shu Fang Lai looks here at "cultural sources of emotion yet to be taken into account" (90), such as artist Charles Le Brun and his 1734 book, *A Method to Learn to Design the Passions*, the influence of which we see in the expressive eyebrows of characters like Jaggers and Matthew Bagnet and the work of scientist Sir Charles Bell, a "leading scientific authority on the nervous system" (93). While we haven't traditionally seen Dickens as a great reader of scientific texts of the period, he would, as John Drew argued in his piece above, have had great familiarity with the work reviewed or mentioned in his journals. Though Dickens was dead at the time of Darwin's 1872 publication of *The Expression of Emotions in Man and Animals*, "Dickens's treatment of emotional expressions, such as his early human-beast analogies, parallels Darwin's thinking" (95). Indeed, Darwin himself mentions the pursuit of Sikes in *Oliver Twist*. Darwin was likely influenced by a French naturalist, Alphonse Toussenel, whose work was reviewed in *Household Words* and *All the Year Round*. Lai argues that the "increased emotional complexity of later characters bears witness to Dickens's intellectual development and awareness of studies of emotion in the art and science of the time" (97).

The particular—and particularly complicated—emotion of resentment forms the subject of Joseph Litvak's engaging essay "Unctuous: Resentment in *David Copperfield*." Taking on the fluid class position of both Dickens and David, Litvak looks at the weird dynamics that stem from the middle-class master "disavowing the servant" so as to disavow "the elasticity of Service as a category, lest he find himself included in it" (133). This is not a situation unique to *David Copperfield*; for, as Litvak notes, "almost every Victorian novel is a Cinderella story" (133). But David is a "resentment-machine" (132), and Litvak explores his complicated relationship with Uriah Heep, who performs a "servant-like masquerade" as a "grotesque parody of David's—and Dickens's—winning ways" (134).

Dickens and/as the Public

In a sample of the critical whiplash that only Dickens 2012 can engender, we move from inside David's head to the Victorian public sphere. In critical overviews this year, such as *The Oxford History of the Novel in English* and *The Cambridge History of the English Novel*, Dickens is as much a public figure at the crossroads of Victorian politics as he is a novelist. Lyn Pykett's chapter in *The Oxford History of the Novel in English*, "Charles Dickens: The Novelist as Public Figure," quotes Dickens's remarks to the Administrative Reform Society in June 1855 that he was "one who lives by Literature, who is content to do his public service through Literature" (202). But, as Pykett's overview of Dickens's career illustrates, he was always deeply involved with his public. The "wider mission as a social critic" was not only sustained throughout his career, but "the development of his narrative technique is interwoven with his exploration and exposure of the political situation in Britain" (187). Pykett makes the important point that to create as Dickens did—through collaboration, in his periodical publications as reporter, writer, and editor, in his "creative appropriation of the forms of popular culture"—was "to write in public" (189). Addressing the question about how effective Dickens was in the political arena, Pykett writes that "Dickens may not have fully understood Political Economy and his targets were occasionally inaccurate or anachronistic, but his conviction that the system did not work for the poor and that it was based on a repugnant view of human nature was persuasive and taken up by influential voices" (193).

In "Dickens, Charlotte Brontë, Gaskell: Politics and its Limits," a chapter in *The Cambridge History of the English Novel*, Amanda Anderson looks at the "political novel," those novels that "treat conditions and crises occasioned by the Industrial Revolution in Britain" (341). Anderson notes that one "consistent feature" of treatments of the political novel is to see "competing narrative foci," such as romantic storylines, as "political evasion that is fundamentally conservative in nature" (342). This point of view, Anderson argues, undervalues non-activist politics by identifying those politics "with quietist forms of economic liberalism or bourgeois modernity" (342). By focusing on the argument "advanced by the narrator and as engaged in by the characters," Anderson shows how *Hard Times* and *Bleak House* resist romantic plot closure and keep alive political questions (343).

We know *Hard Times* to be a critique of utilitarianism; Anderson argues, however, that it is, in its own way, "as formally innovative as *Bleak House*." More like a fable, lacking a typical hero or heroine, and not ending in marriage, this novel suggests that "established novelistic conventions cannot accommodate self-conscious critique of ideology" (343). Through the tortured and only partially redeemed figure of Louisa, the novel is "pulled away from simple moralizing to a more complex understanding of the gap between social critique and moral aspiration" (344). Dickens's "critique of political ideology is also centrally about what lies beyond the horizon of any political or sociological framework" (345). Anderson's reading of *Bleak House* also emphasizes the political significance of its unresolvability. Much of the scholarship on the novel tries to figure out which voice in the famous dual narration emerges as the main voice. But Anderson thinks the point is instead "whether any mediation is possible or desirable between the systemic perspective—the totalizing critique of power, society, and institutions—and the perspective of the embedded social actor" (345). In this reading, the novel becomes "a complex formal enactment of the estranging but also enabling consequences of attempting to think the moral and the sociological perspectives in relation to one another" (346). As such, "it indirectly makes the case for enlisting narrative's formal resources as a way to move beyond limiting conceptual approaches to poverty and social injustice" (346).

Daniel Siegel's chapter "Help Wanting: The Exhaustion of a Dickensian Ideal," in his book *Charity and Condescension: Victorian Literature and the Dilemmas of Philanthropy*, charts a transformation in Dickens's famous concern for the connection between rich and poor. Siegel suggests that the "general benevolence" of his earlier writings gives way to stories that include the revelation of "shared personal histories between rich and poor" that demand some kind of restitution (39). Siegal starts with the "haunted philanthropy" of *Dombey and Son*, *The Haunted Man*, and *Bleak House* and concludes with a thorough reading of *Little Dorrit*. Ultimately, Siegel argues, "restitution presents a serious challenge to the entire philanthropic enterprise" by showing "that philanthropy was an insufficient means of maintaining the social welfare" (39).

The threat to public order of dueling is the concern of David Parker's "Duelling and Public Order in *The Pickwick Papers*." In 1823, four years before the action of *Pickwick* opens, and 13 years before the first number is published, the Association for the Suppression of Duelling is launched (214). *Pickwick* also unfolds in an era which saw the Spa Fields Riot (1816), Peterloo (1819), the "Captain Swing" riots (1830), and the killing of unionized miners in Merthyr Tydfil in 1831. Parker looks at the threatened duel in *Pickwick* in the context of dueling laws and of popular opinion in the 1840s. While there "was general agreement in the House that the custom of dueling was barbarous," Prime Minister Sir Robert Peel thought that "growing public repugnance at the custom was better calculated to put an end to it than legislation" (213–14). Parker looks at the subtext of class warfare here between Mr. Nupkins, defender of "the hegemony of the gentry" and Pickwick, "aspiring Cockney" (226).

Threats to the public order represented by financial speculation are the topic of Silvana Collela's "The Ticklish Topic: Finance and Ideology in *Little Dorrit*." What, Collela asks, does it really look like to "represent" finance? This essay takes us through the backstory to Merdle's speculation: John Sadlier, an Irish MP and financier "whose ruinous speculations were so disastrous that he committed suicide" (7). Given the obvious perils, Collela remarks on the "astonishing resilience of speculation as a popular dream" (9). So while you have Merdle's fall, you also have Pancks's "rise from 'money-grabber' to 'fortune-teller,' speculator, and finally 'partner'" (12). *Little Dorrit* both treats "enormous financial speculations," and makes the small speculator (Pancks) "restored to the centre of the picture" (13). Collela argues that the truth lies somewhere in the middle: "between explicit fantasies and cynical realism lie the more nuanced symbolizations of the economic sphere that are at play in the financial plot and in the story of Arthur Clennam's professional development" (20). Collela concludes that despite our widely held beliefs about Dickens's attitudes towards speculation manifest in *Little Dorrit*, "crucial distinctions between good and bad capitalism can and ought to be drawn" (20).

Biography and Biographical Criticism

There was as much interest in Dickens's private life in 2012 as there was in his public life and this section reviews an eclectic collection of letters, biographies, and works of biographical criticism. Michael Hollington's review in *The Dickensian* of Jenny Hartley's *Selected Letters* suggests that this volume is "destined . . . to become a fixture . . . which everyone, professional and amateur Dickens lover alike, will need to have" (250), and I can only agree. Any Dickens scholar unlucky enough to have to use a college library without the Pilgrim *Letters* knows what back-breaking work it is to secure them through interlibrary loan. Hartley's volume is only a selection: 450 from over 14,000 of the Pilgrim letters (and when one remembers that he burnt almost everything in 1860, "shocked by the misuse of private letters of public men," it boggles the mind). But her choices provide an excellent representation of the pivotal letters and remind us of what a fantastic letter-writer Dickens was. "Letter-writing," Hartley explains, "was an integral part of his writing life, and fortunately for us, the recipients of his letters did not share his habits of destruction" (viii). Hartley notes that the epistolary is "the genre of exuberance" as we see him firsthand as an "indefatigable" editor, an exasperated businessman, a warm friend, and an amateur theater manager (ix). Because "Dickens is primarily known and loved as a novelist," Hartley explains, letters pertaining to the novels have priority (ix). Hartley's "introduction" carefully sets out how each letter is a performance "finely calibrated to the nature of its recipient" (xii). "What the letters give us, then, is not so much inner Dickens as Dickens in motion" (xiii). When Hartley describes, at the end of her introduction, what Dickens these letters represent, it sounds like a table of contents from *Household Words*: "they are also Dickens on Scotland, Paris and Venice; Dickens on child exploitation, Ragged Schools, and soup kitchens; Dickens on the Great Exhibition, women smoking, and dresses for reformed prostitutes; Dickens on ravens, waistcoats, and recipes for punch; Dickens on mesmerism and dreams, and on terrible acting and wonderful children's parties. More than all these, what these letters revive for us is the sheer energy of being Dickens" (xx).

The biographies in 2012 each seemed to have a particular focus—the affair, the theater, the women in his life, his children—rather than attempt to tell the whole story. Michael Slater, who did tell the whole story in his 2009 *Charles Dickens*, here focuses on the now 150-year interest in whether he did or did not have an affair with Ellen Ternan. *The Great Charles Dickens Scandal* chronicles the changing public understanding of Dickens's domestic crisis, and with it Slater shows changes over the century in the attitude towards private lives and how celebrity and the media shape those attitudes. The issue of his affair had more to do with selling papers to an always interested public than any particular question in Dickens studies. This started to change, in part, because two leading intellectuals, George Orwell and Edmund Wilson, wrote essays about Dickens, and Wilson's was particularly interested in the biography (110–11). We still care about this, Slater suggests, because Dickens "is our great national celebrant of hearth, home and family love" (3). So to some degree, this is a bed that Dickens made for himself. But Slater's book also points out ways that the cover-up itself—not only the work of Dickens and his friends in his own life, but in subsequent years by his son or various caretakers of his legacy at the Dickens Fellowship—has taken on a life of its own and fed rather than squelched the scandal.

Slater's book contains two appendices that illustrate the perfect storm of rationalization, self-fashioning, misdirection, and innuendo that characterize this long story. One is Dickens's "Personal Statement" of 1858 that was for public consumption. The other is the "Violated Letter," which he made available to his trusted readings manager Arthur Smith to circulate among, in Dickens's words, "any one who wishes to do me right, or who may have been misled into doing me wrong" (13). While it is beyond the scope of this review to provide the details of the scandal's hearsay fest (indeed, much of the material Slater covers—and clarifies—seems like a century-long game of telephone, where stories are told and retold, often uncited and significantly altered), there are notable moments. By virtue of her long life (she died in her ninetieth year in 1917) and her front-row seat, Georgina Hogarth, the "chief priestess of his cult," and her nephew, Dickens's lawyer son (Henry), maintained a wall of silence that both obscured and contributed to the scandal for over half a century. But it became a much bigger story in the twentieth century, when a *Daily Express* journalist named Carl Eric Bechhofer Roberts wrote a fictionalized account of Dickens's life *This Side Idolatry* (1928). Bechhofer Roberts claimed that he had to write his biography of Dickens as a novel because of a lack of cooperation on the part of the Dickens family (57). Orwell called Hugh Kingsmill's *The Sentimental Journey: A Life of Charles Dickens* (1934) both a "a brilliant book" and "the case for the prosecution" (80). Other figures include alleged accounts provided by Dickens's daughter Kate. Over the years, the scandal was characterized by a tension between new revelations (aided by increased access to letters), some by Dickens's daughter Kate, and the stance of certain standard-bearers like *The Dickensian* to present "Ellen's relationship with Dickens as pure and innocent" (139). Slater concludes by acknowledging that while some of the questions are "unlikely now ever to be resolved" the "frisson and fascination we find in this topic" are "destined to remain with us indefinitely" (191).

I felt grateful for Simon Callow's opening sentence in his *Charles Dickens and the Great Theatre of the World*: "There is a non-stop tsunami of scholarly studies of Dickens from every possible angle" (vii). But Callow's book provides a change, written from the viewpoint of both a fan and as a theater insider, with snappy observations (when Dickens beholds Niagara Falls, "At last: a phenomenon to match him," 121) and insightful summaries: *American Notes* is "a curious mixture of vivid reporting, hard analysis, and personal irritation" (130). Callow's interest is in Dickens's life in the theater, but also, as the title suggests, in the theatrical broadly defined. Even the Blacking Factory episode can be seen as performance: "He was learning to wear a mask, to conceal his inner life, to rise above his circumstances. He had always found acting fun; now he had to learn to do it in deadly earnest. This was character-building, in the most literal sense of the phrase" (21). Some of the scholarship discussed above emphasizes Dickens's collaboration (in his journals) or his fascination with street life (in the *Sketches* or *Pickwick*). Callow sees these as Dickens's sense of the "world-as-theatre, of the charivari, the endless parade, each man in his time playing many parts, absurd, grotesque, battered, damaged, ridiculous, briefly glorious. It is a carnival view of life, in which we are all, like members of a theater company, dependent on each other, all limbs of one body, all human, and therefore all flawed, all beautiful" (83). Callow convincingly sees the theater as an embodiment of Dickens's characteristic "restlessness and recklessness" (184) as well as his need for a "direct line to his readers" in the theater audience.

Callow's book provides a highly readable account of Dickens's varied involvement with the theater from the fateful cold that prevented him from trying out for a spot in the Covent Garden Theatre company to the many benefit performances to the Tavistock House theatricals. He provides an especially engaging account of the transformation of this domestic space into a theater:

> Frustrated by the lack of depth in the room, he removed the bay windows and built a cabin in the garden outside the school-room window, to create what was in effect a thirty-foot stage. Each of the three settings—drawing room, Antarctic hut and, for the last act, cave from which ships in the harbor had to be visible—was individually painted on canvas by Stanfield, who, as well as being the most distinguished marine painter of his time and an RA, had earlier been the chief scene-painter at Drury Lane. (255)

Dickens's public readings were frowned on by his friend Forster and have often been considered in terms of his increasingly desperate financial needs or a quasi-pathological craving for contact with his readers. Callow, however, sees the readings as part and parcel of his life-long involvement in theater. He also gives an insider's sense of the toll that such performances had on Dickens physically: "Every reading was a helter-skelter: the nimbleness of mind, voice and heart needed to pass in seconds from towering emotion to skittishness, from ingénue to gargoyle, from sustained metaphor to verbal fireworks, is peculiarly exhausting, and though Dickens had great natural gifts as an actor, he lacked the steady experience of playing night after night, year in and year out, which alone builds stamina. He entirely relied, every time he performed, on nervous energy—on adrenalin, in fact, and adrenalin is a dangerous drug" (294–95). In a sentence that gestures to the subject of Slater's book, Callow concludes that "literature was his wife, the theatre was his mistress, and to the very end he was tempted to leave the one for the other" (341).

Callow's formulation of Dickens's twin passions does not include his children. Robert Gottlieb's *Great Expectations: The Sons and Daughters of Charles Dickens* provides a partial explanation. But only partial: one's sense from this biography is that Dickens was both a highly attentive and a sadly unsuccessful parent. As Gottlieb writes, "we may fault Dickens for his over-negative view of his boys, but no one can fault him for neglecting his responsibilities towards them: For twenty years he exhausted himself trying to strengthen their willpower and forward their careers" (38). One definitely gets a backstory for *Bleak House*'s Richard Carstone in Gottlieb's descriptions of Dickens's thwarted ambitions for his sons. The book is organized around each child separately; each one gets his/her own section both during the life and after the death of Dickens, with a speculative chapter on the birth of a child with Ellen Ternan. For scholars (like me) for whom the children, other than the oldest ones, have seemed like an indistinguishable mass, Gottlieb provides an extremely useful amount of detail. This is especially true on the emigration of the sons to India, Australia and Canada. One feels especially for Catherine on these plans, largely hatched after their separation, but "she was not consulted: The law gave fathers complete legal control over their children" (18).

The children can be seen, in some measure, as casualties of their father's enormous passions: for writing, for theater, for social reform—and for women. Robert Garnett takes up the latter obsession in his *Charles Dickens in Love*. Tellingly, Garnett does not discuss Catherine Hogarth at any length in this book; he focuses on Maria Beadnell, Mary Hogarth, and Ellen Ternan, with intermittent readings of relevant fictional creations (Agnes, Dora). Garnett's thesis is that "Dickens in love" is a contradiction, a figure trapped between the "virgin icon" (5) of Mary Hogarth and the actress/mistress Ellen. This contradiction is evident in other strains in Dickens's imagination, Garnett explains, "his love of order and fascination with violence often rub against each other in his fiction" (11). Garnett takes up in detail the question of a child born to Dickens and Ellen, and while it must be speculative, it has power (Slater's *Scandal* calls it the "Garnett hypothesis," 190). For this reader, Garnett's extended reading of the passionate devotion to Dickens of Annie Fields, the wife of his American friend and publisher James T. Fields, is the most riveting part of his book. Garnett characterizes their couple-crush on Dickens in a way that both makes incredibly clear the international power of Dickens's celebrity but also that emotions need to be historicized and that it is an act of imagination to understand emotion across a period of time.

While the following essays touch upon everything from shell-shock to Bulwer's bad marriage, they share an interest in Dickens's life and so are grouped together here. In "What Happened to Lucy Stroughill," William F. Long looks at an 1860 "Uncommercial Traveller" piece where the UT is reflecting on "a lost sweetheart" (313). Visiting his childhood home in "Dullborough," "he recalls playing with 'Lucy Green.'" Long speculates that Dickens is drawing on memories of Lucy Stroughill, "a next-door neighbor during his family's stay at Ordnance Terrace in Chatham from 1817 until 1821." Quoting Michael Slater, Long writes that these years "glowed in Dickens's memory as his Edenic period" (314). Like Garnett, Long emphasizes how significant these flirtations were to the young Dickens in shaping his imaginative development. In "Sketches of Boz," Malcolm Andrews reviews three little-known drawings of Dickens, one by John Leech, one by George Richmond, and one by Scottish artist William Allan, which was made during the famous dinner in his honor in Edinburgh "at the height of his early fame" (23). There has been much discussion above about the impact of Staplehurst on Dickens, and Catherine Aird adds to it by diagnosing Dickens with "Railway Spine Neurosis." Railway Spine Neurosis is what might be called shell-shock after WWI. Until the railway, Aird writes, "the effects of major disasters were seldom witnessed by the populace at large" (26). Aird thinks Dickens mainfested symptoms after Staplehurst and cites evidence from his children and Dolby, the manager of his last American tour (28).

Michael J. Flynn looks at a major disaster of another kind in his "Dickens, Rosina Bulwer Lytton, and the 'Guilt' of Literature and Art." Rosina and Bulwer Lytton had perhaps the worst marriage in the nineteenth century. Between *David Copperfield* (1849–50) and *Bleak House* (1852–53), Dickens was working closely with Bulwer on the Guild of Literature and Art, "the most ambitious and high-profile project in a long line of attempts to raise the social status of men of letters in mid-nineteenth-century England" (68). The Guild produced a May 16, 1851, performance of Bulwer's *Not So Bad as We Seem* at the Duke of Devonshire's; Queen Victoria and Prince Albert were in attendance. "Bulwer Lytton's stepping into the spotlight with the Guild theatricals—with the queen looking on, no less—gave Rosina a unique opportunity to humiliate him" (70), Flynn explains. Letters she wrote in the preceding week contain threats to attend "dressed as a beggar girl, distributing parodies" of the play which she titled *Even Worse than We Seem*. Fearing a scene, Inspector Charles Field of Scotland Yard and Dickens's trusty sub-editor and friend, W. H. Wills, ran interference. Flynn suggests that Dickens, who liked to be in control, joined Field and Wills in the intercepting/detaining of Rosina on that evening. Flynn's evidence is that until this time, Dickens was spared her considerable wrath. But about May 16, 1851, she turns on him virulently, and "vent[s] unmitigated spleen upon Dickens" (73) with whom she had no actual acquaintance before or after (according to Bulwer). "Rosina's lifelong loathing of Dickens," Flynn concludes, "would be explicable if he had been personally involved in her being detained" (74).

From the profane to the sacred, Gary L. Colledge's *God and Charles Dickens: Recovering the Christian Voice of a Classic Author* is written from a Christian perspective. Colledge revisits an angle on Dickens scholarship that was central to Chesterton's appreciation, as well as A. E. Dyson's and Angus Wilson's, but is marginalized today: most Dickens scholars and critics "played down the role of religion in the work and life of Dickens" (2). Colledge sees Dickens as a "reformer" rather than a "detractor" in his criticism of organized religion. He writes that "Dickens's Christian voice was sometimes subversive, often prophetic, and always passionate. And he can remind us in humorous, profound, simple, or uncomfortable ways what our faith should look like" (4–5).

Conclusion

In Marsh and Sickmann's review of the Oliver! phenomenon, they mention a "Spirit of London" exhibit at Madame Tussaud's. Tourists can have their pictures taken with the four most recognizable Victorian celebrities: Queen Victoria, Charles Dickens, the Dodger, and Fagin (165). I don't have to point out to anyone who made it this far in the review essay that three of those four have to do with Dickens (and the fourth would have liked to have had more to do with him than she did). After this year in Dickens's world (or at least the world of Dickens scholarship), I am not surprised by the depth of interest in Dickens. It seems both simplistic and correct to echo Archbishop Rowan Williams's idea that we are compelled by Dickens because he makes us understand what it means to be human (113). The irony here is that this year has only confirmed my suspicion that he had superhuman qualities, if only in the energy and imagination departments. Of course, given this aging body and his flaws as a spouse, his humanity was apparent enough. But it is the almost operatic tension between his complicated biography and his vast literary and cultural accomplishments that make you feel as if, in his writing, you can grasp a sense of the range of one's lived experience—even if only fleetingly. And fleetingly is the key word here. While I am aware enough to know that my love for Juliet John's argument against the methodological and intellectual imperialism of "complete knowledge" ("Global Dickens: A Response to John Jordan") is a rationalization of my inability to review *all* of Dickens scholarship in 2012, I do think that my confessed desire to see all of Dickens 2012 is just as suspect as Dickensian omniscience has been to Dickens scholars in recent years. I am not kidding when I say that on the day I was finishing up this review, my husband face-timed me from Whole Foods to show me carolers, decked out in Dickensian garb, singing in the bulk grains aisle, my youngest son brought home an assignment to do a story-board of Dickens's life, and a colleague e-mailed me to see Ralph Fiennes's *The Invisible Woman*. While Dickens would relish the many platforms through which he lives on, I cry Uncle.

Uncle Pumblechook, that is. Resistance is futile.

WORKS CITED

Aird, Catherine. "Dickens and Railway Spine Neurosis." *The Dickensian* 108.1 (2012): 25–28.

Allen, Michael. "Locating Tom-all-alone's." *Dickens Quarterly* 29.1(2012): 32–49.

Amy. Helen. *The Street Children of Dickens's London.* Gloucestershire, UK: Amberly, 2012.

Anderson, Amanda. "Dickens, Charlotte Brontë, Gaskell: Politics and its Limits." *The Cambridge History of the English Novel.* New York: Cambridge UP, 2012: 342–56.

Andrews, Malcolm. "Editorial." *The Dickensian* 108.1 (2012): 3.

———. "Sketches of Boz." *The Dickensian* 108.1 (2012): 22–24.

Bachman, Maria. "Affective Economies and Charles Dickens's *The Haunted Man.*" *Victorians: A Journal of Culture and Literature* 122 (Fall 2012): 51–61.

Bevin, Darren. "Mountain Thoroughfares: Charles Dickens and the Alps" *Dickens Quarterly* 29.2 (2012): 151–61.

Bills, Mark. Introduction and ed. *Dickens and the Artists.* New Haven: Yale UP, 2012. 1–7.

Bledsoe, Robert Terrell. *Dickens, Journalism, Music: Household Words and All the Year Round.* New York: Continuum Literary Studies, 2012.

Boborykina, Tatiana A. "Dickens in Post-Soviet Russia." *Dickens Studies Annual* 43 (2012): 233–60.

Bowen, John. "Ellen Ternan: Traductrice?" *Dickens Quarterly* 29.1 (2012): 81–82.

Boyce, Charlotte, and Elodie Rousselot. "The Other Dickens: Neo-Victorian Appropriation and Adaptation." *Neo-Victorian Studies* 5.2 (2012): 1–11.

Callow, Simon. *Charles Dickens and the Great Theatre of the World.* New York: HarperCollins, 2012.

———. "Playing Dickens." *The Dickensian* 108.1 (2012): 5–8.

Clayton, Jay. "The Dickens Tape: Affect and Sound Reproduction in *The Chimes.*" *Dickens and Modernity.* Ed. Juliet John. 19–40.

Cohen, Marc D. "How Dickens Co-opted the British Theatrical Adaptation Industry in 1844: Part 1" *The Dickensian* 108.2 (2012): 126–40.

———. "How Dickens Co-opted the British Theatrical Adaptation Industry in 1844: Part II." *The Dickensian* 108.3 (2012): 231–47.

Colledge, Gary L. *God and Charles Dickens: Recovering the Christian Voice of a Classic Author.* Grand Rapids, MI: Brazos, 2012.

Collela, Silvana. "The Ticklish Topic: Finance and Ideology in *Little Dorrit.*" *Victorians: A Journal of Culture and Literature* 122 (Fall 2012): 6–23.

Cordery, Gareth. "Remaking Miss Mowcher's Acquaintance." *Dickens Quarterly* 29.1 (2012): 11–31.

de la L. Oulton, Carolyn W. "'Shall memory be the only thing to die?': Fictions of Childhood in Dickens and Jerome K. Jerome." *Dickens Studies Annual* 43 (2012): 111–24.

Dickens, Charles. *The Selected Letters of Charles Dickens.* Ed. Jenny Hartley. New York: Oxford UP, 2012.

———. *Sketches of Young Gentlemen and Young Couples with Sketches of Young Ladies by Edward Caswall.* Ed. Paul Schlicke. New York: Oxford UP, 2012.

Drew, John. Introduction. *Charles Dickens and the Mid-Victorian Press, 1850–1870.* Edited by Hazel Mackenzie and Ben Winyard. Buckingham: U of Buckingham P, 2013.

———. "Texts, Paratexts and 'e-texts': The Poetics of Communication in Dickens's Journalism." *Dickens and Modernity.* Ed. Juliet John. 61–93.

———, Hazel Mackenzie, and Ben Winyard. "*Household Words,* Volume I March 30-September 21, 1850." *Dickens Quarterly* 29.1 (2012): 50–67.

Edwards, Gavin. "Dickens, Illiteracy and 'Writin Large'." *English* 61 (Spring 2012): 27–49.

Elber-Aviram, Hadas. "The Labyrinthine City: *Bleak House*'s Influence on *Perdido Street Station.*" *English* 61.234 (September 2012): 267–89.

Ellison, David. "The Ghost of Injuries Present in Dickens's *The Signalman.*" *Textual Practice,* 26.4, 649–665, DOI: 10.1080/0950236X.2012.696488.

Eslick, Mark. "Agnes Wickfield and Victorian Mariolatry. " *Victorians: A Journal of Culture and Literature* 122 (Fall 2012): 62–76.

Farrar, Aileen. "Charles Dickens and Hablot K. Browne: Cross-narrative Creation and Collaboration in *Bleak House.*" *Victorians: A Journal of Culture and Literature* 122 (Fall 2012): 36–50.

Flanders, Judith. *The Victorian City: Everyday Life in Dickens' London.* London: Atlantic Books, 2012.

Floyd, Stacy. "The Specter of Class: Revision, Hybrid Identity, and Passing in *Great Expectations.*" *Victorians: A Journal of Culture and Literature* 122 (Fall 2012): 100–14.

Flynn, Michael J. "Dickens, Rosina Bulwer Lytton, and the 'Guilt' of Literature and Art." *Dickens Quarterly* 29.1 (2012): 68–80.

Fruhauff, Brad. "The Devil You Know: Sentimentalism and Gothic Threat in *The Pickwick Papers* and *The Old Curiosity Shop.*" *Victorians: A Journal of Culture and Literature* 122 (Fall 2012): 77–88.

Furneaux, Holly. "Dickens, Sexuality and the Body; or, Clock Loving: Master Humphrey's Queer Objects of Desire." *Dickens and Modernity.* Ed. Juliet John. 41–60.

Garnett, Robert. *Charles Dickens in Love.* New York: Pegasus, 2012.

Glavin, John. Introduction. *Dickens Adapted.* Burlington, VT: Ashgate, 2012. xv–xxiv.

Gottlieb, Robert. *Great Expectations : The Sons and Daughters of Charles Dickens.* New York: Farrar, Straus and Giroux, 2012.

Greiner, Rae. *Sympathetic Realism in Nineteenth-Century British Fiction.* Baltimore: Johns Hopkins UP, 2012.

Griffith, Jane. "Such a Labyrinth of Streets: Serialization and the Gendered View of Urban Space in *Bleak House.*" *English* 61.234 (September 2012): 248–66.

Grossman, Jonathan H. *Charles Dickens's Networks: Public Transport and the Novel.* New York: Oxford UP, 2012.

———. "Dickens on Broadway: Future Dickens, Digital Dickens, Global Dickens—a Panel Discussion." Ed. Edward Guiliano. *Dickens Studies Annual* 43 (2012): 1–31.

Hanna, Robert C. "Selection Guide to Dickens's Amateur Theatricals—Part 2." *The Dickensian* 108.1(2012): 33–46.

———, ed. *Dickens's Uncollected Magazine and Newspaper Sketches As Originally Composed and Published 1833–1836.* New York: AMS, 2012.

Hardy, Pat. "Dickens and the Social Realists." *Dickens and the Artists.* Ed. Mark Bills. New Haven: Yale UP, 2012. 154–181.

Hartley, Jenny. Introduction. Ed. *The Selected Letters of Charles Dickens*. Ed. Jenny Hartley. New York: Oxford UP, 2012. viii–x.

Hollington, Michael. "Dickens and the Circus of Modernity." *Dickens and Modernity*. Ed. Juliet John. 133–49.

———. Rev. of *The Selected Letters of Charles Dickens*, ed. Jenny Hartley. *The Dickensian* 108.3 (2012): 250–51.

Holt, Shari Hodges. "Dickens on Broadway: Future Dickens, Digital Dickens, Global Dickens—a Panel Discussion." Ed. Edward Guiliano. *Dickens Studies Annual* 43 (2012): 1–31.

Horrocks, Clare. "Advances in Digitization: The *Dickens Journals Online Project*, 2012." *Victorian Periodicals Review* 45.3 (Fall 2012): 358–362.

Ioannou, Maria. "'Simply because I found her irresistable': Female Erotic Power and Feminism in *Great Expectations*" *Dickens Quarterly* 29.2 (2012): 142–50.

Jackson, Lee. *Walking Dickens' London*. Oxford: Shire, 2012.

Jacobson, Howard. "Dickens: A Birthday Tribute." *The Dickensian* 108.1 (2012): 8–9.

James, Stephen. "Repetition, Rumination, Superstition: The Rituals of *Our Mutual Friend*." *English* 61.234 (September 2012): 214–33.

John, Juliet. "Global Dickens: A Response to John Jordan." *Literature Compass* 9.7 (July 2012): 502–07.

———. ed. Introduction; "Things, Words and the Meanings of Art. "*Dickens and Modernity*. New York: D. S. Brewer, 2012. 1–18, 115–32.

Jordan, John O., and Nirshan Perera. Introduction. *Global Dickens*. Burlington, VT: Ashgate, 2012. xv–xxix.

Jordan, Joseph P. *Dickens Novels as Verse*. Madison, NJ: Fairleigh Dickinson UP, 2012.

———. "Echoes Between the Final Paragraphs of Chapters 1–7 of *GE*." *Dickens Quarterly* 20.3 (2012): 278–84.

Keates, Kim Edwards. "'Wow! She's a lesbian. Got to be!': Re-reading/Re-viewing Dickens and Neo-Victorianism on the BBC." *Dickens and Modernity*. Ed. Juliet John. 171–92.

Kujawska-Lis, Ewa. "Charles Dickens and G. K. Chesterton—Admiration in Many Forms." *Dickens Quarterly* 29.4 (2012): 350–62.

Lai, Shu Fang. "Dickens and Emotions." *Victorians: A Journal of Culture and Literature* 122 (Fall 2012): 89–99.

Laird, Karen. "The Posthumous Dickens: Commemorative Adaptations, 1870–2012." *Neo-Victorian Studies* 5.2 (2012): 12–34.

Lanning, Katie. "Tessellating Texts: Reading *The Moonstone* in *All the Year Round*." *Victorian Periodicals Review* 45.1 (Spring 2012): 1–22.

Lee, Klaudia Hiu Yen. "*A Tale of Two Cities* and Chinese Literary History." *Victorians: A Journal of Culture and Literature* 122 (Fall 2012): 24–35.

Lind, Nancy Engbretsten. "'The Mind of the Heart': Mr Dick's Percipience." *The Dickensian* 108.1 (2012): 19–21.

Litvack, Leon. "Marcus Stone: A Reappraisal of Dickens's Young Illustrator." *The Dickens Quarterly* 29.3 (2012): 214–40.

Litvak, Joseph. "Unctuous: Resentment in *David Copperfield.*" *Qui Parle: Critical Humanities and Social Sciences.* 20.2 (Spring/Summer 2012): 127–150.

Logan, Deborah. "Greetings from the Editor." *Victorians: A Journal of Culture and Literature* 122 (Fall 2012): 4-5.

Long, William F. "What Happened to Lucy Stroughill." *Dickens Quarterly* 29.4 (2012): 313–24.

Mackenzie, Hazel, and Ben Winyard, eds. *Charles Dickens and the Mid-Victorian Press, 1850–1870.* Buckingham: U of Buckingham P, 2013.

———, Ben Winyard and John Drew. *Dickens Quarterly* 29.3 (2012): 251-77.

Mahlberg, Michaela. "Corpus Stylistics—Dickens, Text-drivenness and the Fictional World." *Dickens and Modernity.* Ed. Juliet John. 115–32.

Malik, Rachel. "Stories Many, Fast and Slow: *Great Expectations* and the Mid-Victorian Horizon of the Publishable." *ELH* 79.2 (Summer 2012): 477–500.

Marsh, Joss, and Carrie Sickmann. "The Oliver! Phenomenon; or, 'Please, sir, we want more and more!'" *Dickens and Modernity.* Ed. Juliet John. 150–70.

McKnight, Natalie. "Dickens on Broadway: Future Dickens, Digital Dickens, Global Dickens—a Panel Discussion." Ed. Edward Guiliano. *Dickens Studies Annual* 43 (2012): 1–29.

Meckier, Jerome. "Twists in *Oliver Twist.*" *Dickens Quarterly* 29.2 (2012): 116–24.

Menon, Ayeesha. *The Mumbai Chuzzlewits.* BBC Radio 4. January 1-15, 2012.

Metz, Nancy Aycock, "Recent Dickens Studies: 2010." *Dickens Studies Annual* 43 (2012): 261-358.

Mirmohamadi, Kylie, and Susan K. Martin. *Colonial Dickens: What Australians Made of the World's Favourite Writer.* Melbourne: Australian Scholarly Publishing, 2012.

Mitchell, David. "A Fan Writes to Dickens." *The Dickensian* 108.1 (2012): 9–11.

Moore, Ben. "'When I went to Lunnon town sirs': Transformation and the Threshold in the Dickensian City." *Dickens Quarterly* 29.4 (2012): 336–49.

Naiman, Eric. "When Dickens met Dostoevsky." *TLS.* April 10, 2013. www.the-tls.co.uk/tls/public/article1243205.ece.

Nayder, Lillian. Introduction. *Dickens, Sexuality and Gender.* Burlington, VT: Ashgate, 2012. xiii–xxviii.

———. "Tangible Typography" (excerpted from *Harriet and Letitia: A Novel*). *Neo-Victorian Studies* 5.2 (2012):179–201.

O'Farrell, Mary Ann. "Blindness Envy: Victorians in the Parlors of the Blind" *PMLA* 127.3 (May 2012): 512–25.

Ormond, Leonee. "Dickens and Contemporary Art." *Dickens and the Artists.* Ed. Mark Bills. New Haven: Yale UP, 2012. 35–65.

Osborn, Bryan. "A Note on Costume and Historicity in *Little Dorrit.*" *The Dickensian* 108.1 (2012): 47–51.

Palievsky, Julia, and Dmitry Urnov. "A Kindred Writer: Dickens in Russia, 1840–1990." *Dickens Studies Annual* 43 (2012): 209–32.

Parker, David. "Duelling and Public Order in *The Pickwick Papers.*" *The Dickensian* 108.3 (2012): 213–27.

————. "The *Pickwick* Prefaces." *Dickens Studies Annual* 43 (2012): 67–80.

Paroissien, David. Editorial. *Dickens Quarterly* 29.1 (2012): 7–10.

Patten, Robert L. *Charles Dickens and "Boz": The Birth of the Industrial-Age Author*. New York: Cambridge UP, 2012.

————.Introduction. to *Dickens and Victorian Print Cultures*. Burlington, VT: Ashgate, 2012. xv–xlvii.

————. "*A Tale of Four Cities* Conference." *Dickens Quarterly* 29.2 (2012): 175–77.

Peel, Katie R. "'Make Her Pay': Fanny Dorrit's Disruption in Charles Dickens's *Little Dorrit*." *Dickens Studies Annual* 43 (2012): 125–40.

Peters, Laura. Introduction. *Dickens and Childhood*. Burlington, VT: Ashgate, 2012. xi–xxii.

Petrie, Graham. "A 1919 Hungarian Film of *Oliver Twist*." *The Dickensian* 108.1 (2012): 29–32.

Philpotts, Trey. "Dickens on Broadway: Future Dickens, Digital Dickens, Global Dickens—a Panel Discussion" Ed. Edward Guiliano. *Dickens Studies Annual* 43 (2012): 1–31.

Piggot, Gillian. *Dickens and Benjamin: Moments of Revelation, Fragments of Modernity*. Burlington, VT: Ashgate, 2012.

Preston, Shale, "Existential Scrooge: A Kierkegaardian Reading of *A Christmas Carol*" in *Literature Compass* 9.11 (November 2012): 743–51.

Purton, Valerie. *Dickens and the Sentimental Tradition: Fielding, Richardson, Sterne, Goldsmith, Sheridan, Lamb*. New York: Anthem Press, 2012.

Pykett, Lyn. "Charles Dickens: The Novelist as Public Figure." *The Oxford History of the Novel in English Volume 3: The Nineteenth-Century Novel 1820–1880*. New York: Oxford UP, 2012. 187–202.

Rainsford, Dominic. "Out of Place: David Copperfield's Irresolvable Geographies." *Dickens and Modernity*. Ed. Juliet John. 193–208.

Regis, Amber K., and Deborah Wynne. "Miss Havisham's Dress: Materialising Dickens in Film Adaptations of *Great Expectations*." *Neo-Victorian Studies* 5.2 (2012): 35–58.

Richardson, Ruth. *Dickens and the Workhouse: Oliver Twist and the London Poor*. Oxford UP, 2012.

Rousselot, Elodie. "*A Christmas Carol* and Global Economy: The Neo-Victorian Debt to the Nineteenth Century. *Neo-Victorian Studies* 5.2 (2012): 59–83.

Sage, Victor. "Girl Number Twenty Revisted: *Hard Times*'s Sissy Jupe." *Dickens Quarterly* 29.4 (2012): 325–35.

Schlicke, Paul. Rev. of "The Dickens Bicentenary." *Dickens Quarterly* 29.4 (2012): 378–89.

————. Introduction. *Sketches of Young Gentlemen and Young Couples with Sketches of Young Ladies by Edward Caswall*. New York: Oxford UP, 2012.

Schweizer, Florian. "Afterword: The 2012 Bicentenary." *Dickens and Modernity*. Ed. Juliet John. 209–22.

Sen, Sambudha. *London, Radical Culture, and the Making of the Dickensian Aesthetic*. Columbus: Ohio State UP, 2012.

Sharma, Lakshmi Raj. "Charles Dickens and Me." *English* 61.234 (September 2012): 290–309.

Shaw, Marion. "The Doctor and the Cannibals." *The Dickensian* 108.2 (2012): 117–25.

Shiller, Dana. "The Pleasures and Limits of Dickensian Plot, or 'I have met Mr. Dickens, and this is not him.'" *Neo-Victorian Studies* 5.2 (2012): 84–103.

Shrimpton, Nicholas. "*Great Expectations:* Dickens's Muscular Novel." *Dickens Quarterly* 29.2 (2012): 125–41.

Siegel, Daniel. "Help Wanting: The Exhaustion of a Dickensian Ideal." *Charity and Condescension: Victorian Literature and the Dilemmas of Philanthropy*. Athens: Ohio UP, 2012. 37–74

Slater, Michael. *The Great Charles Dickens Scandal*. New Haven: Yale UP, 2012.

———. Foreword. *Charles Dickens and the Mid-Victorian Press, 1850–1870*. Edited by Hazel Mackenzie and Ben Winyard. Buckingham: U of Buckingham P, 2013. I-iv.

Squire, Lyn. "Two *Drood* Questions." *The Dickensian*. 108.2 (2012): 141–42.

Stearns, Precious McKenzie. "'Sex and the City': Charles Dickens's Working Women in *Martin Chuzzlewit* and *Our Mutual Friend*." *English* 61 (Summer 2012): 137–50.

Stober, Katharyn. "'Another Thing Needful': A New Direction in *Hard Times* Criticism and Pedagogy. " *Victorians: A Journal of Culture and Literature* 122 (Fall 2012): 127–33.

Tambling, Jeremy. "Dickens and Ben Jonson." *English* 61.23 (Spring 2012): 4–25.

———. Introduction. *Dickens and the City*. Burlington, VT: Ashgate, 2012. xi–xxvii.

———. "Dickens, Benjamin and the City: The 'Object Riddled with Error." *Dickens Quarterly* 29.3 (2012): 197–213.

Tarr, Clayton Carlyle. "Knots in Glass: Dickens and Omniscience from Boz to Bucket." *Dickens Studies Annual* 43 (2012):33–66.

Thurston, Luke. *Literary Ghosts from the Victorians to Modernism: The Haunting Interval*. New York: Routledge, 2012.

Tomaiuolo, Saverio. *Victorian Unfinished Novels: The Imperfect Page*. New York: Palgrave Macmillan, 2012.

Underwood, Hilary. "Dickens Subjects in Victorian Art." *Dickens and the Artists*. Ed. Mark Bills . New Haven: Yale UP, 2012. 69–109.

Wagner, Tamara S. "The Making of Criminal Children: Stealing Orphans from *Oliver Twist* to *A Little Princess*." *Victorians: A Journal of Culture and Literature* (Spring 2012): 68–83.

Waters, Catherine. Series Preface. *A Library of Essays on Charles Dickens*. Burlington, VT: Ashgate, 2012.

Williams, Helen. "'Blank Epochs': Narratives of Disability in Charles Dickens's *The Old Curiosity Shop* and Dinah Mulock Craik's *John Halifax, Gentleman*." *Victorians: A Journal of Culture and Literature* 122 (Fall 2012): 115-26.

Williams, Rowan. "Address at The Wreathlaying Ceremony to Mark the Bicentenary of the Birth of Charles Dickens, Westminster Abbey, 7 February 2012."*Dickens Quarterly* 29.2 (2012): 113–15.

Wolfreys, Julian. *Dickens's London: Perception, Subjectivity and Phenomenal Urban Multiplicity*. Edinburgh: Edinburgh UP, 2012.

Wood, Madeleine. "Whispers and Shadows: Traumatic Echoes in Paul Dombey's Life, Death, and Afterlife." *Dickens Studies Annual* 43 (2012): 81–110.

Young, Kay. "'Wounded by Mystery': Dickens and Attachment Theory." *English* 61.234 (September 2012): 234–47.

Zigarovich, Jolene. "Epitaphic Representation in Dickens's *Our Mutual Friend.*" *Dickens Studies Annual* 43 (2012):141–68.

Index

(Page numbers in italics represent illustrations)

Ackermann, Rudolph, 17–18
Adams. James Eli, 126, 129, 131
Adams, William Bridges, 129
Adorno, Theodor, 180, 198, 367
    Aesthetic Theory, 243–44
Aird, Catherine, 390
Alekseev, Mikhail P., and Igor M.
    Katarsky, 342
Allen, Michael, 364
Altick, Richard, 166
Altmann, Rick, 33
American War of Independence, 13–14
Amy, Helen, 362– 63
Analytical Society, 255–56
Anatomy Act (1832), 364
Anderson, Amanda, 230, 384
Anderson, Benedict, 277
Andrews, Malcolm, 31, 390
Arkwright, Richard, 9
Armstrong, Nancy, 127
Arnold, Matthew, 153–54, 230
Ashgate's *Library of Essays on Charles
    Dickens*, 334, 336; *see also* Catherine
    Waters
Association for Preserving Liberty and
    Property against Republicans and
    Levellers, 14
Atwood, Margaret, 374
Auburn System, 115
Austin, Alfred, 179, 180, 182
Axton, William, 160–61

Babbage, Charles, 247–65
    Decline of Science, 253
    Difference Engine, 248–49, 251–52,
        56, 257–58, 261, 264
    Economy of Machinery, 253
Bachelard, Gaston, 301
Bachman, Maria, 382
Bagehot, Walter, 341
Bailey, Peter, 197
Balint, Michael, 140
Barker, Harley Granville, 181, 182
Barnes, David S., 235
Barrie, J. M., 189
    Peter Pan, 177
Bart, Lionel, 373
Beaumont, Gustave de. *See* Tocqueville,
    On the Penitentiary System
Beer, Gillian, 178
Beerbohm, Max, 181
Belasco, David, and John Luther, *Darling
    of the Gods*, 182
Bellamy's Kitchen, 19
Benjamin, Walter, 334, 362, 365–68
Bentham, Jeremy, 66
Bentley, Richard, 24
    Bentley's Miscellany, 30
Benziman, Galia, 95–112
Bernard, Simon, 285, 287
Bevin, Darren, 344
Bickerstaff, Isaac, 15–16
Bizup, Joseph, 259

Bledsoe, Robert Terrell, 352
Blinco, Robert, *Memoir* (1832), 101
Blow, Sydney, 189
Blumenberg, Hans, 155
Boborykina, Tatiana A., 343–44
Bodenheimer, Rosemarie, 102–03
Bolton, Philip, 172
Booth, Michael R., 31
Born, Daniel, 214
Borsa, Marie, 181
Boulton, Matthew, 9–10
Bowen, John, 107, 351
Boyce, Charlotte, and Elodie Rousselot,
    373
Brackbill, Harvey, 162
Bradbury & Evans, 350
Braddon, Mary Elizabeth, *Lady Audley's
    Secret*, 311–12, 316–18, 321–22,
    323–25
Bratton, J. S., 160
Bridgman, Laura, 379
Braudy, Leo, *The Frenzy of Renown*, 47
Braverman, Harry, 259
Briggs, Asa, 4
Brodsky, Joseph, 343
Brontë, Emily, *Wuthering Heights*, 316
Brooke's Soap, 293–95, *294*, 298, 306,
    307
Brooks, Peter, 29, 313, 314
Brown, John, 101
Browne, Hablot Knight ("Phiz"), 55, *55*,
    97, 161. *161*, 352–53
Buckley, Jerome, 82
Bulgakov, Mikhail, 343
Burke, Kenneth, 97
Burnett, Frances Hodgson, *Little Lord
    Fauntleroy*, 177
Burns, Arthur, and Joanna Innes, 4
Byron, George Gordon, Lord, 46
    Childe Harold's Pilgrimage, 168

Callow, Simon, 378–88
Carey, John, 57, 105, 148, 151–52, 154,
    164
Carlisle, Janice, 234–35
Carlyle, Thomas, 130, 132, 162, 248
Cartwright, John, 9
Cassell's Household Guide, 298

Chadwick, Edwin, 235
Chamberlain, Erin D., 293–309
Channing, William, 67–68
Chapman & Hall, 164
Charity Report (1823), 67, 68, 71, 73
Charles Dickens Museum, 336
Chekhov, Anton, 343
Cheney, Edward, 66
Chesterton, G. K., 57, 371
Childhood, 374
Children, abuse of, 99
Chittick, Kathryn, 24
Chute, Hillary, 39
Clarke, Bruce, 313
Claybaugh, Amanda, 214
Clayton, Jay, 380
Clement, Joseph, 250, 251, 259
Cockneys, 1, 7–8, 10, 11–20
Cohen, Marc D., 372
Coleman, Rosemary, 125–45
Coleridge, S. T., 14
Colledge, Gary L., 390
Collela, Silvana, 385
Collins, L. J., 183
Collins, Philip, 149
Collins, Wilkie, 350, 352
    The Moonstone, 353
    The Woman in White, 311–16, 319–21,
        322, 325–26
Conary, Jennifer, 205–28
Corbin, Alain, 234, 235
Cordery, Gareth, 377–78
Corn Laws, repeal of, 5
Cowper, William, "John Gilpin," 11–13,
    16
Craik, George Lillie, 68
Crotch, Walter, 190–91
Cruikshank, George, 25, 26, 27, 162, 301,
    302
Crystal Palace, 206
Curzon, George Nathaniel, 1st baron, 196

Dalyell, Sir John, *Shipwrecks and
    Disasters* (1812), 159
Dana, Henry, 189
Darwin, Charles, 240, 383
Davidoff, Leonore, and Catherine Hall,
    129, 139

Davis, Jim, 197
Death of Nancy Sykes, The (1897), 32
De la L. Oulton, Carolyn, 376
Deleuze, Gilles, 368
Dibdin, Charles, 159, 163
Dickens adaptations, 370–74
Dickens and/as the Public, 383–85
Dickens and the Artists (exhibit 2012), 354
Dickens, Cedric, 191
Dickens, Charles and,
    artists, friendships with, 354
    Australians, 345
    "Autobiography of Boz," 51
    Bicentenary events, 336–38
    bildungsroman, poverty, and self-
      sufficiency, 63–88
    biography and biographical criticism,
      386–91
    "Boz," 348
    celebrity culture, 45–59
    Channel crossings in *TTC*, 275–90
    childhood, 374–77
    dueling in *PP*, 385
    fog and social obscurity in *BH*, 22–36
    Forster opposed to CD and theater, 32
    Humor and social change in *NN*,
      95–109
    moonlighting (Bentley vs. Chapman &
      Hall), 352
    masculinity in *D&S*, 125–40
    nautical literature, 158–59
    odor and social class, 233
    OT, adaptations of, 31–40
    pioneer fiction technique from
      Sketches to *OT*, 23–40
    social problem novel meets
      bildungsroman in *BH*, 205–25
    Squeers, original model for Mr., 97
    stage versions of *DC*, 177
    theater and readings, 387–88
    Tocqueville vs. CD on prisons, 113–19
    Trollope, CD's animosity toward
      Frances, 110n11
    Works written or edited by:
      All the Year Round, 311, 343,
        350–51, 352
      *American Notes for General
        Circulation*, 113–19, 387

"Autobiographical Fragment," 103
Bleak House, 205–25, 229, 231–33,
    236–42, 244, 361, 364, 384
"Calais Night Mail, The," (1861),
    279–80
Chimes, The, 372, 380
Christmas Carol, The, 369; 372
    (1844 play)
Cricket on the Hearth, The, 372,
    378
David Copperfield, 74–77, 79–88,
    103, 168, *176*, *185*, *186*, 175–
    90, *192*, 192–99 (1914 play);
    359, 377–78, 383
Dombey and Son, 40n1, 47,
    125–40, 147–68
Edwin Drood, The Mystery of, 176,
    338 (play), 355
"Flight, A," 281–82
Frozen Deep, The (with Collins),
    346
Great Expectations, 64, 84–88,
    356, 358, 359–60, 361
Hard Times, 103, 361
Household Words, 159, 165, 350,
    352
Letters (Clarendon), 51
Little Dorrit, 214, 229, 230–31,
    236, 237–44, 247–50, 260–65,
    277, 340
Martin Chuzzlewit, 113, 114, 116,
    118,149, 358
Master Humphrey's Clock, 340,
    360
Nicholas Nickleby, 47, 51–59,
    95–109, 160
Old Curiosity Shop, The, 165, 340,
    381
Oliver Twist, 23–40, 65, 69, 72–76,
    78–79, 88, 160, 176, 363–64,
    371 (1919 film); 375
Our Mutual Friend, 335, 358–59,
    368 – 69, 380
"Our French Watering Place"
    (1854), 278–79, 280–81
"Our Watering Place," 165, 167
Pickwick Papers, The, 1–8, 20, 47,
    48–49, 205, 339, 352–53, 381,

385
Reprinted Pieces, 280
"Signalman, The," 368
Sketches by Boz, 7, 18–20, 23–31
"Some Particulars Concerning a
    Lion," 49–50
Tale of Two Cities, A, 177, 183,
    199 (as play *The Only Way*);
    350
Uncommercial Traveller, The, 279,
    389, 90
Works:
    Charles Dickens Edition
        (1867), 3
    Cheap Edition (1847), 2–3, 5
    Library Edition (1867), 3
Dickens Fellowship, 190
Dickens, Henry, 191, 387
Dickens House Museum, 157
Dickens, Kate, 387
Dickens, Mark, 336
Dickens Universe, 335
Dickensian, The, 336, 372
Disability studies, 377–78
Dodd, John, 363
Donskey, Seth, *Twisted* (1996), 38
Douglas-Fairhurst, Robert, 24, 46
Doyle, Sir Arthur Conan, *Waterloo*, 183
Drew, John, 346, 347, 349–50, 351
Dubbey, J. M., 255
Duncan, Archibald, *Mariner's Chronicle*
    (1804), 159

Eastern Penitentiary, 113–19
Edward, Prince of Wales, 179
Edwards, Gavin, 355–56
Eisenstein, Sergei, 32–33
    Battleship Potemkin, 33
Eisner, Will, *Fagin the Jew* (2003), 39
Elber-Aviram, Hadas, 368
Eliot, George, 355
    The Mill on the Floss, 218
Ellis, William, 68–69
Ellison, David, 377
Epping Forest, 16
Eslick, Mark, 359

Falconer, William, 163

Farrar, Aileen, 353–54
Fields, Annie, 389
Finlayson, Geoffrey, 70
Fishing rights, 11
Flanders, Judith, 362
Floyd, Stacy, 361
Flynn, Michael J., 398
Ford, Mark, 57, 97
Ford, Richard, 65
Forster, John, 19, 25, 31, 157, 158, 164
Foucault, Michel, 365
Fraiman, Susan, 216–18, 220, 222
Franco-English diplomatic crisis of 1858,
    277–78
French Revolution's effect on reform
    movement, 14–15; on emigration, 288
Freud, Sigmund, 25–26, 27, 108
Fruhauff, Brad, 381
Furneaux, Holly, 24, 133, 138, 360

Game Act (1831), 17
Game Certificates Act (1827), 17, 18
Garas, Marton, 371
Garnett, Robert, 389
Garrick, David, 165
Gaskell, Elizabeth, *Mary Barton*, 214;
    Ruth, 316
Gautier, Théophile, 148
Giedroyc, Coky, 38
Gilligan, Carol, 84
Gillray, James, 8, 15
Gissing, George, 158
Glavin, John, 370–71
Global Dickens, 338–46
Goodlad, Lauren, 206
Gorky, Maxim, 343
Gottlieb, Robert, 389
Grand Trunk Canal, 10
Greene, Tim, *Boy Called Twist* (2004), 38
Greenwich Fair, 27
Greg, W. W., 69
Greiner, Rae, 382
Griffith, D. W., 32, 33
Griffith, Jane, 361
Gogol, Nikolai, 342
Grossman, Jonathan, 277, 339–40
Guild of Literature and Art, 390
Guy, Josephine, 214

Hackett, Walter, *The Invisible Foe* (1917), 199
Hadley, Elaine, 28–29, 208–09
Hall, William, 6
Hanna, Robert C., 357, 372
Hardy, Barbara, 82
Hartley, Jenny, 386
Hatten, Charles, 129, 138
Heitzman, Matthew, 275–92
Henderson, John, 13
Hendrick, Harry, 99
Henry III, 16
Herbert, Christopher, 210
Herschel, John, 255
Highmore, Anthony, 68–69
Hill, Geoffrey, 148
Hill, T. H., 191
His Majesty's Theatre, 175–99
Hobbes, Thomas, 238
Hogarth, Georgina, 387
Hollington, Michael, 335, 341, 366–67, 370
Holmes, Rupert, 338
Holt, Shari Hodges, 370–71
Hood, Edwin Paxton, 68
Hood, Thomas, 16–17
Hook, Theodore, 30
Hooton, Ellen, 101
Hopkins, Eric, 106
Hornback, Bert, 198
Horrocks, Clare, 347
House, Humphry, 96
Hunting, fox and stag, 11, 16
Hyman, Anthony, 251

Inglis, Fred, 46, 47
Ioannou, Marie, 358
Italian nationalist movement, 351

Jackson, T. A., 32
Jacobson, Howard, 334
Jacobson, Roman, 154
James, Edwin, 285
James, Stephen, 369
Jerrold, Douglas, *Black Ey'd Susan*, 160, 169
John, Juliet, 38–39, 45–46, 341–42, 369–70, 379

Jones, Anna Maria, 312
Jordan, John O., 216, 354–55,
———, and Nishan Perora, 340–41
Joyce, Simon, 208
Justman, Stewart, 97

Keates, Kim Edwards, 360
Kennedy, G. W., 158
Kenyon, Lloyd Tyrell-Kenyon, 1st baron, 11
Kerr, Matthew P. M., 147–73
Kingsley, Ben (as Fagin), 35
Kuskey, Jessica, 247–74

Laird, Karen, 374
Lamerte, George, 364
Langland, Elizabeth, 299
Laplanche, Jean, and J.-B. Pontalis, 25–26, 28
Lardner, Dionysus, 257–58, 264
Lean, David, *Oliver* (1945), 33–34
Leavis, Q. D., 352
Ledger, Sally, 104
Lee, Klaudia Hiu Yen, 344–45
Leighton, Angela, 313
Leitch, Thomas, 370
Lesage, Alain-René, 379–80
Levine, Caroline, 206–7, 213
Lewes, George Henry, 23
Lind, Nancy Engbretsen, 382
Litvack, Joseph, 383
Litvack, Leon, *Marcus Stone*, 352
Lodge, David, 45
Logan, Deborah, 335
London and modernity, 362–70
London Sportsmen, 15
Long, William F., 389–90
Lougy, Robert 233
Lowes Memorial, 70
Lukács, Georg, 83
Lunar Society, 10
Lyell, Charles, 250–51
Lynd, Robert, 190

MacCarthy, Desmond, 180, 181
Macdonagh, Michael, 195
Mackenzie, Hazel, and Ben Winyard, 349–50

Mahlberg, Michaela, 351–52
Malik, Rachel, 356
Manchester Literary and Philosophical
    Society, 10
Marcus, Steven, 136, 138
Markovits, Stefanie, 82
Marryat, Frederick, 158, 162
Marsh, Josh, 46
———, and Carrie Sickman, 373
Martineau, Harriet, 115, 250
Maunder, Andrew, 175–203
Mauss, Marcel, 382
Mayer, David, 178
Mayhew, Augustus, and Henry, *The
    Greatest Plague of Life*, 298–99, 301,
    307
Mayhew, Henry, *London Labour and the
    London Poor*, 66, 234
McDonald, John F., 184
McKnight, Natalie, 335
McLuhan, Marshall, 148, 149
Meadows, Elizabeth, 311–31
Meckier, Jerome, 113–23, 376–77
Mengham, Rod, 186
Metz, Nancy Aycock, 338
Mill, John Stuart, 65
    On Liberty, 208–9, 216, 224
Miller, D. A., 231, 233, 235–36
Miller, J. Hillis, 206
Miller, William Ian, 238
Mirohamadi, Kylie, and Susan K. Martin,
    345
Mitchell, David, 362
Mole, Tom, 46
Montcrieff, W. T., 7–8
Monteiro, George, 153
Moretti, Franco, 83, 216
Morning Chronicle, 6
Morning Herald and Daily Advertiser, 10
Moynahan, Julian, 125–26, 134, 148,
    151–52, 154
Müller, Max, 240–41
"Muscular" novels, 359–60

Napoleon III, emperor, assassination
    attempt on, 275, 277–78, 283–86
Nares, Owen, 180, 186–87, 188, 192, 196
Nayder, Lillian, 358, 373

Neilson, Julia, 178, 179
New Poor Law, 28–29, 34, 63, 205, 364
Nietzsche, Friedrich, *Genealogy of Morals*,
    236
"Nimrod Club," 6–7
Nixon, Jude V., 70
Noddings, Nell, 74

O'Farrell, Mary Ann, 378
Oliphant, Margaret, 319
Orczy, Emma, *The Scarlet Pimpernel*,
    177–78, 183
Orsini, Felice, 278, 285, 286
Orwell, George, 82, 96
Osborn, Bryan, 353
Owen, Robert, 71

Paine, Thomas, *The Age of Reason*, 14;
    The Rights of Man, 14
Palievski, Julia, and Dmitri Urnov, 342
Palmer, William J., 150, 159
Parker, David, 1–21, 352–53, 385
Parker, Louis Napoleon, *176*, 187, 193,
    198
    Drake, 182, 183, 196–97
    Highway, 193–94
    My Lives, 176
Parker's London Magazine, 149–50
Paroissien, David, 334, 369
Patten, Robert L., 51, 336, 347–49
Pearl, Matthew, 46
Pears' Soap, 305, *306*
Peck, John, 150
Pecora, Vincent, 86
Peel, Katie R., 359
Perugini, Kate, 176
Peters, Laura, 374–75
Petrie, Graham, 371
Pettitt, Clare, 254
Phelps, Sarah (*Oliver*, 2007), 36–38
Philpots, Trey, 352
Piggot, Gillian, 366–67, 369
Pitt, William, the Younger, 9
Polanski, Roman (*Oliver Twist*, 2005),
    34–35
Poor Law Amendment Act (1834), 63,
    66–67, 70
Poor Law Commissions, 295

Poovey, Nancy, 81, 177
Pope, Norris, *Dickens and Charity*, 71
Porter, Jane, 183
Preston, Shale, 369
Prison reform in U. S., 114–19
Propp, Vladimir, 64
Public Health Act (1848), 295
Purton, Valerie, 381
Pyat, Félix, 284
Pykett, Lyn, 383–84

Radclyffe, Raymond, 190
Rainsford, Dominic, 276, 345–46
Reed, Carol (*Oliver!* 1968), 35–36
Reform Act (1832). 5, 9, 17–18
Reform movement, 1–19
Reform, promotion of, 1–19
Regis, Amber K., and Deborah Wynne, 373–74
Regnier, François, 286
Reid, Hugo, 71–72, 73
Reitz, Caroline, 333–98
Representation of the People Acts (1869), 5–6
Revelation, Book of, 153
Richardson, Ruth, 363–64
Ricks, Christopher, 147–48
Ritson, Joseph, 14
Roberts, Eric Bechhofer, 387
Roberts, F. David, 70, 77
Robbins, Bruce, 206, 305
Rosen, Michael, 126
Rousselot, Elodie, 374
Rowell, George, 31
Ruth, Jennifer, 81, 254

Sadoff, Dianne F., 23–44
Sage, Victor, 361
Salmon, Richard, 59n4
Samalin, Zachary, 229–45
Savoy, John, 184–85
Schlicke, Paul, 335, 337, 352
Schultz, David, 180
Schweizer, Florian, 335, 336
Scribner, George (film director), *Oliver & Company*, 39
Sedgwick, Eve, 359
Self-help and Samuel Smiles, 67

Sen, Sanbudha, 346, 356
Sensation novels, 311–26, 326n2
Sentiment and affect, 381–83
Servants, Victorian, 293–307
Sexuality and gender, 358–70
Seymour, Robert, 7–8, 20, 353
Shakespeare, William, *Hamlet*, 153, 154; *Henry IV, Pt. I*, 184, 196
Shaw, George Bernard, 179, 198, 361; *Pygmalion*, 181
Shaw, Marion, 346
Shiller, Dana, 373
Shrimpton, Nicholas, 359–60
Shu, Fang Li, 382–83
Siegel, Daniel, 33, 384–85
Slater, Michael, 50, 114, 149, 347, 358, 386
Smiles, Samuel, 67
Smiley, Jane, 45
Smith, Albert, 344
Smith, Arthur, 387
Smith, Grahame, 2, 45
Smith, Sheila, 101
Smithfield, 30
Solitary confinement, 113–16
Spurgin, Timothy, 45–62
Stearns, Precious McKenzie, 358
Sterne, Laurence, 47
Stević, Aleksandar, 63–94
Stewart, Garrett, 151
"Stink of 1858, Great," 235, 242–43
Stirling, Edward, 372
Stober, Katharyn, 361
Stowe, Harriet Beecher, *Uncle Tom's Cabin*, 214
Surtees, R. S., 17–18
Sussman, Herbert, 126, 130

Tambling, Jeremy, 365–66
Tarr, Clayton Carlyle, 379–80
Tennyson, Alfred Lord, "Crossing the Bar," 152–53, 154, 167–68
Ternan, Ellen, 386–87, 389
Thermodynamics, Second Law of, 312–14
Thing theory, 379–80
Thurston, Luke, 368
Tierney, Jacob, *Twist*, 38
Tillotson, Kathleen, 149

Toker, Leona, 103
Tolstoy, Count Lev Nicoleyovich, 343
Tomaiuolo, Savario, 355
Tomalin, Claire, 24
Tonna, Charlotte Elizabeth, 100–102, 104
Tocqueville, Alexis de, 113–19
    Democracy in America, 113
    On the Penitentiary System, 113–15,
        117, 119
Toussenel, Alphonse, 383
Townsend, Joseph, 66
Tracy, Robert, 24
Tree, Sir Herbert Beerbohm, 176–99
Tree, Maud, 189
Trewin, J. C., 184
Trollope, Frances, 100–102, 104, 107,
    304
Trotter, David, 150
Turgenev, Ivan, 343

Urania College, 209

Victorian print cultures, 346–57
Vlock, Deborah, 32

Wagner, Tamera S., 375–76
Waller, Edmund, 156, 160, 165
Warren's Blacking Warehouse, 18, 47
Waters, Catherine, 334, 336
Watt, Joseph, 9–10

Wedgwood, Hensleigh, 240
Welsh, Alexander, 82
Westland, Ella, 163
Westminster Review, 65–66
Whewell, William, 156
Wiener, Martin, 137
Williams, Helen, 378
Williams, Raymond, 238
Williams, Rowan, 334, 391
Wills, W. H., 282
Wilson, Edmund, 2, 96
Winter, Jay, 193
Wolfreys, Julian, 366
Women writers of bildungsromans, 216–17
Wood, Madeleine, 376
Woodward, Sir Llewellyn, 4
Wordsworth, William, 14
    "Ode: Intimations," 153
World War I London plays, 183
Wyvill, Christopher, 9

Yates, Frederick, 372
Yorkville schools, 205
Young, Kay, 377

Zemka, Sue, 33
Zigarovich, Jolene, 380